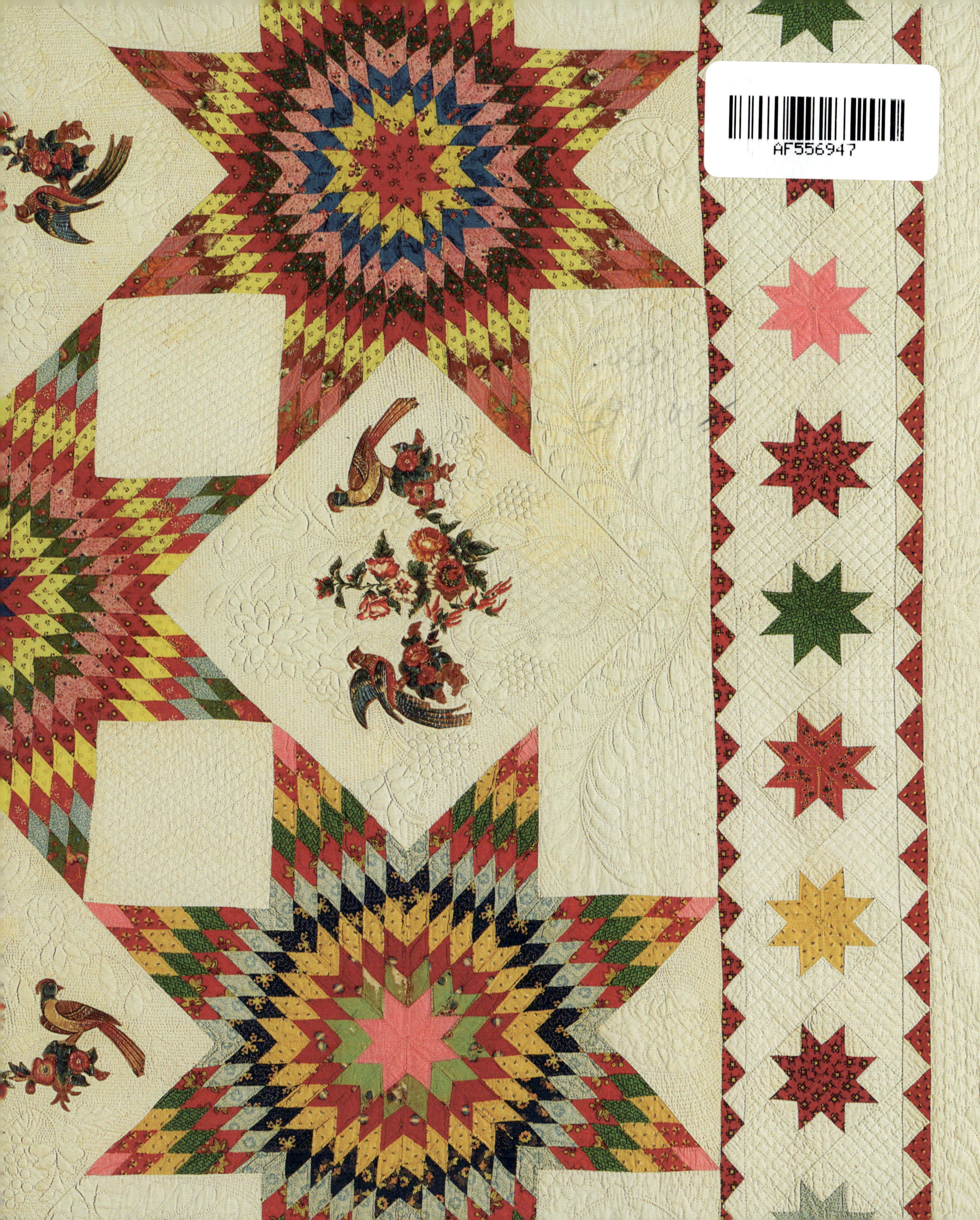

BECOMING AMERICA

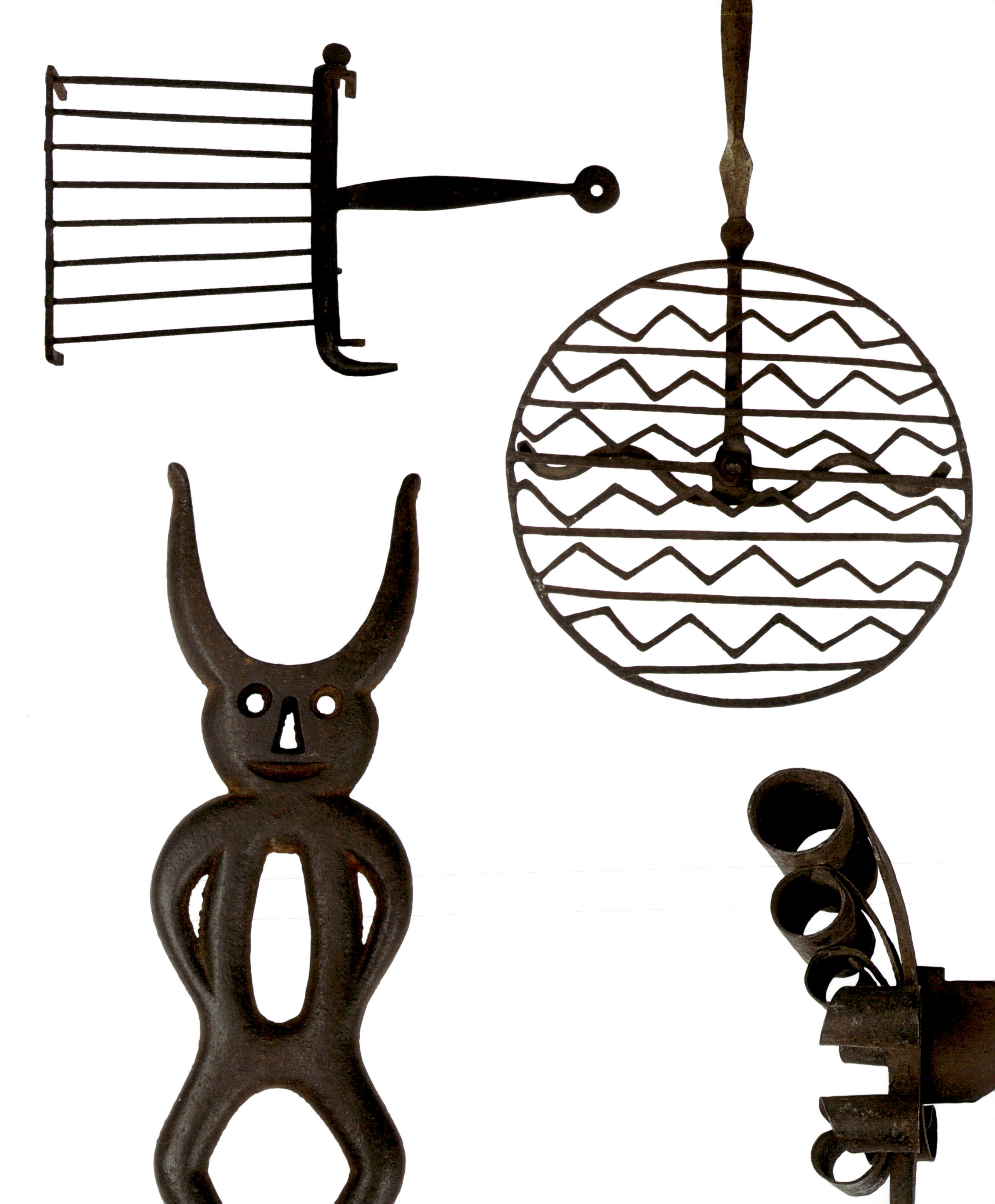

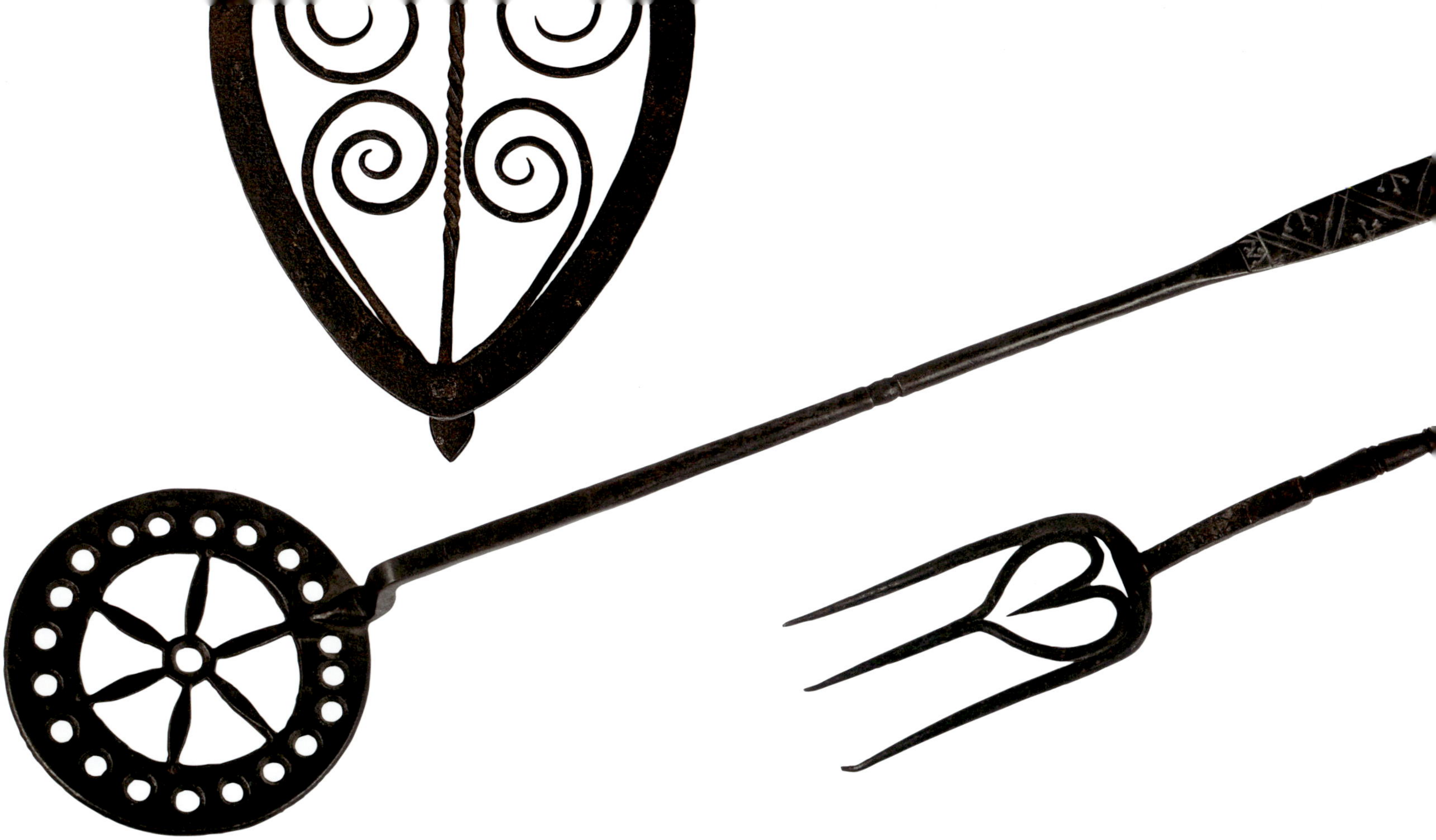

BECOMING AMERICA

HIGHLIGHTS FROM THE JONATHAN AND KARIN FIELDING COLLECTION OF FOLK ART

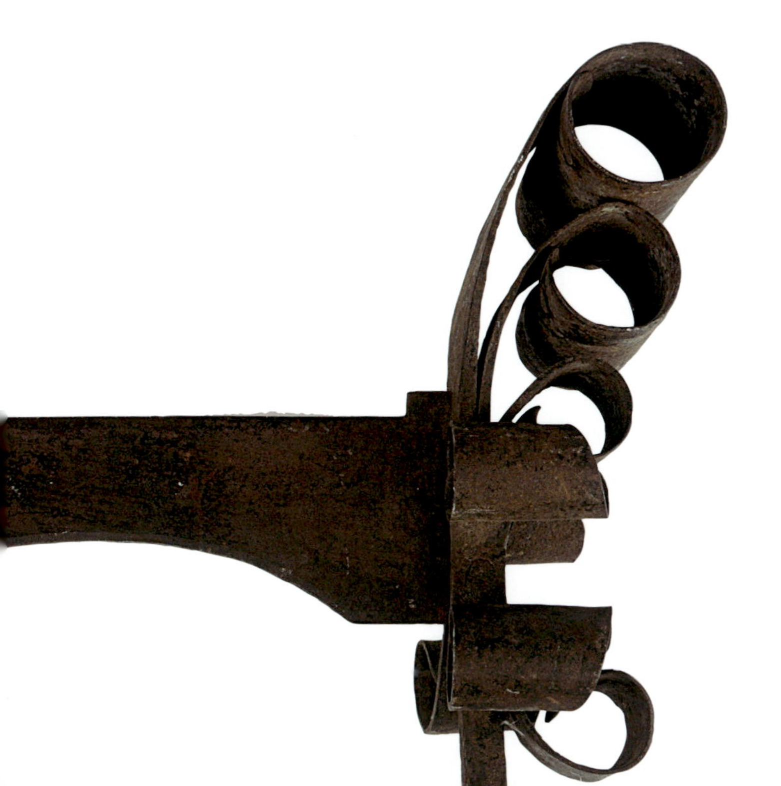

CONTRIBUTORS
John Demos
Jonathan and Karin Fielding
Robin Jaffee Frank
James Glisson, Editor
Stacy C. Hollander
Christina Nielsen
Sumpter Priddy
Elizabeth V. Warren
David Wheatcroft

THE HUNTINGTON LIBRARY,
ART MUSEUM, AND
BOTANICAL GARDENS
SAN MARINO, CALIFORNIA

DISTRIBUTED BY
YALE UNIVERSITY PRESS,
NEW HAVEN AND LONDON

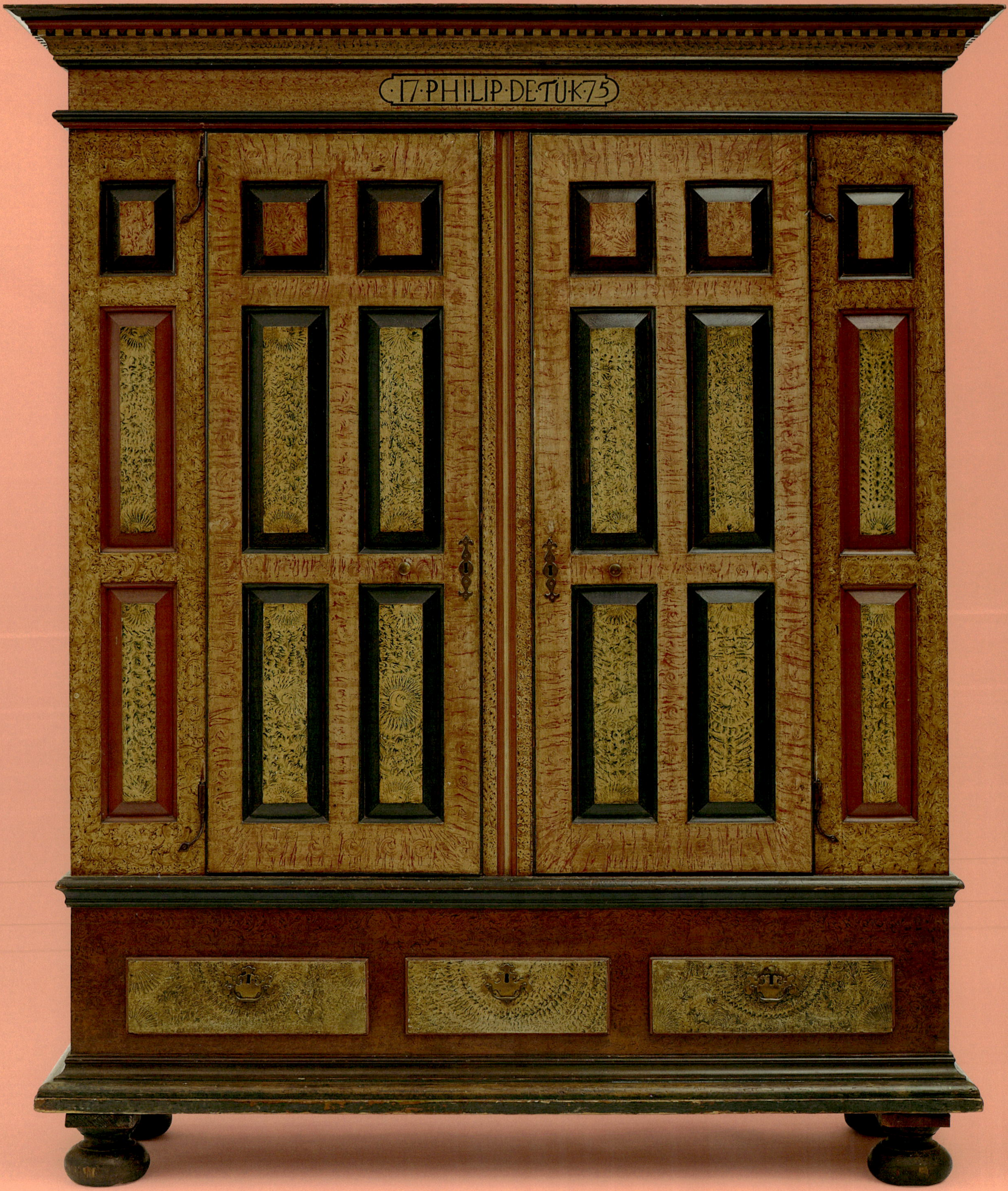

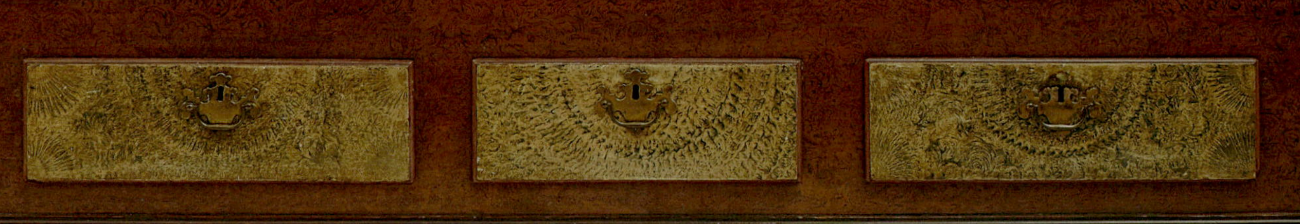
·17·PHI·LIP·DE·TÜ·K·75

Contents

Director's Foreword
CHRISTINA NIELSEN
7

Origins
JONATHAN AND KARIN FIELDING
11

The Old, Forever-New Things
An Introduction to Becoming America
JAMES GLISSON
25

Forty Years in Folk Art
A Conversation with David Wheatcroft
JAMES GLISSON
33

Early American Furniture
Its Making, Its Meaning, Its Pleasures
JOHN DEMOS
55

The Kaleidoscope and the Fancy Style of the Early Republic, 1790–1840
SUMPTER PRIDDY
85

"Husband Every Hour"
Early American Textiles in the Fielding Collection
ELIZABETH V. WARREN
109

In Imitation of Nature
Landscape and Still-Life Painting in Early America
STACY C. HOLLANDER
141

"The Human Heart by Which We Live"
Family Portraits from Cradle to Grave
ROBIN JAFFEE FRANK
171

Acknowledgments
253

Index
255

Illustrations and Photo Credits
263

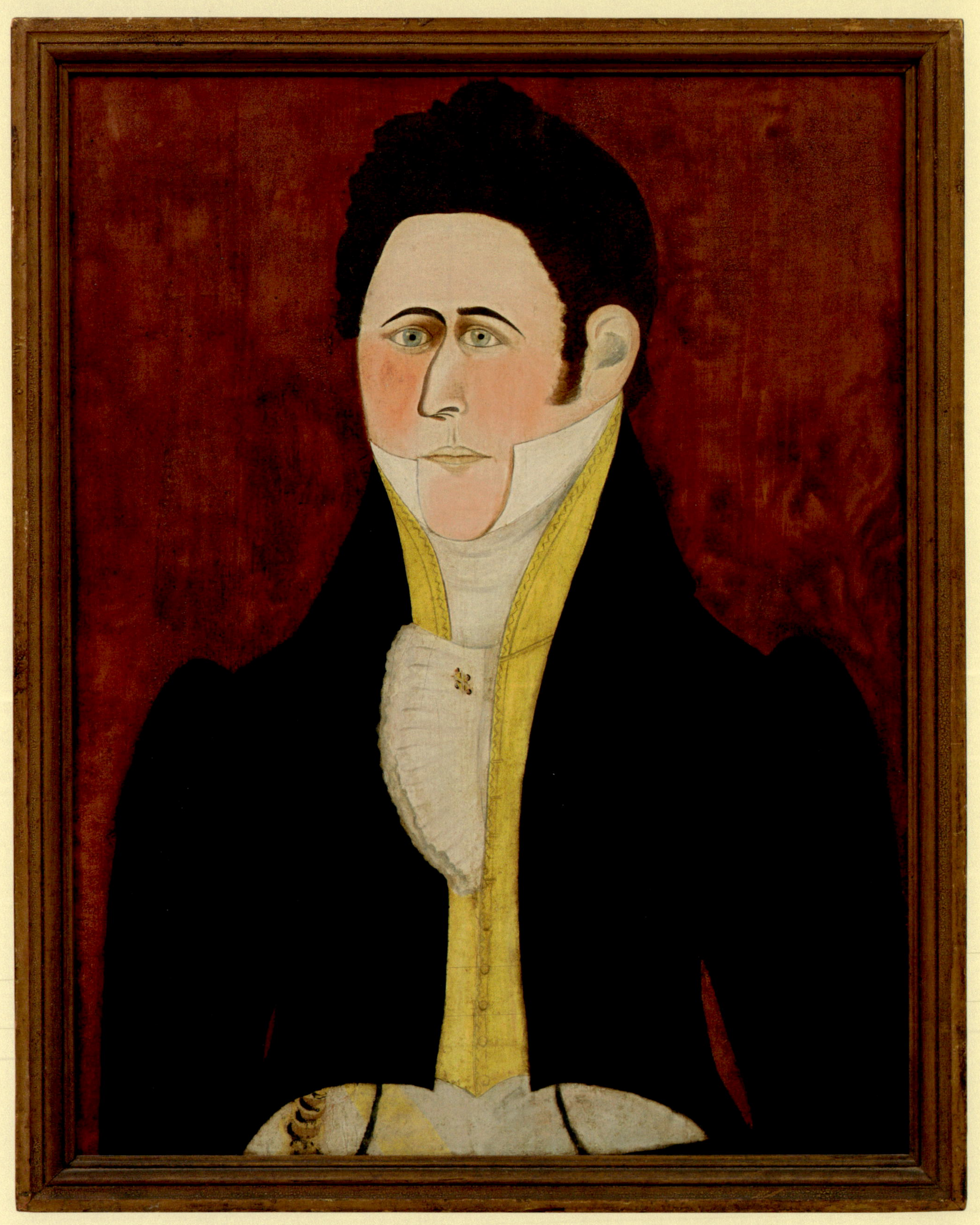

Director's Foreword

PAGE 4:

Painted Schrank

Berks County, Pennsylvania
Late eighteenth century

Poplar and paint
81 × 60 × 21¾ in.

Inscription:
"17 Philip Detük 75"

Details on pp. 46, 48

2018.10

A. ELLIS (ACTIVE 1830S)

Portrait of Albert G. Gilman

Readfield-Waterville area, Maine
1831

Oil on basswood panel
29 × 23 in.

L2015.41.173

The Fielding Collection of early American folk art brings the past to life before our eyes. The objects reproduced in this book and the objects displayed in The Huntington's Jonathan and Karin Fielding Wing of the Virginia Steele Scott Galleries of American Art introduce us to people who lived hundreds of years ago, on the other coast. Some of their names have been lost in the mists of time, like the man who once hauled ice through a field somewhere in New England with a giant pair of tongs (p. 9). Other names have been immortalized by the artworks they made or commissioned. A remarkable sampler stitched by Eunice Hooper, a nine-year-old from Marblehead, Massachusetts, attests to her astonishing skill at embroidery (p. 131). A portrait of Albert G. Gilman, a schoolteacher from Mount Vernon, Maine, speaks volumes about his personality, greeting the viewer with a direct gaze and jaunty attire (opposite page). Such objects hold the memories of the people who once crafted and made them, the people who worked or played with them, and the bystanders who simply marveled at their craftsmanship and their often ingenious or whimsical forms.

The extraordinary collection that Jonathan and Karin Fielding have assembled is widely recognized as one of the finest of its kind. What began as a simple desire to fill a historic home in coastal Maine with appropriate furnishings soon blossomed into a passionate pursuit that has allowed them to bring together an enviable group of outstanding and rare furniture, fine needlework, painted portraits, quilts, and other decorative arts from the late seventeenth to the late nineteenth century. Over the past twenty-five years, these objects have also connected the Fieldings to an astonishing array of people: other collectors, curators, dealers,

Ice Tongs
ca. 1850
Wrought iron
37 × 5¼ × 32⅛ in.
2016.25.129

philanthropists, and scholars, a number of whom have contributed their expertise and their enthusiasm for American folk art to this volume.

The values that have guided Jonathan and Karin in other parts of their lives are equally apparent in their approach to collecting. It should come as no surprise that two people who have dedicated their careers, their time, and their talents to civic, cultural, educational, and public health–related causes should bring a similarly democratizing approach to this passion. Rather than focusing on high art produced for early American elites in Boston, New York, or Philadelphia, they have championed the wondrously and lovingly crafted items owned by the burgeoning middle class of farmers, merchants, and ministers in more rural areas. The Fieldings' natural impulse to do good in the world has also prompted their desire to share the collection with as broad a public as possible and to have it impact the greatest number of lives.

We are enormously grateful that they have chosen The Huntington for such a transformative gift. Over 250 items are now on view in *Becoming America: Highlights from the Jonathan and Karin Fielding Collection*, installed in the Jonathan and Karin Fielding Wing, a substantial addition to the Virginia Steele Scott Galleries of American Art. Designed by Frederick Fisher and Partners, the display showcases early American paintings, furniture, and works of decorative art in dramatic, colorful installations that allow visitors to see the visual links between this material and other parts of the collection. For example, the form and attention to craft displayed in the furniture and decorative arts recall The Huntington's superb Arts and Crafts holdings, while the organic, seemingly free-form designs on the painted wooden boxes foreshadow the turn to abstraction in twentieth-century painting, on view in adjacent galleries.

The Fielding Collection is an unparalleled cultural and educational resource that has catalyzed our ability to tell the story of American art in an unbroken narrative across several centuries, up to the present. It has similarly galvanized our American curatorial team, led by James Glisson, the editor of this catalogue; James has brought his keen eye and his indefatigable intellectual curiosity to bear on this publication. The Fieldings' generosity and unfailing commitment to education have also allowed Elee Wood, former Curator/Educator, Fielding Collection for Early American Art, to design an object-based curriculum that is widely available online. This pedagogical initiative, as with the installation in the Fielding galleries and the presentation of the collection in this catalogue, allows each object at hand to connect the past with the present—all with an eye to the future.

Christina Nielsen
Hannah and Russel Kully Director of the Art Museum
The Huntington Library, Art Museum, and Botanical Gardens

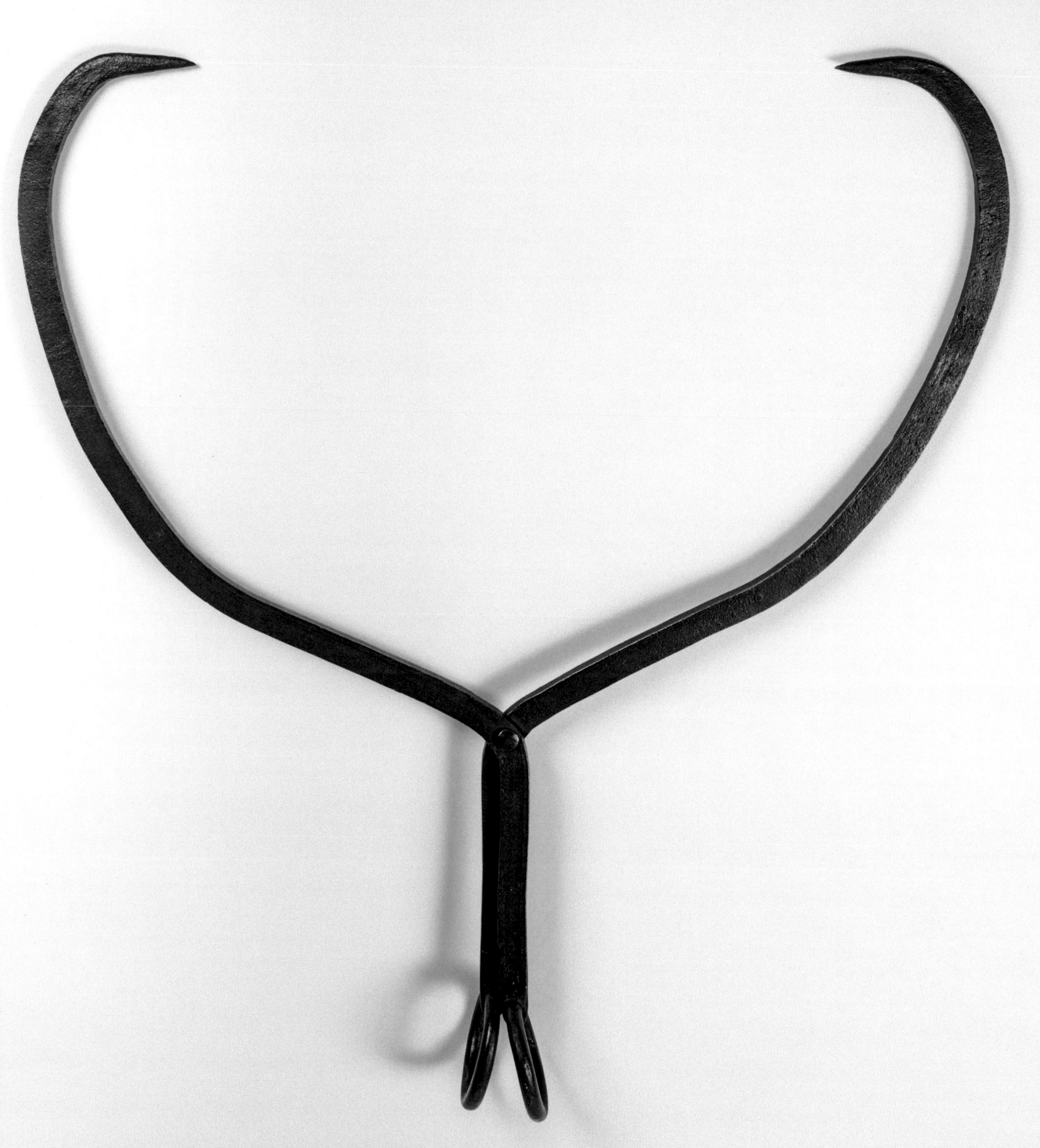

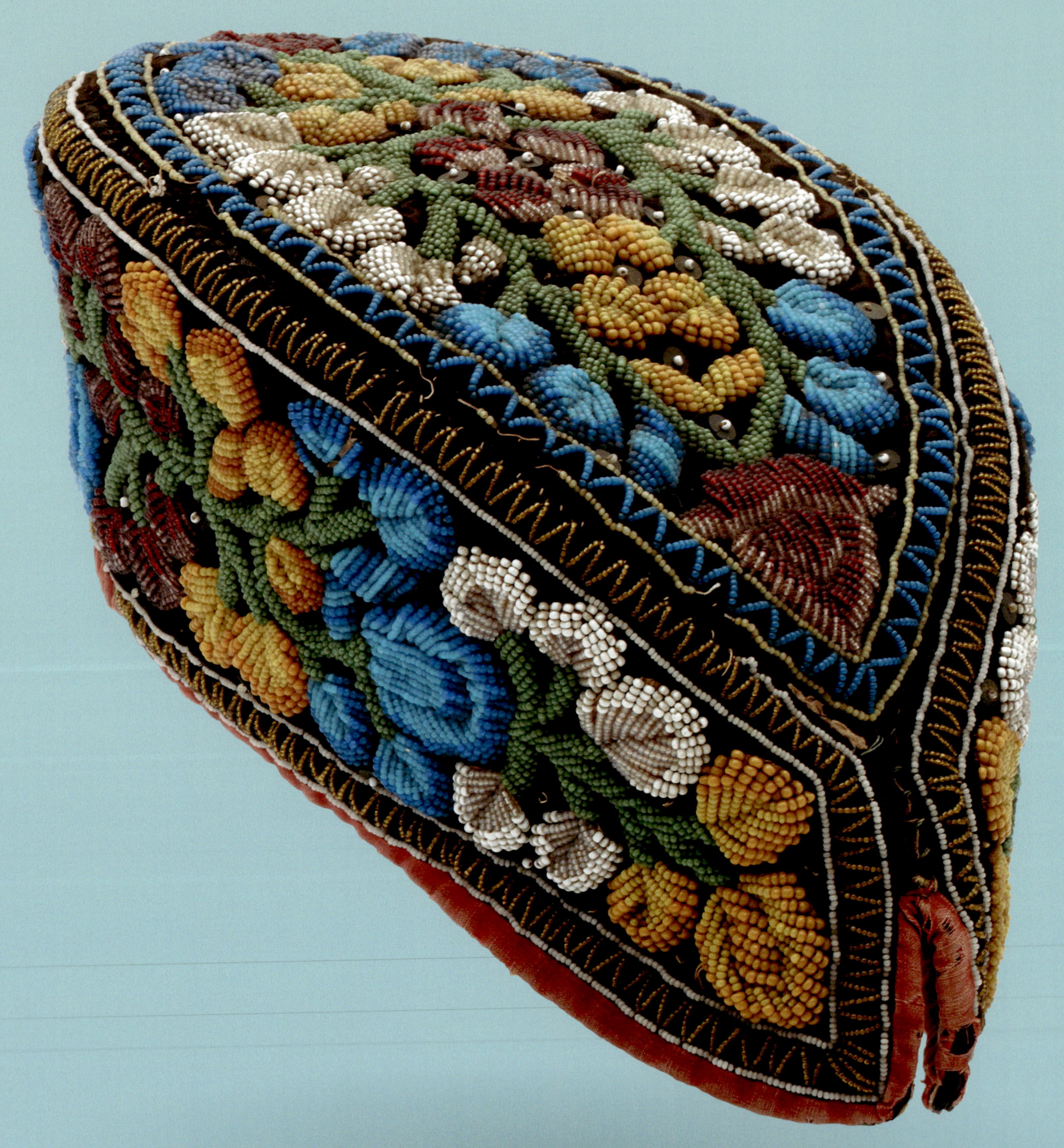

Origins

JONATHAN AND KARIN FIELDING

It all started with a house. While on a trip to coastal Maine in the early 1990s, we were seduced by the charms of a small farmhouse built in 1768 and located on a quiet cove with stunning views of islands and lobster boats. The house, its setting, and the surrounding rural community could not have been more different from our home base in Los Angeles. It was that contrast that may have compelled us to buy it. Our decision certainly had nothing to do with the convenience of getting to Maine from California.

Our first thought about furnishing the home was: Antique house? Let's fill it with antique furniture! We knew almost nothing about antiques when we started down that road. We had begun collecting quilts years earlier, and one of us had, as a student, run an art gallery featuring twentieth-century prints and drawings, but we had never pursued paintings or decorative objects. Undeterred by our lack of knowledge, we began browsing the many antique shops in the area and frequenting local auctions to find pieces from the eighteenth and nineteenth centuries that might work in our home, both stylistically and comfortably.

We summoned our courage and started buying, gravitating toward particular objects for their originality and individuality, rather than their sophistication. Because of the modesty of our home and its rural location, we focused primarily on furniture created and used by people who lived and worked in the country. From furniture, we moved on to paintings, pottery, needlework, ironwork, lighting devices, and other decorative and utilitarian items. In many cases, we knew little about these categories and simply bought objects that appealed to us on a visceral level. For example, we were wowed by what we later found out was a

Niagara Beadwork Hat
Haudenosaunee (Iroquois)
ca. 1850
Beadwork on black cloth and velvet
3¾ × 11 × 6¼ in.
2016.25.5

BOSTON & SANDWICH GLASS COMPANY

Lamps

ca. 1828

Free-blown glass and tin
Maximum height: 4¾ in.

2016.25.87–.90

glengarry hat (p. 10), Scottish in origin but made by the Iroquois people to wear and sell as souvenirs to visitors of Niagara Falls. It appealed to us because of its colorful embroidery using beads and ribbon in a style that we learned was popular with adults and children in the mid- to late nineteenth century. (For more on the glengarry hat, see the discussion by Elizabeth V. Warren in this volume, p. 124.)

Lighting devices also greatly interested us in terms of their innovations in the quest for greater light within the home. Early American households lived in near darkness after sunset, and candles were expensive and time-consuming to produce. Our collection demonstrates the progression of efforts to bring light indoors. It starts with simple flint devices, then moves to mirrored sconces, whale-oil lamps, and glass camphine lamps, which produced a strong light but were apt to explode. Camphine or "burning fluid" was a volatile distilled turpentine product. It became obsolete when kerosene from oil wells in Pennsylvania was introduced around 1860 (p. 28). One lighting device we found, dated from around 1720 (p. 15), provided a way to raise or lower two candles by means of a clever sawtooth ratchet; it is distinctive for its quirky sculptural quality, construction methods, and decorative details. Its maker was motivated not by commercial gain but by the needs of his household. (For more on lighting technology, see the discussion by James Glisson in this volume, p. 26.)

As new collectors, we made mistakes and learned from them, sometimes trading up or selling an item to await one with a better form or finish. We developed a small library, studied its volumes and auction catalogs, visited collections in private homes and museums, and relied on trusted antique dealers to help us hone our skills to recognize quality and decide

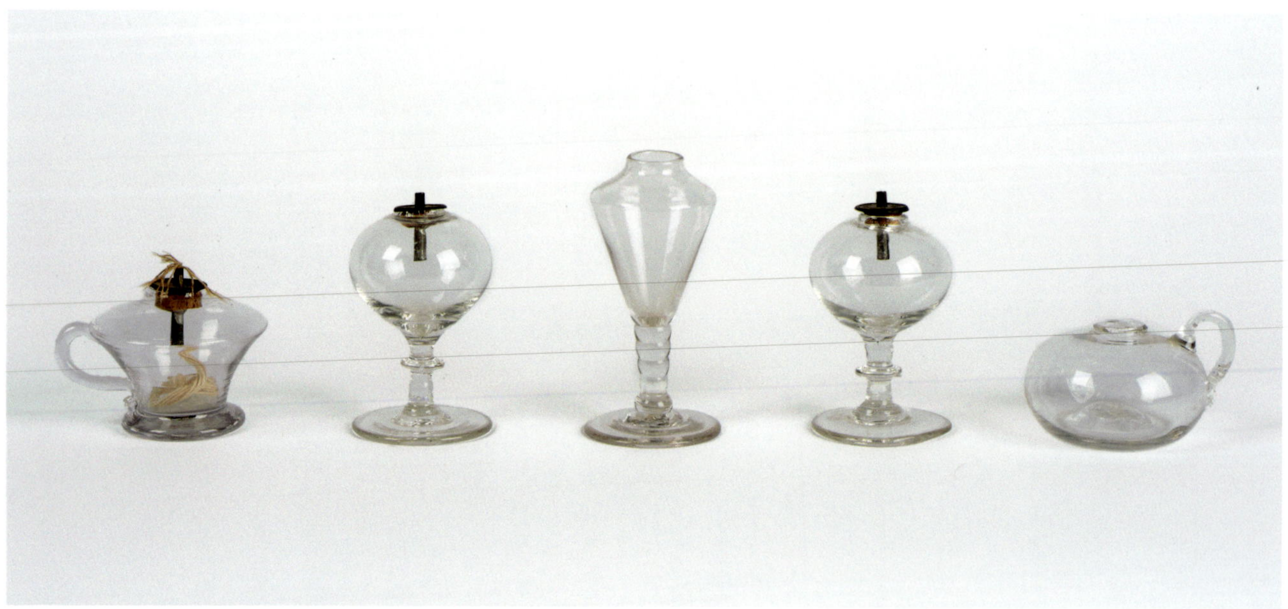

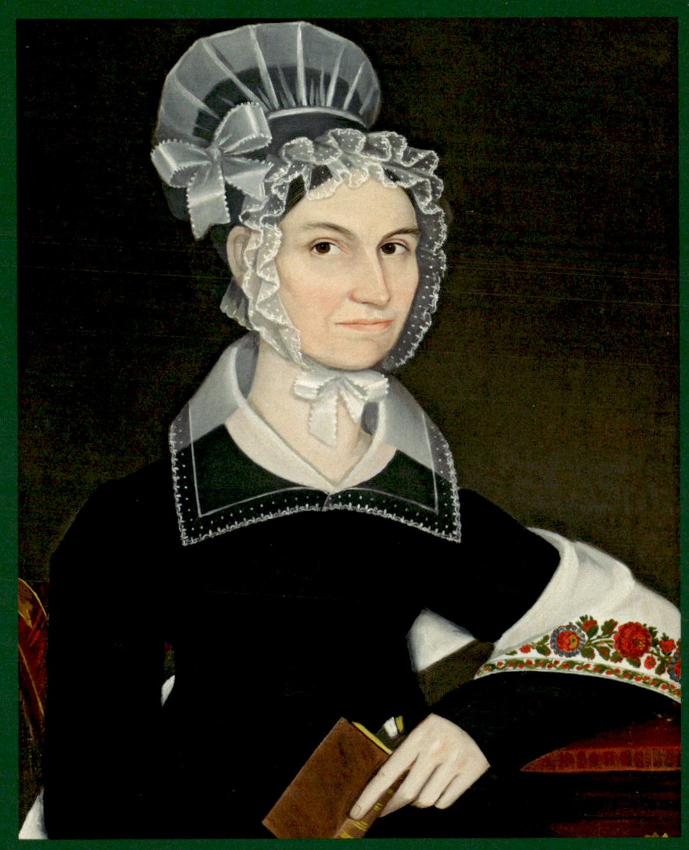

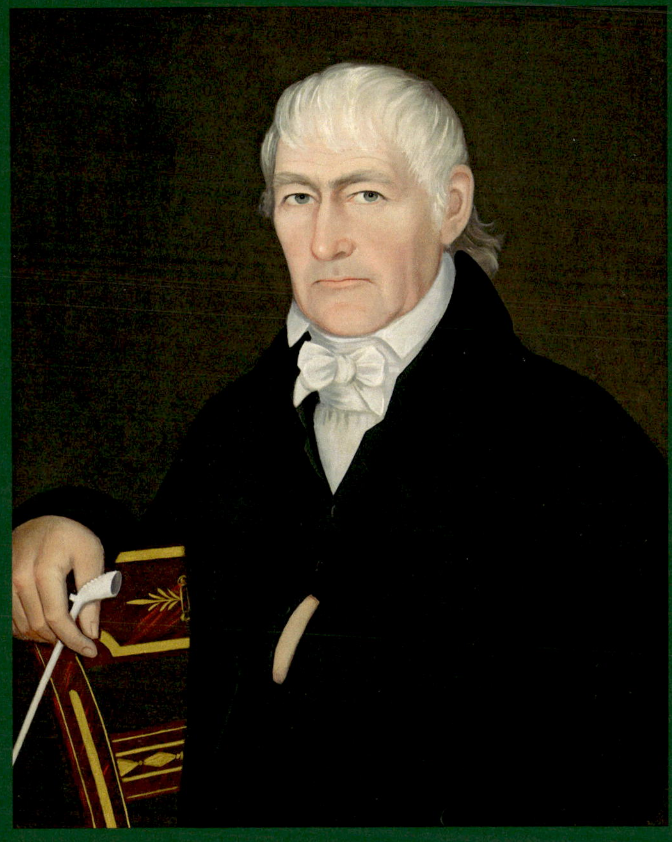

AMMI PHILLIPS (1788–1865)

Portraits of a Man and Woman, Members of the Van Keuren Family

ca. 1825–30

Oil on canvas
Each: 29¼ × 23¼ in.

Detail on p. 23

2016.25.107, .106

what was a fair price. (For more on the collection's formation, see the interview with dealer David Wheatcroft in this volume, pp. 33–53.) Over time, we refined our taste and became better at discerning the quality of form, identifying inconspicuous repairs, and determining whether the surface was original. And we learned that the information provided in auction catalogs can't always be trusted. There is no substitute for being with an object, to feel its essence, gauge its attractiveness, and carefully examine it for "apologies." Finally, we learned to show restraint and discipline, to wait for the best examples of a particular style. But no matter how much we learned, for major purchases—whether through auctions or private dealers—we also consulted the real experts, those with strong reputations, deep knowledge of the material, and an unerring eye.

Though we loved our summer sojourns in Maine, once we returned to Los Angeles, we missed being surrounded by the pieces we had collected. Eventually, our desire to live with our early American art and antiques led us to start bringing our favorite pieces to Los Angeles, where it gave us great joy to constantly see their beauty and to wonder how satisfying they must have been for their makers, who exhibited such imagination, creativity, and skill. That is when it dawned on us that we were no longer just enthusiasts or aficionados, but true collectors.

Bringing our collection to Los Angeles taught us how little people on the West Coast knew or cared about early American folk art. People would come to our home and look around questioningly. They would ask: What is this? Why would you be interested in these old things? Worse still, many said nothing at all, walking past our beloved objects with little interest or appreciation, perhaps thinking to themselves that we had picked them up at yard sales.

That's when we recognized that we wanted people not only to enjoy these uniquely American decorative objects but also to understand and appreciate their importance to the history of our country. We wanted to make our collection widely available as a teaching tool for schoolchildren and adults alike—the objects deserved to be in a place where anyone could experience them.

HIGHLIGHTS AND THEMES

The pieces from our collection that are reproduced in this catalogue date from the late 1600s to the late 1800s; they are primarily from New England, with some examples from Pennsylvania, New York, and New Jersey. A few objects in the collection were made by Native Americans. They are the work of settlers who brought skills from their homelands along with art, books, and other printed materials to serve as inspiration, and then passed those skills on to a new generation. Many of these artists and craftspeople were entirely self-taught, while others learned on the job, some through formal apprenticeships. They were blacksmiths, potters, cabinet makers, house painters, sign painters, sailors, housewives, and schoolgirls. They were itinerant portrait painters, quilt makers, men with a workshop in the

Ratchet Lighting Device
ca. 1720
Oak and maple with paint
30⅜ × 12½ × 7⅛ in.
Inscription: "D. Sherman"
L2015.41.128

barn, teachers, women with skills in needlework and weaving, hooked-rug makers, and young girls learning to read, write, and sew. They shared a quest for beauty and utility as original as their experience in a new, untamed country. Eventually they became Americans with a bold, self-assured view of what constituted quality craftsmanship and attractive art. These innovators forged the way for generations of artists and craftspeople to follow.

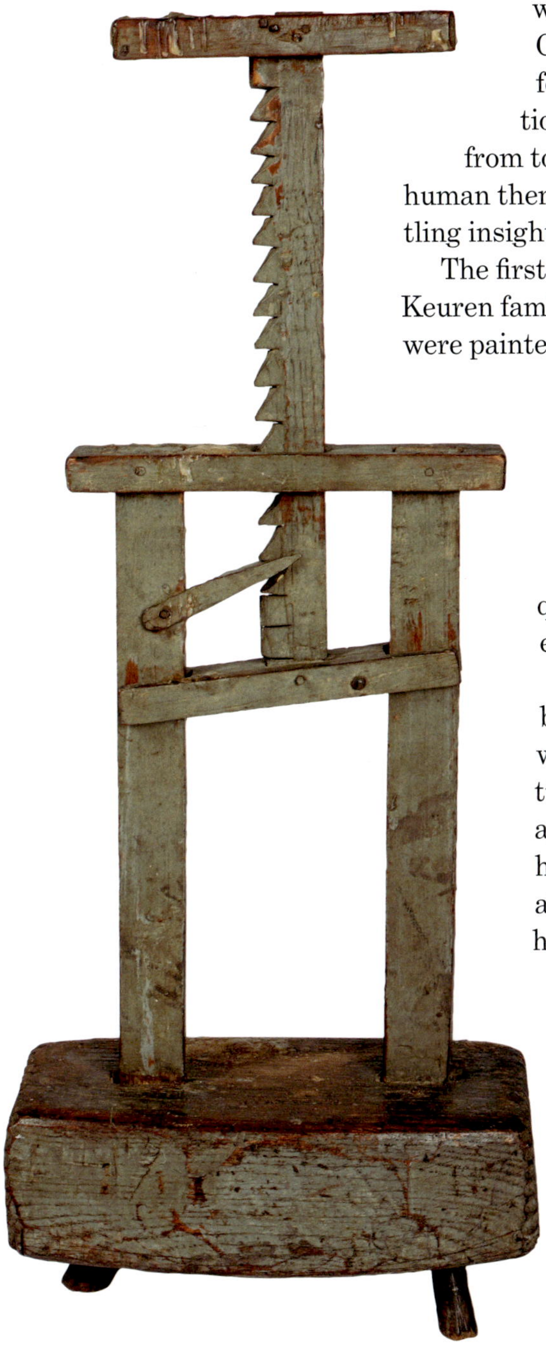

Some of these settlers' faces are familiar to us today. While most museums with early American portraits feature the work of such iconic academic painters as John Singleton Copley, Charles Willson Peale, and Gilbert Stuart, the rural folk paintings we encountered in antique shops and auctions were created by self-taught artists who often traveled from town to town advertising their skills. Their portraits reflect human themes like prosperity, taste, and style, and they provide startling insights into the lives of ordinary people.

The first two portraits we purchased were of members of the Van Keuren family of Upstate New York, most likely Ulster County. They were painted by the itinerant artist Ammi Phillips, who was active in Connecticut, Massachusetts, and New York. He began his career in 1809, when he was twenty-one (p. 13). Phillips is thought to have been entirely self-taught, but he may have served as an apprentice to another artist at a young age. To attract customers, he placed advertisements in rural newspapers to announce that he—a skilled and quick portrait painter with good prices and satisfied customers—would be staying in a nearby town.

The two Van Keuren portraits reflect the style preferred by the artist's customers, the emerging rural gentry. They were painted between 1825 and 1830, before the introduction of the daguerreotype in about 1840. The two subjects appear prosperous and dignified. The distinguished-looking husband wears a dark suit with a white collar, his arm casually resting on the back of a decorated chair and a pipe in his hand, the other hand tucked into his jacket, as was the style at the time. His wife is dressed in black with a diaphanous lace collar, a colorful shawl, and an elaborate bonnet, all at the height of fashion. She holds a book, indicating her literacy. Both appear affluent and refined, showing their family's place in society and reminding future generations of their forebears.

Later, we were excited to add to the collection a portrait of Albert G. Gilman by Maine artist A. Ellis (p. 6). Painted in 1831, this stunning depiction showcases Gilman in a black high-collar cutaway coat, a yellow vest, and a ruffled white shirtfront fitted to his face in the Jacksonian manner. He has an aquiline nose and deep-set blue eyes, a generous shock of brown hair, and long sideburns. Because the painting is relatively flat in its presentation and lacks realism, it has a modern feel. Unusual curves and half-moons, especially in the coat and ruffle, give it a rhythmic, geometric quality, and even evoke the work of the twentieth-century Italian painter Amedeo Modigliani. We know almost nothing about the artist, but we do know that this painting is of his own self-inspired creation and vision and is very abstract and unusual for its time.

Two of our favorite furniture pieces are chests of drawers, but of very different styles. One is a carved cherrywood, bonnet-top Chippendale-style high chest of drawers made about 1774 and attributed to Eliphalet Chapin's workshop in the Connecticut River Valley (opposite page). The top of the chest is highly decorative, with a molded swan-neck crest, an elaborate cartouche, latticework, and finials. The chest rests on graceful cabriolet legs with claw feet. Thanks to family records, we know that its original owners were Samuel and Jerusha Wolcott and that it may have been part of Jerusha's dowry. The Wolcotts were a well-known and wealthy family in East Windsor, Connecticut. Three members of the family served as governors of Connecticut, and Samuel's father, Erastus Wolcott, had been a general in the Revolutionary War.

This elegant, sophisticated Chapin high chest sharply contrasts with the painted lift-top chest of drawers created about 1830 in New York State or Connecticut (p. 57). This country chest in the Federal style is constructed of poplar, a much lighter wood than the Chapin chest. It features a molded top that lifts open over two sham drawers, three working drawers, and bracket feet. While the style is simple, the decoration is anything but. Faux painting was often used by craftsmen to emulate the grain of a more elegant and expensive wood like mahogany. But the finish on this chest goes far beyond trying to make poplar look like a pricier wood. The green-black faux grain detailing on a mustard ground is bold and playful, providing a decorative feature that no one would mistake for wood. Indeed, it is a creative artistic statement all of its own, illustrating the artist's pride in being free to express his creativity in a new and exciting direction.

Throughout our collecting, we have been drawn to everyday objects that have both utility and beauty. Stoneware, for instance, was important to every American household prior to refrigeration. It was used to store a variety of foods, including butter, pickled vegetables, salted meats and fish, water, beer, and wine, and it was a material used to make serving pitchers, milk pans, mugs, and baking dishes. What particularly interested us were the beautiful forms of these pieces, expertly decorated with flowers, animals, and other patterns and designs, all in an arresting cobalt blue.

One of our favorite pieces of pottery is an exceedingly rare stoneware jar with an incised decoration (pp. 20–21). Created around 1750 and found only recently in New York State, it is one of the finest known examples of intact

ATTRIBUTED TO ELIPHALET CHAPIN (1741–1807)

High Chest of Drawers

East Windsor, Connecticut
ca. 1774

Cherry, eastern white pine, and yellow pine
86½ × 39 × 20 in.

L2015.41.97

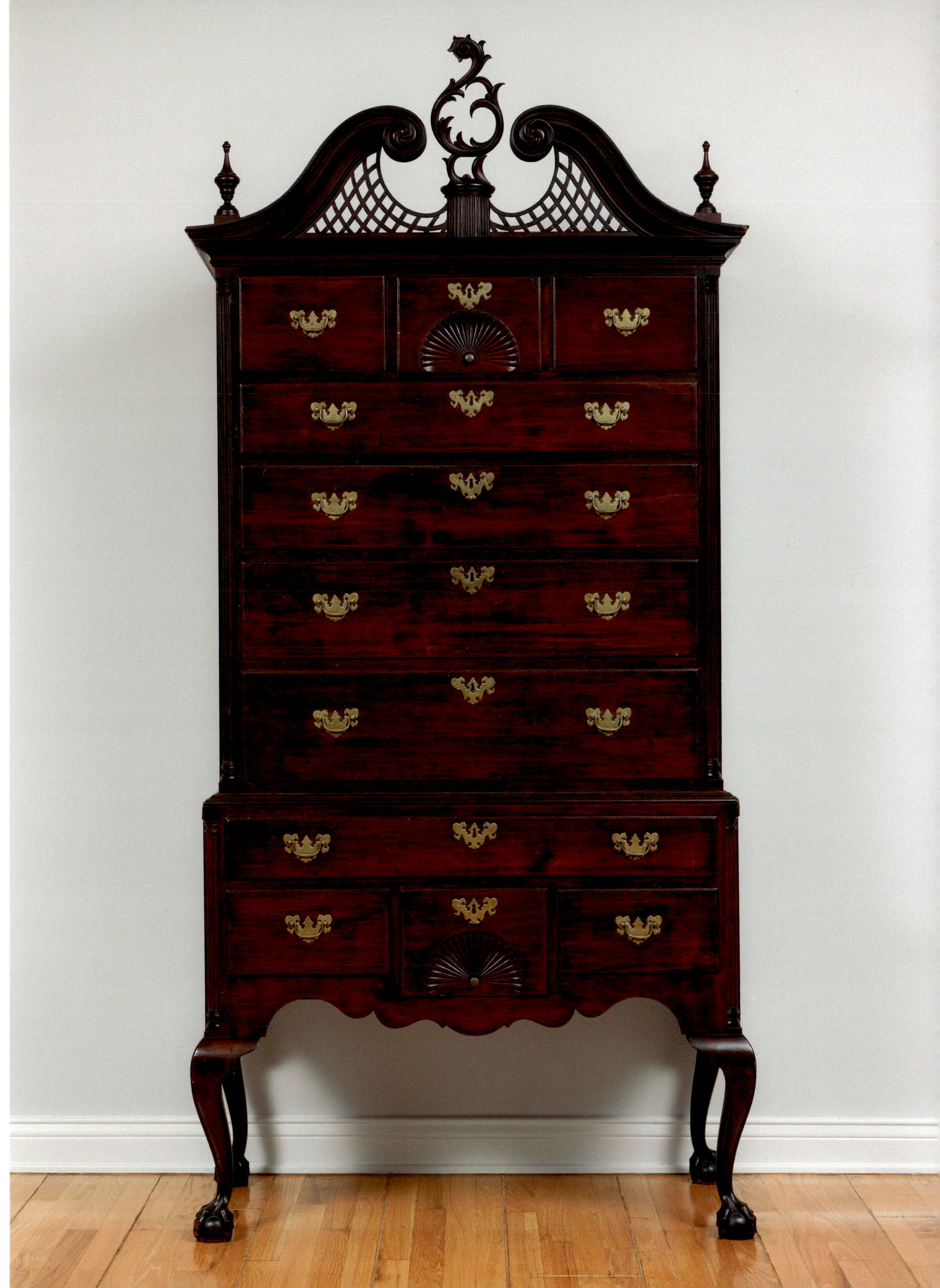

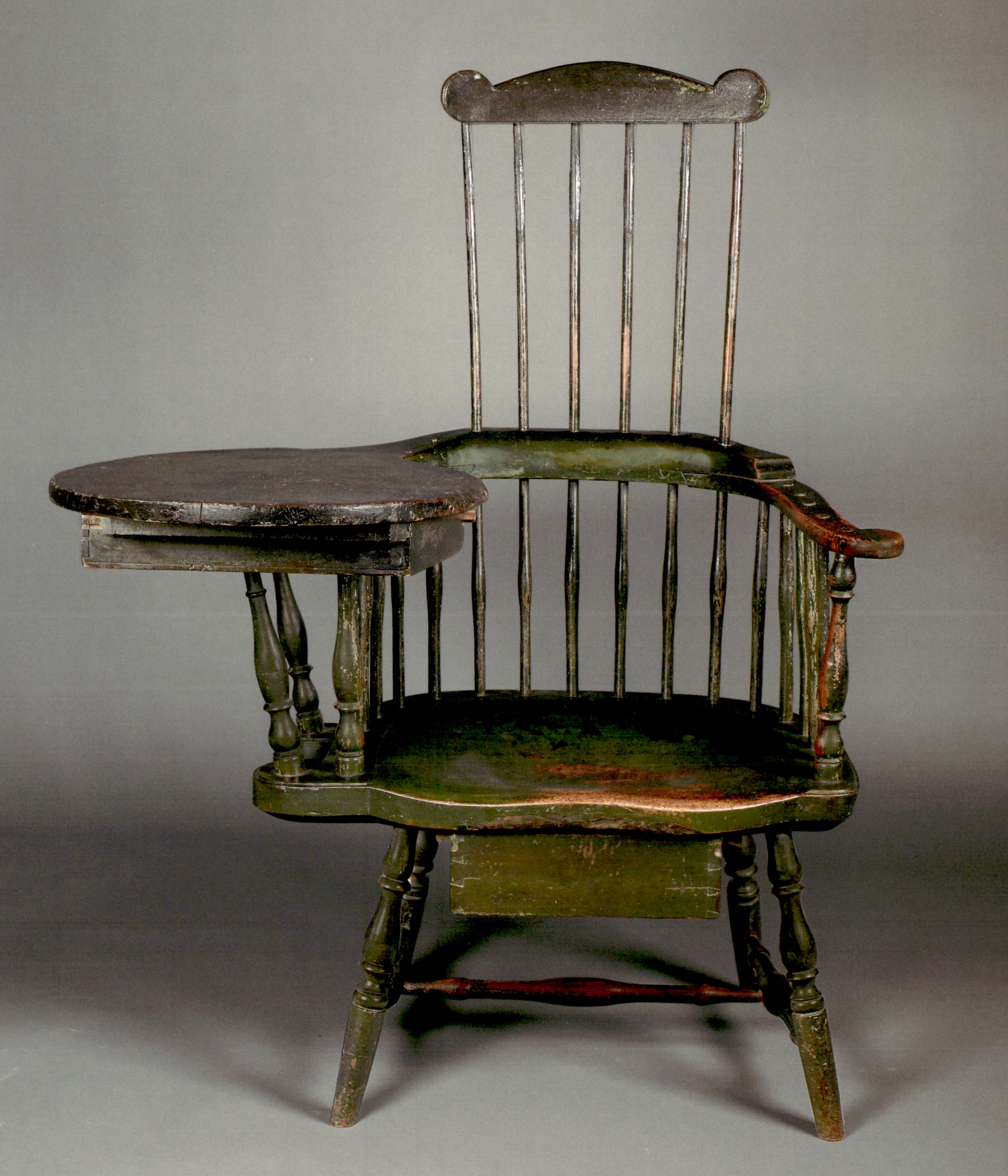

ATTRIBUTED TO EBENEZER TRACY SR. (1744–1803)

High-Back Windsor Armchair with Writing Arm

Lisbon, Connecticut
Late eighteenth century

Wood and green paint
36⅞ × 36¼ × 31 in.

See also p. 78

L2015.41.112

colonial American stoneware. The oval-shaped, thin-walled jar has a rounded foot, a semi-square rim, and ribbed vertical handles. The front has a charming and expansive decoration with a checkerboard-patterned sunflower emanating from an open-handled urn, with the initials "IS" below. On the shoulder is a cobalt heart and circular design, and stripes appear along the rim and base. On the reverse is an incised and cobalt-highlighted daisy and looping line drawing surrounded by an abstract labyrinth design. The side of the jar is incised with the initials "IPR." The piece's distinctive checkerboard design relates to Westerwald stoneware imported from Germany and produced during the period as well as earlier. The use of alternating cobalt-decorated and undecorated incising can also be noted on mid-eighteenth-century shards excavated at the Kemple Pottery of Ringoes, New Jersey; the Morgan Pottery of Cheesequake, New Jersey; and the Remmey and Crolius potteries of Manhattan.

Another beautiful everyday object that caught our attention was the Windsor chair, introduced by English settlers in the first half of the eighteenth century. Its main feature is a solid wooden seat into which the chair back and legs are pushed into drilled holes, in contrast to the standard chairs of the time, in which the back legs and uprights are continuous. The seat was often carved into a saddle shape and then smoothed for comfort. American Windsors were usually painted black, green, or red. As the chair was built to last, an older one might be updated with a new color or with gold-stenciled designs popular in the nineteenth century. The Windsor chair, originally made by hand, is still a popular form today, with both machine-made and handmade versions available in many styles and colors and a wide range of prices.

Our collection has several examples of Windsor chair forms, including comb-back, sack-back, birdcage, and fan-back. But for us, an eighteenth-century writing armchair stands out for its beauty and utility (opposite page). This form of armchair was used by people who did a lot of writing—ministers, lawyers, and teachers. With its stately stance, generous proportions, and assured craftsmanship, the chair is considered a masterpiece of American Windsor chair making. Details in its design and construction point to Connecticut maker Ebenezer Tracy Sr. and suggest that it may be one of his earliest models for a writing armchair. The crest design, with its gentle arch and rounded, upturned terminals, predates those with fully rounded scrolls or pronounced hooks. Thought to have its original finish, it is painted dark green, a popular color at the time of its making. It has an elegant high back with six spindles, swelled turnings below the arm rail, an oversize writing surface with a drawer and candle slide beneath, a deeply shaped seat with a scalloped front profile, and a large drawer beneath the seat for the storage of books, writing paper, ink, and quill pens.

WHY WE CHOSE THE HUNTINGTON

We became increasingly concerned that not too many years from now, it would be extremely difficult to assemble a broad, high-quality collection of early American folk art. Over our twenty-five years of collecting, we found that the market for the best examples of folk art was rapidly diminishing. Because the supply was so limited, we felt a responsibility to democratize our collection. We wanted a permanent home where a portion of the collection's more than nine hundred objects could be displayed in long-term and changing displays and exhibitions. We sought a museum with a substantial number of visitors, adequate resources, and a demonstrated interest and expertise in American art in its many forms and periods. Ideally, we wanted an institution that already had complementary collections and a strong interest in research. It was also important to us to find a location distant from the few museums that already had large, diversified collections and preferably near enough for us to be involved in maximizing its educational impact. And, we wanted a museum that was forward-looking and open to exploring the full range of capacities that digital approaches provide. For example, virtual reality can bring the past to life, and analysis with artificial intelligence can discern patterns and trends in artworks that are imperceptible to humans.

The Huntington met all of our criteria. Gracefully situated on 207 acres with abundant space for expansion, the campus not only housed a significant art collection but also had an area that had not been permanently allocated, the perfect site to build an 8,600-square-foot ground-floor wing adjacent to its existing exhibition space for American art. And The Huntington's location near our Los Angeles home would allow us to be involved with our collection and related educational activities.

The Huntington art galleries already had a collection of American art on display, including some folk art, and an American decorative arts curator. In addition, The Huntington had one of the world's top independent libraries, used by many academic researchers. For example, John Demos, a distinguished Yale Professor of History Emeritus and the foremost authority on life in the early New England colonies, spent many months at The Huntington researching a book project. He is a contributor to this catalogue.

Jar

New York or New Jersey
ca. 1750

Stoneware
15 × 14 × 11 in.

Inscriptions: "IPR" and "IS"

Verso on opposite page

L2015.41.18

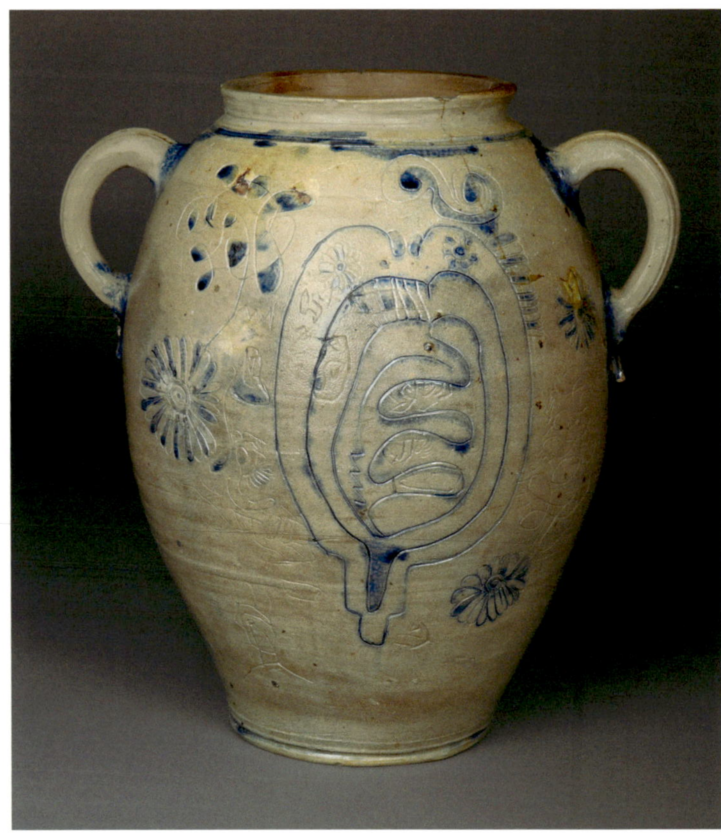

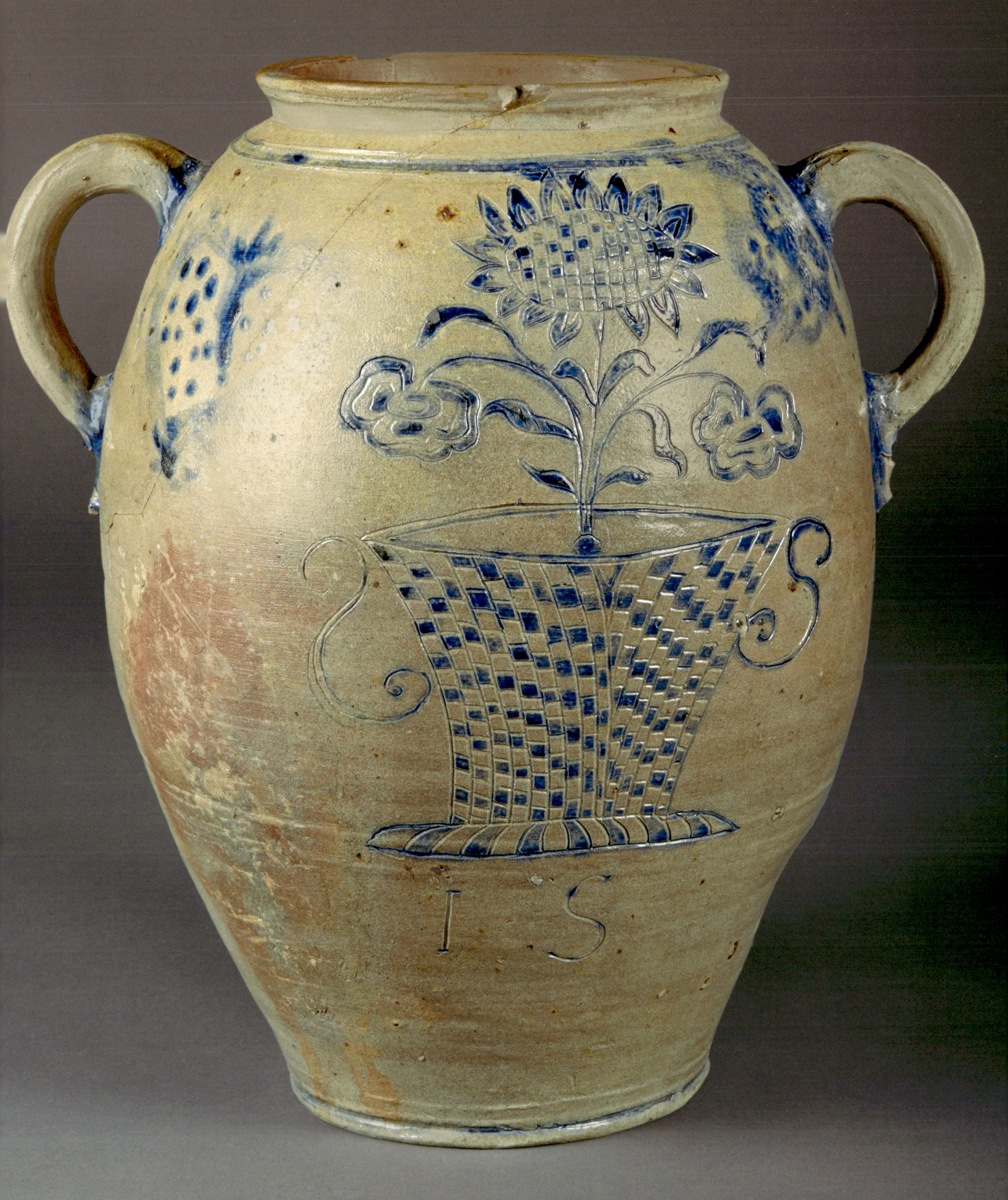
I S

ACKNOWLEDGMENTS

Our journey into the world of early American antiques and art has been exciting and satisfying. But it would have been much more challenging without the help of a number of antiques dealers and other experts. Our principal guide for collecting has been David Wheatcroft, whose fund of knowledge about folk art in its many forms always amazes us. We have also benefited from the keen eye and knowledge of several other antiques dealers, including Ross Levett, Peter Eaton, and Samuel Herrup. We greatly appreciate the assistance of scholars, with special thanks to Stacy Hollander, former Chief Curator of the American Folk Art Museum in New York. Reading her thoughtful and beautifully composed essays has been an invaluable experience in our continuing education about American folk art. We also want to acknowledge the extraordinary vision of Kevin Salatino, former Director of the Huntington Art Collections, who was instrumental in bringing our collection to The Huntington and worked closely with Los Angeles–based architect Frederick Fisher to design the installation that features the pieces in this catalogue. Many thanks go to others at The Huntington, including James Glisson, the Bradford and Christine Mishler Associate Curator of American Art, for his guidance throughout both the exhibition and catalogue design processes, and the extraordinary staff members—from curators to mount makers to registrars and everyone in between—who were part of creating the first display, *Becoming America*, in the new gallery. And a huge thank you goes to all the contributors to this catalogue for their exceptional essays that make the material come alive.

Finally, we thank our sons, Andrew and Preston, who were forced to endure many hours browsing through antique shops and attending auctions in the early years of our collecting when they would have preferred to do anything else. We can still hear them pleading, "Let's go, please," as we replied, "Only another couple of minutes," which usually turned out to be another hour. We hope this catalogue helps them feel that maybe—just maybe—it was actually worth the wait.

Jonathan and Karin Fielding are collectors of American folk art. Jonathan Fielding, MD, is the former Director and Health Officer of the Los Angeles County Department of Public Health and Distinguished Professor at UCLA in the Fielding School of Public Health and the Geffen School of Medicine. Karin Fielding spent most of her career in marketing and communications. Now retired, she is a Trustee of the American Folk Art Museum in New York and Treasurer of the American Folk Art Society. In Los Angeles, she is a member of the Board of Directors of TreePeople, an environmental nonprofit, and a current member and past Director of the Everychild Foundation.

AMMI PHILLIPS

Portrait of a Woman, Member of the Van Keuren Family (detail)

See also p. 13

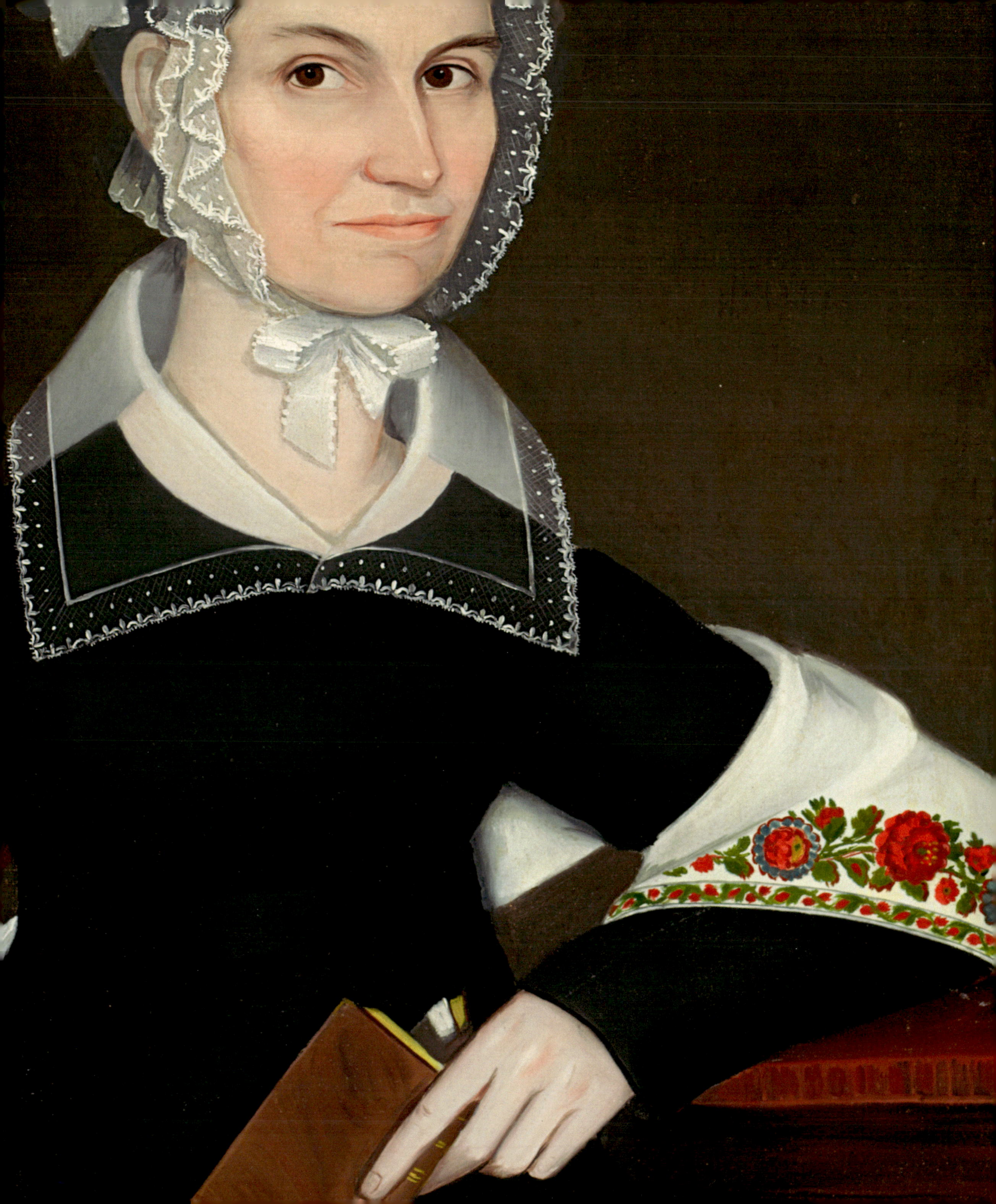

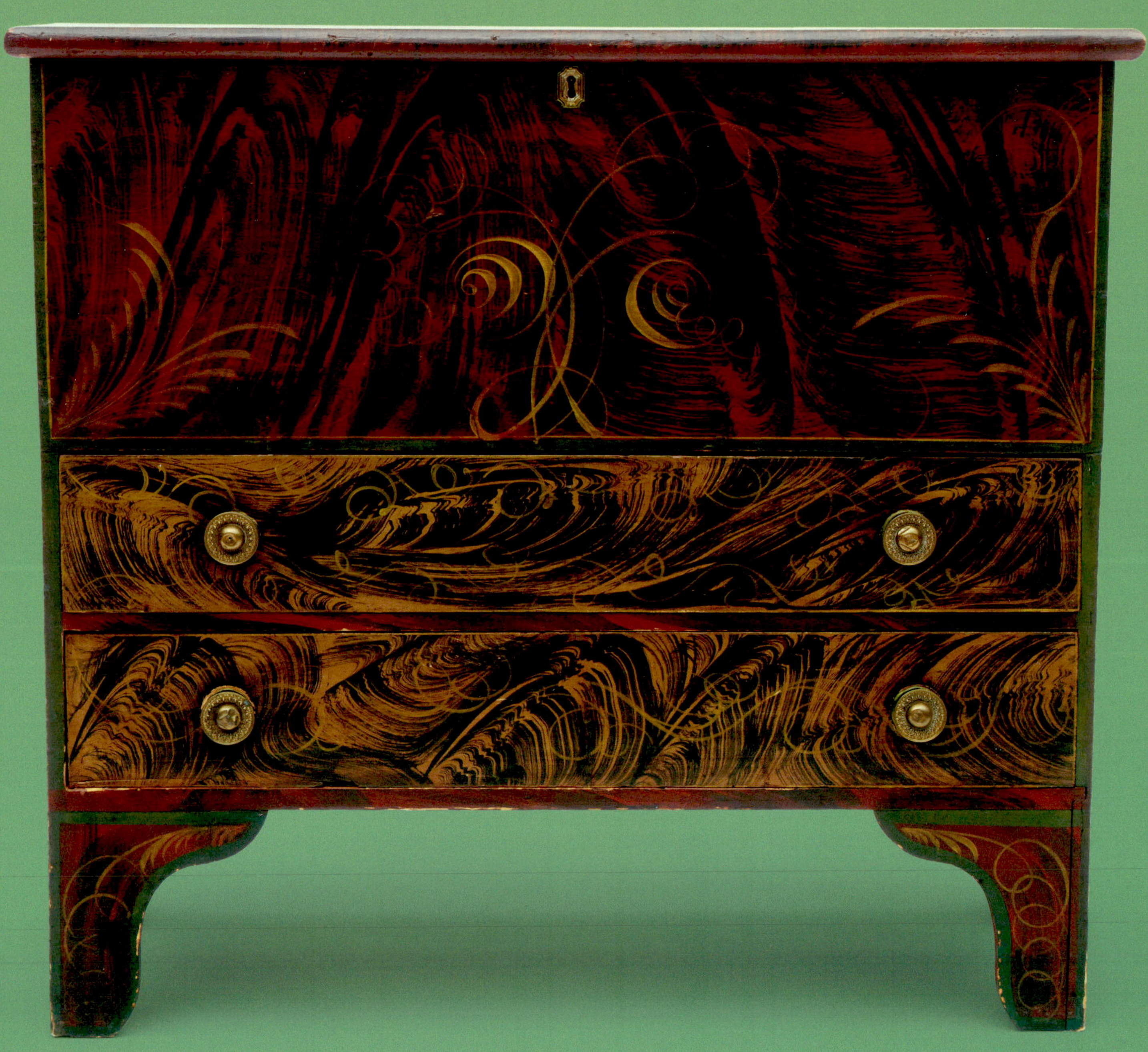

The Old, Forever-New Things

An Introduction to *Becoming America*

JAMES GLISSON

> *Every-day objects, house-chairs, carpet, bed, counterpane of the bed, him or her sleeping at night, wind blowing, indefinite noises,* [. . .]
>
> *City and country, fire-place, candle, gas-light, heater, aqueduct*
>
> —Walt Whitman, "Chants Democratic and Native American," *Leaves of Grass* (1860)

When more than 250 items from Jonathan and Karin Fielding arrived at The Huntington in the summer of 2016, those of us who were involved in the installation of *Becoming America* knew that the American galleries would never be the same again. I had seen many objects in person and, while planning the display, pored over photographs like a greedy online shopper. But it was not until the museum preparators actually unpacked the quilts, chairs, candlesticks, hats, barber pole (p. 26), and baskets that the collection's quality, diversity, and breadth came home.

Before the Fielding Wing opened, the Virginia Steele Scott Galleries of American Art primarily featured artworks made for the elite by artists and craftspeople who were trained or active in such trade centers as New York, Boston, Philadelphia, and London. Rather than the latest fashions for urban elites, the Fielding Wing mostly displays objects from the homes of the emerging middle class of rural New England. The stories of how these Americans lived can now be told. Using objects to learn about everyday life, whether cooking, leisure, sleeping, or rearing children, is known as material culture studies. With the opening of the Fielding

ELISHA MORSE

Lift-Top Blanket Chest

New Portland, Maine
ca. 1830

Pine and paint
38 × 17½ × 41½ in.

L2015.41.99

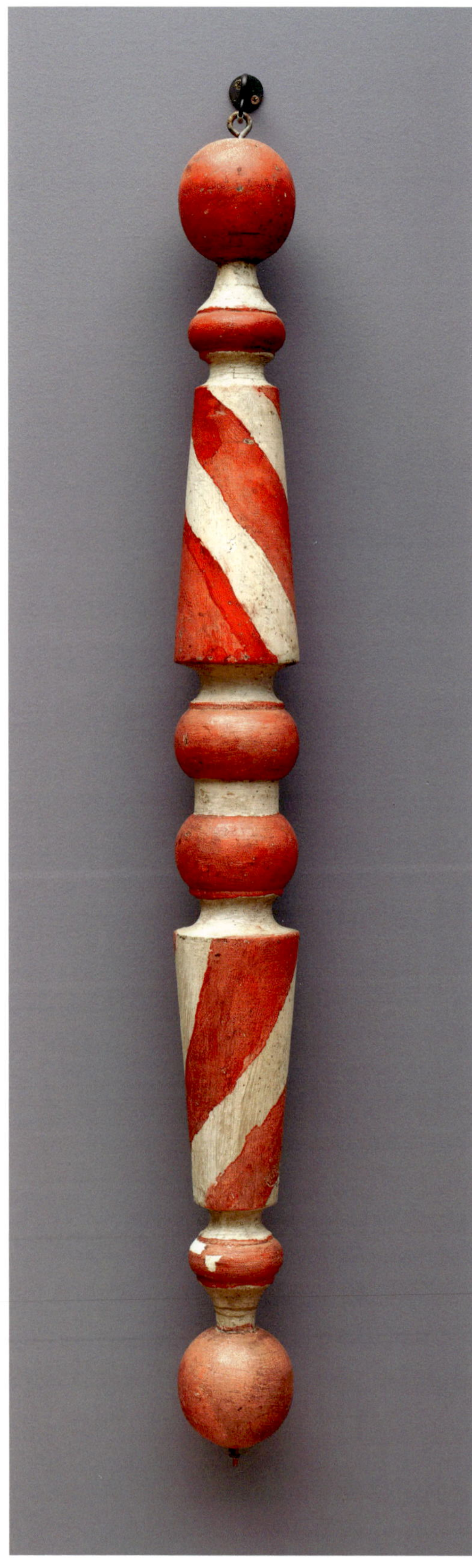

Barber Pole
Wood and paint
49¾ × 5 × 5 in.
2016.25.1

Wing, the Huntington overnight became a West Coast center for this type of research.

The collection's range and its ability to excite the imagination calls to mind Walt Whitman's "Chants Democratic." In this poem, he tried to capture the unruly diversity and energy of the antebellum United States and approached this impossible task by compiling lists. In stanza after stanza, he piles up nouns to describe weather conditions, tools, modes of transport, cities, ships, emotions, types of people, and times of day. Common objects such as chairs, carpets, and beds play a role, too. Whitman understood the power of everyday things to stir memories and emotions. The poem manages the feat of evoking something as big as the nation and as diverse as the American people through objects. With its breadth and variety, the Fielding Collection does the same. In fact, its focus on the eighteenth and early nineteenth centuries coincides with the material world that Whitman, who was born in 1819, knew.

The story of lighting implements is one of the many narratives about American material life that can now be told. On the following pages, candle stands, candleholders, and oil lamps document the ingenuity used to ward off darkness and make good use of precious fuel. In fact, as Marshall B. Davidson in "Early American Lighting" noted, candles were prohibitively expensive, out of the question for everyone except the wealthy. In May 1743, Rev. Edward Holyoke, president of Harvard, recorded that his household made seventy-eight pounds of candles from tallow, or animal fat. To make these candles, Holyoke's

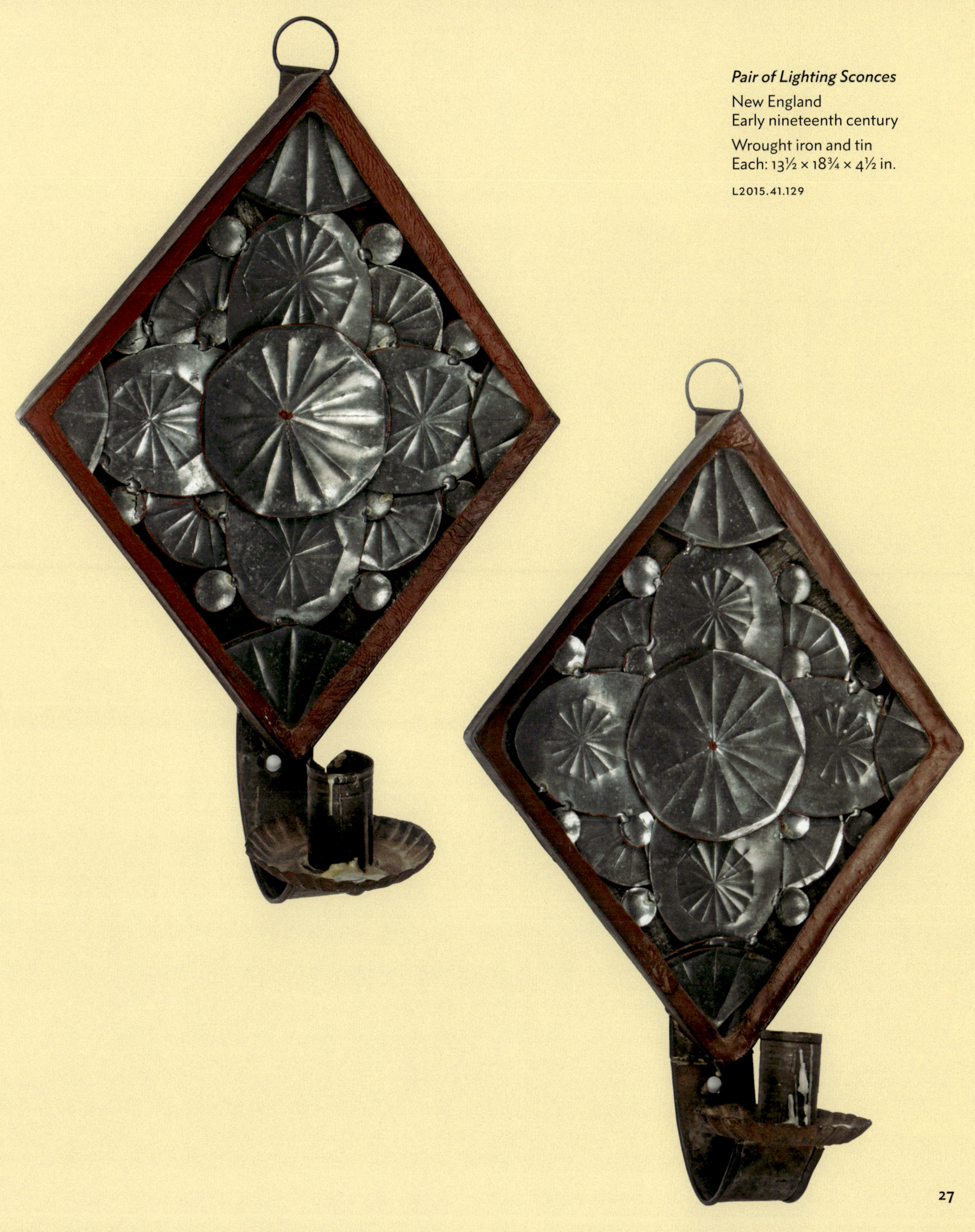

Pair of Lighting Sconces
New England
Early nineteenth century
Wrought iron and tin
Each: 13½ × 18¾ × 4½ in.
L2015.41.129

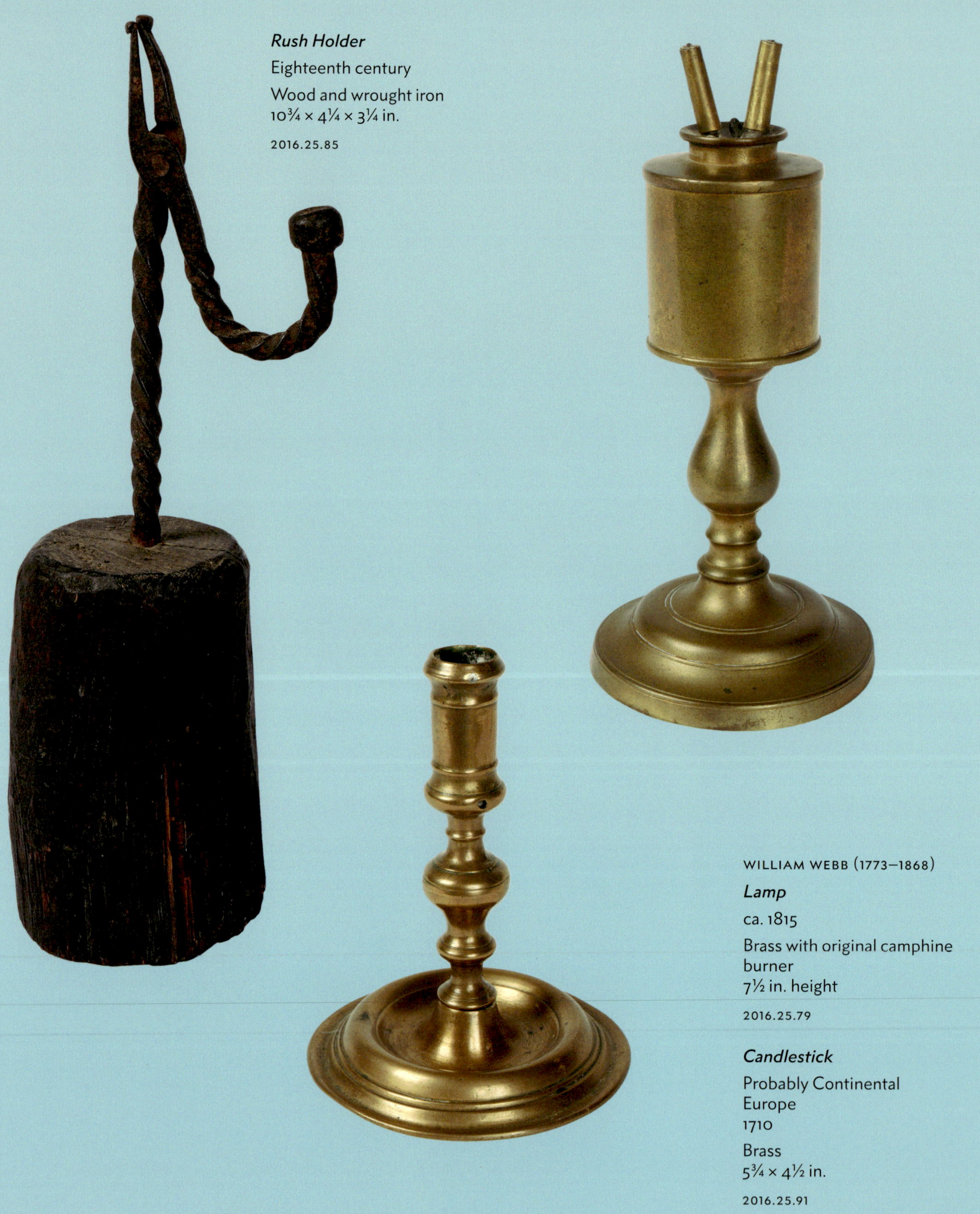

Rush Holder

Eighteenth century

Wood and wrought iron
10¾ × 4¼ × 3¼ in.

2016.25.85

WILLIAM WEBB (1773–1868)

Lamp

ca. 1815

Brass with original camphine burner
7½ in. height

2016.25.79

Candlestick

Probably Continental Europe
1710

Brass
5¾ × 4½ in.

2016.25.91

Candle Stand

Probably England
ca. 1740–1800

Wrought iron, brass, paint, and wood
Fully extended:
43 × 28¾ × 14 in.

2016.25.80

household must have owned or borrowed a candle mold, in which liquid tallow was poured and left to harden (p. 31). These were used up in less than six months, which meant that the household went through about four candles per night, even in the summer months. In 1761, Holyoke figured that it would cost him forty pounds a year—as much as a schoolmaster's annual salary—to supply his home with tallow candles. By contrast, in the 1780s, George Washington, who used more expensive but much longer-lasting and brighter-burning spermaceti for illumination, calculated an annual expense of only eight pounds. (Spermaceti is the liquid wax harvested from the head cavities of sperm whales.) He was one of the wealthiest men in the United States, and yet even he kept an eye on lighting expenditures. Tallow, whale oil, and wax were slowly displaced starting in the early nineteenth century with camphine, a turpentine product mixed with alcohol and camphor. Camphine, sold as "burning fluid" during the period, had a tendency to explode. By the 1860s, kerosene from the oil wells of western Pennsylvania began edging out this liquid. The light bulb, patented by Thomas A. Edison in 1880, would eventually supersede them all.

The lighting implements in the collection show how Americans in the late colonial and early Republican eras managed costly and limited lighting choices. A thin, stork-like candleholder with a penny-foot, tripod base had an adjustable height (left). Its extended arm with four rivet joints brought a single precious candle within inches of a book, piece of sewing, or letter. Other lighting stands are simpler, with only a spring-like curl to gently lock the candle in place along a wrought-iron pole (p. 30). An iron Betty lamp, again with an adjustable height, has a small reservoir for oil or wax (p. 30). These were cheaper to operate and filled with tallow, fish oil, or whatever could be found. Their flames were smoky and stinky. Try to imagine the stench of burnt fish oil and the layer of greasy soot that settled on everything.

In the essays that follow, aspects of the collection are illuminated with the casual reader in mind, one who will dip in and jump around rather than read from cover to cover. The Fieldings talk about their development as collectors and some of their favorite pieces. Their longtime advisor, David Wheatcroft, in a rollicking interview, shares some insights taken from his forty-plus years in the folk art trade and the difficulties of assembling a collection of such quality.

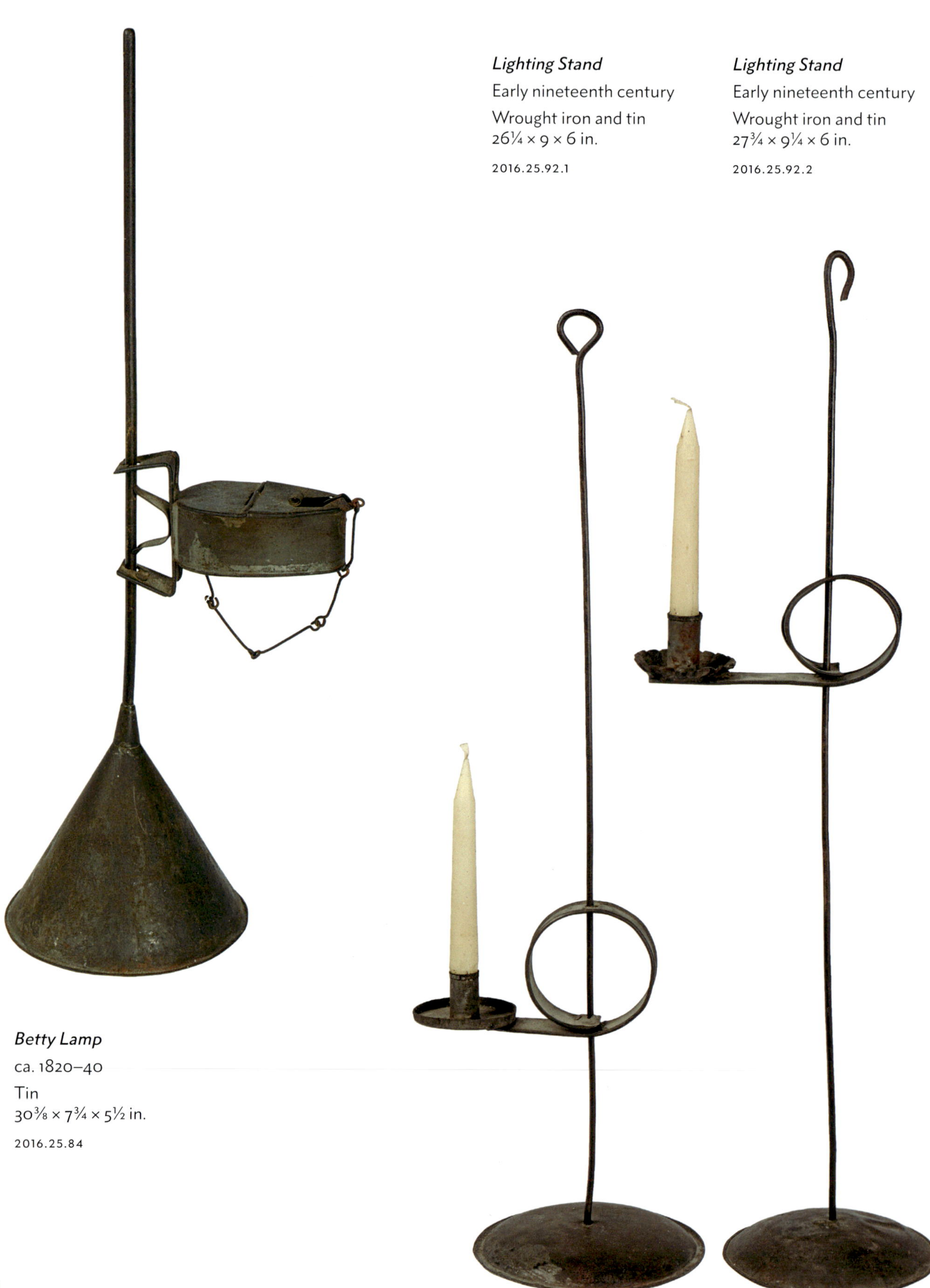

Lighting Stand
Early nineteenth century
Wrought iron and tin
26¼ × 9 × 6 in.
2016.25.92.1

Lighting Stand
Early nineteenth century
Wrought iron and tin
27¾ × 9¼ × 6 in.
2016.25.92.2

Betty Lamp
ca. 1820–40
Tin
30⅜ × 7¾ × 5½ in.
2016.25.84

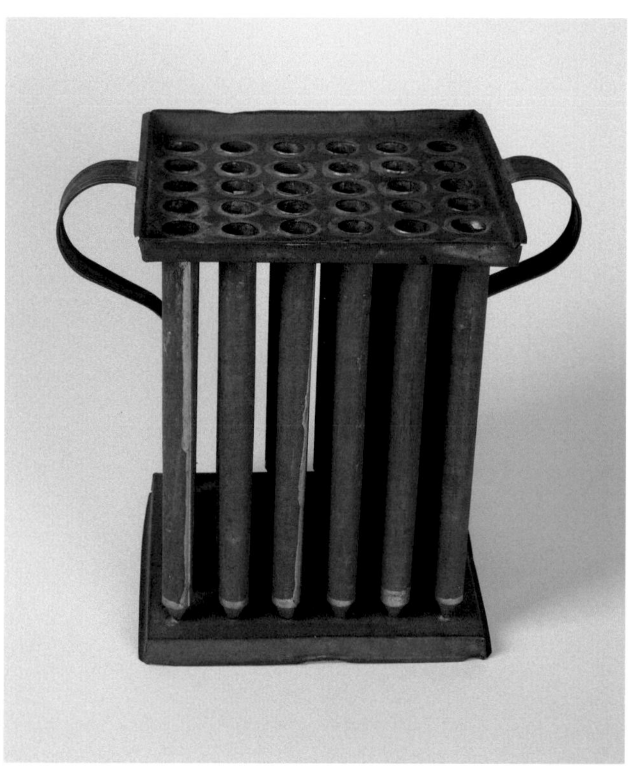

Thirty-Candle Mold
ca. 1800
Tin
10¾ × 11¾ × 8⅝ in.
2016.25.141

Next, John Demos revivifies the furniture workshops of rural Connecticut and Massachusetts during the seventeenth, eighteenth, and early nineteenth centuries. As he shows, craftsmen also farmed, trained apprentices, selected wood, and knew something of the styles produced by high-style, expensive furniture makers in Boston and New York. Textile historian Elizabeth V. Warren lays out the techniques of stitching, piecing, dyeing, and rug making used to make these dazzling quilts, needlework, and rugs.

The remaining essays use the collection to explore Americans' understanding of the natural environment, decoration, and family life. Stacy Hollander writes on the landscapes and still lifes in theorem paintings, watercolors, rugs, and firebacks as a way to examine Americans' changing perceptions of the natural world. Sumpter Priddy delves into the intellectual origins of the exuberant Fancy style of painted furniture and its connections to religion and philosophy. Robin Jaffee Frank turns to portraits of married couples as ways to understand the mores of early nineteenth-century American family life and, especially, the role of women and children in the domestic sphere. She analyzes a pair of John Brewster Jr. portraits as allegorizing pregnancy and motherhood, a portrait of a deceased child playing in a garden, and a New Hampshire couple relaxing at home with their young child.

This catalogue is designed to embody Whitman's idea of "the old, forever-new things." The essays have markedly different writerly voices and perspectives. Accompanying them are close-up photographs, artful cropping, playful layouts, and bold colors, meant to spark connections and encourage further engagement. These objects should act as a stimulus for twenty-first-century people to reimagine the past and keep the Fielding Collection "forever new."

NOTE TO READERS

Throughout this volume, items are identified by unique Huntington loan and accession numbers. Unless otherwise specified, objects are either gifts of Jonathan and Karin Fielding or loans from the Jonathan and Karin Fielding Collection. Loan numbers are preceded by an *L*.

James Glisson, PhD, is the Bradford and Christine Mishler Associate Curator of American Art at The Huntington.

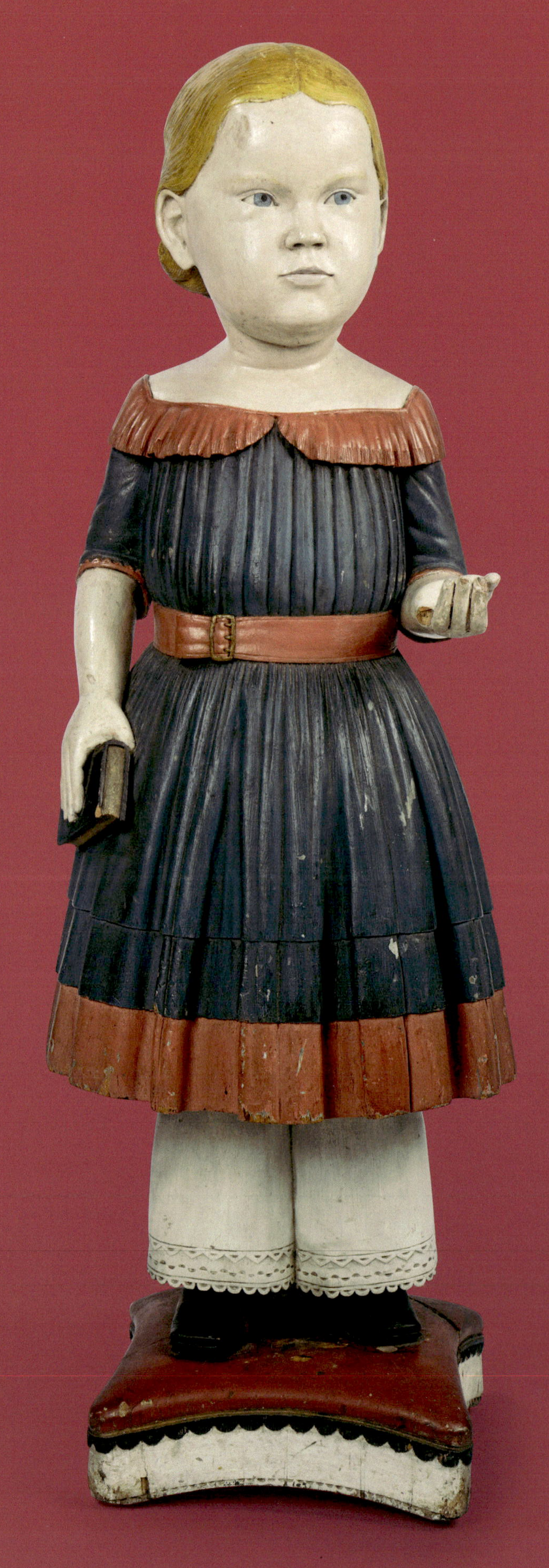

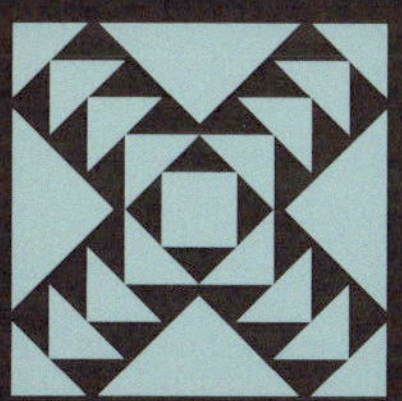

Forty Years in Folk Art

A Conversation with David Wheatcroft

JAMES GLISSON

JAMES GLISSON David, thanks for taking the time to share your story, profound knowledge, and infectious enthusiasm. How did the study and promotion of American folk and decorative art from the eighteenth and nineteenth centuries come to be your calling?

DAVID WHEATCROFT I grew up in central Pennsylvania, where on-site dispersals of estates at live auction was a long-standing tradition. At first, I was a very young, unwitting observer of these events, but by the age of seven, I was considered savvy enough to execute bids for my impatient mother (she had better things to do at home). Much later, I went to art school at the University of Iowa, where I received an MFA in studio art with a focus on drawing, but I took courses in painting and printmaking, too. My interest in art, combined with a long fascination with auctions and the need to generate income, evolved into a business. Buying used contemporary or noncollectible items led to buying the antique and artful, which had much better margins. And artful antiques had even better margins.

JG What sorts of antiques did you start with?

DW The Bicentennial in 1976 saw an upswing in interest in American antiques, especially quilts. The pieced quilt was ubiquitous and highly inventive. Their geometric conceptions showed surprising affinities to the op art and minimalism movements of the 1970s, to artists like Bridget Riley, Richard Anuszkiewicz, and Donald Judd. I saw this strong interest in quilts and made buying and selling them my first attempt at

ASA AMES (1824–1851)
Portrait of Susan Ames
Western New York
ca. 1849
Pine and paint
35 × 10 × 10 in.
L2015.41.183

antique dealing. With undue confidence and the hypnotic chant of the auctioneer planted in my chest, the thrill of the discovery of old, useful objects as art became an unavoidable siren song.

JG So, I take it you really liked the thrill of discovery?

DW Absolutely: the ongoing sorting and sifting of potential purchases, the daily curating of finds, the winnowing down to the most visually exciting pieces while being constrained by what I thought from observation of the market was most likely to sell. During an indenture of nearly a decade in pursuit of quilts, I slowly incorporated into my business other forms of expression, including watercolors, paintings, decorated furniture, and sculptures ranging in date from 1780 to 1950. After forty years, I have a fairly broad knowledge of a variety of objects considered American folk art. My hope is that, over time, I have not only learned a bit of history about the production of folk art but also refined my sense of judgment.

JACOB MAENTEL (1763–1863)

Portrait of Hatter John Mays of Schaefferstown, Pennsylvania

ca. 1830

Watercolor, gouache, ink, and pencil on paper
Framed: 18 × 15 in.

See also p. 245

2016.25.102

JG How long have you worked with Jonathan and Karin Fielding?

DW I have worked with Jon and Karin for about twenty years.

JG What has your role been in shaping the collection?

DW They are the drivers of their collection. They provide the impulse—the passion, as it were—to collect. And they are always the final arbiters. My experience serves as ballast to check the unconstrained love of the object.

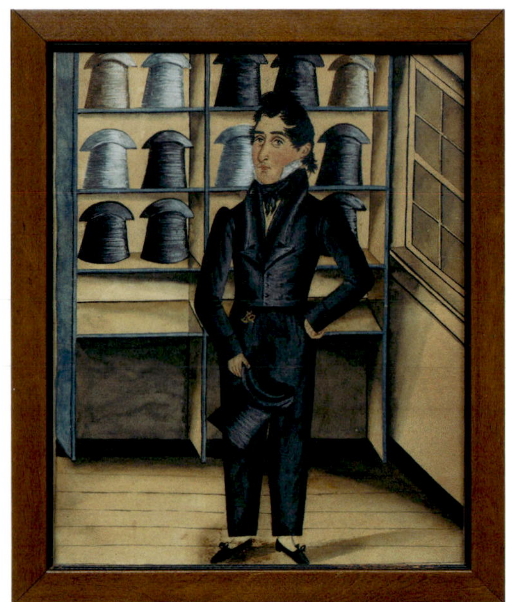

JG You sound like an accountant or attorney tasked with delivering sober facts.

DW I try to offer context. I give opinions about the availability of similar objects and the sale record of related items. I've been in the business long enough to know the market, when something is likely to come up again for sale and when something is truly exceptional—for instance, the Asa Ames full-length carving of a young girl (p. 32). Only two other such depictions of children standing are known. Similarly, the Jacob Maentel portrayal of a hatter (left) is singular, one of a handful of occupational portraits, only two of which are so fully realized. The portrait of Albert G. Gilman by A. Ellis (p. 6) is part of a very small group, perhaps fifteen, that are attributed to this elusive artist. The Gilman portrait has a striking and probably unique red background. And it is in superior condition.

JG It sounds like the thrill of a real find and sharing your knowledge of the market spurs your work.

DW Yes, but never forget that Jon and Karin drive the car; I am in the back seat at times, yelling advice, hopefully without too much waving of arms, best with the top up so that I can be heard.

JG Yelling from the back seat of a convertible?

DW Collecting is filled with the temptation to digress. The Fieldings, however, are patient, and they are willing to wait to find the pieces of great aesthetic or historical merit.

JG Some moments must stand out from these past twenty years.

DW One was the bidding for the *Still Life with a Basket of Fruit, Flowers, and Cornucopia* (p. 140) from the collection of Andy Williams, the singer. It was very competitive. Not completely unanticipated, but I will allow that our tank was hovering on empty by the end of the bidding. The piece from the Williams collection is attributed to Joseph Proctor, an African American whom the 1860 census identifies as an artist; it is by far the largest of a small group of works assigned to him. Moreover, the square format is very unusual. The articulation of the fruit is fulsome yet simple. Note, in particular, the round grapes with the single dot highlight—a simple solution to what is literally a complex reflection of light. And in this context, it does the trick.

The overall composition and size make it especially striking. So I think the appeal at the auction was predictable, but I don't think that the final price was foreseen by many people. It seemed that there was one collector who was especially spirited and competitive in the last third of the bidding. I think the Fieldings' full-throttle approach was well justified. There really is not another American folk art still life that competes with the grandeur of this one.

JG My sense is that, in your field, one must be careful about refinished surfaces, mends, repairs, and uncertain dating—all of which is compounded by the dearth of documentation on these artists and artifacts before the early twentieth century, when the collecting of folk art took off.

DW I try to use whatever skills I have developed in sniffing out the spurious, the counterfeits, and the frauds. I have been taught most effectively by making mistakes, and I have paid for the experience with financial suffering. Fakery comes with the territory of art dealing. Note the more than a dozen fake Jackson Pollocks sold by the heretofore venerable Knoedler Gallery in New York for tens of millions a few years ago.

Especially in the period after the Bicentennial, all kinds of pieces were constructed to fool the collector. For painted pieces, it was commonplace for repairs to be cleverly executed and then further camouflaged with the application of a painted surface made to match the old one, or even a pattern and colors invented whole cloth. The sophistication of this work can make it challenging to recognize. One line of defense is learning the materials and techniques from each period. In the case of furniture, hand tools leave telltale marks. In the case of paintings, there were pigment discoveries (for example, the cadmium colors from the metal) that only became available in the late nineteenth century. They have a different intensity and specific color range that was unachievable using the earlier palette. In the case of quilts, fabric designs evolved. Researching fabric prints and patterns and knowing the dates of their manufacture firms up dates for quilts. Of course, in the field, experience counts for a great deal. And if there are still questions, scientific testing such as microscopy can sometimes provide definitive answers.

I have often thought it best to follow the Euell Gibbons rule. Euell was well known for his natural-eating books and lectures in the 1960s. He was once asked how to recognize the poisonous mushrooms. Euell hushed the crowd and frightened them with his reply, "I don't know the poisonous mushrooms!" Into the breach of the audience's gasp, Euell followed up quickly with, "I only know the ones that are good to eat."

JG You make collecting folk art sound downright dangerous. But I see your point: worry about finding the best, and then the lesser—or toxic—items will drop away. Speaking of folk art, this term is often contested. How would you explain it to a reader just coming to the field?

DW By one definition, folk art is the product of artists who did not train at an academy or apprentice in an urban center. It is often misconstrued as a crudely executed, cartoonish version of refined or professional productions.

JG So, folk artists did not attend the Royal Academy in London (founded in 1768) or apprentice with a fashionable artist, like Joshua Reynolds, the English artist who taught the American painter Benjamin West. The furniture makers represented in the Fielding Collection did not train in Paris, as did Charles-Honoré Lannuier, who set up shop in New York, or Duncan Phyfe, who learned the trade in his native Scotland before moving to the United States.

DW Yes.

ATTRIBUTED TO MARY PETERS HEWINS (1794–1876)

Geometric Hearth Rug

Norfolk County, Massachusetts
ca. 1800

Yarn and shirred wool on linen
34 × 70 in.

Inscription (verso): "J. Hewins"

See also pp. 132–33

L2015.41.84

JG Except you don't think that this lack of training makes folk art crude.

DW Right. As with any art, folk art exists on a continuum. The Fielding Collection is anchored by its focus on collecting the most successful pieces. For example, there are many hooked and sewn rugs that have survived the decades, even centuries. However, few have great merit as art objects. The original geometric patterned yarn-sewn hearth rug (below) in the Fielding Collection by an anonymous artist has bold color and immediate impact.

JG One part of the collection we haven't touched on is the nineteenth-century material. Could you say more?

DW In the early nineteenth century, American makers began to produce objects in larger numbers for a growing middle class; these increasingly served only decorative or aesthetic purposes. New wealth brought anxieties about status and identity, and portraiture in particular was the way in which status, sometimes newly minted, manifested itself, primarily for rural professionals, successful farmers, and businesspeople. The larger and more complex the portrait, the higher the price. After all, relative wealth and respected vocation were, then as now, the root of status. Materials in the eighteenth and early nineteenth century, especially canvas and paint, were often imported from England, and therefore costly.

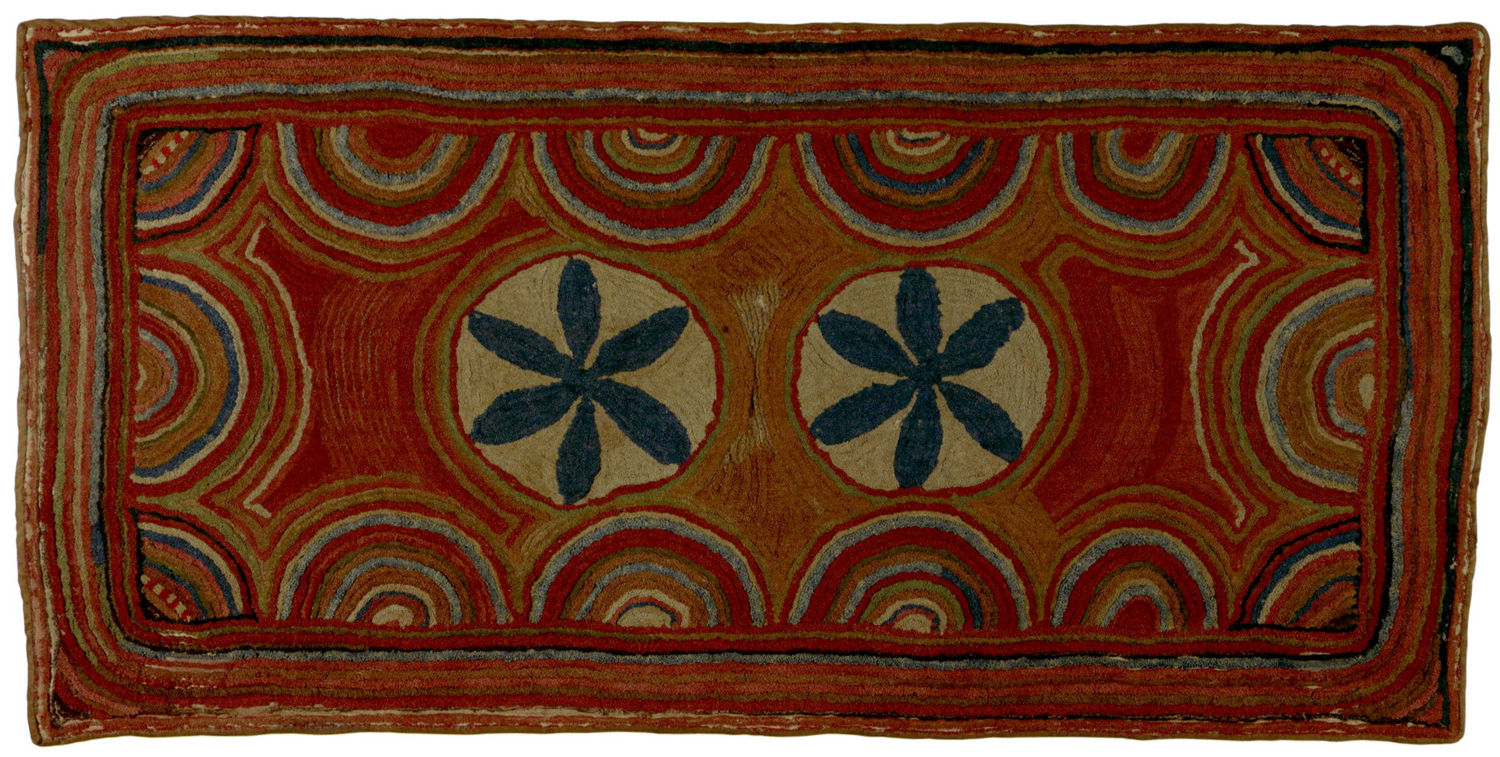

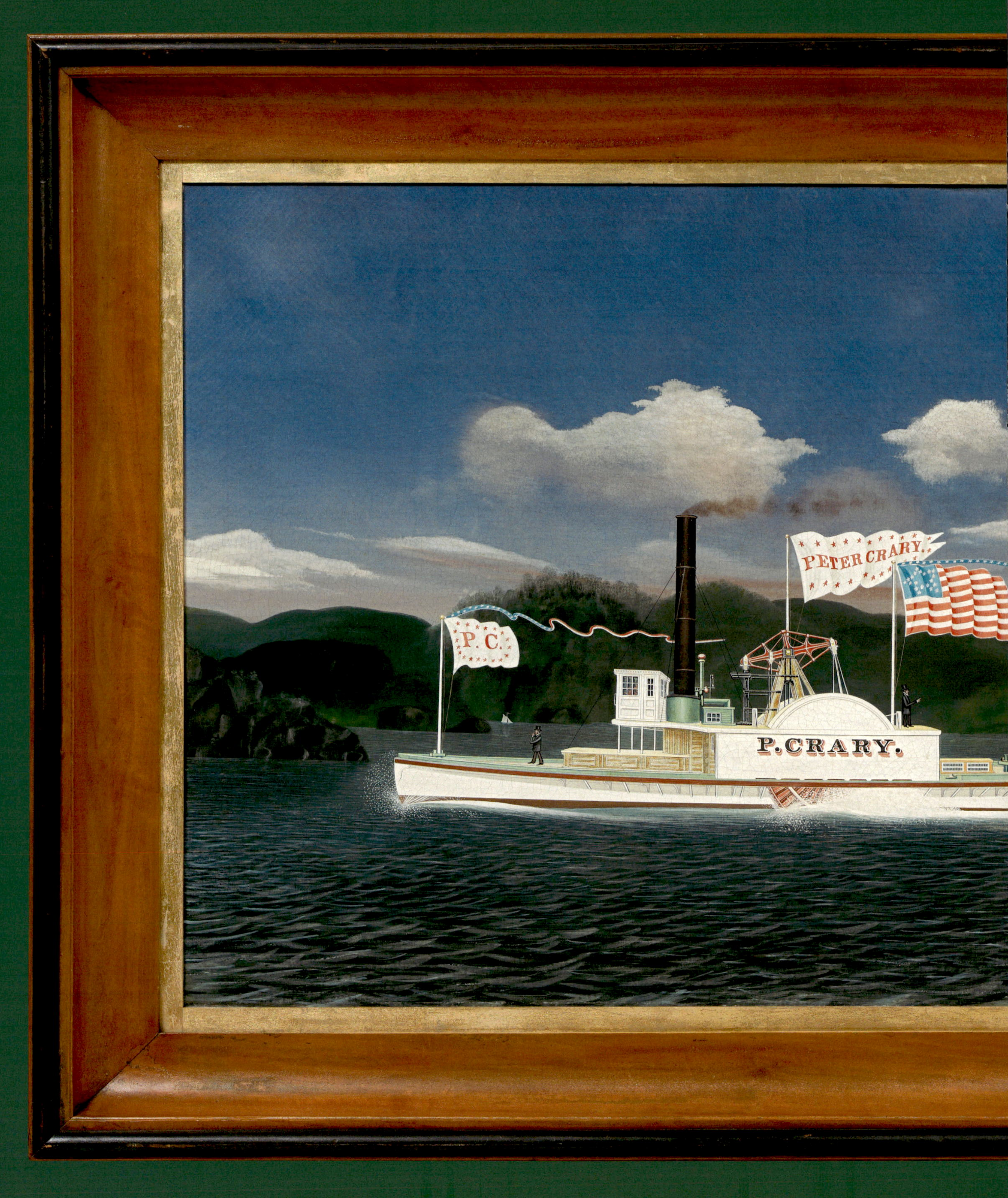
P.C.
PETER CRARY.
P.CRARY.

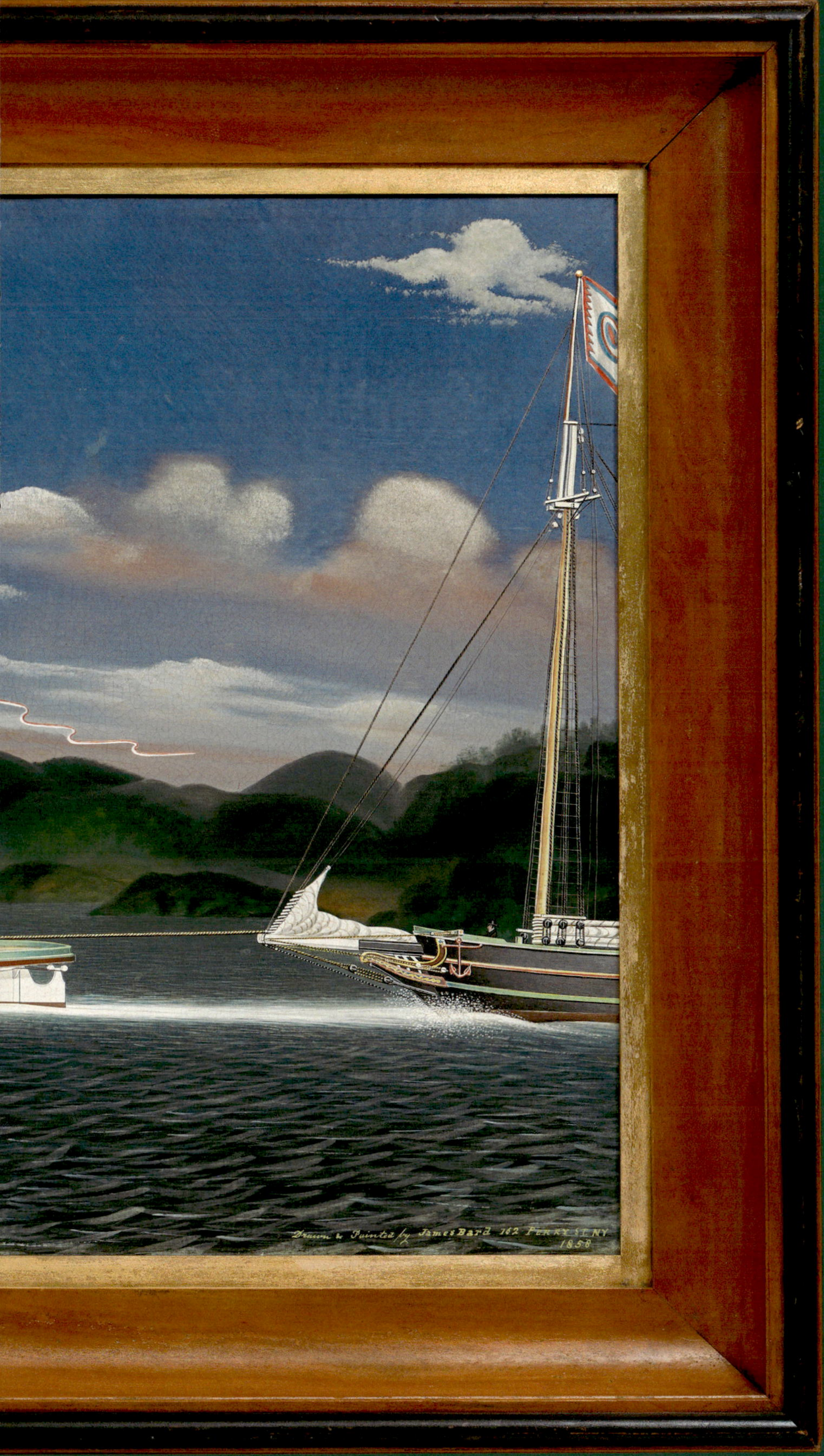

JAMES BARD (1815–1897)

The Steamboat "Peter Crary"

1858

Oil on canvas
Framed: 40 × 61 in.

L2015.41.175

Consider Ammi Phillips's portraits of two members of the Van Keuren family (p. 13). The Van Keurens have the trappings of a comfortable life, with plenty of discretionary income: he holds a clay pipe for smoking tobacco and sits on a richly decorated painted chair, while she wears a frilled bonnet and has a decorated shawl draped over her arm.

Clearly, not everyone could commission a large-scale portrait. On the more affordable end of the scale were the small watercolors executed in profile, like those by Edwin Plummer (p. 187). And the simplest and likely the least expensive were the small silhouettes of heads supported by disproportionate bodies, done in watercolor by a painter known as the "Puffy Sleeve Artist," now identified as Ezra Wood, who lived in western Massachusetts and earned a living as a tavern keeper and woodworker (p. 190).

JG You've talked about folk art, material culture, and the objects acquired by the educated and upwardly mobile middle class. One of the United States' great achievements is its middle class, and these objects help to tell that story. What other stories about the nineteenth century might be told using the Fielding Collection?

DW The collection shows the early transformation of a rural, agrarian nation into an urban, industrial one. New technologies, from the steam engine to the factory-based manufacture of both paper and cloth, influenced folk productions. The steamboat came to be depicted in paintings and watercolors. The Fieldings have a masterful James Bard portrait of a steamboat pulling a sailboat that documents a new technology supplanting an old one (pp. 38–39). This work not only has a clear visual relation to the larger style changes taking place but also is constructed with excellent proportions and embellished with a highly activated paint surface.

JG One of the old yarns about modernization and industrialization is that time sped up. The telegraph and railroad expedited communication and transportation. There still must have been some delay between the city and the country. How might a rural artist find inspiration from a city cousin?

DW Yes, there was often a time lag between the dissemination of a new style in the decorative arts and its reinterpretation in the rural and small-town environment. Some of it was the result of the stickiness of the existing style in a culturally slower environment.

JG The quickness of city life as opposed to the leisurely pace of the country.

DW Yes, exactly. Let's get specific, though. The tall case clock (opposite page) with its original surface decoration is an excellent example of a rural response to an urban-style evolution. The clock is from around 1820 but

Tall Case Clock

RILEY WHITING (1785–1835), CLOCK MOVEMENT

Winchester, Connecticut
ca. 1820

UNKNOWN, PAINTED CASE

Probably Maine
1820s

Pine, glass, wood, and paint
88 × 18½ × 11 in.

Inscription: "R. Whiting Winchester"

Detail on p. 42

L2015.41.23

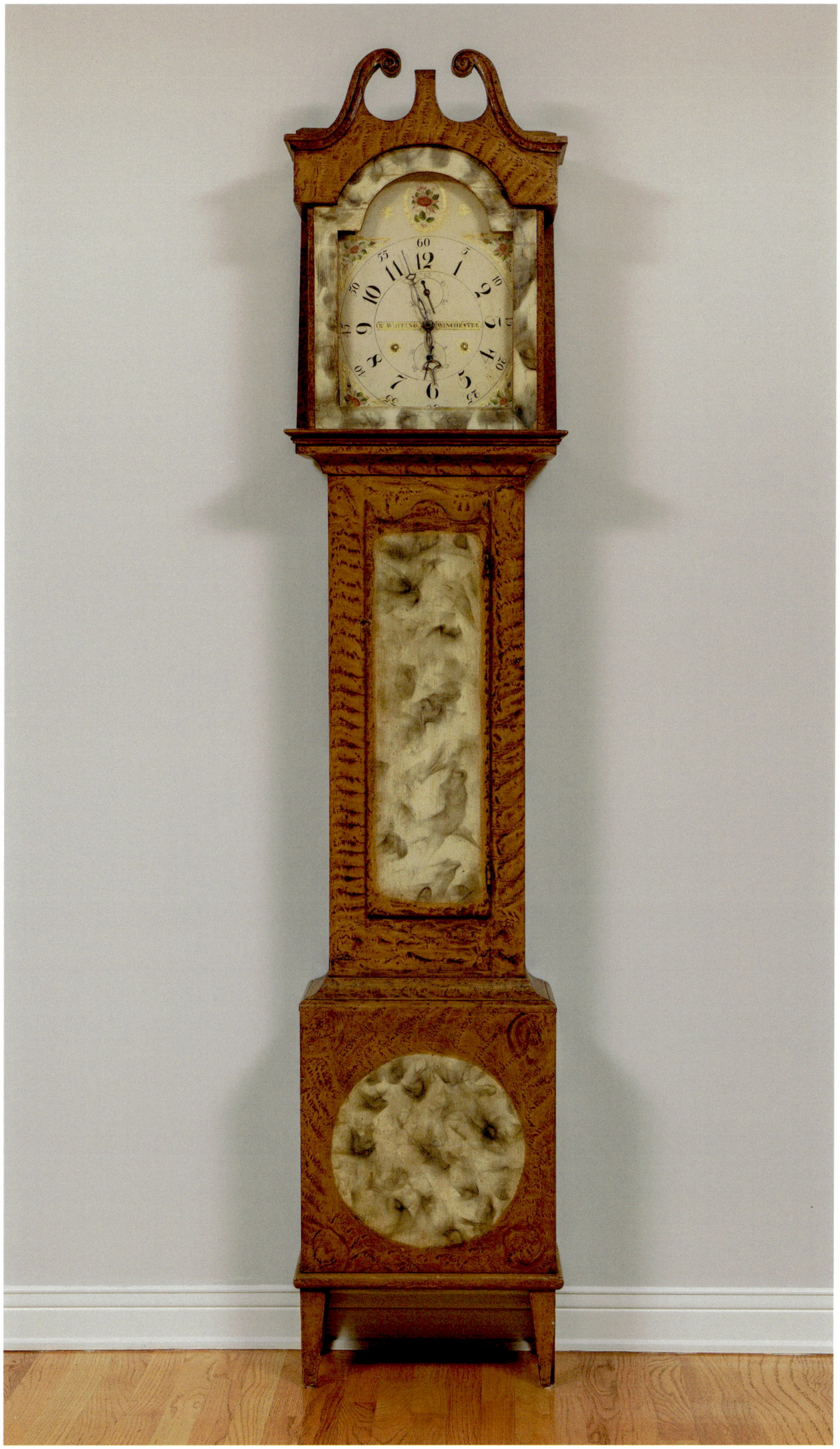

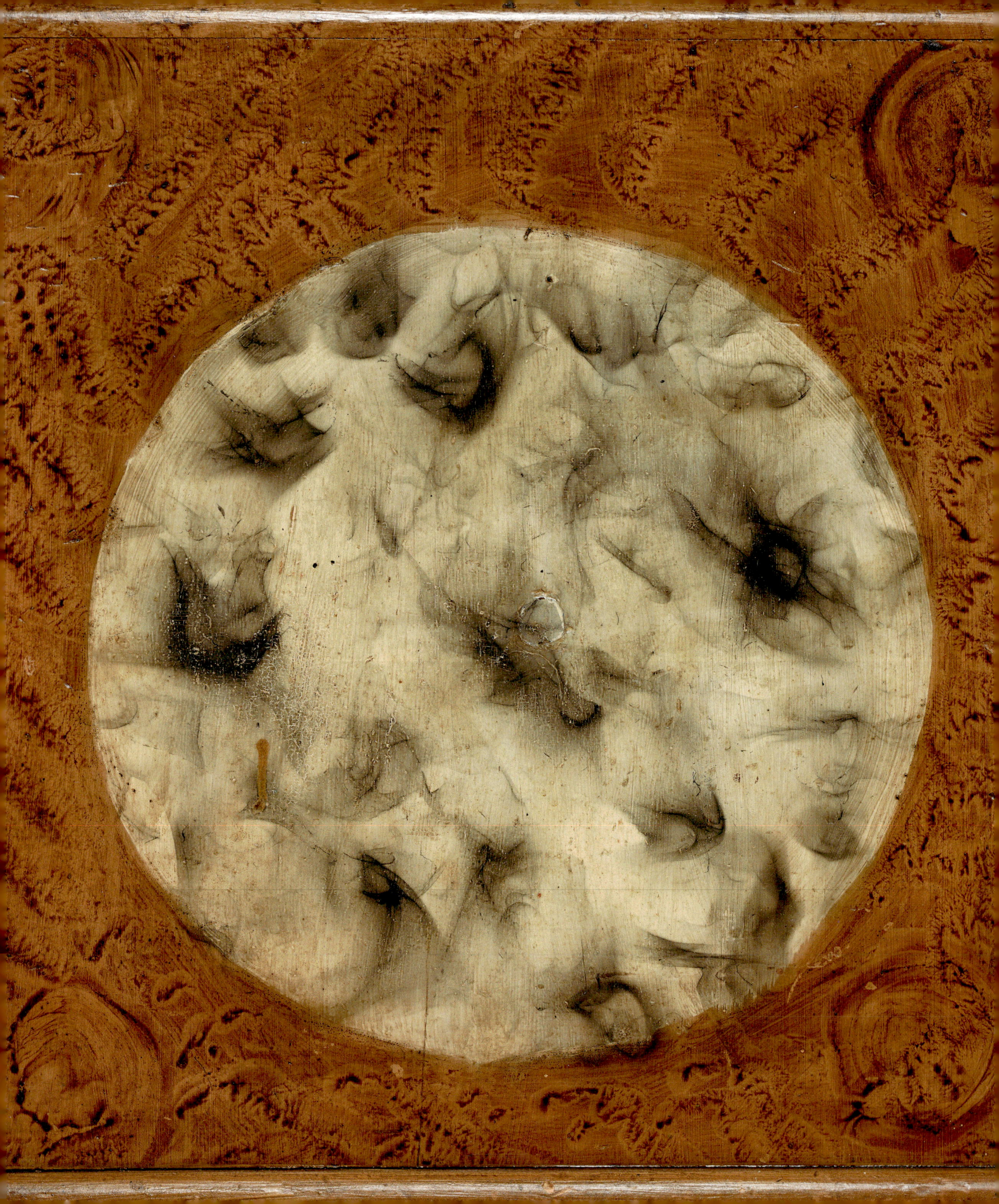

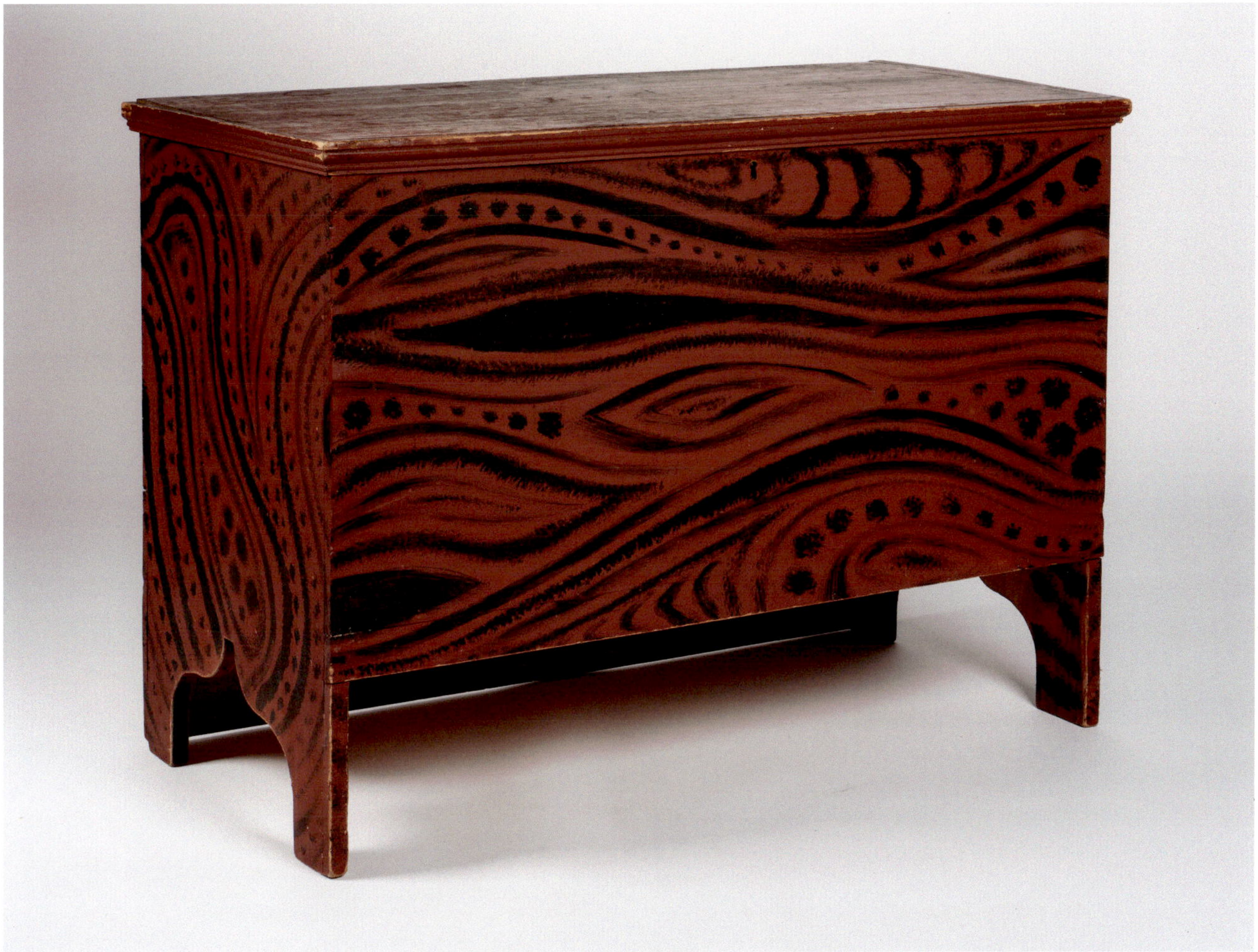

Blanket Chest

Vermont
Nineteenth century

Wood, paint, and metal hinges
28⅜ × 38¾ × 19⅜ in.

Inscription (inside of lid): "The Property of Lena A. Bugbee and Clair Paul Wakefield, Vershire VT"

L2015.41.108

Swirl-Decorated Box

ca. 1820–40

Wood, paint, and iron
8⅝ × 20⅛ × 10 in.

2016.25.28

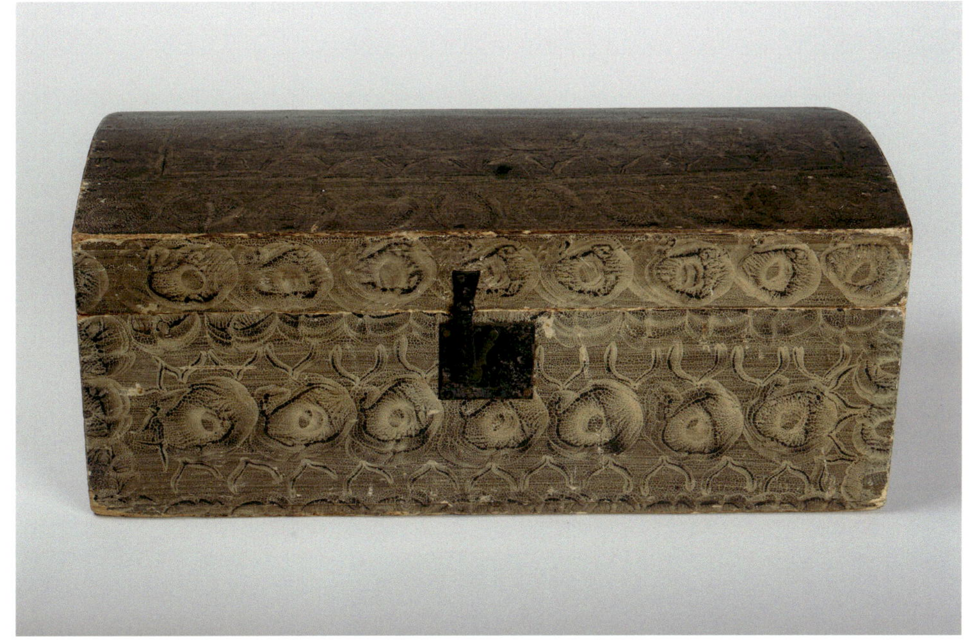

Splayed-Leg Table (and detail)

Southern New Hampshire
ca. 1800

Birch and paint
28 × 22 × 16 in.

L2015.41.115

simulates design trends that became widespread in Federal furniture beginning in the late eighteenth century. It was typical of Federal furniture to use inlay with exotic contrasting woods like mahogany, ebony, or rosewood; high, tapered French feet; round panels; and lozenge-shaped brass handles. In the clock, the rural craftsman simulated expensive wood. Instead of using tiger maple (a striped maple), he made striated lines in the wet paint, umber over a pale yellow base coat. The panels in the door and base have smoke-decorated white paint, probably meant as a stand-in for light birch. The *fumée* effect was achieved by first painting the panel white. Then, while the paint was still wet, a candle was held below, allowing the smoke trail to leave a design on the ground color. The candle was often moved in a swirling motion, and the technique had an unmistakable soft, misty effect. While these faux surfaces clearly mimic birch and maple, other examples of painted furniture in the Fielding Collection often stray far from the literal (p. 43). The patterns on the blanket chest can at best be called wood-like, while the swirls on the decorated box have an eccentric aesthetic that is all their own.

JG The Vermont blanket chest has always read to me like a drawing by the abstract expressionist artist Adolph Gottlieb. Going back to your opening comments on quilts and their link to abstraction, what is the overlap?

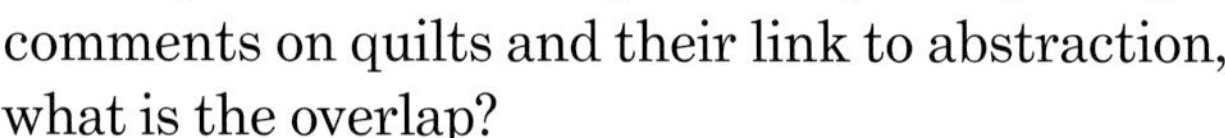

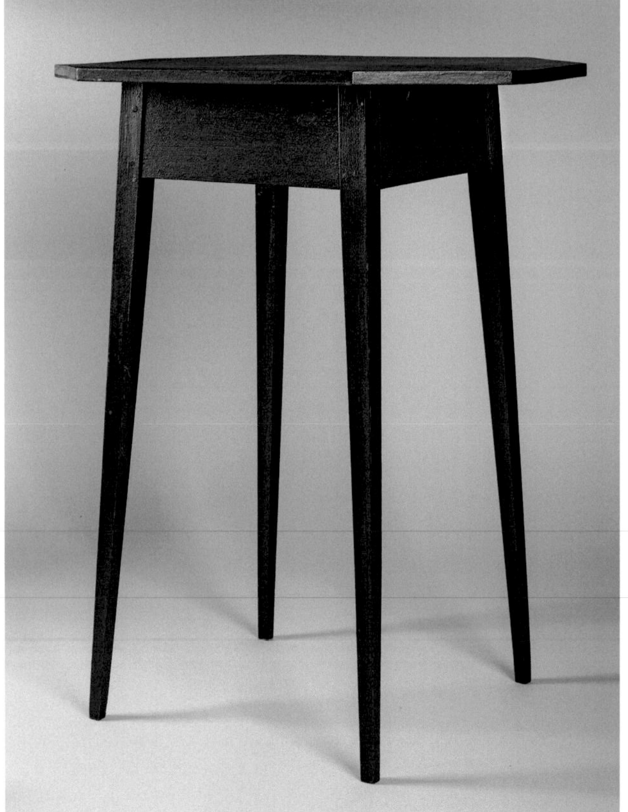

DW It was the use of flat space, strong color, inventive graining and patterning—the soul of traditional folk art—that struck a chord with the modern artists. This strong current of intuitive abstraction became part of a broad stream of visual approaches used by avant-garde artists searching for new means of expression. In fact, the sculptor Elie Nadelman formed a huge collection of American folk art, and Alfred H. Barr exhibited folk material at the Museum of Modern Art in the 1930s and 1940s, when he served as director.

JG One term for this colorful furniture is *Fancy*. Could you say more about when and where this style was popular?

DW The post–Revolutionary War folk artists were influenced by broader cultural trends, including the social/aesthetic movement termed *Fancy*, which spread with fervor in the early

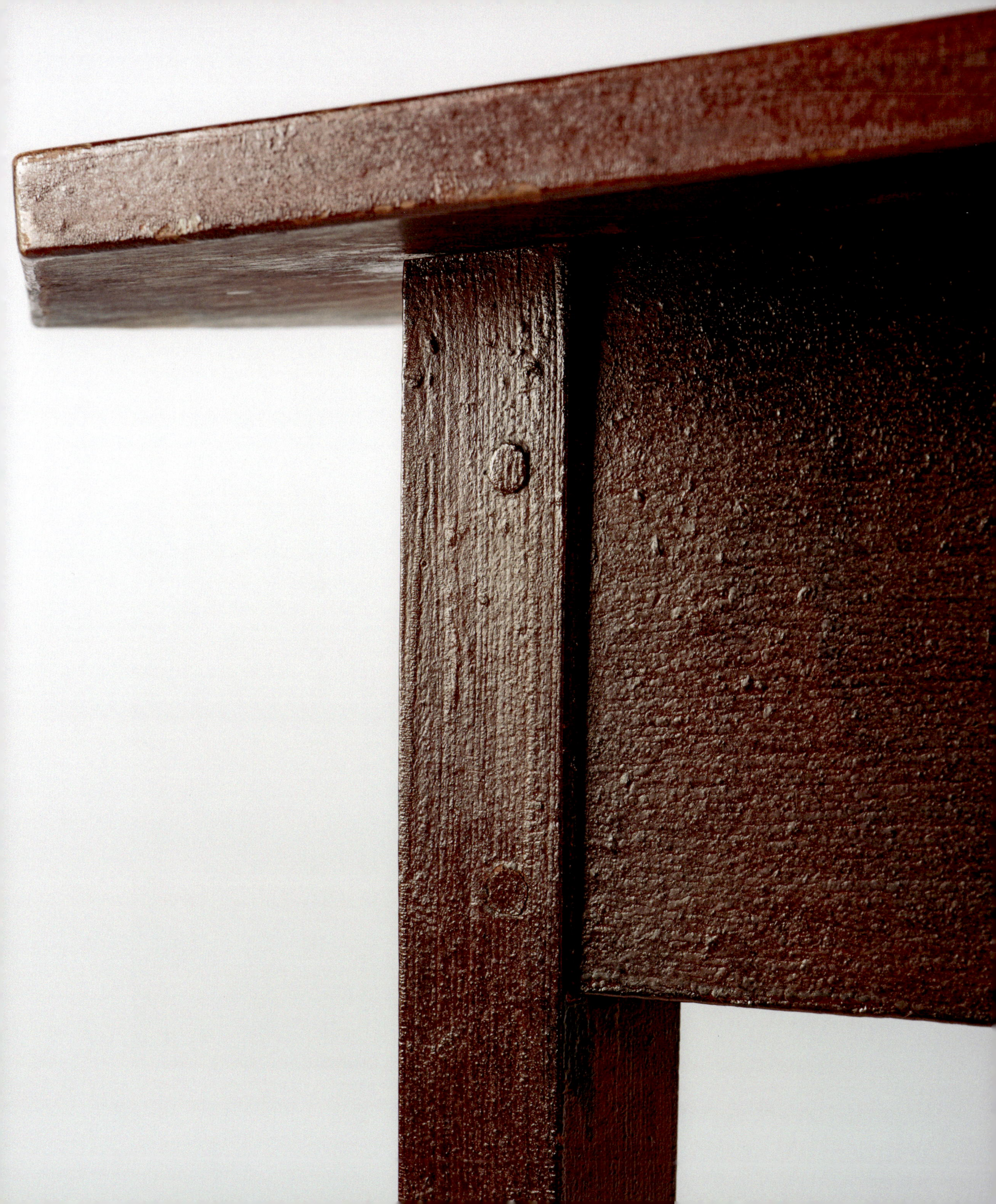

nineteenth century. In the visual and decorative arts, the movement was characterized by increased color saturation and heightened embellishment. No doubt the optimistic outlook of the population of the young republic reinforced a mood that was open to the colorful and expressive—like the red-and-black Vermont blanket chest (p. 43) or the tall case clock I just mentioned.

JG Part of the colorfulness of the Fielding Collection is found in the period surfaces or the surfaces from shortly after the piece's creation. Could you talk about their importance?

DW There is a documentary and aesthetic side to the value of an original surface. To the practiced eye, it is difficult to simulate the changes that have taken place over a long period of time to a painted or clear finish. A repair done at a later date will inevitably have a different surface, perhaps a change in color, texture, or accumulation of particulate matter. Perhaps all three.

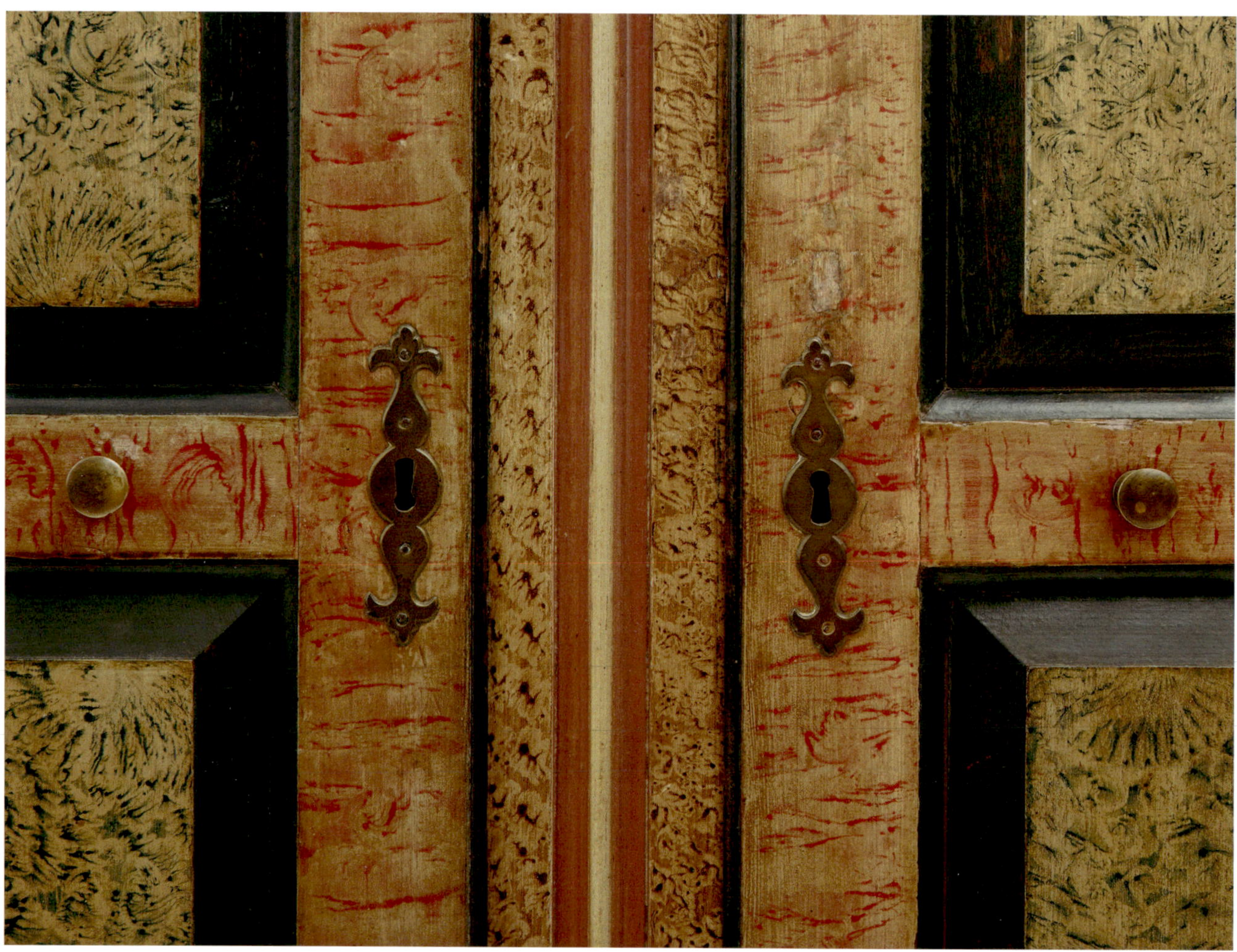

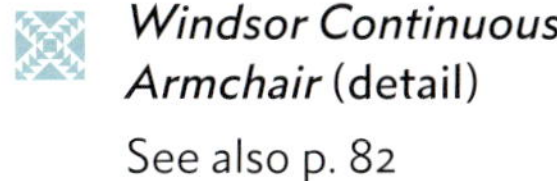

Windsor Continuous Armchair (detail)

See also p. 82

Needless to say, a refinishing—that is, a later finish applied after removal of the old finish—decreases the chances to catch these repairs or restorations. Even more confounding can be a finish in paint or a clear finish that is applied to simulate an old finish. Sometimes only a microscope can resolve questions about the age of a surface. But making such determinations on the fly can be greatly assisted by a well-developed sensitivity to unadulterated finishes. The New Hampshire splayed-leg table with its glowing patina is a good example (pp. 44–45), or the leg and seat of the red Windsor armchair (right).

Furthermore, an undisturbed finish, even with added in-use layers, can provide a window to understanding the taste of each generation—such as the rare green Windsor chair desk attributed to the well-known craftsman Ebenezer Tracy Sr. (p. 18). The generally green Windsors of the eighteenth century were often repainted in more vibrant yellows, reds, light greens, blues, and even shades of pink in the early nineteenth century. And then they were painted black or brown to fit the mid-to-late-nineteenth-century Victorian aesthetic. So, a chair with an undisturbed surface from the 1880s might retain several iterations of changing tastes.

JG So the not-messed-with surface is like a direct line to the past?

DW Yes. A chair with its original paint undisturbed gives us clear documentation of the intended finish that was applied at the time of its making.

JG Tell me, what else can happen to furniture?

DW Simple wear. For instance, in the collection's *Schrank* (p. 48), there is softening around the handles from opening and closing the cabinet. Often, though, it can be hard to know exactly what created a paint effect. Color might have been accidentally applied while the baseboards in the room were being painted, an acidic spill could have dissolved some areas, exposure to

Painted Schrank (detail)

See also p. 4

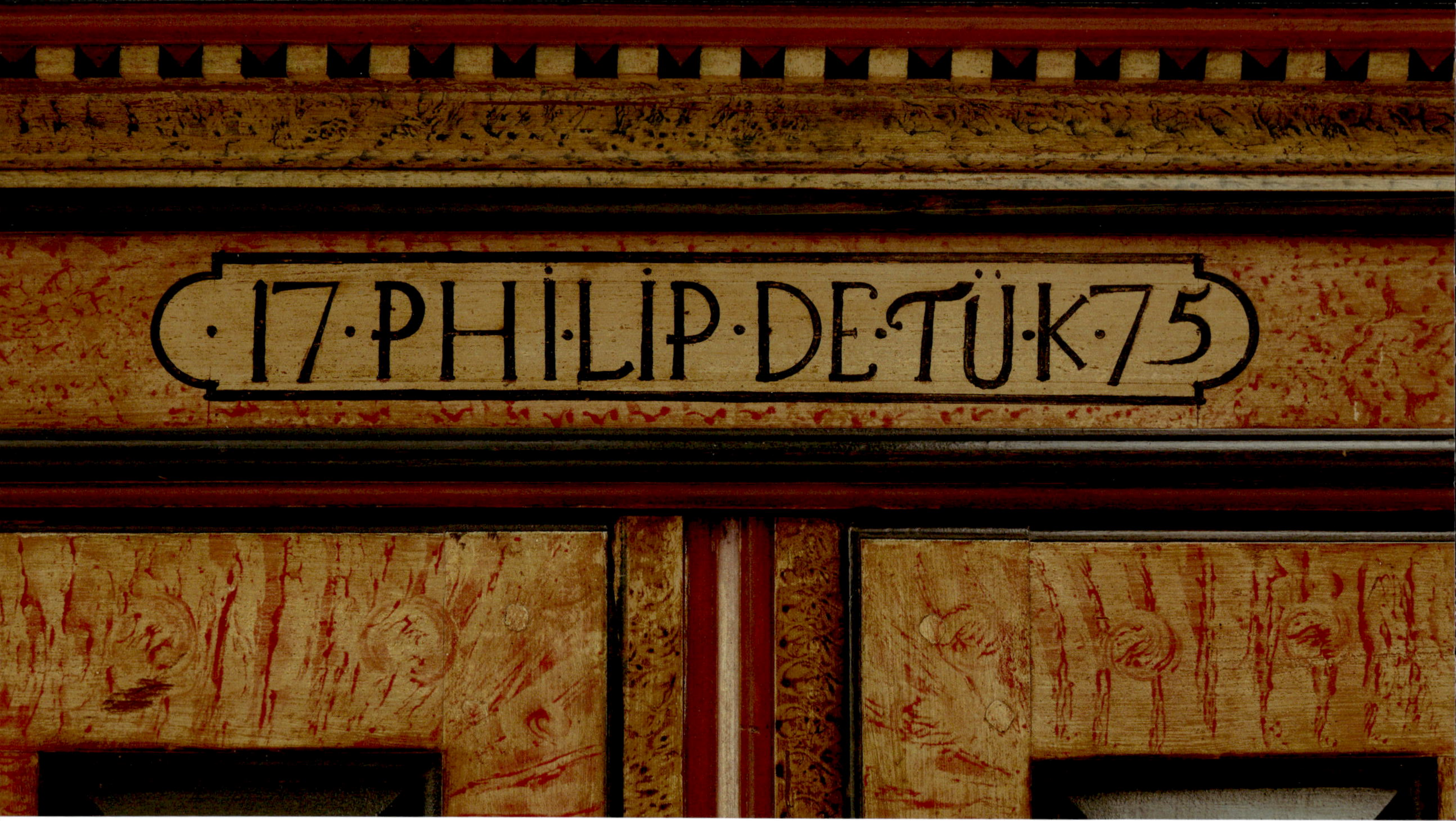

Painted Schrank (detail)
Inscription: "17 Philip Detük 75"
See also p. 4

sunlight might have faded others. Vigorous cleaning might have rubbed away delicate surfaces.

Alternatively, the original finish is an aesthetic delight. Most of the original and intended sheen dulls over time. The texture and buildup of dust, wax, and oils, along with subtle wear from use, can produce a distinctively appealing envelope for the piece. The matte surface more fully absorbs the light. The light also passes through generations of buildup and can achieve the effect of a glaze in an oil painting—a translucent window on the effects of time (pp. 18, 45, 74–75). The variegation of the surface is natural and, in the best of circumstances, has its own logic resulting from decades or centuries of environmental causes that transform the surface's visual effect.

One virtue is that the surface cannot be foreseen by the makers. It is only seen in its archeological fullness by the contemporary examiner. Perhaps the aesthetic side of preserved surfaces is just a romanticism of accumulations of grime and dirt. No matter—the tradition has been formed. For those who see it and are awed, exactly where the magic comes from, they care not. The discovery of an untouched surface aesthetically enhanced by time is a scarce find indeed.

JG This reminds me of contemporary debates around intentionality and artistic meaning. We see with our eyes what the artist did, but working backward to understand exactly what he or she wanted to communicate is harder, if not impossible. We can never see the original surface, only a version of it, like looking at stars through a telescope and knowing the light has traversed the universe over decades or centuries.

DW That's an interesting idea. It is as if a beguiling line of history, at times beautiful, is drawn between the maker then and the discoverer now.

JG Why is the painted *Schrank* such an important acquisition?

DW There are very few large painted case pieces, and even fewer with a wide array of colors and paint application. The Fielding *Schrank* is embellished with a date, 1775, and a name, "Philip Detük," above the doors (opposite page). These give us important pieces of information about its ownership. Like many so-called dower chests (blanket chests), it may have been a wedding gift or part of a dowry. Its highly decorated surface served as a reminder of that bond through many years of usefulness.

The *Schrank* has two doors with raised panels, an applied cornice with dental molding, and generous ball feet. This particular decorator gave us much to see. He employed various paint-application techniques: sponged, dry-brushed, and solid areas of color and multiple contrasting colors (pp. 4, 46). The feet and cornice, commonly replaced, are original, and the paint surface is in an unsurpassed state of condition. To my knowledge, it is the best example of a painted *Schrank* that has been up for sale in the last forty years. Even in museums, there is little to rival it.

The Pennsylvania Germans brought with them from Europe a tradition of the use of strong color. In their hands, imagery was flattened and lacked the plethora of flourishes found on the productions of their European forebears. Even in the more tradition-bound religious sects that avoided ostentation, they found a place in their lives for the novelty and beauty of strong color.

JG In the Fielding Collection, there is tension between decoration and simplicity, or ostentation and restraint. These are proxies for deeper debates about religious observance and secular materialism. Decoration, and the lack thereof, is the manifestation of a theological position or a retreat from the secular world.

DW The Fielding Collection's Amish Diamond in the Square quilt is a good example (p. 50). One of the most conservative, rule-bound religious sects in America is the Old Order Amish. They are easily recognized by their dress, even today. Interestingly, the Diamond in the Square became a widespread pattern in Lancaster County, Pennsylvania, in the late nineteenth century. It seemed to grow out of the plain bordered square (center square), which was likely preceded by an early quilt called the "center medallion."

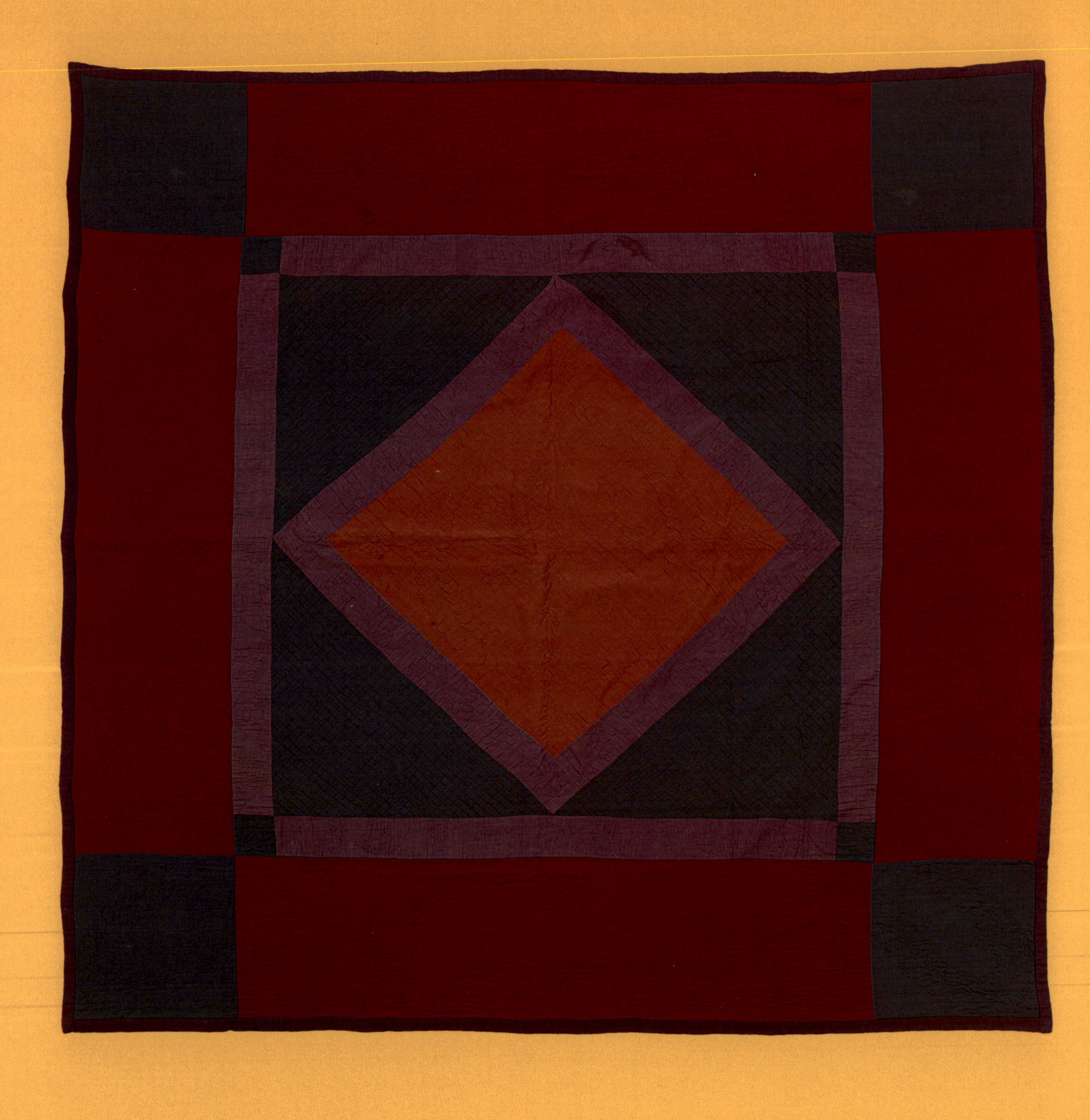

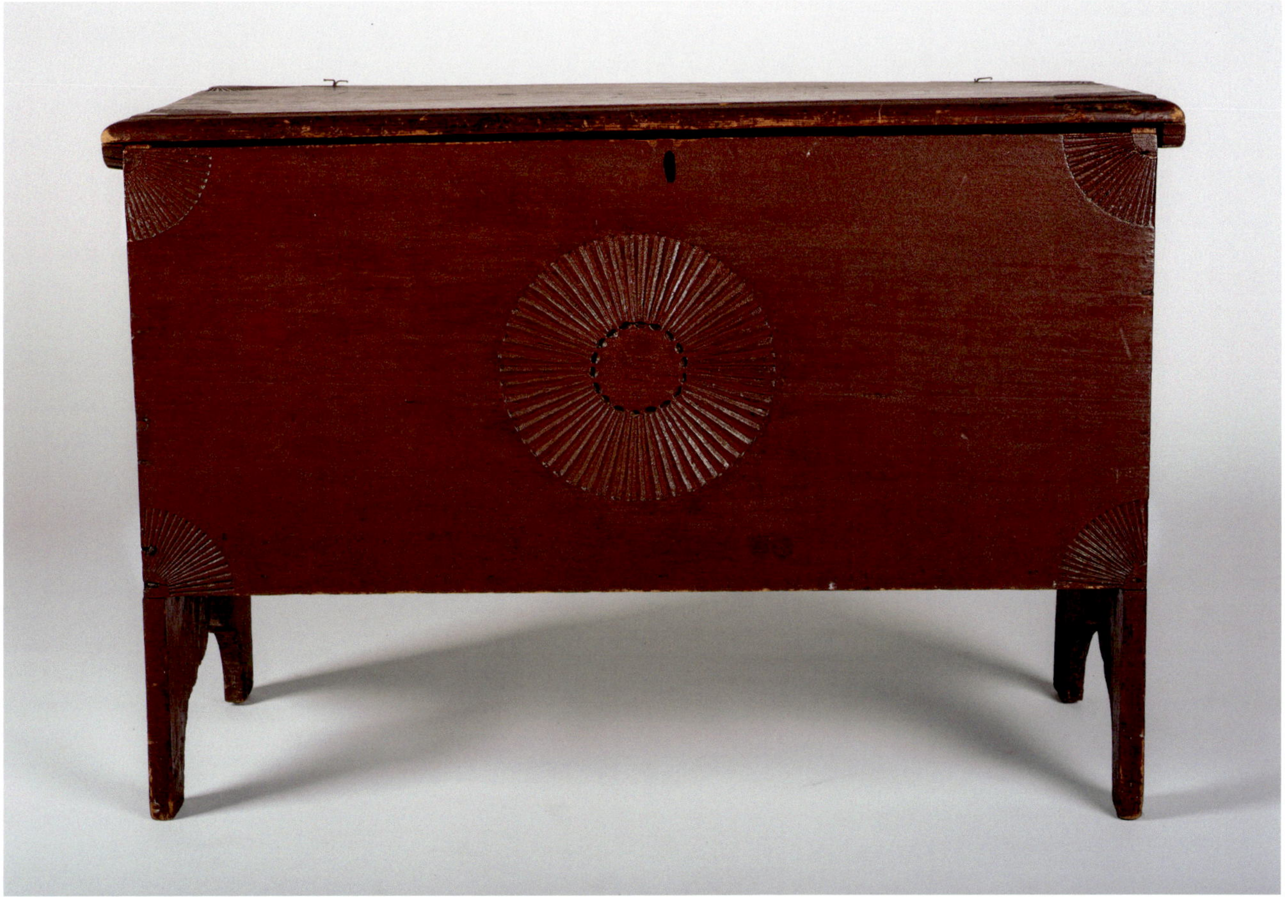

Six-Board Blanket Chest

Hampton, New Hampshire
ca. 1770–85

American white pine with red paint and nineteenth-century clear varnish
25¼ × 36⅛ × 17⅞ in.

Inscription (verso): "S. O. Eaton"

L2015.41.102

Diamond in the Square Quilt

Pennsylvania Amish
ca. 1890–1900

Wool, pieced
76½ × 76 in.

Inscription (verso): "R.S"

2016.25.60

Maybe one way to think about the balancing act between beauty and restraint is to take a detour into Amish clothing. The dresses, capes, and bonnets of Amish women were and still are plain; any printed fabric was forbidden, reflecting the biblical interdictions against graven images and vanity. However, underneath the long, plain dresses, women wore hand-knitted woolen socks with multiple colors and figurative motifs, most often fruit such as strawberries, and on rare occasions, human forms. These fancy socks were not worn on all occasions, but it is interesting to note that even when they were worn, they did not show. It is clear that within the reserve required by religious law, the Amish women who made the quilts and socks found a new vocabulary to express their sense of beauty. Particularly in their quilt production, they unintentionally foreshadowed an entire stream of modern art.

JG David, how did we go from socks to modern art?

DW Well, the Diamond in the Square pattern quilt is a very reductive design related visually to Josef Albers's prolific series of color variations, often called Homage to the Square.

JG I see. The sensuousness of color and the ability of simple patterns to allow the viewer to respond to blocks of color relations—that is what ties these otherwise disparate things together. Let me ask you another question. Can you tell me how objects in the Fielding Collection fit into the larger context of household possessions?

DW Our lives are increasingly complex, with layers of technology interfacing with us in a multitude of ways. So much of our work is digital and unseen. Our living spaces are often relatively uncluttered. The middle-class houses of the colonial period and nineteenth century, however, were often not so large and probably chockablock with the tools that made the things they used. Consider the use of furniture for storage, rather than our built-in closets, and the many, sometimes ungainly, utilitarian objects, like iron tools in the collection (pp. 210–17). Lacking all the various electrical appliances and lighting that are now ubiquitous, they needed to have at hand all of the accoutrements necessary for lighting lamps and stoves for heat: candleholders and oil lamps of all kinds (p. 227), oil for the lamps, wicks and molds to make the candles, snuffers to extinguish the flames, large fireplaces, and all of the brass and iron pots, pokers, spatulas, and flesh forks. All this made for a busy visual environment—not to mention firewood.

Their lives were slower, and in that sense, simpler. They had no consumer culture such as ours, no fountain of ever-novel entertainments, or clever ways to record themselves. Their access to the past and an imagined future was much more limited. Records were on paper, in logs and books that consumed real space. Fewer choices, we can assume, made colonial and post-Revolutionary America a simpler place.

JG That makes sense. One imagines laundry, preserved foods, items being mended, and worn-out items recycled. The pace of life was based on the seasons, the weather, and the amount of daylight. This leads me to a final point: In your vivid responses, you talk about being a dealer, watching the market, knowing what you're buying, carefully looking for signs of alteration. But you often shuttle from that to how these objects embody philosophical ideas and cultural outlooks. They become tinctures filled with the concentrated essence of another time. What do these objects tell us in broad strokes about the formation of a distinct American national identity no longer in the shadow of Europe?

DW European settlers brought cultural and craft traditions to North America that were naturally changed by the new environment. The objects they produced have more in common with the centuries that preceded settlement. In relation to northern Europe, the small-town and rural American decorative art products were less embellished and distinctly less burdened by pretentious materials. American immigrants created a relatively restrained art that reinforced their ideals of egalitarianism. They rejected aristocratic and complex systems of royalty. Americans were constrained by limited access to fine materials—mahogany and expensive brass fittings. They were often a long way from coastal urban centers, like Boston or Philadelphia, where the latest styles were imported from Europe.

JG Distance is a theme that has run through our conversation. And we, today, are light-years away from the culture that made these objects, a world only beginning to mechanize, a world where religion and family ties determined so much about a person's life path. The objects assembled in the Fielding Collection help visitors to imagine a long extinct way of life, but, perhaps, one whose lessons will be more relevant as we learn to live with less to save the planet. Thank you so much for sharing your passion and profound knowledge of the period. The collection is a testament to the incredible collaborative endeavor—one based on mutual trust—between you and the Fieldings.

From 1980 to 2018, David Wheatcroft was the owner of David Wheatcroft Antiques in Westborough, Massachusetts. He has advised the Philadelphia Museum of Art, the Museum of Fine Arts, Boston, and the American Folk Art Museum. His opinions on American folk art have been sought out by the *New York Times*, *Wall Street Journal*, and *Art & Auction*. Now living in Pennsylvania, he continues to work with clients.

 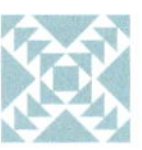 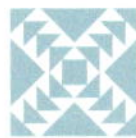

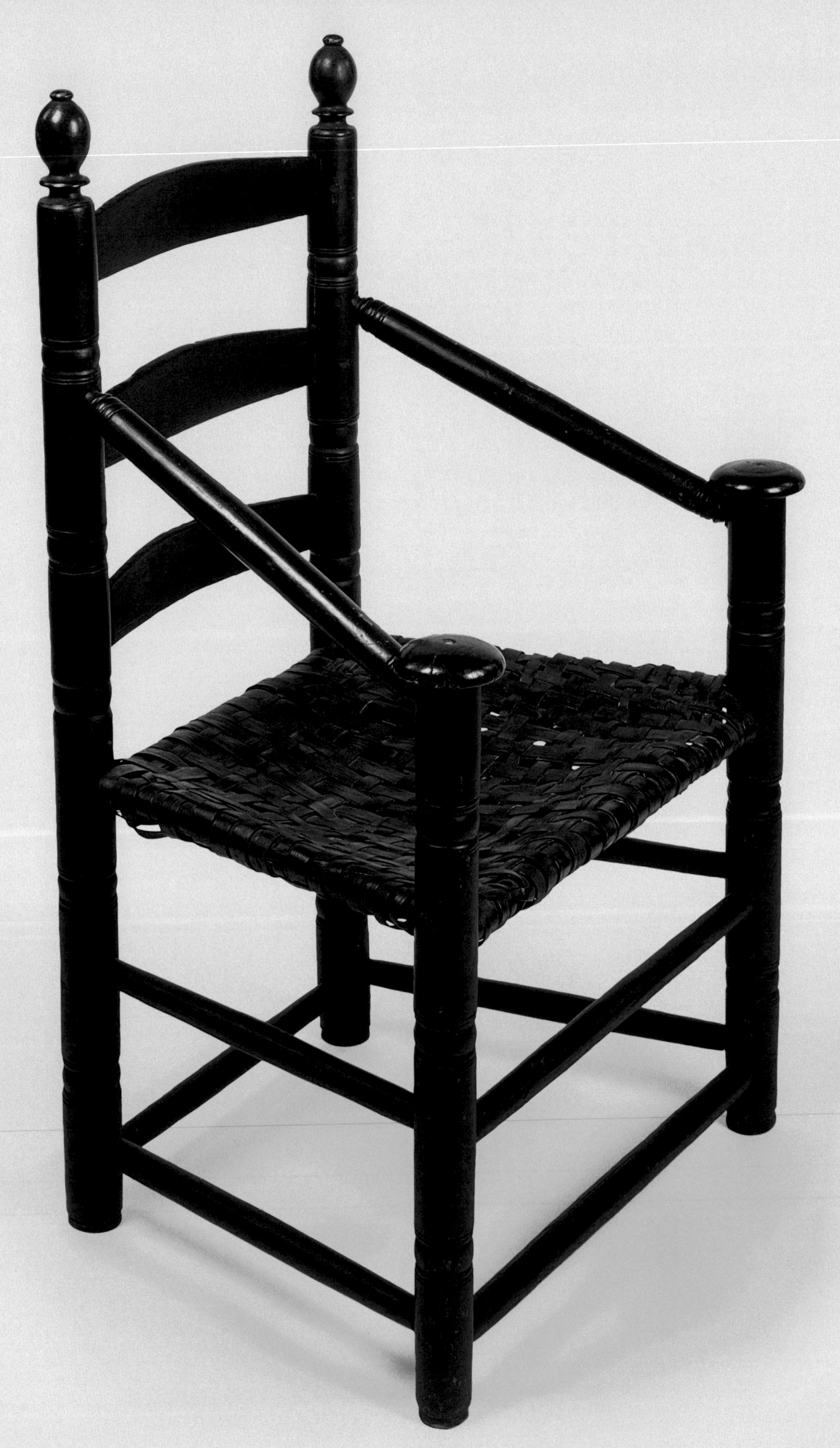

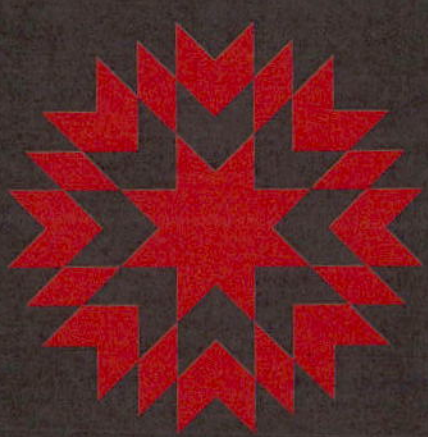

Early American Furniture

Its Making, Its Meaning, Its Pleasures

JOHN DEMOS

If only antique furniture could talk, what would it tell us? For a generation and more, scholars of material culture have worked hard to create such talk. In this they are joined by collectors like Jonathan and Karin Fielding and antiques dealers like David Wheatcroft, a chief source for the Fieldings and an interview contributor to this volume. The result is, indeed, a sort of conversation. Though ostensibly one-way, it nonetheless feels real. When we ask the right questions, the furniture answers. Its response is helped along by various kinds of documentation from the period—account books, estate inventories, occasionally a diary or a piece of personal correspondence.

The questions we could ask of any particular piece of furniture are relatively straightforward: How was it made? When, where, and by whom? How was it used? What did it mean over time, in the minds, hearts, and lives of its makers and users? How has it survived the passage of centuries? Finally, how is it meaningful to us today?

MAKING

We must start by acknowledging the factors of time and space. The core of the Fielding Collection dates from the late seventeenth, eighteenth, and early nineteenth centuries, with provenance in the northeastern part of what would become the United States. Its focus, with some important exceptions, is early New England.

Even this degree of narrowing, of specifying, leaves much room for change and difference. Between, say, 1670 and 1830, furniture making passed through a sequence of style periods: Jacobean (1660–1700), William and Mary (1690–1740), Queen Anne (1730–70), Chippendale

Chair

New London, Connecticut, or Long Island
ca. 1690–1700

Maple, ash, rush, and black paint
41½ × 26¾ × 20½ in.

L2015.41.107

(1760–1800), Federal (including Hepplewhite and Sheraton, 1790–1830), and Empire (1820–50), to name the leading, if somewhat old-fashioned, categories. The variance between them is large. A tall, black-painted, bannister-back chair from the William and Mary period (p. 82), to take just one example, bears little resemblance to its angular, colorful, Sheraton counterpart (except, of course, that both served as seating).

There is also some crosscutting between "high-style," "country," and "primitive." This trio corresponds very roughly to what we now call class difference, upper, middle, and lower; in short, they reflect different levels of wealth and social rank. Another kind of crosscut must also be mentioned: location, urban versus rural. The highest of the high-style would have appeared mainly in the households of affluent city dwellers (in Boston, New York, and Philadelphia), the most basic of the primitive among simple folk in the hinterland. The majority of the Fielding Collection qualifies as country, while occasionally (since these boundaries somewhat overlap) pushing toward high-style. (Antiques dealers might collapse the two by referring to "high country.") The term *country* does not mean of lesser interest or value—or beauty. To the contrary, some of the finest of all early American furniture is country through and through.

The men (invariably men) who made such furniture were well-established artisans—woodworkers, residents of mid-sized towns (Salem or Northampton, in Massachusetts; Hartford, in Connecticut; Portsmouth, in New Hampshire), and likely to be prominent in local affairs. They kept what they called a "shop" as the locus of their production—a room attached to the home, or sometimes a small outbuilding nearby. Wherever found, it was a busy, cluttered place, full of hand tools, furniture parts, rude containers of paint pigments and varnish, a long bench with attached vises and clamps, foot- and hand-powered lathes, and worktables scarred with the markings of the trade. It was, too, a showroom where customers would come to examine, order, and then carry off a finished product. The shop's crew would often include a journeyman, another woodworker hired by the day, and an apprentice or two, boys learning the craft under the tutelage of the master. (Apprentices were a subcategory of servants, bound by contract for a stated period, and members of the master's household. The master was, in every sense, their boss, and he stood in loco parentis—if he was not, in fact, their actual parent.)

Furniture making was unspecialized, low-technology work. The master was in charge of every aspect, from conception through all phases of construction to sales. In the seventeenth century he might even have had to cut the trees, trim the logs, and saw the boards—before starting actual construction. Later on, in a more developed environment, he could resort to local mills and lumber merchants for materials. In all periods, however, he would have known wood in very deep ways: its many species (oak, maple, white pine, and cherry were New England favorites), the intrinsic properties

Federal Lift-Top Chest of Drawers

Probably New York State or Connecticut
ca. 1830

Poplar and paint with metal pulls
47¼ × 43 × 19¾ in.

Detail on p. 71

L2015.41.104

of each, its growth patterns, its subtle gradations. Wood was the very stuff of his work—and life.

He did not, however, operate in an ad hoc way; he followed habits and methods passed down from generation to generation. Many woodworkers were part of a family line: a father training and then succeeded by a son, a grandson, and so on. Within the larger community, woodworkers formed their own subgroup, which enabled them to consolidate capital and reputation, and to control training. Working separately, they nonetheless influenced each other. So it was that a town or region might evolve a distinctive style. The preferences of clients—almost all of them local—were shaped accordingly; this, too, weighed on the side of continuity. There was innovation, but only to a degree and mostly with the details.

To be sure, furniture making was not wholly shut off from outside influence. One broad current ran from city to countryside. Rural shops, aiming to please rural customers, might adapt a stylish urban form. For example, the graining painted on a chest might simulate the surface of a high-style piece

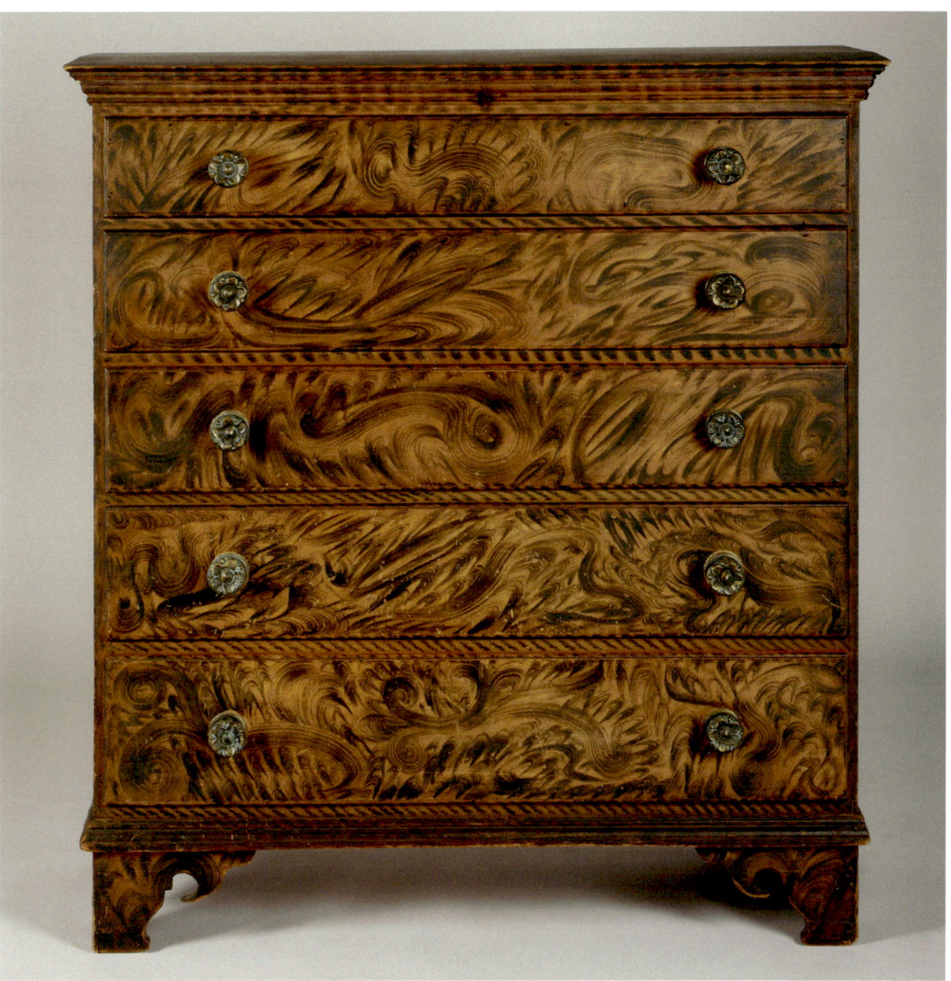

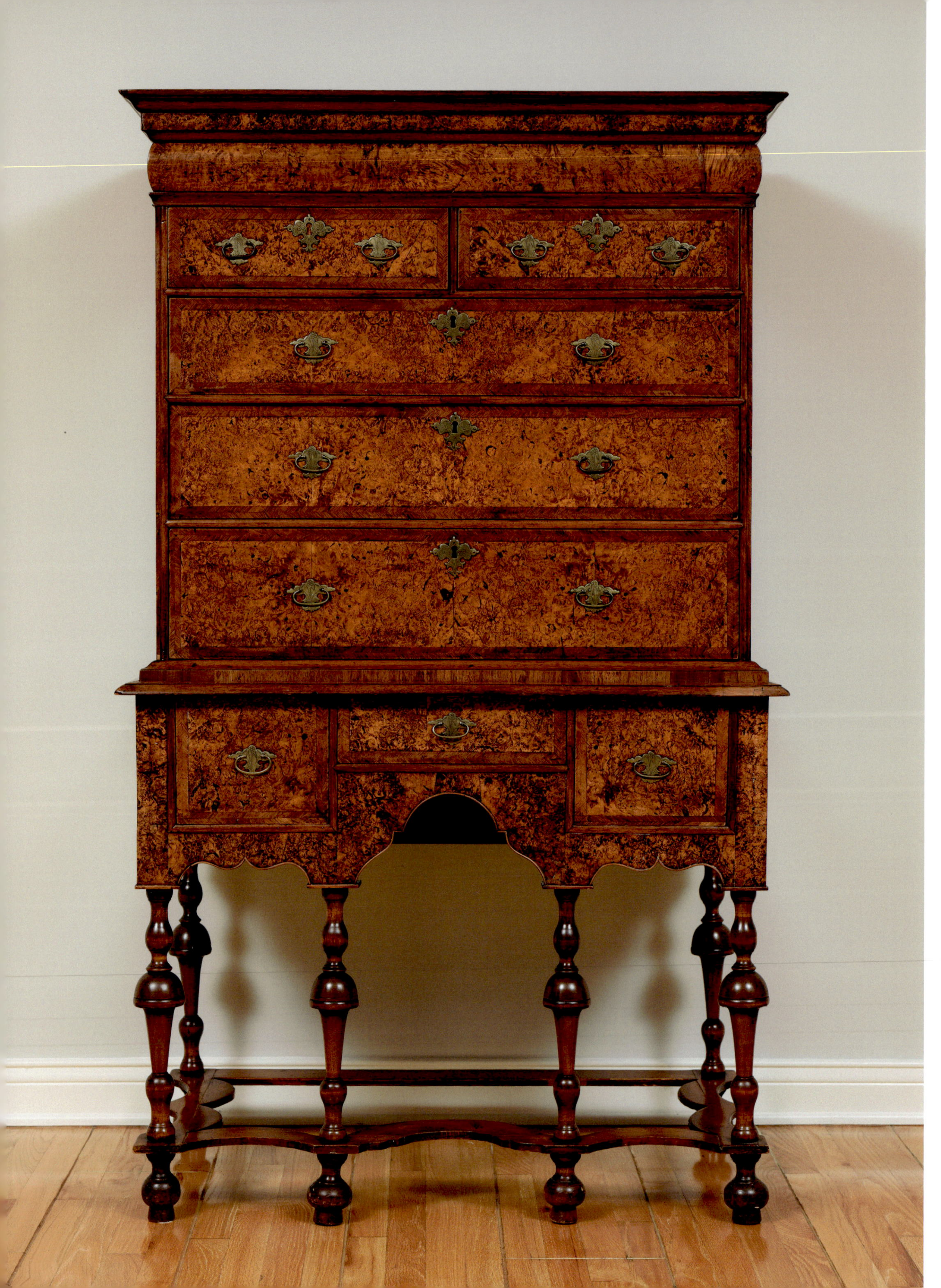

High Chest of Drawers
Boston area
ca. 1720
Maple, pine, ash, and mahogany with brass hardware
66½ × 39½ × 23 in.
Detail on pp. 60–61
L2015.41.91

in walnut or mahogany made for an urban clientele (p. 84). Or another kind of paintwork might mirror a much fancier carved design.

Makers and customers made decisions together and in person. Thus, when a farmer needed side chairs for his expanding family, he went directly to the shop. He expected to purchase a set of perhaps a half dozen. The shop would offer several alternatives, with a range of price and workmanship. These might be "bespoke" (commissioned) or, later on, ready-made; in the former case, the customer could exercise a degree of choice over size and style (for the back, bannisters, an urn-shaped "fiddle," or graduated slats; for the seat, a weaving of rush or splint; for the legs, curved "Spanish" scrolled feet or turned balls). Often enough, a maker had already stockpiled a number of each of the necessary parts; what remained, then, was their assemblage. To this limited extent, furniture making was a form of mass production.

It was also seasonal. Most woodworkers, certainly those outside the cities, were part-time farmers. They grew much of their own food on land they owned and tended; they kept livestock for fieldwork, and milk, and butchering. Like their neighbors, they planted in the spring and harvested in the fall. Winter was the main time for furniture making (but also, to a lesser extent, midsummer). It was then that they created most of what became their stock-in-trade.

The work was often called *joinery*, and the workers themselves *joiners*. These age-old terms had long described a particular skill, the essential process of fastening together adjacent furniture members. The classic device was a mortise-and-tenon joint, with a tenon, or "tongue," on one piece driven into a mortise, or slot, in another. A peg or "pin" would hold them in place. An alternative was the dovetail, in which one part is tapered (to something like a dove's tail in shape) and fitted into a corresponding wedge-like recess.

Another important skill was *turning*, the shaping of wood parts by applying a cutting edge as they rotate on a lathe; its practitioners were called *turners*. There was also carving, especially in the earliest years. Adept use of special tools—chisels, gouges, files—might yield a three-dimensional design; flowers, vines, and compass-drawn geometric shapes were favorite motifs. But these distinctions seem to have faded over time. Most woodworkers could perform joinery, turning, and carving—all three. *Carpentry* and *carpenter* were terms of more general purpose, covering anything that involved nailed construction. This might even extend to building houses and ships—additional roles of woodworkers, at least occasionally. In sum, furniture making was just a part, albeit a central one, in a broad array of woodcraft. It is a wonder that so many did it so well.

Indeed, something more must be said of the sheer beauty created by these various methods. A chest from the shop of a skillful joiner (opposite page) would show its fine proportions: height, length, and width in perfect alignment. A chair, with front legs, rear posts, and topmost finials shaped

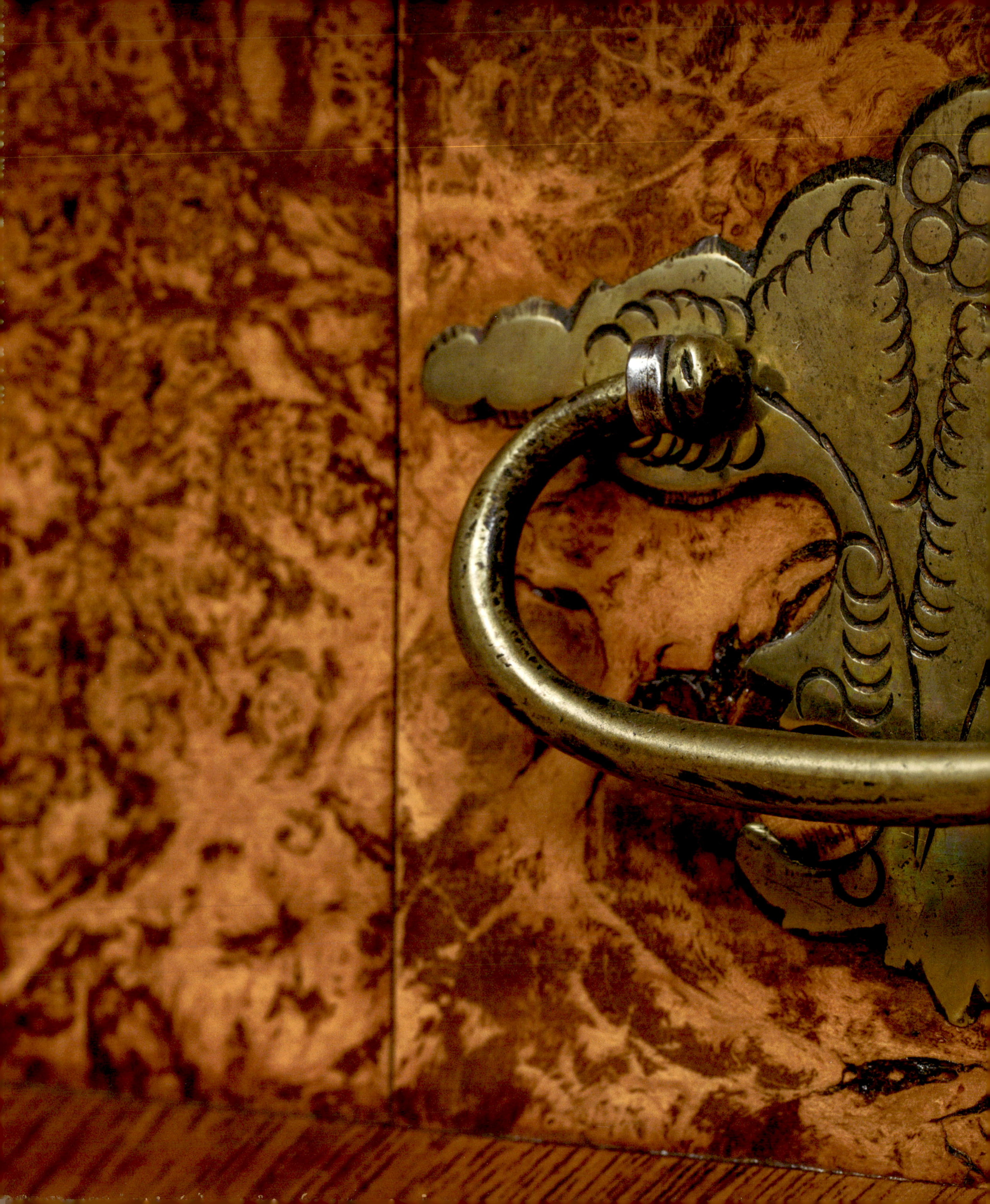

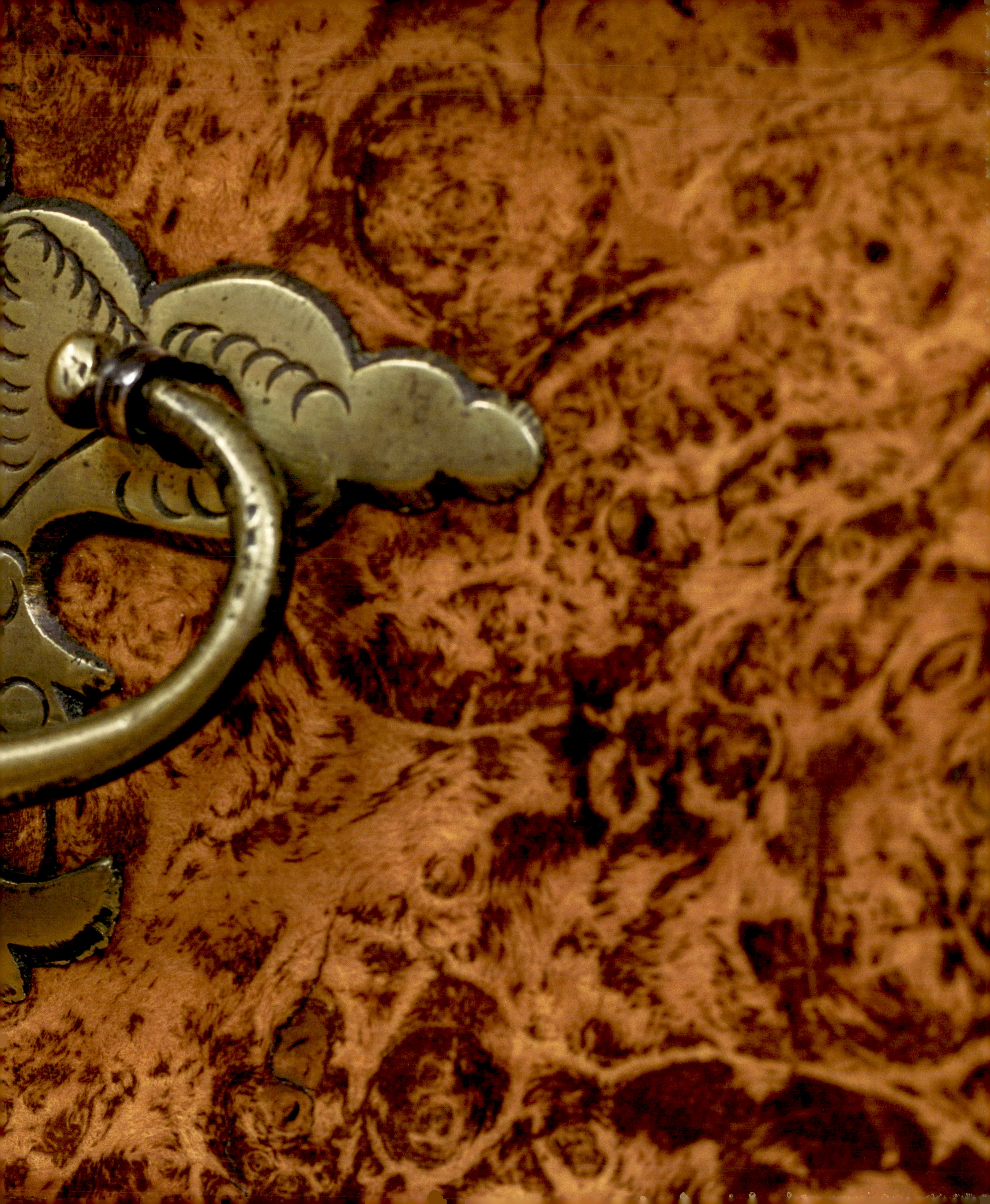

by turning—each part a procession of rounded balusters (pp. 79, 82), compressed balls, narrow rings, and delicate, vaselike platforms—was made to be eye-catching. A tabletop hand-planed to a surface like hard butter was lovely to touch. We sometimes imagine our forebears in centuries past as being too limited, too busy, too unaware, to appreciate fine decoration. Nothing could be further from the truth, and nothing makes the point more clearly than their furniture. They, like us, knew the pleasures of the senses, especially look and feel.

USING

Furniture then and now can be grouped under two broad headings defined by purpose: support, on the one hand; storage, on the other. The former includes chairs, benches, stools, tables, and bedsteads; the latter, chests, trunks, and cupboards of all kinds. Estate inventories, careful records of household possessions tabulated following an owner's death, are especially helpful in sorting out the details of usage and terminology. Sometimes these listings went room by room. In an average case, this would mean a "keeping room" (our closest equivalent would be a living room), a parlor or "best room" (a space reserved for receiving visitors or for other, more formal, occasions), a kitchen (sometimes, but not always, present), and bedchambers (usually on an upstairs floor). The furniture was distributed accordingly.

The keeping room was the site of most everyday activities: cooking on the hearth (if there was no separate kitchen), meals, and domestic crafts (spinning, sewing, candle making, churning, among others; pp. 31, 135–36). Hence it would certainly have had chairs and benches, a dining table, probably a worktable or two, a cupboard, and a variety of craft accoutrements (wheels, buckets, and more esoteric devices like yarn winders).

Space was always at a premium; furniture was made and arranged with that in mind. A conspicuous example was what we now call a *chair-table*, a hybrid form in which a table's top could be swiveled upright and thus become a chair's back, with a small platform underneath serving as the seat. A different kind of table, the so-called drop-leaf, held folding extensions, or leaves, on opposite sides that could be opened and supported by rotating gates, most likely at mealtimes—thus the alternate term *gateleg table* (pp. 76, 77). Either type could be reduced in size when not in use and pushed against a wall, at rest. The middle of a keeping room was precious space, through which various furnishings would be moved in and out, depending on the activity immediately at hand.

The parlor, with its more ceremonial aspect, was a place for displaying a family's most valuable possessions, not least its furnishings. A fine chest of drawers (p. 67) or a so-called press cupboard might hold pride of place, with pewter or silver plate spread out on top. Perhaps there would be some impressive seating furniture, a turned or carved settee (pp. 74–75), or what was commonly called a *great chair*. This last would be for the master, an

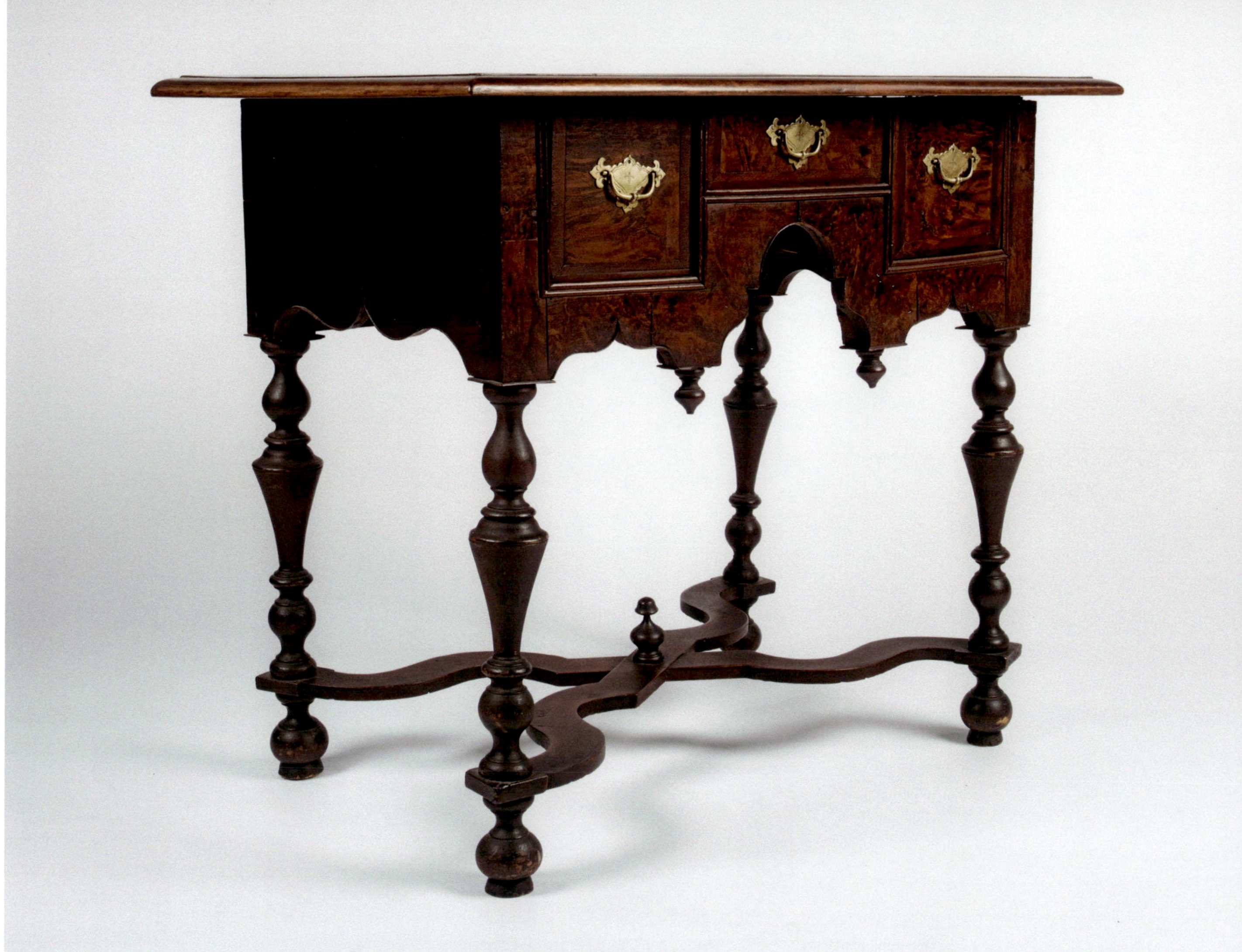

Dressing Table
Boston area
ca. 1710–20
Walnut, walnut veneer, and pine with brass hardware
30 × 33½ × 23¼ in.
Detail on p. 65
L2015.41.95

armchair of large size and stately proportions. A handsome bedstead, hung with embroidered curtains, might also have its own spot in the parlor.

The kitchen, if there was one, was women's space—men took no part in food preparation—and its furnishings were modest and functional. A simple chair or two (though most cooking was done standing up), a rough-hewn table on which to set platters and cookware, a cupboard in the corner: this was the likely extent of it. Upstairs rooms were used mainly for sleeping and storage, and thus had little or no daytime occupancy. Furnishings there were correspondingly sparse: barrels, trunks, and bedding. A country bed was of simple design: a frame composed of head- and footboards and a pair of side rails, with roped netting in between to hold a mattress, which in their minds was the actual "bed."

There was, of course, more variance than this brief sketch can show. Estate inventories record a wide range in the number and quality of furnishings: from greater to fewer, from "fine" to "common." Furniture was always a marker of rank and prosperity.

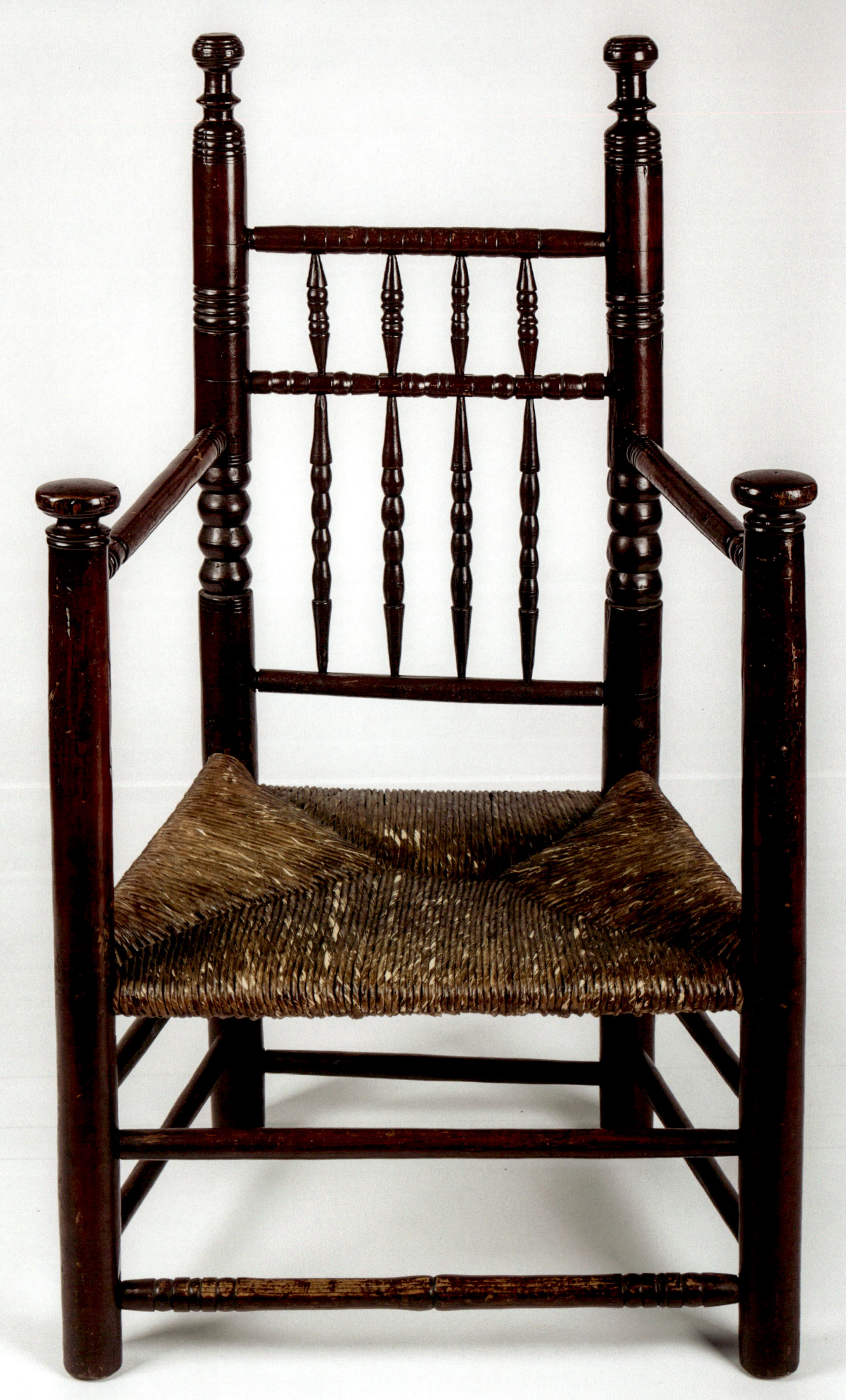

MEANING

Going further to interpret what furniture meant to its makers and users is a difficult task. We enter what is, by and large, a realm of inference, of possibilities. We can start with the obvious point that theirs was a world of hand-wrought, as opposed to machine-made, objects—of things taken from, but not entirely removed from, nature. Did a chest (a table, a chair) placed in a room evoke, at some level, the trees that supplied the material from which it was fashioned? Conversely, did trees suggest the possibility of a chest? Was there not, then, a feeling of closeness, even intimacy, between men or women and their furnishings? Perhaps this gave added meaning to ownership; to own and use was to possess in a more than ordinary sense. On a good many surviving objects we find initials—and yearn to know more. What kind of personal linkage did such inscriptions imply? Wills sometimes mention particular furnishings: a great chair bequeathed from father to son, a dower chest from mother to daughter. These legacies are the source of the word *heirloom*, and surely they were freighted with emotion. The deceased would live on in the things that had—in a sense both literal and figurative—supported them.

Chairs, in particular, invite thoughts of connection. They are so humanlike; they have backs, seats, arms, legs, feet. They mirror our bodies. In fact, this was clearer then—of every chair—than is the case today. (Our own chairs have such varied designs, some quite different from the traditional form.) And there is more. Consider the matter of finials, a small but significant feature of most (not all) premodern chair making. A finial is a distinctively fashioned element at the top of each of a chair's rear posts. On some quite modest examples, it is the only part to which the maker has given special attention, most often by turning. Why is this? What makes it important? The most likely answer is the human face. Finials are positioned so as to frame the sitter's head (p. 80). And in a cultural setting where face-to-face exchange was the

Carver Chair
Maine
ca. 1690
Maple, ash, and red stain
45 × 26½ × 20 in.
L2015.41.98

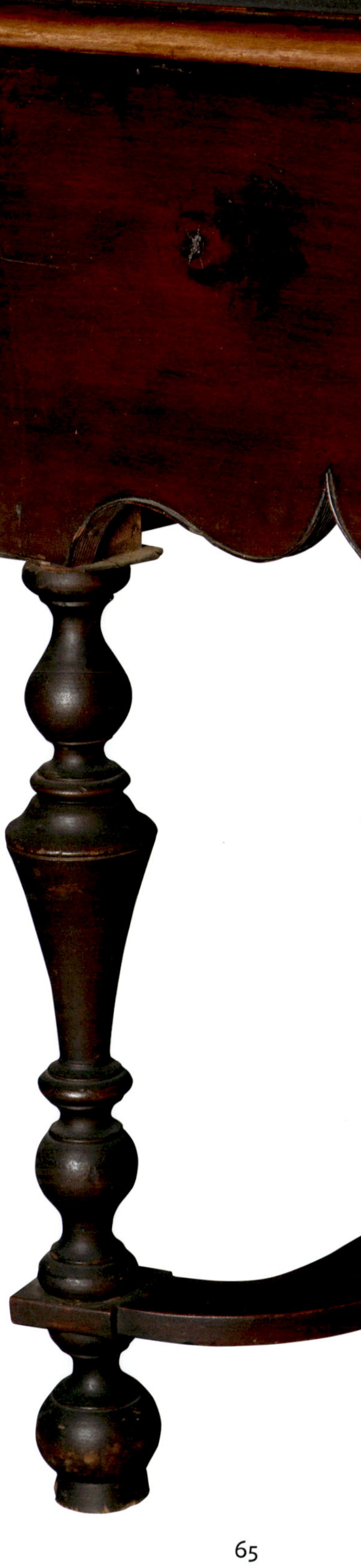

Dressing Table (detail)
See also p. 63

ATTRIBUTED TO THE SHOP OF SAMUEL DUNLAP (1752–1830)

Chest on Chest

Southern New Hampshire
ca. 1780–1810

Tiger maple and brass
82½ × 43 × 23 in.

2016.25.67

norm, this cannot have been coincidental. The face was the person, nothing less. Much on-paper evidence makes the same point more explicitly.

In addition, chairs tell their own story about the power of social rank. A great chair, as mentioned previously, would express the importance of a household "head" (the husband, the father). You need to try sitting in one to appreciate this. The vertical back insists that you assume a ramrod, upright posture. Your arms push forward along those parts of the chair; if there are handholds, you must grip them. Your knees break at the seat front, legs going straight down, feet settling solidly on the floor. (No slouching.) You assume, all told, a highly authoritative pose, indeed throne-like. (A monarch's throne was simply the greatest of all the great chairs in the realm.)

When a seventeenth-century family gathered for dinner at a long, rectangular table, a great chair would rest at one end; there sat the paterfamilias (p. 64). Other seating furniture—consisting, in that earliest period, of unbacked benches and stools—would be ranged down, and "below," on either side; these were meant for women, children, and visitors who were of lower standing—thus the context for the idiom "below the salt." As time passed, the benches were replaced by side chairs, but the principle of center and periphery, of higher and lower, remained.

Only when tables became circular or oval in shape—a gradual change, spanning the early and middle decades of the eighteenth century—was a different, more egalitarian, pattern established. By this point, too, chairs had become less constricting and more comfortable. A prime example was the Windsor form, with a row of spindles creating a rounded back, and a sculpted seat bottom. Drawn from English prototypes, it was soon recast in a simpler American style. Because they were inexpensive to make and appealing to all, Windsors soon became the "democratic" choice of numerous American households (p. 72).

We cannot recover the full range of such meanings for early American folk because we cannot go right inside their heads. But it seems safe to say that furniture was threaded into all parts of their thinking, values, and practice.

SURVIVAL

As the colonies achieved independence and remade themselves as a nation, furniture traveled alongside. Old was out; new was in. New, new, new: thus the cry in all quarters. Chairs, tables, chests, and many other kinds of inheritance from the centuries preceding became passé; what had once seemed stately was now stodgy. Some old pieces were simply tossed out, others consigned to attics or cellars. Still others remained in use but in a compromised condition (feet cut down, seats replaced, to remove decay; the paint surface faded and scuffed). Occasionally, one with remarkable workmanship or strong connections (to ancestors, for example) might be lovingly preserved. But these carried a flavor of the quaint, the peculiar—no longer fully

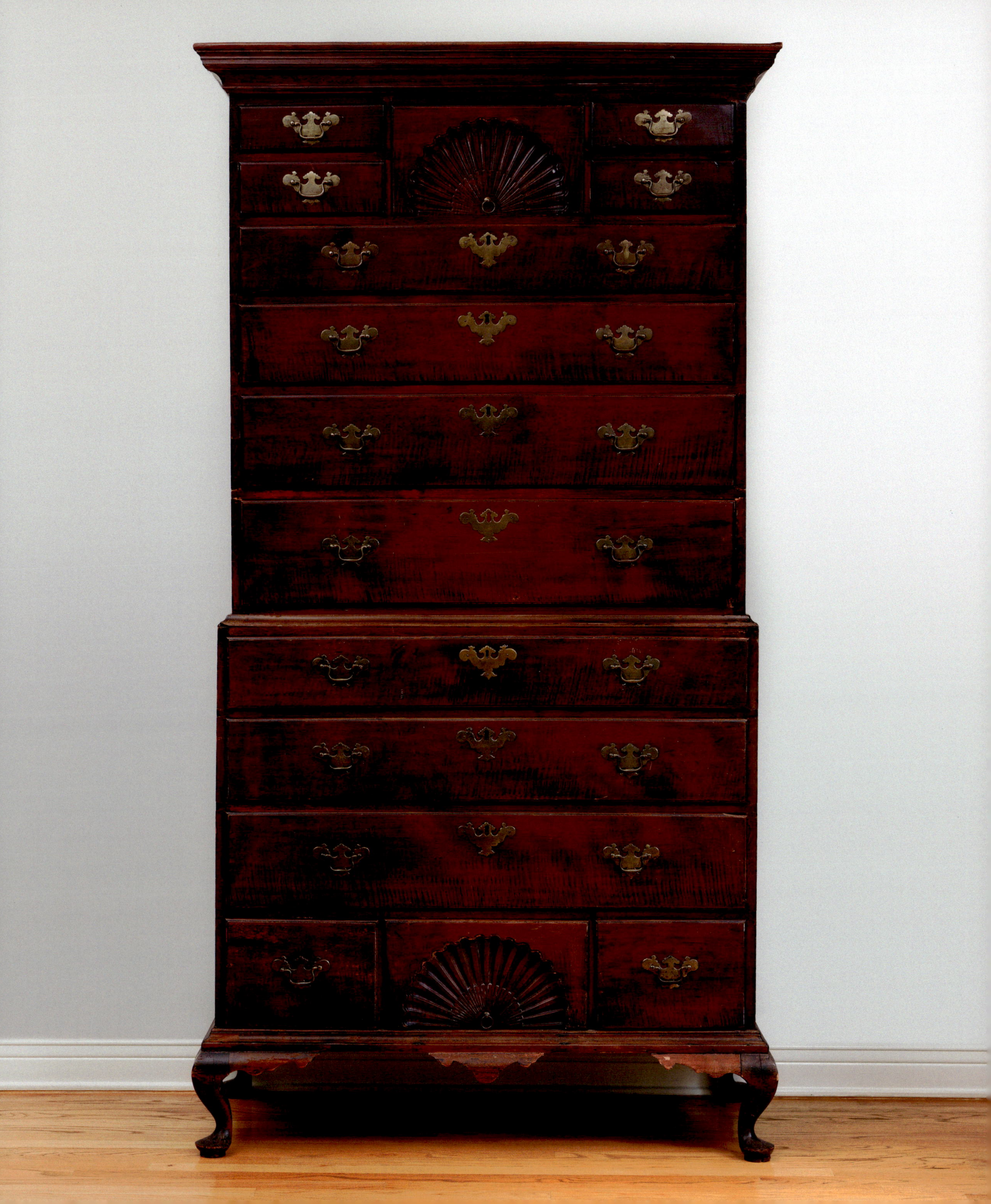

embraceable. Looking back from the modern era, we can see a winnowing process here. The finest, the "best," survived much more than the common. The antiques world of today is skewed accordingly. Great chairs are relatively abundant in collections and museums, and on the market—the seat forms of humble folk a rarity. The Fielding Collection is unusual in its focus on rural and country objects.

To be sure, the craft of woodworking continued apace. But style preferences changed dramatically. Much of the furniture made in the first decades of the new (nineteenth) century expressed a spirit of excitement, not to say exuberance. The term we give to it now is *American Fancy*. Color and vivid design ruled the day, consistent with the hopeful, expressive tenor of what many called "Young America." This was especially true of "country" work, painted case pieces (boxes, trunks) most of all (pp. 102–7).

Meanwhile, another category of furniture making—cabinetry—rose to prominence, especially in the ranks of elite society. Starting as far back as the early decades of the eighteenth century, cabinetmakers created highboys, dressing tables, and similarly elegant pieces, typically made from imported mahogany, to grace the homes of the most affluent. Indeed, many would say that cabinetmaking was the apex of woodworking craft.

Then came what we know as the Industrial Revolution, a sea change for all sorts of productive enterprise. Most furniture making moved out of traditional shops and into factories. Handmade gave way to machine-made. And the survivors from an earlier time became exactly that—survivors—and thus more "quaint" than ever.

But further twists and turns still lay ahead. The approach of the nation's centennial—1876, one hundred years after the Declaration of Independence—birthed a substantial "Colonial Revival." Quite suddenly, Americans began looking back on their origins with feelings of special fondness, even reverence. Furniture followed the trend—and itself nourished the trend—well into the twentieth century. Much of this Revival furniture was factory-made, with motor-driven machines creating copies of, say, an early Windsor chair or a Chippendale-style highboy. Thus a new term entered the antiques world: *repro*, for reproduction. A Connecticut clergyman-turned-entrepreneur named Wallace Nutting led the way there. Furniture, produced in factories organized and financed by Nutting, became the keystone of his broad-gauge campaign to re-create what he called Old American Life. As he once said, succinctly and sweepingly, "Whatever is new, is bad." The irony is that he was making the old new again.

Even as Nutting and others pursued their Revival agenda, antiques—the Real Thing, not repros—began to spark renewed interest. By the 1920s one could speak of an "antiques market"—with auctions and dealer shops and shows proliferating. Major museums followed suit, offering "period" rooms stocked with early furniture. Old pieces emerged from attics, barns, and other sites of neglect; dusted off, scrubbed, repaired, "restored," they entered the domain of commerce. Too often, alas, they were stripped of their original paint surfaces; buyers of that era preferred the look of "natural wood." Scholars—more from the museum world than from academia—turned furniture history into a serious field of research. Thus well before the Second World War, antiques had claimed, and filled, their own cultural and commercial niche.

From that point on, the trend lines have followed a broadly consistent course. Market preference has zigged and zagged—what is hotly sought after in one year or decade may be "down" in the next. Values fluctuate accordingly, in response to larger economic conditions. (The Great Recession of 2007–9 hit the antiques business especially hard.) Dealers worry that their clientele is aging, without sufficient reinforcement by the young. But, for all that, no one expects a general collapse.

TODAY

This brings our story to the present, and the nagging question of why. Why do we care? What does old furniture mean to us? Surely there are complex reasons, and just as surely they vary from one individual or group to the next. Still, when an interest has spread so widely, it must have tapped some quite general set of motives.

Shall we begin by acknowledging the less attractive of these—and thus get them out of the way? The pride of acquisition, control, self-enhancement. (Most collectors would admit, if only in a whisper, to having tasted greed.) The competitive instinct. (Shall we compare?) Hoarding. (Better buy now; soon there won't be any left.) Investment profit. (Perhaps a boom in Chippendale-style chairs is just around the corner?) Depth psychologists have gone further, positing a range of "infantile projections." (These can be left unspecified.)

Enough. There is much else to say on the positive side. Antique furniture may be an acquired taste, but with time and experience it can come to feel irresistible. Again, there is the matter of its look—its sheer beauty. Damn! These makers, these creators, knew what they were about. Shape, surface, proportion, color: the best of them, the most skilled, had mastered all. Another point: handmade meant personal, and so, too, is our appreciation personal—that is to say, heartfelt, emotion-driven. And another: the care invested in them, the cherishing over many generations, humbles us—and, at the same time, uplifts us. And yet another: think time travel. Early furniture is a spaceship, pointed in reverse.

Finally: the pleasures, and duties, of stewardship. We do not truly own these things; they lie beyond such claims. They both precede and outlive us. We receive them from the past, preserve them as best we can, and pass them along to the future. We partake of their journey. Is this not its own reward?

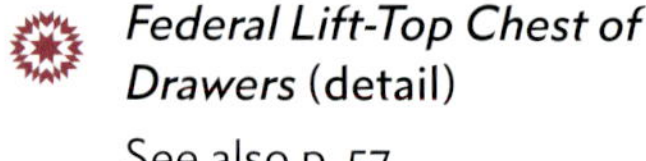

Federal Lift-Top Chest of Drawers (detail)

See also p. 57

I wish to thank Philip Zea, president of Historic Deerfield, Inc., and a leading authority on furniture history, for his careful, critical reading of an early draft of this essay.

The following works have been useful in the preparation of this essay. All can be recommended to readers wishing to pursue matters of furniture history in a more detailed way.

Nancy A. Smith, *Old Furniture: Understanding the Craftsman's Art; A Guide to Collection, Appreciation, and Preservation*, 2nd ed. (New York: Dover, 1991), provides a useful introduction to the whole subject.

John Fiske, *When Oak Was New: English Furniture & Daily Life, 1530–1700* (Ipswich, Mass.: Belmont Press, 2013), explores the English background of early American furniture making.

Jonathan L. Fairbanks et al., *New England Begins*, exh. cat., 3 vols. (Boston: Museum of Fine Arts, 1982), is the catalogue for the finest of all museum exhibitions of early New England furniture and decorative arts, replete with illustrations and short and long essays by experts in the field.

Robert Tarule, *The Artisan of Ipswich: Craftsmanship and Community in Colonial New England* (Baltimore, Md.: Johns Hopkins University Press, 2004), offers an up-close look at the life and work of a single, highly important furniture maker in seventeenth-century Massachusetts, authored by an accomplished furniture maker in our own time.

Edward S. Cooke, *Making Furniture in Preindustrial America: The Social Economy of Newtown and Woodbury, Connecticut* (Baltimore, Md.: Johns Hopkins University Press, 1996), is a detailed study of furniture making in two early Connecticut towns, with emphasis on social and cultural questions as well as those about craft.

Thomas Andrew Denenberg, *Wallace Nutting and the Invention of Old America* (New Haven, Conn.: Yale University Press, 2003), examines the "revival" impulse in American furniture making during the late nineteenth and early twentieth centuries.

John Demos, the Samuel Knight Professor of History Emeritus at Yale University, is the author of ten books on early American history and culture and was twice a finalist for the National Book Award.

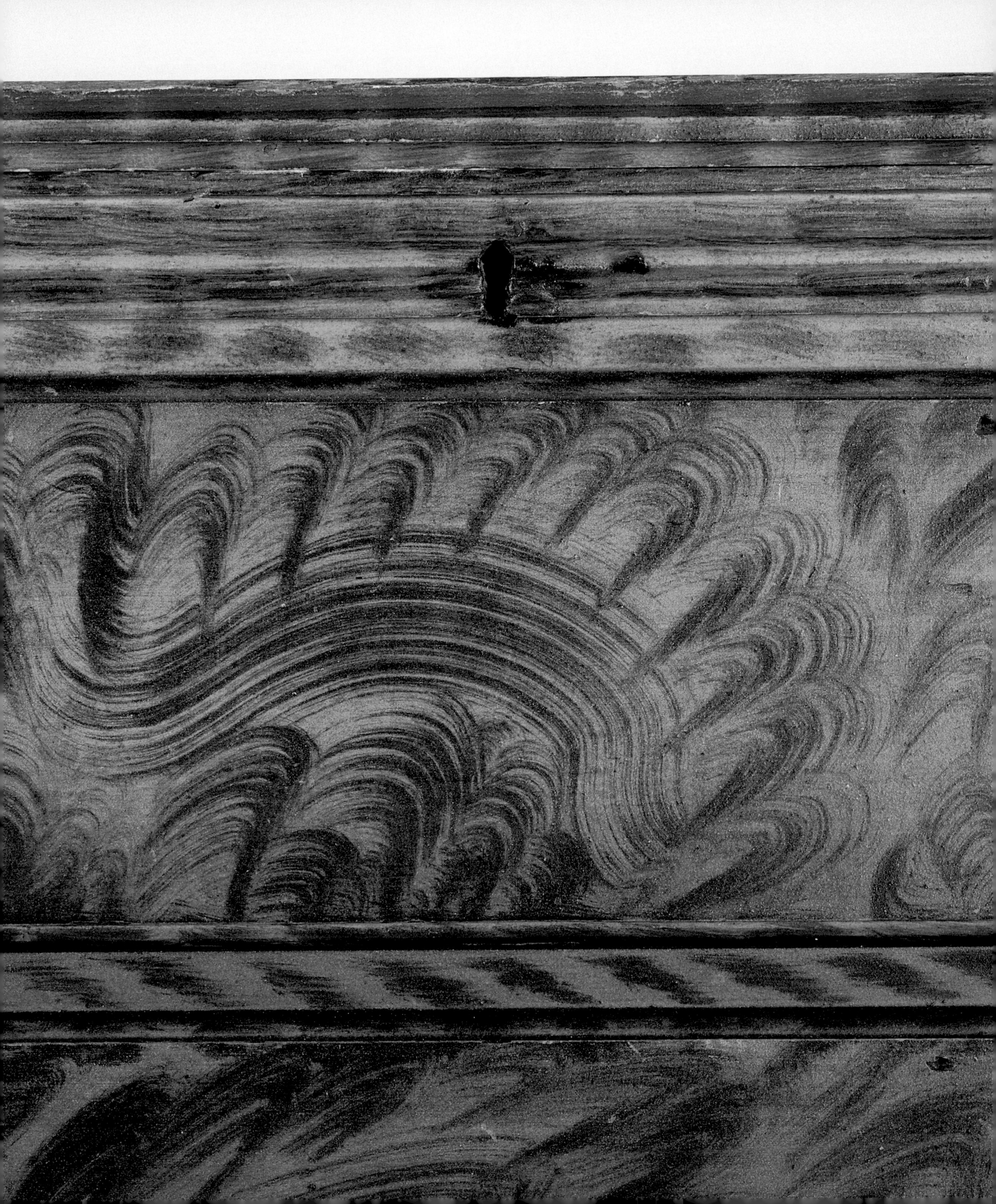

WINDSOR CHAIRS

Windsor chairs like the one shown below feature a solid seat joined to the spindles, arm posts, and legs either by mortise and tenon or by a snug fit into drilled holes. By contrast, other chairs in the Fielding Collection, such as the child's chair at lower right or the slat-back armchair on page 80, have a vertical stile—or back post—that runs from top to bottom as a single piece of wood and an upholstered or woven seat. Other than the seat, which is carved, nearly all the Windsor's components are turned on a lathe. Often called "stick chairs" in the eighteenth century, Windsors became popular in Britain during the 1720s. By the late 1760s, Massachusetts alone exported over a thousand chairs a year to the southern colonies. Their ubiquity cannot be overemphasized: everyone from Thomas Jefferson and Benjamin Franklin to common tradesmen owned them, and they graced homes, workplaces, and public areas like theaters and courtrooms. The comb-back writing armchair on page 18, with its original green paint and two drawers, matches the style of Ebenezer Tracy Sr., whose workshop in Lisbon, Connecticut, produced chairs now considered exemplary.

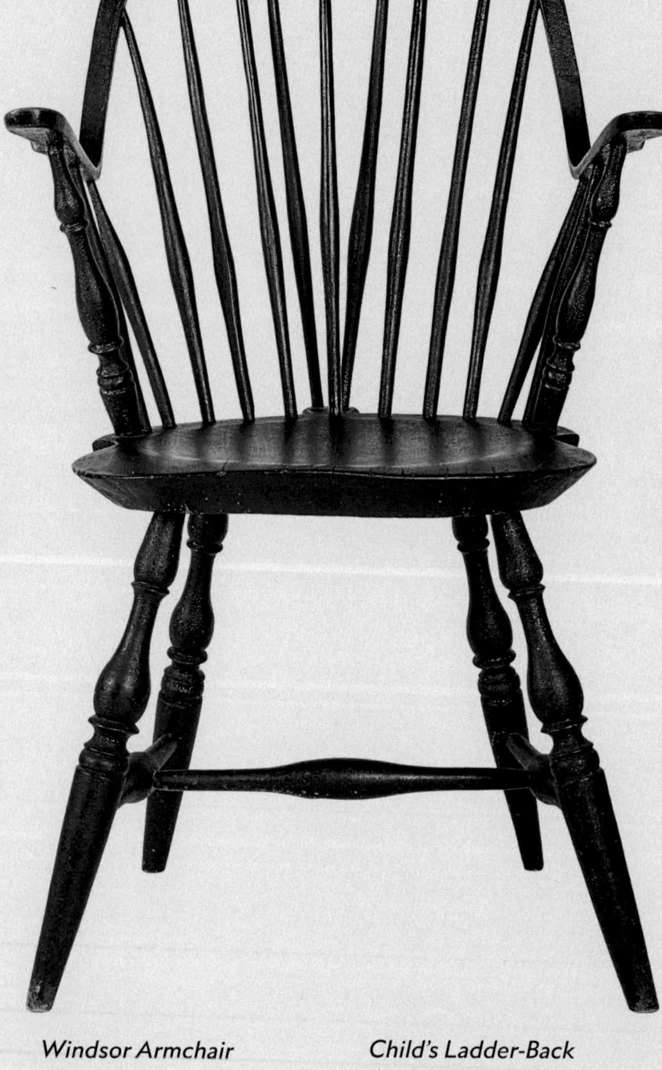

Windsor Armchair
Rhode Island
Oak with hickory spindles
40⅛ × 21⅞ × 20⅞ in.

2016.25.71

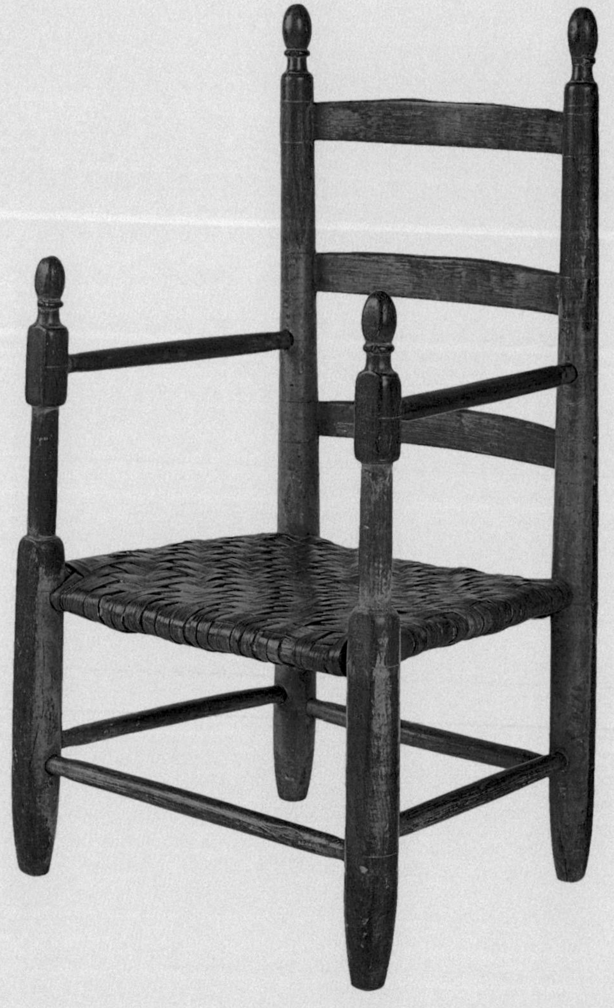

Child's Ladder-Back Armchair
Probably Maine
ca. 1800
Wood, reed, and green paint
23½ × 13 × 11¼ in.

2016.25.72

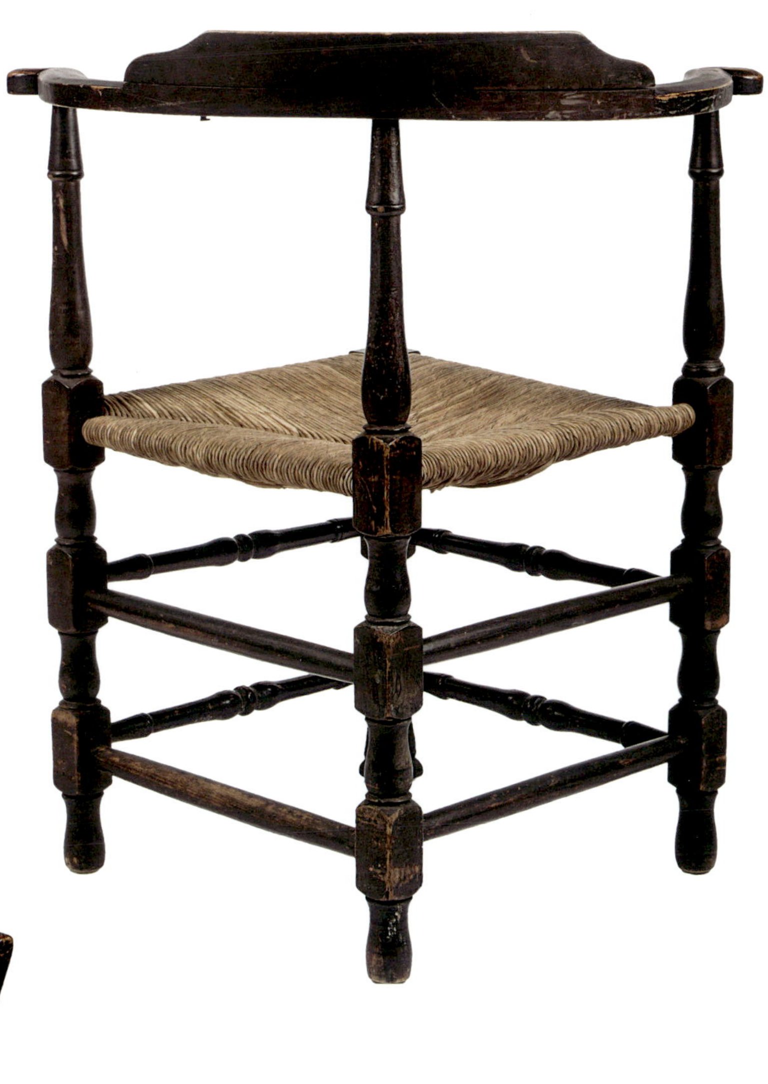

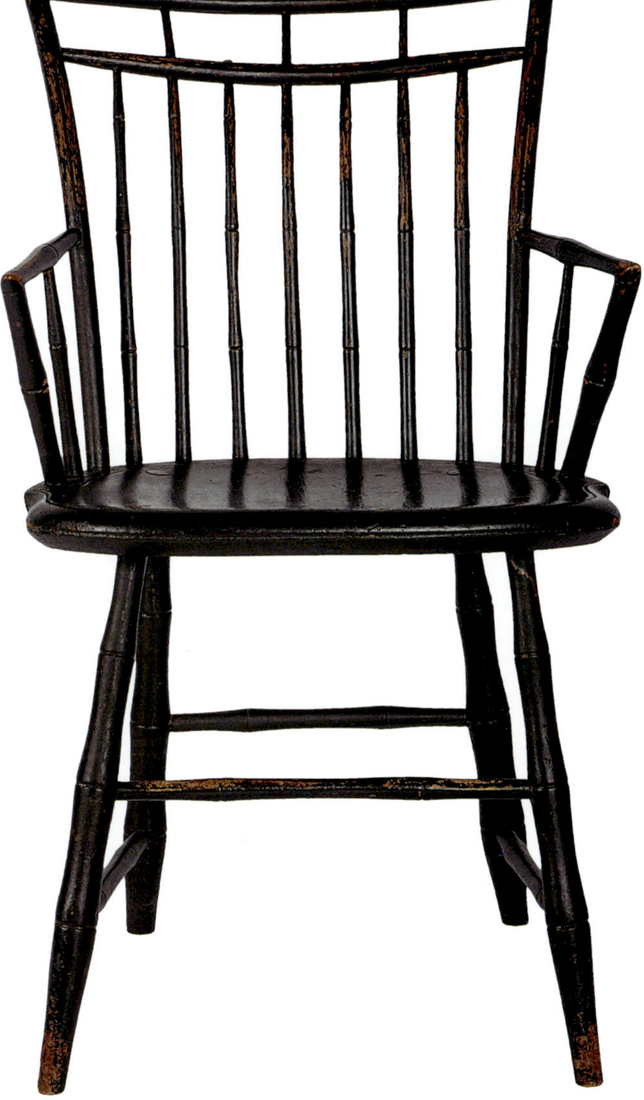

Birdcage Windsor Armchair

Plymouth, Massachusetts
ca. 1800

Wood
34½ × 20½ × 22 in.

2016.25.73

Corner Chair

Eastern Massachusetts or
Rhode Island
Eighteenth century

Maple, rush, and red varnish
31 × 27 × 25 in.

2016.25.62

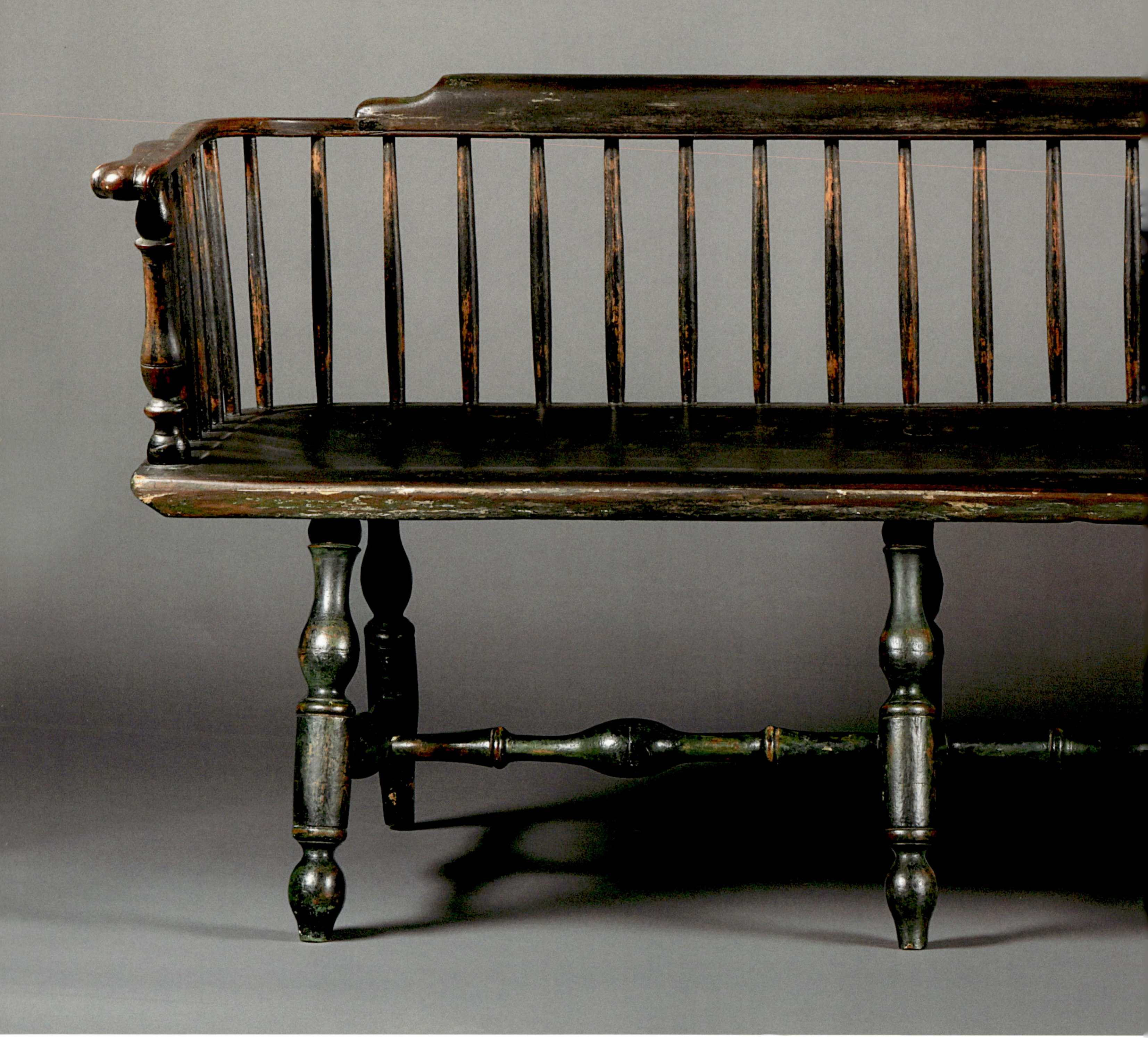

Windsor Low-Back Settee

Lancaster County, Pennsylvania
ca. 1760–80

Wood with black and green paint
30 × 81 × 24 in.

L2015.41.100

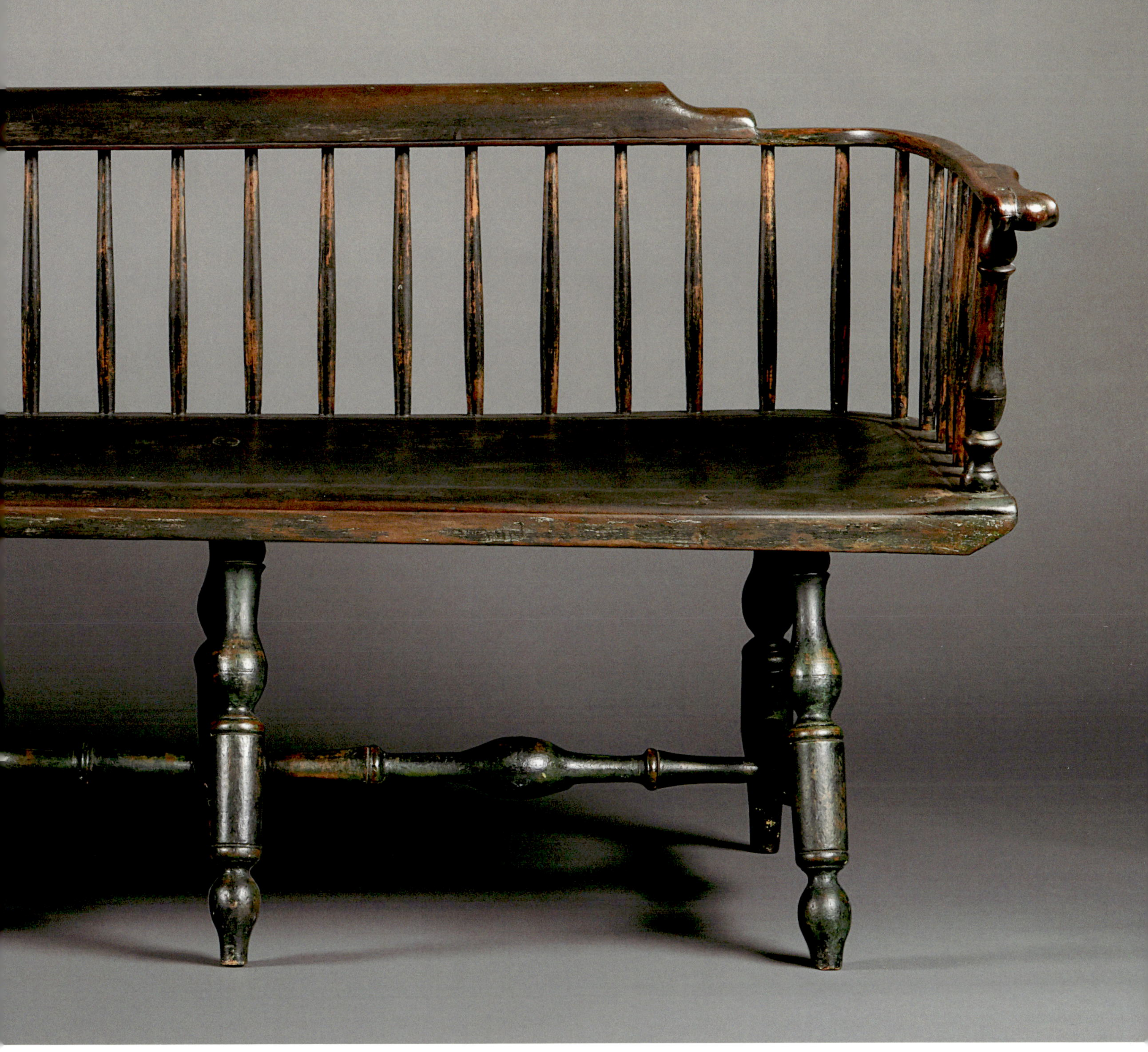

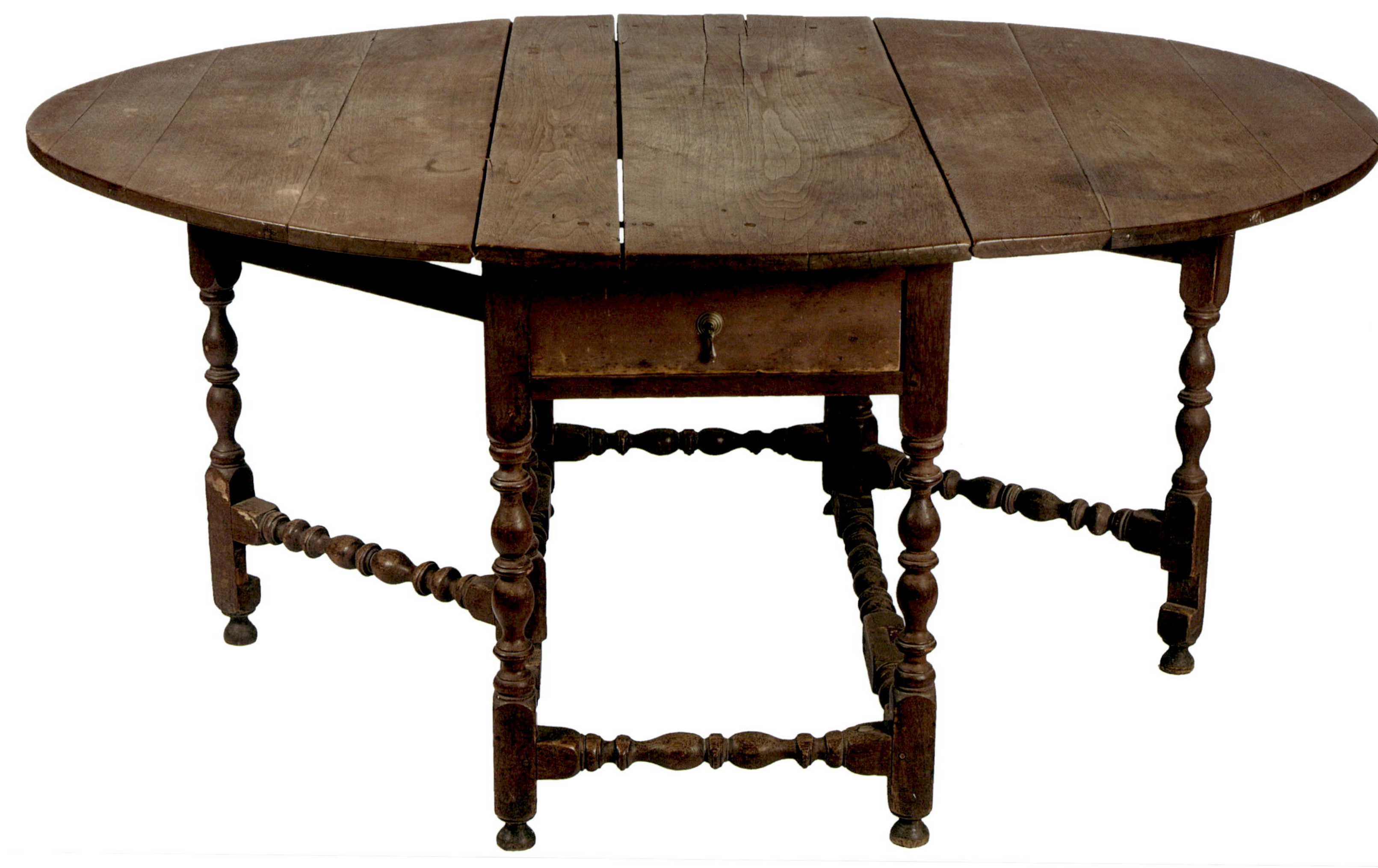

Gate-Leg Table with Drop Leaves

Boston area
ca. 1710–25

Walnut and red paint
Extended: 29 × 63½ × 50 in.
Closed: 29 × 22½ × 50 in.

L2015.41.93

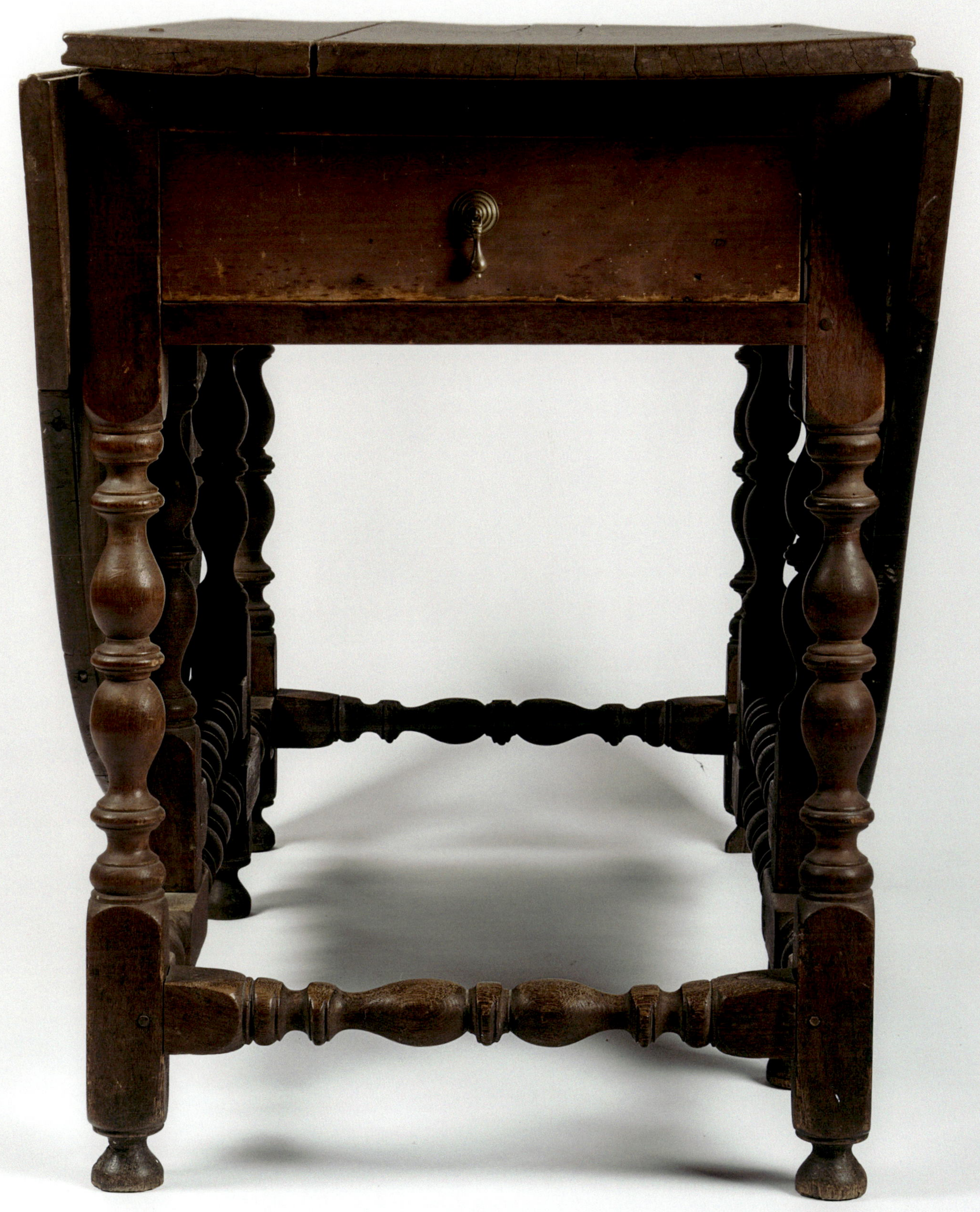

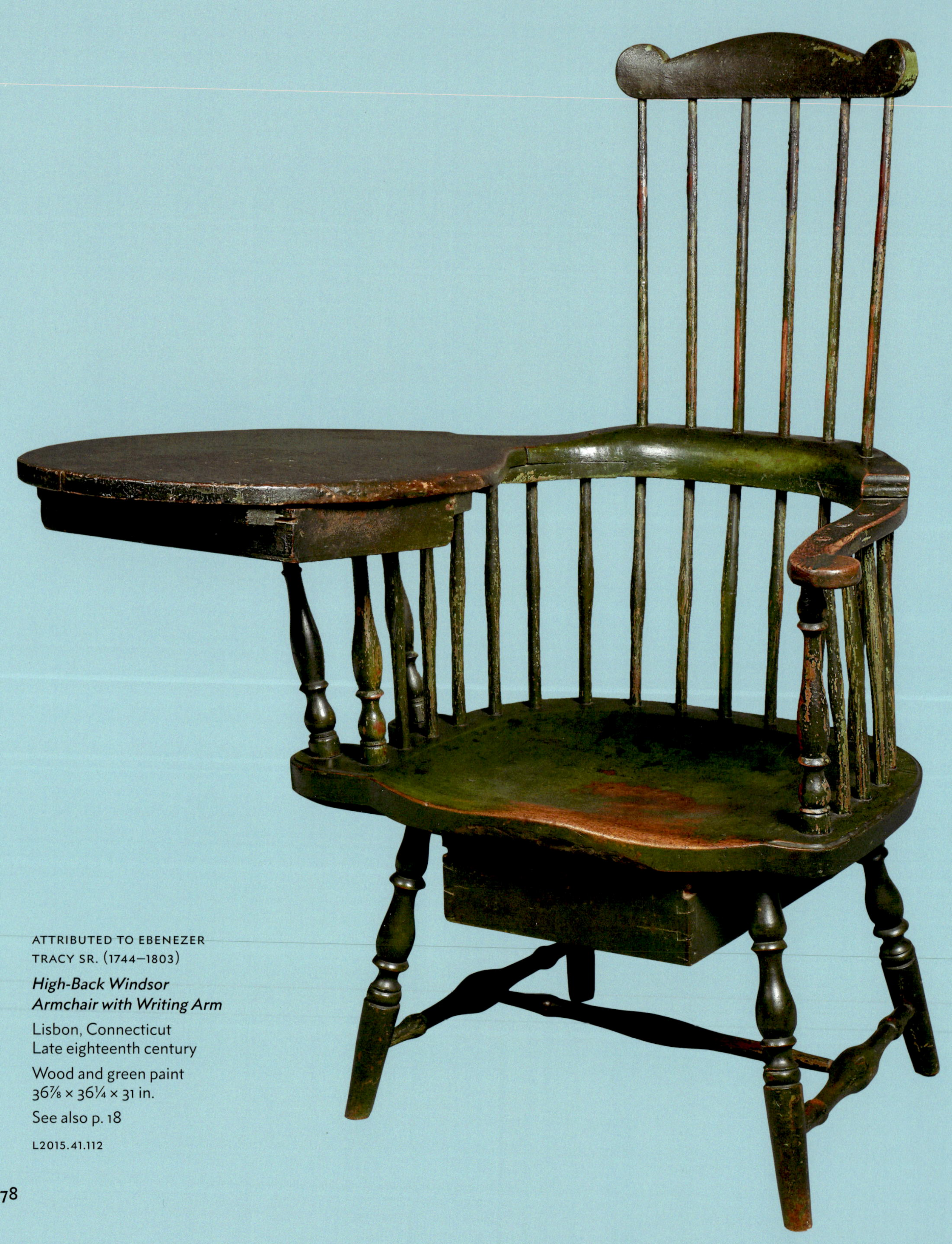

ATTRIBUTED TO EBENEZER TRACY SR. (1744–1803)

High-Back Windsor Armchair with Writing Arm

Lisbon, Connecticut
Late eighteenth century

Wood and green paint
36⅞ × 36¼ × 31 in.

See also p. 18

L2015.41.112

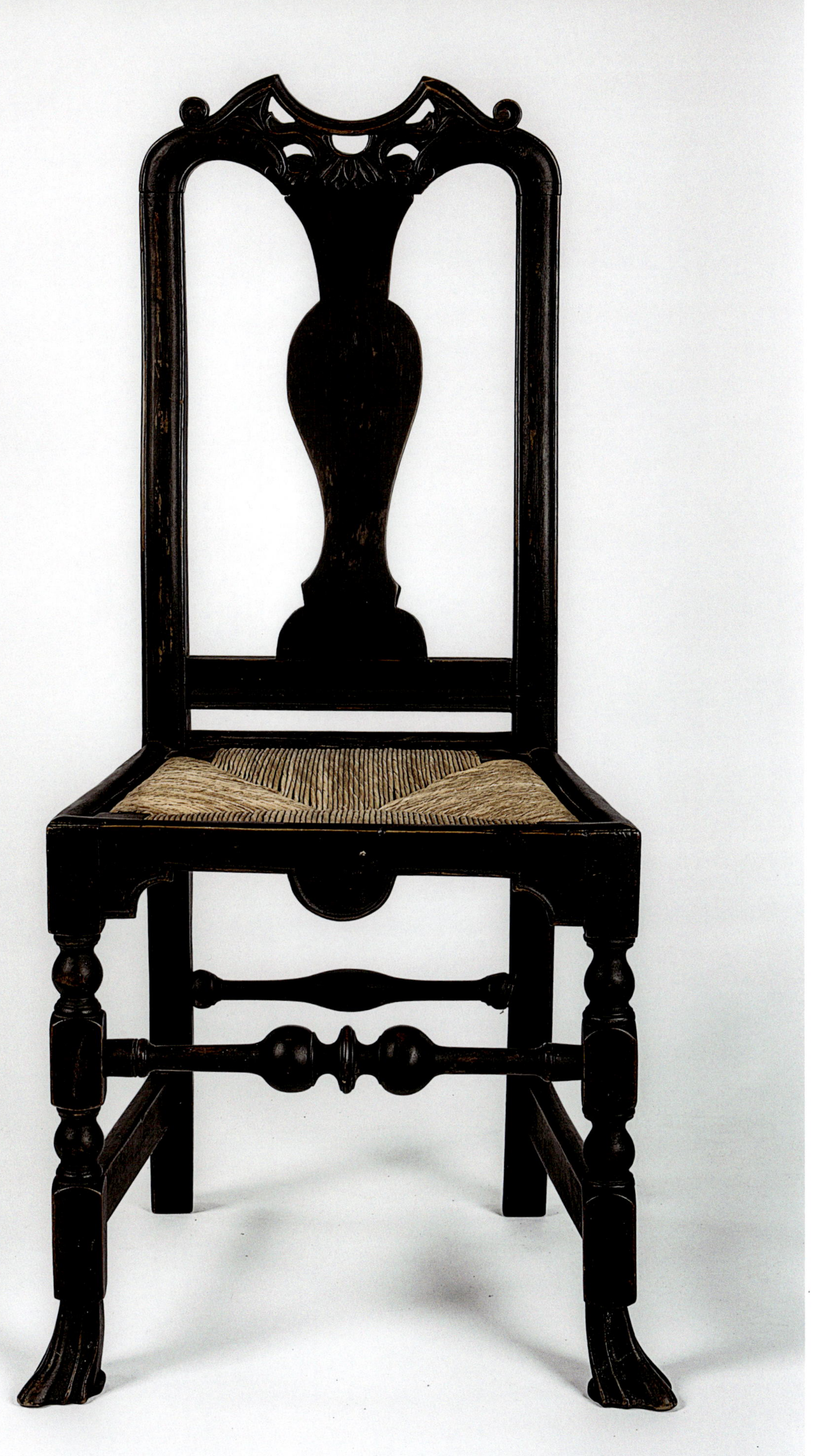

ATTRIBUTED TO JOHN GAINES III (1704–1743)

Side Chair

Portsmouth,
New Hampshire
ca. 1735–43

Wood and rattan
41½ × 20½ × 20 in.

L2015.41.89

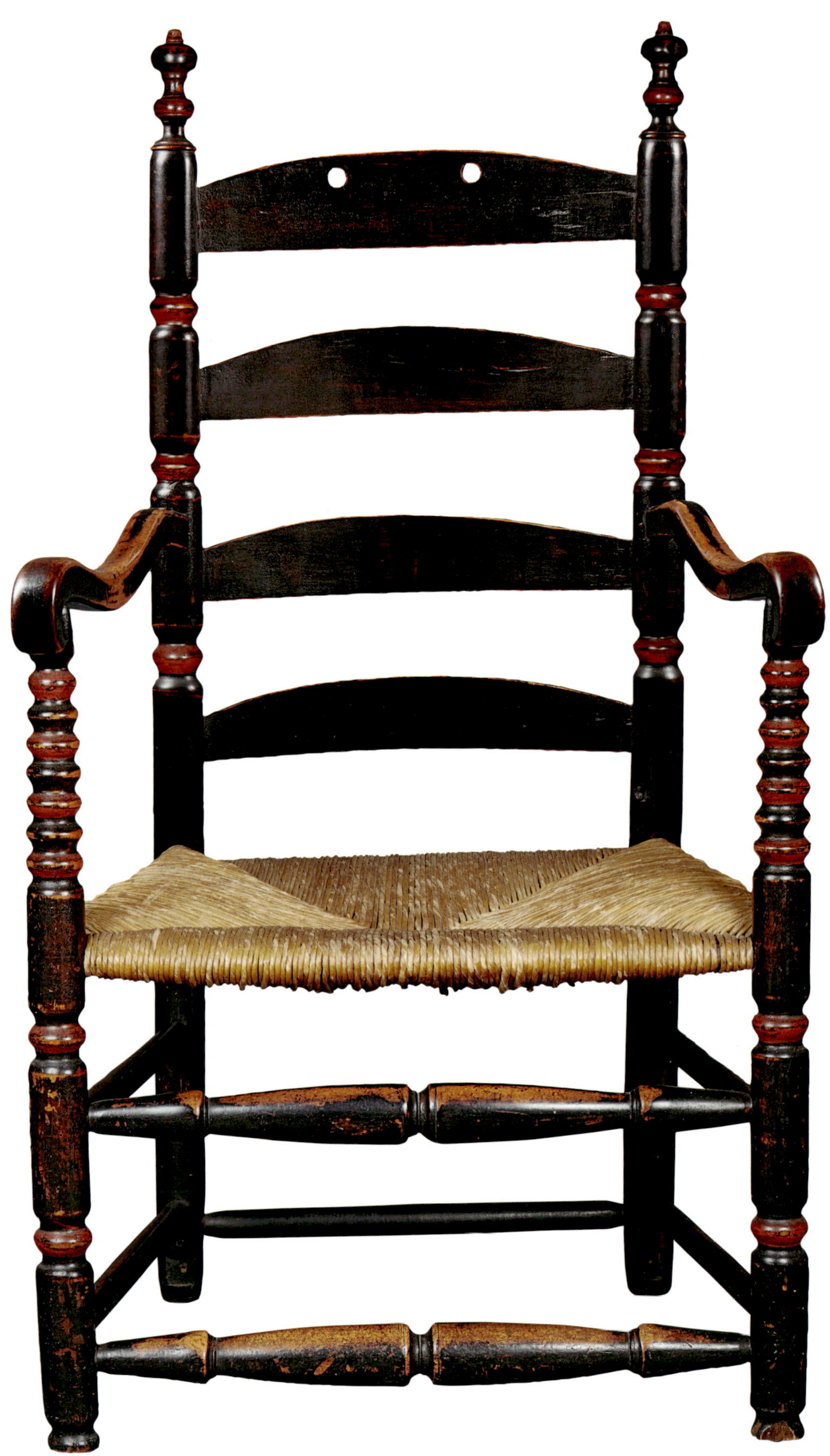

Slat-Back Armchair

Probably New York
ca. 1740

Wood with red
and black paint
47 × 25½ × 23 in.

2016.25.65

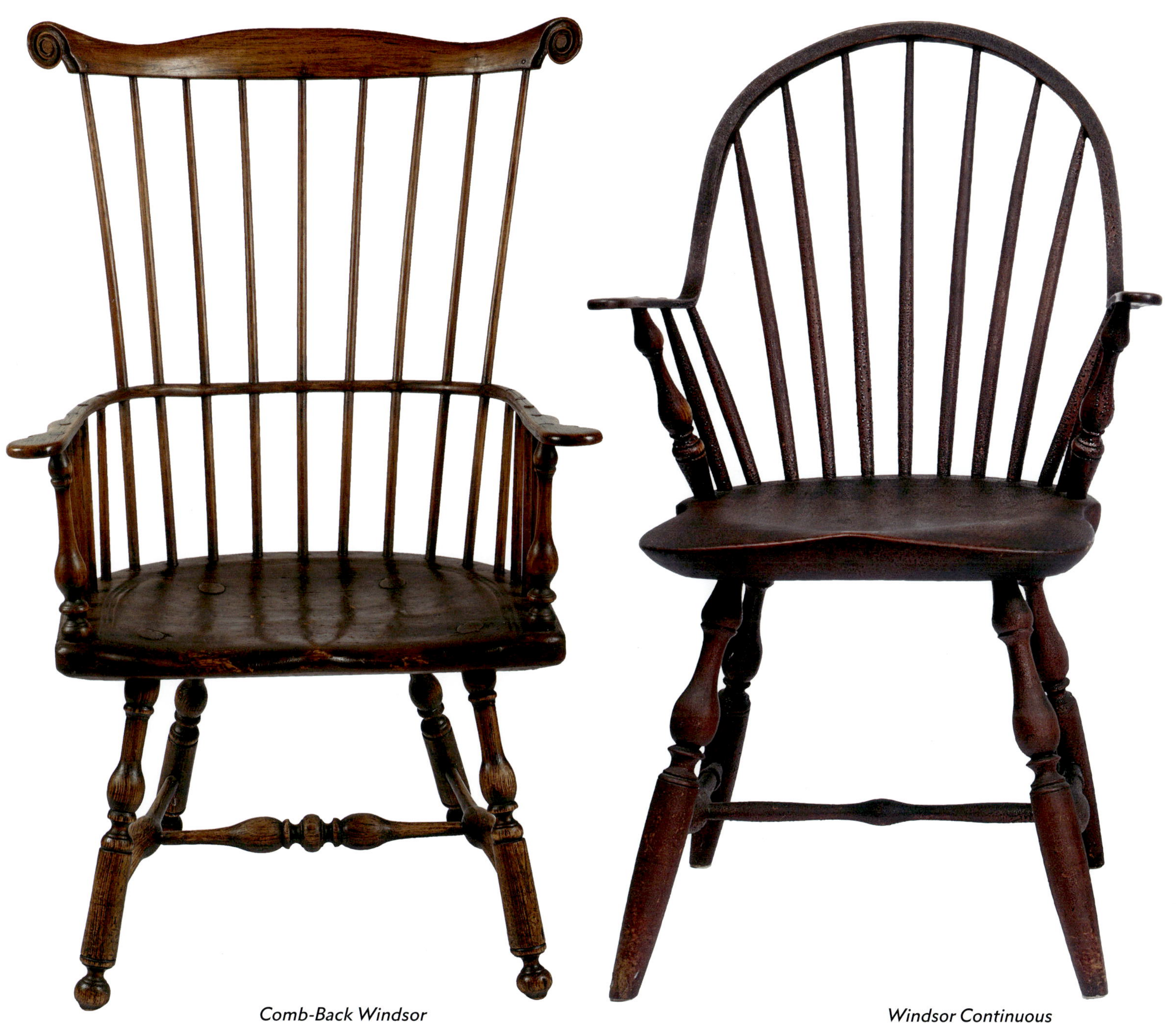

Comb-Back Windsor Armchair with D Seat

Philadelphia
ca. 1760

Wood with early red wash and later green paint
46 × 27¾ × 23 in.

2016.25.74

Windsor Continuous Armchair

ca. 1780

Wood and red paint
36 × 21½ × 20 in.

2016.25.63

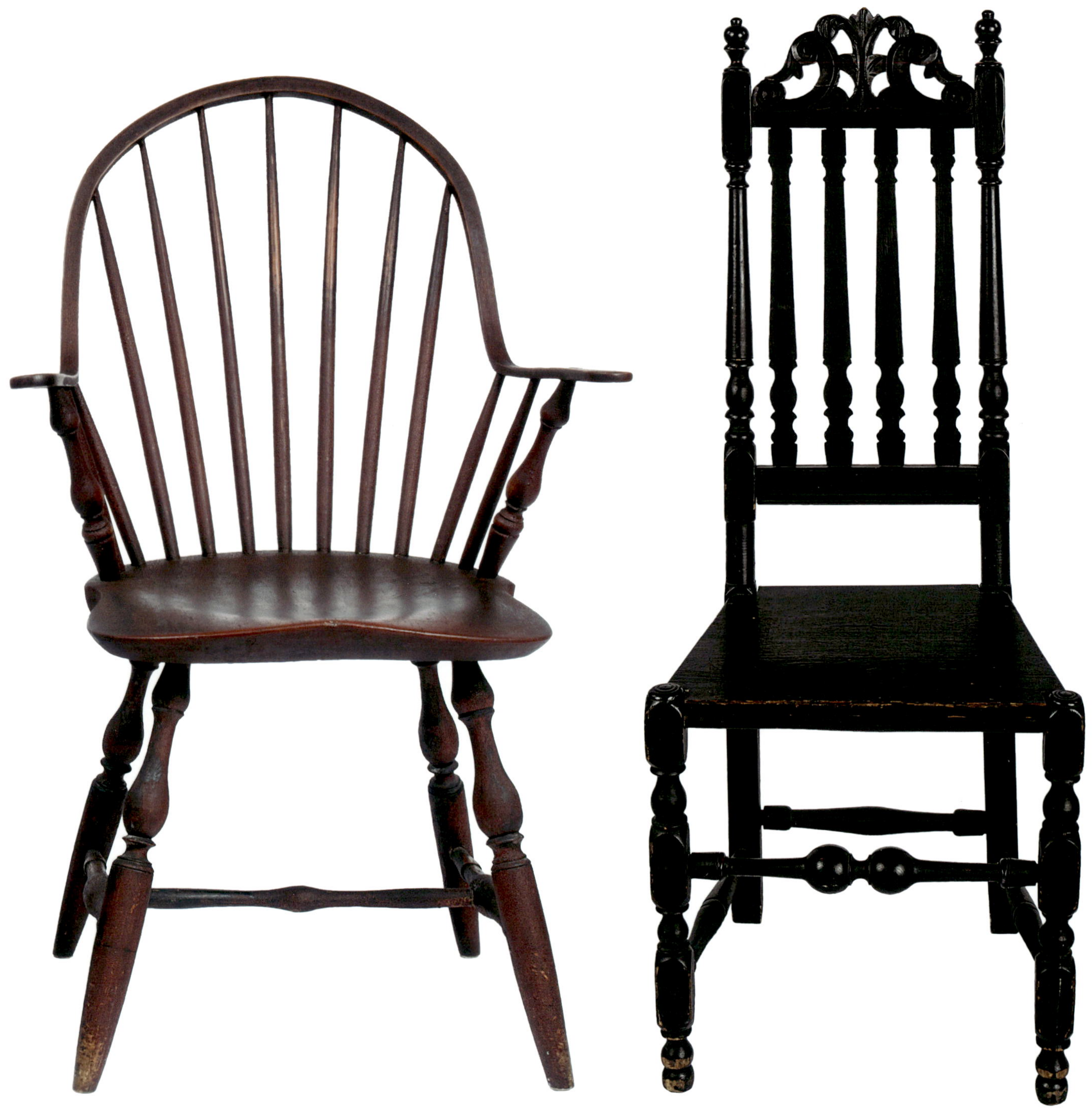

Windsor Continuous Armchair

ca. 1780

Wood and red paint
36 × 21½ × 20 in.

Detail on p. 47

2016.25.64

Banister-Back Side Chair

Boston or North Shore, Massachusetts
ca. 1710–25

Maple and black paint
47 × 19½ × 21 in.

2016.25.66

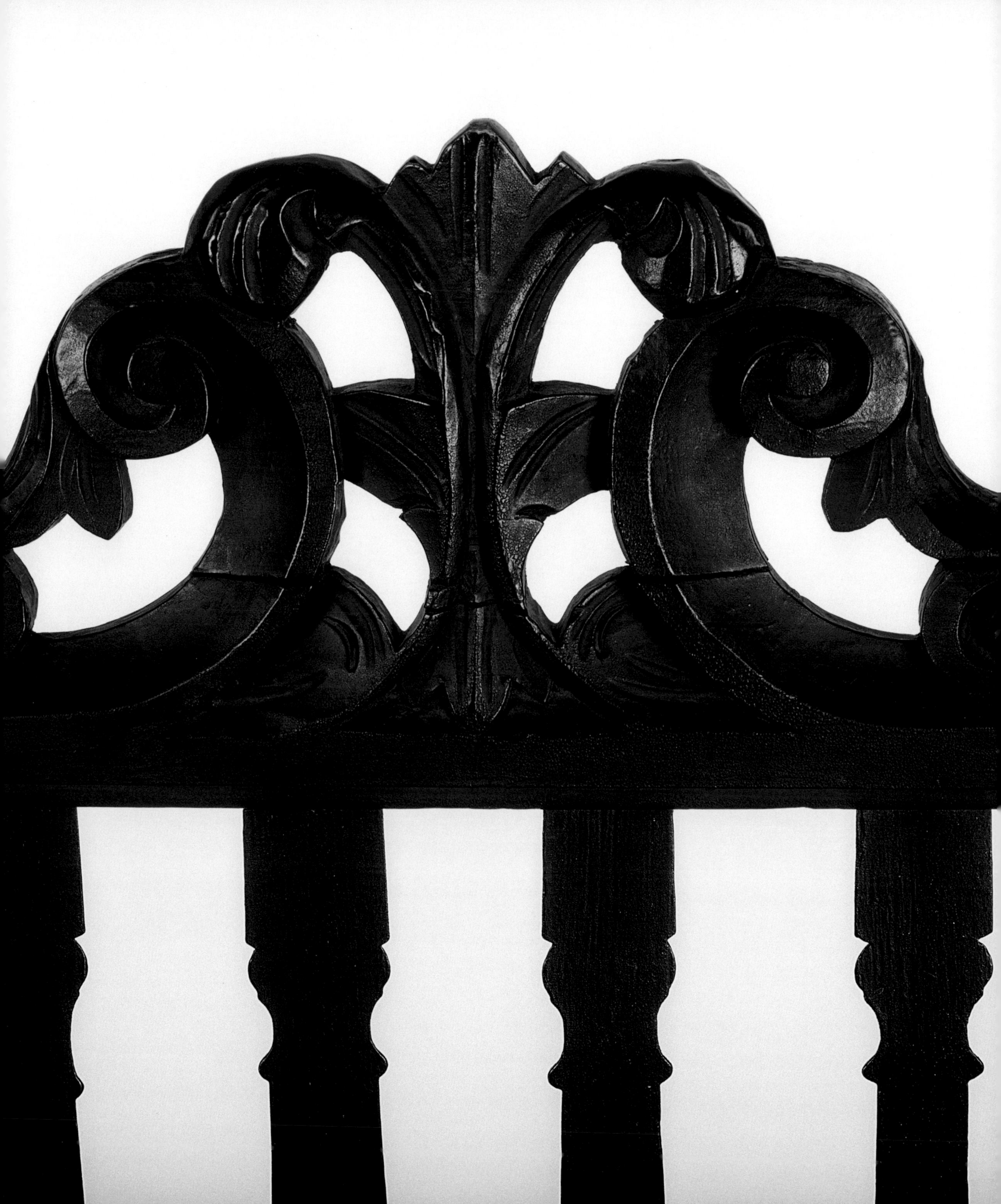

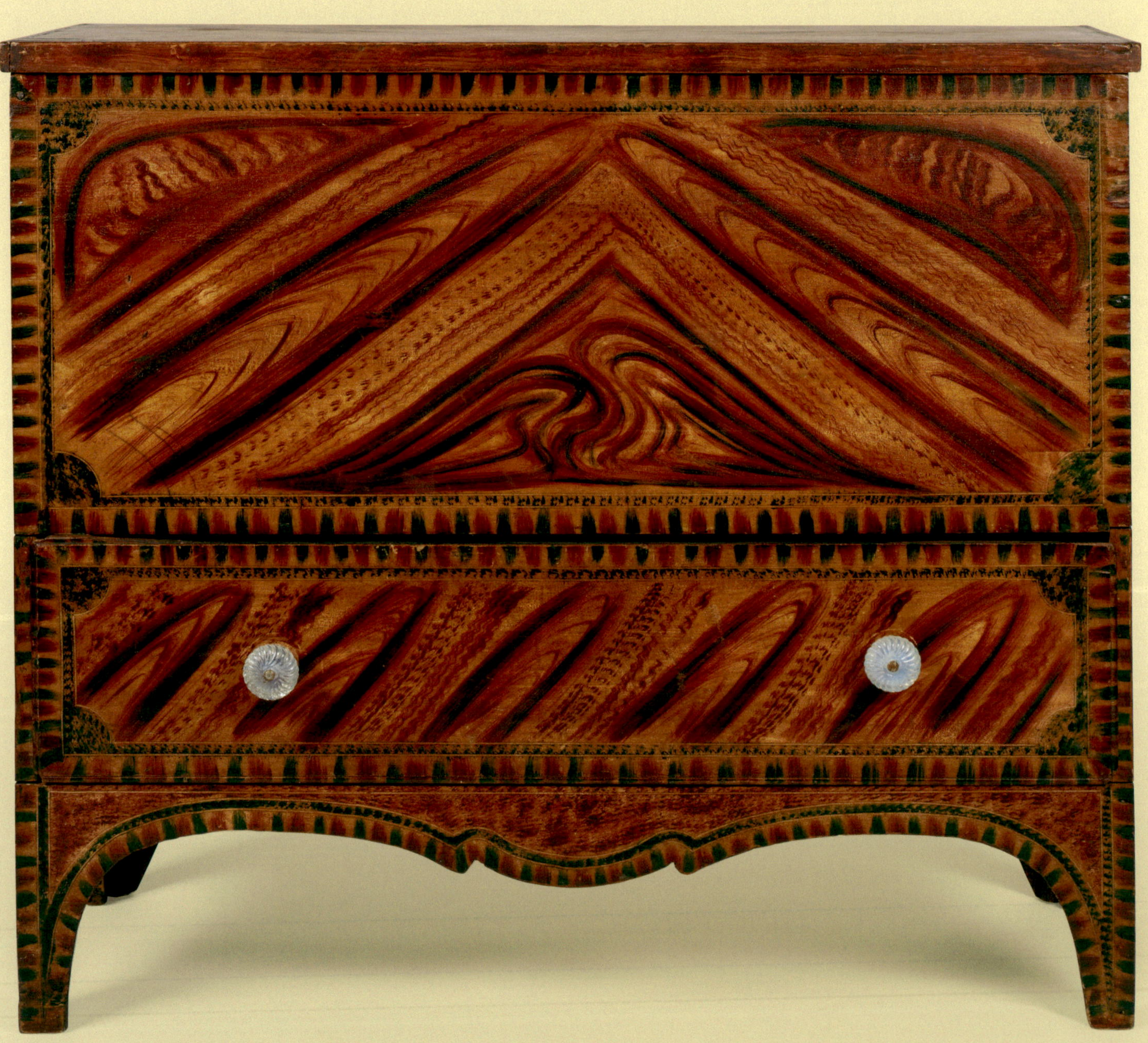

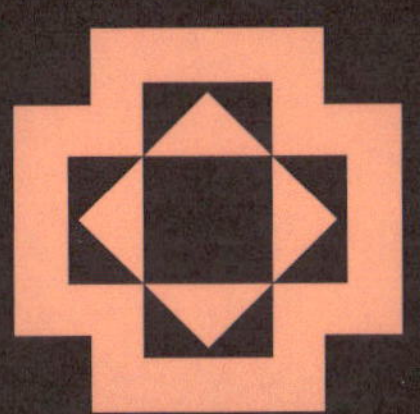

The Kaleidoscope and the Fancy Style of the Early Republic, 1790–1840

SUMPTER PRIDDY

Few realms within American art history have attracted greater attention than the broad range of artifacts in the category of "folk art." Scholars periodically observe that these objects have an *engaging* character or an *immediacy* that reflects the spontaneity of makers from centuries past and resonates today with American collectors, such as the Fieldings, and museum visitors. Many consider folk art to embody the inherent virtue and untutored genius that emerged among everyday Americans during the late eighteenth and early nineteenth centuries. They view these attributes as refreshing contrasts to the formal styles and lofty aspirations that often dominate academic taste—whether expressed in the emotion-laden sentiments and detailed morality of Victorian design or the understated restraint of streamlined modernism.[1] But there is another perspective that conveys the character of American taste, particularly for the transitional era that followed the American Revolution, when the nation's identity coalesced to reflect emotional outlooks and aesthetic standards that were quite different from anything known in Europe. That new outlook, encapsulated by the term *Fancy*, began to emerge shortly after the Declaration of Independence, and it had a growing influence among Americans during the three-quarters of a century that followed—and in some instances, far beyond.

The terms *Fancy-style* and *Fancy* were once regularly used by Americans to describe colorful and exuberantly patterned objects of the kind seen in the Fielding Collection (for example, pp. 57, 88, and opposite page). As I explain, the style flourished outside of art academies and far from the workshops of urban craftsmen who imitated the latest French and English imports. Rather than following the strictures of European

Grain-Painted "Matteson" Blanket Chest
New Shaftsbury, Vermont
ca. 1820–25
Pine, paint, and glass
36 × 40¾ × 18 in.
See also p. 87
L2015.41.114

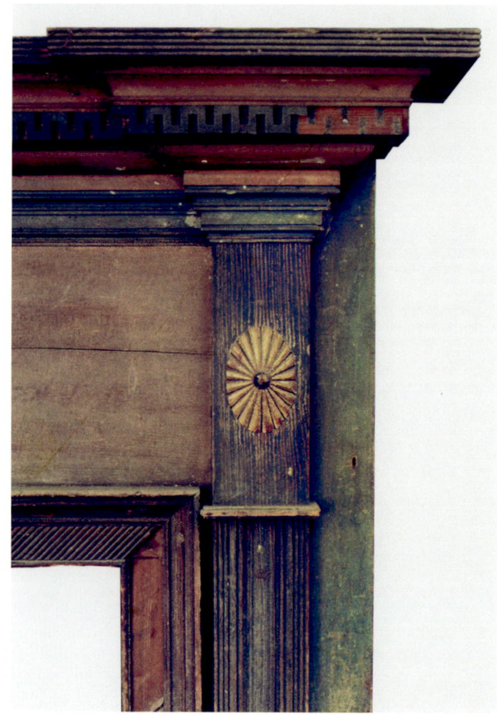

Detail of parlor mantelpiece from Snow Hill, Surry County, Virginia
ca. 1836

PHOTOGRAPH BY THE AUTHOR

arts tradition and borrowing classical Greco-Roman motifs, these Fancy artists gave their imaginations free rein. In what follows, I sketch out the rich but nearly forgotten intellectual context that during the eighteenth and nineteenth centuries surrounded these Fancy-style objects.

I stumbled upon the intriguing term *Fancy* during my graduate courses at Winterthur, and it guided me toward the intellectual concepts and emotional dimensions that define the boundaries of the strikingly patterned objects within the Fielding Collection. Yet rather than invoking the modern concept of *folk art*, the objects led me down a different path for exploring and experiencing the past. They compelled me to see the world through the cultural lenses of the individuals who made and used them. These lively objects embodied not only the subjectivity and emotionalism of the Romantic Era but also a reflection of the United States' youthful optimism.

At the time, I was researching an 1836 farmhouse, Snow Hill, near the headwaters of Blackwater River, in Surry County, Virginia. Though not a large structure, it stood tall on high brick piers—five bays wide, one room deep, with a staircase that spiraled upward through the center passage.[2] I had admired the house since childhood and had watched it fall into decay in a cornfield. Residents had long since departed, the paint had cleaved from the wood siding, glass had fallen from the windows, and its sole inhabitants were the swallows beneath the rafters and the breeze that claimed the passages. It was a taunting symbol of the tattered economy and depressed mood of the rural South for decades following the Civil War.

Though the house was in derelict condition, its parlor contained surprising, wildly painted woodwork. The mantel had carved and gilded sunbursts with moldings of green and orange (above), and the wainscot adjoining it sported bright yellow panels with lively red frames. A closer look revealed the woodwork's surface to emulate beautifully striped mahogany and birdseye maple—yet entirely in paint on inexpensive yellow pine. On the stairway, the riser beneath each approaching tread sported a swirl of black and white and gray paint replicating marble.

When I entered graduate school in 1975, I was determined to learn more about these practices of marbling and graining. In early American and British painter's manuals, I learned that the practice of painting woodwork to emulate eye-catching woods and marbles was popular from about 1680 until the mid-nineteenth century. Artisans and consumers sometimes referred to marbling and graining as "fancy painting"—particularly in the early nineteenth century. The term seemed logical enough, for the painted surfaces were sufficiently decorative to merit the name.

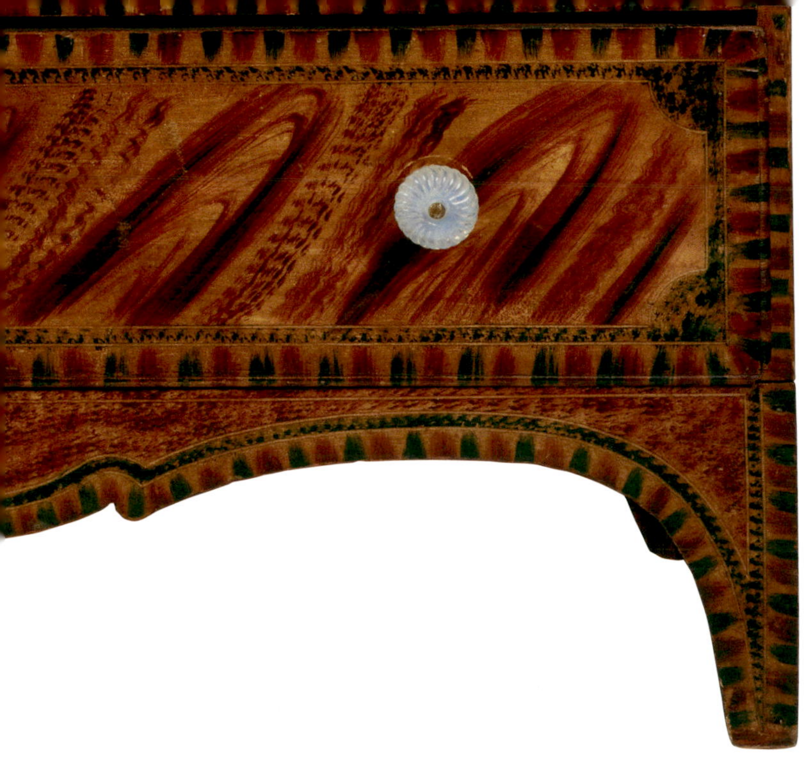

About that time, I visited an early New England home in which the owner proudly displayed her collection of historical furnishings and textiles, including a wildly patterned Jacquard coverlet in an array of colors. It had a six-inch square in each of the lower corners, where the early weaver had left telling messages for potential customers. My mind began to whirl when I noticed that the maker had included his name, "Archibald Davidson," followed by "Fancy Weaver."

The use of the word *Fancy* triggered memories of the painted interiors of the Surry farmhouse. And on the square to the left he had woven the words "Fancy Coverlet," followed by "1836"—the year of the farmhouse. It dawned on me that Davidson was not a decorative weaver but an imaginative weaver and that *Fancy painting* might also mean *imaginative painting.*

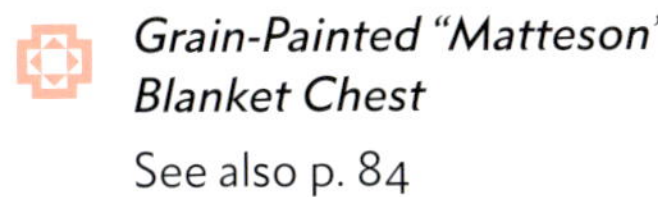

Grain-Painted "Matteson" Blanket Chest

See also p. 84

The meaning of *Fancy* had apparently changed dramatically in a century and a half. It had originally emphasized the positive influence of emotions on human creativity, particularly in the making of objects. This positive outlook evolved, however, to reflect the modern view of the "ornamental" or "decorative"—often with a negative connotation. When I consulted the *Oxford English Dictionary*, I found two full pages allotted to its definitions, with a variety of meanings that seemed to shift, expand, and then contract again through the decades. They reflected changing moral perspectives, as they moved from negative to positive—and then back again to negative.

The primary definition of *fancy* through the generations was "imagination," and Americans understood it in that way between 1750 and 1850, a period that encompasses much of the Fielding Collection. When used as an adjective, *fanciful*, it had a parallel significance: "rather guided by imagination than reason."[3] The term *decorative* was absent.

In Victorian-era dictionaries, not a single lexicographer linked the concept to ornamentation until 1860. Joseph Worcester assigned *fancy* a moral value: "Ornamental, rather than useful."[4] The connection of fancy with the ornamental, and the ornamental with excesses, augured the end of Fancy style. But up until that time, artisans spoke of ornament as essential. Its liveliness sparked creativity, caught the viewer's eye, heightened emotional awareness, elevated one's spirit, and filled the storehouse of memory with vivid images that were easily recalled. For instance, the swirling patterns of Fancy chests of drawers, such as these blanket and six-board chests (p. 88 and above), entrance the viewer with their striking color contrasts and animation.

I set out to define the spectrum of objects that would have been considered "Fancy" between 1790 and 1840, the era in which this concept played a

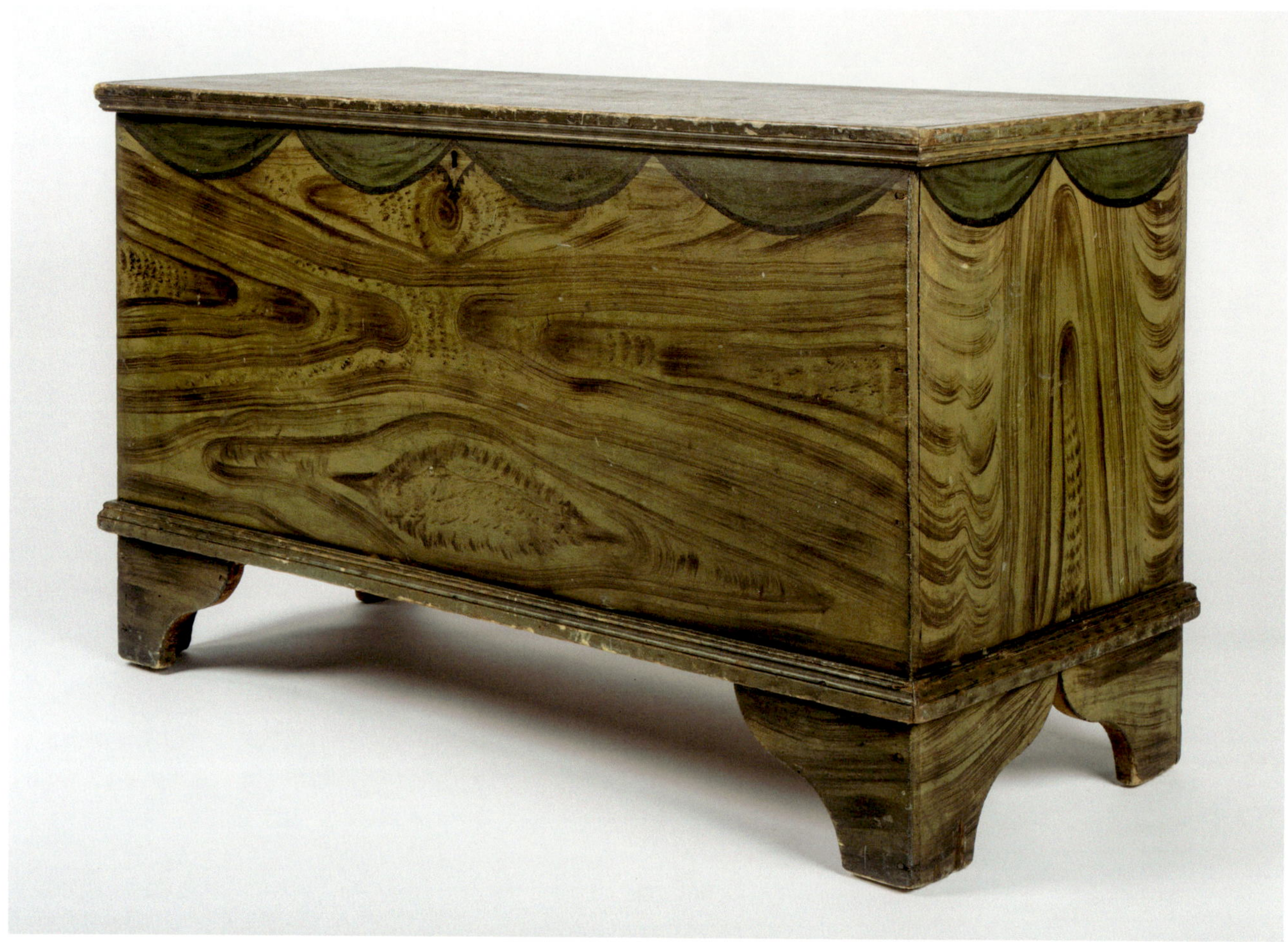

Six-Board Chest

Probably New York State
Early nineteenth century

Pine and paint
25 × 42½ × 18 in.

Inscriptions: "E. M. S." on lid exterior; "Cyrus Sherwood 1825" on the underside of the top

L2015.41.86

vital role within American culture. Above all, the style defined imaginative things that Americans aspired to make, to learn from, and to own during a crucial period of transition. The agrarian world that dominated American life from shortly after the Revolution changed in the second quarter of the nineteenth century, when traditional artisans who were under tremendous pressure from inexpensive, factory-made goods pursued creative solutions for making household goods to compete in the market.

The philosophical and cultural underpinnings of the Fancy style had emerged in Britain during the early eighteenth century, when educators and philosophers discussed the merits of the imagination—and the feelings that accompanied it—as keys to learning. As the eighteenth century progressed, educators weighed the capacity of rich experience to fuel the storehouse of memory with images that elicited delightful emotions. The experience of immersing oneself in the world, and of savoring the objects that filled it, complemented such rational endeavors as mathematics, science, and physics. Middle-class Americans gravitated toward this engaging new style of Fancy as a metaphor for garnering wisdom from practical experience, as opposed to formal education.

Still Life with Fruit Theorem Painting

ca. 1830

Stenciled watercolor on paper
14 × 18 in.

Stamped: "De La Rue & Co Extra London," a London-based paper maker

2016.25.100

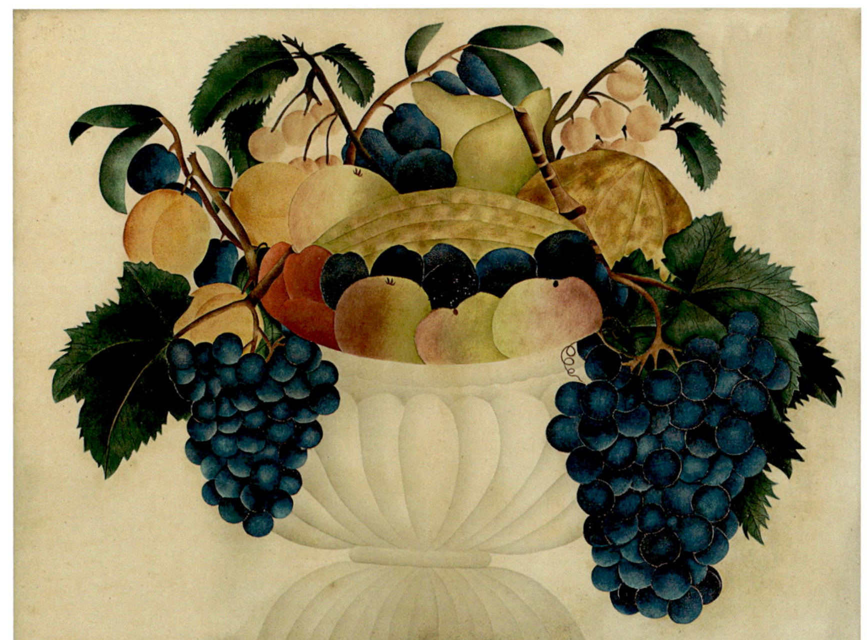

LIGHT, COLOR, MOTION

Two visual stimulants—light and color—had long been recognized for their role in conveying images to the eye and mind. The seventeenth-century British engraver Alexander Browne found them key to the visual experience of fancy: "Light . . . is the cause . . . whereby coloured things are seen, whose *Shapes* and *Images* pass to the *phantasie*."[5] In the early eighteenth century, the English philosopher Joseph Addison further explored the power of color to "paint" images into the storehouse of memory and experience: "Among these several kinds of Beauty the Eye takes most Delight in Colours," Addison wrote. "Colors paint themselves on the Fancy."[6]

The appeal of light and color found a further complement in the power of motion. Addison described its appeal: "We are quickly tired of looking . . . where every thing continues fixt and settled in the same Place and Posture, but find our Thoughts a little . . . relieved at the Sight of such Objects as are ever in Motion."[7]

The growing acknowledgment of fancy's role was reflected in the process of teaching young students—especially female students—to make theorems or theorem paintings. *Theorem* was the word for stencil, and the process of using paper cutouts to construct a "painting" was more mechanical than creative. To produce a still-life painting using theorems, a student followed the teacher's instruction for cutting paper stencils that provided the outlines for the table, the bowl, each piece of fruit that separately filled it, and ultimately—in more ambitious designs—a colorful parrot that usually completed the composition (above). For students, the process of carefully arranging fruit in a bowl offered a compelling parallel to filling the memory's storehouse with vivid experiences.[8]

Americans also had a penchant for motion, as reflected in the popularity of the rocking chair—a form that was largely unknown in Europe, where it was reserved for the aged and infirm, or for mothers with infants. Chair maker Lambert Hitchcock of western Connecticut produced beautifully contoured "Boston rocking chairs" with scrolled arms, decorative crest rails, and lean spindles that were carefully contoured to the human form. Working between 1818 and 1843, Hitchcock painted these chairs in brilliant colors or emulated rosewood, then stenciled designs of fruit baskets or flowers on the most visible surfaces. He could produce them so efficiently that he sold the chairs for as little as a dollar apiece.[9]

During the 1820s and 1830s, almost every American householder had one in the parlor. When British writer Harriet Martineau encountered painted rocking chairs in an American hostelry during an 1838 visit, she was appalled by the conduct they encouraged, especially among the ladies: "In these small inns the disagreeable practice of rocking in the chair is seen in its excess. In the inn parlors are three or four rocking chairs in which sit ladies who are vibrating in different directions at various velocities, so as to try the head of a stranger.... How this lazy and ungraceful indulgence ever became general, I cannot imagine."[10] Conversely, when the New England educator Heman Humphrey visited England in 1835, he found that rocking chairs were hardly known among the "staid and upright" British, who considered the energetic seesawing back and forth a vulgar "Americanism."[11]

Visual motion—or more specifically, a plethora of surface ornamentation—characterized the furniture of the period, and there was scarcely a plain surface in sight. A close inspection of even simple surfaces often reveals that the artist *scumbled* the ornament—that is, used a nearly dry brush to apply a thin and irregular overcoat of paint, or a lightly tinted varnish, to add depth or variety. This is particularly evident in a tall case clock from the Fielding Collection (p. 41) in which the artist carefully applied paint and varnish to a simple pine case to add visual interest and suggest expensive bird's-eye maple. Lively patterns created by scumbling can also be observed in the *Dome-Top Trunk* (p. 107), *Blue Box with Oyster-Shell Graining* (p. 102), and most extravagantly on the *Painted Schrank* (p. 4).

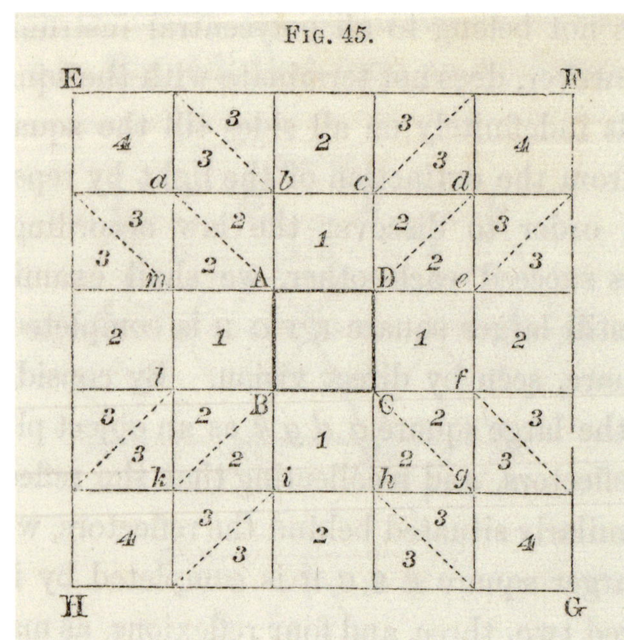

"On combinations of four mirrors forming a square" in David Brewster, *The Kaleidoscope: Its History, Theory, and Construction* (London, 1858), figure 45

COURTESY, THE WINTERTHUR LIBRARY: PRINTED BOOK AND PERIODICAL COLLECTION

THE KALEIDOSCOPE

Few objects have played a greater role in underscoring the combined power of light, color, and motion than the kaleidoscope. It was invented in 1816, quite by accident, during experiments with the polarization and refraction of light by the

Drunkard's Path Quilt
ca. 1880–90
Cotton, pieced
87 × 87½ in.
2016.25.55

Scottish physicist Sir David Brewster (1781–1868). In an early phase of his research, he placed several long mirrors in a narrow brass cylinder to reflect an image as it traveled from its source to the viewer's eye.[12] When Brewster peered into the tube, he found that it transformed reality in unimaginable ways. He called his invention the "kaleidoscope," from the Greek words for "beautiful image viewer." Before Brewster could patent his design, competitors had purloined the concept and were selling inexpensive versions of cardboard and mirror plate to passersby on the street.[13] The invention was an instant success, for it provided the perfect tool for understanding the powers of fancy and for demonstrating how light, color, and motion caught the eye and imprinted stunning images in the mind, where they could fuel the creative process.

British academics were intrigued by the charming images, but the colorful scenes provoked a much stronger response in America. There, the kaleidoscope seemed an ideal tool to whet one's appetite for learning. This ingenious device would help Americans understand the power of the imagination in ways that were far removed from the literary sources that had long dominated British understanding of the subject.

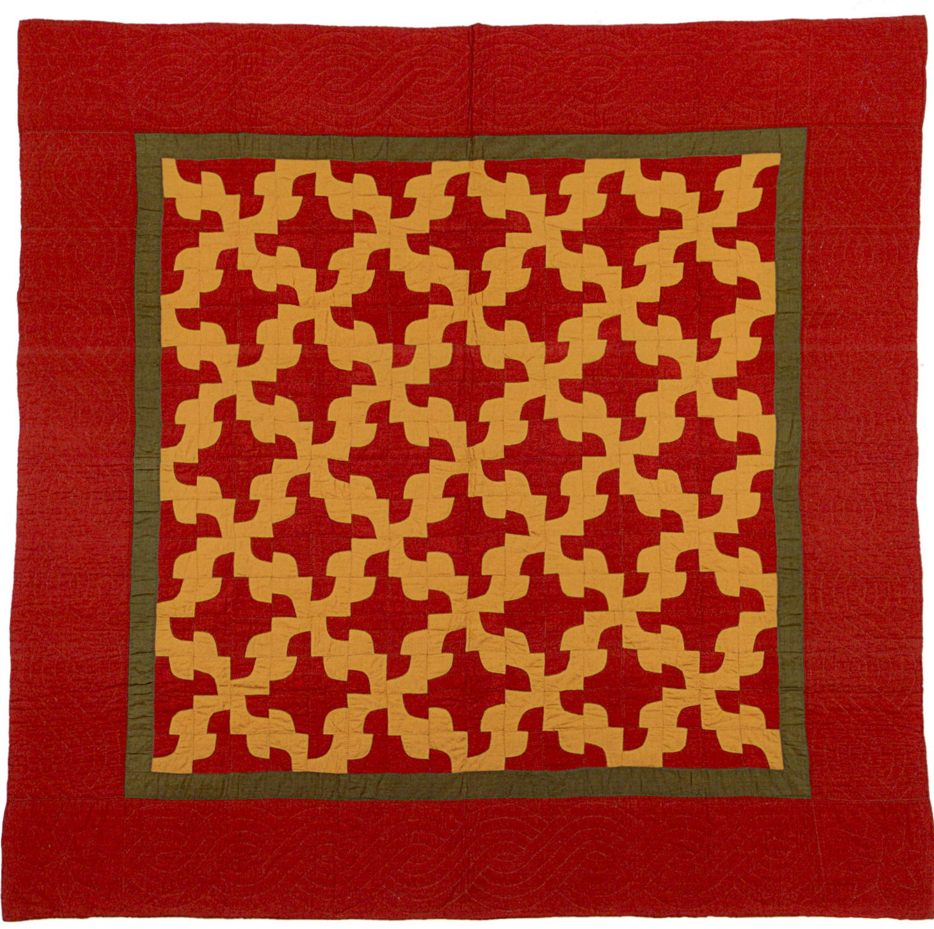

In 1819 Brewster published *A Treatise on the Kaleidoscope*, in which he presented diagrams of distinct kaleidoscopes—those having two, three, or four mirrors grouped together in the tube—to show how a varied arrangement of mirrors would alter the image. He discussed the device's ability to produce patterns for household decoration in record time: "It will create, in a single hour, what a thousand artists could not invent in the course of a year."[14] It could be used for a variety of objects, from stained-glass windows for cathedrals to household carpets and floorcloths. It was no longer necessary to devote significant time to drawing an entire design on paper. Rather, one could sketch a segment of the pattern and rely on the kaleidoscope to quickly expand the design into a variety of options.

Several of the diagrams that Brewster included had such a strong geometric character that they spurred public interest in an entirely new range of orderly design (p. 90). The kaleidoscope had its greatest impact on American quilts (p. 91 and below). Whereas quilt makers on both sides of the Atlantic had traditionally focused on classical subjects or elegant foliage derived

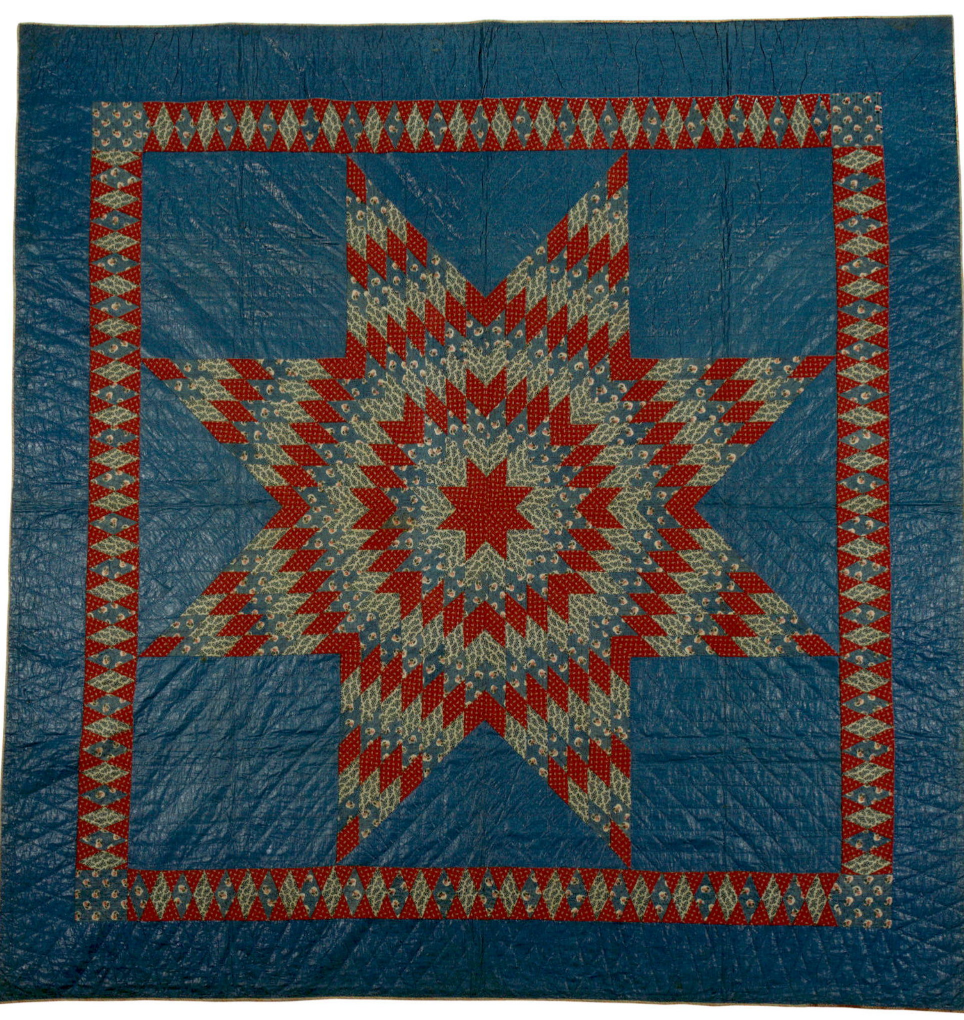

Lone Star Quilt—Red, White, and Blue

ca. 1850

Glazed cotton, pieced

96½ × 94 in.

See also back endpapers

2016.25.58

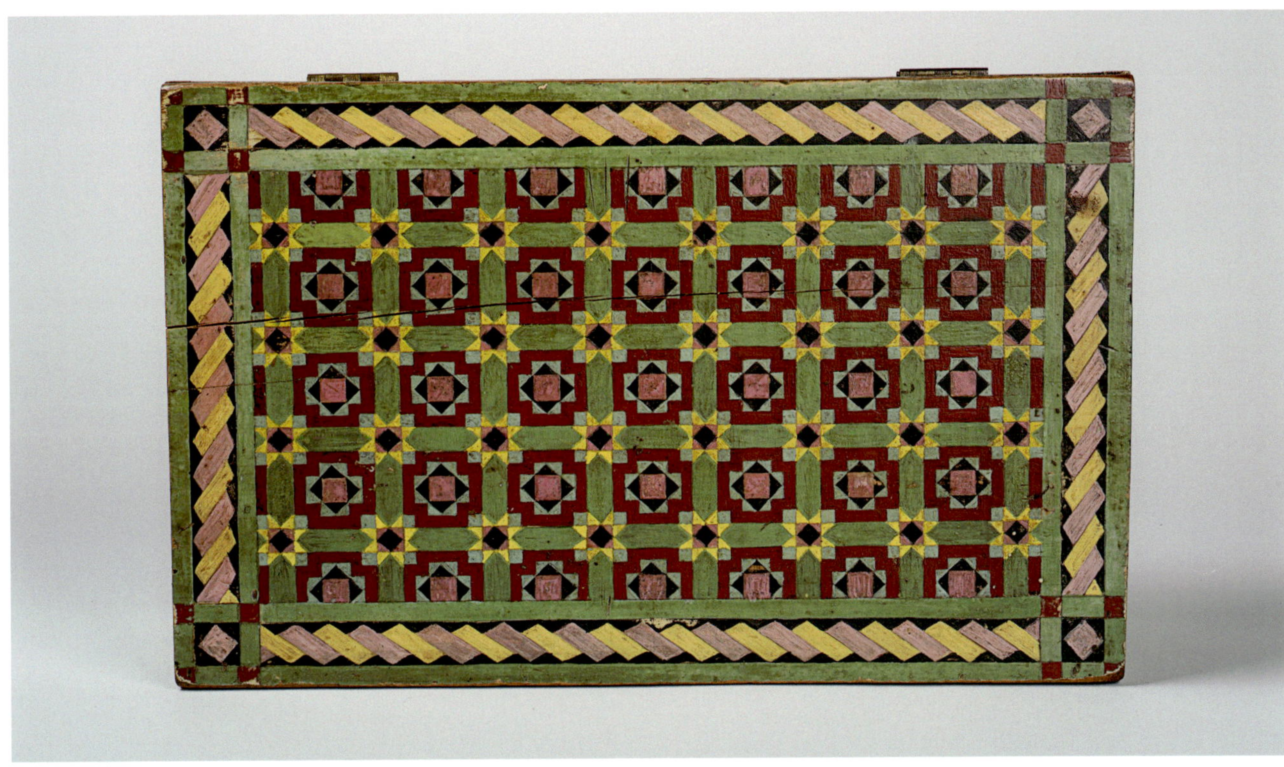

Box with Painted Geometric Design
New England
ca. 1840
Pine and paint
6½ × 14⅛ × 9 in.
2016.25.43

from nature, once the device was invented, they created a variety of innovative geometric designs that either emulated a kaleidoscopic view or looked to Brewster's published diagrams for inspiration. Kaleidoscopes with two mirrors created a pattern that exploded outward from the center toward the edges in a large starburst. This was particularly obvious in the visual lines that radiated outward from the center of the quilt. In quilts of this type, the seams of adjoining wedges replicate where the image abuts a mirror—to create the star. Kaleidoscopes with a three-mirror system, joined together in a 30-60-90-degree triangle, likewise replicated the design, yet with subtle variety. Brewster depicted the pattern within an octagonal format—a diagram to which quilt makers often looked for octagonal piecework.

Influenced by the kaleidoscope, women moved away from relying on large pieces of fabric and toward the use of tiny, multicolored pieces, carefully stitched together, to emulate the bits of glass in a kaleidoscope—and they expanded the quilts to completely cover a bedstead. It was only a matter of time before house painters transferred the patterns to canvas fabric to produce eye-catching floorcloths and table covers, expanding Fancy's influence on American homes from wall to wall.[15]

In addition to producing kaleidoscopes with two mirrors that created stunning explosions with colored glass, makers created examples with three and four mirrors, each of which produced a distinct design. Kaleidoscopes with a three-mirror system, joined together in a 60-60-60-degree triangle, repeated the image at the end of the tunnel time and again in a diagonal grid—thereby assuring that multiple replications of the image were firmly imprinted in the storehouse of memory. Indeed, kaleidoscopes with four mirrors facing inward in a square replicated the image in the center as an eight-pointed star. This produced even further options, not only for quilt makers but also for decorative painters. For example, a box from the Fielding Collection with a pink, green, red, and black palette evokes kaleidoscopic patterns (p. 93).

In this way, the kaleidoscope shaped Americans' expectations for non-representational design and transformed middle-class homesteads. Although British kaleidoscopes were expensive devices made with hollow brass cylinders and highly polished mirrors, Americans were so infatuated by the device that they produced inexpensive examples of pasteboard or tinned sheet iron, and they relied on simple mirror plate rather than polished lenses. Foreign visitors to America were astounded to find that middle-class Americans were inspired by this "philosophical instrument."[16]

Although kaleidoscopes of two, three, and four mirrors produced their respective designs according to the dictates of geometry, their patterns were open to nearly endless interpretations by the viewer. Equally important, the range of ornament produced by the kaleidoscope embodied a new type of creativity that Addison had envisioned more than a century before when he observed the human capacity to "fancy to it self Things more Great, Strange, or Beautiful, than the Eye ever saw."[17] The kaleidoscope's broad appeal in America helped its middle classes embrace abstract ornament.

DEMISE

Whereas light, color, and motion typified the Fancy aesthetic in the 1820s and 1830s, with the Panic of 1837 and the economic crash that followed, the ebullient style seemed oddly out of place. Just three years later, Edgar Allen Poe summed up society's disdain for the outmoded concept of Fancy. Although he singled out floorcloths as particularly onerous, he was equally critical of other household furnishings that embodied the precepts of Fancy, particularly those that reflected the kaleidoscope's influence:

> *Those antique floor-cloths which are still seen occasionally in the dwellings of the rabble—cloths of huge, sprawling and radiating devices, stripe-interspersed, and glorious with all hues, among which no ground is intelligible—are but the wicked invention of a race of time servers and money lovers... worshippers of Mammon... who,... to save trouble of thought and exercise of fancy,... cruelly invented the Kaleidoscope.*[18]

The Fancy style that had dominated popular taste since the 1790s fell rapidly from favor after 1840, as tastes shifted toward darker, more introspective colors and eventually to greatly simplified furniture forms and minimal ornament. The renowned designer Gustav Stickley (1858–1942)—a dominant figure of the Arts and Crafts movement—denigrated the style to advance the understated aesthetic that became his hallmark. "'Fancywork' was a cruelly right name for the old time decoration so labeled," he noted with disdain. "It was fancy, superfluous, and very hard work, and the burden fell alike upon those who made it and those who beheld it."[19]

The emotions associated with Fancy had run full cycle, from a period of awakening into—and through—an era of widespread popularity, before slowly retreating as middle-class attitudes toward animated behavior and expectations for learning shifted yet again. Americans would abandon the vestiges of the expressive emotions and vibrant styles of the nineteenth century and embrace the sleek new styles and restraint that defined the twentieth.

Sumpter Priddy is an antiquarian and consultant in Alexandria, Virginia.

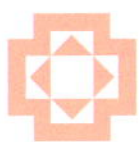 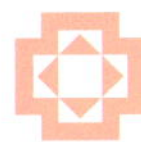 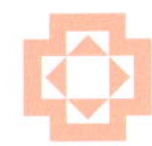

NOTES

1 A number of American museums have sponsored exhibitions and published catalogues pertinent to folk art ever since the term surfaced in the early twentieth century.

2 The Tidewater planter Samuel Booth (1795–1876) and his wife, Sarah Ellis, began the house for their family in 1836; they named it "Snow Hill" for the bitter winter that delayed its completion until spring the following year; see "090-0040 Snow Hill," Virginia Department of Historic Resources website, https://www.dhr.virginia.gov/historic-registers/090-0040/.

3 Samuel Johnson, *A Dictionary of the English Language* (London: Printed by W Strahan for J. and P. Knapton, 1755), s.vv. "FANCY" and "FANCIFUL."

4 The earliest dictionary in which the word *fancy* appears as an adjective is Joseph E. Worcester, *A Dictionary of the English Language* (Cambridge, Mass.: H. O. Houghton, 1860), s.v. "fancy," 537.

5 Alexander Browne, *Ars Pictoria: or an academy treating of drawing, painting, limning, and etching*, 2nd ed. (London: Arthur Tooker, 1675), 40; quoted in *OED Online*, s.v. "fantasy | phantasy, *n*.," March 2019, Oxford University Press.

6 Joseph Addison, *The Spectator*, no. 412 (June 23, 1712): 69; no. 411 (June 21, 1712): 64.

7 Addison, *The Spectator*, no. 412 (June 23, 1712): 67.

8 For more on theorem painting, see the discussion by Stacy Hollander in this volume, pp. 149–51.

9 For more on the Boston rocking chair, see Nancy Goyne Evans, "The Genesis of the Boston Rocking Chair," *The Magazine Antiques* 123, no. 1 (January 1983): 252.

10 Quoted in Ellen Denker and Bert Denker, *The Rocking Chair Book* (New York: Mayflower, 1979), 38.

11 Denker and Denker, *The Rocking Chair Book*, 37.

12 For more on the original concept and publication, see David Brewster, *A Treatise on the Kaleidoscope* (Edinburgh: Archibald Constable and Co., 1819); and Brewster, *The Kaleidoscope; Its History, Theory, and Construction, with Its Application to the Fine and Useful Arts* (London: John Murray, 1858).

13 Brewster, *Treatise on the Kaleidoscope*, 7.

14 Brewster, *Treatise on the Kaleidoscope*, 116.

15 For more on the quilts in the Fielding Collection, see the essay by Elizabeth V. Warren in this volume, pp. 109–19.

16 Brewster, *Treatise on the Kaleidoscope*, 6.

17 Joseph Addison, *The Spectator*, no. 418 (June 30, 1712): 92; see also E. H. Gombrich, *The Sense of Order: A Study in the Psychology of Decorative Art* (Oxford: Phaidon, 1979), 151.

18 Edgar Allan Poe, "The Philosophy of Furniture," *Burton's Gentleman's Magazine and Monthly American Review* 6 (May 1840): 244.

19 Gustav Stickley, quoted in Lizabeth A. Cohen, "Embellishing a Life of Labor: An Interpretation of the Material Culture of American Working Class Homes, 1885–1915," in *Material Culture Studies in America*, ed. Thomas J. Schlereth (Nashville, Tenn.: American Association for State and Local History, 1982), 189.

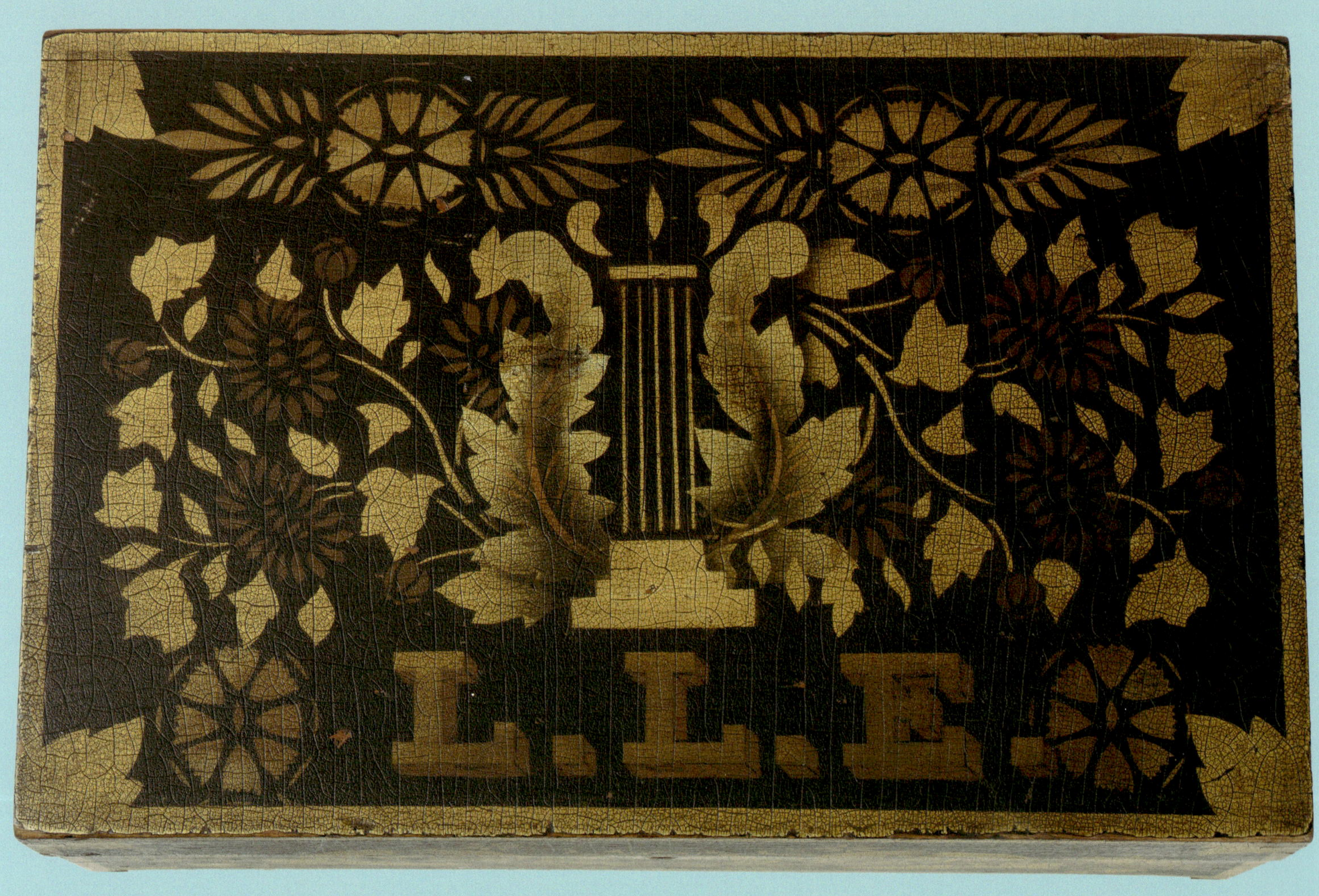

Stenciled Box
(view from above)

Connecticut or New York
ca. 1835

Wood, metal, and paint
5 × 12 × 8 in.

Inscription (top): "L. L. E."

2016.25.44

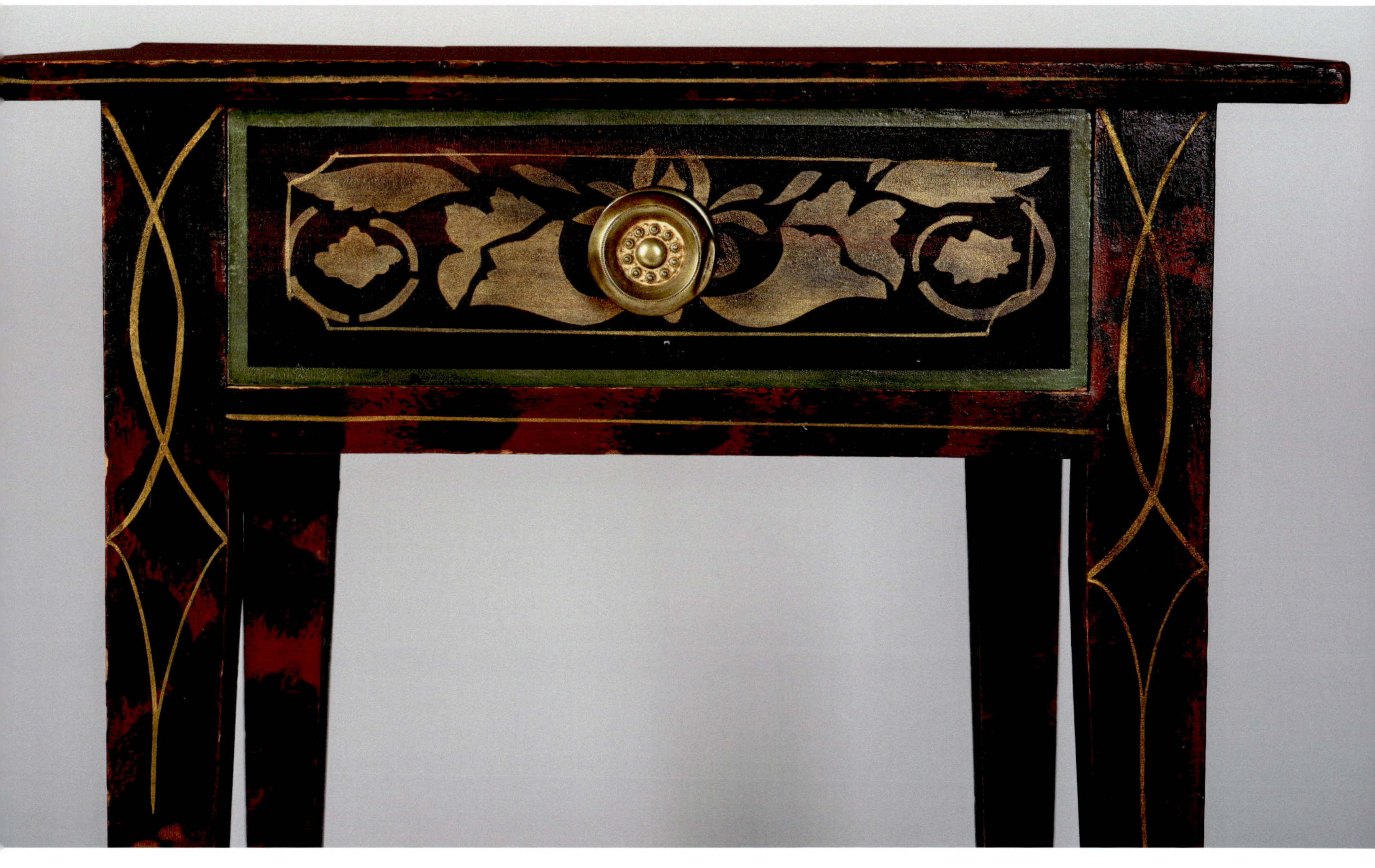

One-Drawer Stand

Near Paris, Maine
ca. 1830

Basswood, paint, and brass
28½ × 17⅛ × 18⅞ in.

L2015.41.111

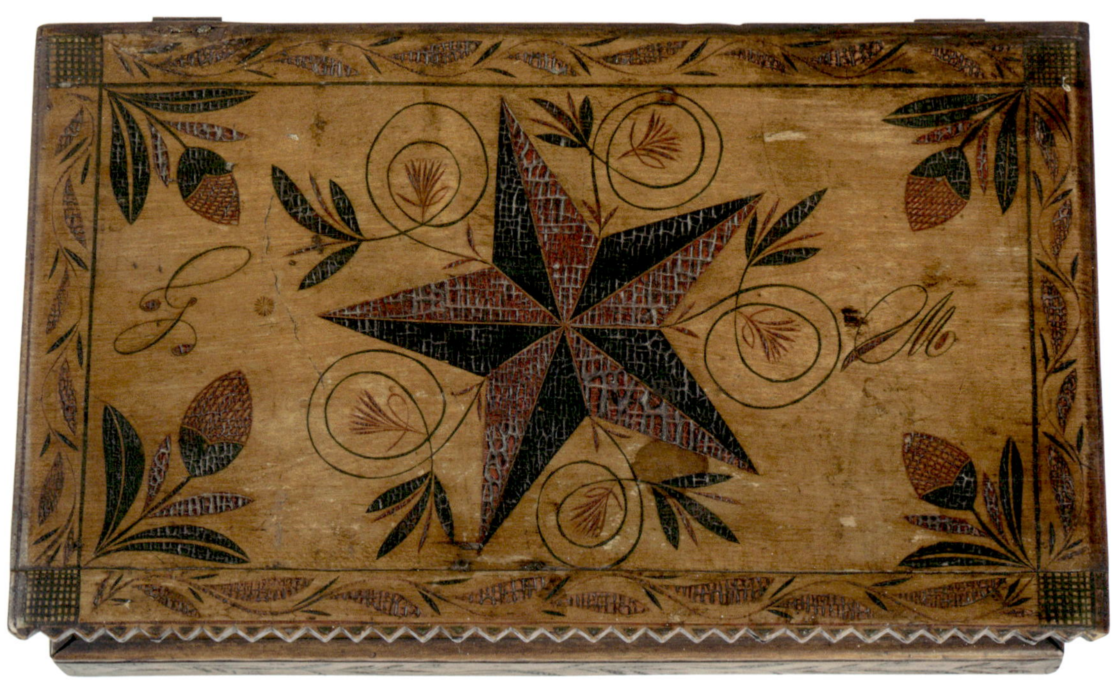

Sailor's Trinket Box
(view from above)

ca. 1830

Pine with wax inlay
4 × 11½ × 6½ in.

Inscription (top): "G M"

L2015.41.28

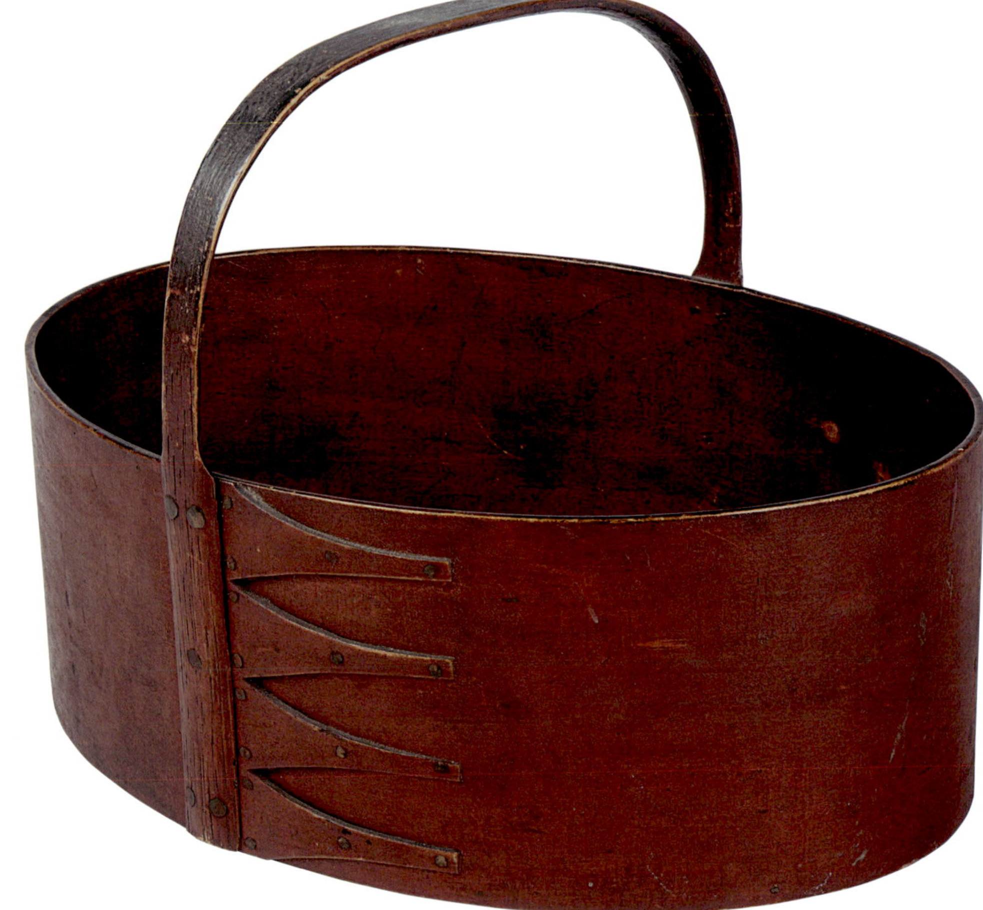

Red Shaker Carrier

ca. 1820–40

Maple or pine with red stain
11 × 8 × 4 in.

L2015.41.36

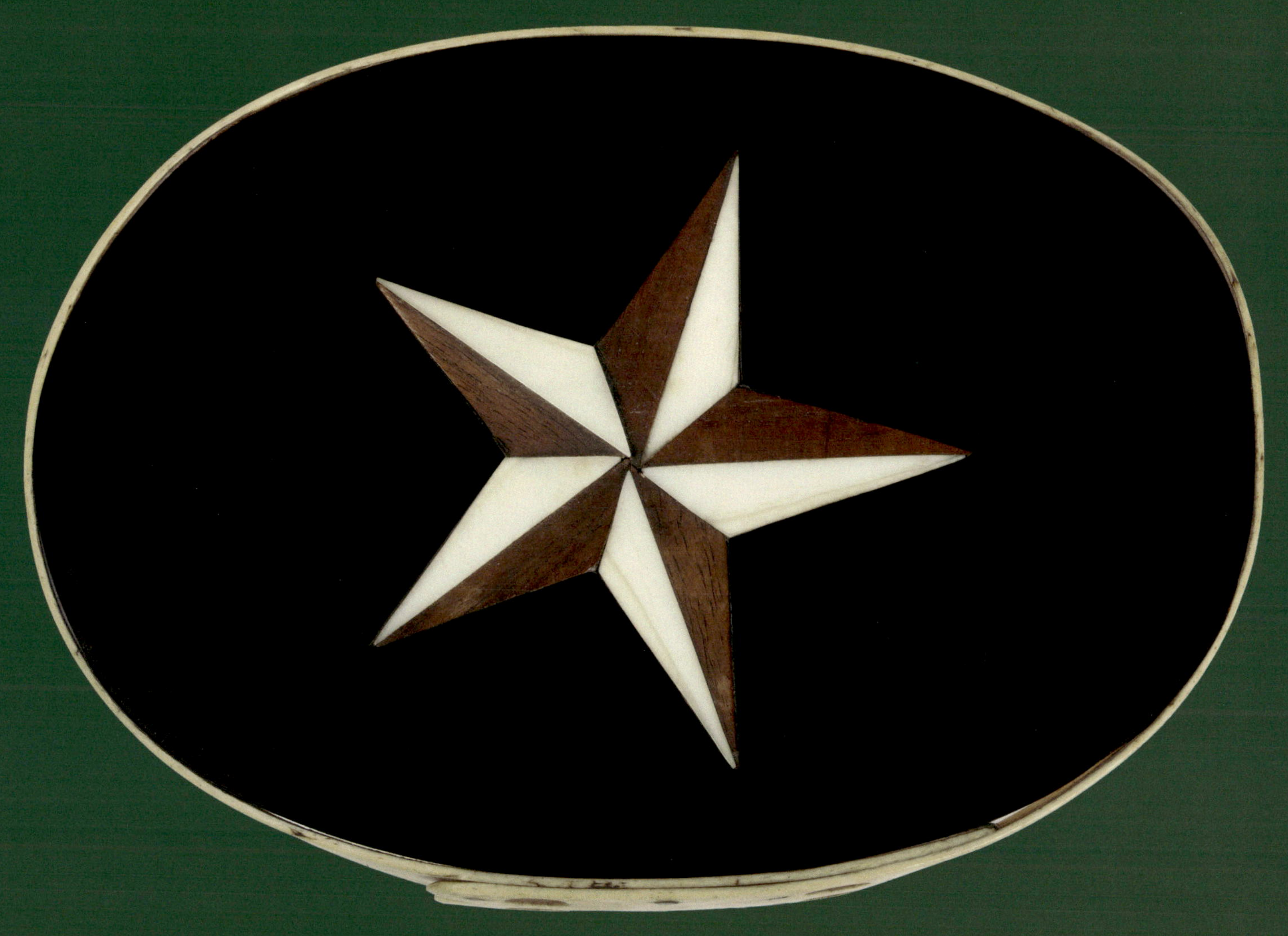

Scrimshaw Oval Box with Inlaid Five-Point Star
(view from above)

ca. 1840

Whalebone ivory and hardwoods
3 × 6½ × 4½ in.

2016.25.47

SHAKER BOXES

The United Society of Believers in Christ's Second Appearing, better known as the Shakers, is a Christian sect whose membership peaked with a couple thousand adherents between 1840 to 1860. Like a monastic community, the Shakers require celibacy, a life of prayer, and communal property. For commercial sale, they produced furniture, buckets, baskets, medicines, and seeds. Their craftsmanship reflects their beliefs in simplicity and the rejection of ostentation. This set of colored bentwood boxes was meant to be nested, one box inside another, like Russian dolls. Their maple sides comprise a single piece of wood secured by metal tacks with swallowtail joints that clasp together like interlocking fingers. Maple could be sliced into thin sheets and then shaped with steam over an oval form without splitting. Pine, a light wood, formed the tops and bottoms. Complete sets in such vibrant colors are rare. The yellow box below is an unusually fine example.

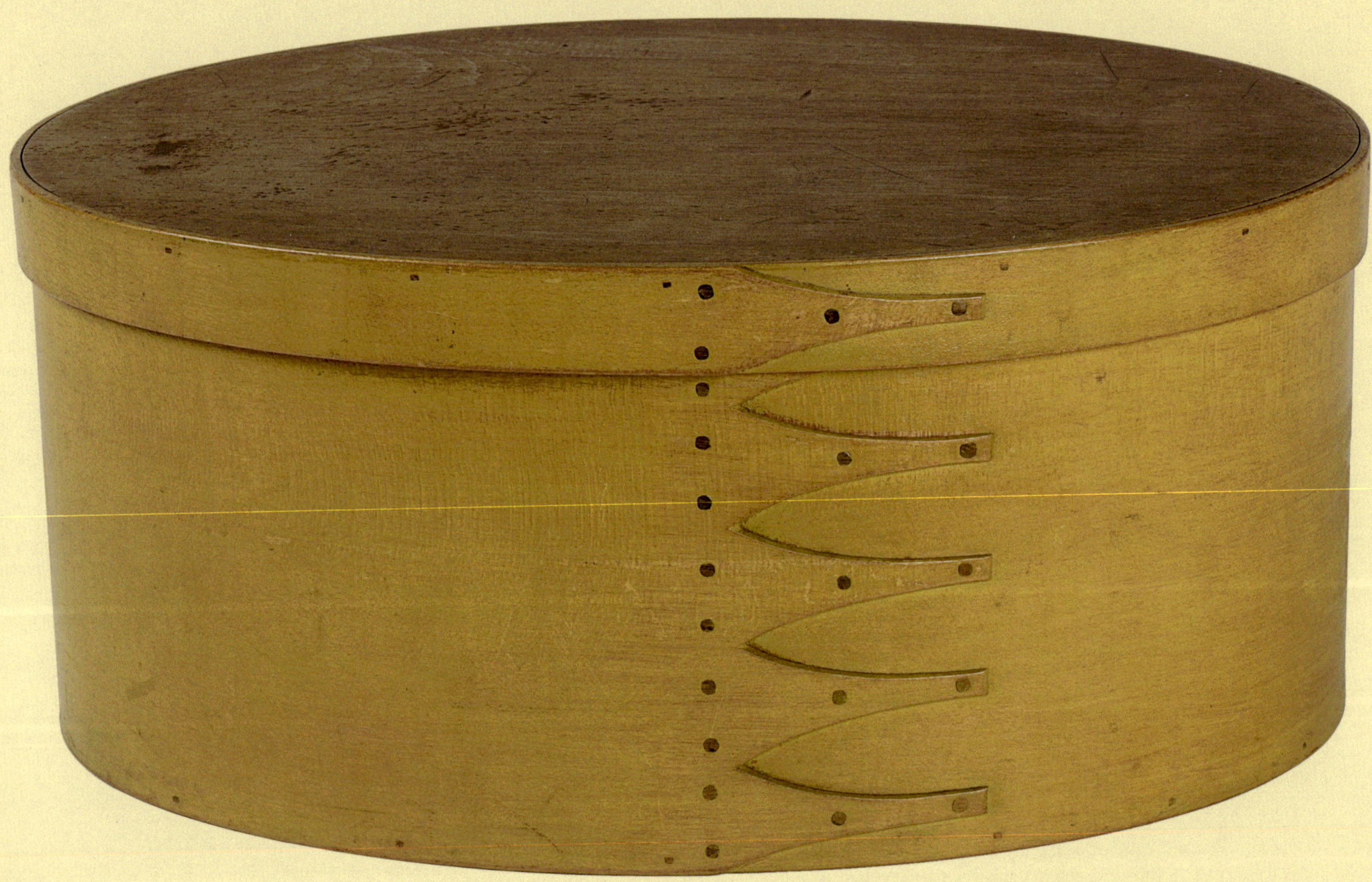

Chrome Yellow Oval Box

Probably New Lebanon, New York
ca. 1820–40

Pine, maple, tacks, and chrome yellow finish
6½ × 15 × 11 in.

L2015.41.27

Shaker Boxes

Possibly Canterbury, New Hampshire
ca. 1820–60

Pine, maple, stain, shellac, and copper tacks
Maximum size:
3⅝ × 9⅜ × 7 in.

Inscription (lid of smallest box): "Presented by Eld'r Grove to Martha Johnson"

2016.25.46

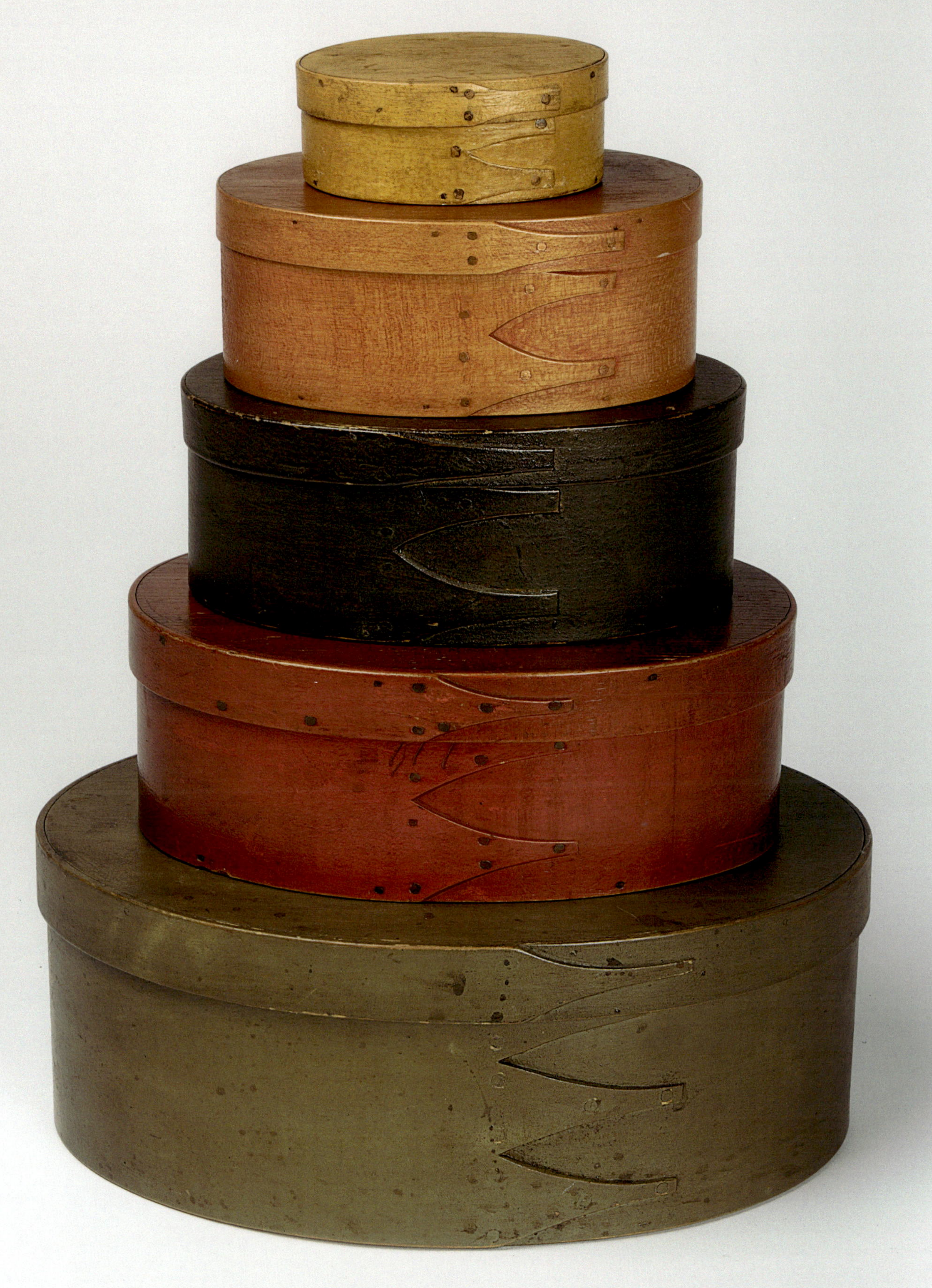

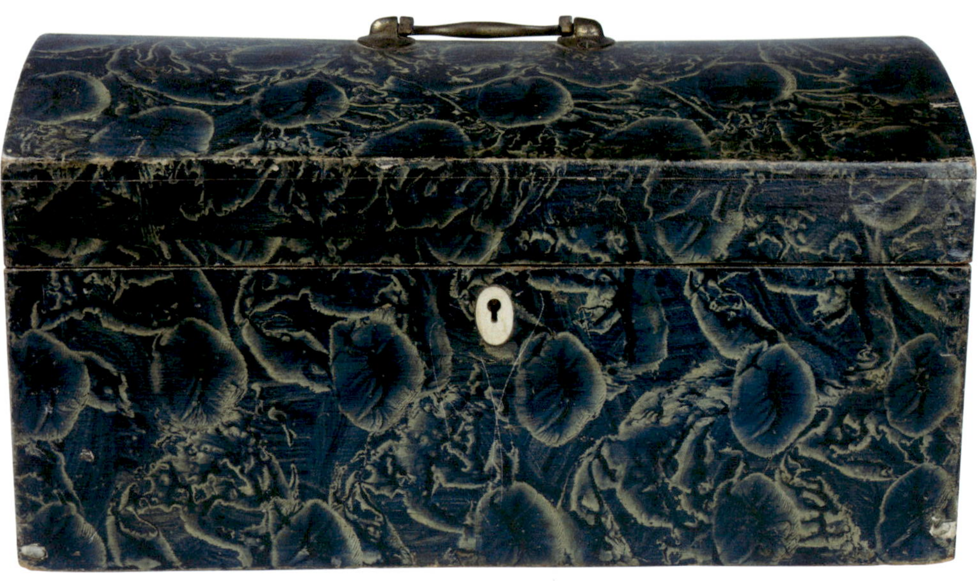

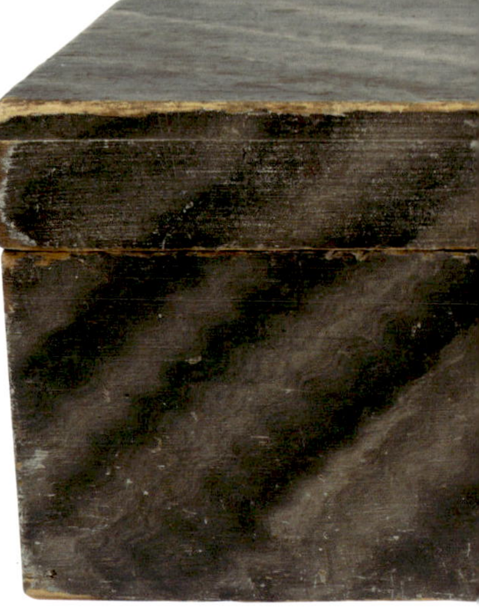

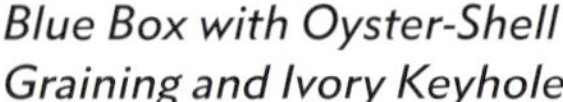

Blue Box with Oyster-Shell Graining and Ivory Keyhole
ca. 1820–40
Wood, paint, ivory, and iron
6½ × 11⅞ × 7 in.
2016.25.29

Flat-Top Diagonally Decorated Box
ca. 1820–40
Wood and paint
6½ × 13 × 9⅞ in.
2016.25.33

Decorated Box
Paris Hill, Maine
ca. 1820–40
Wood, paint, and iron
5⅛ × 11⅞ × 5⅞ in.
2016.25.32

Blue Smoke-Decorated Box
ca. 1820–40
Wood, paint, and iron
5½ × 12⅜ × 6¼ in.
2016.25.37

Decorated Box
ca. 1820–40
Wood and paint
5½ × 9⅞ × 5⅛ in.
2016.25.31

Writing Box
New England
ca. 1800
Wood, paint, and brass
4½ × 14¾ × 11 in.
2016.25.26

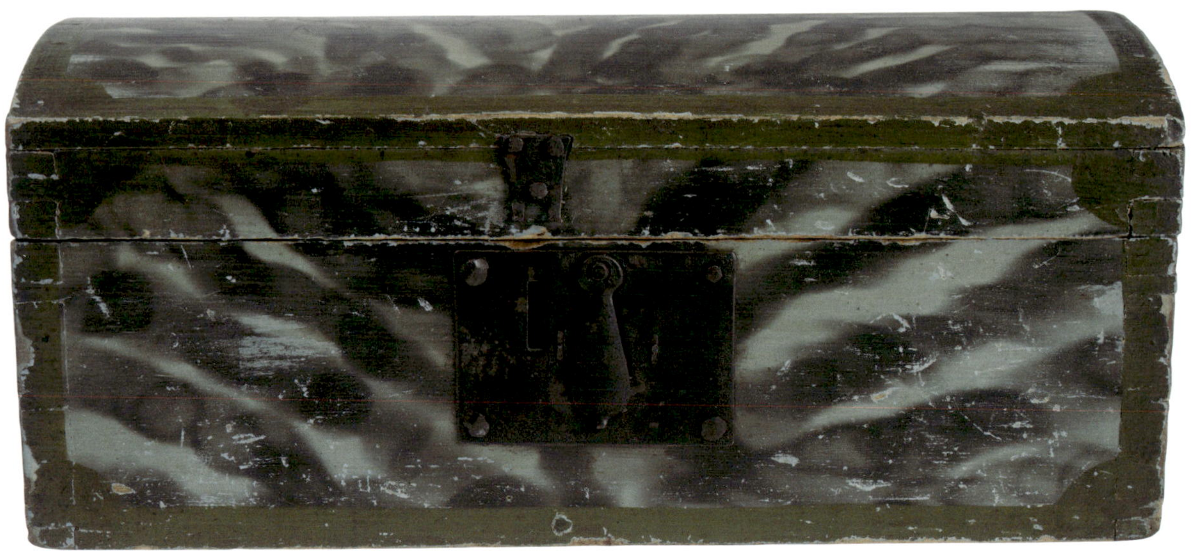

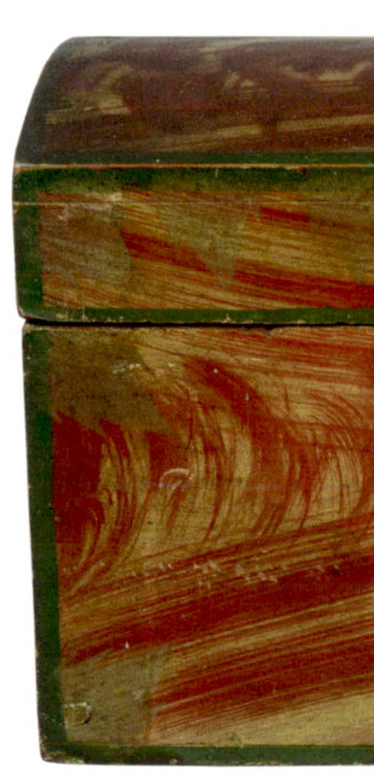

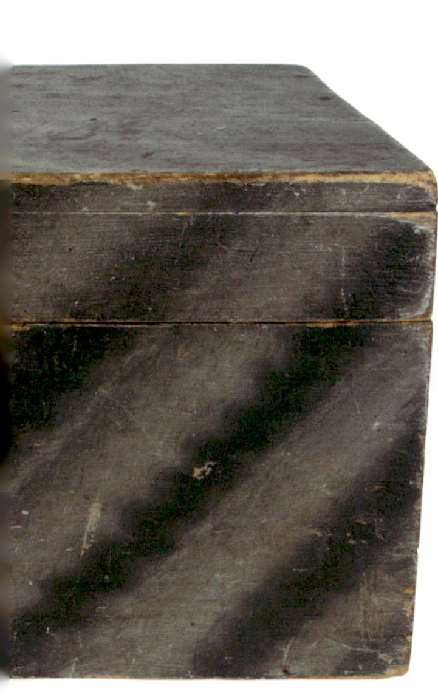
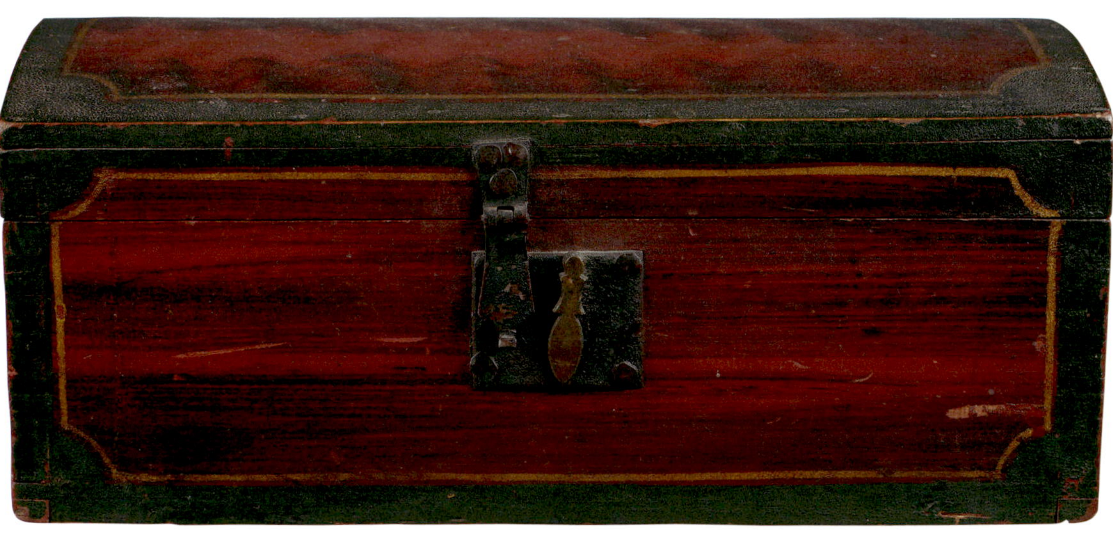
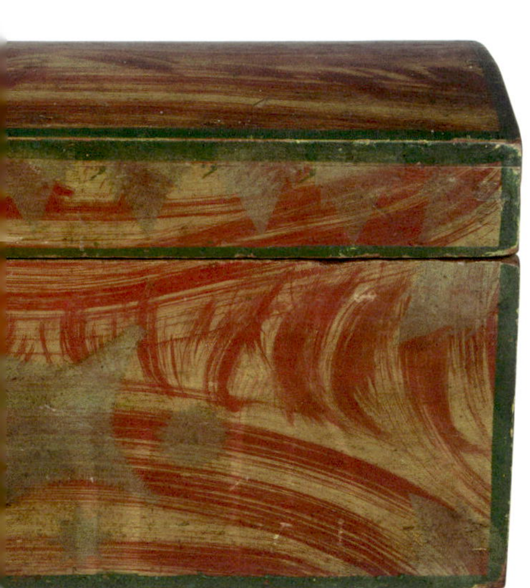
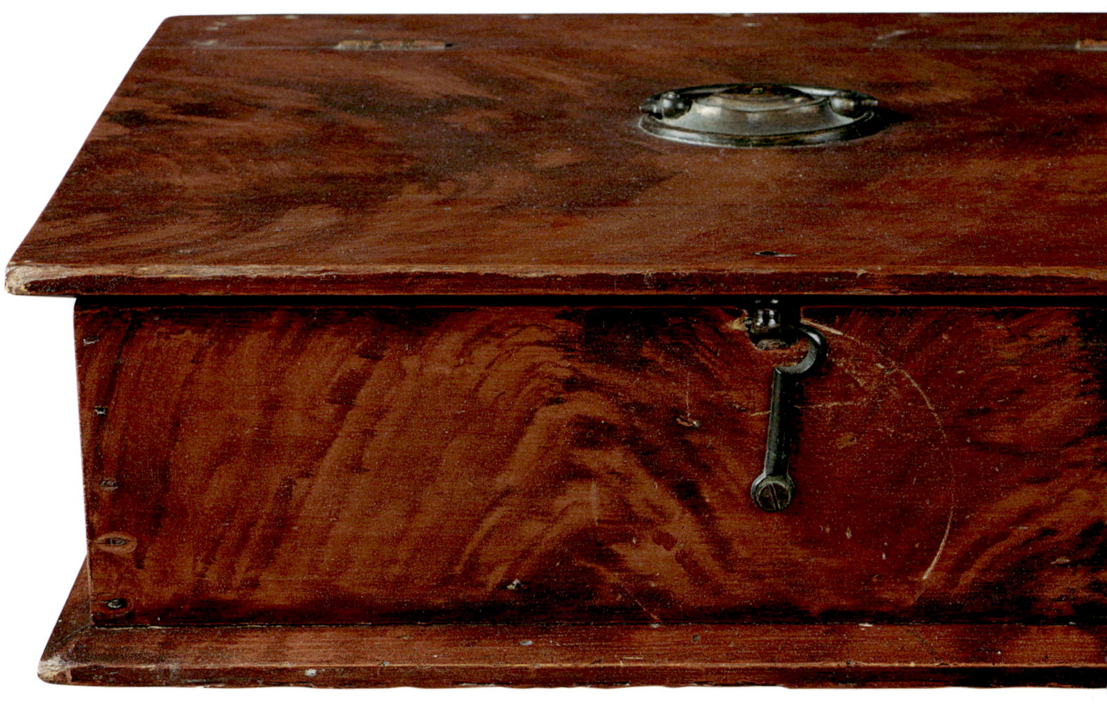

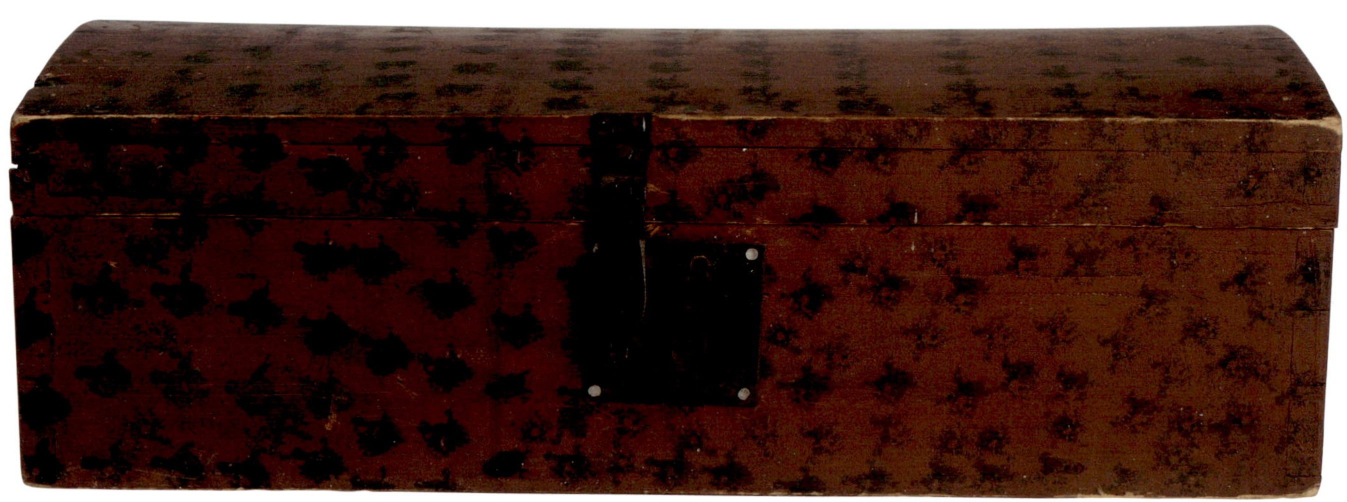

Red-Spotted Box with Shallow Dome Top

ca. 1820–40

Wood, paint, and iron
5⅛ × 15 × 8 in.

2016.25.34

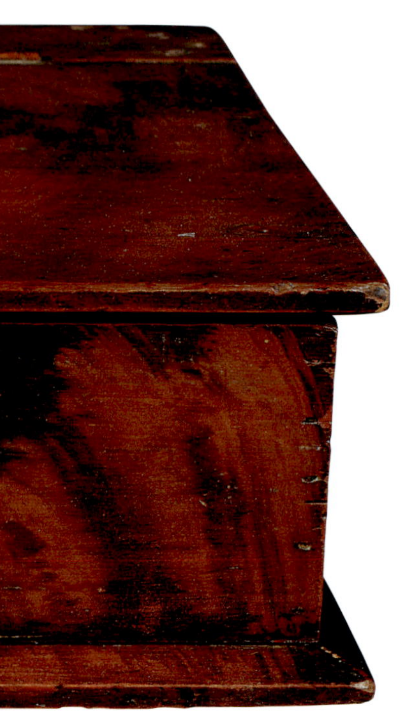

Arch-Decorated Box

ca. 1820–40

Wood, paint, and iron
9 × 18⅝ × 9¼ in.

2016.25.41

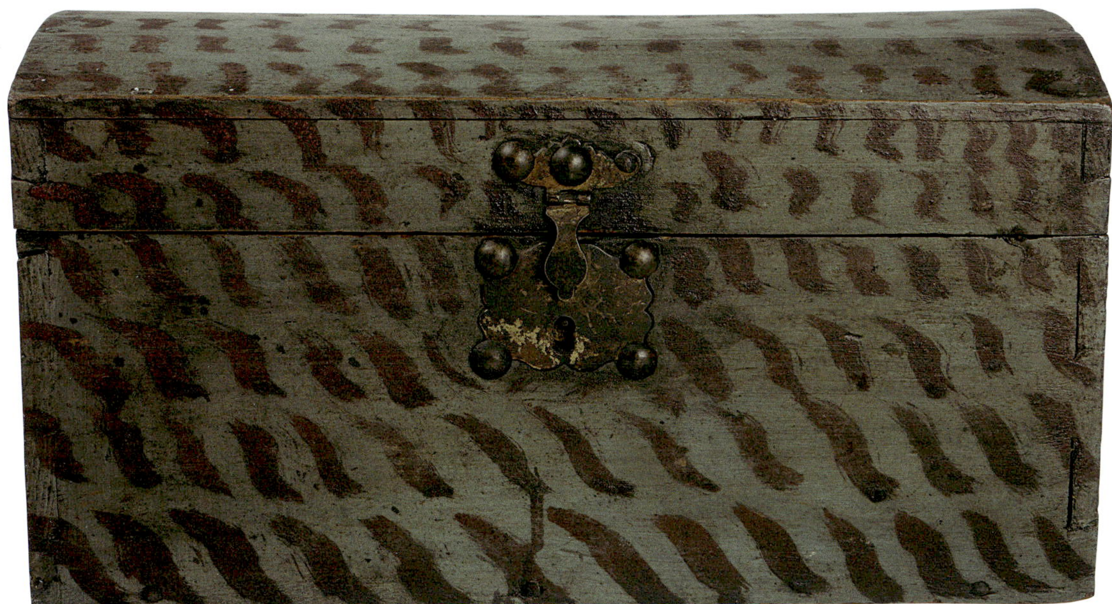

Green Dash-Decorated Box

ca. 1820–40

Wood, paint, and brass
6⅜ × 11¾ × 6¼ in.

2016.25.40

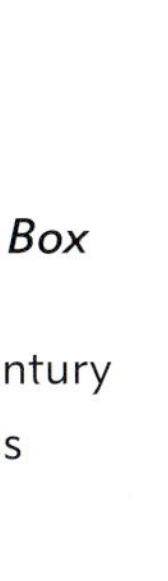

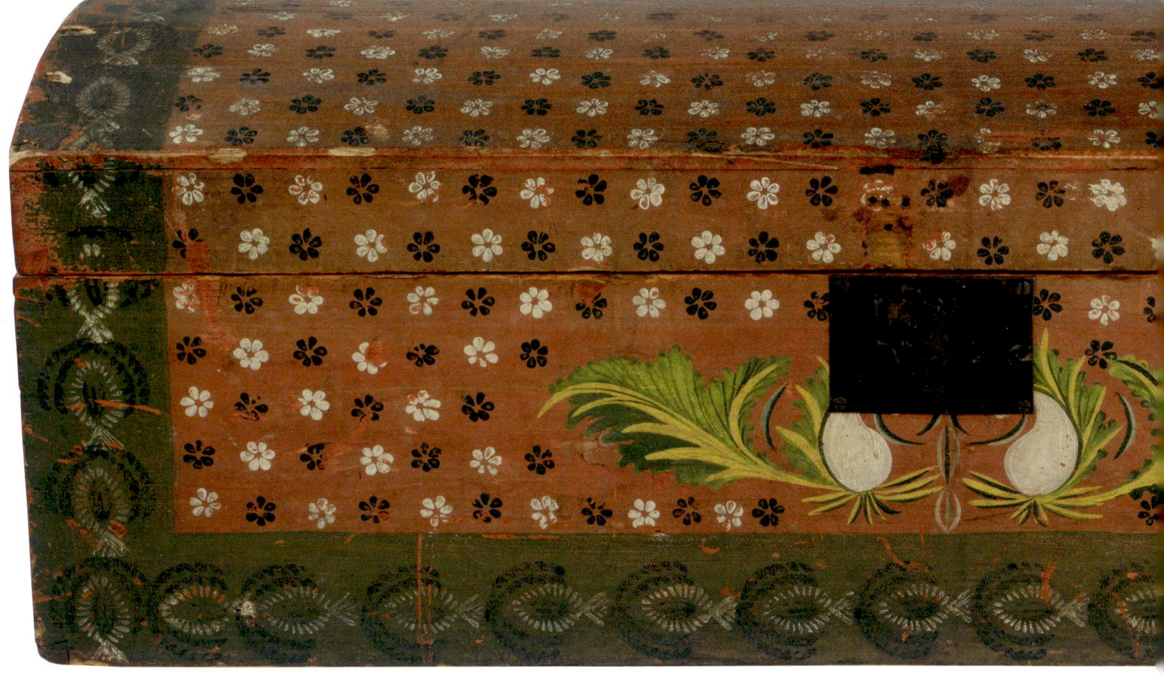

Painted Dome-Top Box

Possibly Vermont
Early nineteenth century

Pine, paint, and nails
10½ × 29⅝ × 12 in.

2016.25.42

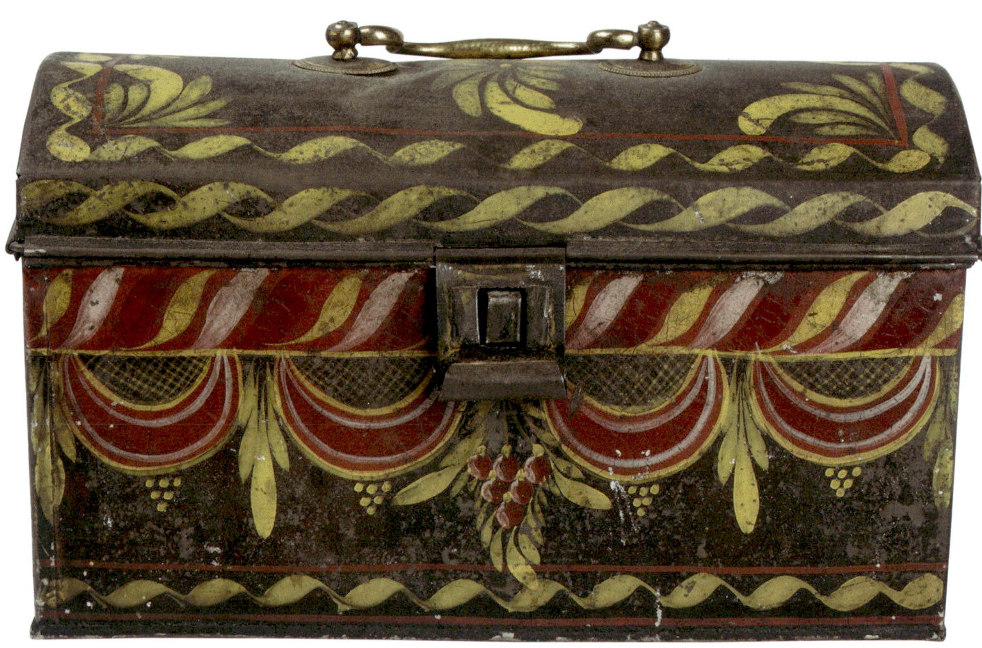

ATTRIBUTED TO ELIJAH AND ELISHA NORTH

Decorated Document Box

Stevens Plains (now Westbrook), Maine
ca. 1806–40

Tin, brass, and paint
5½ × 9 × 4½ in.

2016.25.45

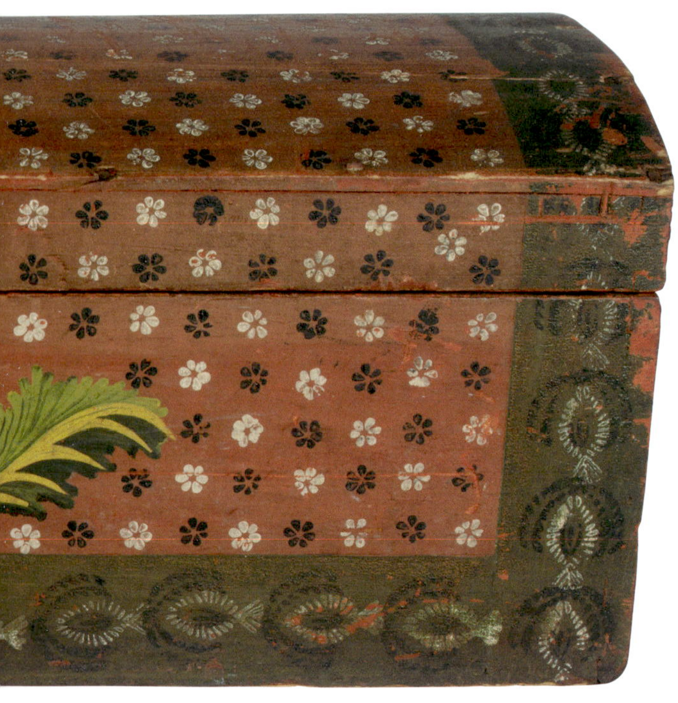

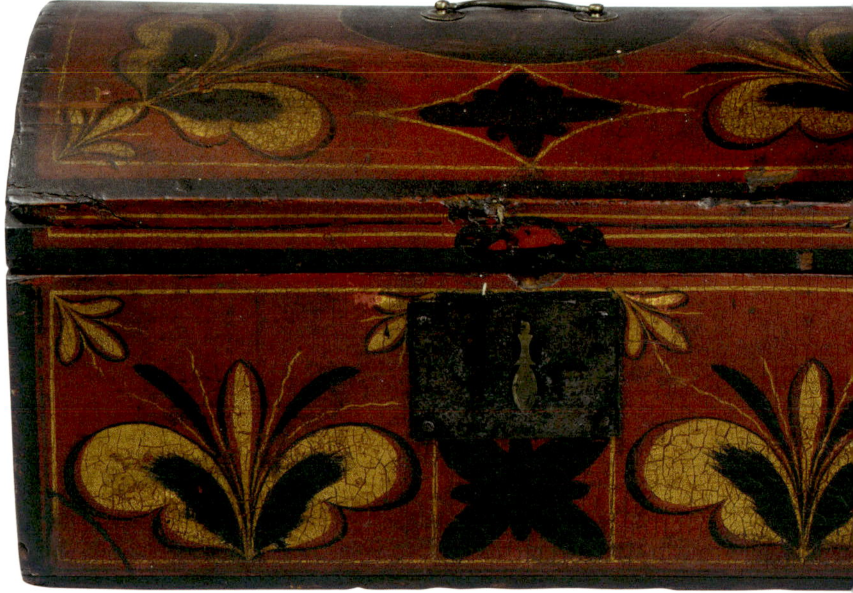

Painted and Decorated Dome-Top Box

New York State
ca. 1820–30

Basswood or pine and paint
9½ × 17½ × 10½ in.

Inscription (lid): "A.D."

L2015.41.63

Decorated Box
ca. 1820–40
Wood, paint, iron, and wallpaper lining
6¼ × 12⅜ × 6⅜ in.
2016.25.38

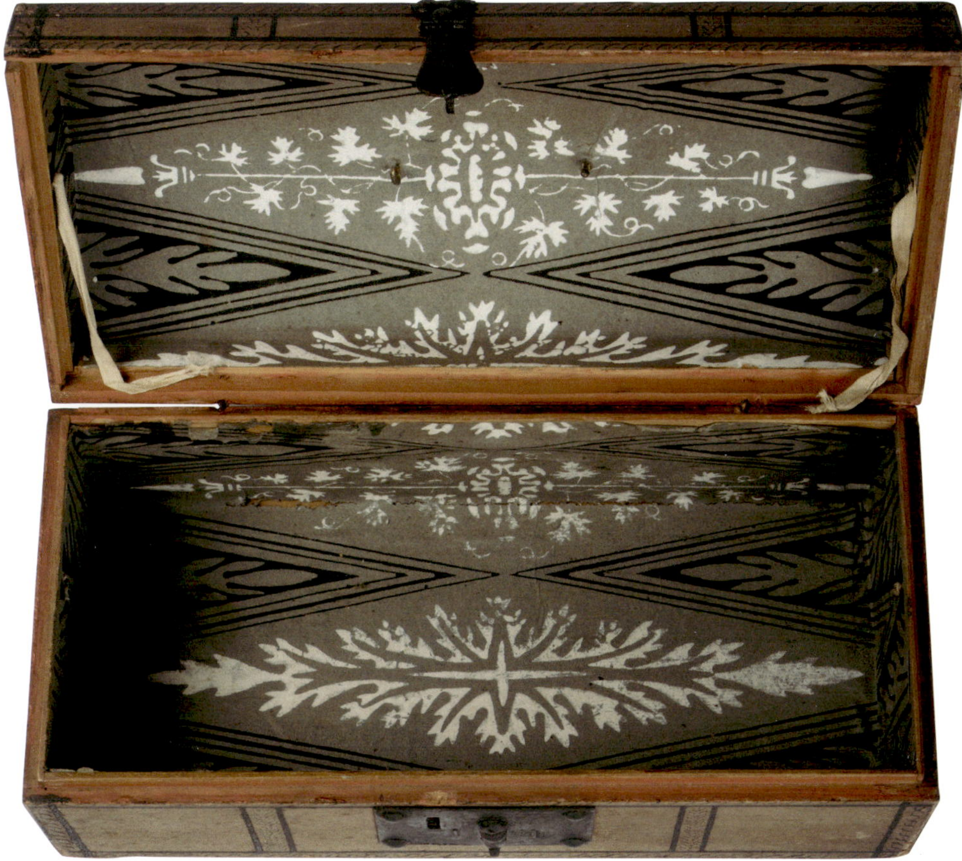

Dome-Top Trunk
Maine
ca. 1850
Wood, iron, and paint
12¾ × 28¼ × 15 in.
2016.25.69

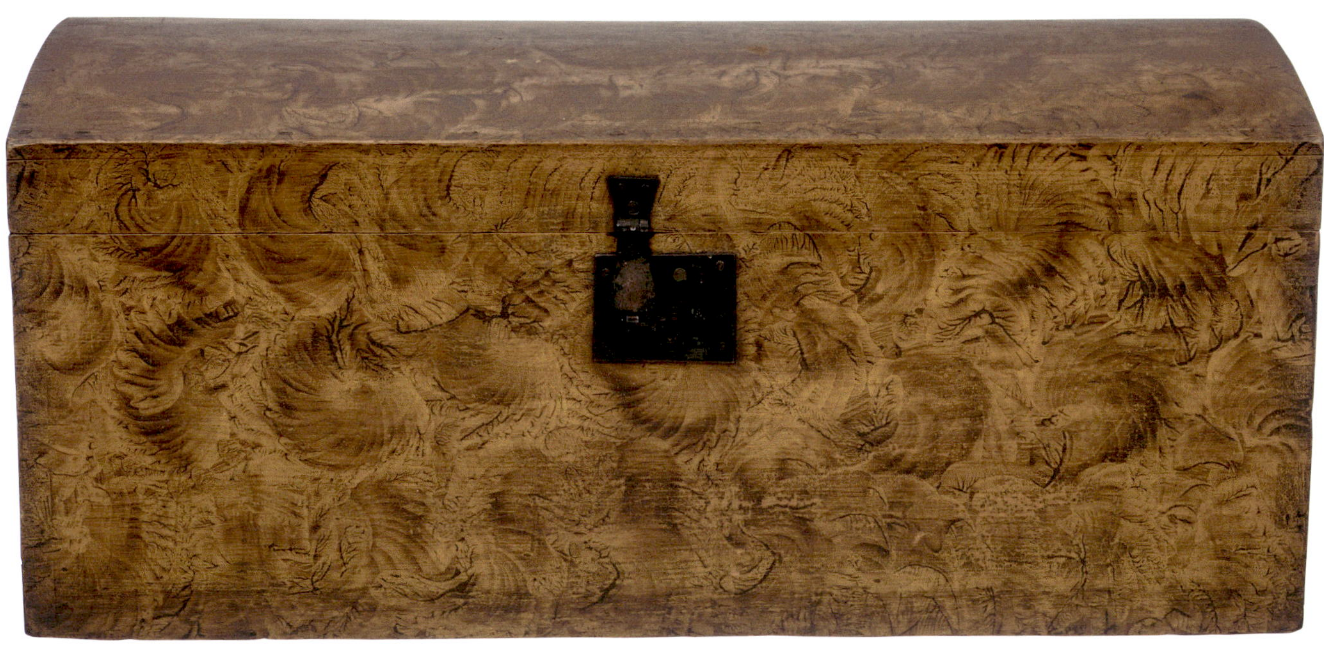

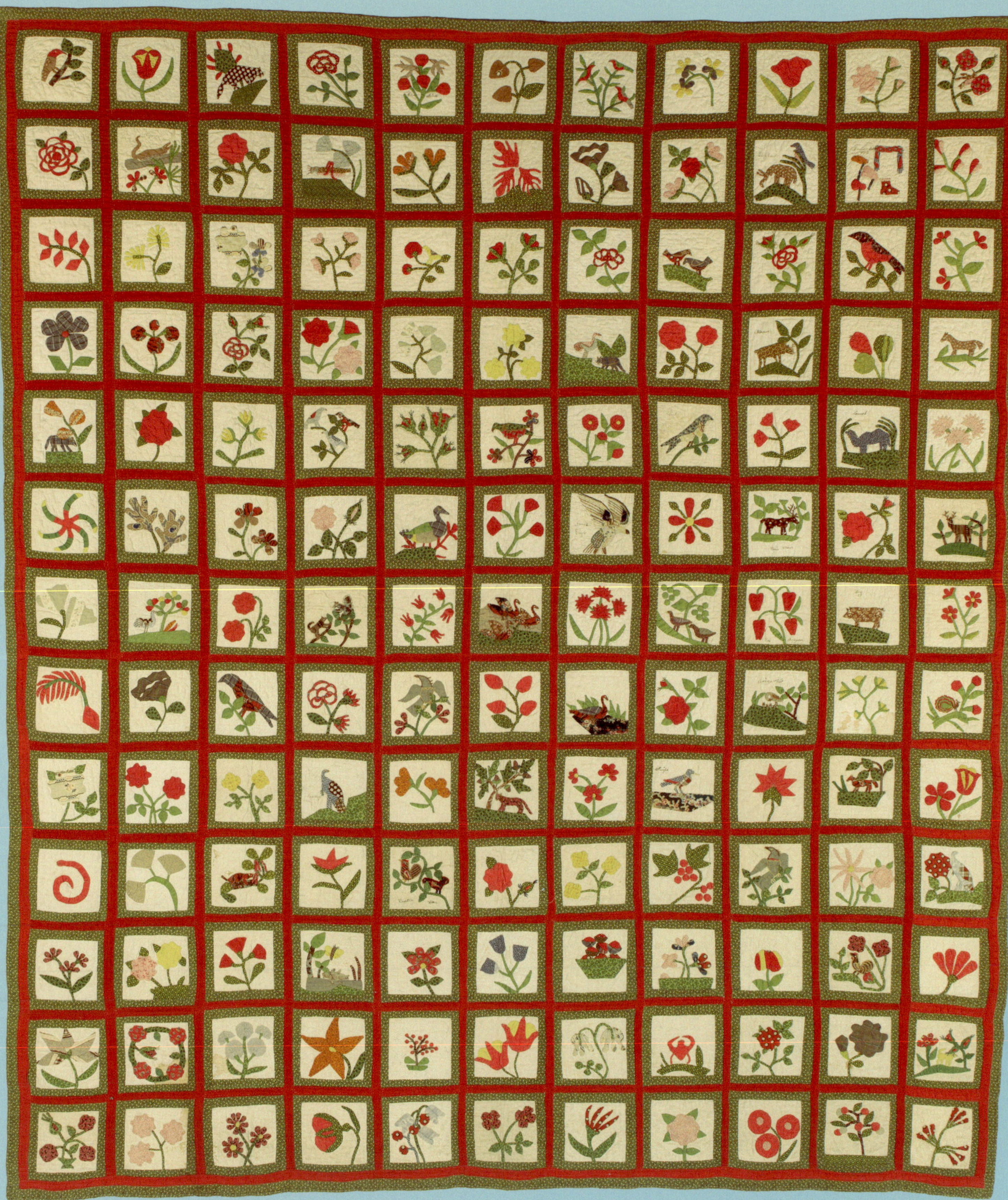

“Husband Every Hour”

Early American Textiles in the Fielding Collection

ELIZABETH V. WARREN

In the first years of America’s settlement, textiles were often the most expensive and important household possessions. Bedcovers were sometimes worth more than beds, for instance, as shown by estate inventories of the period. Since fabric was produced by hand, usually at home, the process was extremely labor-intensive. Imported fabric was rare and expensive, and found only in the dwellings of the wealthy. And as the raw material was so costly, inventive artists tended to recycle materials.

The beautiful examples of early American textiles in the Fielding Collection reveal a remarkable range of resources and creativity. These works of art were usually created by women, many of whom have not been identified. By closely examining the textiles in the collection—quilts, samplers and needlework embroideries, hooked and sewn rugs, embroidered pockets and pocketbooks, Native American beadwork—this essay presents an overview of needle arts in the eighteenth, nineteenth, and early twentieth centuries, primarily in the Northeast.

QUILTS

Women without means had precious few minutes to devote to sewing. For some, creating a quilt was an expression of creativity—a rare chance to make something beautiful and colorful to enhance their lives. By the early nineteenth century, textile mills in New England were producing a wide range of fabrics for household use, including quilts. Some of the fabric that women used for quilt making was recycled or left over from other uses, including clothing, but a remarkable number of quilts were made from material that was specifically purchased to make a bedcover. These were intended to be used as “best” bedcovers, only put out for visitors,

Album Quilt
New York
ca. 1850
Cotton, pieced and appliquéd
87¼ × 74½ in.
L2015.41.220

ATTRIBUTED TO MARY SEEDS MOON (1806–AFTER 1880)

Lone Star Quilt

Baltimore
ca. 1840

Cotton, pieced and appliquéd
128 × 129 in.

See also front endpapers

L2018.3.1

which is part of the reason they still exist today. Everyday bedding, often made from scraps, simply wore out from hard use and the wash, and no longer survives.

Quilts comprise the largest category of the Fieldings' textile collection, but not the earliest. There are currently thirty-five quilts in the collection, most dating from the second half of the nineteenth century. Many of them were made like a traditional sandwich: a pieced top, cotton batting, and a fabric backing, with stitches running through all three layers to hold the bedcover together. And while the makers of most of these quilts remain unidentified, the artist behind the *Lone Star Quilt* (opposite page) was very likely Mary Seeds Moon of Baltimore, Maryland.[1] Both family history—the quilt was passed down through Mary's daughter Emily Quail Moon—and examination of the materials and techniques used in making the quilt help to date it to around 1840. Moon used a combination of *piecing,* designs created out of fabrics that are seamed together side by side, and *appliqué*, decorative patches cut from assorted textiles and sewn onto a contrasting background fabric, to construct her quilt. She also used cut-out chintz appliqué, a practice that was popular in the late eighteenth century and the first half of the nineteenth. This technique involves carefully cutting printed motifs from fabric and applying them to a ground fabric. (In the second half of the nineteenth century, the term *broderie perse,* French for "Persian embroidery," was used for this method.) These chintz floral motifs can be seen between the lone stars on the quilt top. Often the chintz fabric was manufactured specifically for home-furnishing projects, with designs printed with the intention that they would be cut out and then sewn on a contrasting background. On this quilt, a second chintz fabric has been used as a border for the bedcover.

The spectacular mid-nineteenth-century *Album Quilt* (p. 108) also combines the techniques of piecing and appliqué. Each of its 143 blocks contains a handmade appliqué image of a plant or animal, and each is unique. Many of the blocks have been labeled: an "Alegator," "Red Pepper," "Rain Deer," "Great Eagle," and "Elephant" are among the plants and animals depicted. Some of the images have also been enhanced with embroidery. It is highly unlikely that the maker of this quilt would have seen firsthand all of the exotic animals depicted, but the images could have been copied from contemporary publications.

Friendship quilts such as the red-and-white example shown here (pp. 112, 113) are often similar to album quilts and are sometimes known as *single-pattern albums* or *single-pattern friendship quilts*, terms that indicate that all or most of the blocks are made of the same design. This quilt, dated 1855, features white crosses on red backgrounds. The signature in each cross indicates either the maker of the square or the person who donated money to have it sewn. While many friendship and album quilts were made to celebrate a particular event, to honor a distinguished member of the

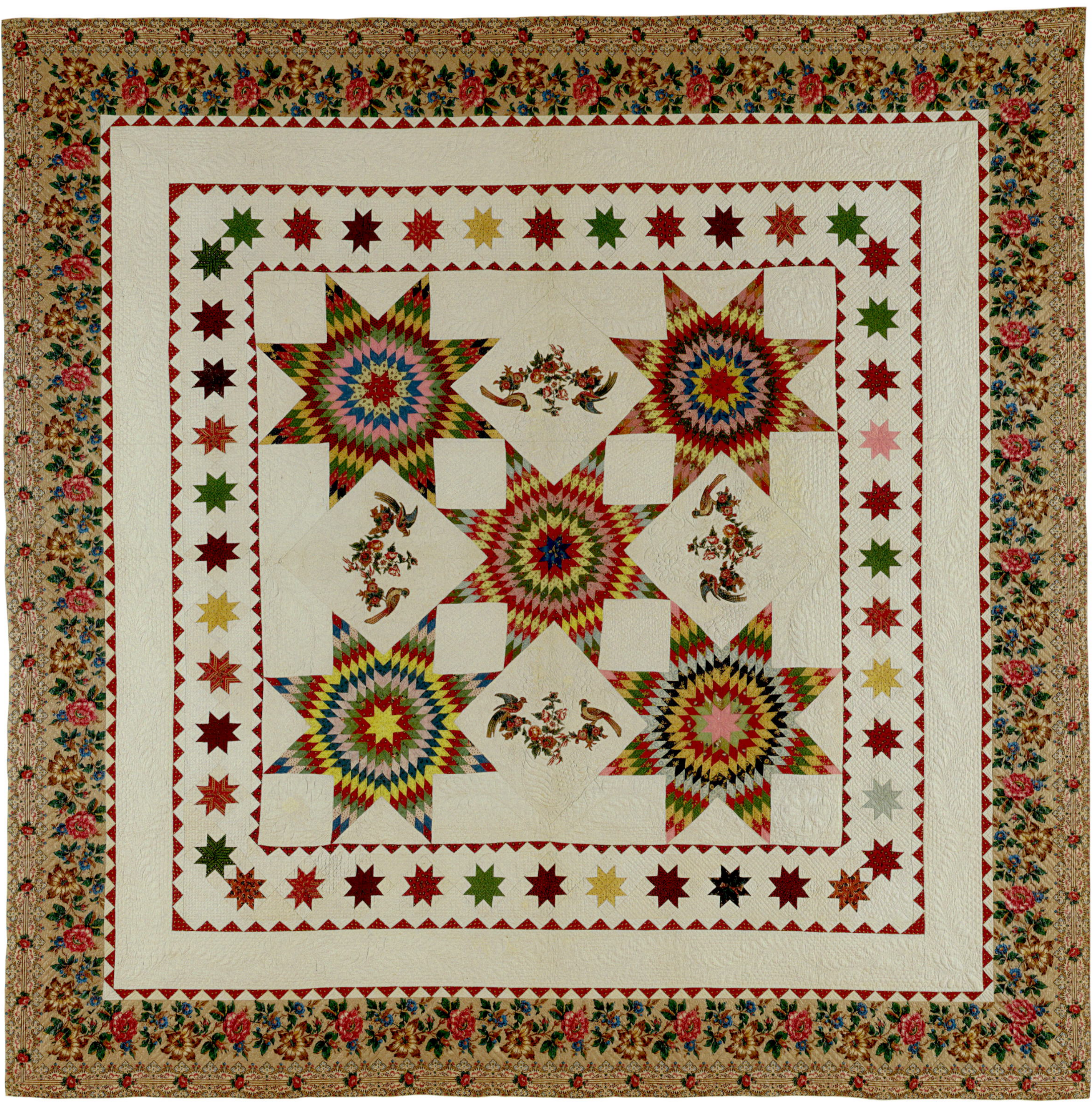

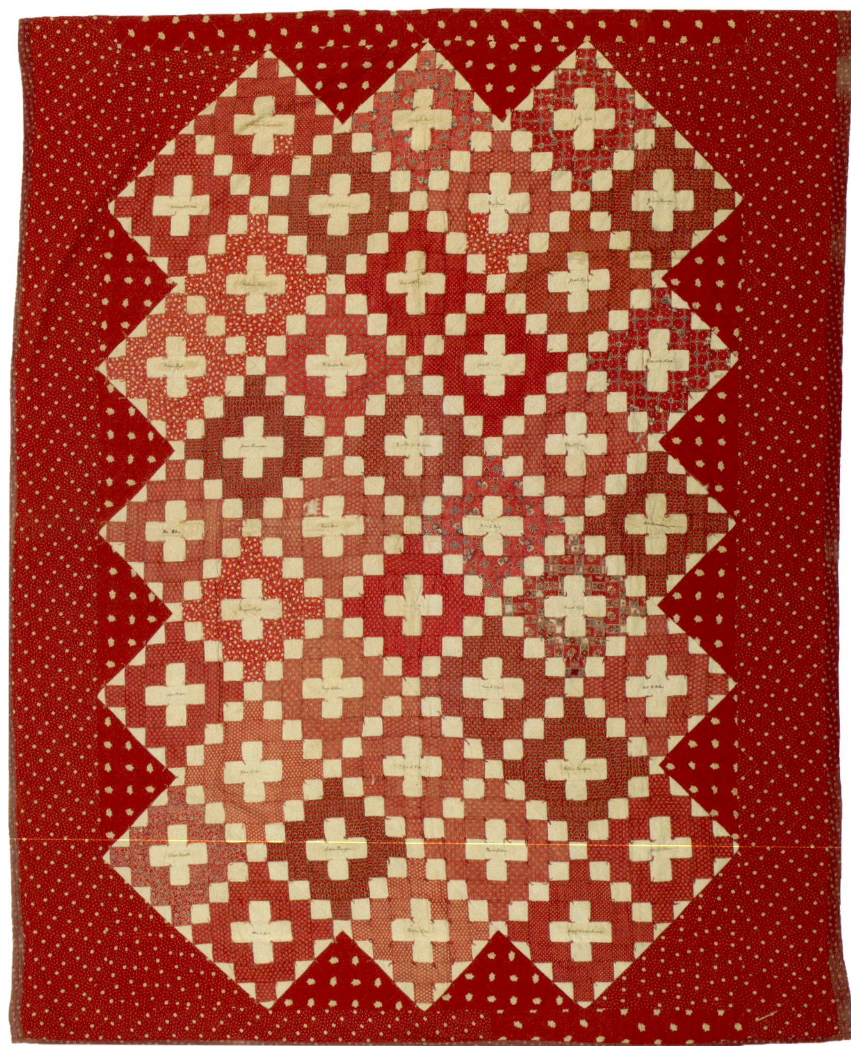

Red Friendship Quilt
1855
Cotton, pieced
87¼ × 69½ in.
Varied inscriptions
Detail on opposite page
2016.25.54

community, or to give to a departing family member or friend, others were created simply as an expression of community. Sometimes they were used to raise funds, and people would pay to have their names included on the quilt. Album quilts were also sold or raffled to raise money.

In the nineteenth century, piecing was the most common method of making a quilt. The clever needleworker had at her disposal an almost infinite variety of pieced-quilt patterns that could be devised based on geometric designs. Squares, rectangles, diamonds, triangles, and circles could be combined and recombined in original ways or in variations on an existing pattern. The names these quilts are called today are often no more than descriptive titles or romantic, if unreliable, titles that were created by late nineteenth- or early twentieth-century needlework editors and designers. Among the popular nineteenth-century geometric designs included in the Fielding Collection are Jacob's Ladder (p. 114), Wild Goose Chase (p. 115), and Geese in Flight (p. 138). Clearly there is great similarity among these

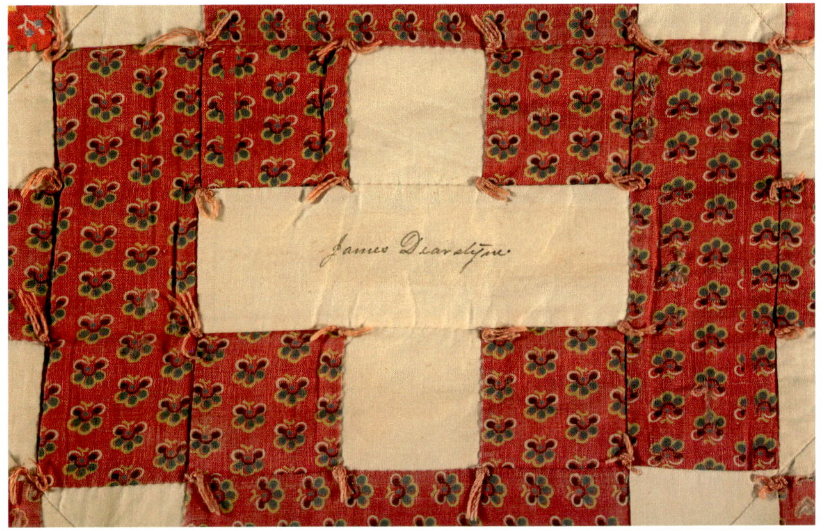

designs, and unless there is supporting documentation from a quilt maker, it is often impossible to know what the pattern was originally called.

Quilt making was the most democratic of the needle arts. Fine pocketbooks, samplers, and silk embroidery involved not only a substantial cost for the materials and frame but also the school fees and other expenses incurred in attending a female seminary. In contrast, most girls could learn simple sewing and quilt making at home, and patterns were often passed down through families or shared at community events.

Red Friendship Quilt
Inscription: "James Dearstyne"

Typically, a quilt maker would piece the top of the quilt herself, but often the "quilting," the stitches required to hold the three layers of the quilt together, would be done around a frame at a quilting bee. This type of gathering was often an important social event for quilt makers, providing time for women to gather for companionship, gossip, and quilt-pattern sharing. Quilting bees were held in the home or at a local meeting place, such as a Grange Hall or church. Many of the quilting groups had religious affiliations, and it was common for women to create quilts as gifts for their ministers. On some occasions, the party could last into the evening, as husbands and families joined the ladies for dinner. Many of the social functions of a quilting bee are continued today by the quilt guilds that exist all around the world.

Godey's Lady's Book, a popular periodical of the nineteenth century, began publishing patterns for quilts in 1835. By the end of the century, magazines and newspapers around the country were printing patterns (often the same ones but with different names) in an effort to satisfy their female readership. The Ladies Art Company, believed to be the first mail-order quilt-pattern company, was founded in St. Louis in 1889 and was soon followed by many competitors. Though quilt patterns continued to be shared among friends and family, and sometimes pattern names can be identified by region, quilt making had become big business, and companies invented mythical "grandmas" and "aunts" to sell their designs.

The Log Cabin quilt rose in popularity in the United States in the mid-nineteenth century. This type of quilt is important in American textile history not only because of the sheer number of examples made in the many variations of this pattern but also because it introduced a method of construction called *foundation piecing*. In this technique of quilt making,

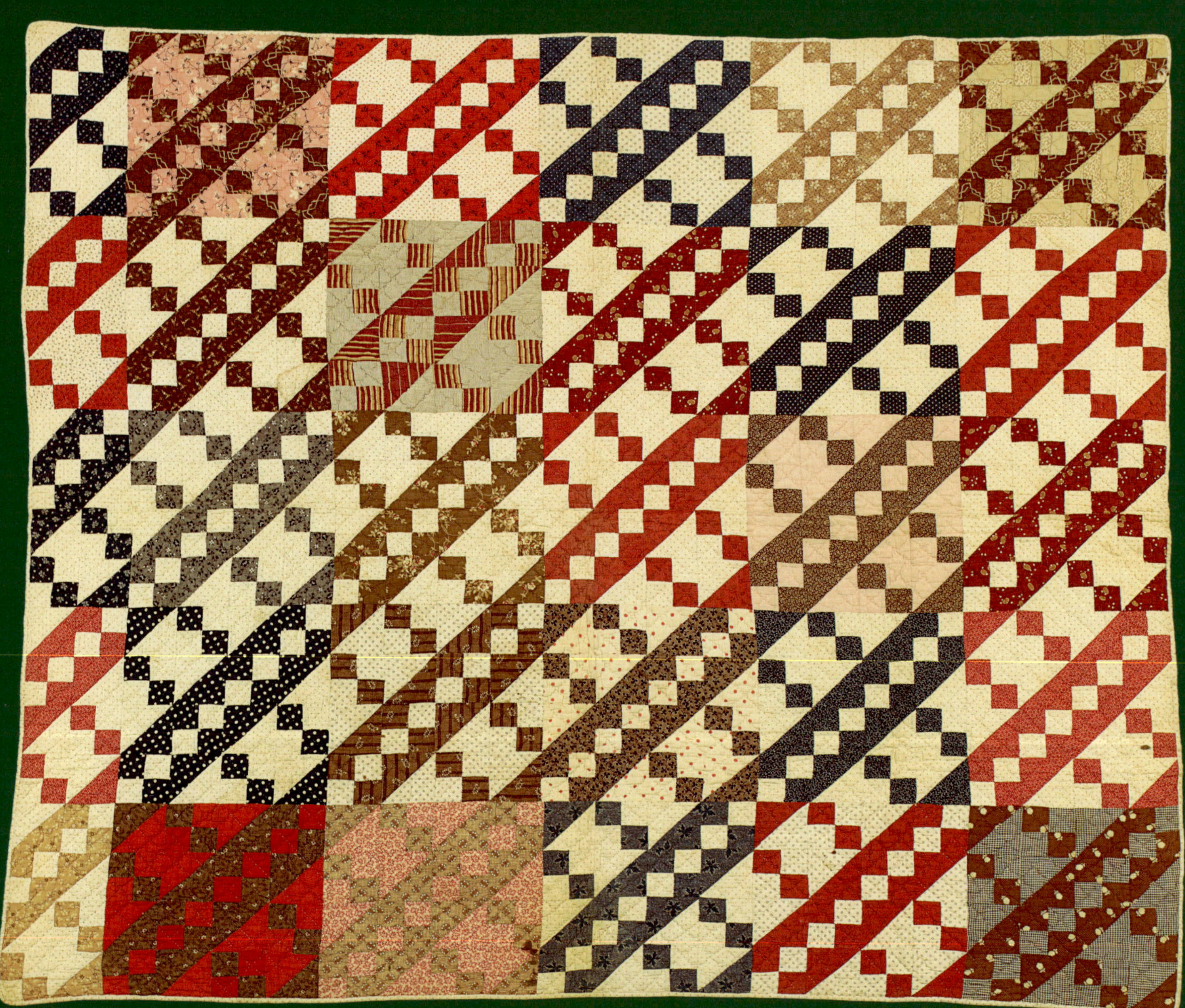

Jacob's Ladder Quilt
Lehigh County, Pennsylvania
ca. 1880
Cotton, pieced
73½ × 63 in.
2016.25.52

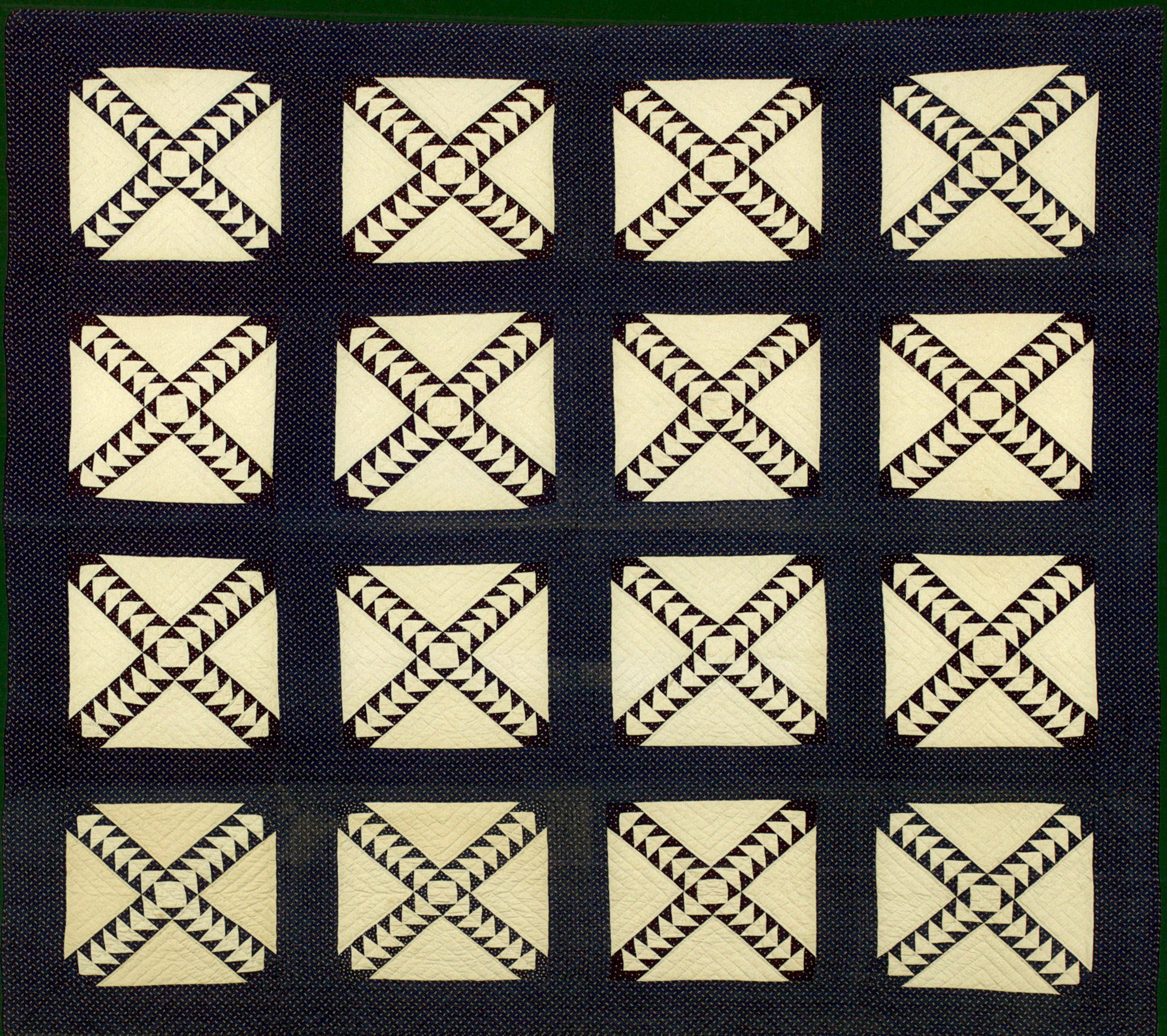

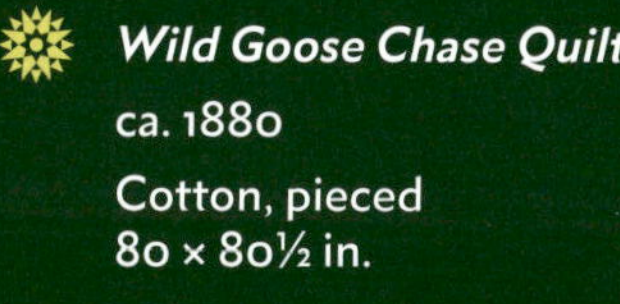

Wild Goose Chase Quilt

ca. 1880

Cotton, pieced
80 × 80½ in.

2016.25.56

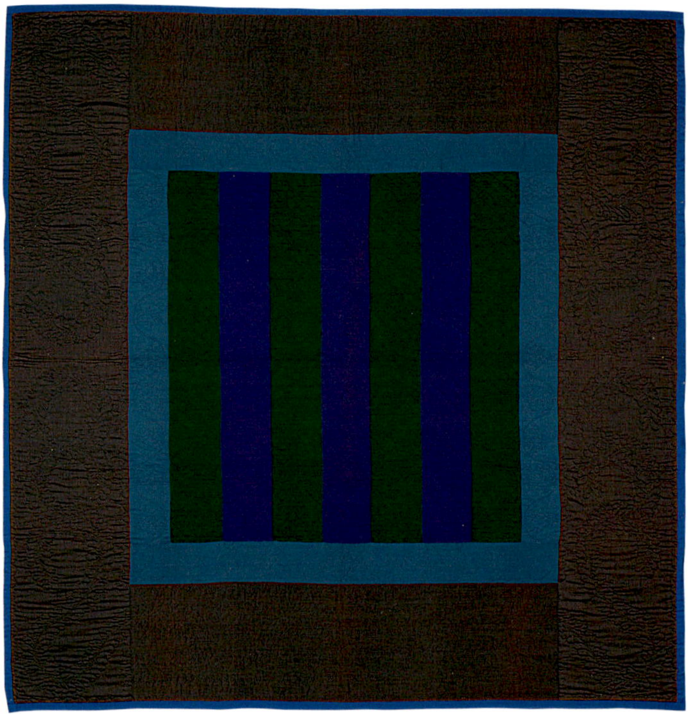

Bars Quilt

Probably Lancaster County, Pennsylvania, or Holmes County, Ohio
Early twentieth century

Cotton, pieced
81 × 78 in.

L2018.3.3

individual pieces of fabric (the logs of the cabin) are sewn to an underlying piece of fabric, or foundation, as well as to each other. Frequently, the foundation fabric is the size of an individual block, and the block is constructed by working outward from the center. Often, a red square representing the hearth of the cabin is placed at the center of the block. Typically, foundation-pieced quilts consist of only two layers, as there is no need for batting. There is also no need for quilting stitches to hold the three layers together: most Log Cabin quilts are tied to their backing, although some examples are not.

Varieties of Log Cabin quilts are created by the arrangement of the blocks, which are often composed of half light fabrics and half dark fabrics. The *Log Cabin Quilt* (p. 139) is a typical example of blocks sewn together to create alternating light and dark diamonds. The *Folk Art Crazy Quilt* (p. 134), made by Helen E. Hatch in 1885, is actually not a real "crazy," in which pieces are sewn together randomly, but combines a Windmill Blades or Pineapple Log Cabin variation center with pieced strips of concentric rectangles. In the Windmill Blades/Pineapple variation, the ends of the center strips are clipped at an angle to create the illusion of motion or to suggest the spiky leaves of a pineapple. The larger rectangles of this quilt do contain some randomly shaped pieces, but the whole has a more regular appearance than a crazy quilt. Quilts made of silk, such as this example, are known as *show quilts*, as their fragile fabrics make it unlikely that they were ever used as bedcovers. They usually served as throws or decorative objects.

For some immigrants, quilts were unknown in their homeland. Unlike their English-speaking neighbors in Pennsylvania, the Amish (and other Germanic groups) did not bring a tradition of quilt making to America with them. Blankets, featherbeds, and woven coverlets were more typical styles of bedding. The quilt-making tradition, learned from their "English" neighbors, seems to have taken hold among the Amish in the 1870s and 1880s, and the majority of Amish quilts collected today were made between the 1880s and the 1950s. The Fieldings' two Amish quilts (p. 50 and above) are archetypal designs of this community and among the first styles of quilts made by the Amish. As befitted their conservative lifestyle and their religious prohibition against naturalistic images, the Amish used only geometric designs. Realistic motifs such as flowers, hearts, and baskets could be stitched into the quilt, however, as those stitches were necessary to hold the three layers

Quilt with Concentric Circles

Lenhartsville, Pennsylvania
ca. 1870

Cotton, pieced and appliquéd
84 × 84½ in.

L2015.41.221

of the quilt together. The earliest Amish quilts were made of large pieces of solid color fabric (either cotton or wool). By the end of the nineteenth century, these monochromatic quilts were followed by examples with more colors and more complex design elements, although large geometric pieces of solid color fabric were still the norm. Printed fabrics, while sometimes found on the back of a quilt, were considered too worldly to use on the front.

The *Diamond in the Square Quilt* (p. 50, sometimes called *Center Diamond*) is made in the typical jewel-tone colors that the Amish favored for their quilts and for the clothes they wore under their black coats and capes. The fine wool fabrics indicate that the quilt was probably made in Lancaster County, Pennsylvania. Although the maker's name is unknown, she stitched the initials "R.S" on the reverse of the quilt. These initials could be the

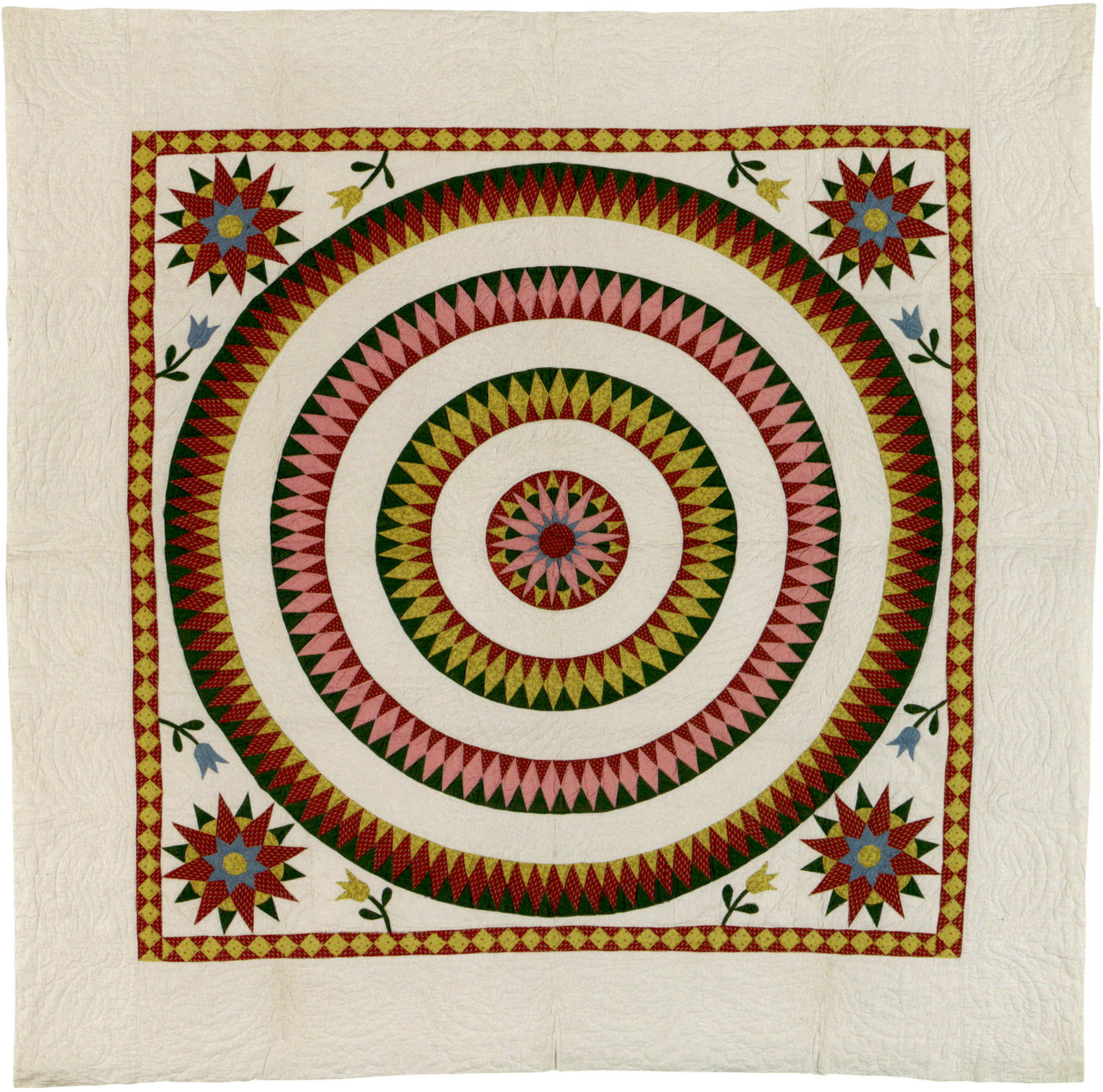

Lone Star Quilt Top—Red and White

1880–1910

Cotton, pieced
79 × 78 in.

2016.25.59

maker's own, or those of the recipient of the quilt. The fabrics, simple pattern, and initials on the reverse are all typical of Amish quilts made at the end of the nineteenth century and the very beginning of the twentieth.

The *Bars Quilt* (p. 116) is based on another favorite Lancaster County pattern. Like the Diamond in the Square, it is constructed with a center design surrounded by a narrow inner border and a wide outer border. As this quilt is made of cotton and not the wool usually found on the early Lancaster County quilts, it probably was created either in the mid-twentieth century or in another Amish settlement, most likely Holmes County, Ohio. Holmes County is home to the largest group of Amish in the United States, and their quilts are typically made of cotton. Black and blue were also favored colors in Holmes County at the beginning of the twentieth century.

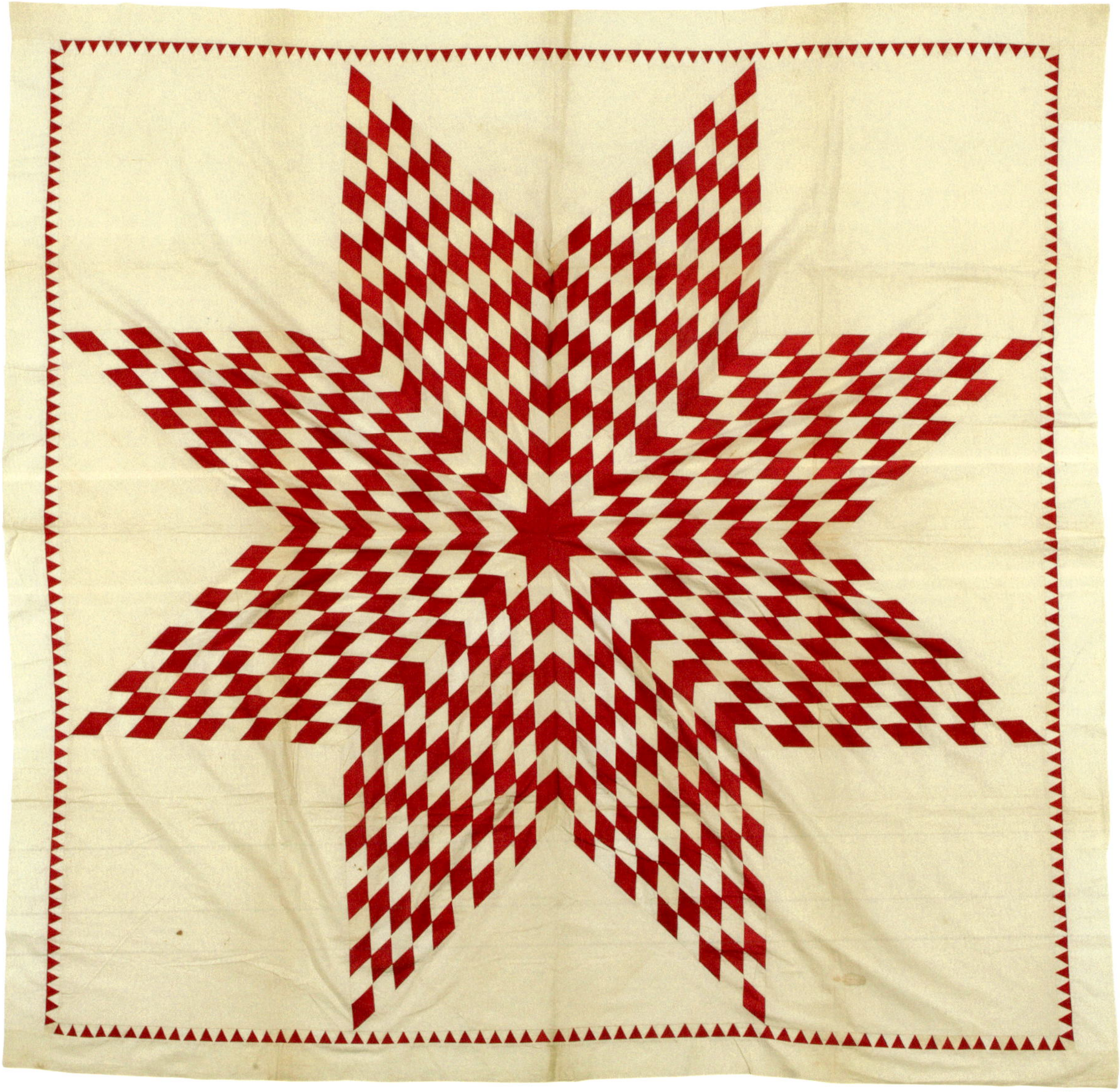

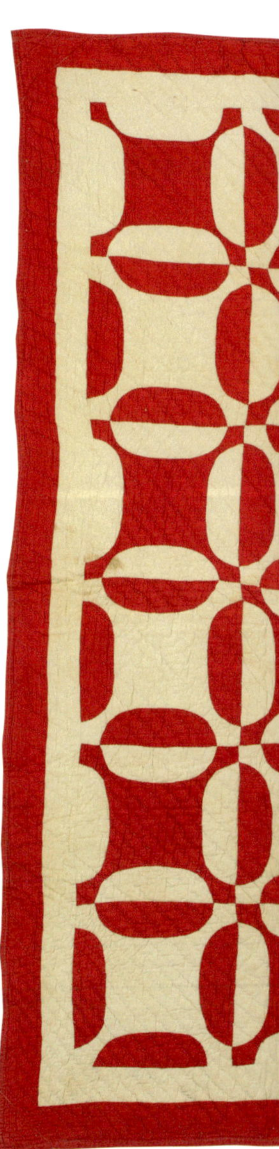

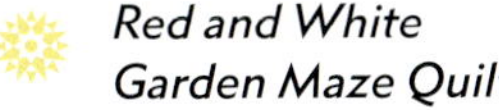

Red and White Garden Maze Quilt
1880–1910
Cotton, pieced
73 × 72½ in.
2016.25.53

Other Germanic settlers in Pennsylvania did not have the same religious proscriptions as the Amish, and their quilts tend to be more complicated. These feature combinations of piecing and appliqué (forbidden among the Amish, as appliqué is considered a decorative technique) and brightly patterned fabrics. The Bulls Eye or *Quilt with Concentric Circles* (p. 117) is a typical example of this truly joyous expression in quilt making. The bedcover is similar to a group of quilts that were made in a Germanic enclave of Berks County, Pennsylvania, between the last quarter of the nineteenth century and the beginning of the twentieth. Meticulous sewing skills were required to piece this quilt so that the many diamonds and triangles of the concentric circles would lie flat.

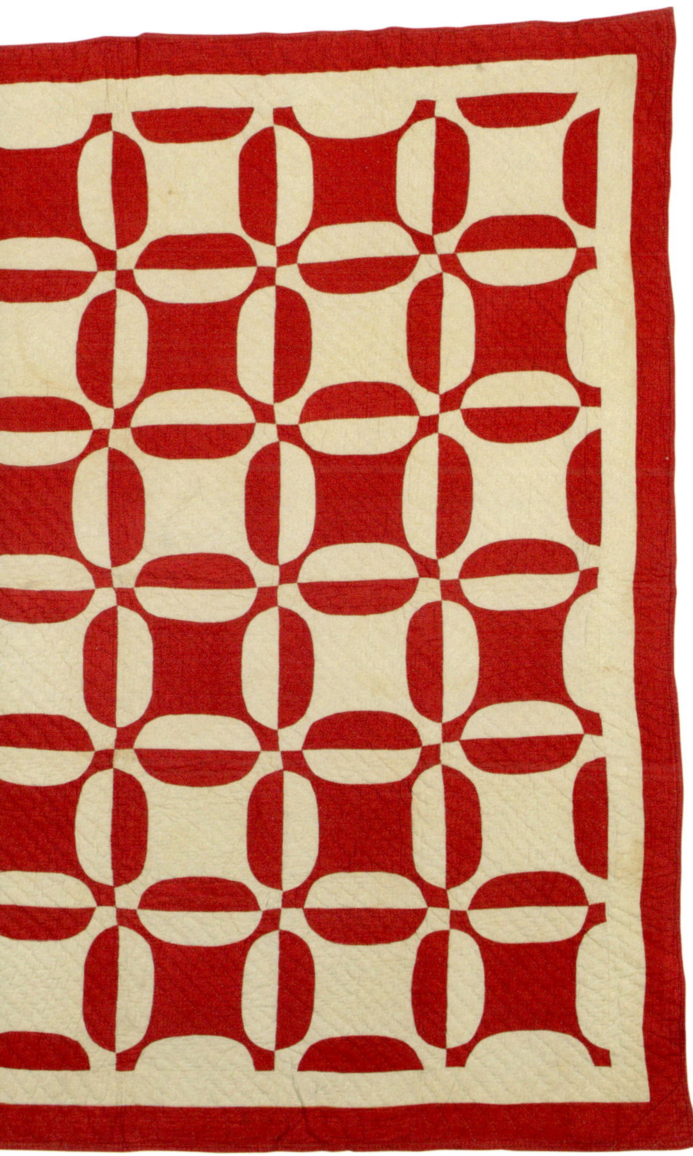

Red and white has been a classic color scheme for American quilts since the early nineteenth century. The popularity of this deceptively simple combination, apart from its intrinsic aesthetic appeal, can be traced to a basic scientific reality: the remarkable colorfastness of Turkey red dye. At a time when most colored fabrics tended to run or fade when washed or exposed to the light, Turkey red cotton was known for its reliability. Derived from madder root, Turkey red dye came to Europe from the eastern Mediterranean in the 1750s, hence the name. Producing it was a long and expensive process, and the fabrics dyed with it were correspondingly costly. In 1868, however, a synthetic version of the dye became available, simplifying the process and enabling the production of Turkey red cotton by American mills. One result of this invention was an explosion in the number of quilt patterns created to take advantage of this colorfast fabric. Both the *Red and White Garden Maze Quilt* and the *Lone Star Quilt Top* (left and opposite page) were probably made at the end of nineteenth century, when red-and-white quilts were at the height of popularity.

NEEDLEWORK AND SAMPLERS

Few quilts made in the American colonies in the eighteenth century have survived. In all likelihood, they were used up, worn out over the years. A number of forms of needlework from the colonial and early Federal periods, however, have been preserved. The Fielding Collection includes four examples of eighteenth-century canvas work—including a pair of pockets (p. 130) and a worked pocketbook (pp. 120, 121)—as well as several schoolgirl embroideries (pp. 122, 123, 131).

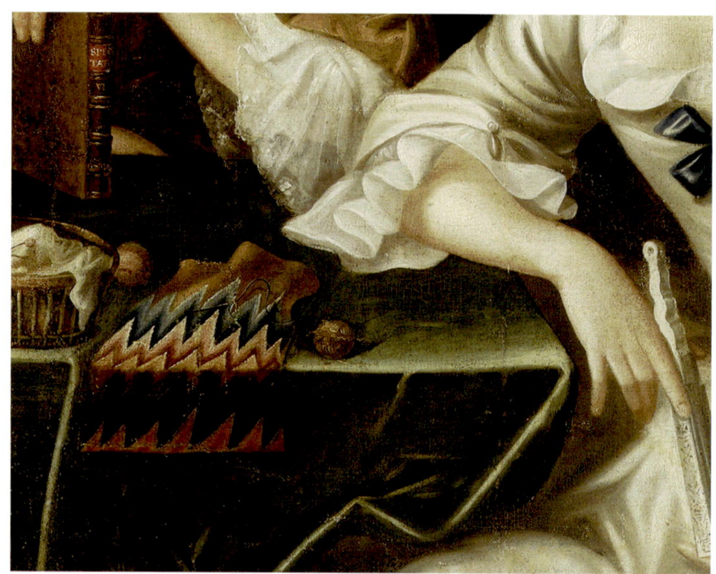

JOHN GREENWOOD
(1727–1792)

The Greenwood-Lee Family (detail)

ca. 1747

Oil on canvas
55½ × 69⅛ in.

BEQUEST OF HENRY LEE SHATTUCK IN MEMORY OF THE LATE MORRIS GRAY, 1983.34, MUSEUM OF FINE ARTS, BOSTON. PHOTOGRAPH © 2020 MUSEUM OF FINE ARTS, BOSTON

In the eighteenth and nineteenth centuries, “pockets,” as people today consider them, were not part of ladies’ garments. Instead, most women wore one or a pair of fabric bags tied to the waist and hidden underneath the skirt. These pockets served much the same purpose as a handbag, and they were accessed by openings in the side seams of petticoats.[2] These bags could be pieced of bits of fabric, much like quilts, or embroidered on canvas with a very fine, two-ply worsted wool known as crewel. The pockets shown on page 130 were probably made between 1760 and 1790, when this latter type of canvas work was most popular. They were sewn in shades of red, green, blue, and yellow crewel in the Irish stitch, today often called flame stitch or bargello. A similar type of flame-stitch canvas work appears in a mid-eighteenth-century portrait of the accomplished women of the Greenwood and Lee families (above).

Worked pocketbooks, such as the one shown below, were similar to today’s wallets and were carried by both men and women, although women often put valuables in their pockets. Leather was actually a more common material for pocketbooks, but over the years the needlework was saved, perhaps because of personal associations, whereas relatively few leather examples still exist.[3] A handwritten note found inside one pocketbook reads:

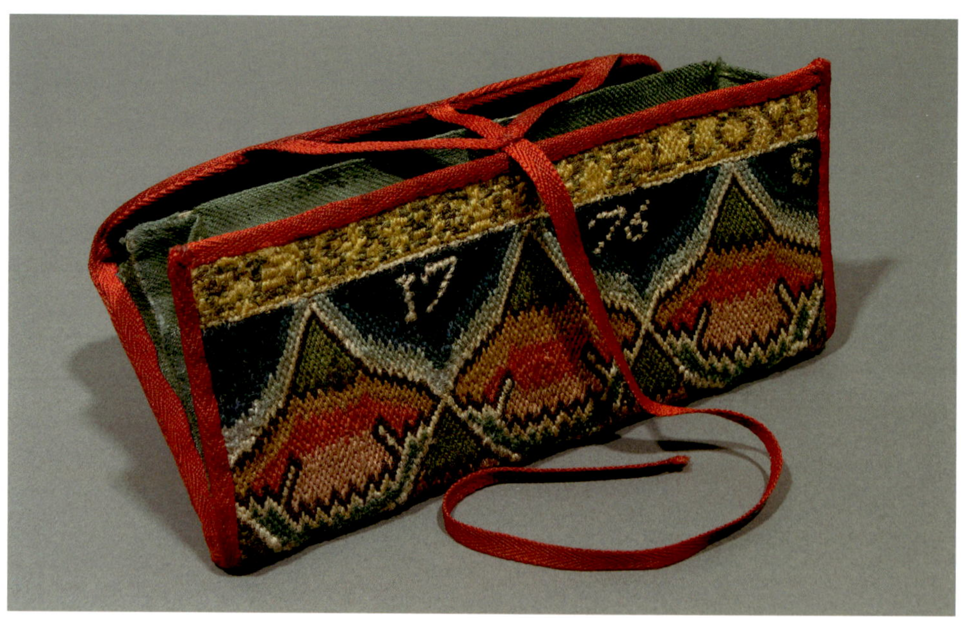

ELISABETH FELLOWS

Pocketbook

ca. 1776

Wool on linen, cotton trim
4¼ × 8⅝ × ⅞ in.

See opposite page for verso of pocketbook

L2015.41.68

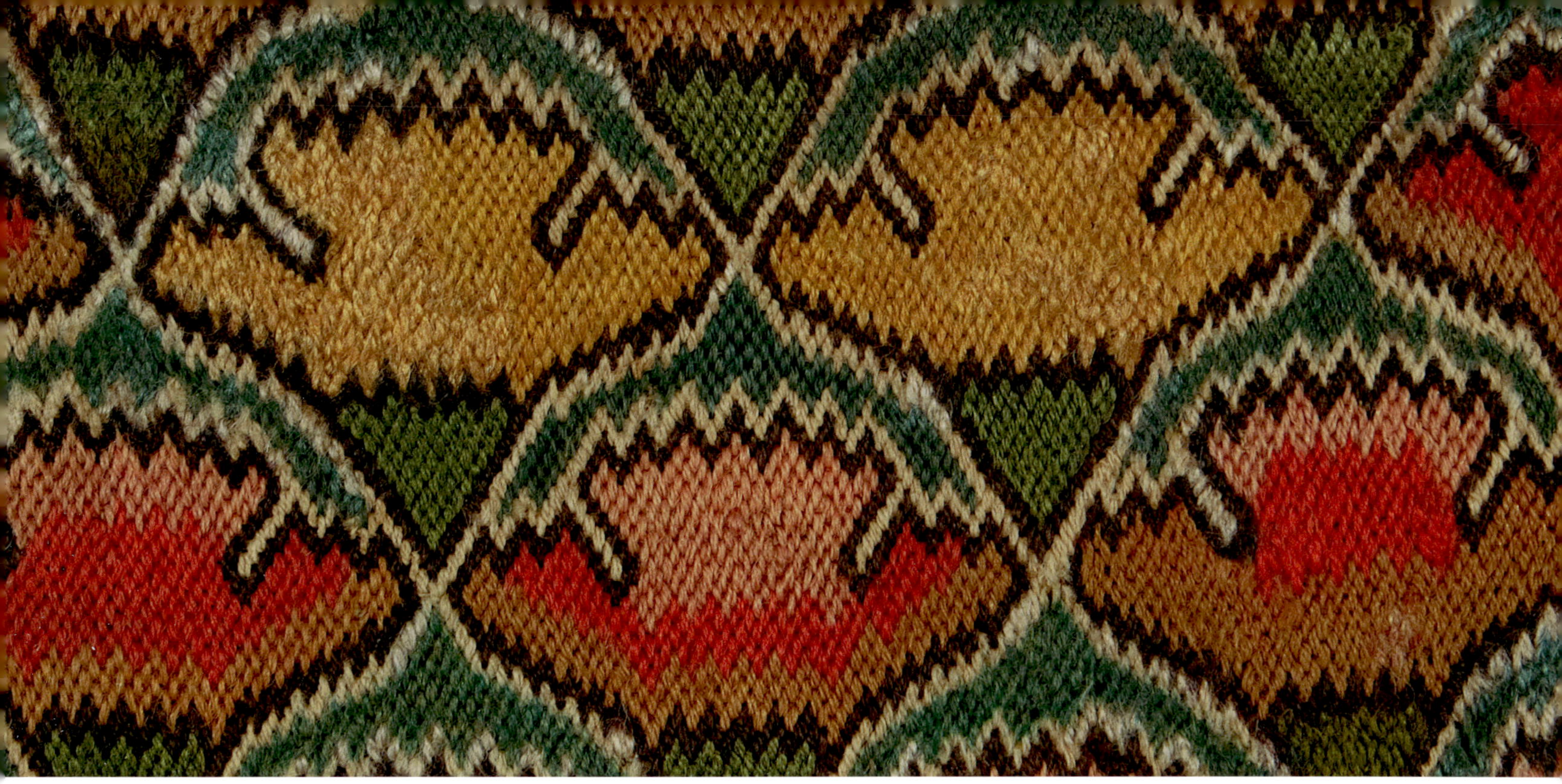

"Pocket Wallet / Carried through the American Revolution by / Captain Nehemiah Emerson of / Haverhill - Mass. / (Great Grandfather of Sallie / B. Thomas) Wolcott Covington, Kentucky." The pristine condition of the pocketbook indicates that it was probably not carried in the war, however; it was more likely a courting present from Captain Emerson's future wife, Mollie Mary Whittier, before their marriage in 1784. The pocketbook was handed down in the family of their daughter Mary Emerson Smith.

Elisabeth Fellows clearly stitched her name on the flap of the pocketbook that she made, although she failed to leave enough room on one line, so the *S* in *FELLOWS* is placed below the *W*. The date 1776 is also clearly worked on the front of the object, but whether this indicates the date that Elisabeth made the pocketbook or a commemoration of the start of the American Revolution or some other occasion cannot be determined. Elisabeth also favored the Irish stitch in a flame pattern.

Samplers and silk embroideries made by girls at school are much more likely to have survived than canvas-work pockets and pocketbooks. Until about 1840, when public schools became more common, almost every girl who received any amount of education was taught to embroider linens for her future household, and she produced a sampler to showcase her needlework skills. Often, these samplers were framed and hung in the parlor or best bedroom, but sometimes they were carefully stored away, ensuring that their colors remained bright and fresh. And because samplers were signed by the girls (who usually included their ages and sometimes their hometowns), it is often possible to locate the young makers in family genealogies.

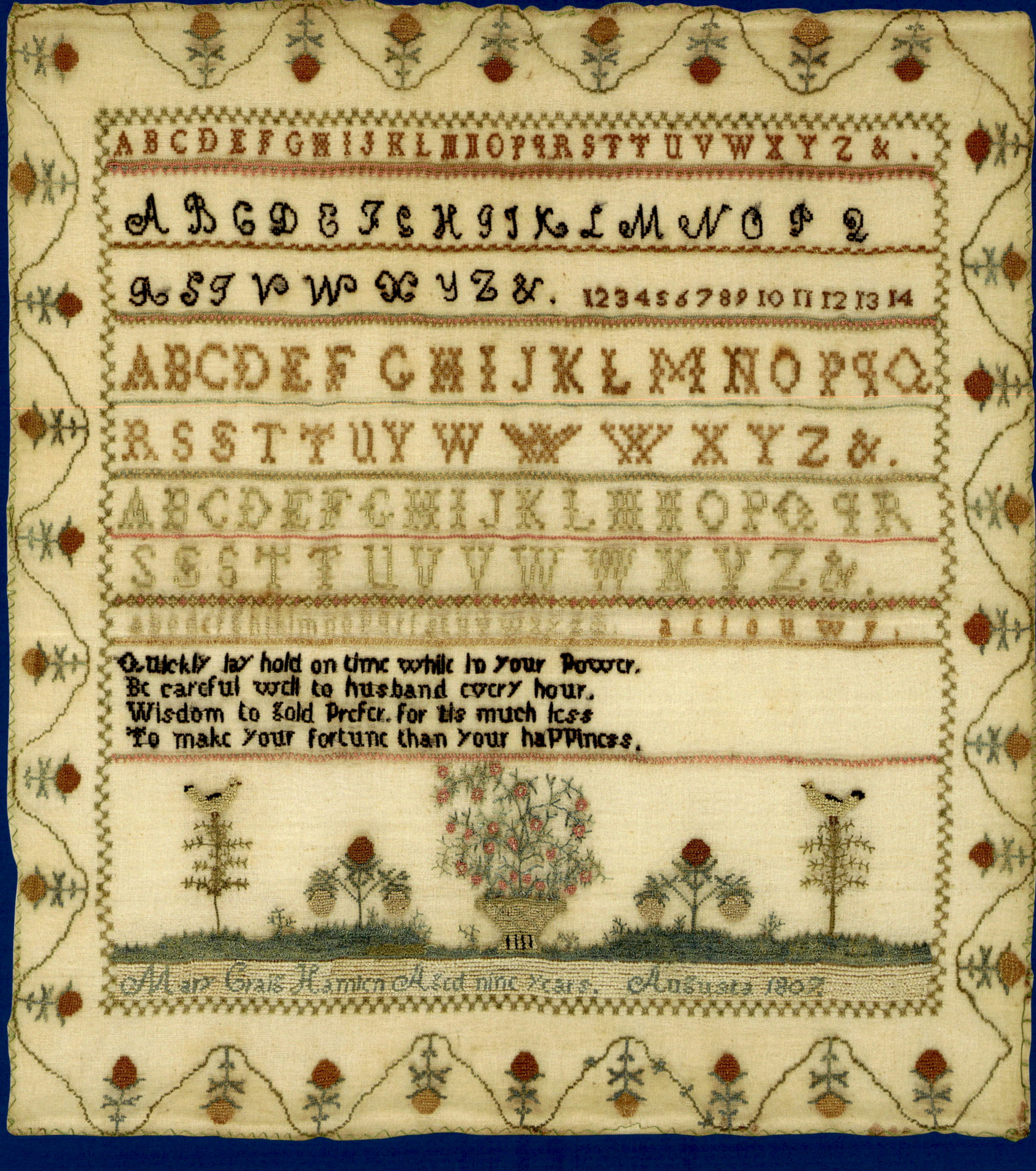
ABCDEFGHIJKLMNOPQRSTTUVWXYZ&.
ABCDEFGHIJKLMNOPQ
RSTUVWXYZ&. 1234567891011121314
ABCDEFGHIJKLMNOPQ
RSSTTUVWWWXYZ&.
ABCDEFGHIJKLMNOPQR
SSSTTUUVVWWXYZ&.
Quickly lay hold on time while in your Power.
Be careful well to husband every hour.
Wisdom to Gold Prefer. for tis much less
To make your fortune than your haPPiness.
Mary Craig Hamilton Aged nine years. August 1807

MARY CRAIG HAMLEN
(1798–1881)

Sampler

1807

Cotton on fabric
17¼ × 15½ in.

Inscription: "Mary Craig Hamlen Aged nine years. Augusta 1807"

L2015.41.67

ABIGAIL M. ANDREWS
(B. 1818)

Sampler

Woonsocket Falls, Rhode Island
ca. 1831

Silk on linen
16¼ × 17¼ in.

Inscription (verso): "A. E. Todd 33 Middle Street, Woonsocket"

2016.25.61

Samplers made in Marblehead, Massachusetts, "represent American girlhood embroidery at its best,"[4] writes needlework scholar Betty Ring in her two-volume opus on the subject. Nine-year-old Eunice Hooper's work (p. 131) is part of a group of samplers that were probably made under the direction of schoolmistress Martha Barber,[5] who most likely designed the work of her young pupils. The instructor might have drawn the design directly on the linen background or provided an image for the girls to copy. Eunice's work is similar to samplers made by twelve-year-old Hannah Hooper in 1790 and teenaged Sukey Jarvis Smith in 1791, around the time Eunice made her piece.[6] All three needleworks feature distinctive black backgrounds and scenes of domesticity and nature. Sukey's embroidery has the same yellow house that is seen in Eunice's work.

Mary Craig Hamlen was also nine years old when she stitched her sampler at a still-unidentified school in Augusta, Maine, in 1807. Though needlework from Augusta is less well known than that made at schools in Portland and other towns along Maine's coast, the town did have at least one prominent girls' school, the Cony Female Academy.[7] Mary's sampler (opposite page) is not as pictorial as Eunice's,[8] but it does contain the alphabet in a number of styles, along with didactic verses that may have been proposed by Mary's teacher or parent: "Quickly lay hold on time while in your power / Be careful well to husband every hour / Wisdom to gold prefer, for tis much less / To make your fortune than your happiness."[9]

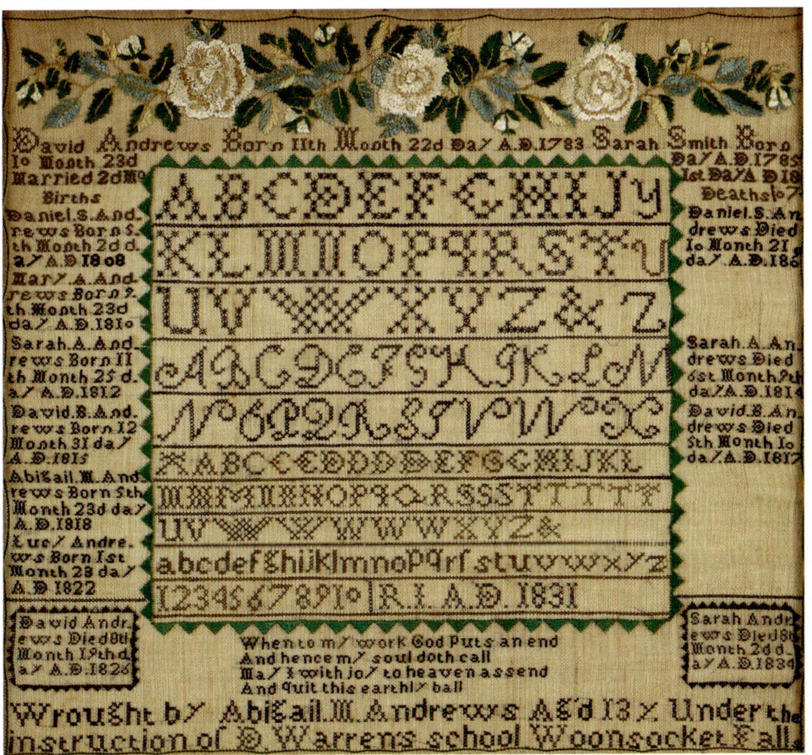

The family record sampler, such as the example made by Abigail M. Andrews (left), became popular at girls' schools during the second quarter of the nineteenth century. Abigail's needlework contains not only the birth, death, and marriage dates of most members of her immediate family but also the name and location of the school where she was a pupil: "D. Warren's school Woonsocket Falls." Abigail found room for a decorative floral border at the top of the sampler as well as a number of versions of the alphabet and a suitably poignant verse: "When to my work God puts an end / And hence my soul doth call / May I with joy to heaven assend / And quit this earthly ball." Abigail, born in 1818, is found in the records of the coeducational

Friends' Boarding School (now known as the Moses Brown School) in Providence, Rhode Island, in 1837. Both she and her sister Lucy, along with two other Andrews girls who are not on the family register, are listed in the Catalogue of the Officers and Pupils of the school, and it is noted that their home is in Smithfield, Rhode Island.[10] It is possible that by age nineteen, Abigail was a teacher at the school, but her attendance accompanied by her sister and other relatives makes it more likely that they were all students.[11]

One of the most intriguing canvas works in the Fielding Collection was made not by a schoolgirl but by a Native American. The *Niagara Beadwork Hat* (p. 10) represents a blending of needlework styles and cultures. The basic hat, called a "glengarry," was derived from traditional Scottish Highland dress, familiar to nineteenth-century Wabanaki and Haudenosaunee (Iroquois) people from military uniforms worn by British soldiers in Canada. The Hudson's Bay Company of Canada imported large quantities of hats for trade with the First Nations. Many of the hats were then transformed with traditional beadwork and moose-hair embroidery into colorful objects that would be sold as souvenirs at Niagara Falls or kept for private use. The example in the collection includes a red ribbon binding and is worked in what has come to be called the Niagara floral style. The sale of hats and other decorated objects provided economic support for the native peoples of the area, as they were particularly popular with tourists in the second and third quarters of the nineteenth century.[12]

RUGS

Before the late eighteenth century, the term *rug* in America was used only for bed or table coverings. The high cost of textiles (in terms of both time and money) kept them off the floors of all but the extremely wealthy. Hooked, yarn-sewn, and other types of homemade rugs did not become popular until the nineteenth century, when fabric for their construction became more affordable.

Yarn-sewn rugs, probably the earliest form of homemade coverings, were used on both the bed and the floor. These were created using woolen design yarn that was sewn through a linen ground canvas in a series of short stitches. Rugs made using this technique are easily identified by the separate stitches on the back.[13] Most of the yarn-sewn pieces would have been worked on a linen, wool, or cotton foundation with needle and yarn.[14]

The *Pictorial Hearth Rug* (pp. 126–28), initialed "PS" and dated 1824, is believed to be the earliest-known yarn-sewn rug in America with a recorded date.[15] Although the motifs on the surface—birds, trees, flowers and flowerpots, sheep—may appear random at first glance, they are actually symmetrically arranged around a central wreath. The sheep on the right side of the rug are balanced by what might be a building (perhaps a barn) on the left, and the initials on the left are balanced by the date on the right. These designs from nature and farm life are not unlike the appliqués seen on quilts and needlework pictures of the same period.

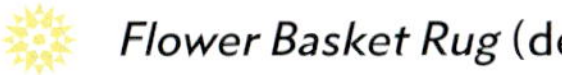

Flower Basket Rug (detail)

Illustration of the bias-shirring technique of rug making. Note the white stitches that hold the brown strip of irregularly edged cloth to the rug's beige linen foundation. For the recto of the rug, see pp. 166 and 169.

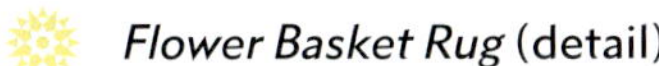

Flower Basket Rug (detail)

Verso showing the stitches that affix the strips of fabric, like the one shown above, to the rug foundation. For the recto, see pp. 166 and 169.

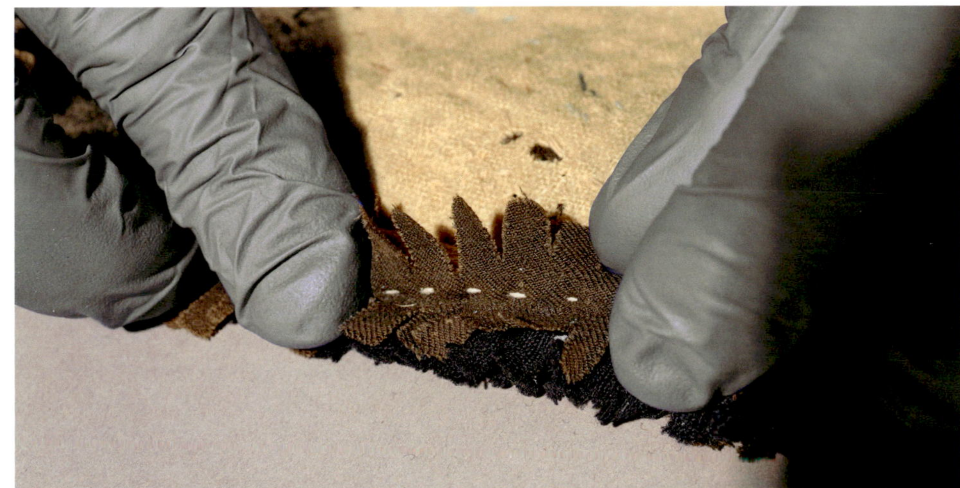

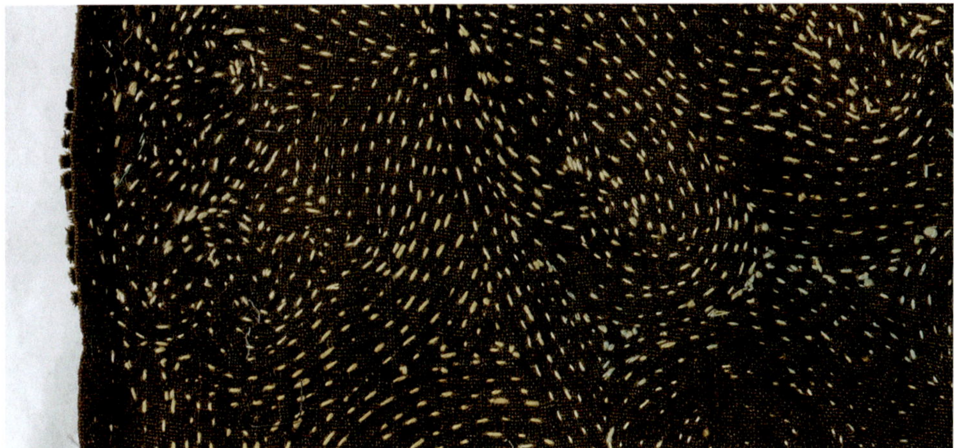

Shirring, another type of rug making, was most popular from the 1830s to the 1860s.[16] Shirring is essentially an appliqué technique that developed using strips, made from scraps of fabric, that were thicker than yarn and could not be sewn through a woven linen or cotton base.[17] With this method, the strips were shirred or gathered with a needle and sewn to the foundation. The needle stitches, but no design yarn, could be seen on the reverse.[18]

The Augustine W. Phillips *Yarn-Sewn Rug* (p. 167) features a flat background that is yarn-sewn, whereas the flowers are chenille-shirred, so that they have a raised, almost three-dimensional appearance. With this method, according to rug scholars Joel and Kate Kopp, "strips of cloth one-half inch to one and one-half inches wide were sewn down the center with a running stitch. The cloth was then gathered into folds by pulling the thread, after which the gathered cloth strip resembled a fabric caterpillar. These 'caterpillars' were then stitched to a base of linen, cotton, or even a rough grain bag."[19] Augustine Washington Phillips was probably the recipient of the rug, not its maker.[20] It is likely that the rug was made, perhaps as a wedding gift, by one of his wives or possibly by one of his daughters.

Pictorial Hearth Rug
1824
Yarn-sewn wool on linen
25 × 77½ in.
Inscriptions: "PS" and "1824"
L2015.41.82

Bias shirring, the technique used to make the *Flower Basket Rug* (p. 125), is even more complicated and therefore rarely found in American rugs. This style of rug is created with an appliqué technique using fabric strips cut on the bias (at a forty-five-degree angle to the fabric's warp and weft) and stitched lengthwise down the center of the strip to a ground fabric. The strips are closely sewn, side by side, with the edges folded up to create the pile, creating a wavy look in the design. Dating from 1820 to 1840, bias shirring is the earliest and most challenging of the shirring techniques.[21]

The *Geometric Hearth Rug* (pp. 132–33) was also created using both yarn-sewing and shirring techniques. The long, narrow shape of this rug indicates that it was made to be placed in front of a hearth during the summer months. It was passed down with an attribution to Mary Peters Hewins and the supposition that "J. Hewins," written in brown ink on the back of the rug, refers to her husband, James Hewins.[22]

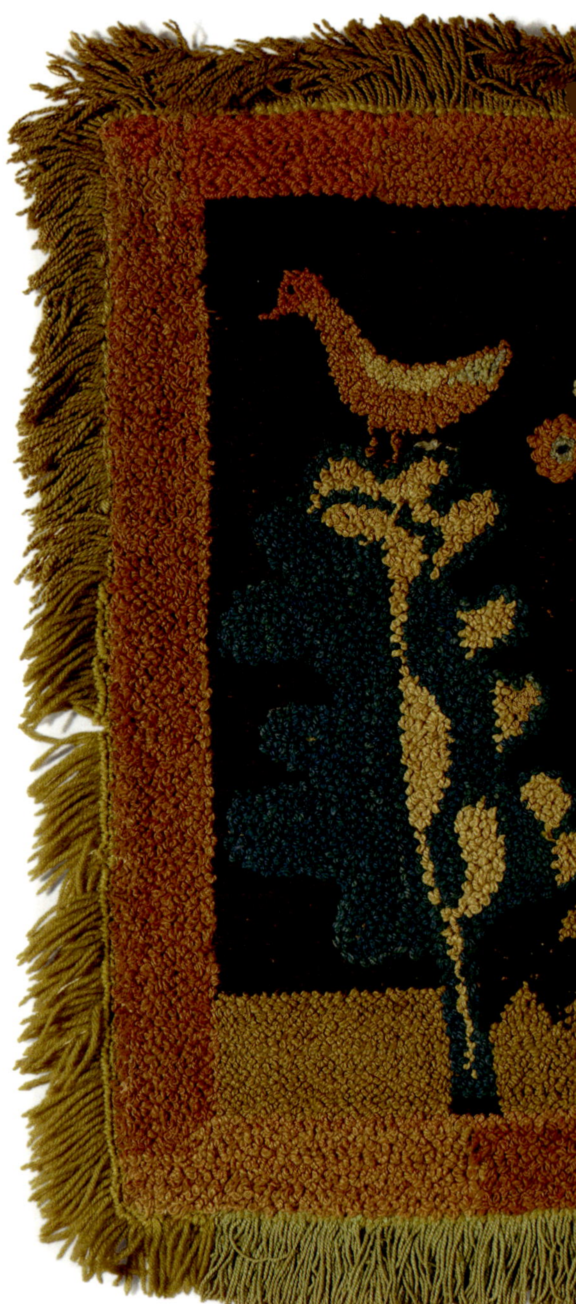

The colors of this rug were probably derived from natural sources, based on recipes for dyeing fabric and yarn at home. Many of these materials would have been locally available, but some came through channels of established trade. The red seen here, for example, was likely derived from madder, mentioned above. This dye was made from the roots of a plant cultivated by the Dutch in Zeeland but was also propagated in the United States. Indigo, probably used for the blue, came not only from Bengal, the East Indies, and South America but also (with greater impurities) from the Carolinas and New Orleans.[23] Much of the beauty of this rug derives from its simplicity. The hand-drawn semicircles and six-leaved flowers are imprecise yet charming. Two similar geometric hearth rugs of the late eighteenth or early nineteenth century exist (one is in the collection of Old Sturbridge Village in Massachusetts), and both are believed to have been made in New England.[24]

These evocative examples of quilts, embroideries, samplers, and rugs of eighteenth- and nineteenth-century America were more than simply useful everyday objects. They were expressions of beauty in the lives of women who frequently had no other socially acceptable outlet for their creativity. Whether made as a gift for a loved one, or as a means to bring color and joy in the home, the textiles presented here went far beyond necessity. They are truly works of art.

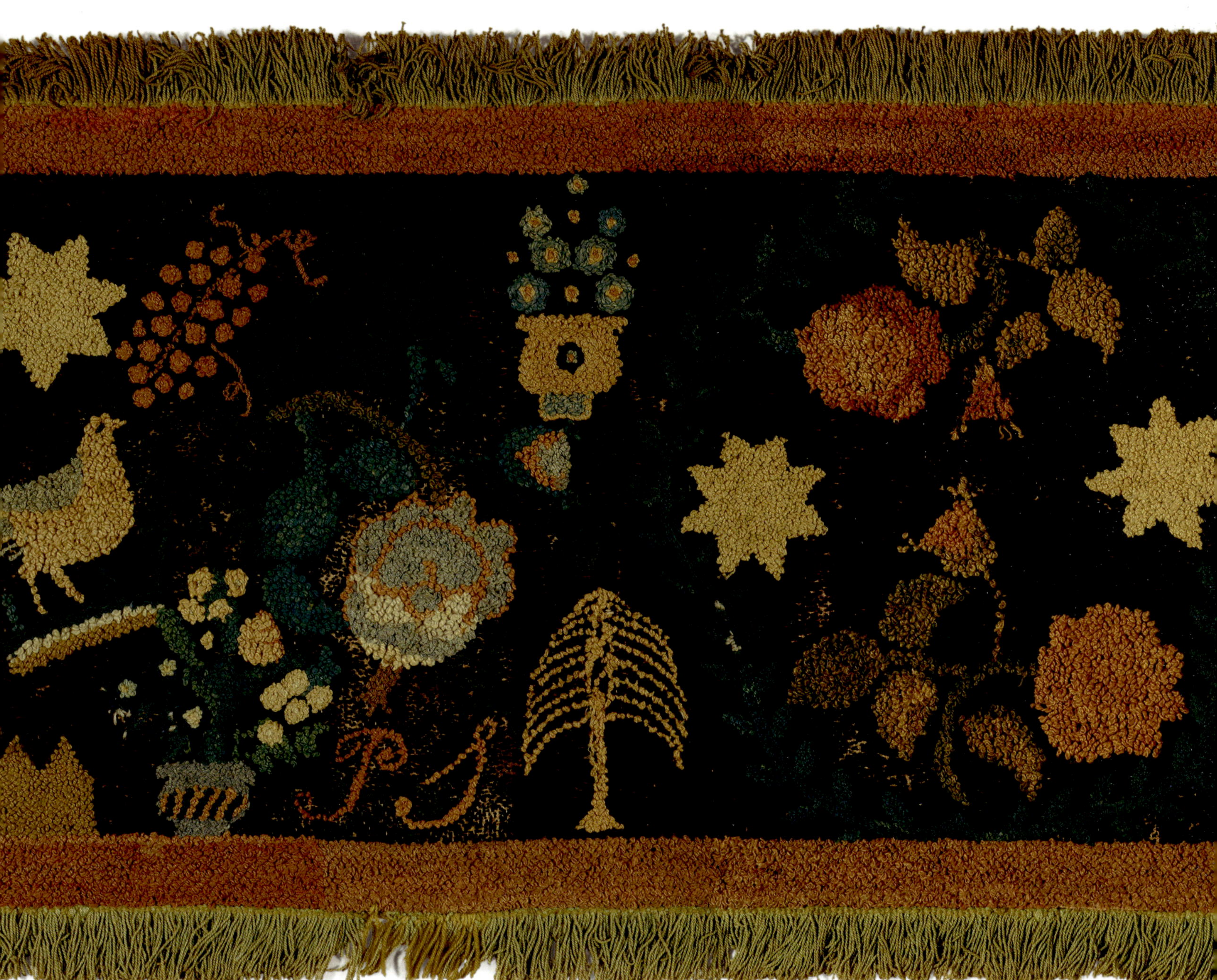

Elizabeth V. Warren is an author, collector, independent curator, and leading authority on textiles and folk art.

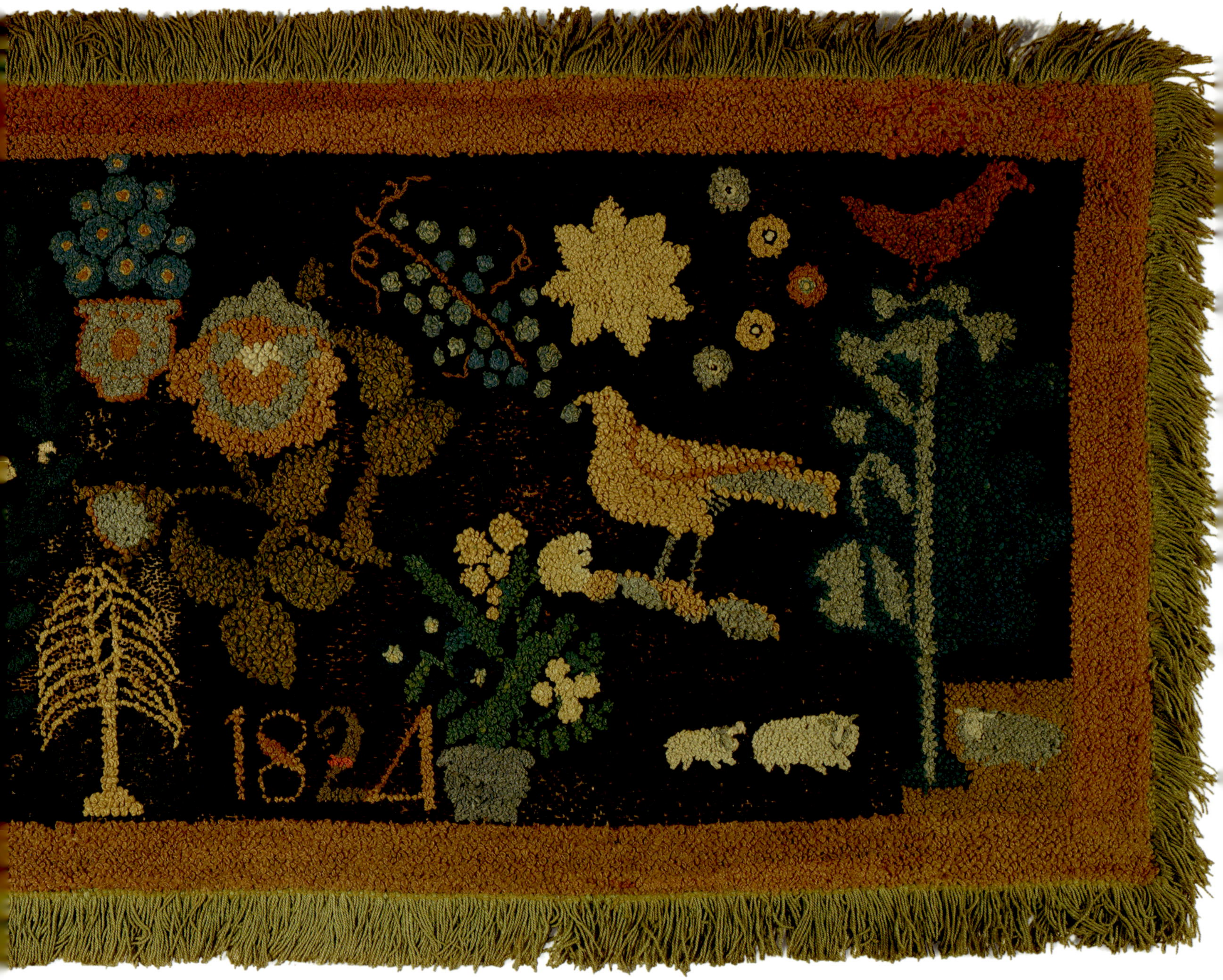

NOTES

1 Mary Seeds Moon was born in England in 1806. She married Edward Moon in 1826 in Baltimore. By the 1850 U.S. census, she was living in Baltimore with her husband, Edward, and their ten children. By the 1880 census, Moon was a widow, and sick, due to old age. Year: 1880; Census Place: Baltimore, Baltimore (Independent City), Maryland; Roll: 504; Page: 651B; Enumeration District: 181, Ancestry.com.

2 "A History of Pockets," Victoria and Albert Museum, http://www.vam.ac.uk/content/articles/a/history-of-pockets/.

3 Susan B. Swan, "Worked Pocketbooks," in *Needlework: An Historical Survey*, ed. Betty Ring, Antiques Magazine Library 1 (New York: Main Street/Universe Books, 1975), 53, https://openlibrary.org/works/OL15838641W/Needlework.

4 Betty Ring, *Girlhood Embroidery: American Samplers and Pictorial Needlework, 1650–1850*, 2 vols. (New York: Knopf, 1993), 1:131.

5 Ring, *Girlhood Embroidery*, 1:134. Eunice Hooper was born in Marblehead in 1781. She married John Hooper there in 1799, and together they had nine children. Eunice died in 1866.

6 Ring, *Girlhood Embroidery*, 1:135–36.

7 The Cony Academy did not open until 1815, however, so Mary could not have been a student there when she made her sampler.

8 The Mary Craig Hamlen sampler is similar in design to samplers made by girls at schools operated by the Society of Friends (Quakers). See, for example, the sampler worked by Mary Starbuck in 1808 at Lydia Gardner's school in Nantucket, illustrated in Ring, *Girlhood Embroidery*, 1:150.

9 The first two lines of verse appear, among other places, in various editions of William Mather's educational text *The Young Man's Companion*, first published in 1681. The last two lines appear in John Gregory, *A Father's Legacy to His Daughters*, 2nd ed. (Worcester, Mass.: Isaiah Thomas, 1796). Hamlen, or Hamlin, was a common name in Augusta in the eighteenth and nineteenth centuries, so Mary cannot definitely be identified in genealogical records. However, it is likely that she is the Mary Craig Hamlen (1798–1881) identified in *Hamlin Family: A Genealogy of James Hamlin of Barnstable, Massachusetts*; that Mary Hamlen was born in Augusta in 1798 and died there in 1881. She married Levi Page in Augusta in 1824 and had two children. The Hamlin Family; a Genealogy of James Hamlin of Barnstable, Massachusetts, Ancestry.com.

10 U.S., High School Student Lists, 1821–1923, Ancestry.com.

11 Abigail Maria ("Abby") Andrews married Albert Todd in 1839 in Smithfield and died there in 1871. Rhode Island, Vital Extracts, 1636–1899, Ancestry.com.

12 Getty Biron, "19th Century Iroquois and Wabanaki Beaded Hats," *Historic Iroquois and Wabanaki Beadwork* (blog), April 29, 2011, http://iroquoisbeadwork.blogspot.com/2011/04/19th-century-iroquois-and-wabanaki.html.

13 Anthony N. Landreau, *America Underfoot: A History of Floor Coverings from Colonial Times to the Present* (Washington, D.C.: Smithsonian, 1976), 39.

14 Tracy Jamar, "A Few Loops of Hooked Rug History," New Pathways into Quilt History, http://www.antiquequiltdating.com/Hooked_Rugs-Jamar.html.

15 Joel and Kate Kopp, *American Hooked and Sewn Rugs: Folk Art Underfoot* (New York: Dutton, 1975), 23.

16 Landreau, *America Underfoot*, 39–40.

17 Kopp and Kopp, *American Hooked and Sewn Rugs*, 28.

18 Landreau, *America Underfoot*, 40.

19 Kopp and Kopp, *American Hooked and Sewn Rugs*, 28.

20 Augustine Phillips, born in Hawley, Massachusetts, in 1823, married Hannah Rosina Maynard in 1845. Hannah died shortly thereafter, and Augustine married Maria Nutting in 1851. Augustine died in Amherst, Massachusetts, in 1899. U.S., Find a Grave Index, 1600s–Current, Ancestry.com.

21 "The First Exhibition of Rare Early-American Sewn and Hooked Rugs at the Art Museums of Colonial Williamsburg to Open in September 2018," press release, ArtfixDaily, July 30, 2018, http://www.artfixdaily.com/artwire/release/4025-the-first-exhibition-of-rare-early-american-sewn-and-hooked-rugs-.

22 Dr. James Hewins, born in Sharon, Massachusetts, in 1782, was an 1804 graduate of Harvard College. He married Mary Peters in 1814 in Medfield, Massachusetts, and died there in 1846 from complications of disease. The couple had two sons, and Mary died in Medfield in 1876. "Dr James Hewins," FindaGrave.com, https://www.findagrave.com/memorial/90970483.

23 Nina Fletcher Little, *Floor Coverings in New England before 1850* (Sturbridge, Mass.: Old Sturbridge Village, 1967), 35.

24 Little, *Floor Coverings*, fig. 35; Landreau, *America Underfoot*, 39.

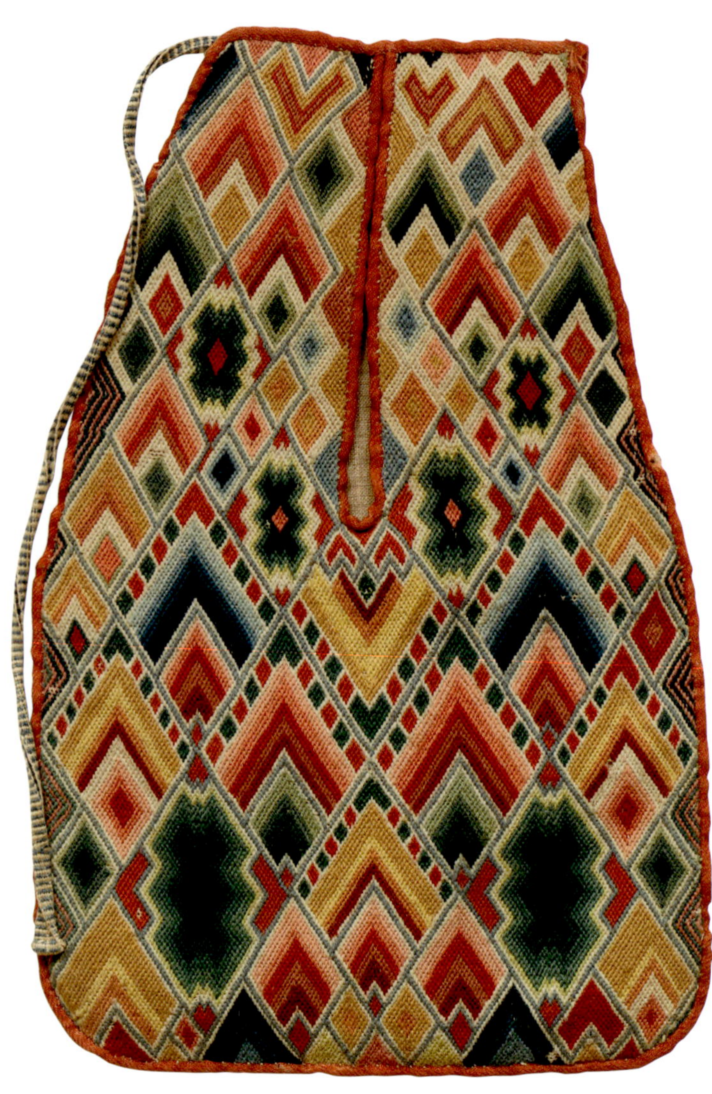

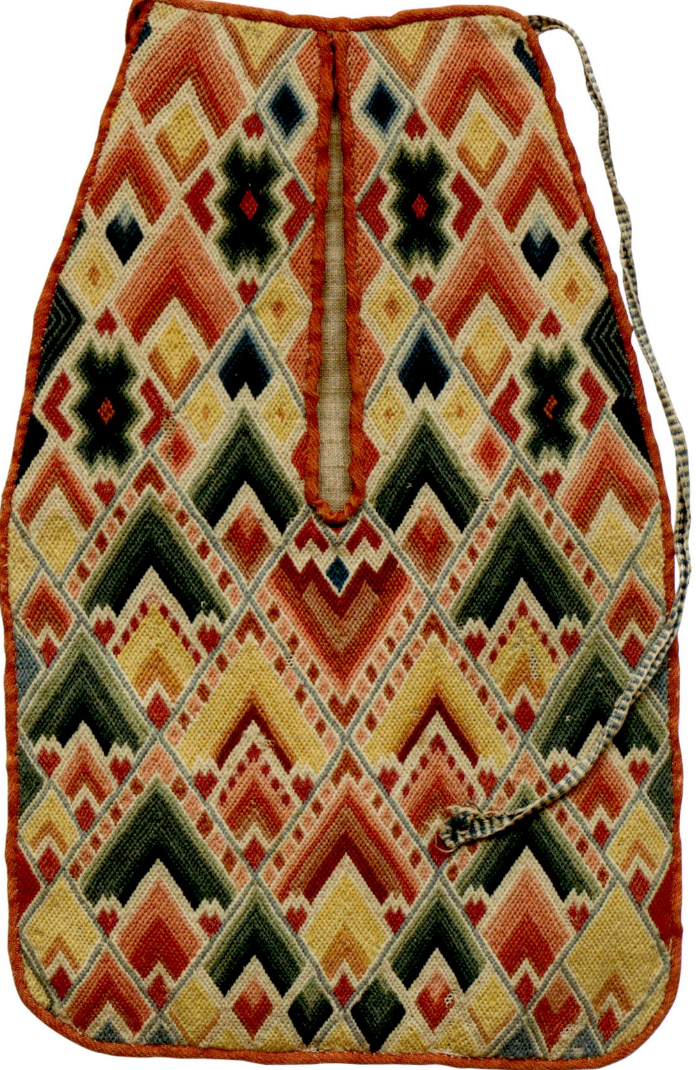

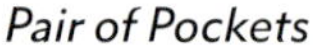

Pair of Pockets

ca. 1775

Wool, linen, and cotton canvas
Each: 14¼ × 9½ in.

L2015.41.64

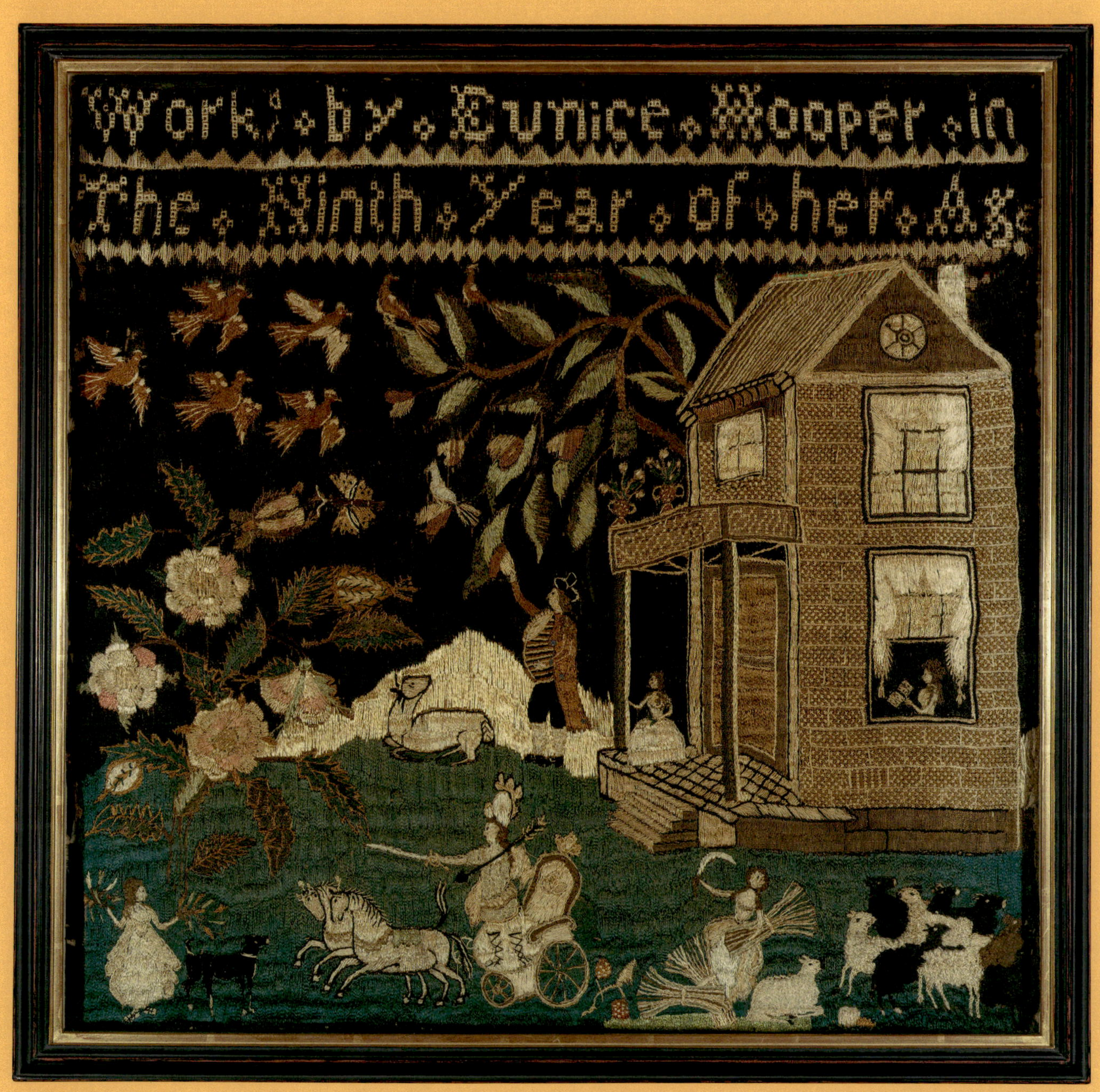

EUNICE HOOPER (1781–1866)

Sampler

Marblehead, Massachusetts
ca. 1790

Silk on linen
Framed: 23 × 23½ in.

Inscription: "Work by Eunice Hooper in The Ninth Year of her Age"

L2015.41.65

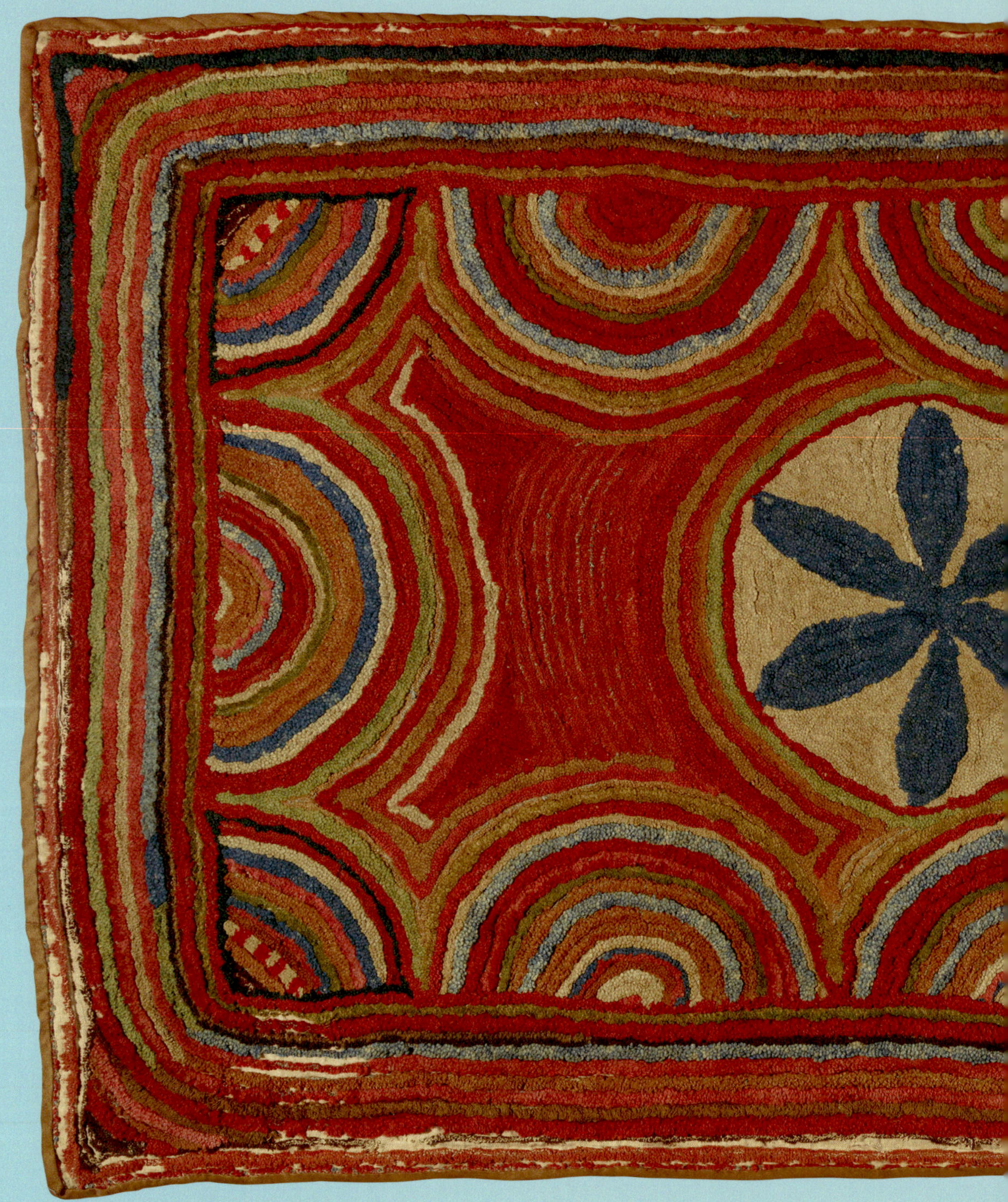

ATTRIBUTED TO MARY PETERS HEWINS (1794–1876)

Geometric Hearth Rug

Norfolk County, Massachusetts
ca. 1800

Yarn and shirred wool on linen
34 × 70 in.

Inscription (verso): "J. Hewins"

L2015.41.84

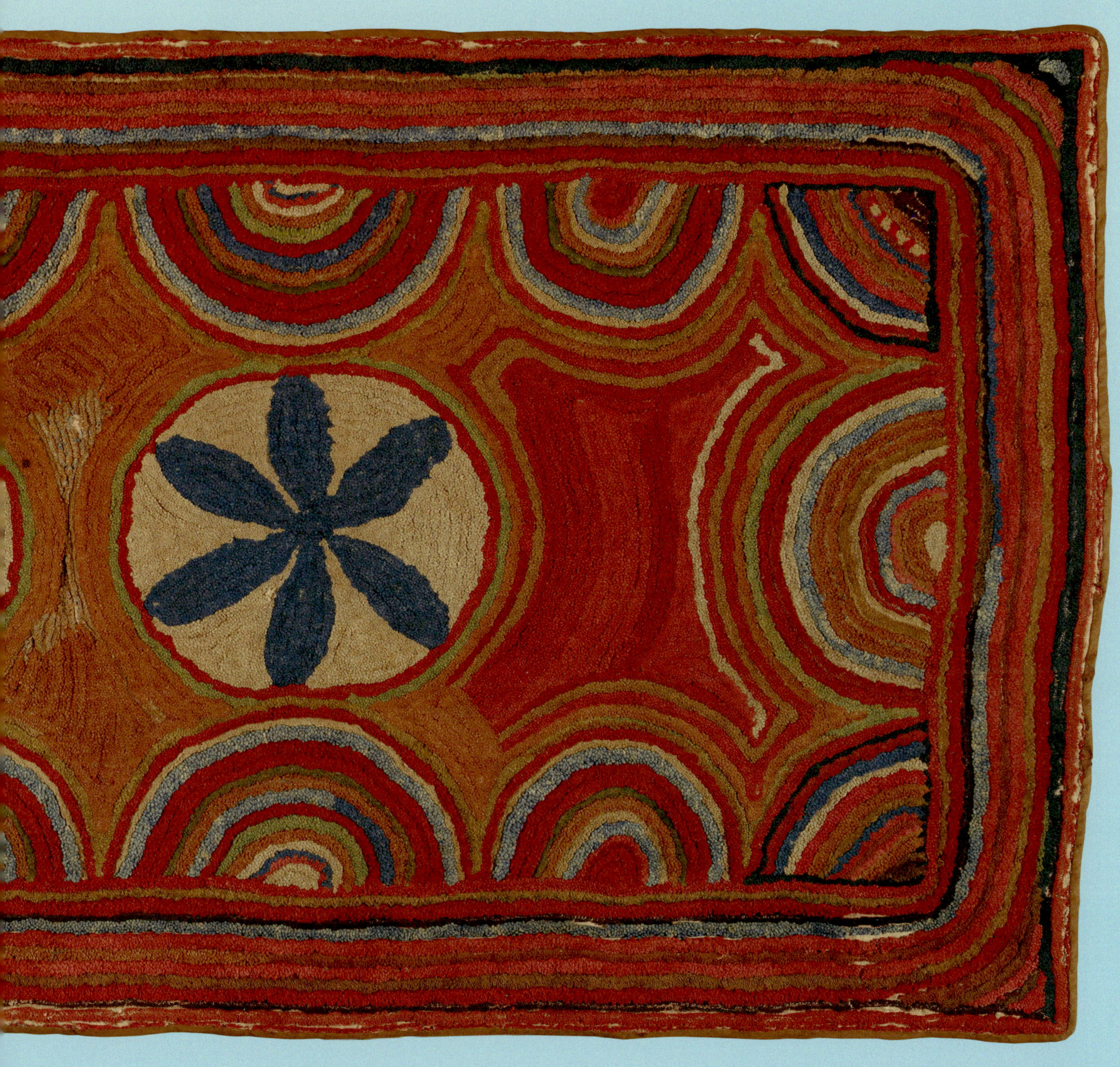

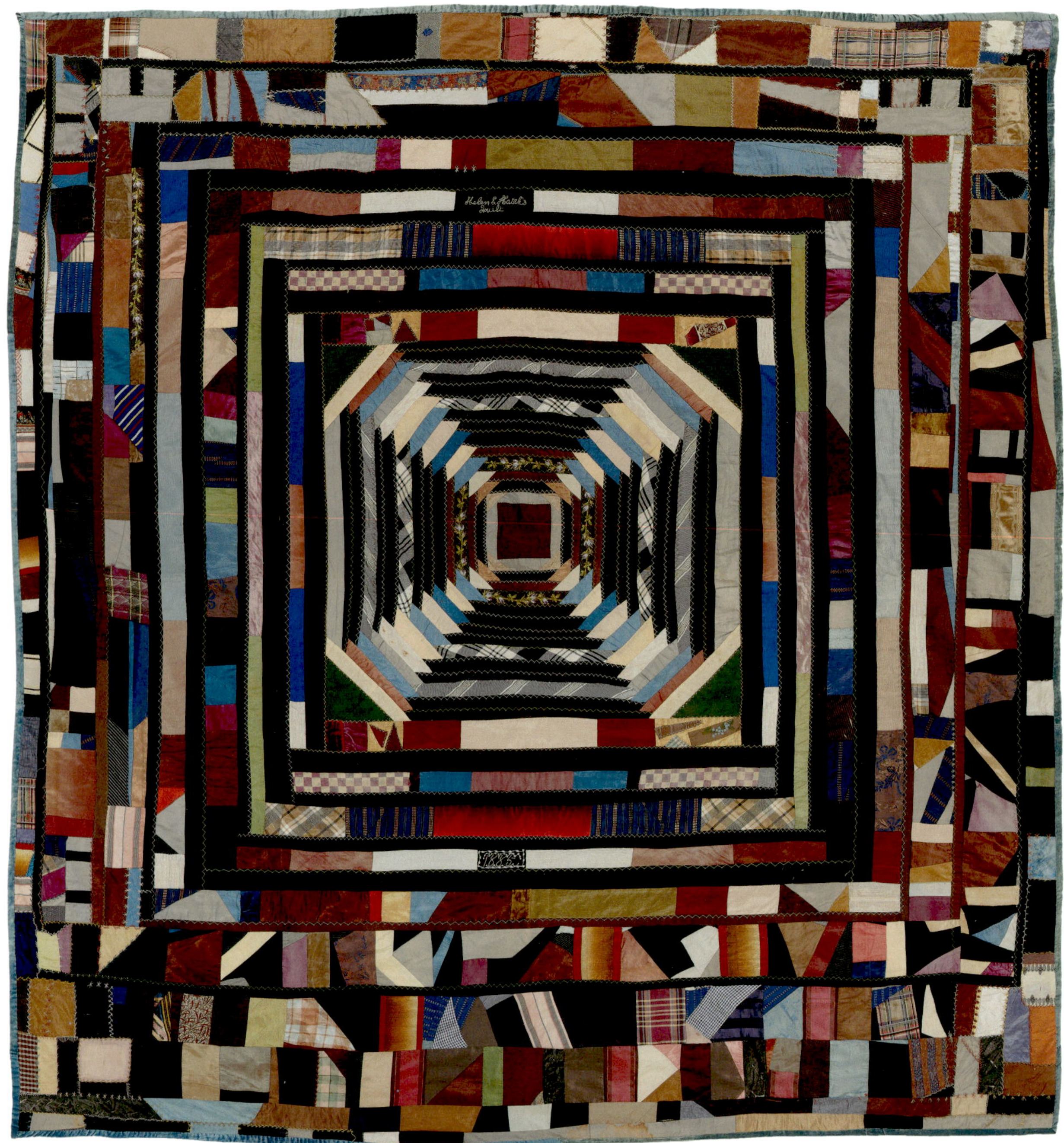

HELEN E. HATCH

Folk Art Crazy Quilt

Winterport, Maine
1885

Silk and velvet, pieced
77½ × 82½ in.

Signed in stitch: "Helen E. Hatch's quilt / 1885"

2016.25.51

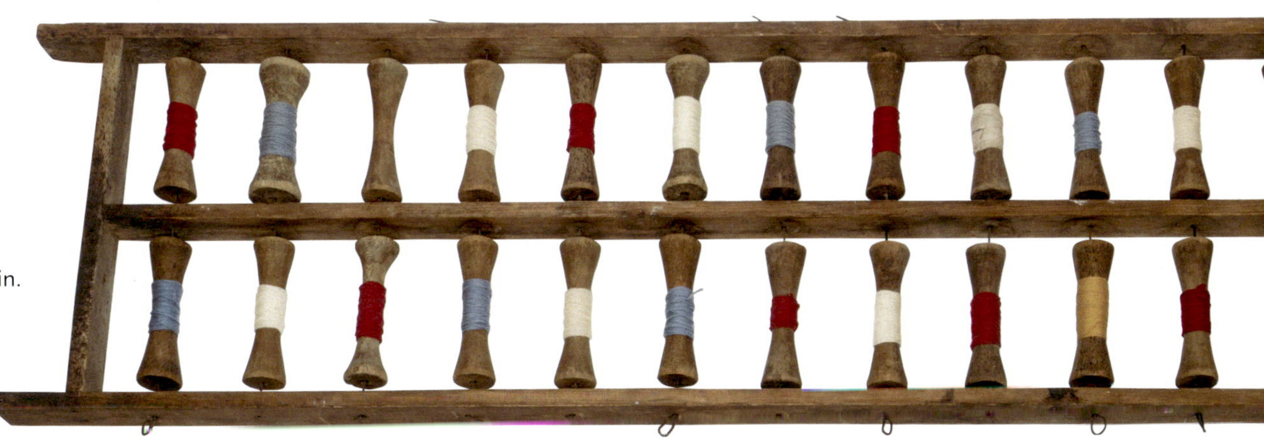

Yarn Rack
Northern New Hampshire
ca. 1850
Wood, wire, and modern fiber
24½ × 75¼ × 2⅝ in.
2016.25.143

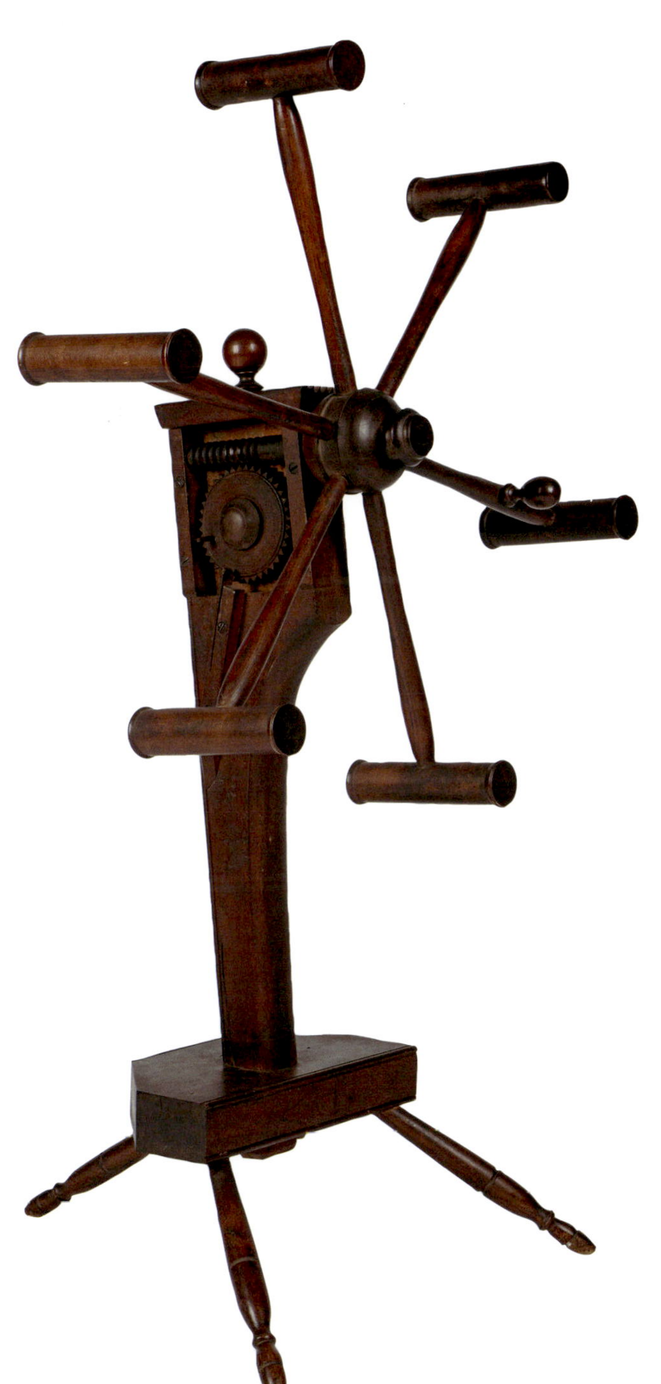

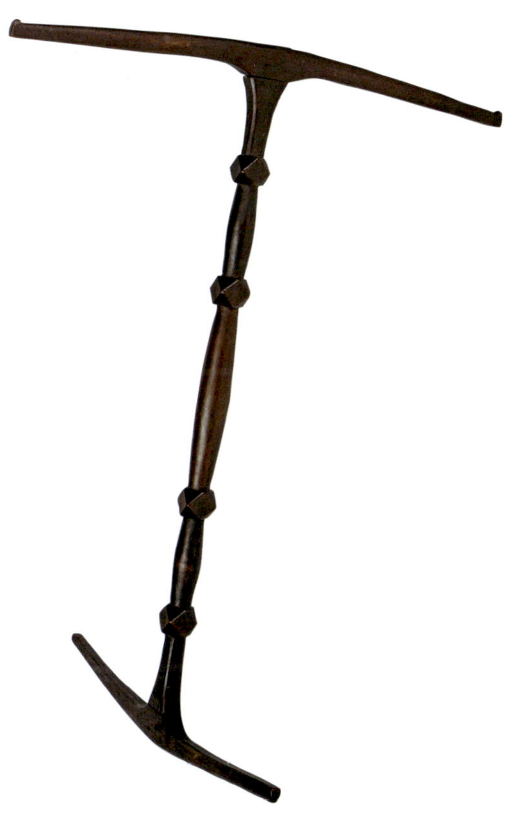

Yarn Winder
Massachusetts
ca. 1790
Cherry, metal, and traces of red paint
40½ × 19½ × 25½ in.
2016.25.148

Niddy-Noddy
ca. 1800
Walnut
14 × 18¼ × 13¾ in.
2016.25.144

HOMESPUN

These tools relate to domestic yarn making: yarn produced for sale, exchanged for credit, or used at home. Governor Bernard of colonial Massachusetts reported in 1763 that while people from cities wore clothes imported from Great Britain, "the poor laboring people in the country towns wear their own common clothes principally of homespun linens and woolens."

Wool yarn was once spun on this giant wheel, then wrapped around a niddy-noddy to make a skein (p. 135). Like the niddy-noddy, the winder prepared the yarn for weaving or knitting, while this rack (p. 135) of twenty-four bobbins stored it or perhaps fed it to a hand- or water-powered loom.

Probate records from 685 homes in Connecticut and Massachusetts show that by 1674, 50 percent of homes owned a spinning wheel, whether large for wool, or small for linen. Fewer than one in ten households owned a loom. This discrepancy reflects the fact that yarn spinning required substantially more labor than weaving on a loom.

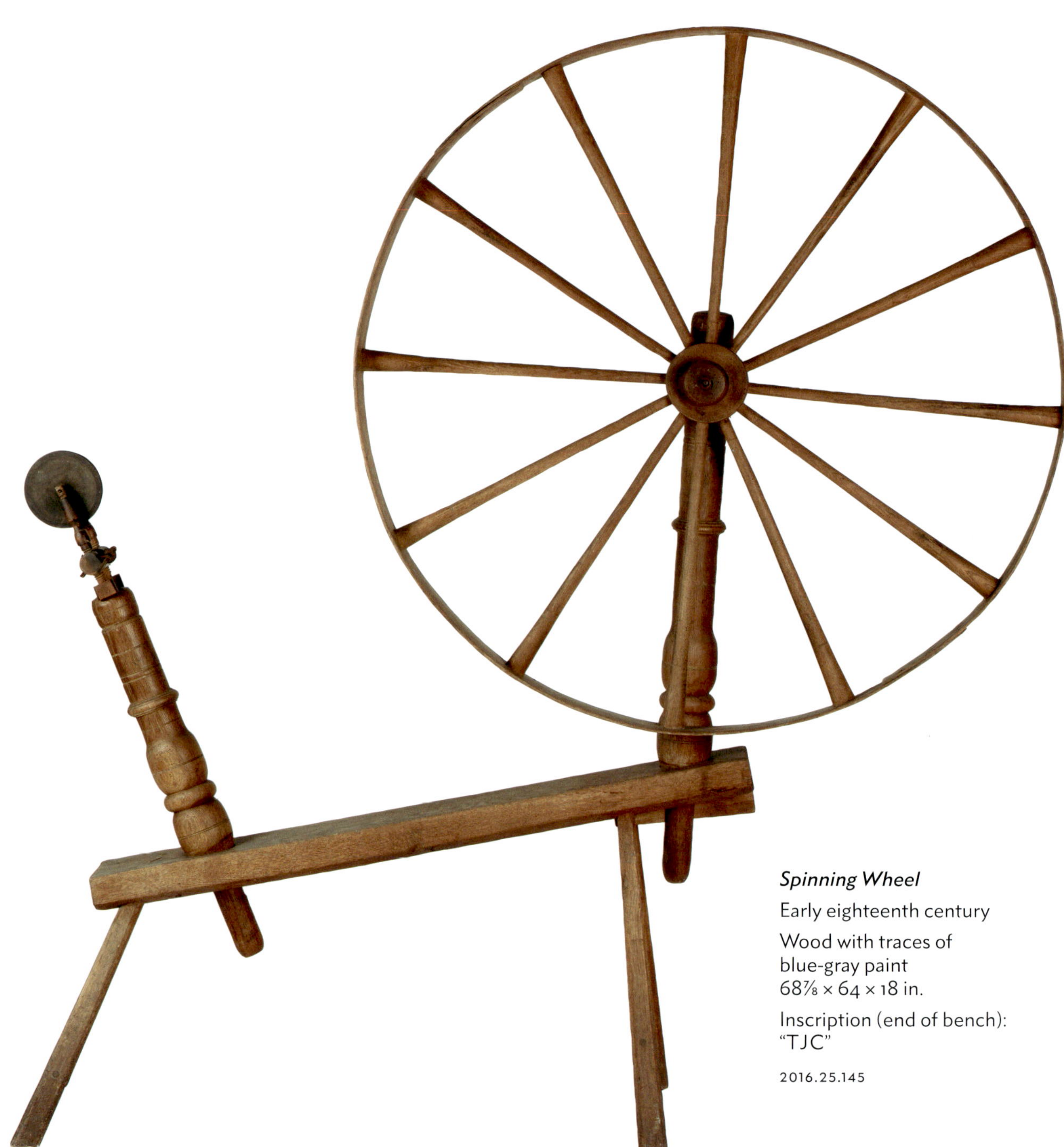

Spinning Wheel

Early eighteenth century

Wood with traces of blue-gray paint
68⅞ × 64 × 18 in.

Inscription (end of bench): "TJC"

2016.25.145

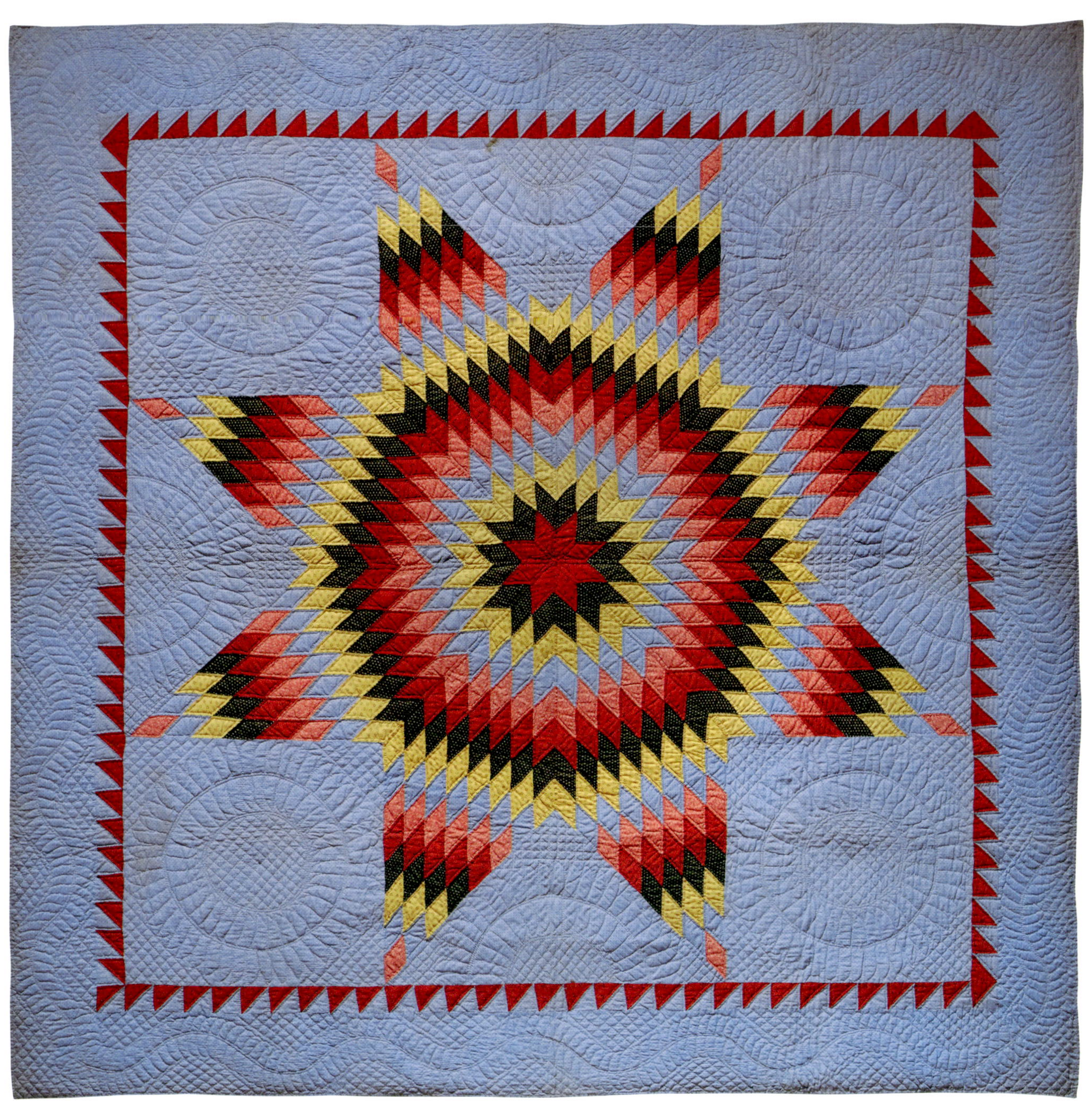

Lone Star of Bethlehem Quilt

ca. 1880–1900

Cotton, pieced
78 × 78 in.

L2018.3.2

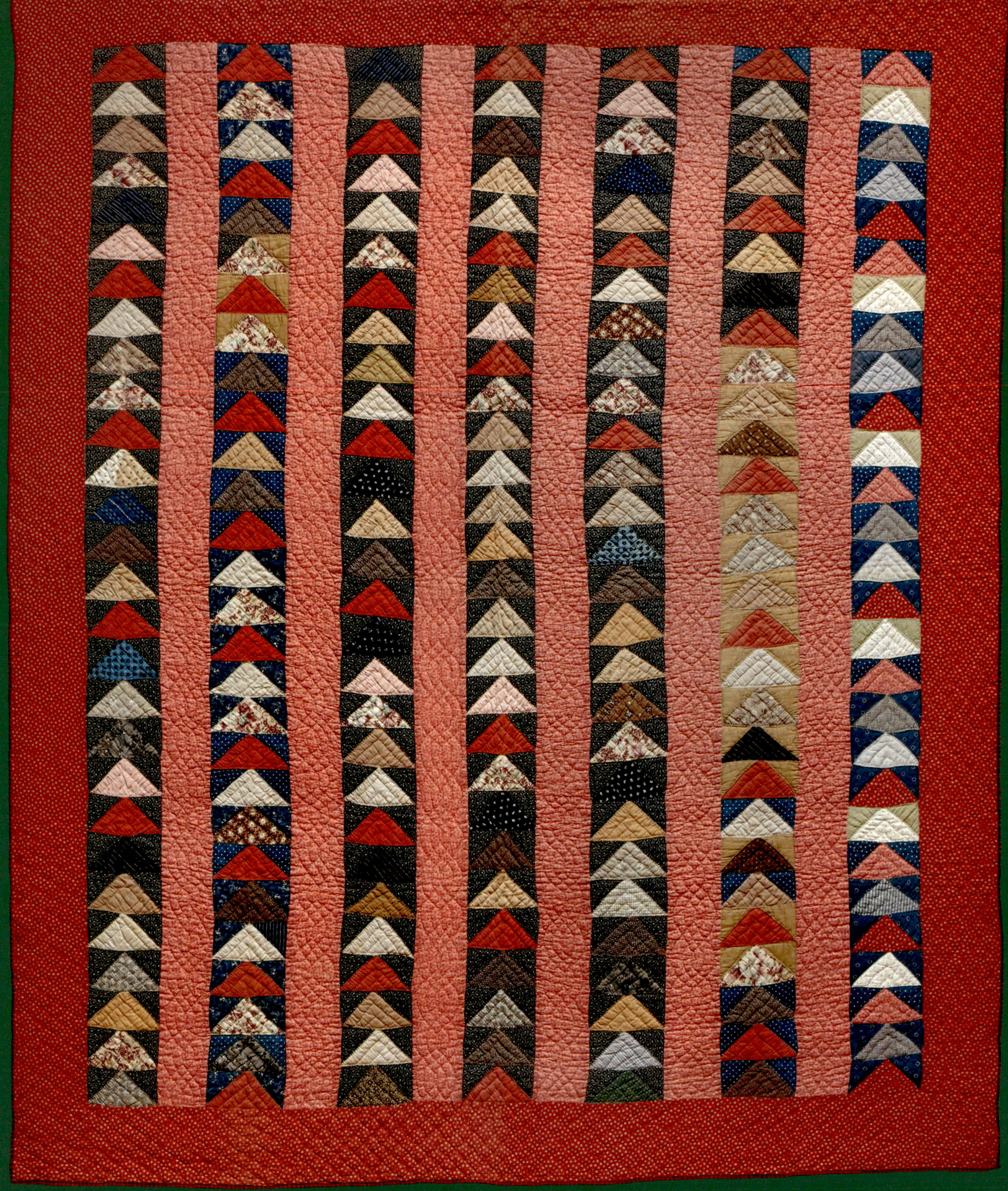

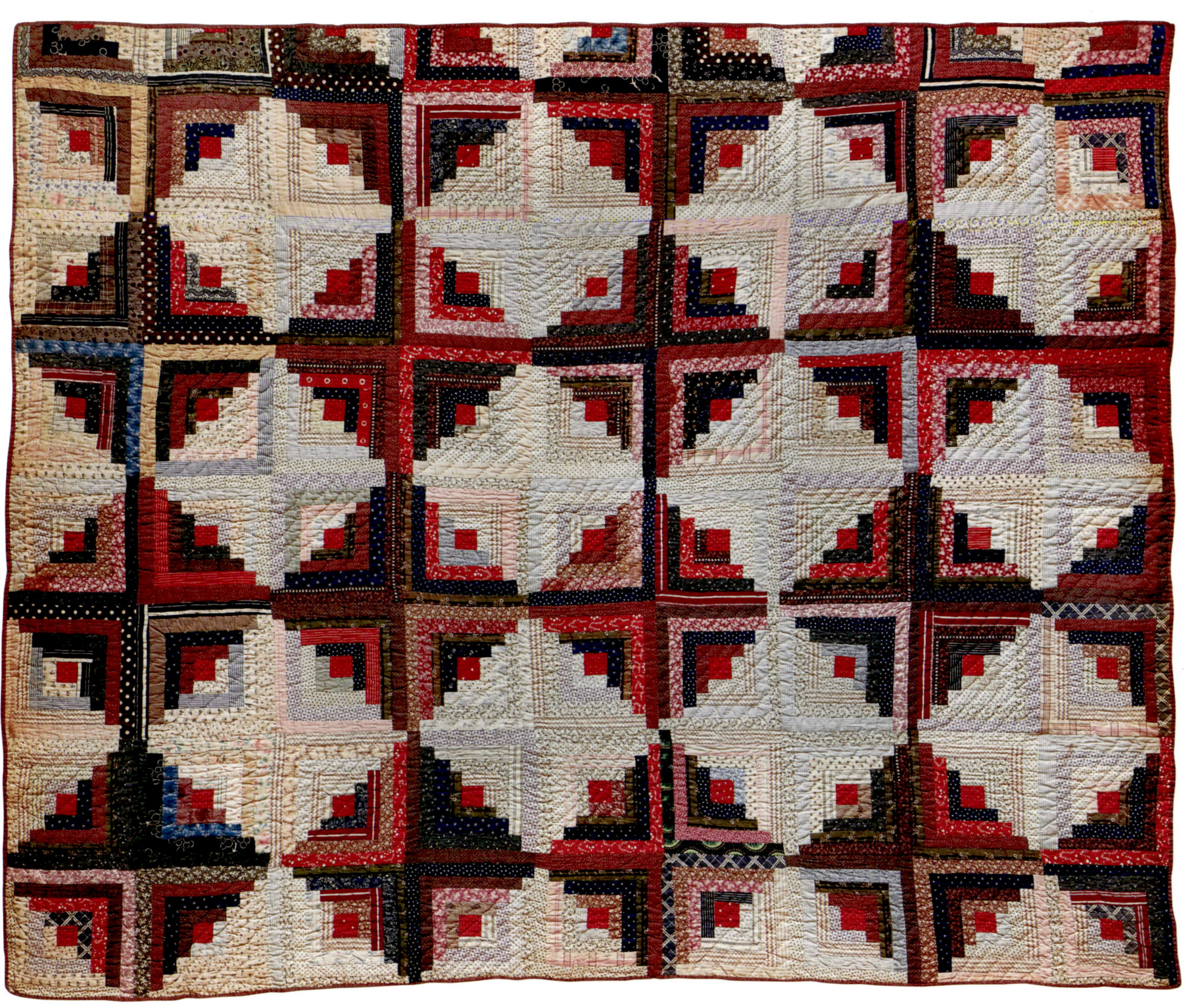

Geese in Flight Quilt

Pennsylvania
ca. 1880–90

Cotton, pieced
77 × 64½ in.

L2018.3.5

Log Cabin Quilt

Boston area
ca. 1870

Cotton, pieced
72 × 83 in.

L2018.3.4

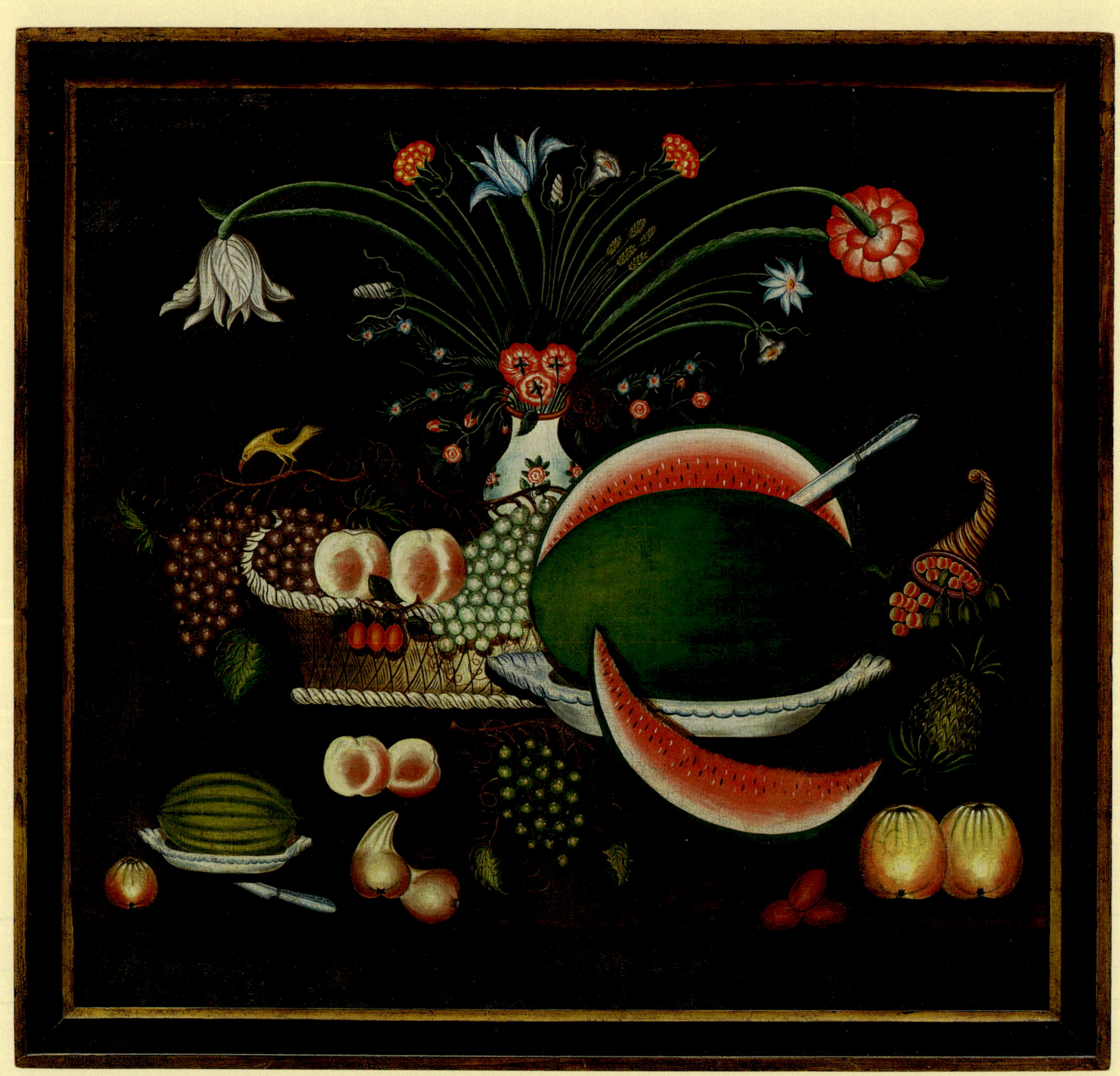

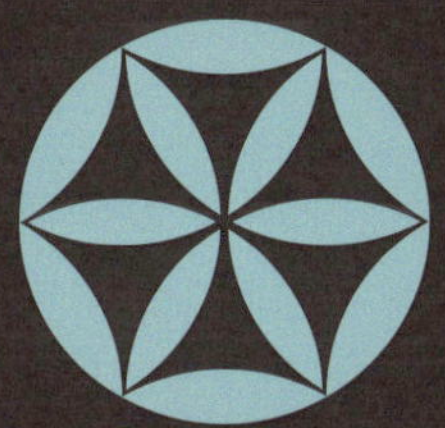

In Imitation of Nature

Landscape and Still-Life Painting in Early America

STACY C. HOLLANDER

In 1836, when Charles and Comfort Caverly of New Hampshire had their portrait painted by the artist Joseph H. Davis, they gave some truth to a pronouncement made by the American critic and author John Neal a few years prior, regarding the development of artistic appreciation in the young republic: "Pictures of worth are beginning to be relished—by and by they will be understood; after that, they will soon become not merely an article for the rich, a luxury for the few, but things for every body, familiar household furniture. Already are they quite as *necessary* as the chief part of what goes to the embellishment of a house, and far more beautiful than most of the other furniture."[1]

The Caverlys were not a young couple when they commissioned this work (p. 176). Comfort, at age forty-four, holds her sixth baby, Isaac, on her lap. Charles, at age fifty-two, is a farmer and blacksmith who would represent his community in the state legislature ten years later.[2] A Fancy rural landscape hangs on the wall above them. An elaborate flower arrangement on the table obliquely refers to the increasingly popular still-life tradition while speaking to the perfect love in this household through the selection of blossoms and, more explicitly, the heart outlined on the vase. There is little or no hierarchical distinction drawn between the Caverlys themselves and the rich patterning and material comforts of their home; the art, table, floor carpet—indeed, their own portraits—are all part of the furniture. The whole is designed to titillate the senses through exuberant and colorful designs, while affirming the stolidity of the Caverlys. More broadly, it demonstrates America's growing conversance with and acceptance of an urbane market for art that held the promise of advancing beyond the "painter of fire-buckets,

ATTRIBUTED TO JOSEPH PROCTOR (ACTIVE NEW YORK CITY AND STATE)

Still Life with a Basket of Fruit, Flowers, and Cornucopia

Mid-nineteenth century

Oil on canvas
46 × 48 in.

L2015.41.171

Family Mansion of David Thayer

Bainbridge, New York
1830

Pencil, watercolor, and ink on paper
17 × 22⅛ in.

Inscription: "FAMILY MANSION of DAVID THAYER *BAINBRIDGE*"

2016.25.101

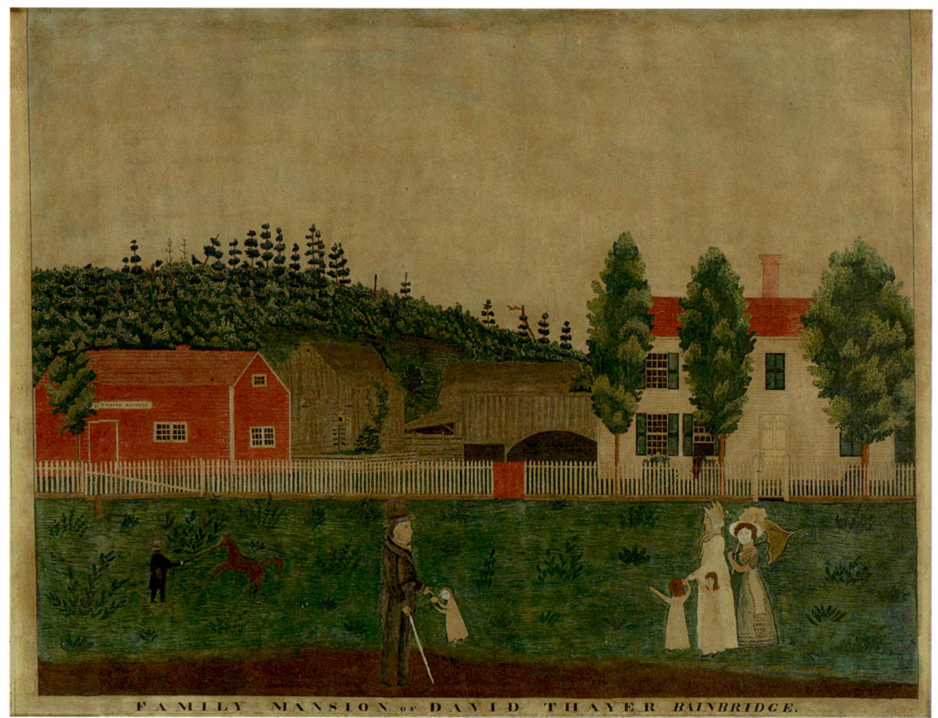

looking-glass tablets, or militia standards."[3] As the taste for art matured, it was accompanied by a marked desire for displays of personal attainment that paralleled the growth of the nation itself. The self-taught landscape and still-life paintings in the Fielding Collection span more than two centuries, from mere notes in colonial portraits—a partial scene glimpsed through a window, a bowl of cherries spilling across a lap (p. 164)—to detailed renderings that situate buildings and activities in time and place. Beginning in the eighteenth century, American homes revealed a lively delight in and pocketbook for portraits of houses and lands, descriptions of place that were necessarily connected to the life of man.

The story of American landscape painting is, in part, one of changing perspectives both literal and metaphorical. The earliest landscapes were embedded in the very architectural structures they might portray in the form of overmantels and fireboards. As time went by, the eye was raised from level gazes in personal portraits that depicted the home and those who resided within, such as the *Family Mansion of David Thayer* (perhaps an overstatement for his modest property and saddlery) in Bainbridge, New York, painted in 1830 (above), to lofty and expansive birds-eye views that highlighted complexes such as the large and orderly farm belonging to Sarah and Daniel Leibelsperger in Berks County, Pennsylvania, drawn in 1882 (p. 156). Landscapes even functioned as a kind of precursor to photojournalism, as evidenced in John Hilling's series of paintings relating the shocking burning in 1854 of a Catholic church in Maine as an act of religious intolerance (pp. 158, 159).[4]

In some sense, the paintings in the collection reveal a telling dichotomy in the American character as it developed in the years just before and following the Revolution: a push-pull between stubborn iconoclasm and the need to prove worth in European eyes. Much of the art revels in the intimate particularity of expression emerging from the self-taught genius of early American citizenry. At the same time, it also highlights the growing divergence of this popular art with the aspirations of those, like Neal, who would have American art shed the taint of artisanship associated with the self-taught and ornamental painter and instead embrace the grandeur and authenticity of America's natural bounty: "People have done with nature.... The standard for landscape is no longer what we see outstretched before us, and on every side of us, with such amazing prodigality of shape and colour. We have done with the trees of the forest and the wilderness... and of all the painting of that master who used to be looked up to as authority in landscape—God."[5]

ARCHITECTURAL LANDSCAPES
OVERMANTELS AND FIREBOARDS

It was not God that the earliest painters sought in the American landscape, when colonists were "hacking and hewing" their way to settled respectability, as the nineteenth-century English travel writer Frances Trollope later observed. Rather, they looked for reminders of the life they had left behind, primarily through Dutch- and English-inflected motifs, followed by their own reflections in landscapes improved for the usefulness of man.[6] As early as 1688, Samuel Sewall, the Boston diarist, noted seeing "Landscips of Oxford Colledges and Halls," most probably engravings, while visiting a friend. Alexander Stewart advertised in Philadelphia in 1769 that he would paint "Landskips, sea pieces, perspective views of gentlemen's country seats, &c." for those who had "picture panels over their chimney pieces, or on the sides of their rooms, standing empty."[7] "Picture panels" referred to overmantels, also known as "chimney paintings" or "chimney pieces." These were paintings on wood that were typically integrated into the surrounding architectural paneling over a fireplace, the most important feature of the room. Images were portraits of the homestead and properties; "deception paintings," or trompe-l'oeil; or depictions based on European prints and engravings of hunting parties, pastoral scenes, prospects, and town views.

The earliest overmantel in the Fielding Collection was painted for civil engineer and surveyor Ebenezer Waters (1739–1808) in Sutton, Massachusetts (pp. 144–47).[8] It is one of around a dozen such panels by the artist Winthrop Chandler, who is best known for more than thirty-five portraits painted for family, friends, and neighbors in Connecticut and Massachusetts.[9]

The artist had portrayed Ebenezer's brother Samuel and his wife, Prudence, in 1779, and it is likely that the overmantel was painted between that date and his own death in 1790. It was mounted above the fireplace

WINTHROP CHANDLER
(1747–1790)

Landscape with Riding and Walking Figures, a River, and a Village (Overmantel)

ca. 1770–80

Oil on pine panel
23 × 61 × 1¼ in.

L2015.41.159

in the lower southwest parlor of the home, which was built in 1767, and framed by a raised molding in a room that was entirely grained and marbleized, as was the fashion after around 1750.[10] The panel shares characteristic motifs with other overmantels painted by Chandler around this time, such as houses with white-painted corner boards, window frames, and cornices, and black-painted doors. A pastiche of figures forms a kind of panoply across the bottom foreground. This is probably derived from English prints of the period, engraved after such British artists as James Seymour (1702–1752) and John Wootton (ca. 1682–1764). The traveler with a sack over his shoulder was a familiar type from Boston needlework pictures and chimney pieces. Also featured in the scene are diverse figures (including two pairs of lovers), a grandmother holding a kerchief to her nose and walking with her little granddaughter, various animals, and several figures mounted on fine steeds, singly or in pairs. A dark-skinned figure riding a nag is of particular interest; he wears a bright red turban and an exotic and fancy suit of clothes, suggesting that the original copy source may have depicted an enslaved member of an aristocratic English household.[11] The Waters home came into the possession of a Dr. Bullard, whose daughter Eunice was married to the famous preacher Reverend Henry Ward Beecher (1813–1887) in the very room with this overmantel. The homestead was graced in front by a majestic elm tree made famous in Beecher's novel *Norwood; or Village Life in New England* (1868). It is perhaps the tree depicted in the left middle ground.[12]

The finest landscapes through the 1830s might still have adorned fireplaces or decorated the broad rectangular tablet tops of chairs and suites of furniture, even as aspiring artists struggled to gain acceptance for the genre as easel painters.[13] But in 1825, a revolutionary approach to landscape painting played into the Yankee love of innovation, expediency, and economy. It was introduced by the self-taught polymath Rufus Porter (1792–1884) in his publication *A Select Collection of Valuable and Curious Arts, and Interesting Experiments*. The volume continued a legacy of manuals descended from medieval sourcebooks known as "books of secrets," which were essentially compilations of alchemical recipes, practical crafts, medicinal and culinary recipes, magic tricks, and other esoteric lore. The lay public was not privy to the mysteries of the early painters and stainers, remnants of a European guild system designed to protect trade secrets from becoming general knowledge. By this time, however, the alluring "secret knowledge" contained in such

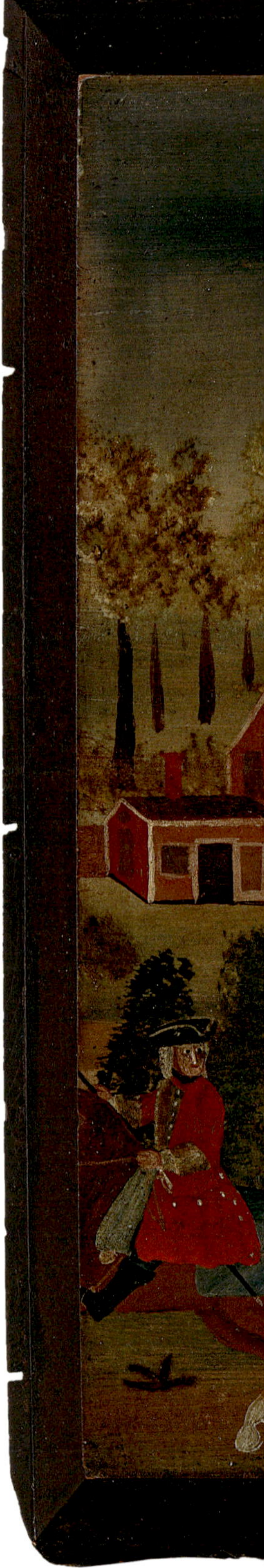

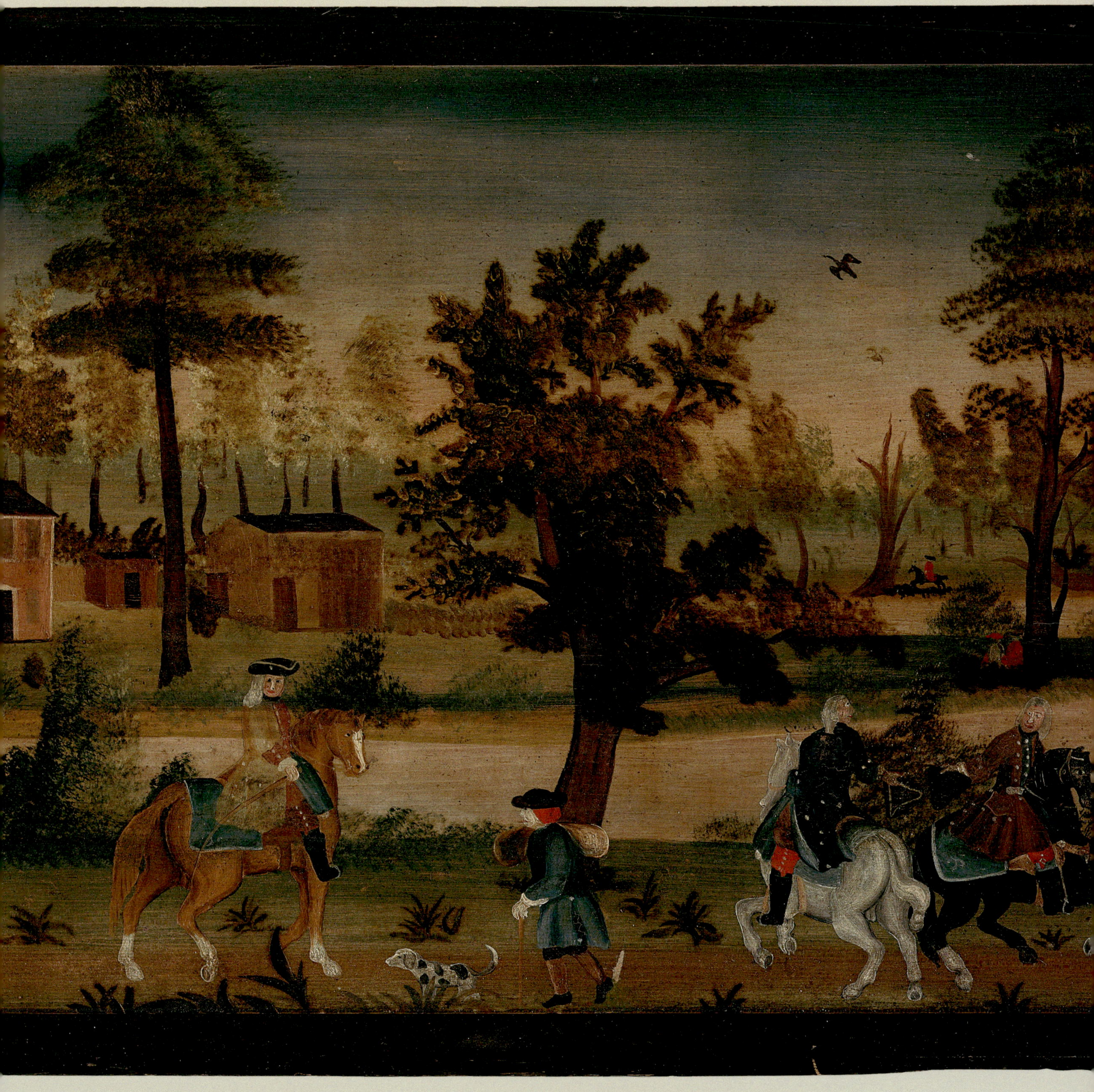

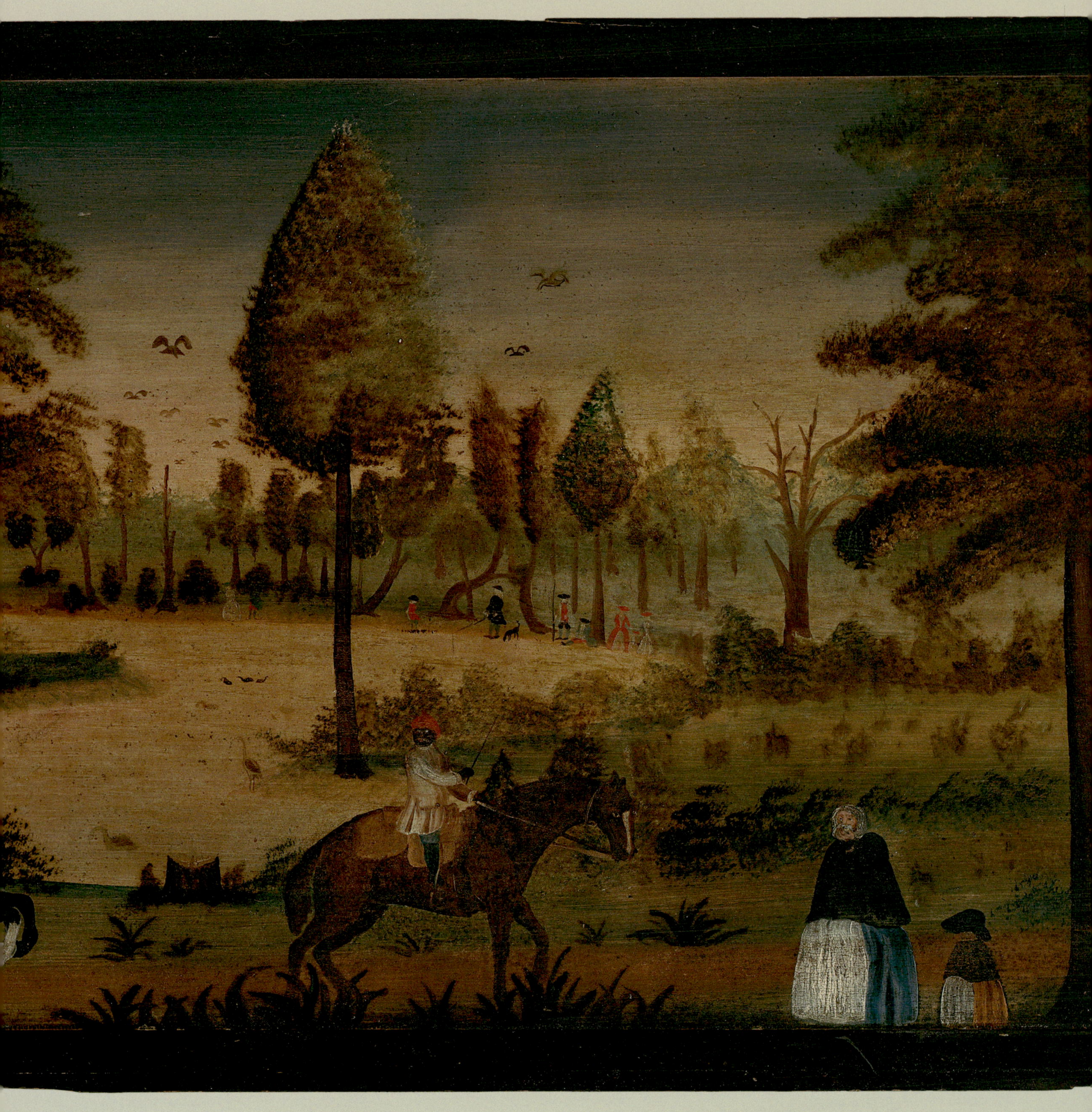

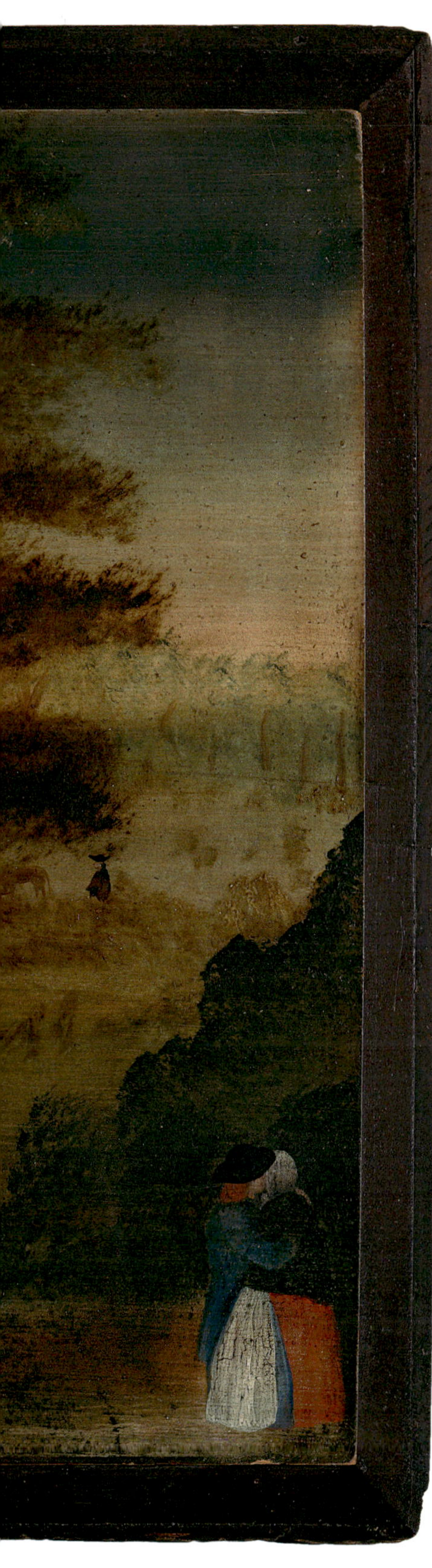

publications was more valuable as a marketing strategy than as a source of actual forbidden wisdom.

Porter's approach to interior mural painting brought the expansive air of the outdoors into the confined interiors of homes throughout New England. Of probably hundreds of rooms that received frescoed and dry-painted decoration, most were influenced by Porter's reductive scheme of a horizon line around the four walls of a room, with a foreground, middle ground, and distance. A proponent of the American scene, the design typically contained a body of water and forested land, and it was further enlivened by such details as sailing vessels, animals, human figures, and activities. The resulting vista displayed a neat and logical world that thrummed with productive order.

Coastal Landscape brings just such a breath of fresh air indoors (p. 160). It belongs to a group of land- and seascapes by an as-yet-unidentified artist whose distinctive work is found in southern New Hampshire homes.[14] Occurring as fireboards, overmantels, and wall paintings, they notably share the composition of a central tree flanked by leaning trees that bleed off the edges of the board. The trees exhibit elegant, sweeping branches that are heavily highlighted along one side in black. Repeated elements include lighthouses, residences, and sailing vessels on choppy waters, among other motifs. Each example features a stratified arrangement of colors, including a glowing sunset that specifically recalls Porter's instructions: "Strike a line around the room, nearly breast high; this is called the horizon line: paint the walls from the top to within six inches of the horizon line, with sky blue (composed of refined whiting and indigo, or slip blue), and at the same time, paint the space from the horizon to the blue, with horizon red, (whiting, coloured a little with orange lead and yellow ochre,) and while the two colours are wet, incorporate them partially, with a brush."[15]

Although this vibrant landscape has been termed an overmantel, the breadboard ends (narrow vertical pieces adjoined to each side of the panel) are characteristic of fireboard construction. A fireboard, or chimney board, sealed the open fireplace during the warm months, when it was not in use to heat the room. The board would be cut to the exact dimensions of the opening, so that it nestled snugly on all four sides. It might have had cutouts for andirons (pp. 213–14), a wide base molding, or a turn knob at the top to stabilize it within the fireplace. The simplest construction was wooden boards battened together at the back with strips of wood and painted on the front surface. Sometimes canvas was stretched over the wooden boards, tacked around the edges, and painted; other fireboards were more like conventional paintings of stretched canvas that was painted in oils, covered with wallpaper, or embellished with paper cutout appliqués.[16]

More typical of fireboard imagery are examples that feature an urn of flowers. This trope imitated the practice of placing an actual vase of flowers in the open hearth. In 1723, Colonel John Custis of Williamsburg, Virginia, wrote to his brother in England: "Get me two pieces of as good painting as you can procure. It is to put in ye summer before my chimneys to hide ye fire place. Let them bee some good flowers in potts of various kinds.... Done on canvas this is the exact dimensions of ye chimneys. I send this early that the painter may have time to do them well and the colors time to dry."[17]

A chimney board in the Fielding Collection from around 1825 represents an illusionistic space suggesting that the urn is placed within the fireplace (p. 163). It combines two conventions associated with the hearth: in addition to the flowers seemingly standing inside the fireplace, it includes a border in imitation of Delft tiles. These tin-glazed faience tiles were produced in several Netherlands pottery centers by the seventeenth century, but the factories in Delft were so numerous that the tiles came to be known generally as "delftware."[18]

Dutch delftware tiles were exported to the American colonies in New Amsterdam and the Hudson River Valley from at least the seventeenth century; they were used, as in Europe, to surround the fireplace. They were found throughout North America by the turn of the eighteenth century, when advertisements for the sale of Dutch tiles appear in newspapers in major cities, including Boston, New York, and Philadelphia. By 1761, English delftware had entered the American market advertised as "English Chimney Tiles."[19] The Fielding Collection chimney board is one of a number of similar examples that feature a painted vase of flowers and tiles surrounding the fireplace. In each, the exact configuration of tiles and imagery used is different, though most of them display trees and some landscape elements.

STILL LIFES AND ORNAMENTAL PAINTING

Another fireboard with a flower arrangement (opposite page) makes no attempt to simulate a real vase of flowers; instead, it is treated as a still-life painting set within a smoke-decorated and marbleized "frame." As such, it is on trend with the growing taste for still lifes in American homes. The still life emerged from several impulses at the end of the eighteenth century. It resonated with a widespread desire to gain an understanding of God's created world through an investigation of natural history in all its manifestations. Advances in scientific techniques and innovations in classifying the natural orders had led to a global movement to examine all geological and life forms. In botany, the sexual system of flower classification devised by Swedish botanist Carl Linnaeus (1707–1778) inspired professionals and amateurs alike to inventory all the flowering plants in an area by collecting specimens in the form of herbaria.

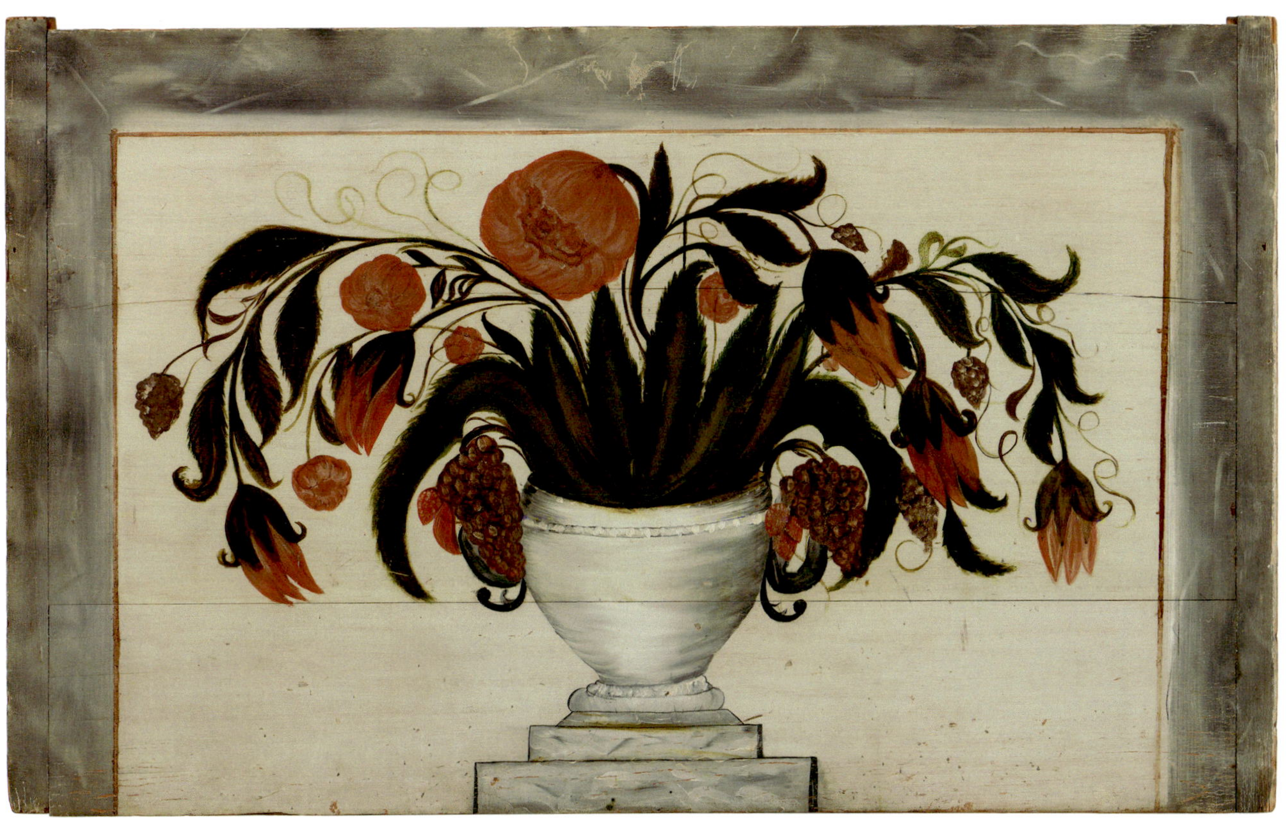

Fireboard
Probably Cape Ann, Massachusetts
ca. 1825
Polychrome pigment on pine
38½ × 60 × 1½ in.
L2015.41.133

In 1786 the American artist, patriot, and entrepreneur Charles Willson Peale (1741–1827) opened the first natural history museum in his Philadelphia home on Lombard Street. In 1794 it moved to Philosophical Hall, where he displayed specimens gathered from America and around the world as well as his own portraits of prominent Americans. The following year, his son Raphaelle Peale (1774–1825) exhibited a number of paintings at the Philadelphia Columbianum, including still lifes.[20] Despite the long history of still-life painting in the Netherlands and even more ancient representations in Greco-Roman mosaics, the form was not welcomed in America at a time when most art was held in some suspicion unless it served a practical or edifying purpose. Raphaelle Peale is credited with introducing the still life into the American art-historical canon, even as his own father derided "the painting of objects that have no motion, which any person of tolerable genius, with some application may acquire."[21] To the elder Peale, the elevation of such quotidian forms held no moral, enlightening, or even technically impressive implications. Yet the early still-life tradition symbolized the worth of everyman in the early American republic by examining the specificity of the humble and everyday and finding beauty and meaning in its very existence.

By 1829 John Neal was able to write "our portrait, our landscape and our still-life painters, if not too numerous to mention, are much too numerous to particularize."[22] In part, he was responding to the proliferation of botanical and still-life prints that demanded the presence of a still-life picture in every home of refinement. The growing popularity of abundant displays of fruit and flowers had also spawned a number of painting techniques that circulated in amateur circles, including an art primarily practiced by women and known at the time as either *Poonah painting*, deriving from a type of brush associated with Poonah, India, or *Oriental tinting*, because of a Chinese technique of painting with stencils. Today it is known as theorem painting.

This type of still life was executed with the use of stencils—theorems—on paper or velvet. It was one of a number of ladies' ornamental arts that relied on earlier techniques that were once the sole domain of the decorative painter. Stenciling was a well-established and respected method of ornamentation used in a variety of applications, from interior painting on walls and floor carpets to the embellishment of furniture, objects, and wares. It was not until it was applied to wall-hung art in the form of theorem painting that stenciling earned utter derision as an art requiring no talent. Its mechanical nature was at once deplored and extolled in such instruction manuals as *The Artist, or, Young Ladies' Instructor in Ornamental Painting, Drawing, & c* (1835).[23] This manual took the form of a conversation among a mother, daughter, and the cousin who is employed to teach the young girl a variety of arts for the benefit of contributing to fancy fairs. In the chapter on Oriental tinting, "Mamma" mentions the poor reputation held by an art that is accomplished merely by "cutting out holes in pieces of paper and then scrubbing a quantity of colour through them without any more care than a mere novice will at once bestow." Cousin Charlotte disabuses her of this concern, pointing out that "This art may be viewed as a study of light, shade, and colour, but not of form; and when the form has once been obtained, the expedition with which the shade and colour are put on is certainly a recommendation."[24] Nevertheless, the instructions were complex, demanding, and time-consuming, from numbering each tiny element of the composition to be copied, preparing the paper with oil and varnish, cutting and registering multiple stencils, one for each color, and even preparing the paints. The technique of pouncing, or dabbing dry powdered pigment through the hollow-cut stencil using a stiff bristle brush, required practice to give clarity and modulation to the form, and details such as veins in leaves were drawn with a fine brush.

Still Life with Fruit from around 1830 is an example of the subtle effects that could be achieved in the hands of a skilled

Still Life with Fruit
Theorem Painting
ca. 1830
Stenciled watercolor on paper
Framed: 20½ × 24½ in.
Stamped: "De La Rue & Co Extra London," a London-based paper maker
2016.25.100

practitioner (opposite page). The transparency of the vase, the careful toning and mottling of the rounded forms of the fruit, and the balanced composition indicate a level of experience on the part of the unidentified artist. The use of stencils is betrayed by the hard, defined edge of each element, produced as the color-laden brush hit against the inside cut pattern. Although the copy print on which this composition is based has not yet been identified, the paper itself retains a stamp from the storied company of Thomas De La Rue (1793–1866), a Guernsey-born London manufacturer. This helps to date the watercolor sometime between around 1820 and 1828–32, when De La Rue turned his interests primarily to printing playing cards.[25]

Instructions in the art of Poonah painting were advertised in *La Belle Assemblée* as early as 1817 and continued to be offered in manuals throughout the nineteenth century.[26] Its popularity and longevity may lie in the long lineage of association between women and botanical studies, both scientific and artistic. Flowers and fruit had figured in needlework since at least the fifteenth century, based on illustrations in herbals and needlework pattern books. Baskets of flowers and fruit were common motifs in pictorial needlework, samplers (p. 122), bed rugs, quilts, hearth rugs (pp. 126–28), and also in watercolor accomplishments acquired as part of a girl's education.[27] These included original and copied compositions painted on furniture, boxes, hand screens, reticules, and albums. Botany was considered especially appropriate for the feminine sensibility, and, as a theological basis underlay much of the early consideration of natural history, it was morally apt as well. Botanical studies were offered as a regular course in a girl's academic education, and some of the standard textbooks were written by women such as Almira Hart Phelps (1793–1884), whose *Familiar Lectures on Botany* went through multiple printings from 1829 to 1869.

STILL LIFES AND AMERICAN BOUNTY

As the nineteenth century progressed, opulent still lifes had little to do with "humble truths," as William H. Gerdts termed the early American still life in his seminal study, and instead assumed significance as a metaphor for American bounty and consumerism.[28] By this time, the interior organization of homes had expanded to include specialized private and public spaces, and rooms dedicated to taking meals. "Dining room pictures," in the form of original oil paintings or brilliantly colored chromolithographs, displayed spectacular towers of fruit and flowers overflowing their vases, baskets, and other vessels, and spilling onto a dining table or other surface. A large and unusual example in the Fielding Collection is the highly stylized *Still Life with a Basket of Fruit, Flowers, and Cornucopia*, painted around 1860, probably in New York City (p. 140). There is no illusionistic space; each form is sharply delineated and heavily shaded in black. Flowers and fruit stack vertically on the canvas against an undifferentiated background. Small flowers painted onto the vase metamorphose into real flowers inside the vase; there

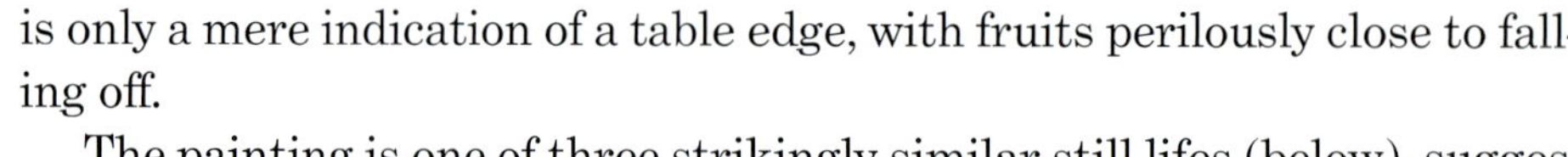

is only a mere indication of a table edge, with fruits perilously close to falling off.

The painting is one of three strikingly similar still lifes (below), suggesting a common source for the compositions, though differences in technique and spatial manipulation indicate that two artists were at work. The still life has generally been attributed to Joseph Proctor, an African American artist born in Maryland in 1786; he married Sophia Plater, also born in Maryland, in Washington, D.C., in 1814.[29] Their whereabouts are not known until 1850, when Joseph and Sophia appear in the New York City Federal Census with a seven-year-old named George Stewart, born in New York City, as part of their household.[30] Proctor's occupation is listed as "artist" or "painter," which is how he characterized himself in the New York City directories at various addresses on Mercer, Laurens (now West Broadway), and Elizabeth Streets in Lower Manhattan from 1851 through 1856, then again from 1858 through 1862.[31] Little George is no longer listed in the 1860 census, suggesting that he died in the intervening years. After 1860, the family is no longer to be found in the New York City census records or directories.

Despite the bright colors of the fruit and flowers, a somber palette casts a melancholy pall on the composition, relating it to the early Dutch tradition of *vanitas* that used the still life as a contemplation on the certainty of

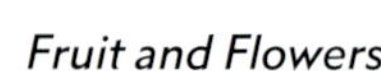

Fruit and Flowers
Mid-nineteenth century
Oil on canvas
26 3/8 × 41 5/16 in.
NATIONAL GALLERY OF ART, GIFT OF EDGAR WILLIAM AND BERNICE CHRYSLER GARBISCH, 1966.13.7

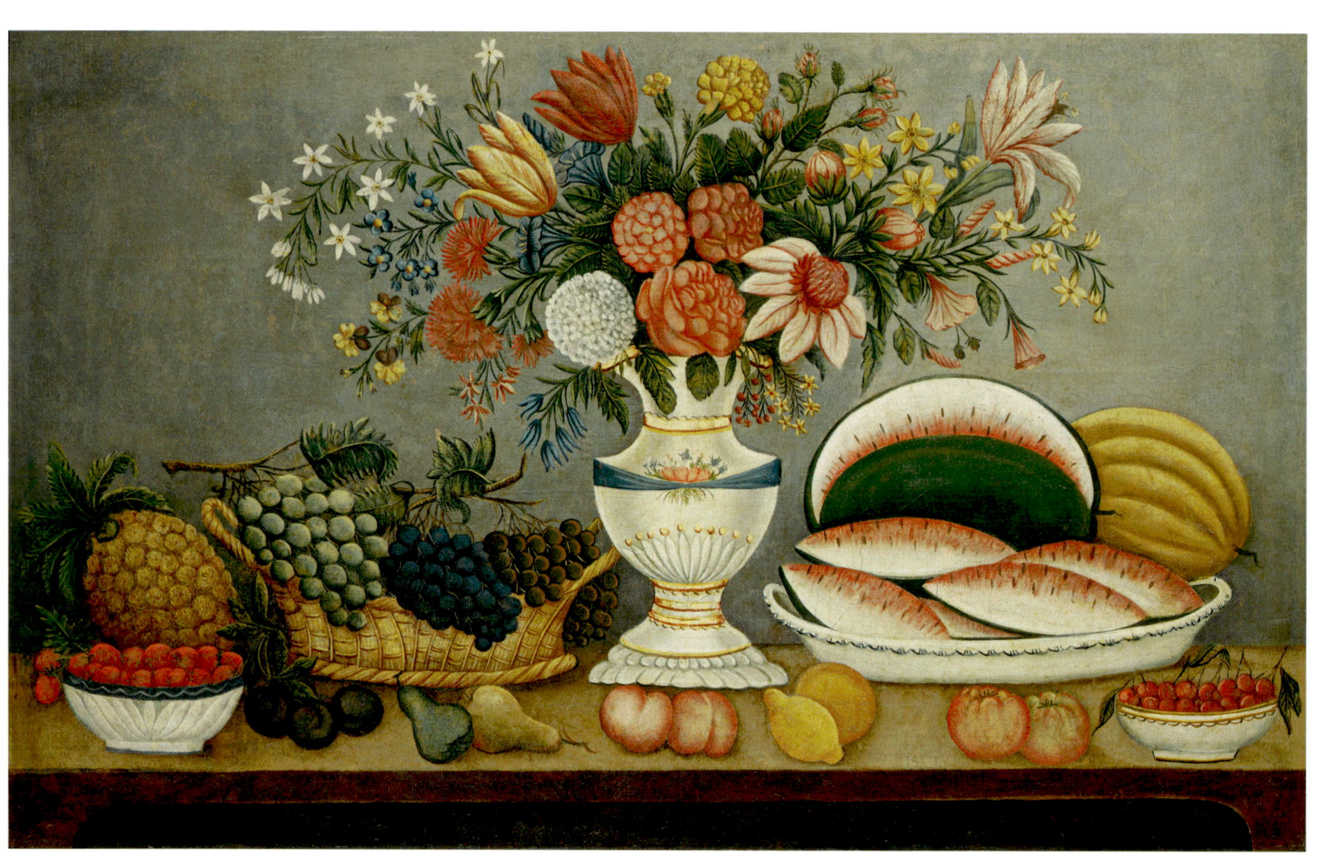

death. The bouquet includes flowers that betoken mourning, such as morning glories and forget-me-nots; a goldfinch, sometimes associated with resurrection, perches meaningfully on a bunch of purple grapes, recalling its presence in another type of still life represented in the Fielding Collection, the posthumous portrait of Cynthia Mary Osborn, painted by Samuel Miller (p. 186).

In a series of articles on the art of painting that appeared in the inaugural issues of *Scientific American,* the publication he founded in 1845, Rufus Porter wrote that it was "neither necessary nor expedient, in all cases, to imitate nature," lending credence to John Neal's plaint.[32] In the hands of the self-taught artist, early American landscape and still-life painting enjoyed a malleability that subscribed to no single convention. The contract between artist and viewer was not always bound to represent literal truth in art or nature but instead held a deeper truth: a growing consensus of American identity rooted in a multiplicity of experiences and expressions. This new model of unity deriving from diversity was an experiment, one that would, as observed in 1837, ultimately be judged by the "aggregate formed from the culture of individual minds."[33]

Stacy C. Hollander is the former Deputy Director for Curatorial Affairs, Chief Curator, and Director of Exhibitions, American Folk Art Museum, New York.

NOTES

1 John Neal, "American Painters—and Painting," *Yankee and Boston Literary Gazette*, n.s., no. 1 (July 1829): 46–47.

2 Robert Boodey Caverly, *Genealogy of the Caverly Family, from the Year 1116 to the Year 1880, Made Profitable and Exemplified by Many a Lesson of Life* (Lowell, Mass.: G. M. Elliott, 1880), 77, http://books.google.com/books?id=7fQZAQAAMAAJ.

3 Neal, "American Painters," 47. In deriding the work of the ornamental painter, Neal refers to typical products of their artistry that satisfied a variety of purposes, including fire buckets, such as those in the Fielding Collection (pp. 234–35), and "looking-glass tablets," rectangular mirrors that were ornamented with reverse-painted glass panels at the top showing landscapes, classical figures, and urns of flowers. The same ornamental painter might paint militia standards, the insignia associated with specific branches of the military, for a variety of purposes, including parade banners, flags, or oil on canvas to hang on a wall.

4 A wave of anti–Irish Catholic sentiment swept the eastern United States from the 1830s to the 1850s. One nativist group opposed to Catholics and the Irish who immigrated to the United States during the potato famine was a secret society called the Know-Nothings. The paintings depict a violent attack on Bath's Old South Church, which had been sold to Catholics, after a crowd of more than two thousand had attended night rallies over several days, listening to harangues against Catholics and foreigners. John Hilling, an English-born local sign- and housepainter, was probably an eyewitness to the event because he was also a firefighter in Bath and may have been called to the scene.

5 John Neal, "Landscape and Portrait-Painting," *Yankee and Boston Literary Gazette*, n.s., no. 3 (September 1829): 113.

6 Frances Milton Trollope, *Domestic Manners of the Americans* (London: Whittaker, Treacher, & Co., 1832), 243, https://archive.org/details/domesticmanners000troliala.

7 Abbott Lowell Cummings, "The Beginnings of American Landscape Painting," *Metropolitan Museum of Art Bulletin* 11, no. 3 (1952): 93–99 at 93, 94, doi:10.2307/3258297.

8 Nina Fletcher Little, "Recently Discovered Paintings by Winthrop Chandler," *Art in America* 36 (April 1948): 81–97. Chandler painted a second overmantel for the Waters residence around the same time, featuring a river view with fort.

9 "Winthrop Chandler, Limner of Windham County, Connecticut," *Art in America* 35 (April 1947): 84, 90, 112–13, 162. Members of the Chandler family were among the founders of Woodstock, Connecticut, where the artist was born. In 1762, several years after his father's death in 1754, young Winthrop seems to have been apprenticed, perhaps to a Boston decorative painter, as he returned to Connecticut around 1770, where he painted important portraits of Reverend Ebenezer Devotion and his wife, Martha. By 1775, Chandler had a growing family but was experiencing financial difficulties in the unrest of the impending War of Independence. His own family was divided between ardent Loyalists and members who fought on the Patriot side: Chandler carved a coat of arms of Great Britain and Ireland for his cousin Gardiner Chandler in Worcester, Massachusetts, and he painted a portrait in Woodstock of his brother Samuel Chandler, who fought in the Revolutionary War. After 1785, the artist moved to Worcester, where, in addition to painting portraits and overmantels, he kept a shop that offered house painting. He returned to Woodstock, impoverished and sick, near the end of his life. Chandler's obituary in Worcester's *Massachusetts Spy* remembers him as a house painter but notes "many good likenesses on canvas show he could guide the pencil of a limner."

10 Little, "Winthrop Chandler," 91. Whether Chandler was responsible for the imitative painted graining and marbleizing is not known, though he would have possessed the requisite skills to produce decorative finishes.

11 Sukhdev Sandhu, "The First Black Britons," BBC Online Archives, last updated February 17, 2011, http://www.bbc.co.uk/history/british/empire_seapower/black_britons_01.shtml.

12 William Addison Benedict and Hiram A. Tracy, *History of the Town of Sutton, Massachusetts, from 1704 to 1876: Including Grafton until 1735; Millbury until 1813; and Parts of Northbridge, Upton and Auburn* (Worcester, Mass.: Sanford, 1878), 200, http://books.google.com/books?id=OnMNAQAAIAAJ.

13 For an in-depth consideration of the struggle to make the transition from ornamental painter to easel painter, see Jessica Nicoll, "'The Real Pioneer of Art in this City': Charles Codman and the Rise of Landscape Painting in Portland, Maine," in *Charles Codman: The Landscape of Art and Culture in 19th-Century Maine*, ed. Caroline Sloat (Portland, Maine: Portland Museum of Art, 2002), http://www.tfaoi.com/aa/3aa/3aa654.htm.

14 Linda Lefko, email message to author, November 25, 2018. I am grateful to Linda Lefko for sharing her insights into this fireboard, especially as it relates to examples of painted New England wall murals of the period.

15 Rufus Porter, *A Select Collection of Valuable and Curious Arts, and Interesting Experiments, Which Are Well Explained, and Warranted Genuine, and May Be Performed Easily, Safely, and at Little Expense* (Concord, N.H.: Rufus Porter, 1825), 27–29.

16 Nina Fletcher Little, *American Decorative Wall Painting, 1700–1850* (New York: E. P. Dutton, 1989), 66.

17 Little, *American Decorative Wall Painting*, 66.

18 Josslyn Kay Stiner, "Piecing It Together: The Introduction of Delftware Tiles to North America and Their Enduring Legacy in Charleston, South Carolina" (MS thesis, Clemson University, 2010), https://tigerprints.clemson.edu/all_theses/828.

19 Stiner, "Piecing It Together," 49–50. The early tiles had monochromatic designs in blue and white or purple and white. Designs might incorporate Chinese-influenced motifs, portraits of famous people, soldiers, or more generic images of fruit and flowers. As tastes changed, these were replaced by landscapes, biblical scenes, and depictions of daily activities. Tiles were especially popular for encasing fireplaces in Dutch homes because they were easy to clean, reflected heat into the room, and provided a measure of fire safety. Delft-type tiles were produced in England as well, introduced through émigré Dutch potters and centered in Liverpool and Bristol. Although the earliest examples are similar to true delftware, these areas developed their own distinctive images and painting techniques over time.

20 The Columbianum was the first association in the United States to promote the fine arts. It was conceived in Philadelphia by Charles Willson Peale, Benjamin Rush, Joseph Ceracchi, and others as an academy of art and science, and as a platform to exhibit works of art. The first and only exhibition occurred in 1795.

21 Carol Troyen, "Fruit, Flowers, and Lucky Strikes: The Still Life in American Culture," in *The Art of American Still Life: Audubon to Warhol*, ed. Mark D. Mitchell (Philadelphia and New Haven, Conn.: Philadelphia Museum of Art in association with Yale University Press, 2015), 25.

22 Neal, "American Painters," 46.

23 B. F. Gandee, *The Artist, or, Young Ladies' Instructor in Ornamental Painting . . . and Manufacturing . . . Articles for Fancy Fairs* (London: Chapman and Hall, 1835), 126–62.

24 Gandee, *The Artist*, 128, 129–30.

25 Simon Wintle, "Printing of Playing Cards," The World of Playing Cards, last updated February 24, 2011, http://www.wopc.co.uk/cards/printing; Adam Wintle, "Thomas de la Rue: A Brief History of De la Rue's Playing Cards," The World of Playing Cards, last updated November 5, 2018, http://www.wopc.co.uk/delarue/index. Coincidentally, until De La Rue introduced letterpress printing, playing cards were hand stenciled and colored in watercolors, similar to theorem painting.

26 *La Belle Assemblée; Being Bell's Court and Fashionable Magazine*, n.s., 1817. See also *London Examiner*, April 29, 1821, 272. As late as 1898, author William Makepeace Thackeray derided Poonah painting as a "rank villainous deception," showing that it was an art still being practiced.

27 *The Young Lady's Book: A Manual of Elegant Recreations, Exercises, and Pursuits* (London: Vizetelly, Branston, and Co., 1829) gives an idea of the full range of refinements necessary in order for a young woman to be considered truly accomplished. The chapters comprise moral deportment, botany, minerology, conchology, entomology, embroidery, writing, archery, dancing, music, and the ornamental arts, among others, calling to mind this passage from Jane Austen's *Pride and Prejudice*: "No one can be really esteemed accomplished who does not greatly surpass what is usually met with. A woman must have a thorough knowledge of music, singing, drawing, dancing, and the modern languages, to deserve the word; and besides all this, she must possess a certain something in her air and manner of walking, the tone of her voice, her address and expressions, or the word will be but half-deserved."

28 William H. Gerdts, *Painters of the Humble Truth: Masterworks of American Still-Life, 1801–1939* (Columbia, Mo.: University of Missouri Press, 1981).

29 District of Columbia, Marriage Records, 1810–1953, Ancestry.com. This attribution is based on oral history of a similar signed example whose present location is not known.

30 Year: 1850; Census Place: New York Ward 8 District 1, New York, New York; Roll: M432_541; Page: 119B; Image: 245.

31 Irma and Paul Milstein Division of United States History, Local History and Genealogy, The New York Public Library, "New York City directory," New York Public Library Digital Collections, http://digitalcollections.nypl.org/items/e669fcd0-52b8-0134-cae4-00505686a51c.

32 Jean Lipman, "Rufus Porter 1792–1884," in *American Folk Painters of Three Centuries*, ed. Tom Armstrong and Jean Lipman (New York: Hudson Hills Press in association with Whitney Museum of American Art, 1980), 152.

33 G. V. H. Forbes, "Female Education," *The Ladies' Garland* 1, no. 5 (July 15, 1837): 75.

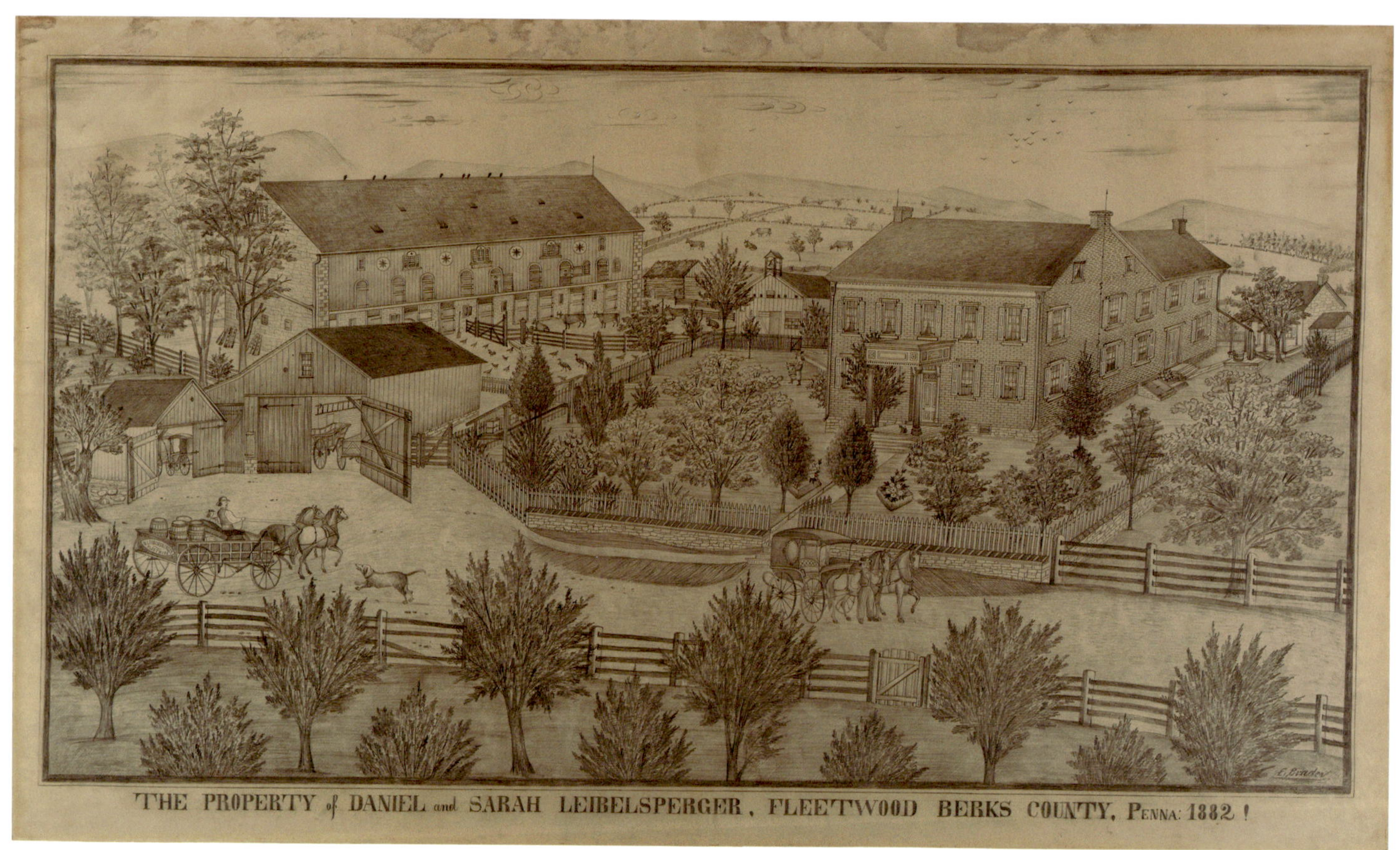

FERDINAND A. BRADER
(1833–1901)

The Property of Daniel and Sarah Leibelsperger, Fleetwood, Berks County, Pennsylvania

1882

Graphite on wove paper
30⅝ × 51 in.

Inscription:
"THE PROPERTY of DANIEL and SARAH LEIBELSPERGER, FLEETWOOD BERKS COUNTY, PENNA: 1882!"

2016.25.98

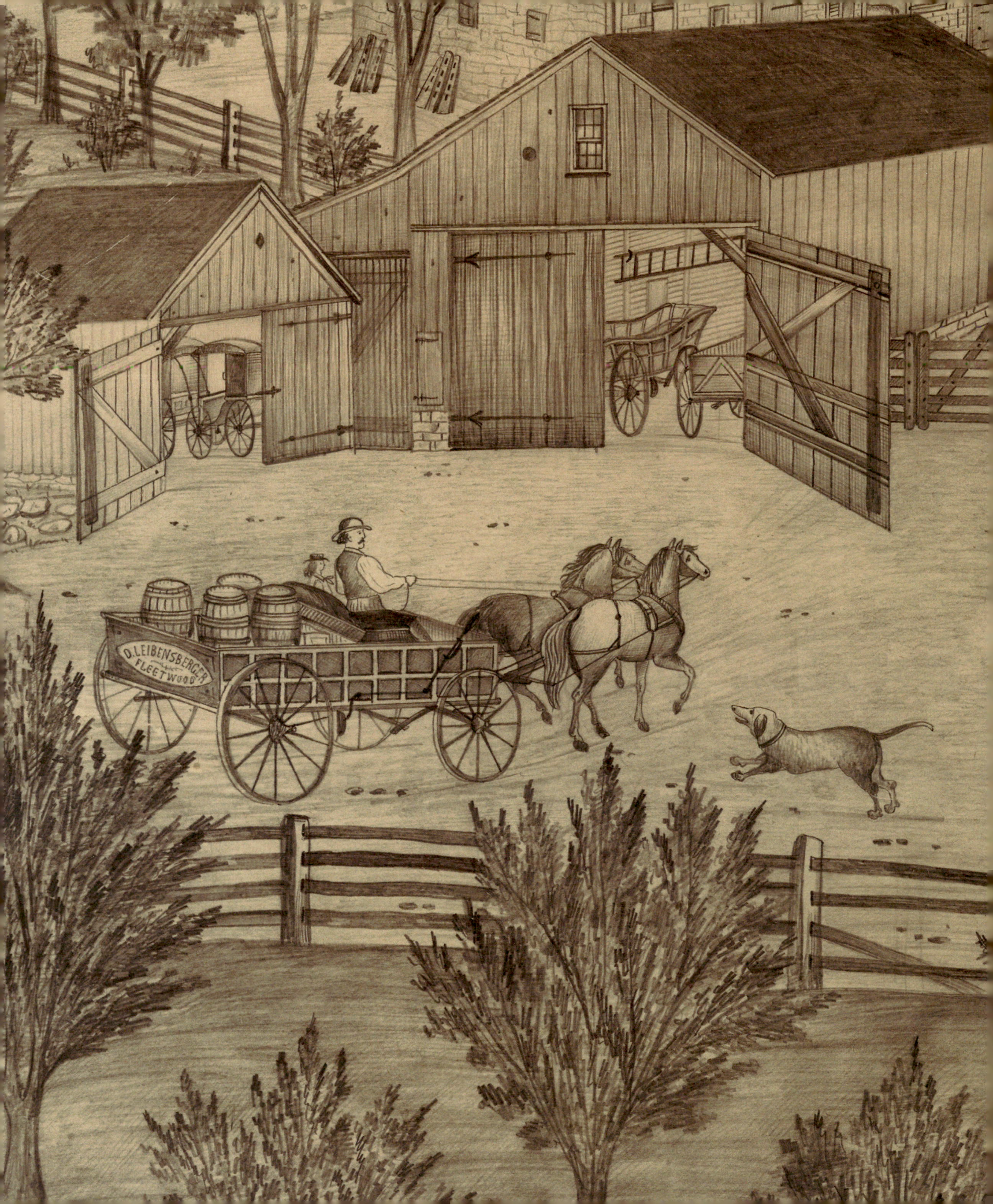
D. LEIBENSBERGER
FLEETWOOD

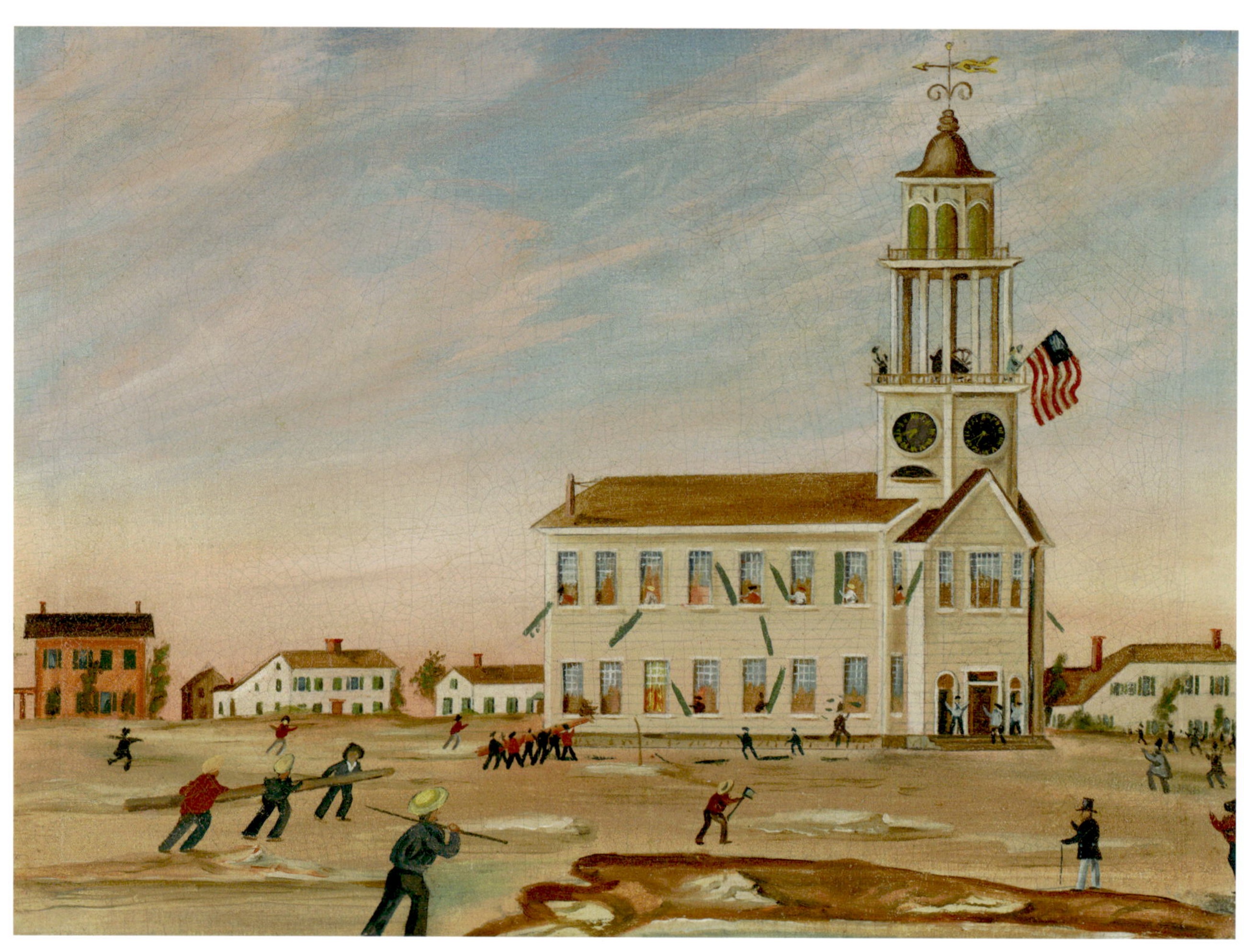

ATTRIBUTED TO JOHN HILLING (1822–1894)

Before the Burning of Old South Church in Bath, Maine

ca. 1854

Oil on canvas
17 × 23 in.

L2015.41.177.1

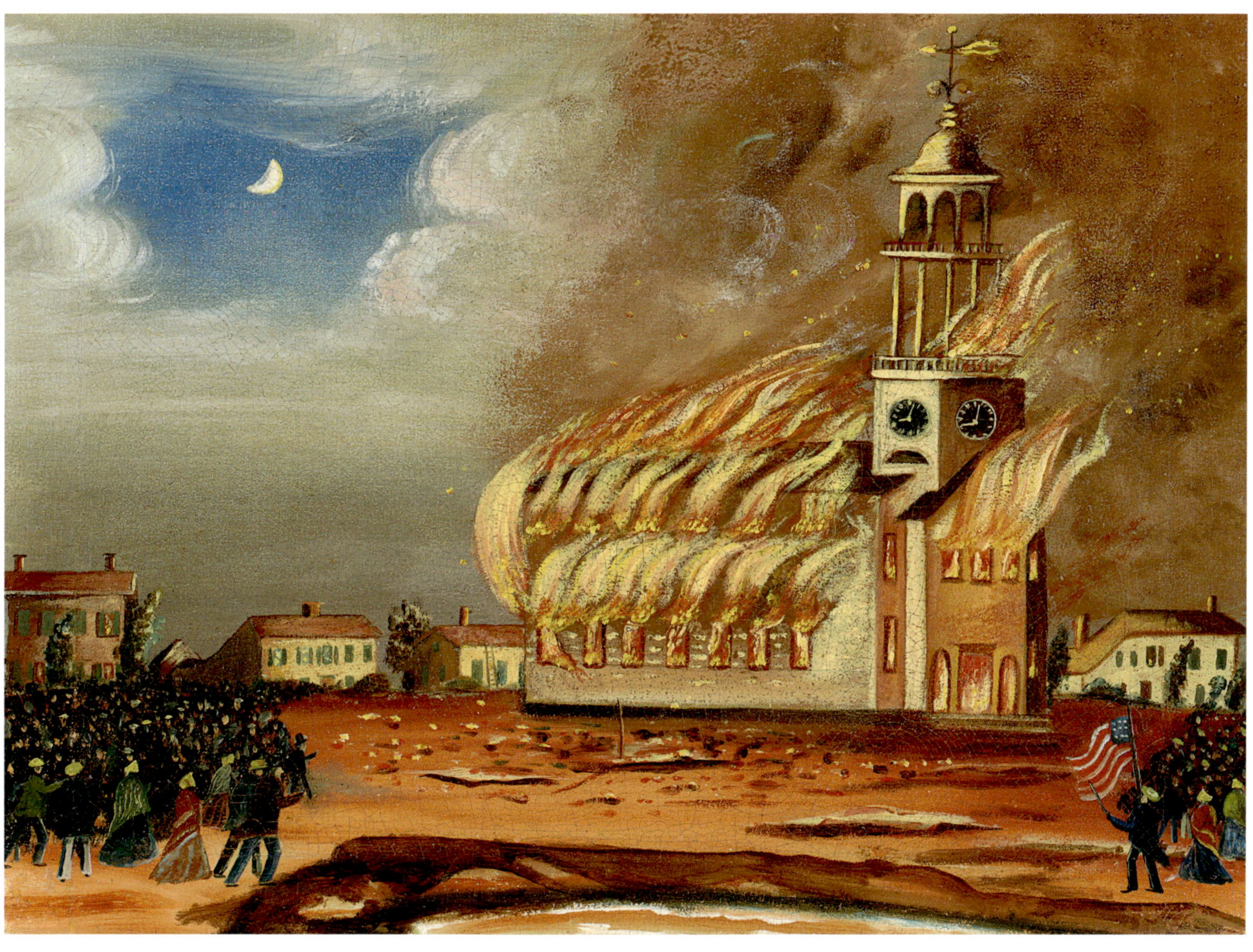

JOHN HILLING

This artist was a jack-of-all-trades. An 1867–68 directory published in Bath, Maine, advertised his skills as a "house, sign, and fancy painter, grainer and paper hanger." He chronicled the destruction of Bath's Catholic Old South Church on June 6, 1854, by an anti-Catholic and anti-Irish mob.

During the 1850s, the United States saw the growth of anti-immigrant and anti-Catholic sentiment primarily directed at Irish Catholics escaping the Potato Famine (1845–52). A rabble-rousing representative of the Know-Nothings, a vehemently anti-immigrant American political party, gave a speech that stirred up a crowd.

On the following evening, they looted and burned the church. The clock and moon mark the rioters' destructive progress, while pews tossed from windows, a makeshift battering ram, and an American flag saved from the flames give the paintings a reportorial quality.

ATTRIBUTED TO JOHN HILLING (1822–1894)

The Burning of Old South Church in Bath, Maine

ca. 1854

Oil on canvas
17½ × 23½ in.

L2015.41.177.2

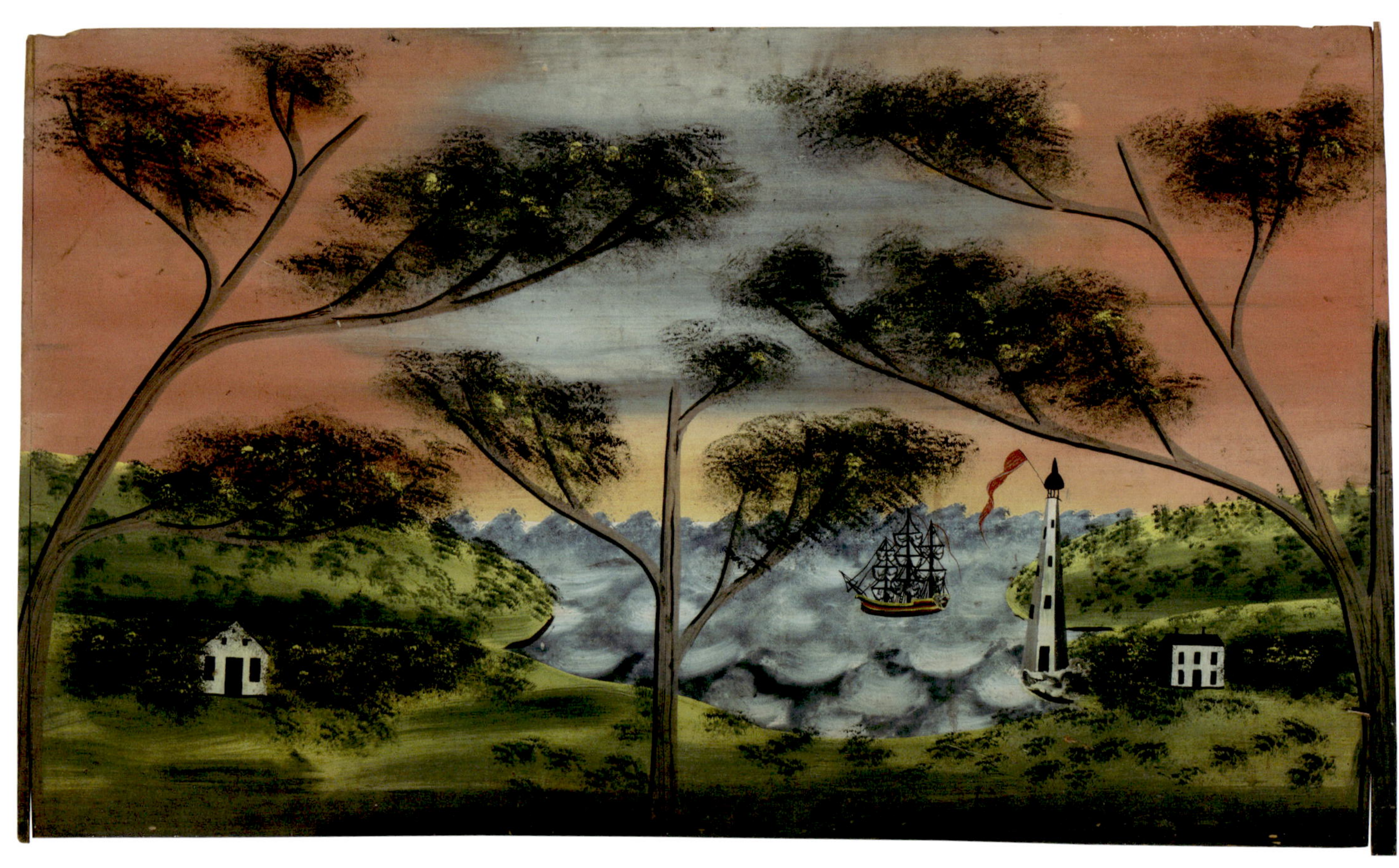

Overmantel:
Coastal Landscape

Early nineteenth century

Oil on pine panel
overmantel
29 × 48 × 3/8 in.

2016.25.109

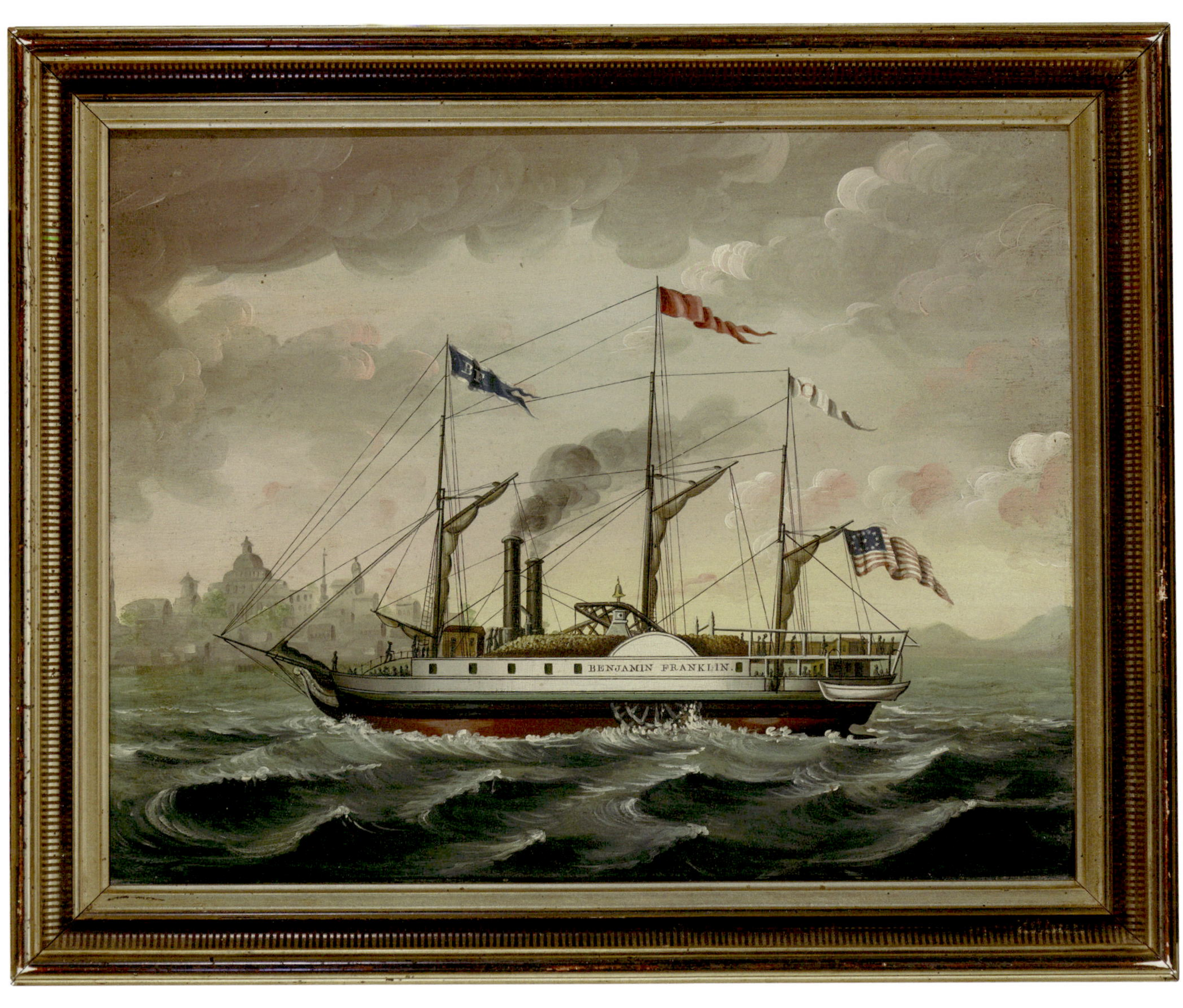

THOMAS G. CHAMBERS
(1808–1869)

The "Benjamin Franklin"

Mid-nineteenth century

Oil on board
Framed: 14¾ × 17¾ in.

L2015.41.174

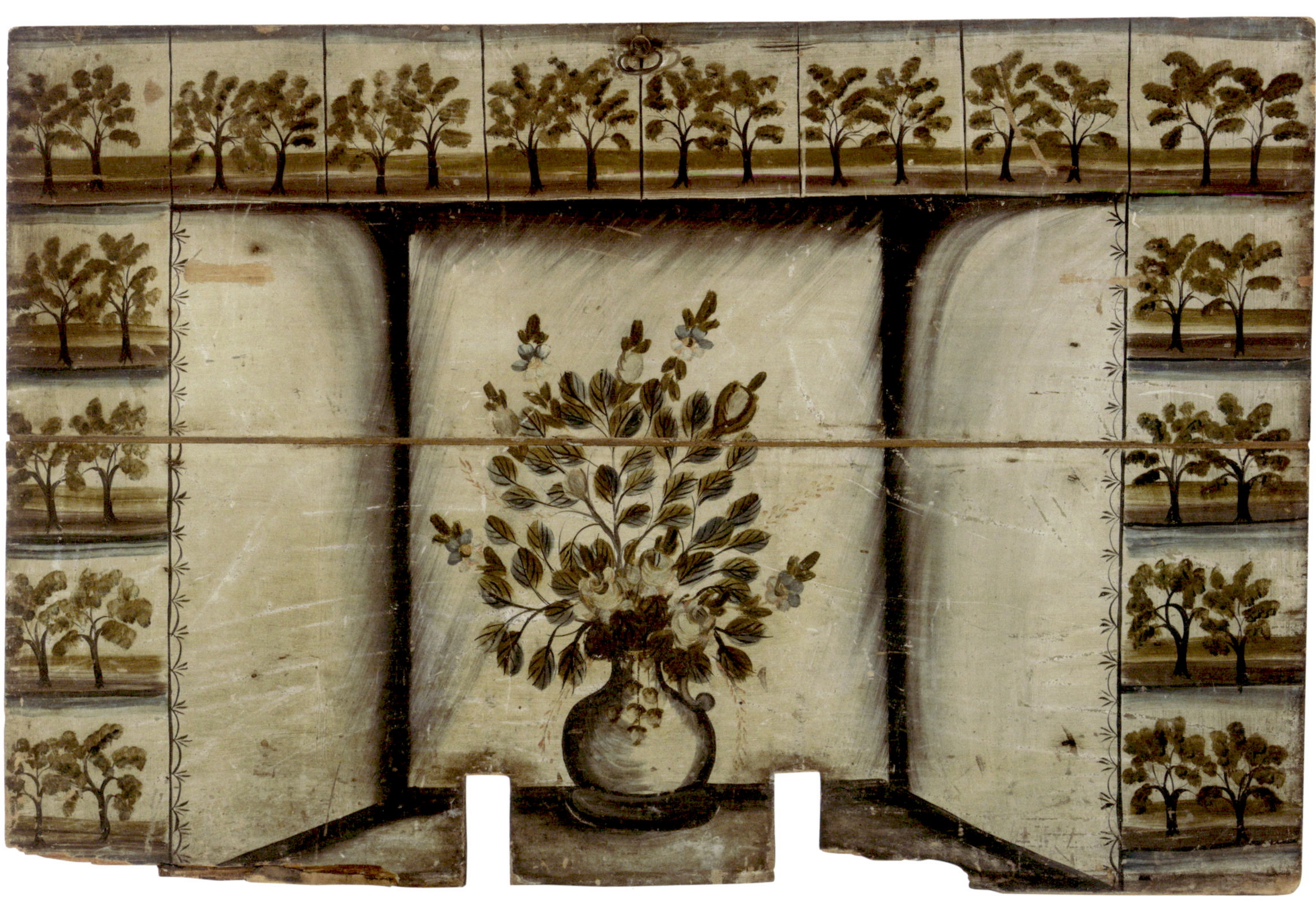

Adam and Eve Fireback

Boston
ca. 1770

Puddle-cast iron
34½ × 23 × ½ in.

2016.25.94

Fireboard

New England
ca. 1825

Polychrome pigment on
pine with brass hardware
33¼ × 49 × 2 in.

2016.25.93

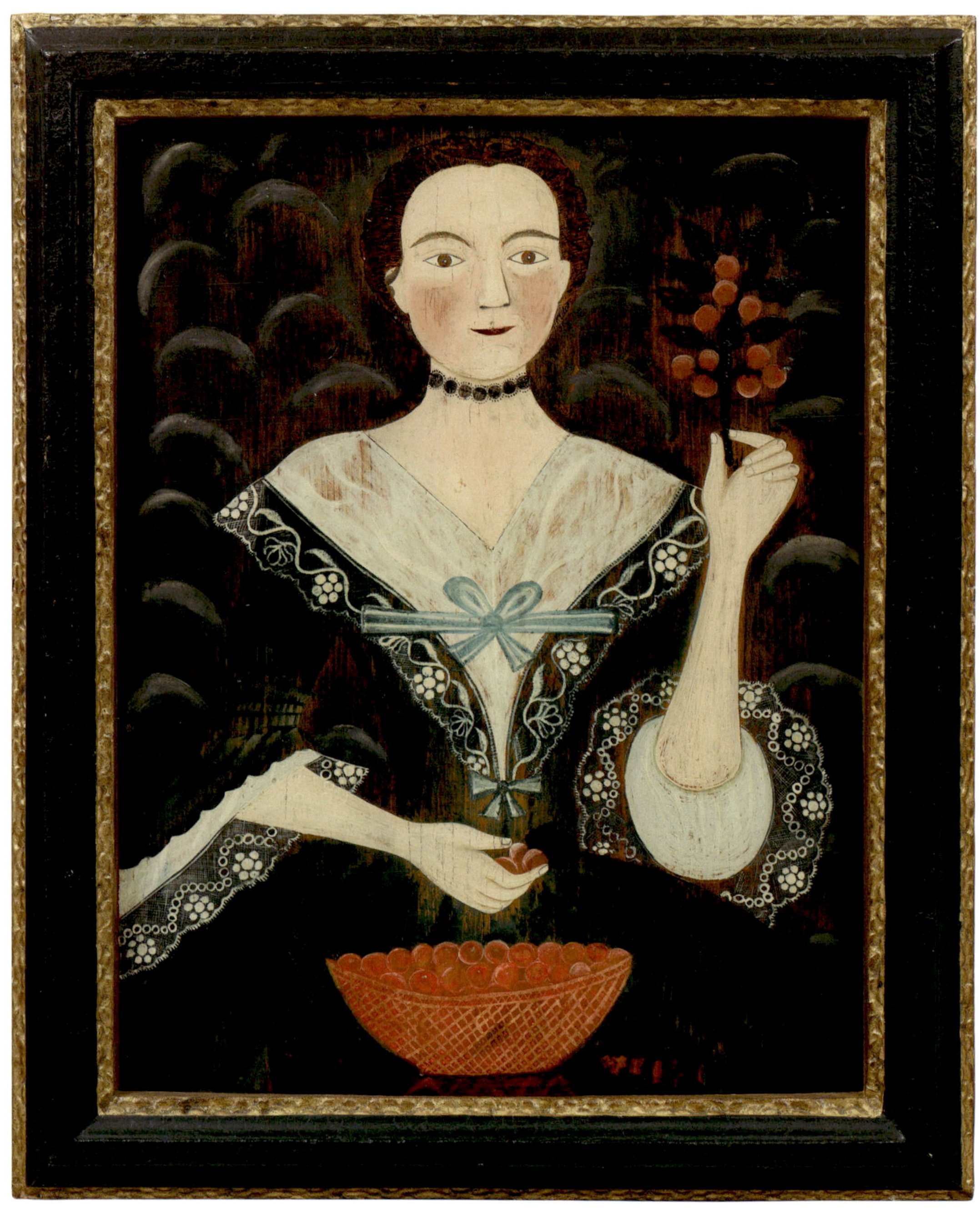

Portrait of a Woman with a Bowl of Cherries

Connecticut or New York
ca. 1770–80

Oil on panel
Framed: 28 × 23 in.

L2015.41.172

MILTON W. HOPKINS (1789–1844; ACTIVE IN NEW YORK STATE; RICHMOND, VIRGINIA; AND OHIO)

Girl with Flowers

Probably New York State
Early to mid-nineteenth century

Oil on canvas
Framed: 43½ × 29½ in.

2016.25.112

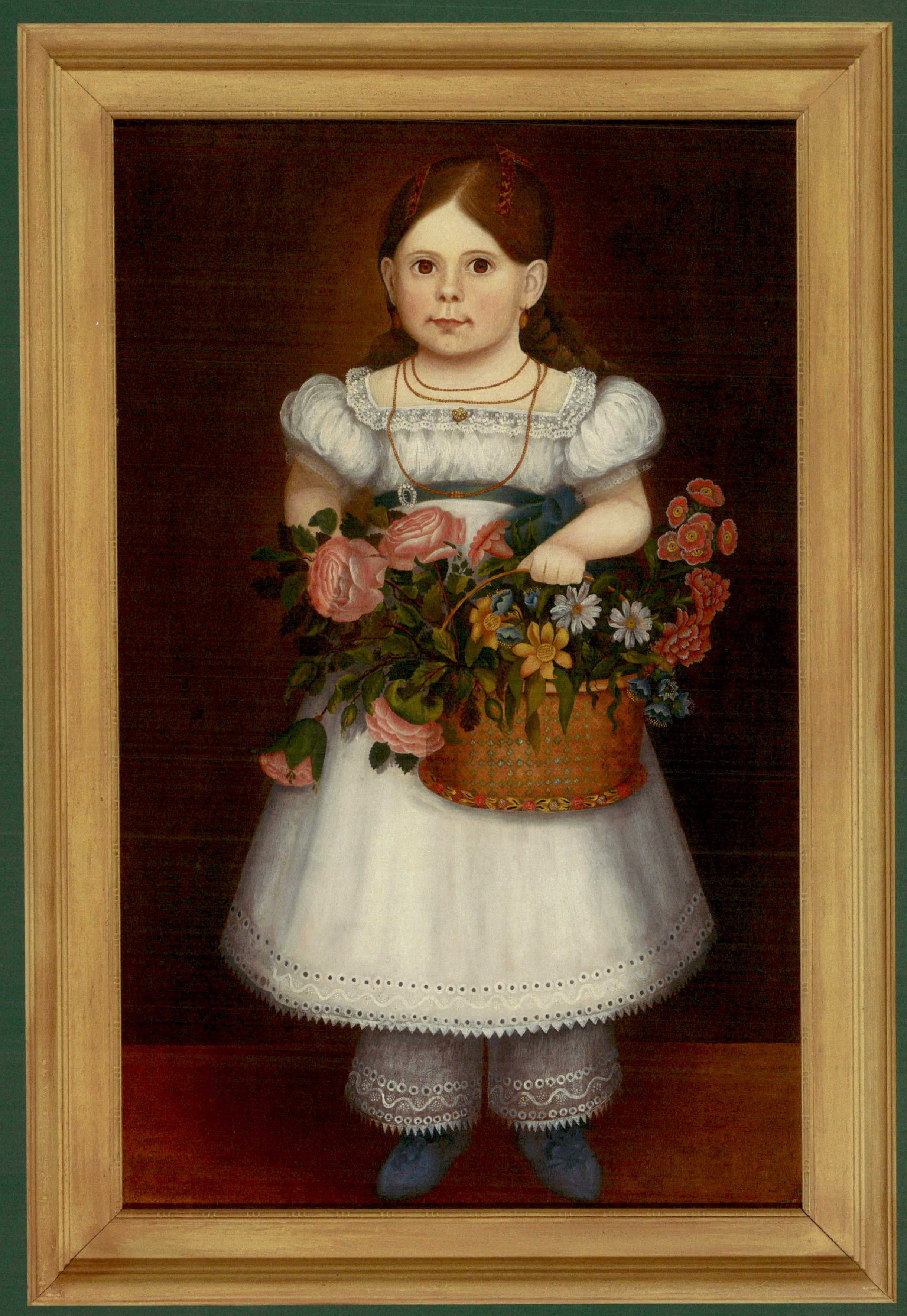

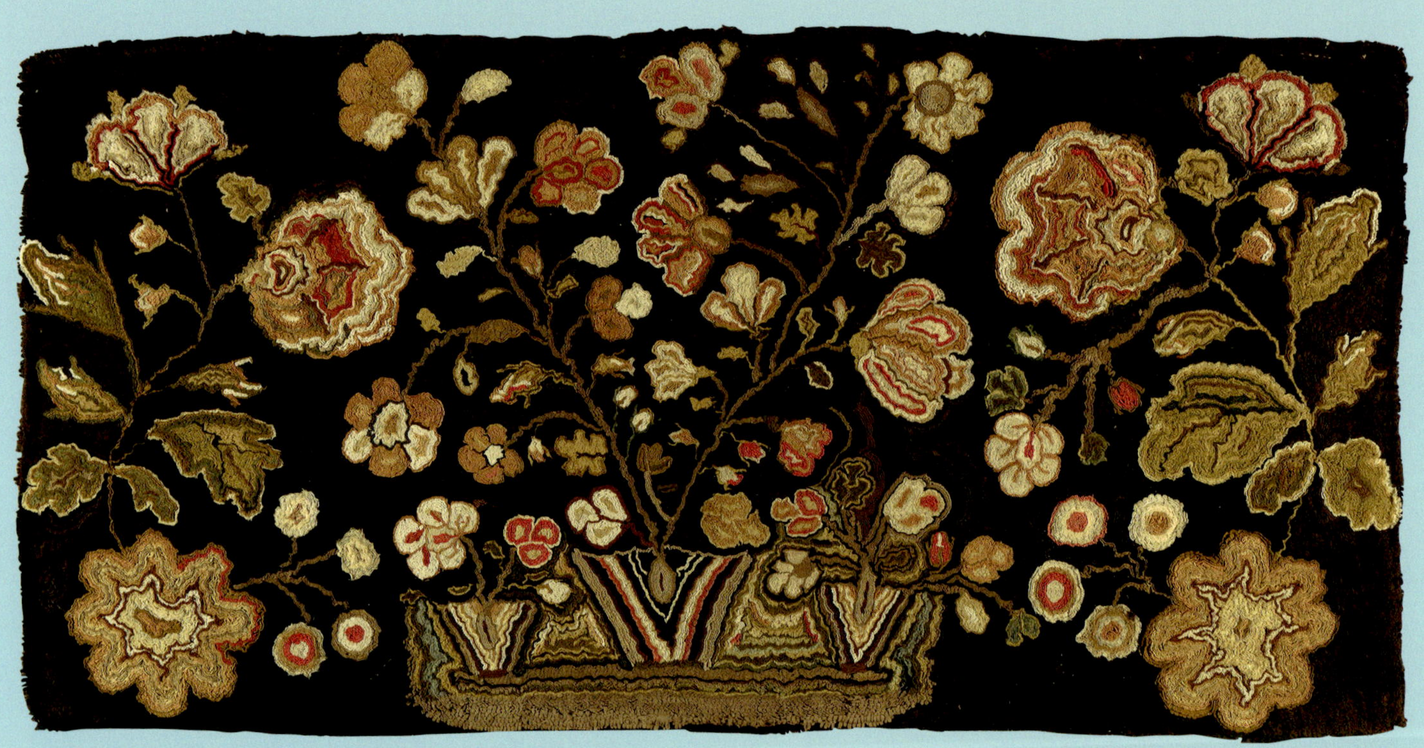

Flower Basket Rug

New England
1810–30

Bias-shirred and vegetable-dyed wool on linen
33½ × 66½ in.

Detail on p. 169

L2015.41.81

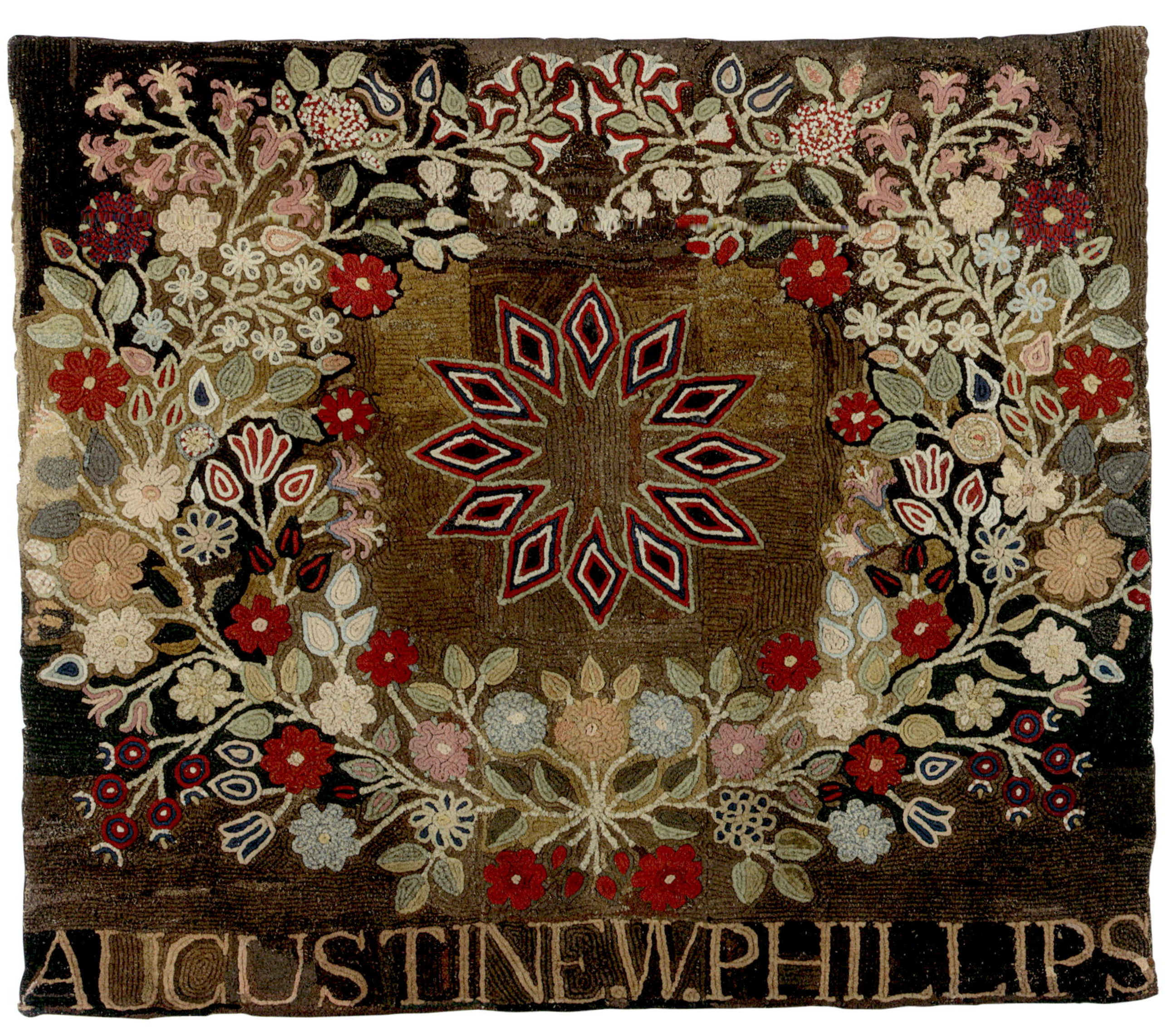

Yarn-Sewn Rug

Probably Maine
ca. 1845

Yarn-sewn, chenille-shirred wool on linen
54½ × 63 in.

Inscription: "AUGUSTINE. W. PHILLIPS"

L2015.41.83

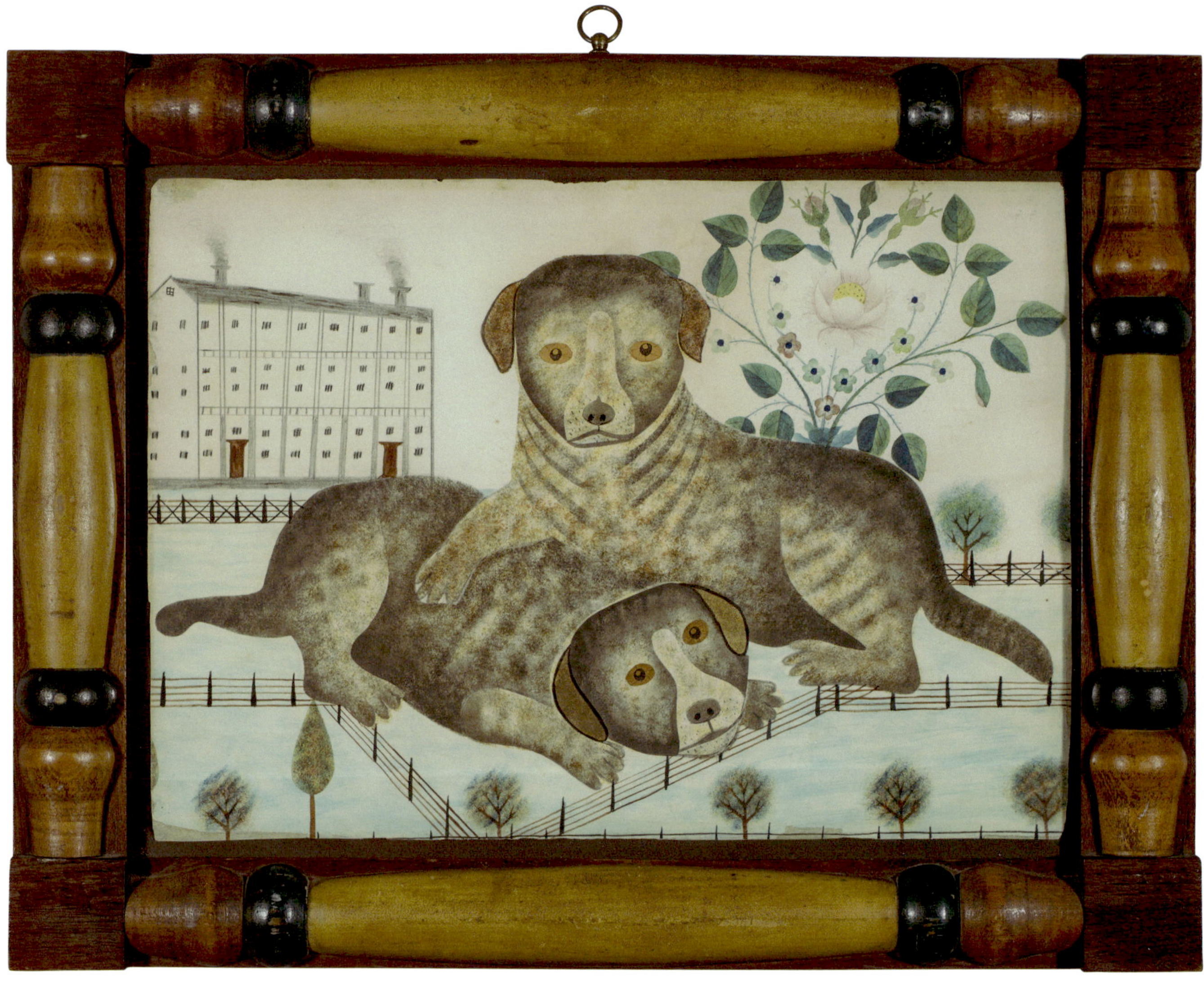

Puppies
1846–47
Watercolor on paper
Framed: 11 × 14 in.
L2015.41.156

Flower Basket Rug (detail)
See also p. 166

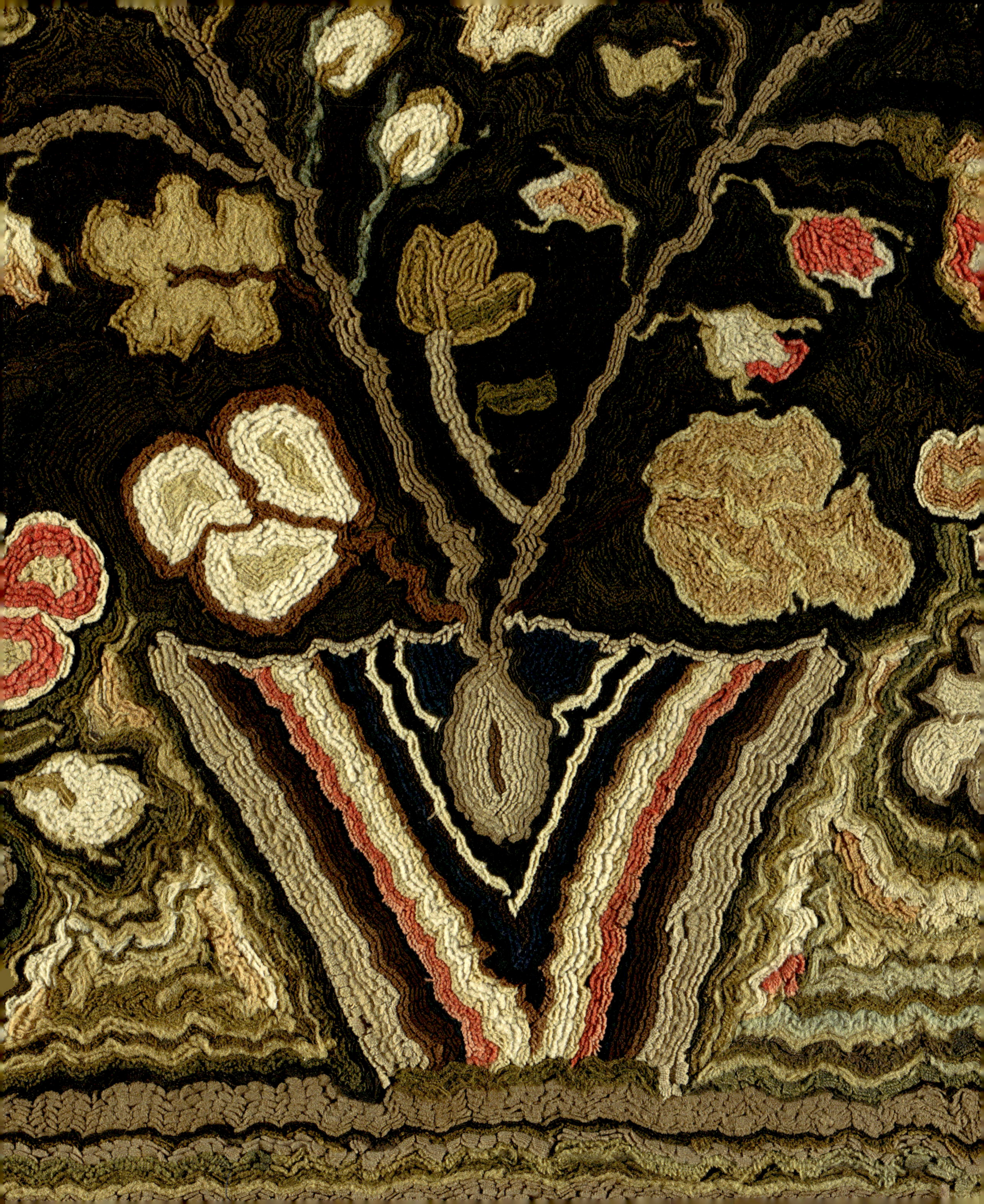

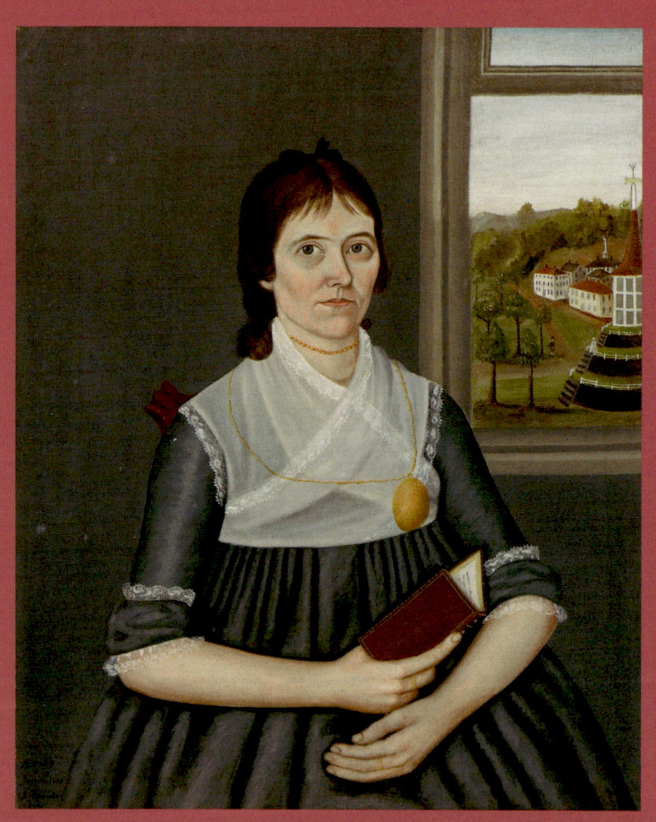

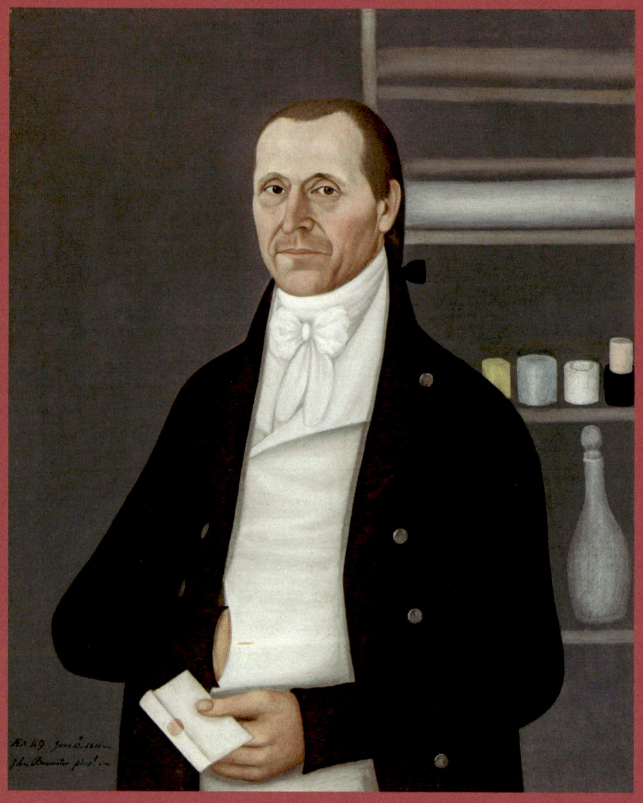

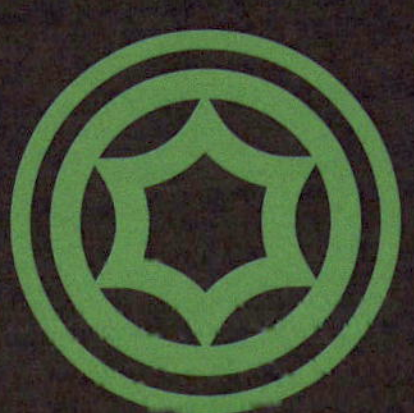

"The Human Heart by Which We Live"

Family Portraits from Cradle to Grave

ROBIN JAFFEE FRANK

Portraiture, the dominant form of painting in nineteenth-century America, offered a sense of not only how the subjects actually looked but also how they wanted to be seen by their peers and remembered by posterity. Affluent sitters, and increasingly members of the middling classes, commissioned portraits as an expression of social position and material aspirations. Portraits also served as a visual record of family members during a period when mortality rates were high. Beyond conveying status, they embodied the yearning to capture likenesses of loved ones who might die young, and to keep those who did within the circle of the living. These memorial and sentimental functions of early American portraiture are the primary concern of this essay.

Drawn from the Fielding Collection, the portraits discussed here explore family ties, especially maternal bonds of affection. John Brewster Jr. portrays a married couple in the midst of their eighth pregnancy; Joseph H. Davis, parents at home with their youngest infant; and Samuel S. Miller, a deceased child pictured as healthy. Together, these artists create a vivid portrait of a young nation by imbuing their compositions with details personal to the sitters yet resonant with the era's attitudes about family life from cradle to grave.

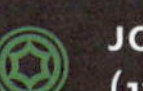

JOHN BREWSTER JR. (1766–1854)

Portraits of Elizabeth Stone Coffin and Major David Coffin

Newburyport, Massachusetts
1801

Oil on canvas
Each: 33¾ × 26¾ in.

Detail on p. 172

L2015.41.164, .165

"DUTY AND HAPPINESS"
JOHN BREWSTER JR.'S PAIRED PORTRAITS OF EXPECTANT PARENTS

An evocative portrayal of a long-married couple at the dawn of the nineteenth century, John Brewster Jr.'s paired portraits likely depict Major David Coffin (1763–1838) and his pregnant wife, Elizabeth Stone Coffin

(1767–1811).[1] Born in Hampton, Connecticut, Brewster was the son of a prominent physician and a direct descendant of Mayflower pilgrim William Brewster. Although deaf and mute, the artist became a leading itinerant portraitist of the region's elite merchant class through his prodigious talent and family social connections.[2] He possessed the ability to communicate through both writing and a rudimentary sign language, before its standardization, but also made his voice heard through art.

In 1796, Brewster settled in his brother Royal's home in Buxton, Maine, and traveled from there to fulfill commissions across New England. During 1801–2, he lodged with the affluent family of James Prince in Newburyport, Massachusetts, where he probably painted the portraits of David and Elizabeth Coffin. Family ties facilitated the connection between the sitters and the artist: David Coffin was the nephew of Paul Coffin, the minister of the Church of Christ in Buxton; his daughter Dorcas had married Royal Brewster in 1795.

In Brewster's time, Harvard-educated Congregational ministers like Reverend Coffin transmitted a vision of American society as a well-ordered patriarchal hierarchy. The Coffins' paired portraits reflect this gendered worldview. Women were subordinated legally to men, but they did hold power in the home, where they were responsible for the family's legacy through their role as mothers.

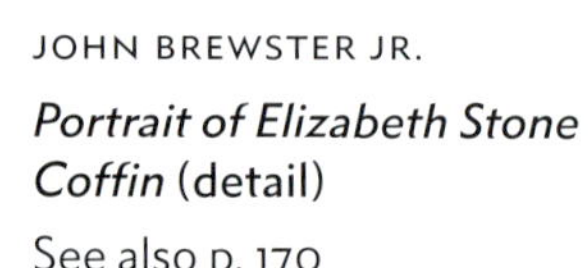

JOHN BREWSTER JR.

Portrait of Elizabeth Stone Coffin (detail)

See also p. 170

The two canvases lend equal size and visual importance to husband and wife, who are nonetheless differentiated by gender-specific attributes and gestures that reflect contemporary assumptions about their separate spheres (p. 170). The merchandise in David's portrait indicates his attainments in business; the prayer book and locket in Elizabeth's portrait, her role as guardian of morality and fount of affection. The deaf artist has translated his sensitivity to nuances of gesture and gaze—vital means of communication for him—into the language of paint with quiet eloquence. David's hand-in-waistcoat pose identifies him as a well-mannered gentleman;[3] the position of Elizabeth's hand resting on her belly suggests pregnancy. Both sitters regard the artist and viewer with calm solemnity.

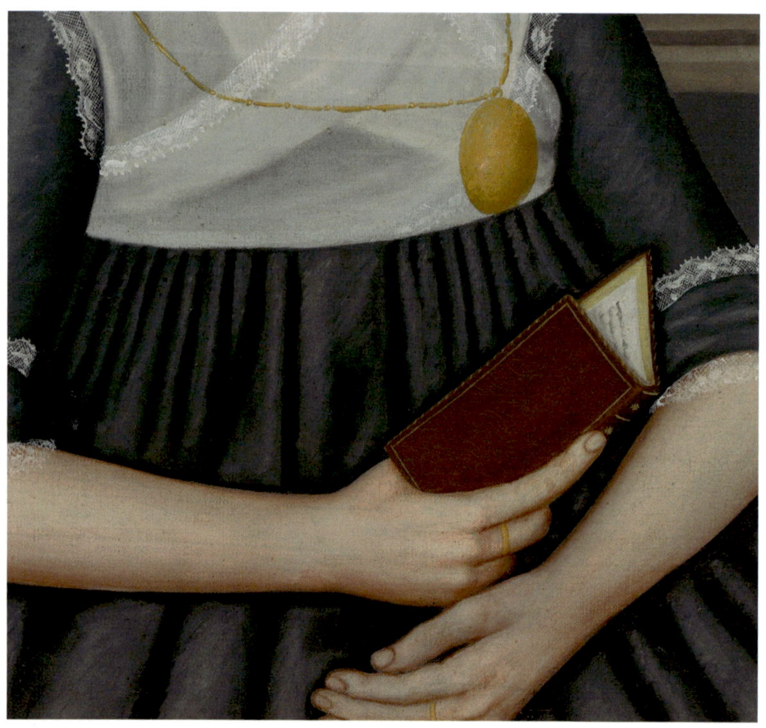

Before reliable contraception and modern medicine, a large family would have seemed inevitable, and well-founded fears of death in childbirth filled diaries and letters.[4] David Coffin had married Elizabeth Stone on February 9, 1786. Thirteen weeks later, their son Nathaniel was born. Premarital sex between engaged couples was common, revealing that the boundaries of conduct at the turn of the nineteenth century were not as narrow as we might believe.[5] By the time Elizabeth sat for Brewster's portrait, she was carrying her eighth baby. Ebenezer Stone Coffin, born on October 11, 1801, would grow up to become a shipmaster, inventor of improved steering wheels, and manufacturer of shipping materials. The couple ultimately had twelve children.[6] Two of them died in infancy: Richard Pike at age one, in 1793; John Stone, the day he was born, in 1807.[7] In Elizabeth's portrait, her fashionable dress conceals her condition because the popular high-waisted style was well suited to both pregnancy and breastfeeding. The voluminous fabric characteristic of the period accommodated her body as her belly grew; once the baby arrived, crisscrossed removable bibs at the bustline permitted breastfeeding.[8]

Whereas childbearing and child-rearing dominated Elizabeth's life, business dominated her husband's. In the portrait of David Coffin, Brewster's spare still life of horizontal and vertical bands of flat color reveal his ability to find beauty in abstractly arranged objects executed with an economy of detail. An entrepreneurial shipmaster, investor, and owner of approximately fifty ships, David Coffin stocked his store with merchandise from his own cargoes.[9] The decanter might have contained spirits from Coffin's Distillery. On the shelves above, the bolts of fabric resonate with the European and Caribbean textiles the sitter advertised, among them "Coloured Cotton Cambrick," "Blue Broadcloth," and "FRESH LINENS." Spools of "coloured Threads" punctuate the neutral environment. In Elizabeth's portrait, "White edgings" adorn her clothing.[10]

In addition to communicating her role as mother and his as entrepreneur, Brewster's props honor the Coffins' marital intimacy. Interpreted in the context of a long history of secret letters and lockets in literature and art, the letter David tantalizingly holds toward the viewer and the locket Elizabeth wears contain hidden secrets. David appears to have just broken the sealing wax, verifying that the letter has remained unopened until now. Is it from Elizabeth? Does it convey private feelings, or mere commercial information? The locket so decisively pinned over Elizabeth's heart and breast declares its centrality in her affections. At the time, lockets frequently enshrined portrait miniatures painted in watercolor on ivory. Brewster, who painted miniatures, might have made small images of David and Elizabeth at the same time he painted their larger likenesses. They would serve as surrogates while David was away at sea—not unlike the small portraits in the Fielding Collection of a sea captain and his wife (p. 174). Men often carried tiny framed portraits of their loved ones tucked in a vest pocket or as a pendant hidden under an intricately knotted cravat. Women publicly displayed on their bodies the family's wealth and affections in one

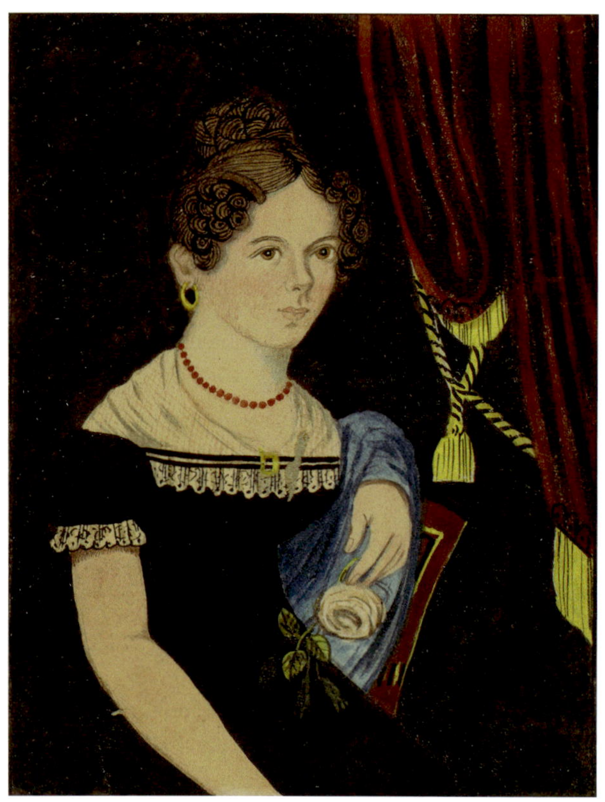
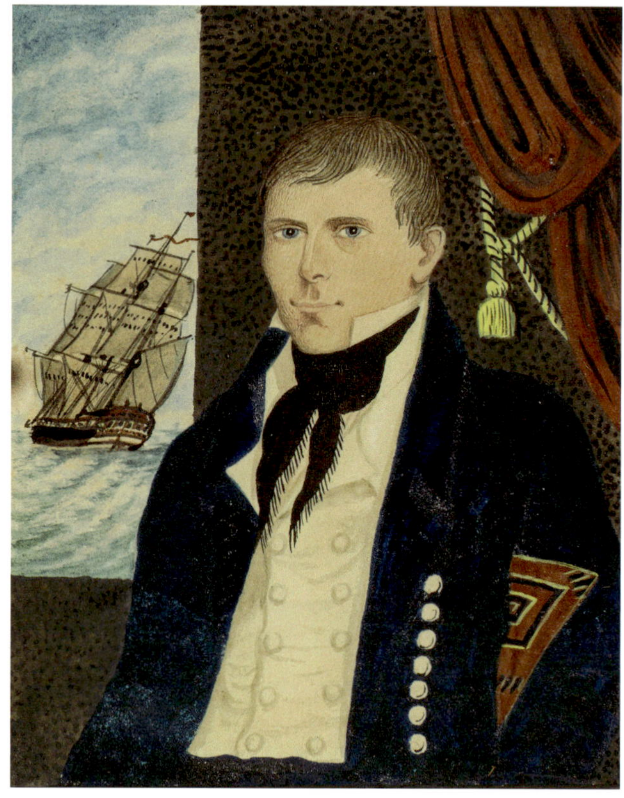

Portrait Miniatures of a Sea Captain and His Wife
Early nineteenth century
Watercolor on paper
Each: 5 × 3⅞ in.
L2015.41.142.1, .2

potent symbol, the miniature. In many eighteenth- and nineteenth-century oil paintings, the sitter excludes the viewer from her inner circle by showing only the portrait miniature's covering case, as Elizabeth does here. We yearn to be invited to hold the locket, but its size and placement demand that it be viewed and exchanged in a way that excludes us.[11]

The view over Elizabeth's shoulder also intrigues us by suggesting hidden meanings. Since the Renaissance, Western portraitists have frequently depicted sitters posed near large windows affording pleasurable prospects. Brewster not only continued this tradition in Elizabeth's portrait but also lavished exceptional attention on the enigmatic vista. He likely borrowed elements from actual structures and invented others. A devastating fire in Newburyport in 1811 hampers identification of buildings that had stood in 1801. Notwithstanding, Brewster's pleasing arrangement of large buildings speaks of prosperity—as do the densely packed white-clapboard buildings in a Newburyport townscape dated 1774 (opposite page). The tall spires, representing three churches, proclaim the town's piety.[12] In Elizabeth's portrait, a garden folly, crowned with a white spire, soars above the landscape, much like Newburyport's churches. Brewster visually links the church-like structure with the sitter through their shared pyramidal shape and palette: the terrace's alternating tiers echo the folds of her dress; the white circling fences, the white lace circling her sleeves; the white tower's translucent windows, her translucent white fichu. The visual association accords with the

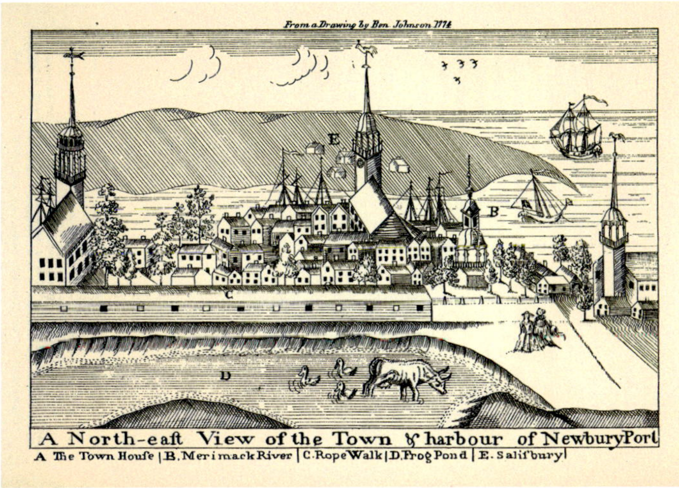

S. W. CHANDLER & BRO. LITHOGRAPHERS, BOSTON, AFTER A DRAWING BY BEN. JOHNSON

A North-east View of the Town & harbour of NewburyPort

1774

Reproduced in John J. Currier, *History of Newburyport*, vol. 1 (Newburyport, Mass: Published by the author, 1906), 80.

era's elevated view of mothers as guardians of spirituality in the domestic sphere.

During the early American republic, mothers were urged to sacrifice their own desires, comfort, and even health to ensure the growth and success of the new nation by bearing and raising many virtuous citizens.[13] Six years after Brewster painted the portraits of David and Elizabeth Coffin, their youngest child, Frances Boyd, arrived on Christmas Day in 1810. Only six weeks later, Elizabeth passed away after a "short illness." Mothers often suffered lingering complications in the weeks after giving birth. In harmony with Brewster's characterization, Elizabeth's obituary praised her "high veneration for religion: Influenced by its dictates, she has ever found duty and happiness in a diligent attention to the concerns of a beloved and numerous family; to promote their present and future happiness."[14] In the tumultuous years that followed, the sea claimed two sons: David drowned near Boston in 1815; Nathaniel died at Port-de-Paix, Haiti, in 1833. Daughter Sarah died in 1836.[15] Two years later, Major David Coffin died. His epitaph proclaims his faith: "Through all the changing scenes of life / In trouble and in joy: / The praises of my God shall still / My heart and tongue employ."[16]

"HATH ANY BEING ON EARTH, A CHARGE MORE FEARFULLY IMPORTANT, THAN THAT OF THE MOTHER?" JOSEPH H. DAVIS'S PORTRAIT OF A FAMILY

Much like Brewster's portraits of the Coffins, Joseph H. Davis's small watercolor depicting Charles and Comfort Caverly with their baby, Isaac, illuminates social assumptions about American family life over three decades later (p. 176). While Elizabeth Coffin protectively places her hand over her pregnant belly, Comfort Caverly holds her son tenderly, yet securely, in her lap. As opposed to showing husband and wife in separate drawings, in their distinct commercial and domestic domains, Davis unites the family members on a single sheet of paper, positioning them at home, seated around a table.

But the gender divisions persist. Charles reads the *Dover-Gazette* and—as the quill pens with inkwell and his notes on the paper attest—responds to the news, demonstrating engagement with the outside world nearly a century before women won the right to vote. His top hat rests on the table, suggesting that he has recently returned home. The family Bible and psalm book, placed in front of Comfort, define her spiritual role at home. Davis directs our attention to Isaac by outlining his profile in pencil and leaving the cream wove paper untouched to represent his pale skin illumined

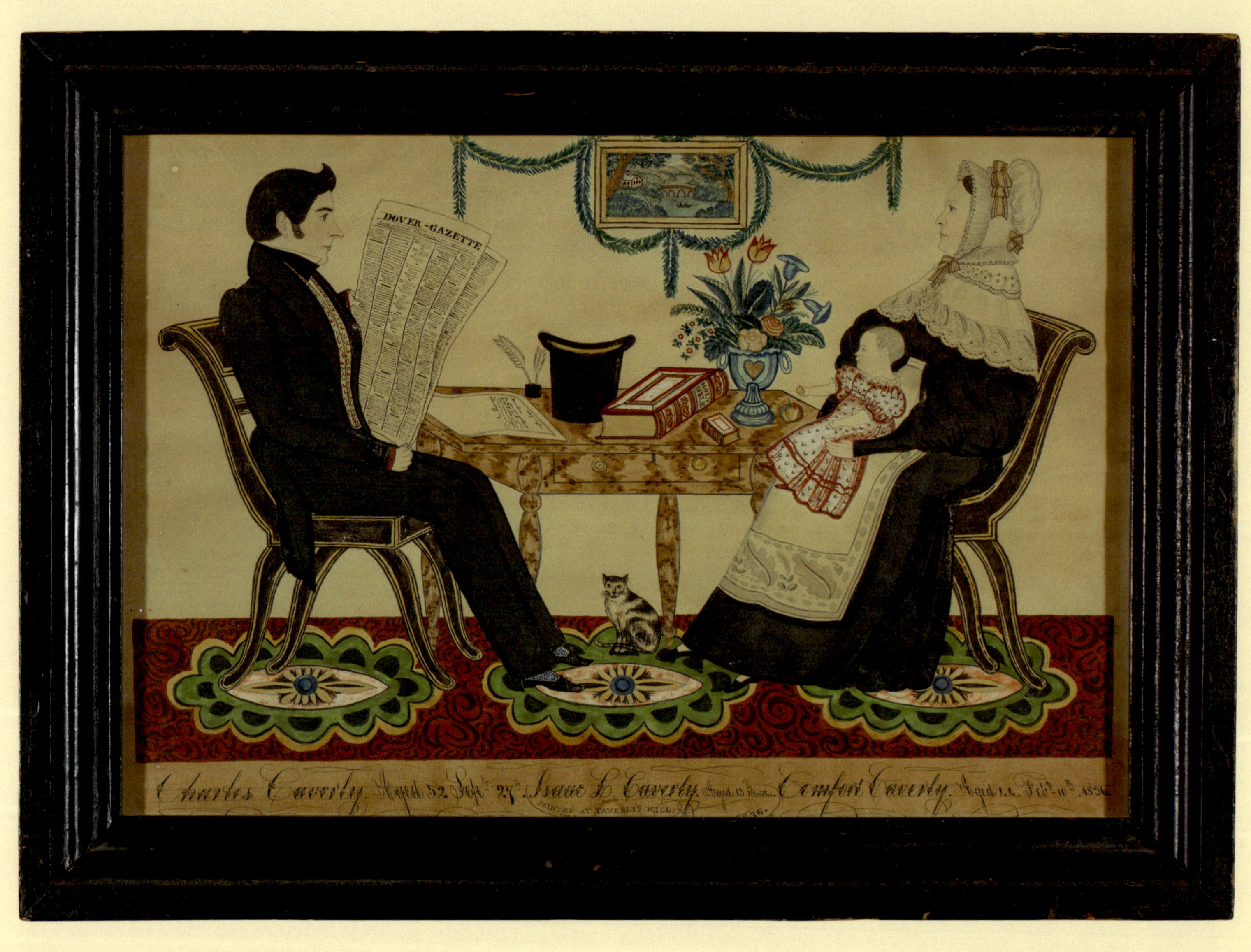
DOVER-GAZETTE
Charles Caverly
Isaac L. Caverly
Aged 13 Months.
Comfort Caverly
PAINTED AT CAVERLY'S MILL

JOSEPH H. DAVIS (1811–1865)

Family Portrait of Charles and Comfort Caverly and Their Son Isaac

Caverly's Hill, New Hampshire
1836

Watercolor, pen, and ink
Framed: 12½ × 17 in.

L2015.41.144

against his mother's dark dress. The nearby apple, a common emblem of fertility, and the baby on her lap celebrate motherhood.

As the nineteenth century advanced, mothers' duty to protect their children's bodies, characters, and souls—and by extension the nation itself—became codified as the "cult of domesticity," with its emphasis on piety and purity.[17] Social commentators like Catharine Beecher and Lydia Sigourney encouraged intense bonding within the nuclear family to link generations together through maternal love rather than patriarchal authority. In an increasingly commercial society, mother and child served as signs of stability and comfort—the name of the sitter—in contrast to the hostile world outside.

Here, Davis has used brilliant white outlined in red to illuminate the family Bible, psalm book, and Isaac's heart-festooned gown—visually associating the Word of God with the blessed child. Children were seen as being in an ideal state, free of sin, close to God, in stark opposition to the older doctrine of infant depravity based on Scripture. "But trailing clouds of glory do we come / From God, who is our home: / Heaven lies about us in our infancy!" popular poet William Wordsworth exclaimed.[18] The pervasive elevation of the mother-and-child bond found expression in paintings, prints, fiction, and poetry extolling maternal devotion. A proliferation of sermons and popular child-rearing magazines promoted the education of women in the belief that they should devote themselves with near-religious fervor to preserving the godliness of their children. By the 1830s, mother and child had ascended to the throne of domestic virtue. In *Letters to Mothers* of 1838, Sigourney preached: "You are sitting with your child in your arms. So am I.... Ah! How much have we to learn, that we may bring this beautiful and mysterious creature, to the light of knowledge, to the perfect bliss of immortality! Hath any being on earth, a charge more fearfully important, than that of the Mother?"[19]

Like David and Elizabeth Coffin decades earlier, Charles and Comfort Caverly still lived in an era when parents had reason to fear that their offspring might not live to adulthood. Similar to Elizabeth, Comfort was pregnant when she wed; her first child, Eliza Jane, was born on November 1, 1812. Sadly, Eliza died on March 3, 1826, at age thirteen and a half. Only "E. J." appears on her gravestone at Caverly Cemetery.[20] Conflicting historical records make it difficult to know for certain whether the couple had more daughters, with one source listing Lavinia D and no life dates, and another recording Eliza Jane (1834–1866).[21] Typically, the life dates of unmarried females are difficult to confirm, given the restrictions on their legal and economic rights. Comfort safely delivered four boys—Joseph, Leonard, Charles, and Cyrus—between 1815 and 1825. The youngest, Isaac, held on Comfort's lap in Davis's watercolor, was born a full decade after the couple lost their firstborn.

Davis's vignettes of family groups like the Caverlys, presented in profile, convey a generalized ideal of family life in the rural areas of New Hampshire and Maine that this itinerant artist roamed in the years 1832 to 1838. He often received commissions from members of the same extended family, including the Caverlys.[22] With a strong sense of flat pattern typical of non-academically trained artists, Davis painted watercolors that share similarities in the style and props of the interior scenes. He delineated his sitters' profiles in precise pencil and watercolor on paper. These profiles record a likeness without foreshortening or shading, making this format a preferred choice of many self-taught artists. The stiff poses suggest that Davis may have used the aid of a time-saving mechanical device that transferred the outline of a sitter onto a piece of paper to ensure a correct likeness.[23] Among the other distinguishing features of Davis's work are exuberantly colorful carpets, delight in costume details, elaborate calligraphic inscriptions below the image that provide details about the sitters, and props that articulate their roles as upstanding members of a community that shared the values communicated by the artist.

In the inscription below the Caverlys' portrait, Davis recorded each subject's name, date of birth, and age at the time the picture was completed: "Charles Caverly. Aged 52 Sep^{tr} 27th. Isaac L. Caverly. Aged 13 Months. Comfort Caverly. Aged 44. Feby 10th. 1836." Based in part on the exquisite calligraphy that the left-handed Davis used to embellish scenes like this, scholars have surmised that he probably was both an itinerant artist and a writing master who offered instruction when rural schooling was erratic.[24] Thus Davis, who was in his mid-twenties and had recently married in 1835, regularly interacted with families who had children and valued education.

In addition to expertly penned captions, Davis also frequently included pets in his watercolors. The Caverly family's whimsically delineated calico cat gazes up at its master. Popular picture books of the period often featured engravings of children playing with pets to teach boys and girls that these animals were "created by the same benevolent hand as humans."[25] Emphasis on the gentle training of pets echoed parents' gentle approach to child discipline, in comparison with earlier eras.

Hearts—ancient symbols of human emotions that attained their greatest popularity during the nineteenth century—adorn the vase of flowers, Charles's vest, and—as mentioned—baby Isaac's dress.[26] Wordsworth recollected a joyous childhood, marred by the loss of his mother when he was only eight, in poetry colored with hearts and flowers:

Thanks to the human heart by which we live,
Thanks to its tenderness, its joys, and fears,
To me the meanest flower that blows can give
Thoughts that do often lie too deep for tears.[27]

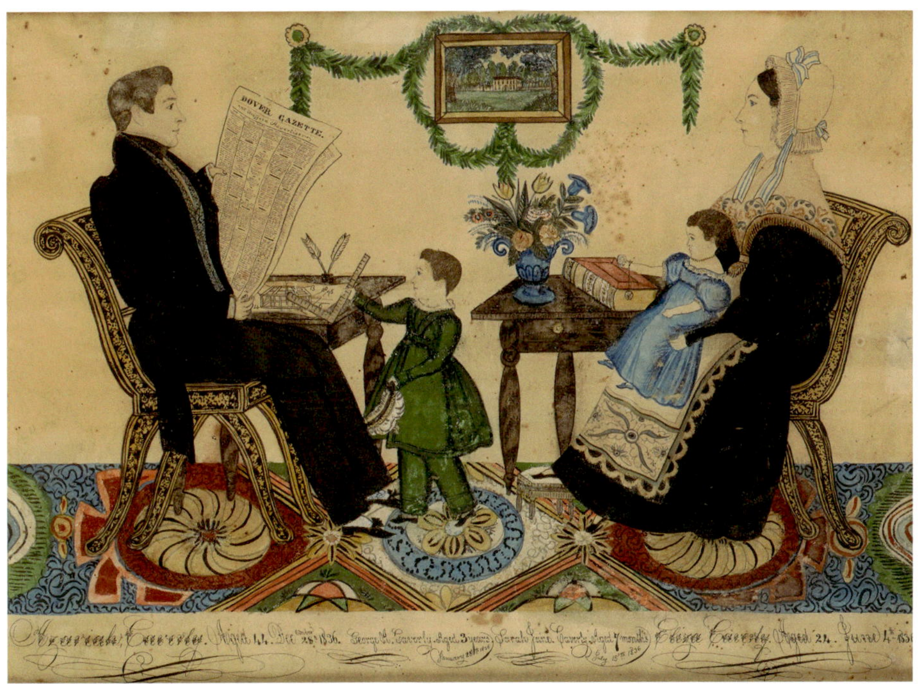

ATTRIBUTED TO JOSEPH H. DAVIS (1811–1865)

The Azariah Caverly Family

1836

Watercolor and pencil on paper

11 × 15 in.

FENIMORE ART MUSEUM, COOPERSTOWN, NEW YORK, JEAN AND HOWARD LIPMAN COLLECTION, GIFT OF STEPHEN C. CLARK., N0061.1961. PHOTOGRAPH BY RICHARD WALKER

Despite their stiff poses, Charles and Comfort are drawn together by slight smiles and gazes—and by Isaac's endearing gesture of reaching toward his father. As Wordsworth acknowledged, flowers, like those blooming in the Caverlys' heart-decorated vase, will fade—all the more reason to paint portraits celebrating the tenderness of the human heart.

As noted, Davis painted numerous members of the Caverly clan. In *The Azariah Caverly Family*, three-year-old George holds a carpenter's square in emulation of his father, Azariah, whose drawing identifies him as an architect, engineer, or carpenter; seven-month-old Sarah, held in her mother Eliza's arms, sits near the family Bible (above). Davis's props reflect a widespread perception of children as malleable instruments who could be encouraged to develop into adults with certain qualities, signified by prescribed attributes considered gender-appropriate.

In both Caverly family groupings, the children's engagement with their parents epitomizes the family structure that began to emerge in the late eighteenth century, when a less-authoritarian style of parenting joined new notions of the innocent nature of childhood. By the early nineteenth century, child-rearing manuals were published to guide parents—especially mothers—in fostering their young ones' development through play. Social commentators, instructors, and parents embraced the conviction of John Locke and other Enlightenment philosophers that children were inherently good, full of potential, and capable of learning through play and imitating parental behavior.[28] In Davis's family scenes, the children are celebrated within families stiffly posed yet linked by bonds of affection. The child's moral and religious coaching by mothers—and practical instruction by fathers for sons—was deemed vital in a nation that depended upon a public-spirited and entrepreneurial citizenry. The lessons learned at home provided the foundation not only for the children pictured here but also for a young democracy that was growing into a mature republic.

But the Civil War would ravage the nation. Isaac's brother Cyrus Caverly, who fought for the Union, was among the approximately 620,000 American soldiers killed in battle. Many others died of disease. Isaac—the baby held by his mother in Davis's watercolor—also died during the war, although the cause remains unknown.[29] After outliving their two young adult sons, Charles died on June 6, 1872, aged eighty-seven; Comfort on March 30, 1876, aged eighty-five.[30]

SAMUEL S. MILLER
(1807–1853)

Portrait of Cynthia Mary Osborn (1834–1841)

Cambridge, Massachusetts
After 1841

Oil on canvas
49 × 26⅝ in.

See also p. 186

L2015.41.170

"THE ROSE STILL IS FRAGRANT, THOUGH BROKE FROM THE STEM"
SAMUEL S. MILLER'S PORTRAIT OF A GIRL

In the mid-nineteenth century, American infants accounted for 17 percent of all deaths; children, more than 38 percent. These mortality rates had remained nearly unchanged since colonial times.[31] Notwithstanding, child-rearing by mothers was routinely touted as joyful. Physicians stressed nutrition, fresh air, and proper dress. Although helpful, such advice compounded parental guilt, for before modern medicine, even the most devoted care rarely saved a seriously ailing child. Many parents commissioned posthumous portraits to keep the semblance of their beloved, departed child present for family and friends, to preserve their memory beyond the lives of those who knew them, and to perpetuate family ties.[32]

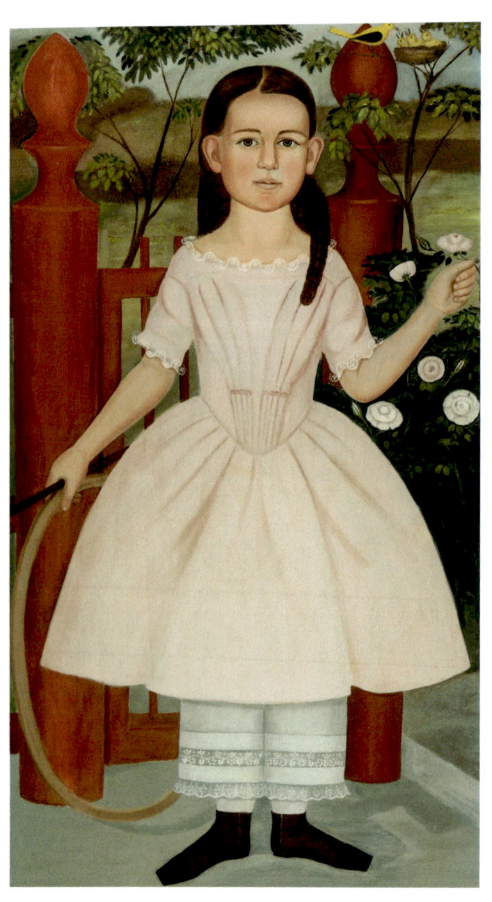

Seventeen portraits painted in the 1840s and 1850s, fourteen of them depicting children, can be attributed to Samuel S. Miller based on style. The artist preferred flat frontal figures standing in the foreground, with the feet pointing in opposite directions. Besides bold colors and attention to details in clothing, he included flowers and trees as Christian symbols of death, mourning, and resurrection. When such a portrait was displayed inside the home, friends and family seeing it hanging beside other family pictures knew that the child had died, lending the image its ineffable sadness.

Little is known about Miller's life or why he focused much of his practice on death. He was born in 1807 in Boston to Robert and Ann Wait Miller. His father passed away when Samuel was fourteen, and he appears to have been an only child—unusual at the time. Perhaps like so many of his era, he had experienced the deaths not only of his elders but also

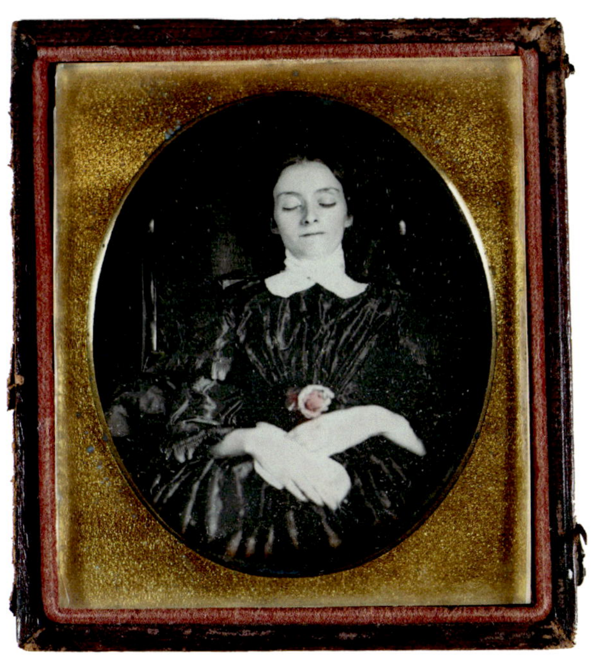

Young Woman with Rose
ca. 1844
Tinted sixth-plate daguerreotype

of siblings at a young age. The artist and his wife, Elvira Wait Miller, lived in Charlestown, Massachusetts, where their son Samuel was born in 1850 and their daughter Elvira Anna two years later. The artist would die of heart disease in 1853; his wife, Elvira, the following year of consumption, leaving behind their two young children.[33]

Among Miller's most poetic posthumous portraits is *Cynthia Mary Osborn* (opposite page). Based on city death records, the subject is probably the Cynthia M. Osborn who died on April 27, 1841, in Cambridge, Massachusetts, at approximately six to eight years of age. Other family members passed away in June and July.[34] The cluster suggests that a contagious illness claimed their lives. Illustrated narratives of the time attempted to address children's intimate experience of disease and death by promising young readers a reunion with their families, especially their mothers, in a domesticated heaven.[35] Such promises might have comforted Cynthia before her death. Her loss would have devastated both parents. But the mother likely ministered to her child throughout the sickness and prepared the small body for burial.

Miller's posthumous portrait of Cynthia partially granted to the bereaved their most fervent wish by picturing the dead as a living presence in tangible form. To conjure her person, Miller could have painted her likeness directly from the corpse, based it on verbal descriptions, or modeled it after a recently painted portrait or—given that she died soon after the invention of photography—a daguerreotype. Her evenly illuminated, delicately painted, expressionless face possesses an otherworldly quality. Not convincingly situated in space, Cynthia stands in the foreground of the canvas, close to the viewer, on a pathway before a gate—an emblematic passage from the land of the living to the hereafter. The scene resonates with funerary references.

Cynthia wears a pale pink gathered dress over pantaloons shirred and embellished with lace with inset bands of flowers. She resembles the rose of innocence that she plucks from a rosebush. The setting evokes the rural cemetery movement that arose in response to a growing sentimentality about death. Cynthia died in Cambridge, Massachusetts, where in 1831 the first garden cemetery, Mount Auburn, had opened. There mourners communed with regenerative nature—like the rosebush in Miller's portrait. Roses also enhance postmortem photography, which offered an inexpensive alternative to the painted portrait as a tangible memento. In a daguerreotype taken around the time of Cynthia's death, a seemingly sleeping woman likewise holds a hand-tinted, pale pink rose (above).[36]

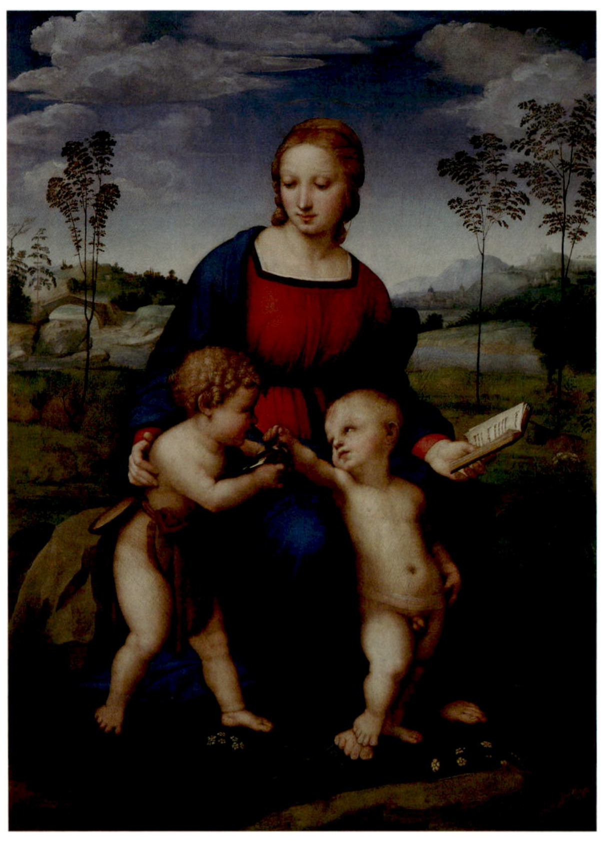

RAPHAEL (1483–1520)
Madonna of the Goldfinch
1505–6
Oil on panel
42 × 30¼ in.
UFFIZI GALLERY

Roses appear in many examples of mourning poetry found in popular magazines in nineteenth-century America. The compilation *Our Little Ones in Heaven*, published at midcentury in Boston, opens with a declaration by the Protestant Church of its belief in the salvation and eventual resurrection of deceased children. Throughout, as in Cynthia's portrait, roses are common emblems of the transience of life. The poem "O Mourn Not, Fond Mother" offers consolation in harmony with Miller's imagery:

The plant that you reared to smile on earth's gloom,
Has fastened its roots in the soil of the tomb;
It smiled in your garden, so bright and so fair,
It has climbed o'er the wall, and is blossoming there. . . .
The rose still is fragrant, though broke from the stem,
The setting is ruined, but safe is the gem.

Then gird thee to labor, to trial and love,
The treasure once thine shall await thee above;
Be faithful, be earnest, night soon will be riven,
And the lost ones of earth, be thy jewels in heaven.[37]

The dead will live again. Miller's painting expresses the triumph of love and faith over life's most formidable foe.

If roses suggested the transience of life, then the goldfinch—which Miller positions at the closest elevation to the sky, or heaven, in his scene—symbolized the new life promised by "O Mourn Not, Fond Mother." In Christian theology, the bird alludes to the Resurrection of Christ. In the context of nineteenth-century America, specifically, its use by the artist may also reflect the evangelical Great Awakenings that swept the nation, reinvigorating belief in Christ's Resurrection—and in the conviction that the saved would come back from the dead, with their bodies intact. The goldfinch frequently appears in Renaissance paintings (above), reproduced in prints, of the Christ Child playing with the bird. In Renaissance times, and still in the nineteenth century, birds were popular pets for children. Thus, the goldfinch not only emphasized Christ's divinity but also humanized him by alluding to his childhood.[38]

Cynthia is likewise shown playing as she waits for her family in a semi-enclosed garden—a domesticated heaven where she is forever entertained by a hoop. A favorite outdoor activity of children for centuries, hoops were frequently included in illustrations of children's games in the late eighteenth and nineteenth centuries—with boys usually shown racing hoops, while girls posed beside them, as Cynthia does. New England toymakers and woodenware factories made wooden hoops. Cynthia would have propelled hers by stroking it along the top with her stick. While the pastime could be solitary, children also held contests for both the fastest and the longest hoop rollers. Another competitive game pitted one player rolling a hoop in a straight line along the ground against others trying to slip their sticks through the hoop as it passed them without knocking it down.[39] In the context of this memorial portrait, the hoop's circular shape—without beginning or end—signifies eternal life.

By 1900 American women had half as many children as they did in 1800, and those children were twice as likely to live through infancy as they were in 1850, thanks to advancements in medicine. But even today, parents worry about protecting their children. As we look back upon the history of parenthood and childhood—expressed in a language beyond words in these portraits—we wonder at how much, or how little, family life has changed.

Robin Jaffee Frank is the Director of the Silvermine Arts Center in New Canaan, Connecticut, and Vice Chair of the Board. She also is an independent museum curator, having formerly served as Chief Curator at the Wadsworth Atheneum Museum of Art and Senior Associate Curator of American Paintings and Sculpture at the Yale University Art Gallery. She has organized numerous exhibitions throughout the United States, lectured extensively, and published widely on American visual culture from the colonial through contemporary periods. Dr. Frank holds a PhD in the history of art from Yale University.

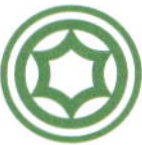 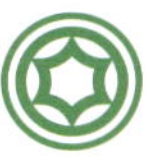 

NOTES

For research assistance at The Huntington, I warmly thank Elee Wood, former Curator/Educator, Fielding Collection for Early American Art, and Lily Allen, Curatorial Assistant in American Art.

1 Huntington Art Museum, object file for L2015.41.164. See Jeanne-Marie Zebrowski, "Just Plain Folk," *Maine Antique Digest*, January 1981, 22A; Marguerite Riordan, advertisement, *The Magazine Antiques*, November 1992, 626–27; *The Collection of Susan and Mark Laracy: Distinguished American Furniture and Folk Art* (New York: Sotheby's, 2007), lot 174. In the lot description, Paul S. D'Ambrosio identifies the sitters and dates the portraits to June 1801: "These portraits are the earliest documented portraits of Brewster's extended 1801 sojourn in Newburyport, which suggests that the Coffins played a role in bringing the artist to the town. Brewster's nine documented 1801 Newburyport portraits include: this pair, executed in June; portraits of Captain and Mrs. William Wise, painted in August, and five well-known portraits of the James Prince family painted in November." The

portraits of Captain and Mrs. William Wise are in a private collection; *James Prince and Son William Henry*, *James Prince, Jr.*, and *Benjamin Prince* are in the collection of the Historical Society of Old Newbury. *Portrait of Sarah Prince* (also known as *Silver Moon* or *Girl at the Pianoforte*) is in the collection of the Yale University Art Gallery, New Haven, Conn. It must be noted, however, that two William Jennys portraits from 1807 that are allegedly of Major David Coffin and Elizabeth Stone Coffin, now in the collection of the Smith College Museum of Art (SC 1995:2-1 and 1995:2-2), do not resemble the couple portrayed by Brewster, now in the Fielding Collection.

2 On Brewster, see especially Nina Fletcher Little, *John Brewster, Jr., 1766–1854: Deaf-Mute Painter of Connecticut and Maine* (Hartford, Conn.: Connecticut Historical Society, 1960); Harlan Lane, *A Deaf Artist in Early America: The Worlds of John Brewster, Jr.* (Boston: Beacon Press, 2004); and Paul S. D'Ambrosio, *The World of John Brewster, Jr., 1766–1854*, exh. cat. (Cooperstown, N.Y.: Fenimore Art Museum, 2006).

3 Arline Meyer, "Re-dressing Classical Statuary: The Eighteenth-Century Hand-in-Waistcoat Portrait," *Art Bulletin* 77 (March 1995): 45–63.

4 On childbirth anxieties expressed in letters and diaries, see Elisabeth Donaghy Garrett, *At Home: The American Family 1750–1870* (New York: Abrams, 1989), 227–31.

5 For premarital pregnancy rates in New England, see Gloria L. Main, "Rocking the Cradle: Downsizing the New England Family," *Journal of Interdisciplinary History* 37, no. 1 (Summer 2006): 35–58, esp. 45, fig. 5.

6 Some sources state either ten or eleven children; however, an examination of various records reveals that David and Elizabeth had twelve children, including two sons, Richard Pike and John Stone, who did not live to adulthood: Nathaniel (1787–1833), David (1788–1815), Mary (1790–1864), Richard Pike (1792–1793), Richard Pike or Richard Pitt (1794–1844), George (1797–1865), Isaac Stone (1798–1855), Ebenezer Stone (1801–1870), Elizabeth (1803–1858), Sarah Miller (1805–1836), John Stone (1807–1807), and Frances Boyd (1810–1881). The following genealogical sources were consulted: W. S. Appleton, *Coffin Gatherings: Five Generations of Descendants of Tristram Coffin of Newbury and Nantucket* (Boston: David Clapp and Son, 1896), 34; Louis Coffin, *The Coffin Family*, introduction by Will Gardner (1884; reprint, Nantucket, Mass.: Nantucket Historical Association, 1962), 155; Massachusetts Vital Records, 1620–1988, Ancestry.com; Massachusetts, Town and Vital Records, 1620–1988, Ancestry.com; Massachusetts, Marriage Records, 1840–1915, Ancestry.com; Massachusetts Death Records, 1841–1915, Ancestry.com; North America, Family Histories, 1500–2000, Ancestry.com; New England Historic Genealogical Society, Boston; FindaGrave.com, https://www.findagrave.com/memorial/, database and images: "Maj David Coffin," 101757406; "Richard Pitt Coffin," 101757407; "Richard Pike Coffin," 85727348; "Sarah Coffin *Miller* Stevens," 101758763; "Ancestors of ACB [Anna Coffin Benedict]," http://rgm3.net, entry 56; *Town and Vital Records of Newbury, Essex, Massachusetts to the Year 1849* (Salem, Mass.: Essex Institute, 1911).

7 Richard Pike's life dates are July 1, 1792–October 24, 1793. See previous note.

8 On the connection between the high-waisted style and maternity, see Linda Baumgarten, *What Clothes Reveal: The Language of Clothing in Colonial and Federal America* (Williamsburg, Va., and New Haven, Conn.: Colonial Williamsburg Foundation in association with Yale University Press, 2002), 152; and Elizabeth Mankin Kornhauser, *Ralph Earl: The Face of the Young Republic*, exh. cat. (Hartford and New Haven, Conn.: Wadsworth Atheneum and Yale University Press, 1991), 220. On removable bibs, see Ann Buermann Wass and Michelle Webb Fandrich, *Clothing through American History: The Federal Era through Antebellum, 1786–1860* (Santa Barbara, Calif.: Greenwood, 2010), 108.

9 Frances Geisewite Reiland, *Footprints in History: Bradstreet, Brocklebank, Coffin, Dudley, Greenleaf, Johnson, Pierce, and Richardson Families in America* (Newburyport, Mass.: Museum of Old Newbury, 2015), 74–77. For this reference, and for responding to my numerous inquiries and generously sharing research on the history of the Coffin family and Newburyport, I am enormously grateful to the Newburyport Public Library Archival Center. I especially and warmly thank Sharon Spieldenner, senior librarian/archivist, as well as Dana Echelberger, staff librarian/assistant archivist, and their research volunteers: Linda Tulley, Bob Richard, Carrie Poirier, and Sue Connell. I also thank Susan Edwards, executive director, and Emily Lawrence, assistant director, Museum of Old Newbury.

10 For the distillery, see *Newburyport Herald and Country Gazette*, April 18, 1800, 4; for other goods, see September 27, 1799; April 8, 11, 15, and 25, 1800; May 16, 1800; and May 7, 1802.

11 On full-scale portraits of women wearing miniatures, see Robin Jaffee Frank, *Love and Loss: American Portrait and Mourning Miniatures*, exh. cat. (New Haven, Conn.: Yale University Art Gallery in association with Yale University Press, 2000), 21–35.

12 At left is the North Church, Central Congregational, with the fish weather vane and three-pronged trident, on Titcomb Street; in the middle, the Religious Society, rebuilt on Pleasant Street in 1801; at right, the Old South Church, First Presbyterian, with a weathercock. Identifications courtesy of Sharon Spieldenner, Newburyport Public Library Archival Center.

13 On "republican motherhood," see Linda K. Kerber, "The Republican Mother: Women and the Enlightenment—An American Perspective," in *Toward an Intellectual History of Women: Essays by Linda K. Kerber* (Chapel Hill: University of North Carolina Press, 1997), 41–62.

14 Elizabeth died on February 6, 1811; *Newport Herald*, February 8, 1811, 3. My thanks to Elee Wood.

15 Reiland, *Footprints in History*, 74–77; Coffin, *Coffin Family*, 155; "Ancestors of ACB," entry 56; "Sarah Coffin

Miller Stevens," FindaGrave.com, https://www.findagrave.com/memorial/101758763/sarah-coffin-stevens.

16 Reiland, *Footprints in History*, 74–77; Coffin, *Coffin Family*, 155; "Ancestors of ACB," entry 56; "Maj David Coffin," FindaGrave.com, https://www.findagrave.com/memorial/101757406/david-coffin.

17 Barbara Welter, "The Cult of True Womanhood: 1820–1860," *American Quarterly* 18, no. 2, pt. 1 (1966): 151–74.

18 William Wordsworth, "Ode: Intimations of Immortality from Recollections of Early Childhood," in *The Complete Poetical Works of William Wordsworth*, ed. A. J. George (Boston: Houghton Mifflin, 1904), 354, https://catalog.hathitrust.org/Record/001428231; first published in *Poems, in Two Volumes* in 1807.

19 Lydia Howard Sigourney, *Letters to Mothers* (Hartford, Conn.: Hudson and Skinner, 1838), vii, viii.

20 "Eliza Jane 'Ej' Caverly," FindaGrave.com, https://www.findagrave.com/memorial/162572627/eliza-jane-caverly.

21 Robert B. Caverly, *Genealogy of the Caverly Family, from the Year 1116 to the Year 1880, Made Profitable and Exemplified by Many a Lesson of Life* (Lowell, Mass.: George M. Elliott, 1880), 61, New Hampshire Historical Society; and Ancestry.com, which includes dates for Eliza Jane but does not record Lavinia. Life dates gleaned from both sources.

22 See Esther Sparks, "Joseph H. Davis," in *American Folk Painters of Three Centuries*, ed. Jean Lipman and Tom Armstrong, exh. cat. (New York: Hudson Hills Press, 1980), 66–69; and Arthur and Sybil Kern, "Joseph H. Davis: Identity Established," *The Clarion*, Summer 1989, 46–65, https://issuu.com/american_folk_art_museum/docs/clarion_14_3_sum1989. Also see Robin Jaffee Frank, "Portraits of Children," in *Expressions of Innocence and Eloquence: Selections from the Jane Katcher Collection of Americana*, vol. 1, ed. Jane Katcher, David A. Schorsch, and Ruth Wolfe (Yale University Press in association with Marquand Books, 2006), 104–21.

23 See Peter Benes, "Machine-Assisted Portrait and Profile Imaging in New England after 1803," in *Painting and Portrait Making in the American Northeast*, ed. Benes (Boston: Boston University, 1995), 118–50.

24 See Sparks, "Joseph H. Davis," 66–69.

25 Laura Wasowicz, "The Child's Picture Gallery: Picture Books from Nineteenth-Century Massachusetts," in *The Worlds of Children, 1620–1920*, ed. Peter Benes (Boston: Boston University, 2004), esp. 151.

26 See Robert Shaw, "United as This Heart You See: Memories of Friendship and Family," in Katcher, Schorsch, and Wolfe, *Expressions of Innocence and Eloquence*, 84–101. Shaw quotes Wordsworth's poem.

27 Wordsworth, "Ode: Intimations of Immortality," 356.

28 On family history, see Philippe Ariès, *Centuries of Childhood: A Social History of Family Life*, trans. Robert Baldick (New York: Vintage, 1962); Carl N. Degler, *At Odds: Women and the Family in America from the Revolution to the Present* (New York: Oxford University Press, 1980); and Lawrence Stone, *The Family, Sex and Marriage in England, 1500–1800* (New York: Harper and Row, 1983).

29 K. Torp and B. Ziegenmeyer, "New Hampshire Civil War Soldiers," genealogytrails.com/newham/civilwarsoldiers_c.html.

30 Torp and Ziegenmeyer, "New Hampshire Civil War Soldiers." See also Caverly, *Genealogy of the Caverly Family*, 61.

31 Catherine M. Scholten, *Childbearing in American Society, 1650–1850* (New York: New York University Press, 1985), 10–11, 70–71; Sally G. McMillen, *Motherhood in the Old South: Pregnancy, Childbirth, and Infant Rearing* (Baton Rouge, La.: Louisiana State University Press, 1997), 164–67, tables III, V, VI, VII, VII. Regarding mortality statistics, Scholten states that "mortality rates for children under age ten approached 50 percent" in the colonial era (p. 11); the physician who in 1844 appended a supplementary chapter to the first American edition of Louisa Barwell's *Infant Treatment* confronted infant mortality statistics very similar to those Benjamin Franklin had observed a century earlier (p. 71).

32 For a thoughtful discussion, see Stacy C. Hollander, *Securing the Shadow: Posthumous Portraiture in America*, exh. cat. (New York: American Folk Art Museum, 2016), esp. 138–39 on Miller. Also see Phoebe Lloyd, "Posthumous Mourning Portraiture," in *A Time to Mourn: Expressions of Grief in Nineteenth Century America*, ed. Martha V. Pike and Janice Gray Armstrong, exh. cat. (Stony Brook, N.Y.: Museums at Stony Brook, 1980), 71–89; Robin Jaffee Frank, "Small Portraits to 'Cheer the Lonely Heart,'" in *Expressions of Innocence and Eloquence: Selections from the Jane Katcher Collection of Americana*, vol. 2, ed. Jane Katcher, David A. Schorsch, and Ruth Wolfe (Yale University Press in association with Marquand Books, 2011), 46–59.

33 Massachusetts, Town and Vital Records, 1620–1988, Ancestry.com.

34 Edward, aged thirty-four, in June; Eliza, aged nine, in July; see Massachusetts, Town and Vital Records.

35 On children's deathbed literature, see Jacqueline S. Renier, *From Virtue to Character: American Childhood, 1775–1850* (New York: Twayne, 1996), 90–95.

36 Stanley B. Burns, MD, "Postmortem Daguerreotypes: The Burns Family Collection," in Hollander, *Securing the Shadow*, 193, 220–21.

37 Rev. F. S. Smith, "O Mourn Not, Fond Mother," in Walter Aimwell, *Our Little Ones in Heaven* (Boston: Gould and Lincoln, 1870), 133.

38 Herbert Friedmann, *The Symbolic Goldfinch: Its History and Significance in European Devotional Art* (Washington, D.C.: Pantheon Books, 1946); Philip Johnson, "Goldfinch: Symbol for Resurrection," blog post, https://animalsmattertogod.com/2012/06/03/goldfinch-symbol-for-resurrection/.

39 "Antique Toys: Rolling Hoop," *Victoriana*, http://www.victoriana.com/antiquetoys/rollinghoop.html.

SAMUEL S. MILLER
(1807–1853)

Portrait of Cynthia Mary Osborn (1834–1841)

Cambridge, Massachusetts
After 1841

Oil on canvas
49 × 26⅝ in.

L2015.41.170

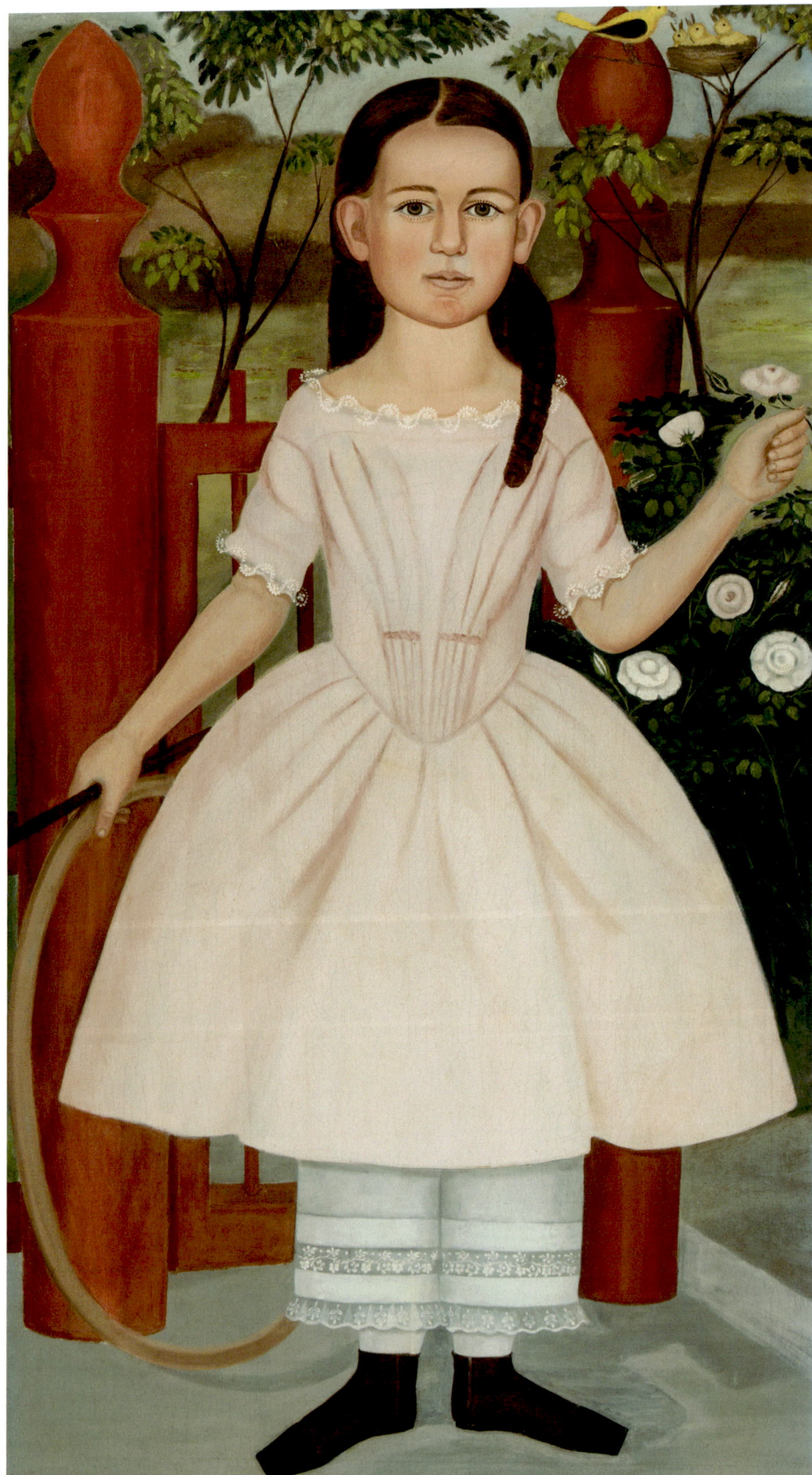

EDWIN PLUMMER
(CA. 1802–1880)

Four Portraits of Children

Massachusetts
Mid-nineteenth century

Watercolor and gouache on paper
Framed: 13 × 10½ in.

L2015.41.143

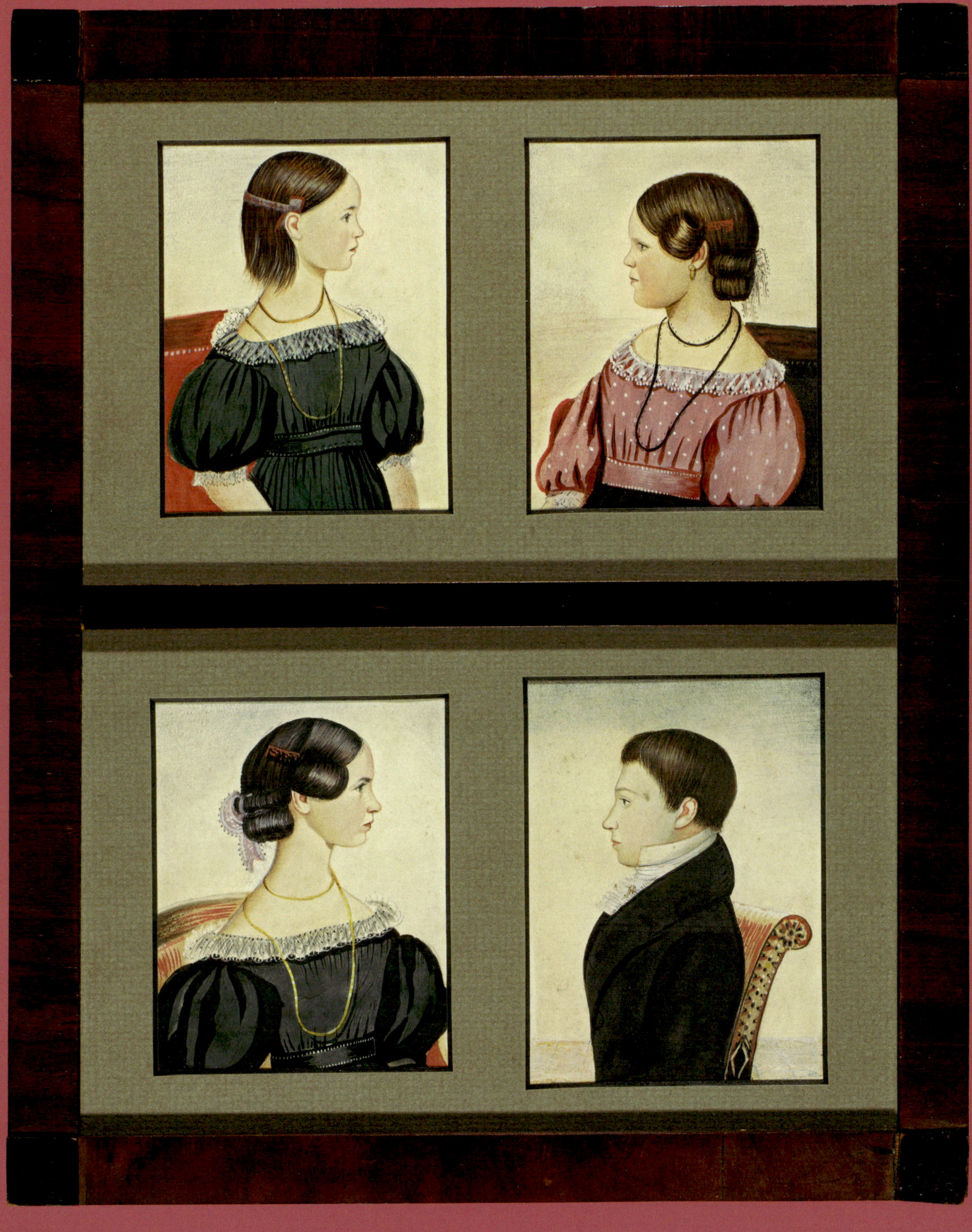

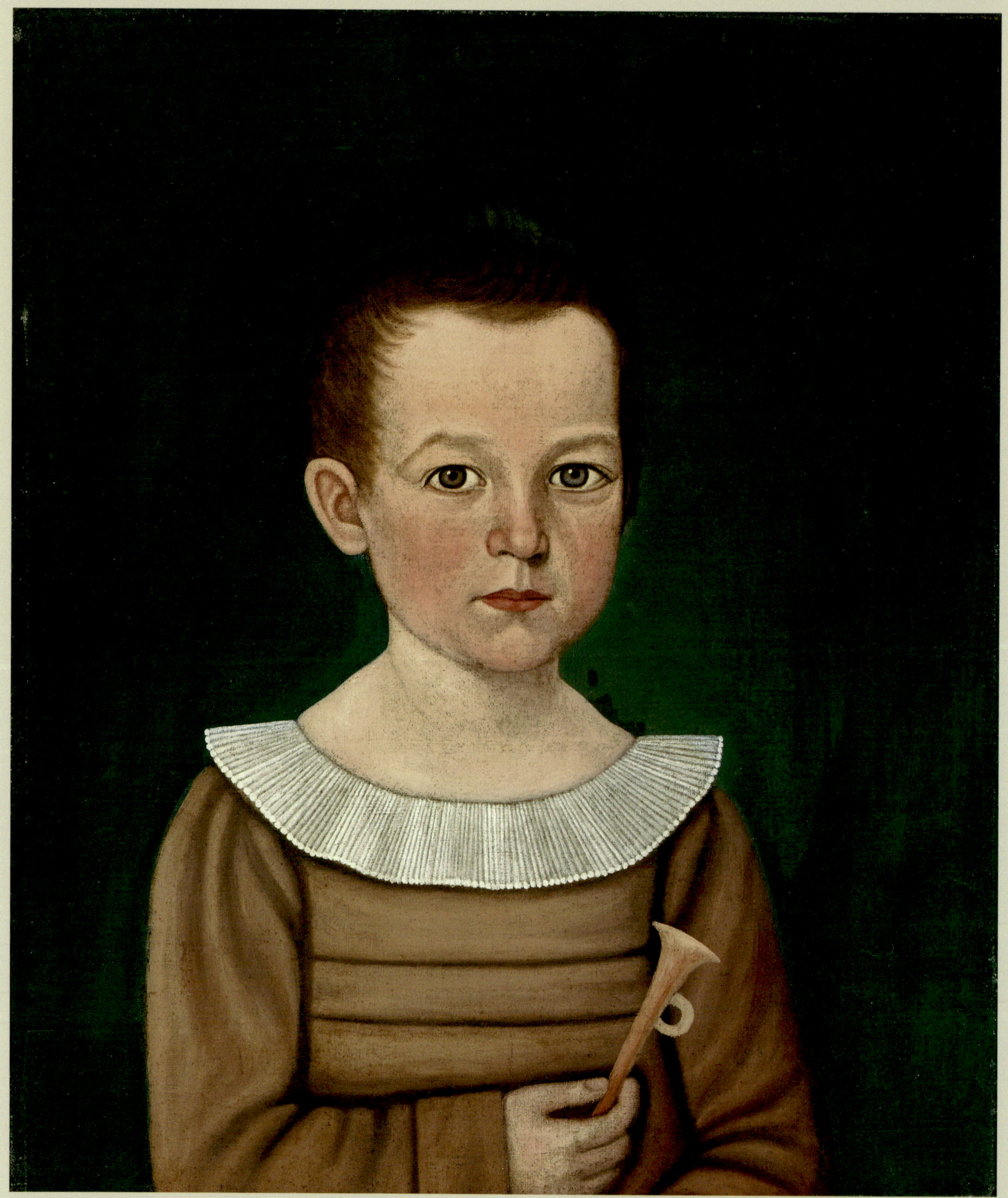

PERIPATETIC

A successful itinerant portrait painter, John Brewster Jr. was also deaf and mute. Brewster studied art under Reverend John Steward and pursued a successful career, traveling throughout New England. In 1820, he moved to Hartford to enroll for three years at the recently founded American School for the Deaf, where, in his fifties, he finally learned formalized sign language. Brewster completed the portrait of Henry Sayward (opposite page) of Alfred, Maine, after leaving the school. Distracted by his toy horn long enough to sit still, the boy has lively eyes and rosy cheeks, suggesting a picture of health—not to be taken for granted in a period with high rates of child mortality. In fact, Henry lived a long life, passing away in 1901 after a career as an express-man, a courier for shipments of gold and hard cash.

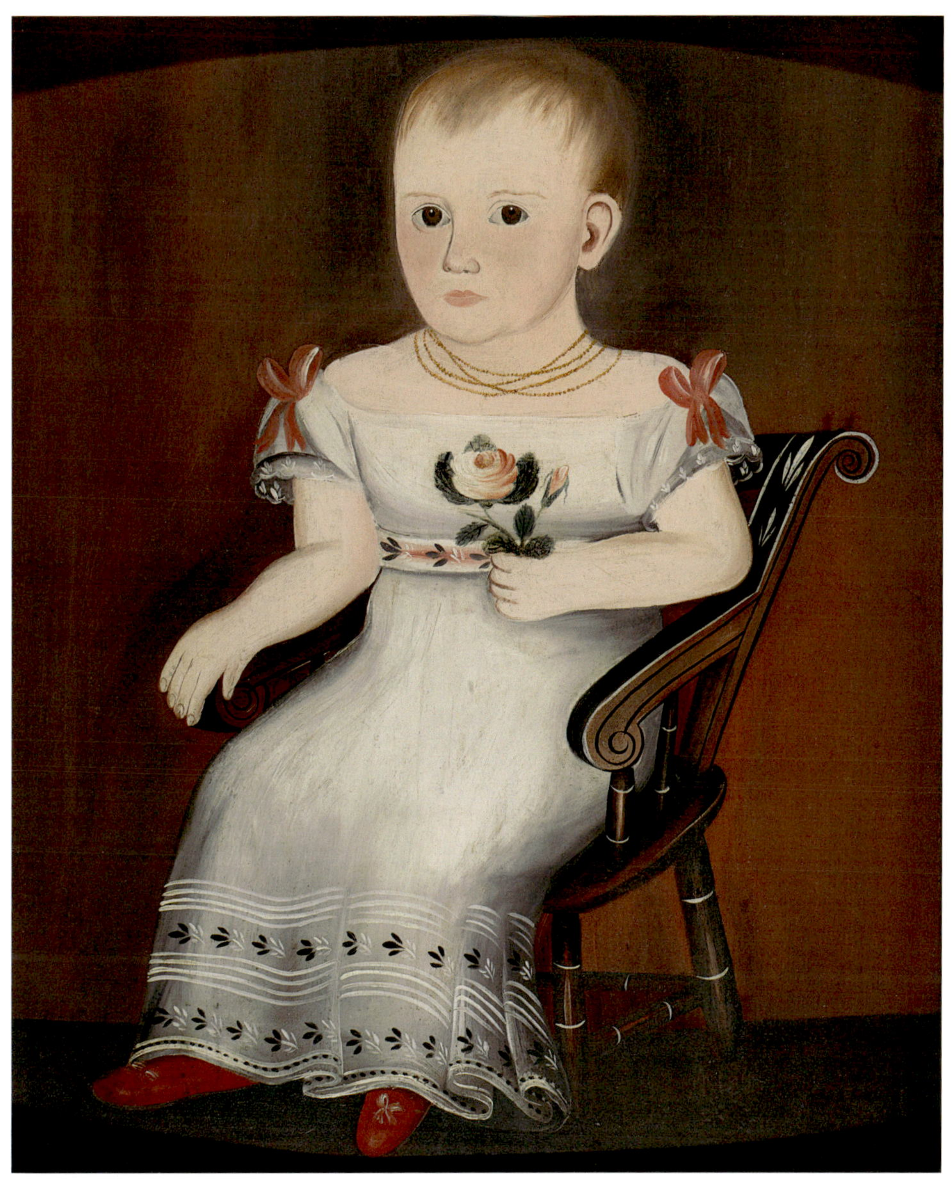

JOHN BREWSTER JR. (1766–1854)

Portrait of Henry Sayward

York County, Maine
1820

Oil on canvas
20 × 16½ in.

L2015.41.167

ATTRIBUTED TO SHELDON PECK (1797–1868)

Little Girl in a Windsor Armchair

ca. 1827–32

Oil on panel
23 × 18½ in.

L2015.41.169

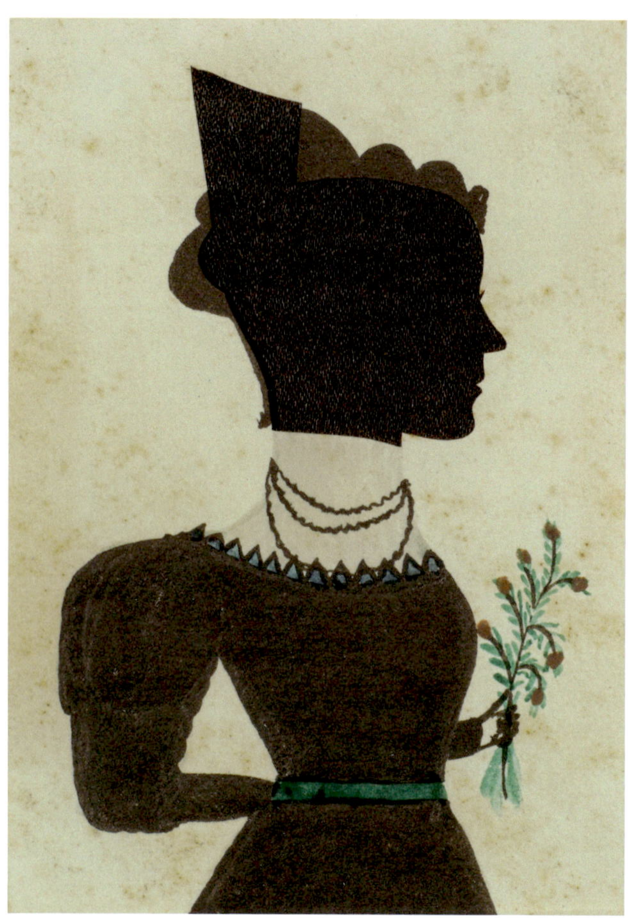

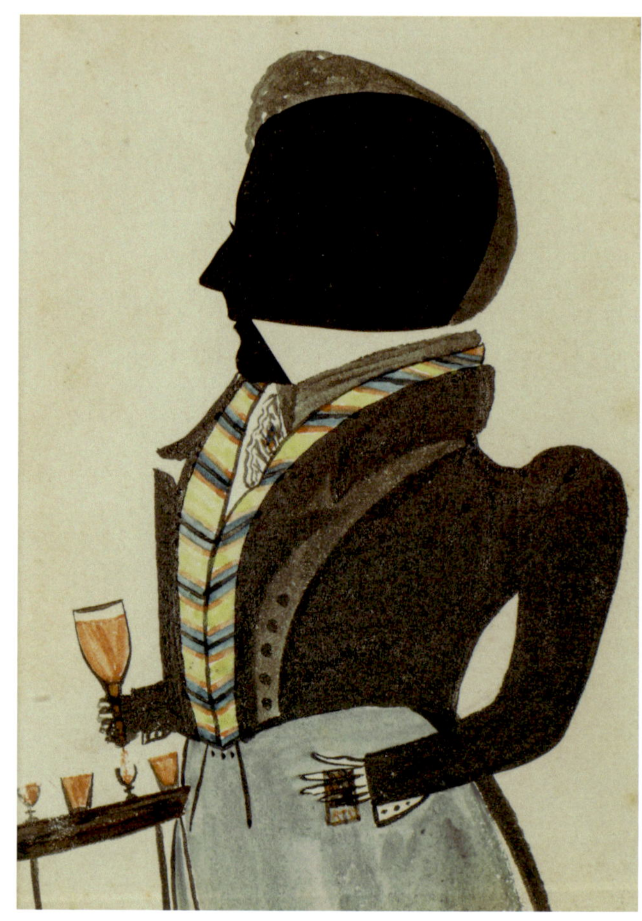

MINIATURISTS

Before the invention of photography in 1839, silhouettes and miniature portraits were a more affordable, though by no means inexpensive, way to memorialize someone. In Boston, William M. S. Doyle set up a shop, while itinerant silhouettists traveled the country advertising in local papers. The term *silhouette* only came into use gradually, and Americans called such a work a "shadow portrait," "shade," "shadow graph," or, simply, "likeness." The portrait pair of Samuel and Elvira Fish could have been a wedding portrait. Both are dressed formally, and Samuel holds a glass with wine or rum, while a row of glasses points to a festive occasion.

On the following spread, the portraits of Hannah and Stephan Spear were also probably made for their wedding and were formerly attributed to an artist known as Mr. Boyd. They are more likely by Jasper P. Miles, an artist and sign painter active in northern Pennsylvania, New York's Finger Lakes, and later, northern Ohio. Miles is known to have painted on wood, used a neutral gray background, and captured likenesses with delicate brushwork.

POSSIBLY EZRA WOOD (1798–1841), "PUFFY SLEEVE ARTIST"

Portraits of Samuel and Elvira Fish

ca. 1810

Watercolor and ink on paper
Each: 3½ × 2⅞ in.

Inscription (verso): "Samuel / Mrs. Elvira Fish / (Gov. Wentworth Family—N.H.)"

L2015.41.148

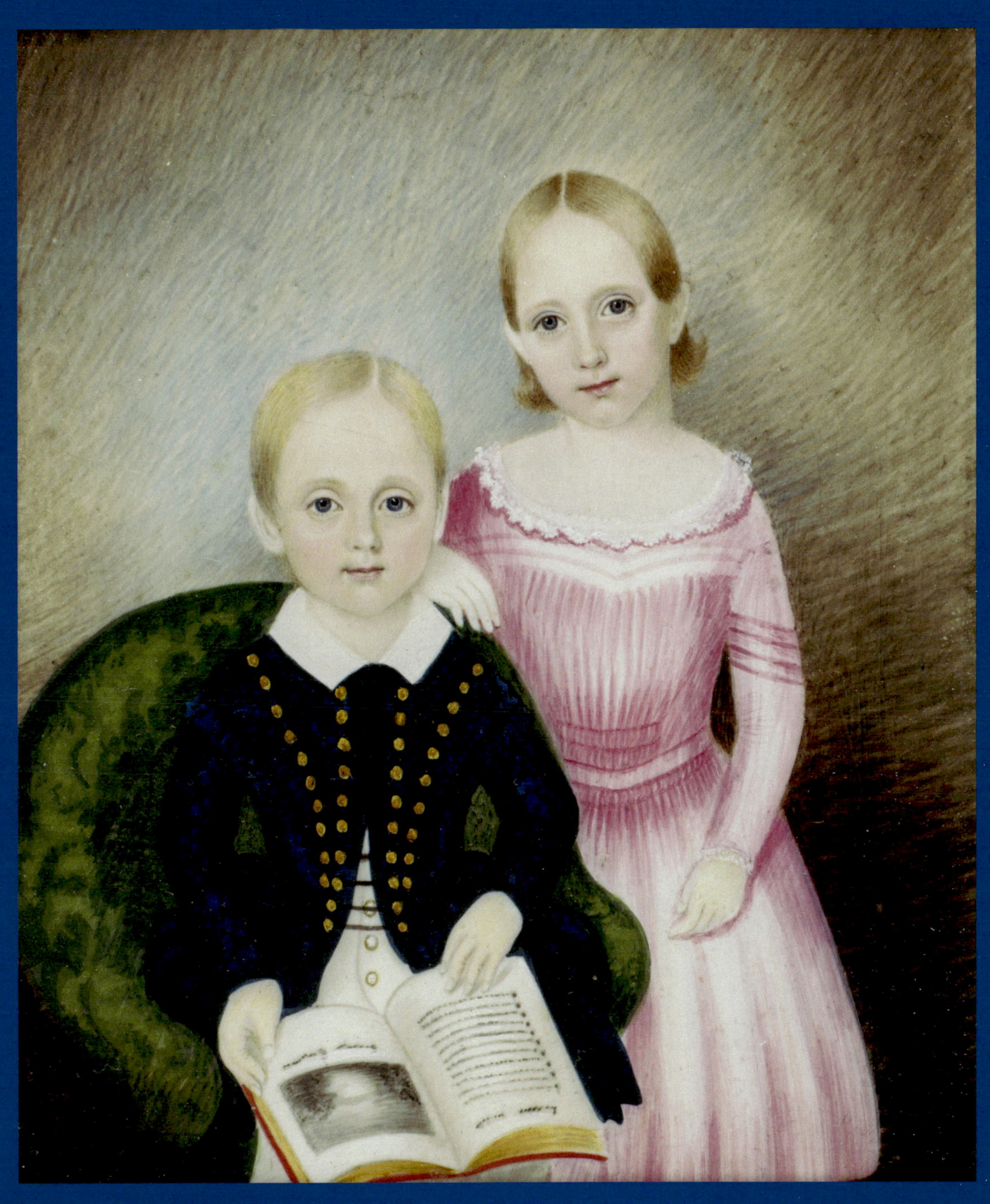

MRS. MOSES RUSSEL

Children in Pink and Blue

1840

Watercolor on ivory
5 × 3⅞ in.

L2015.41.181

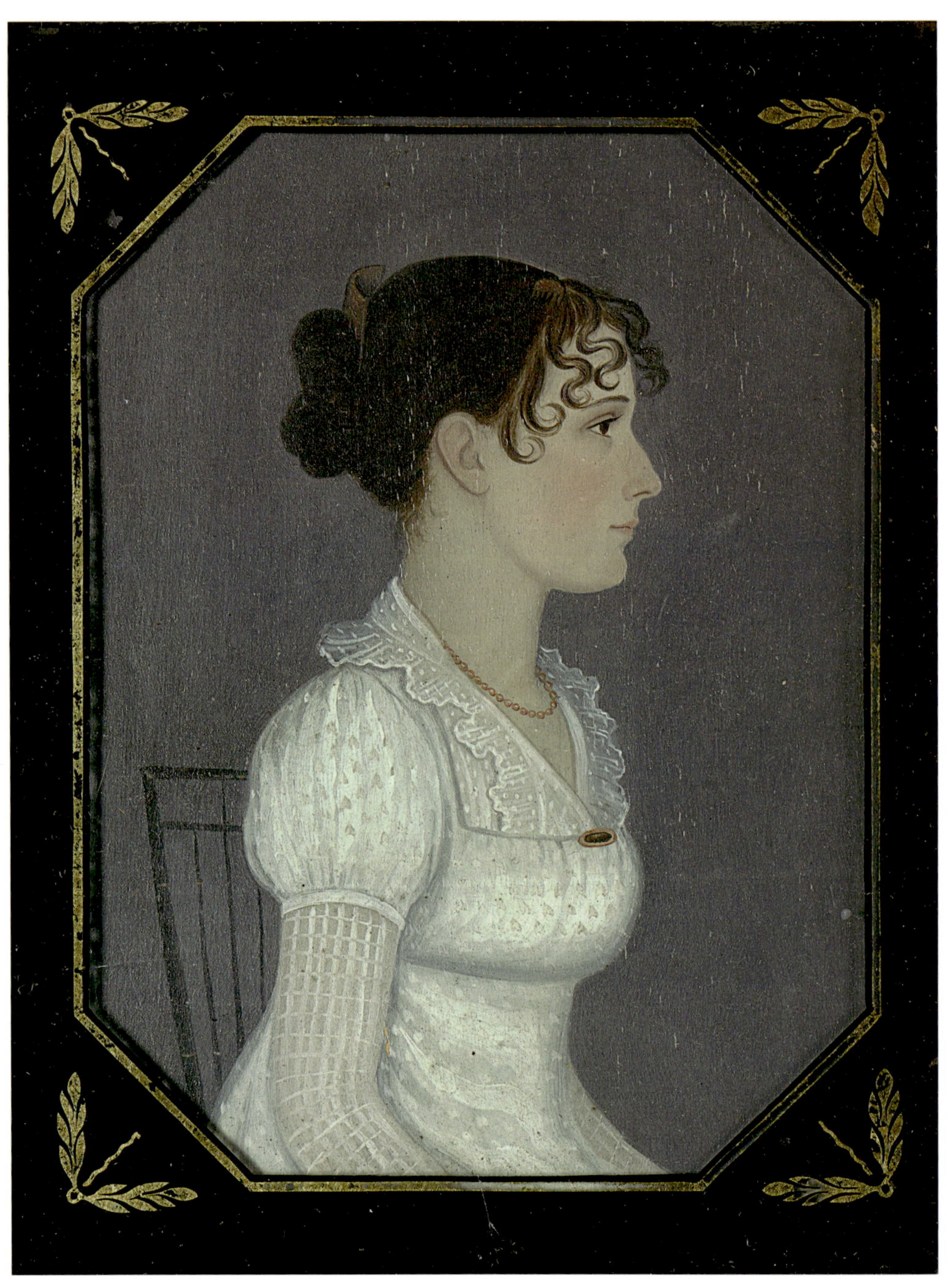

JASPER P. MILES (1782–1849)

Portrait of Hannah Spear

ca. 1820–25

Oil on tulipwood panel
8½ × 6¼ in.

L2015.41.158.2

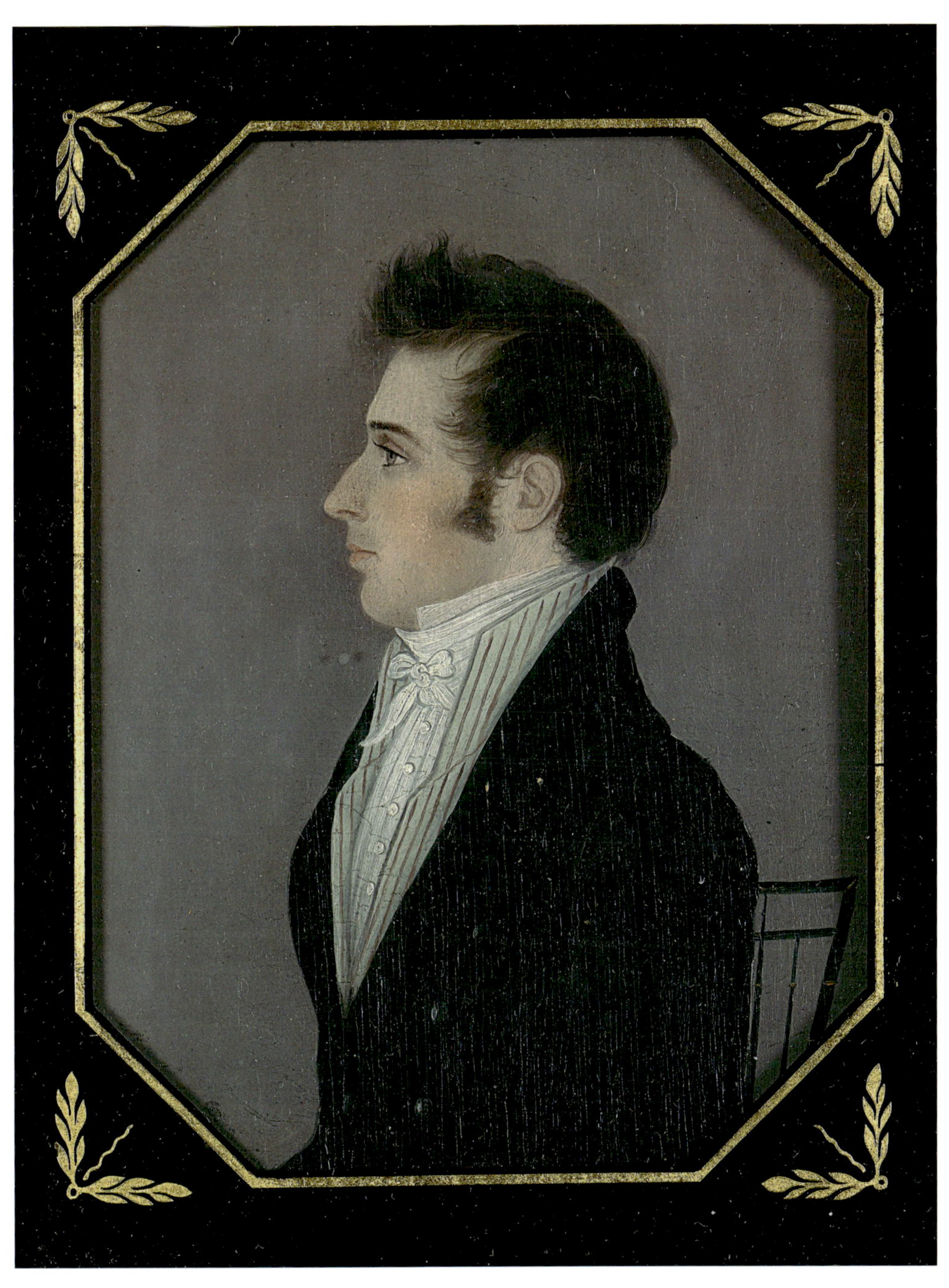

JASPER P. MILES (1782–1849)

Portrait of Stephan Spear

ca. 1820–25

Oil on tulipwood panel
8½ × 6⅜ in.

L2015.41.158.1

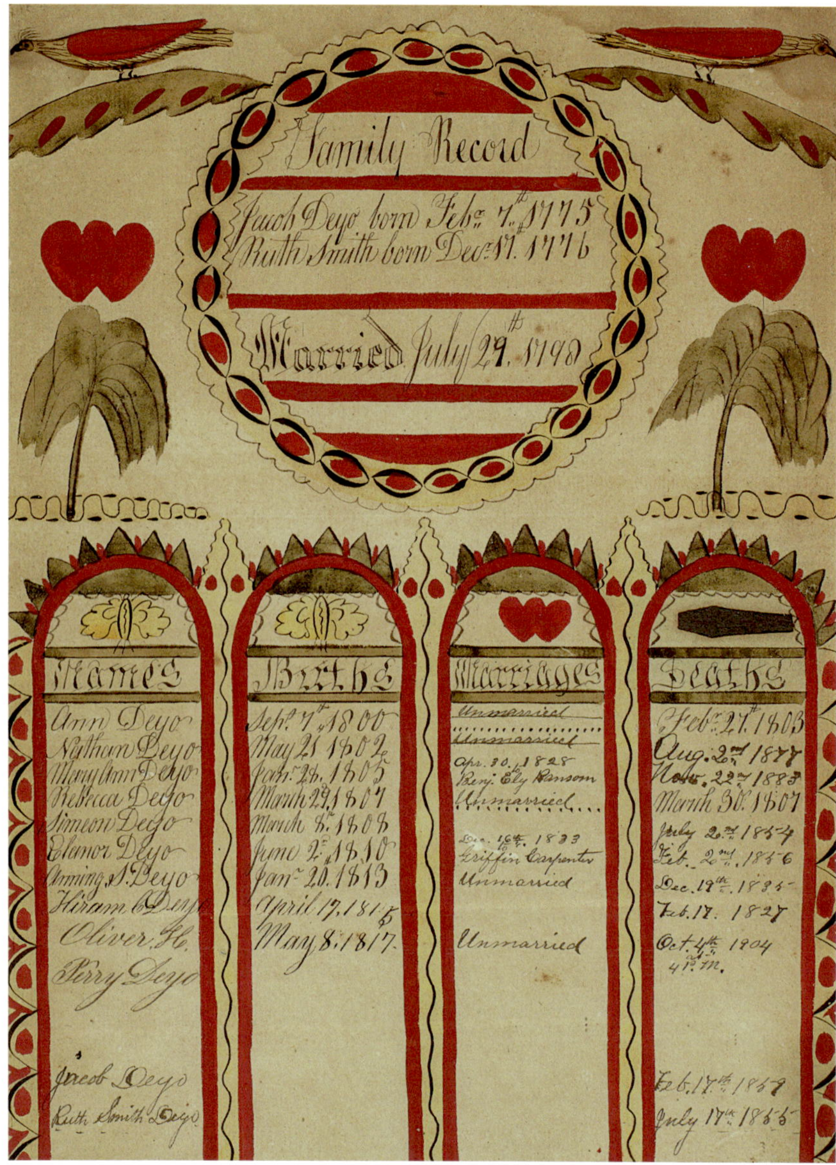

Jacob Deyo–Ruth Smith Family Record

Connecticut
ca. 1813

Watercolor and ink on paper
13½ × 9½ in.

2016.25.104

GENERATIONS

Illuminated family registers of births, marriages, and deaths began appearing in the United States after the Revolutionary War. Before that time, the family Bible served as the genealogical archive. The dedication to maintaining these records across generations is touching. The Deyo-Smith register spans three centuries, from the parents' births in the 1770s until the death of an unmarried son, Oliver, in 1904. Across New England, these registers have consistent emblems and symbolism. The double heart signified marriage and its indissoluble bond, an association driven home in this register by the marriage column's double-heart header. Tree and vine imagery was also common, and present in all the registers illustrated in this catalogue. In the Acrostic "Portrait" on the following spread, delicate vines run along the sides, while the lithographed border of the *Tracy Family Register* on page 198 has curling morning glories and stylized boughs. Trees and fruits as metaphors for lineages can be found in the Bible. Printers began to turn out empty registers like the Tracy one en masse by the 1820s and 1830s.

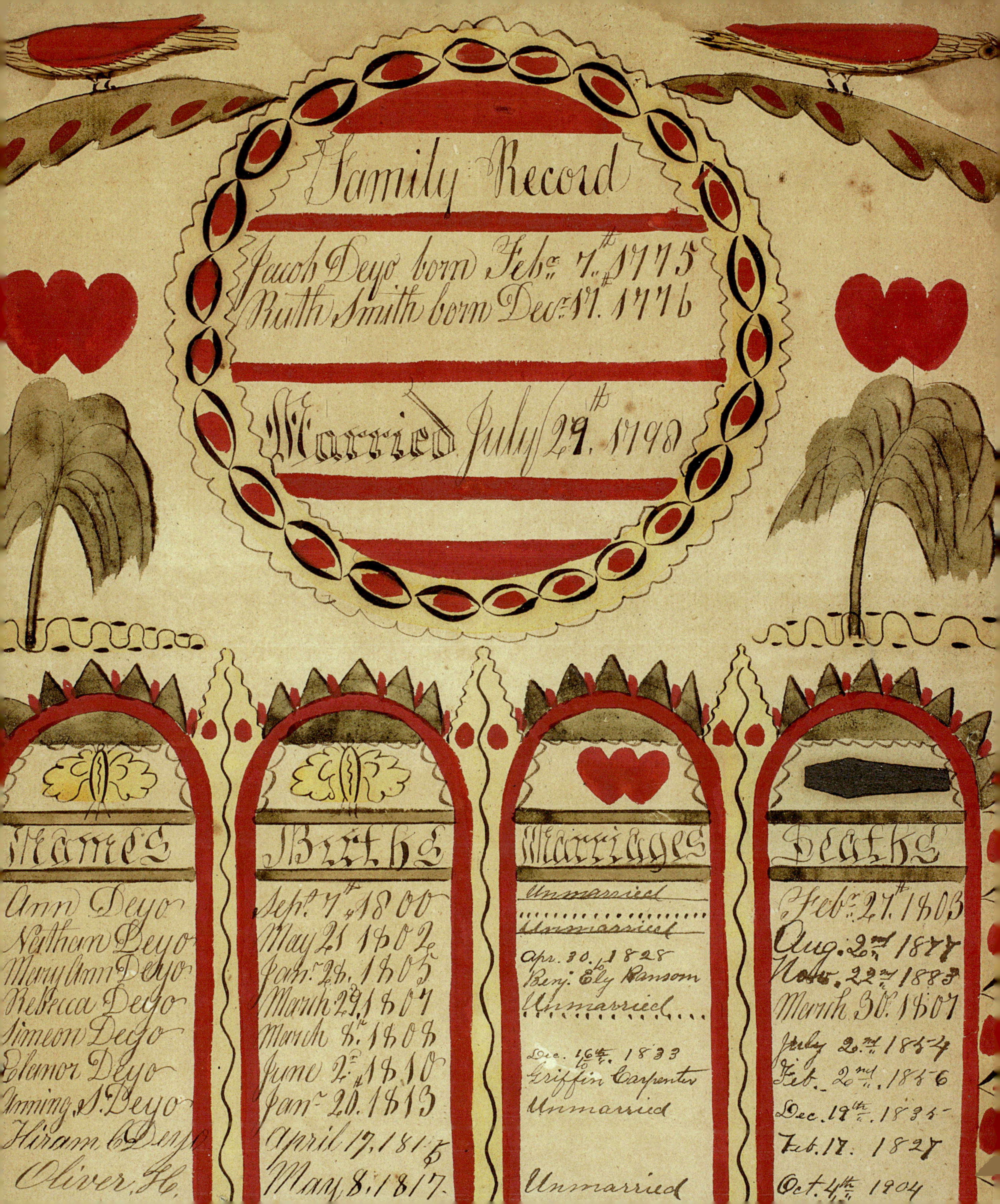

Family Record
Jacob Deyo born Febr. 7th 1775
Ruth Smith born Decr. 11th 1776
Married July 29th 1798
Names
Births
Marriages
Deaths
Ann Deyo
Nathan Deyo
Mary Ann Deyo
Rebecca Deyo
Simeon Deyo
Eleanor Deyo
Anning S. Deyo
Hiram C. Deyo
Oliver H.
Sept. 7th 1800
May 21 1802
Jan. 28. 1805
March 29, 1807
March 8th 1808
June 2d 1810
Jan. 20. 1813
April 17, 1815
May 8, 1817
Unmarried
Unmarried
Apr. 30. 1828
Benj. Ely Ransom
Unmarried
Dec. 16th 1833
Griffin Carpenter
Unmarried
Unmarried
Febr. 27th 1803
Aug. 2nd 1877
Nov. 22nd 1883
March 30. 1807
July 2nd 1854
Feb. 2nd 1856
Dec. 19th 1835
Feb. 17. 1827
Oct. 4th 1904

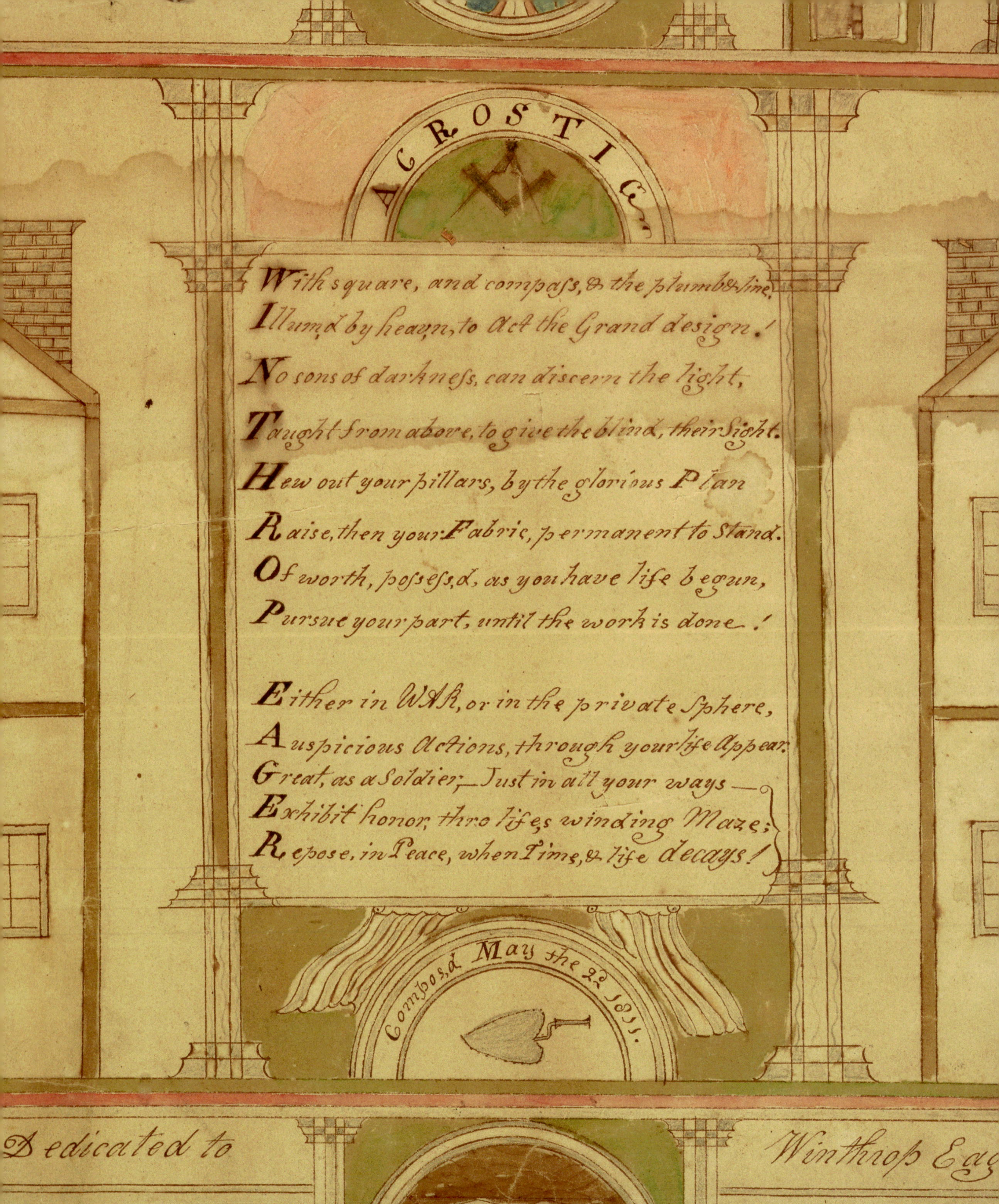
ACROSTIC
With square, and compass, & the plumb & line,
Illum'd by heav'n, to Act the Grand design!
No sons of darkness, can discern the light,
Taught from above, to give the blind, their Sight.
Hew out your pillars, by the glorious Plan
Raise, then your Fabric, permanent to Stand.
Of worth, possess'd, as you have life begun,
Pursue your part, until the work is done!
Either in WAR, or in the private Sphere,
Auspicious Actions, through your life Appear.
Great, as a Soldier,—Just in all your ways—
Exhibit honor, thro life's winding Maze;
Repose, in Peace, when Time, & life decays!
Compos'd May the 2d 1835.
Dedicated to
Winthrop Eag

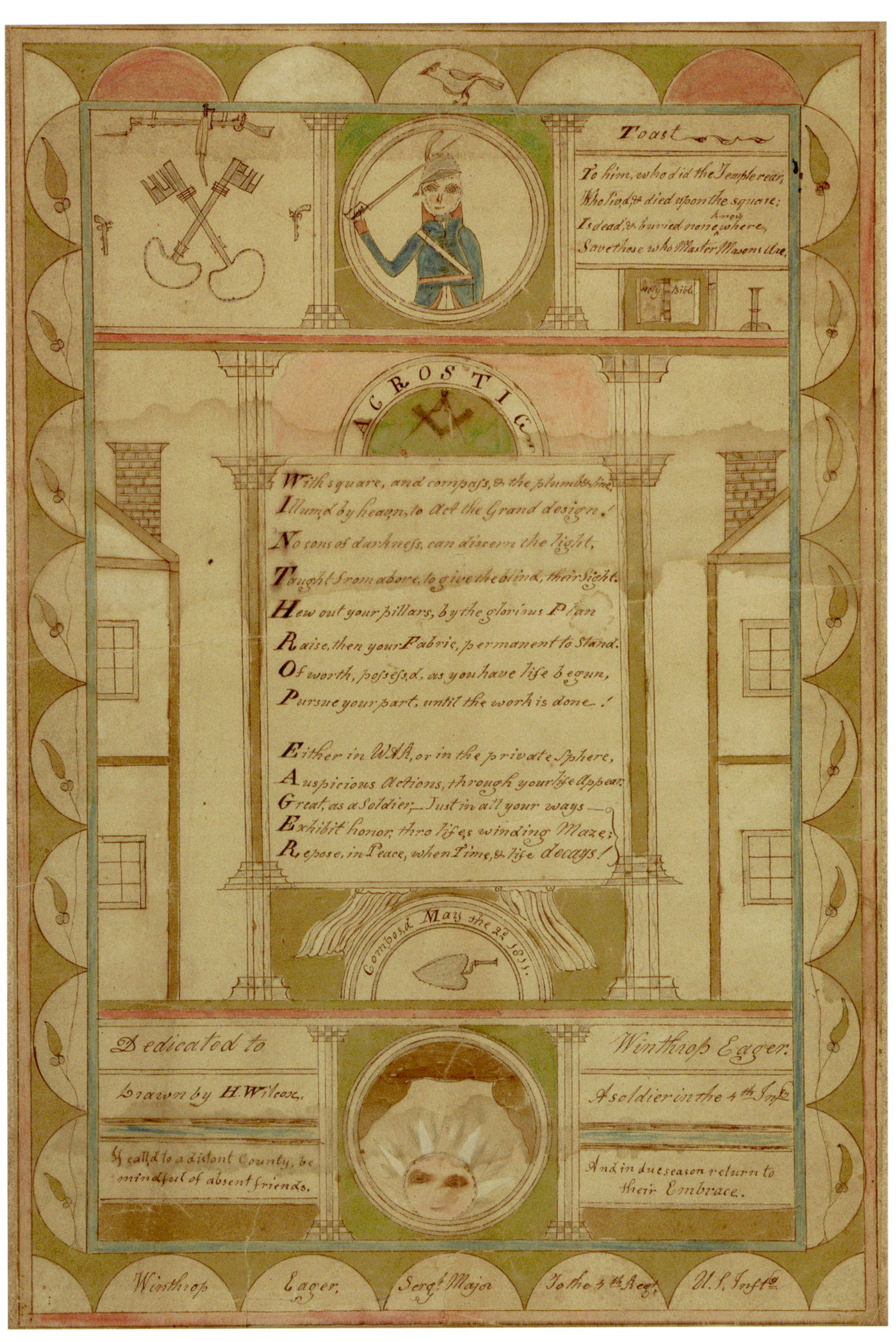

DRAWN BY H. WILCOX

Acrostic "Portrait" Dedicated to Winthrop Eager

Massachusetts
1811

Watercolor and ink on paper
18¼ × 12⅞ in.

Inscriptions: "Dedicated to Winthrop Eager. / Drawn by H. Wilcox, A soldier in the 4th Inftry"

"Winthrop Eager, Sergt Major To the 4th Regt. U.S. Inftry"

2016.25.103

Tracy Family Register

Durham, New Hampshire
Kellogg & Comstock, Lithographic Firm (active 1849–50)

Hand-colored lithograph

"Heart and Hand Artist" (active 1850–55)

Watercolor and ink on lithograph
Framed: 12⅜ × 16½ in.

2016.25.105

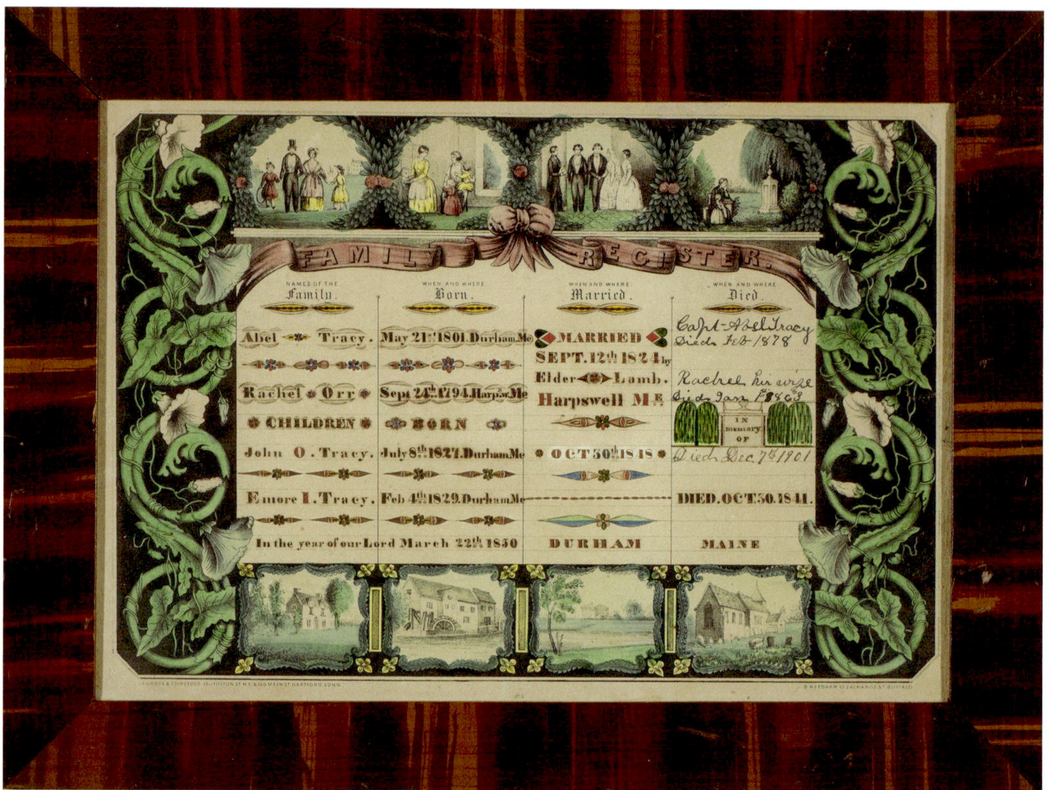

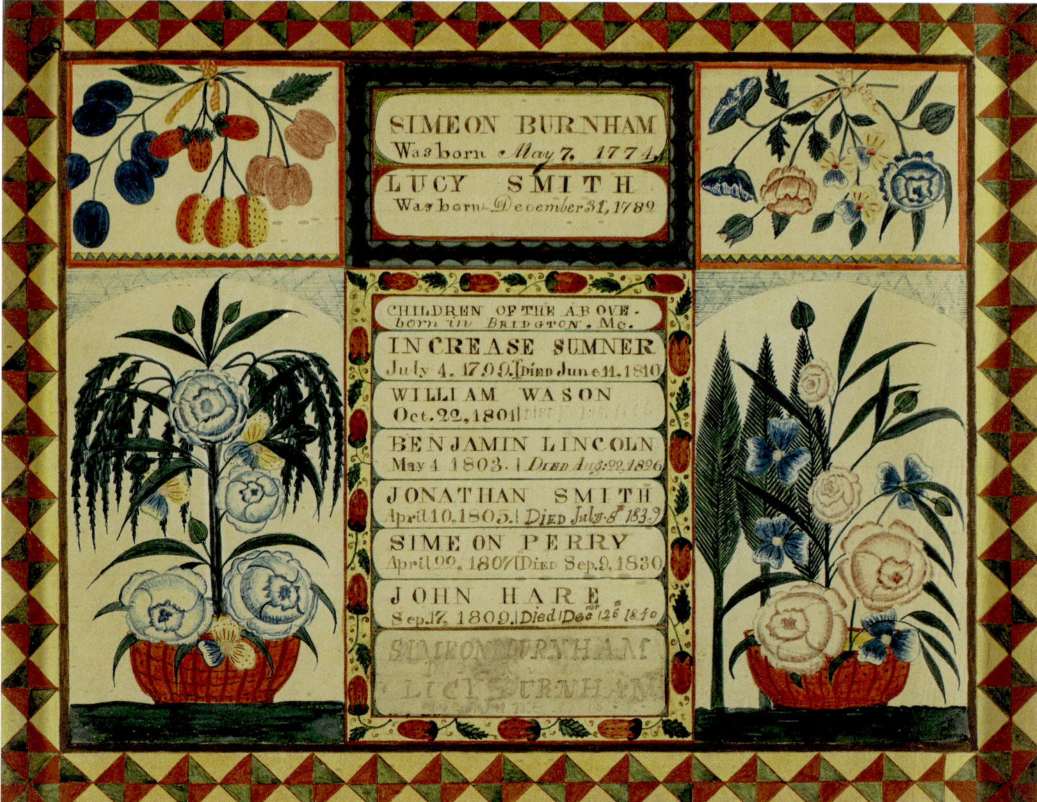

Simeon Burnham & Lucy Smith Family Record

Bridgton, Maine
ca. 1830

Watercolor and ink on paper
7½ × 9½ in.

L2015.41.149

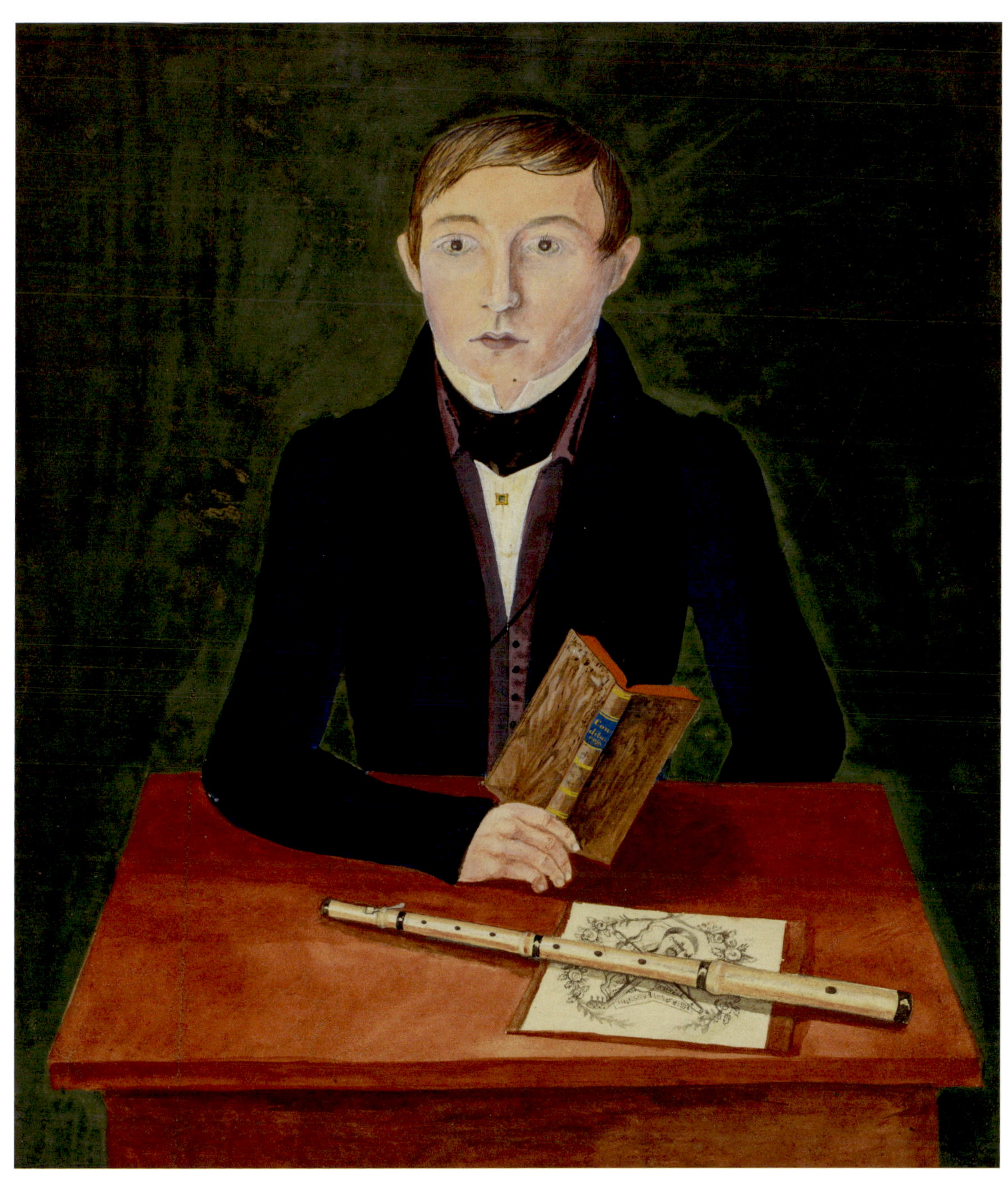

Boy with a Book and a Flute

ca. 1830

Watercolor and gouache on paper
13¾ × 11½ in.

2016.25.99

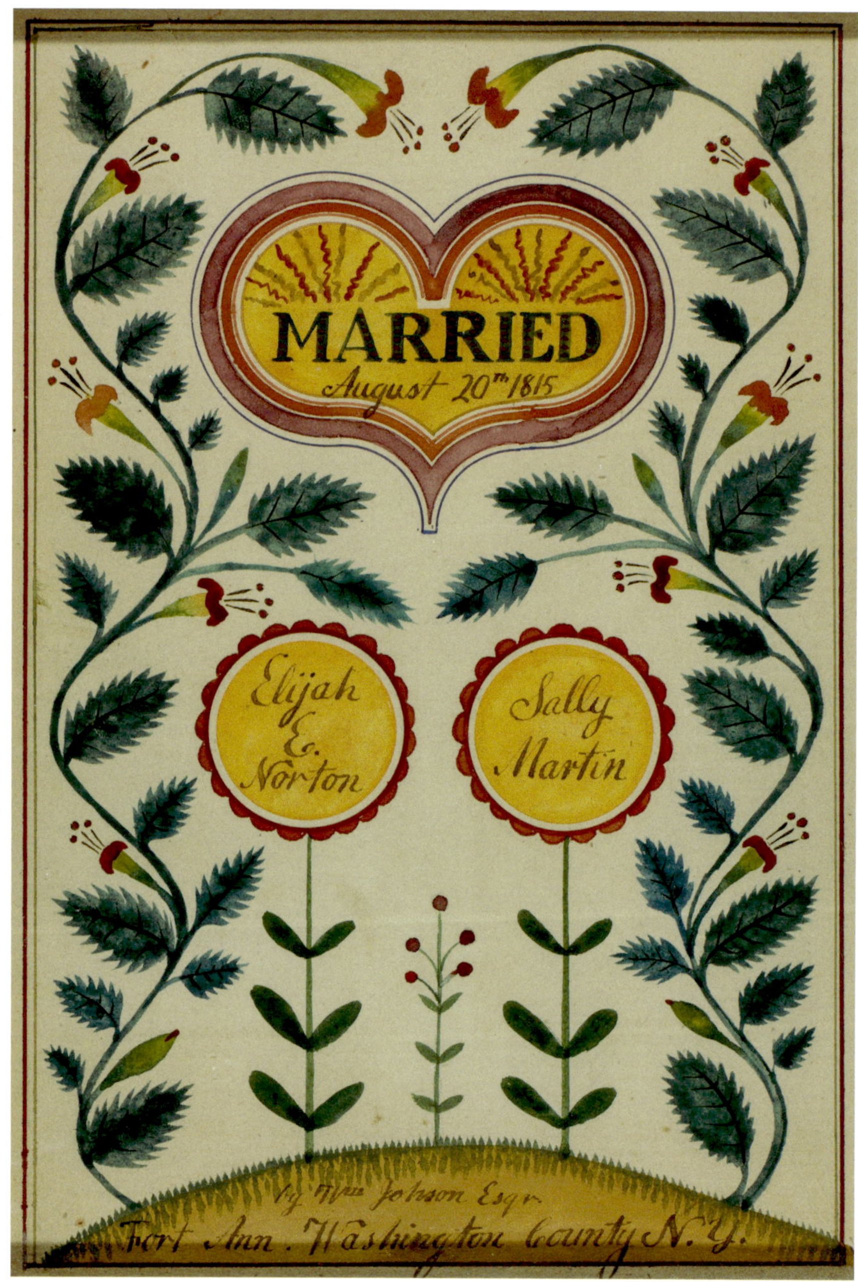

WILLIAM JOHNSON, ESQ.

Elijah E. Norton and Sally Martin Marriage Certificate

1815

Watercolor and ink on paper
9 × 6¼ in.

Inscription: "by Wm Johnson Esqr. / Fort Ann. Washington County N.Y."

L2015.41.155

A Record of the Family of Ensign Jacob Chamberlain of Alton, in the County Strafford, and State of New Hampshire

1800

Watercolor and ink on paper
15 × 12 in.

L2015.41.157

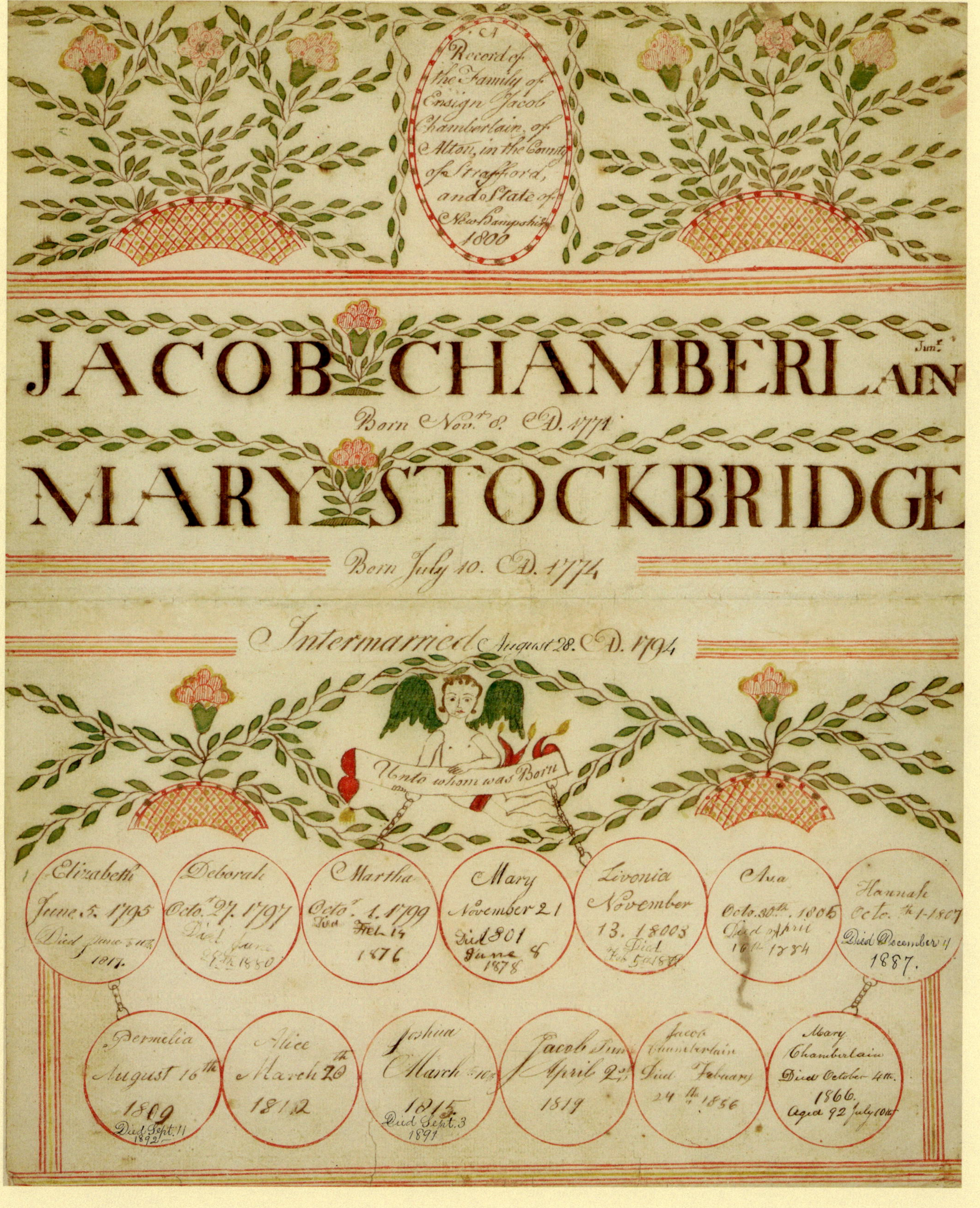

A Record of the Family of Ensign Jacob Chamberlain, of Alton, in the County of Strafford, and State of New Hampshire 1800
JACOB CHAMBERLAIN Jun.r
Born Nov.r 8. AD. 1771
MARY STOCKBRIDGE
Born July 10. AD. 1774
Intermarried August 28. AD. 1794
Unto whom was Born
Elizabeth June 5. 1795 Died June 11th 1817.
Deborah Octo.r 27. 1797 Died June 1880
Martha Octo.r 1. 1799 Died Feb 14 1876
Mary November 21 1801 Died June 8 1878
Livonia November 13. 1803
Asa Octo. 30th. 1805 Died April 16th 1884
Hannah Octo. 1-1807 Died December 1887.
Permelia August 16th 1809 Died Sept. 11 1892
Alice March 20th 1812
Joshua March 10th 1815. Died Sept. 3 1891
Jacob Jun April 2d 1819
Jacob Chamberlain Died Febuary 24th 1856
Mary Chamberlain Died October 4th. 1866. Aged 92 July 10th

AMMI PHILLIPS (1788–1865)

Portrait of Betsy Brownell Gilbert

Columbia County,
New York
ca. 1820

Oil on canvas
29 × 22¾ in.

Comb shown below

L2015.41.162

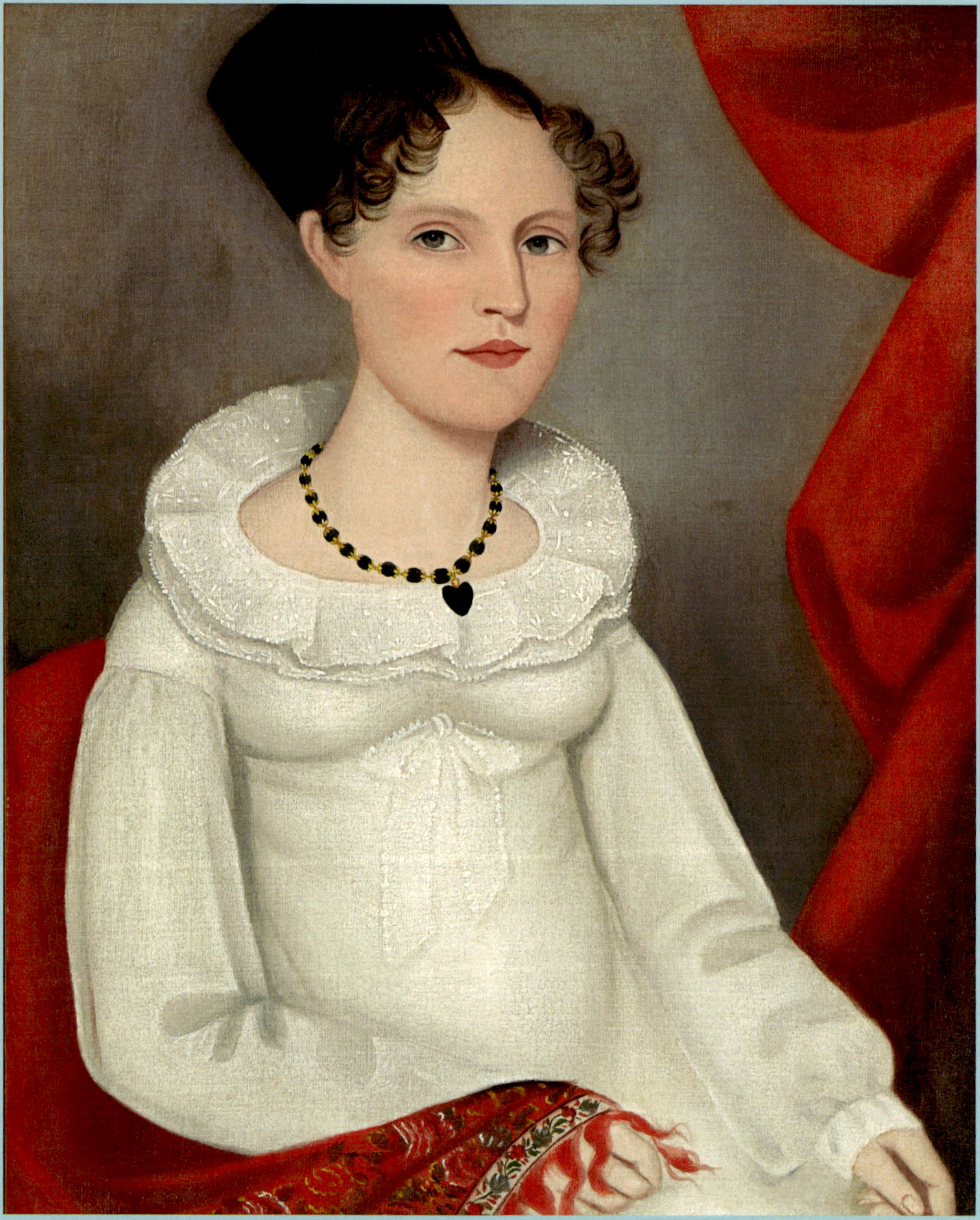

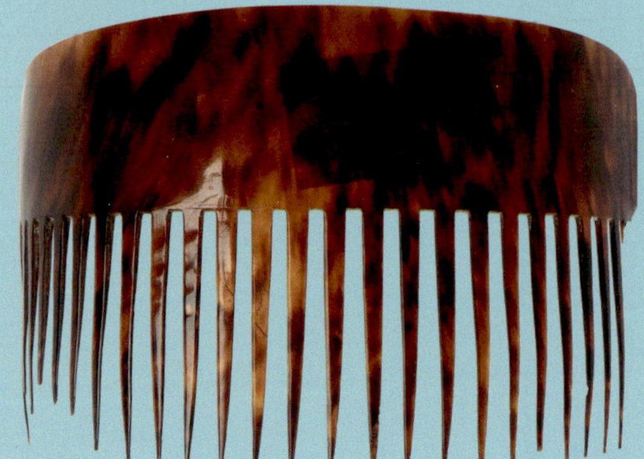

Comb

ca. 1820–30

Possibly tortoiseshell
4 × 5½ × 2¼ in.

L2015.41.26

SHELDON PECK (1797–1868)

Untitled (Portrait of a Young Man with Red Curtain)

ca. 1827–30

Oil on poplar panel
23 × 19¼ in.

L2015.41.160

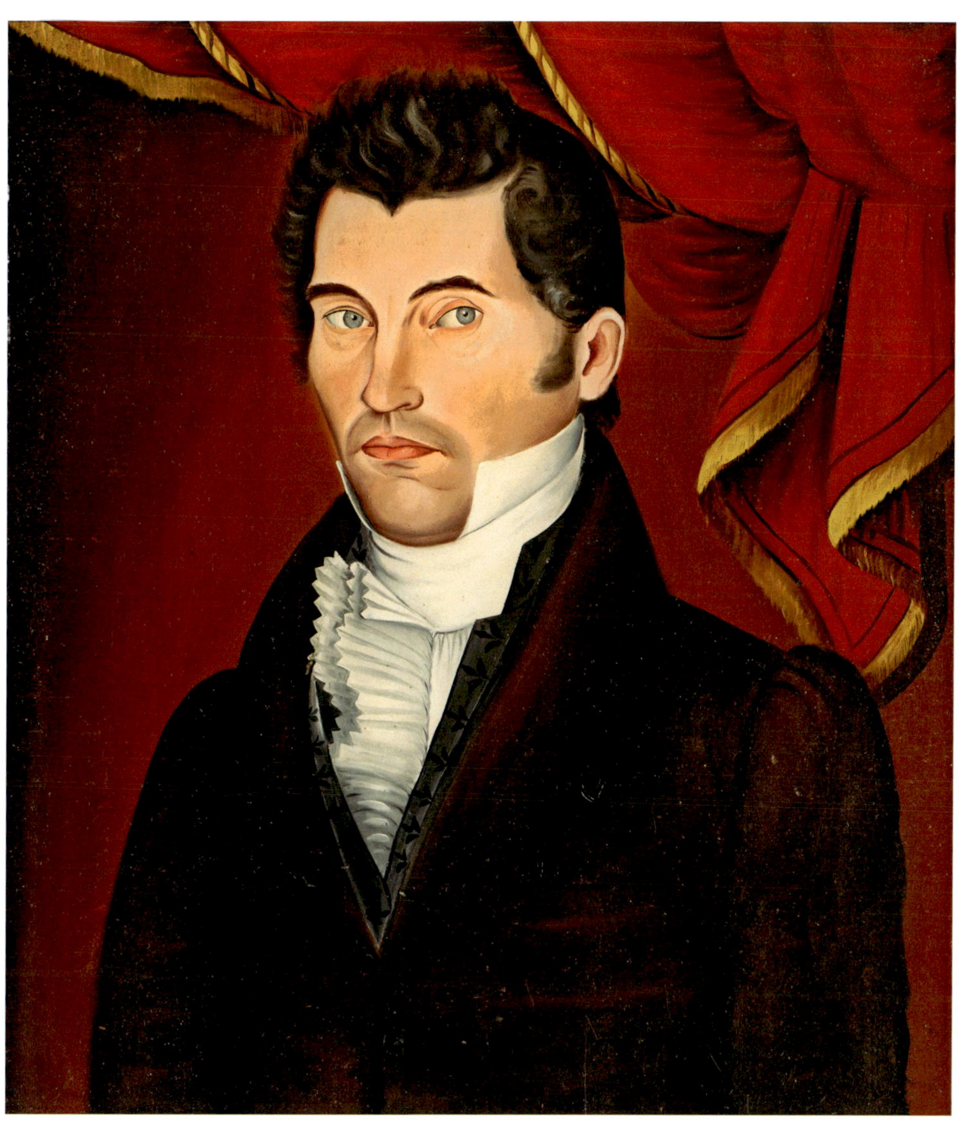

SHELDON PECK

This striking portrait of a fashionably dressed blue-eyed man by Sheldon Peck was rediscovered under a nineteenth-century print during the filming of the PBS series *Antiques Roadshow* in 1997. The artist's decision to slightly misalign the focus of the sitter's eyes—as if he were looking in different directions at once—heightens the picture's dramatic intensity. Born in Vermont but later moving west, Peck straddled numerous careers, painting portraits while homesteading in Illinois and perhaps dabbling in real estate speculation in Chicago. A radical abolitionist and active in the Liberty Party, Peck opened his home in rural DuPage County outside Chicago as a stop on the Underground Railroad.

A telltale symbol of the artist is the trefoil, or rabbit's foot, seen here in the gray band between the brown jacket and brilliant white cravat, and on the following page in the embroidery on the dress of Eunice Judkins.

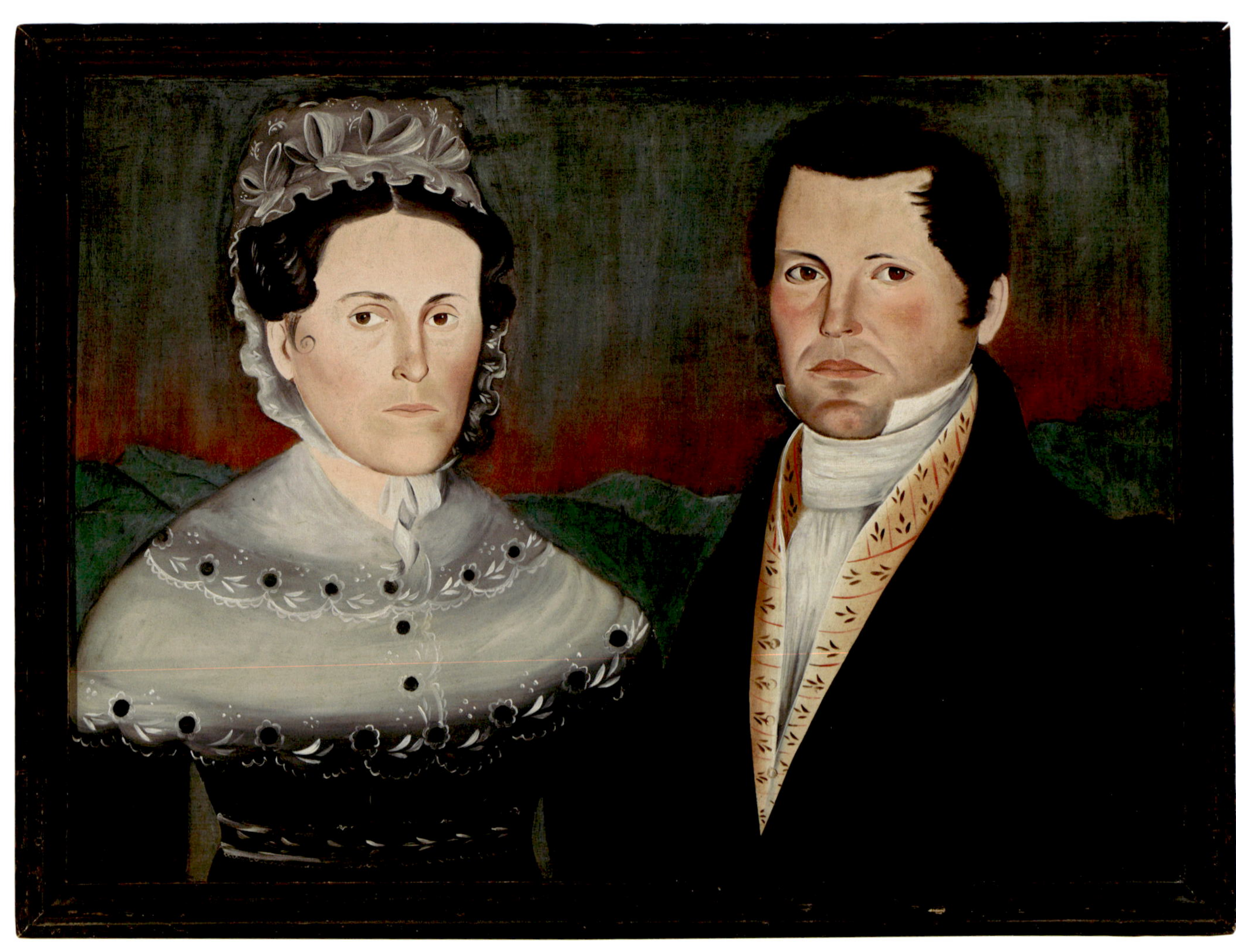

SHELDON PECK (1797–1868)

Portrait of Samuel and Eunice Judkins, Ulster County, New York

ca. 1834

Oil on wood panel
Framed: 23 × 30 in.

Inscription: "SAMUEL JUDKINS ORIGINALLY FROM ~~NEW HAMPSHIRE~~ VERMONT OF OHIOVILLE, ULSTER CO. N.Y. AND HIS FIRST WIFE WHO PAINTED THE PICTURE / EUNICE DAUGHTER OF CONSTANT / AND DEBORAH SAMUEL JUDKINS DIED SEPT 7TH 1844 / AGED 50 YRS 4 MO AND 10 DAYS."

L2015.41.168

PRIOR-HAMBLIN SCHOOL

Prior-Hamblin School is an attribution given to American folk portraits in the style of William Matthew Prior (1806–1873) and Sturtevant J. Hamblin (active 1837–56), brothers-in-law who worked together. Sturtevant's sister, Rosamond, married Prior. The three lived together in Portland, Maine, and later in Boston. By the 1850s Sturtevant probably left painting to work with his brother Joseph. Prior continued as a portraitist in a studio at 36 Trenton Street, Boston, until 1873.

Paintings of this school have direct frontal poses, bright colors, and confident, unfussy brushwork, which is most evident in the deft treatment of the lace and trimmings in the children's clothing.

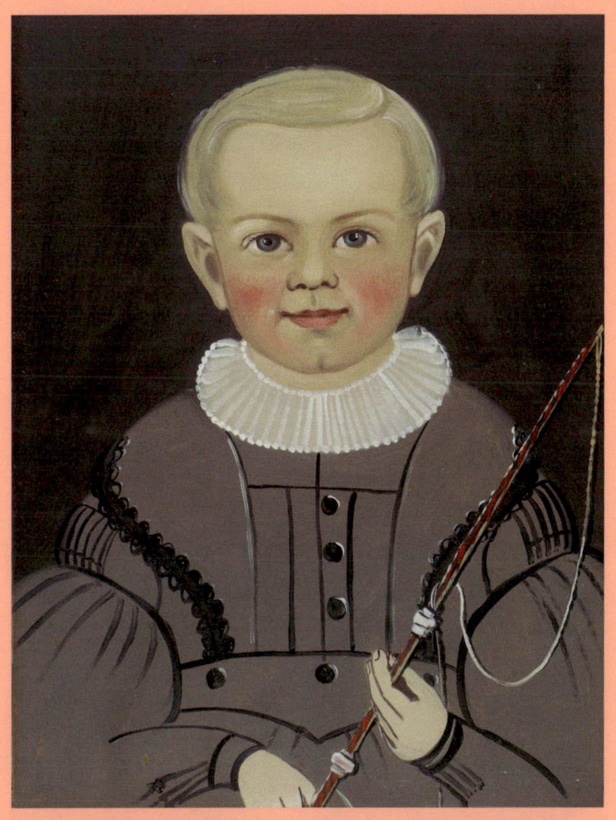

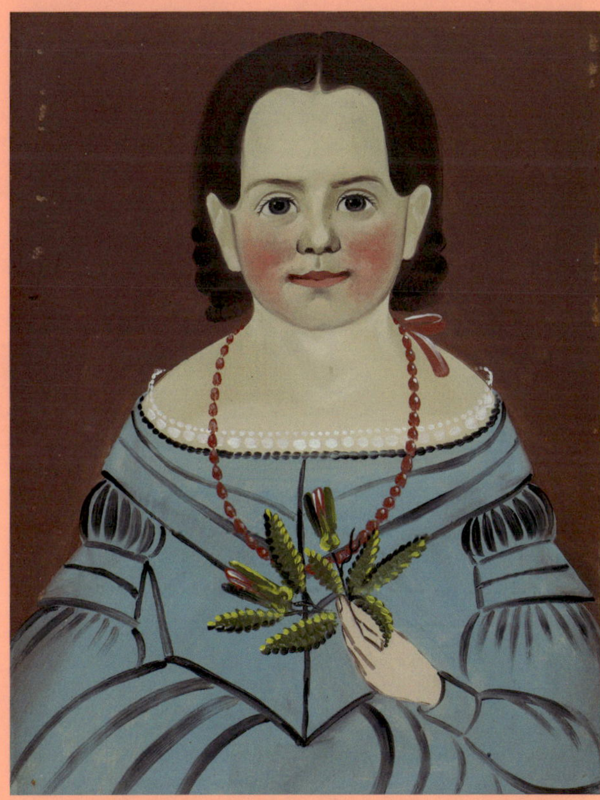

PRIOR-HAMBLIN SCHOOL

Portraits of Boy and Girl

ca. 1840–50

Oil on heavy paper (paper laminate)
Each: 14¼ × 10¼ in.

2016.25.110, .111

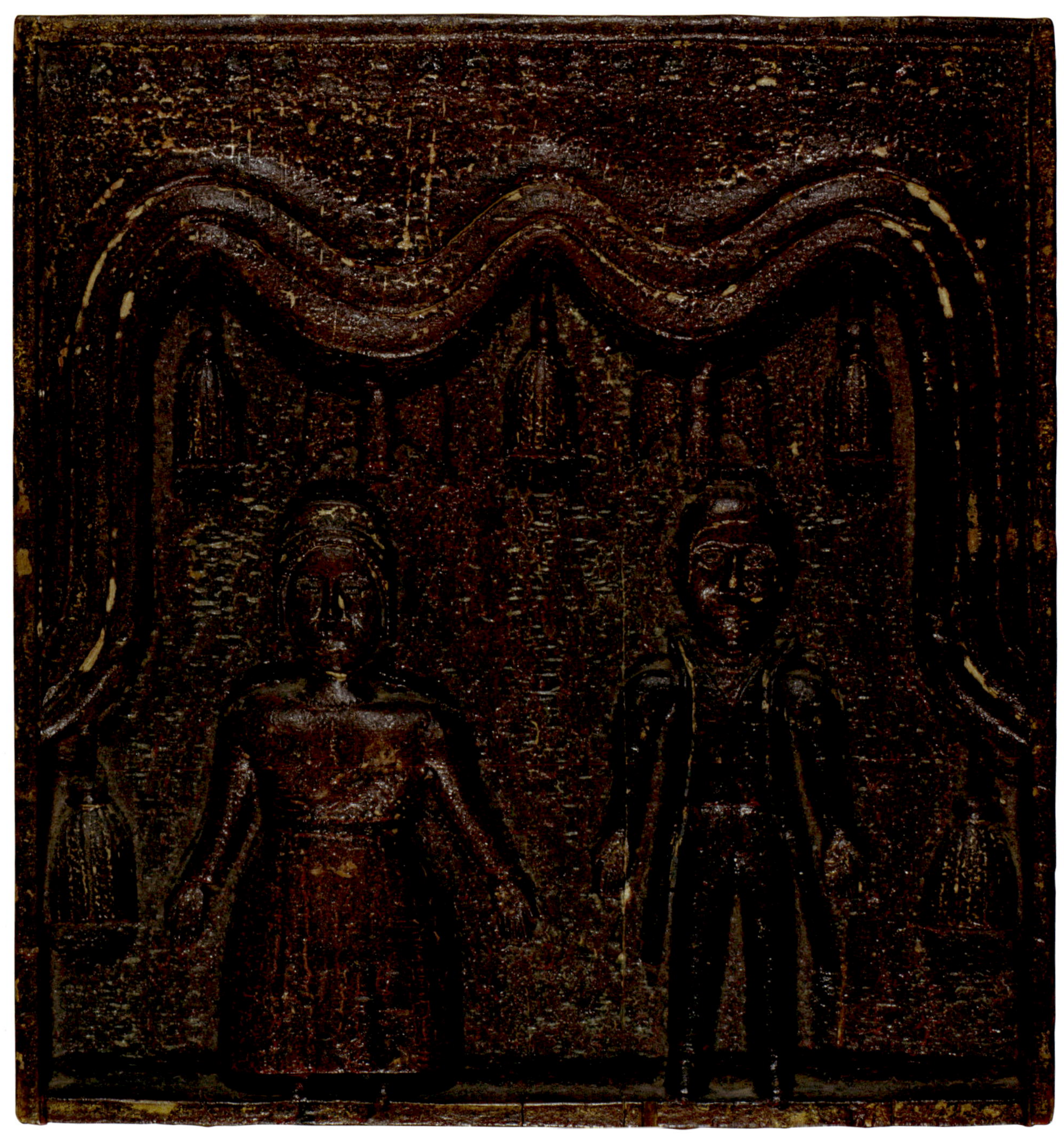

Plaque with Bas Relief of a Man and Woman

Maine
ca. 1830

Pine, paint, and shellac
15 × 14 × 1 in.

2016.25.113

STURTEVANT HAMBLIN (1817–1884)

A Portrait of Two Children

Boston
ca. 1845–50

Oil on canvas
Framed: 39½ × 32½ in.

2016.25.108

PAGE 208:

Boot Scraper (detail)

See also p. 214

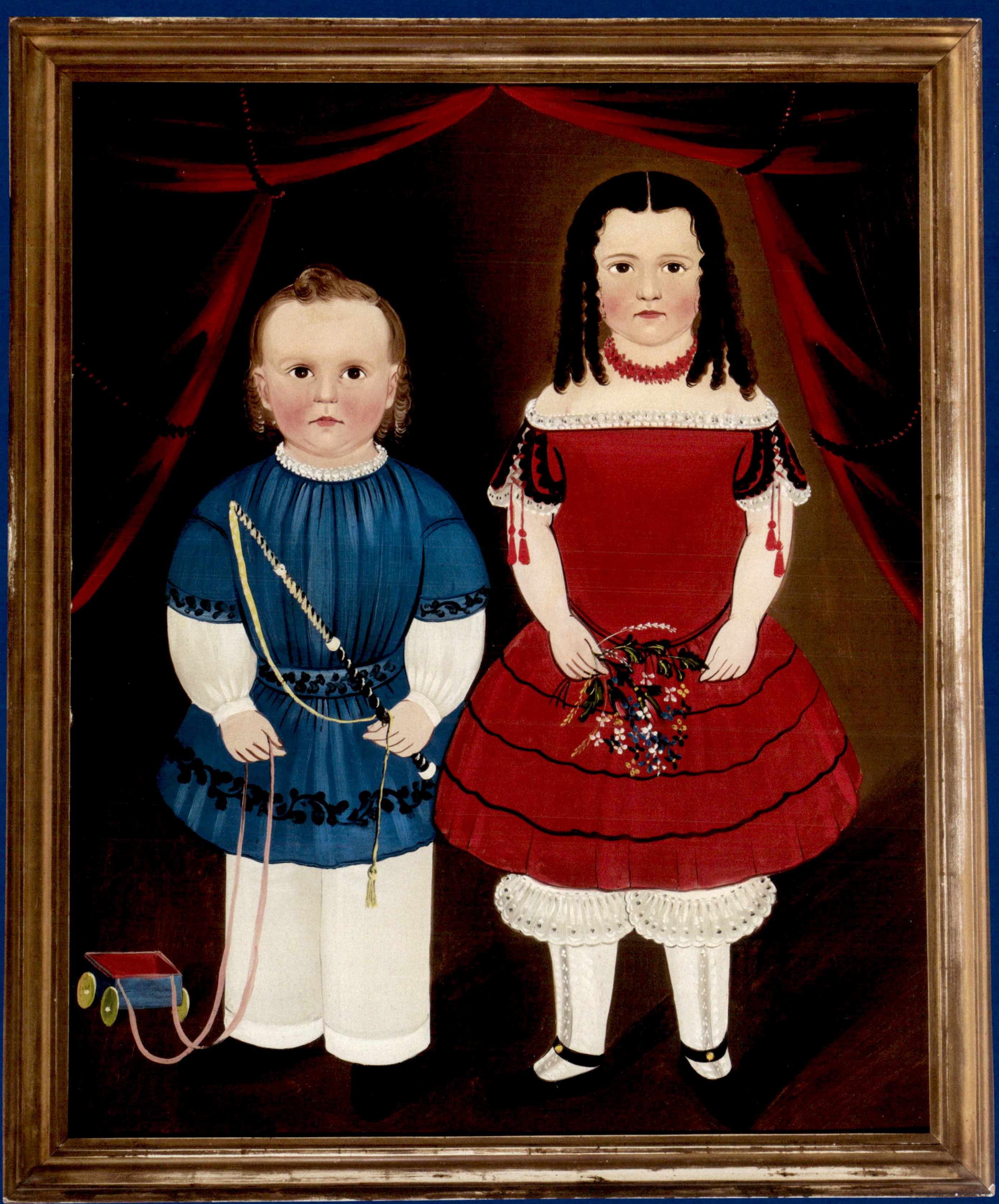

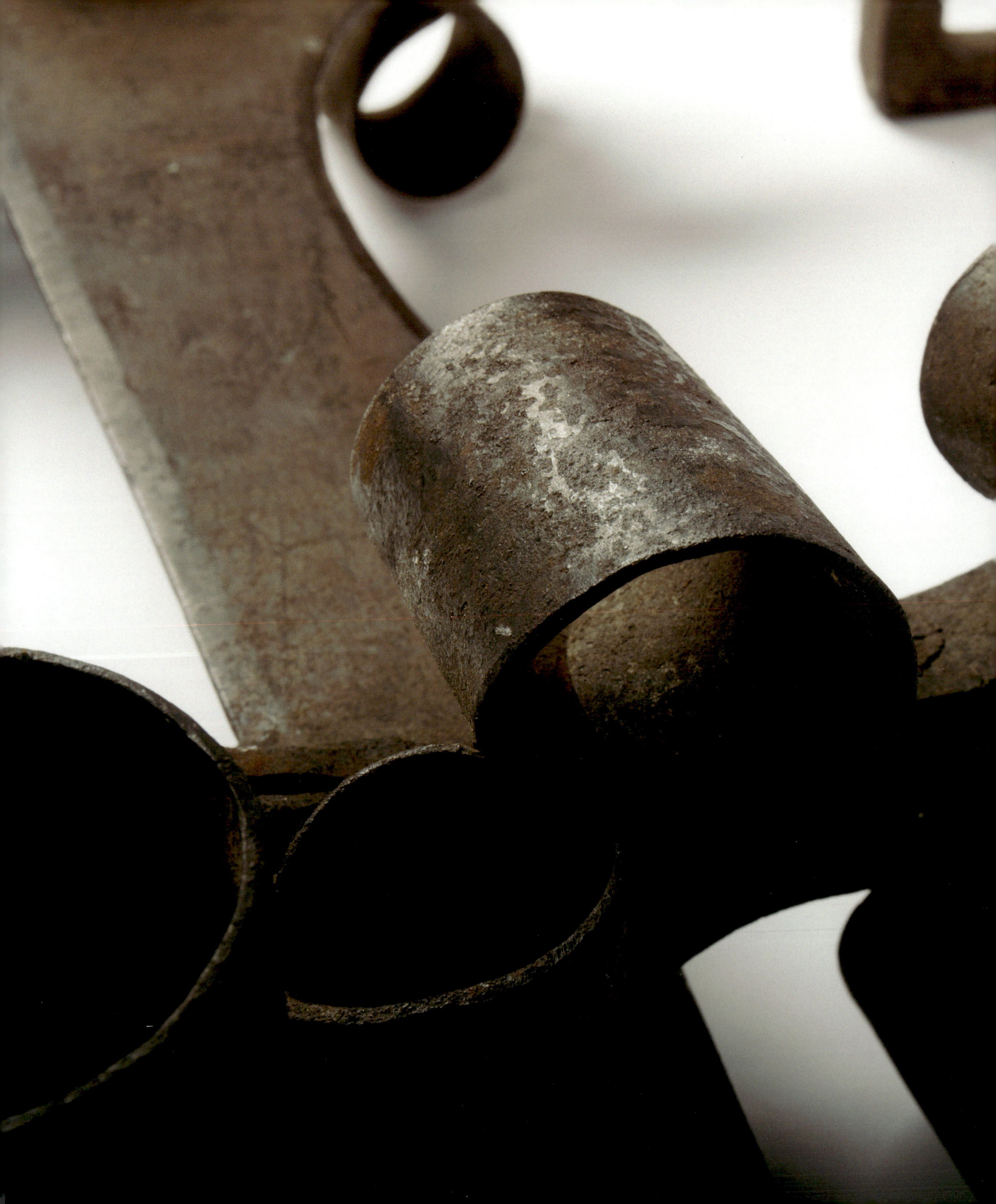

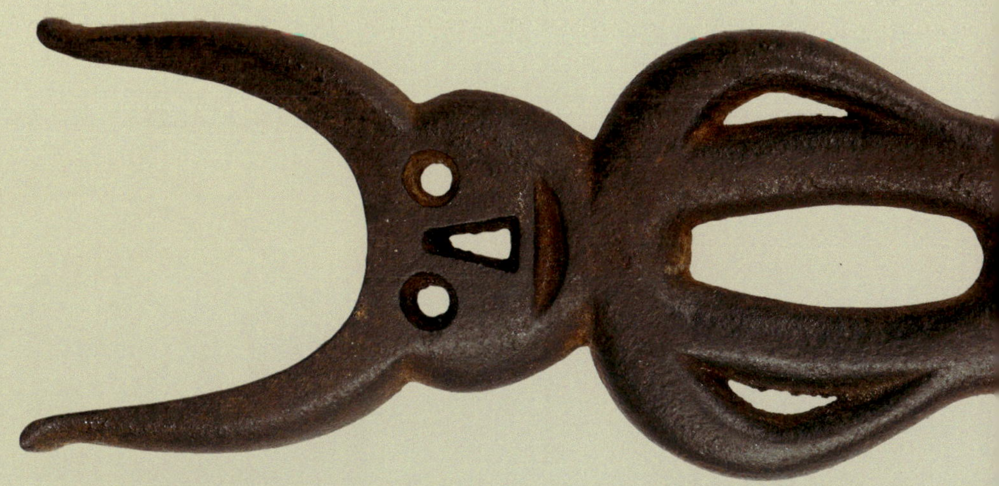

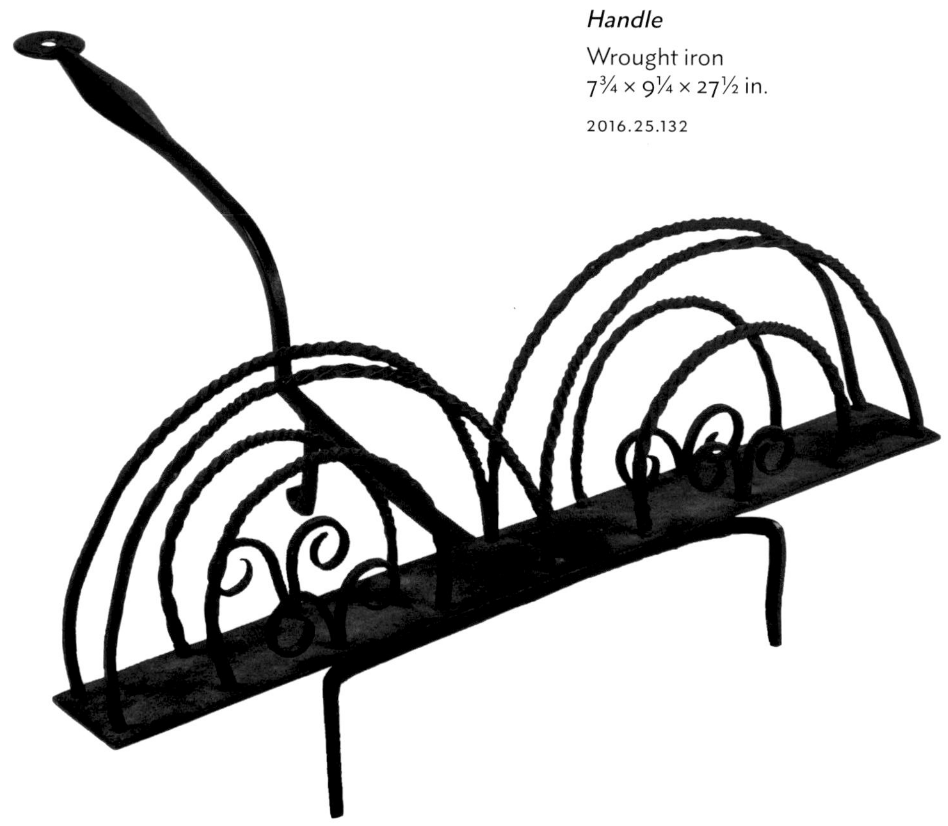

Toaster with Shoulder Handle

Wrought iron
7¾ × 9¼ × 27½ in.

2016.25.132

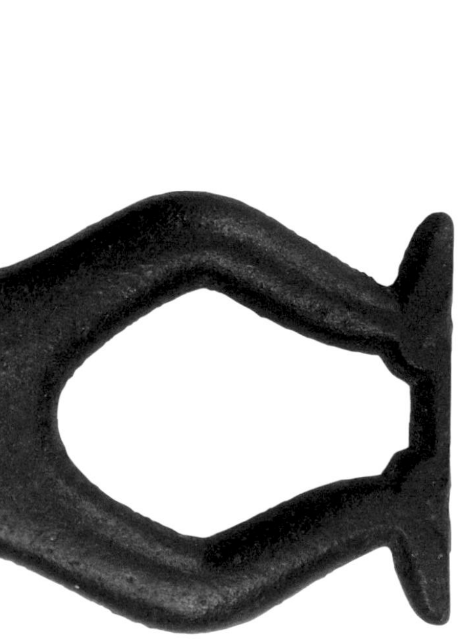

Devil Bootjack

ca. 1850

Cast iron
2¼ × 10½ × 3⅜ in.

2016.25.114

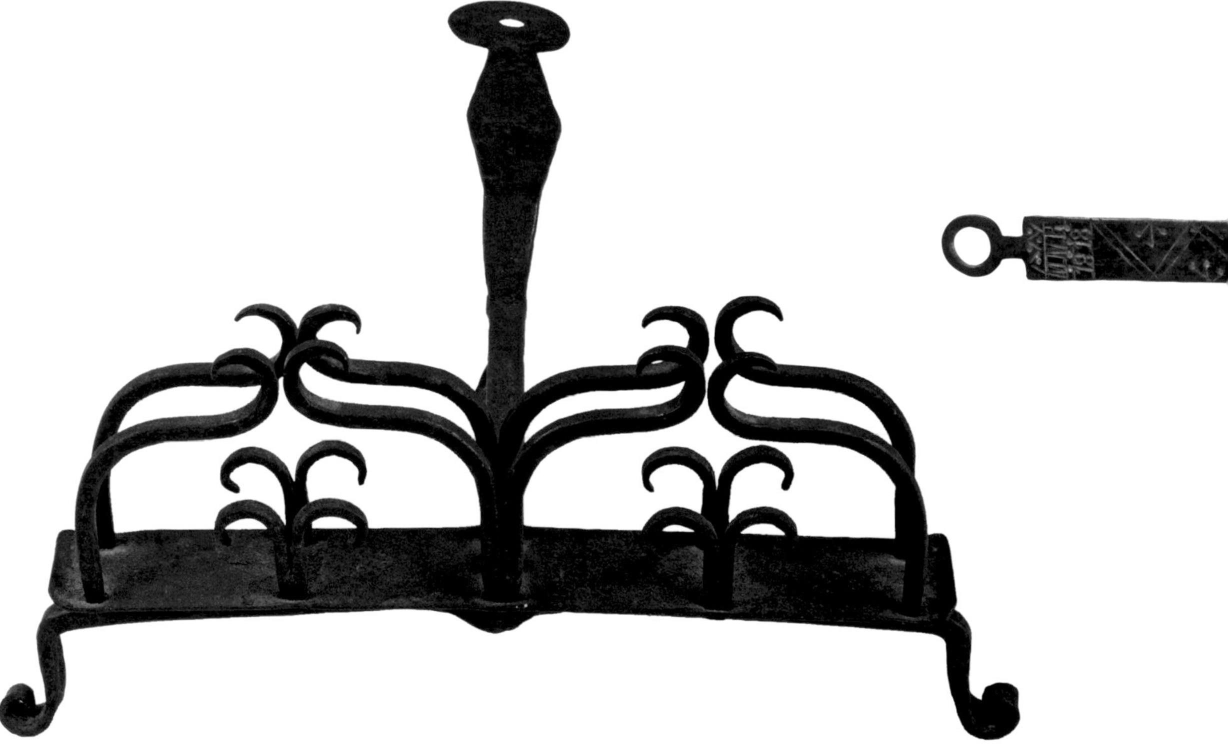

Toaster

Eighteenth or nineteenth century

Wrought iron
7 × 18 × 14 in.

2016.25.128

Heart-Shaped Trivet

Wrought iron
1⅝ × 5¼ × 9 in.

2016.25.133

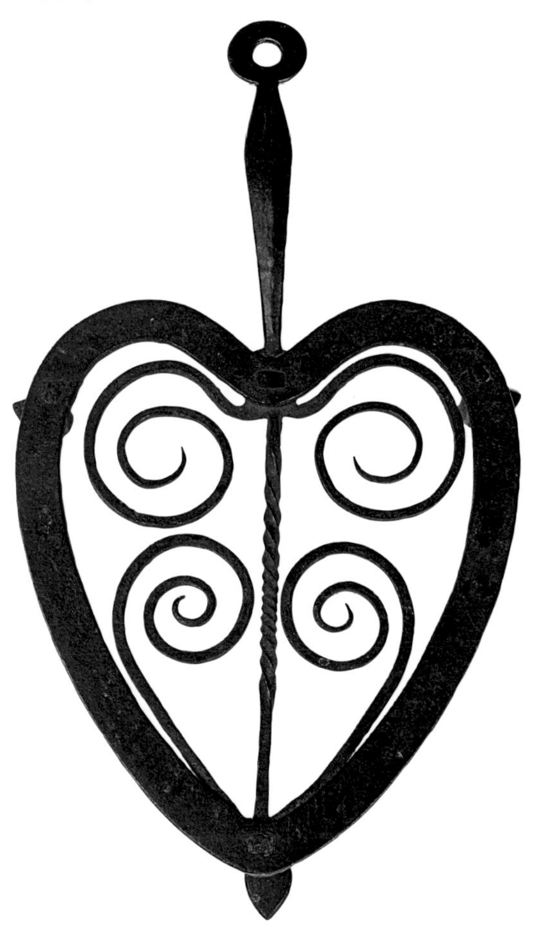

Horse Tool

ca. 1850

Cast iron
¾ × 15½ × 9⅛ in.

2016.25.142

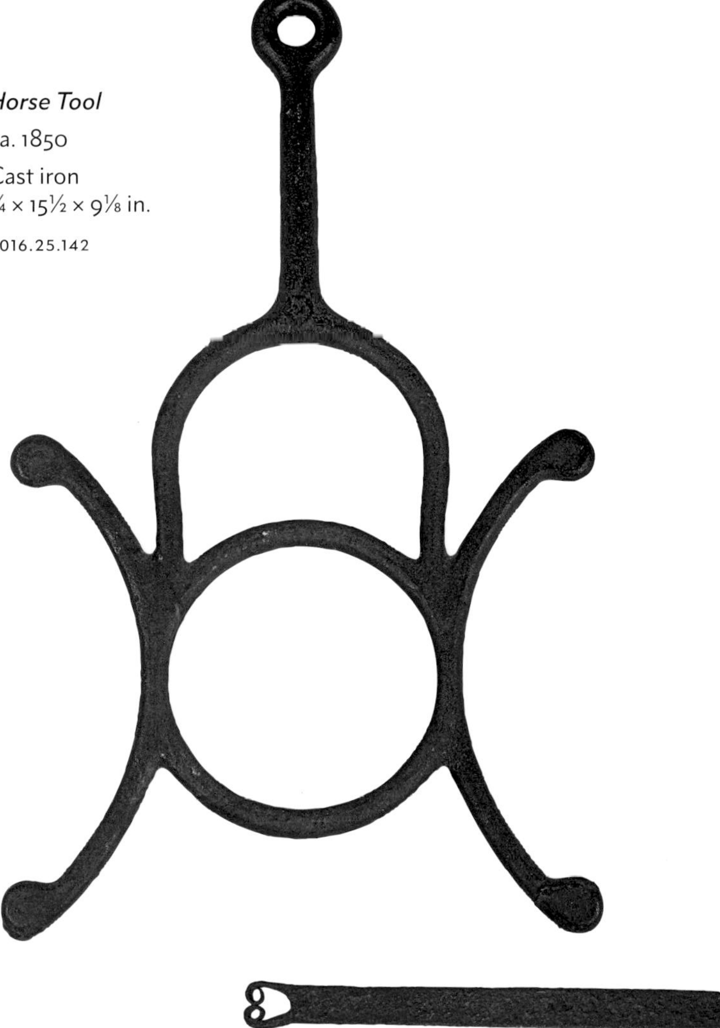

FIRE AND IRON

The kitchen was central to homes in early America, and the focal point of the kitchen was the hearth. Toasters placed next to hot coals crisped brown bread, a mixture of rye and corn that colonists preferred because wheat was expensive. Skimmers (p. 216) could have lifted doughnuts frying in a cauldron of boiling lard. Trivets or broilers once held pieces of meat while they grilled over hot coals. Smokers grasped embers with pipe tongs (p. 217) and dropped them into long clay pipes. The typical New England hearth was deep, with pots suspended above the fire on a lug pole and later a swinging iron crane. This kettle tilter's hook at one time attached to a crane (p. 217). Firebacks, like the one on p. 162, grew hot and radiated heat into the room, recapturing some lost heat. A long-armed oven peel (p. 215) enabled a cook to retrieve bread from a deep beehive oven built into the hearth's thick sides. By the 1830s and 1840s, factory-made cast-iron cook stoves requiring far less fuel began to replace hearths and removing the need for tools like these.

Pierced Spatula

1818

Wrought iron
25¼ × 4½ × 1⅜ in.

Inscription: "MMK 1818"

2016.25.130

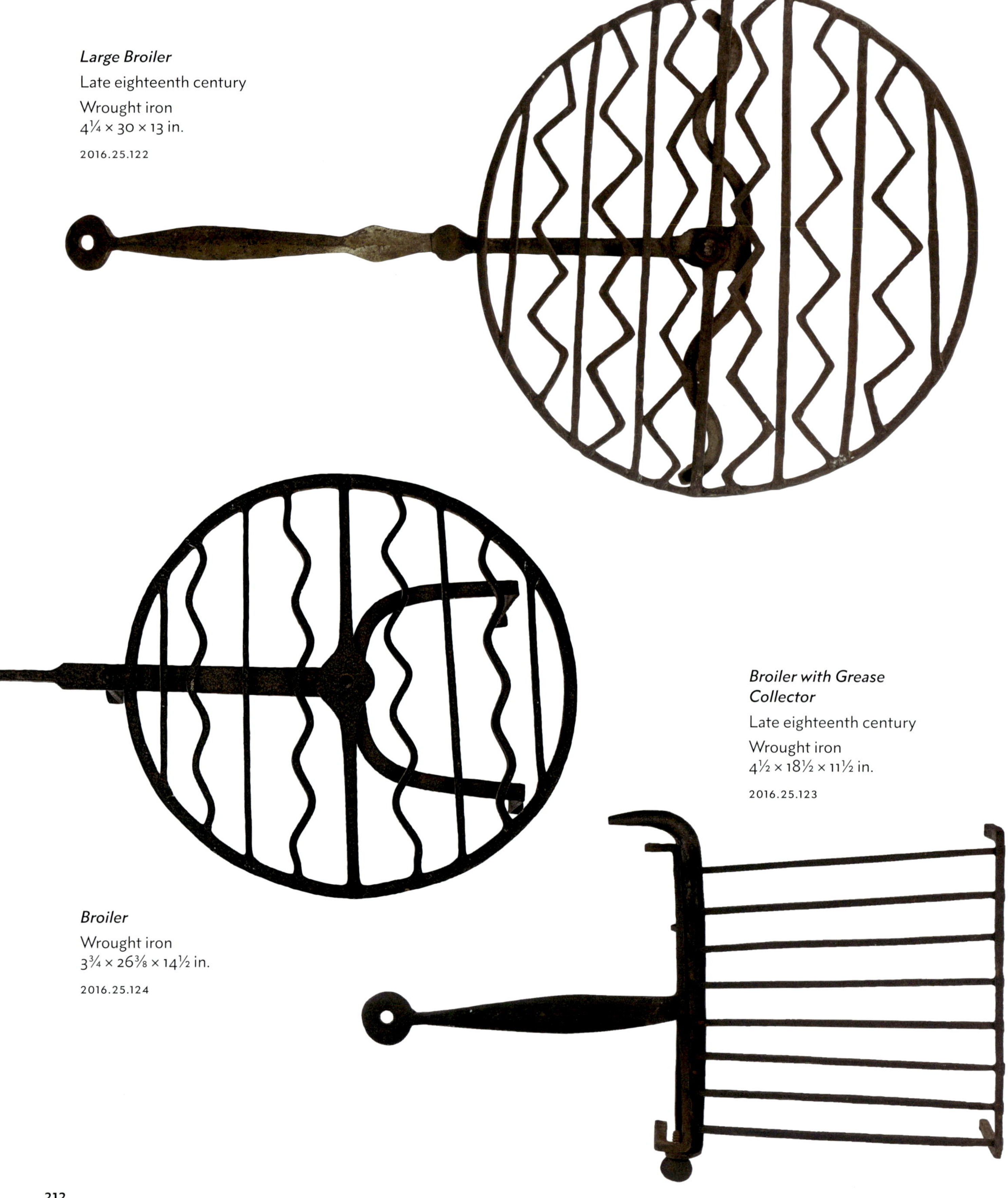

Large Broiler
Late eighteenth century
Wrought iron
4¼ × 30 × 13 in.
2016.25.122

Broiler with Grease Collector
Late eighteenth century
Wrought iron
4½ × 18½ × 11½ in.
2016.25.123

Broiler
Wrought iron
3¾ × 26⅜ × 14½ in.
2016.25.124

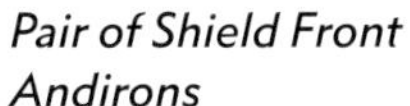

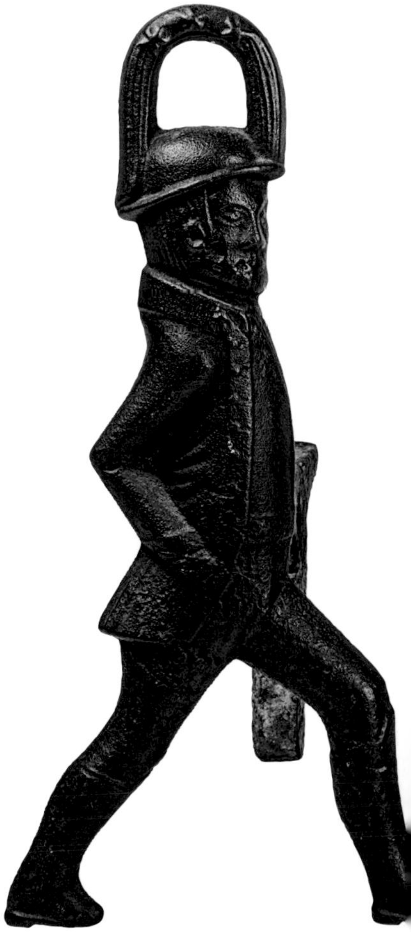

Pair of Shield Front Andirons

ca. 1790

Wrought iron
14½ × 11 × 17 in.

2016.25.7

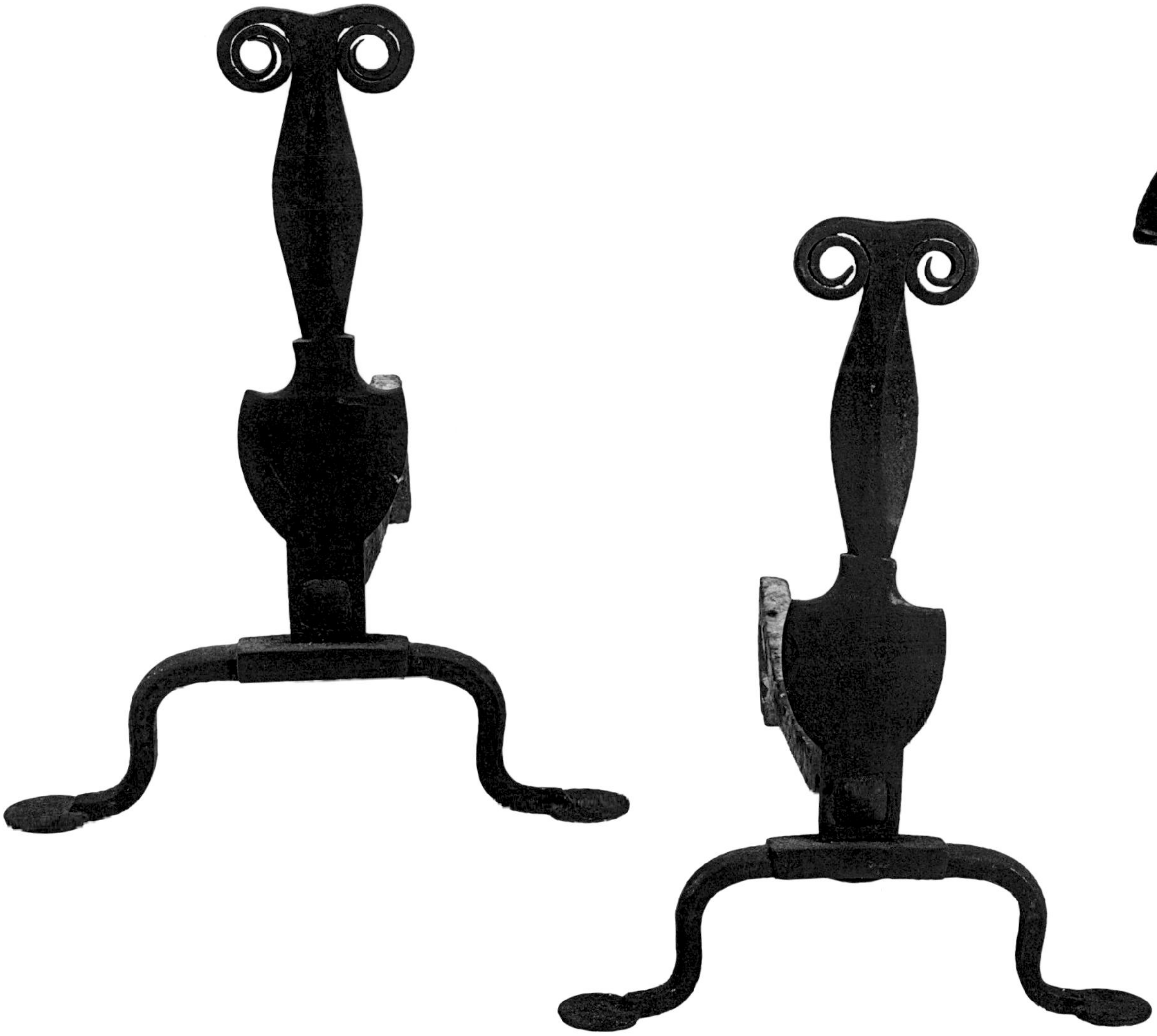

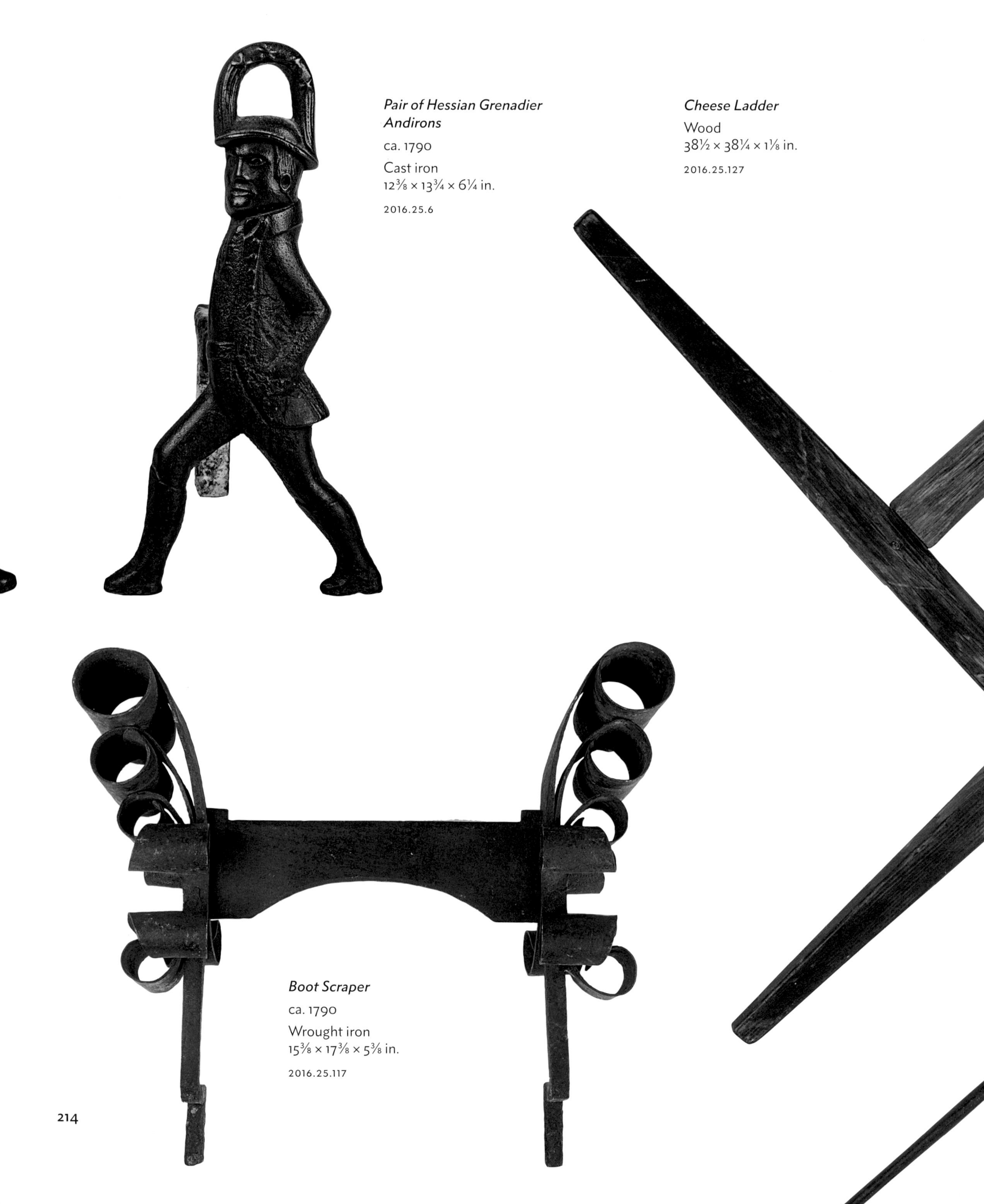

Pair of Hessian Grenadier Andirons

ca. 1790

Cast iron
12⅜ × 13¾ × 6¼ in.

2016.25.6

Cheese Ladder

Wood
38½ × 38¼ × 1⅛ in.

2016.25.127

Boot Scraper

ca. 1790

Wrought iron
15⅜ × 17⅜ × 5⅜ in.

2016.25.117

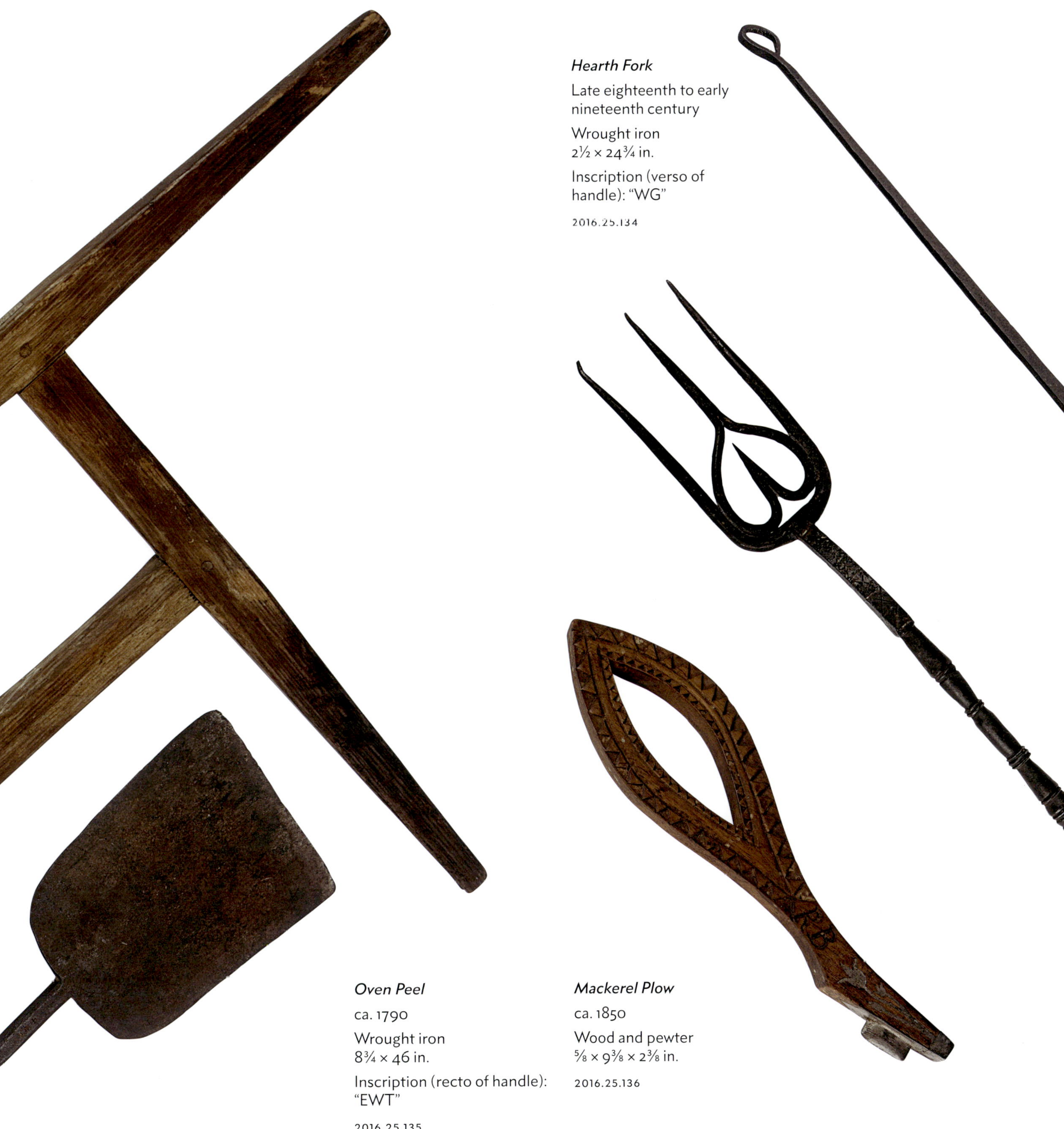

Hearth Fork

Late eighteenth to early nineteenth century

Wrought iron
2½ × 24¾ in.

Inscription (verso of handle): "WG"

2016.25.134

Oven Peel

ca. 1790

Wrought iron
8¾ × 46 in.

Inscription (recto of handle): "EWT"

2016.25.135

Mackerel Plow

ca. 1850

Wood and pewter
⅝ × 9⅜ × 2⅜ in.

2016.25.136

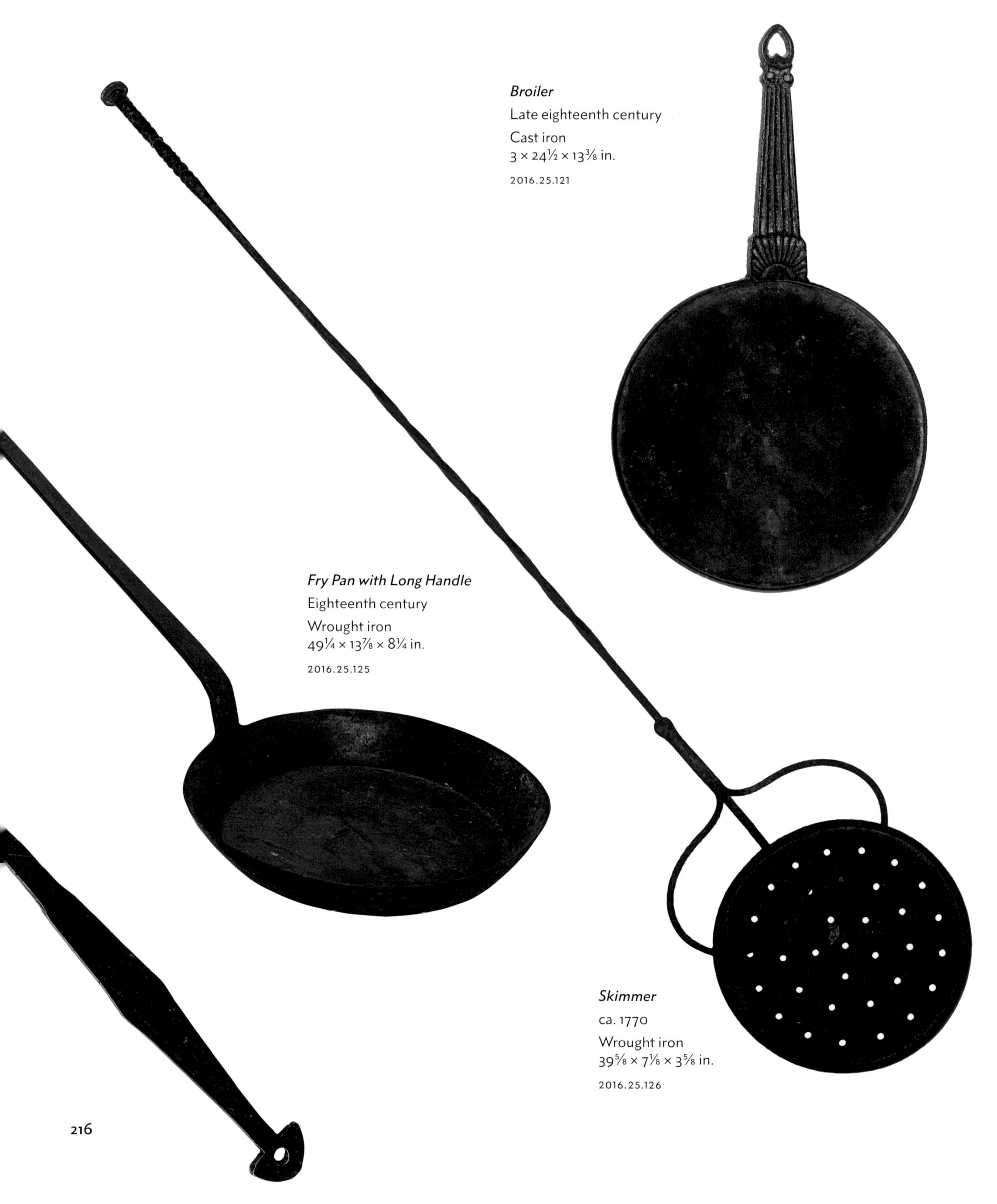

Broiler
Late eighteenth century
Cast iron
3 × 24½ × 13⅜ in.
2016.25.121

Fry Pan with Long Handle
Eighteenth century
Wrought iron
49¼ × 13⅞ × 8¼ in.
2016.25.125

Skimmer
ca. 1770
Wrought iron
39⅝ × 7⅛ × 3⅝ in.
2016.25.126

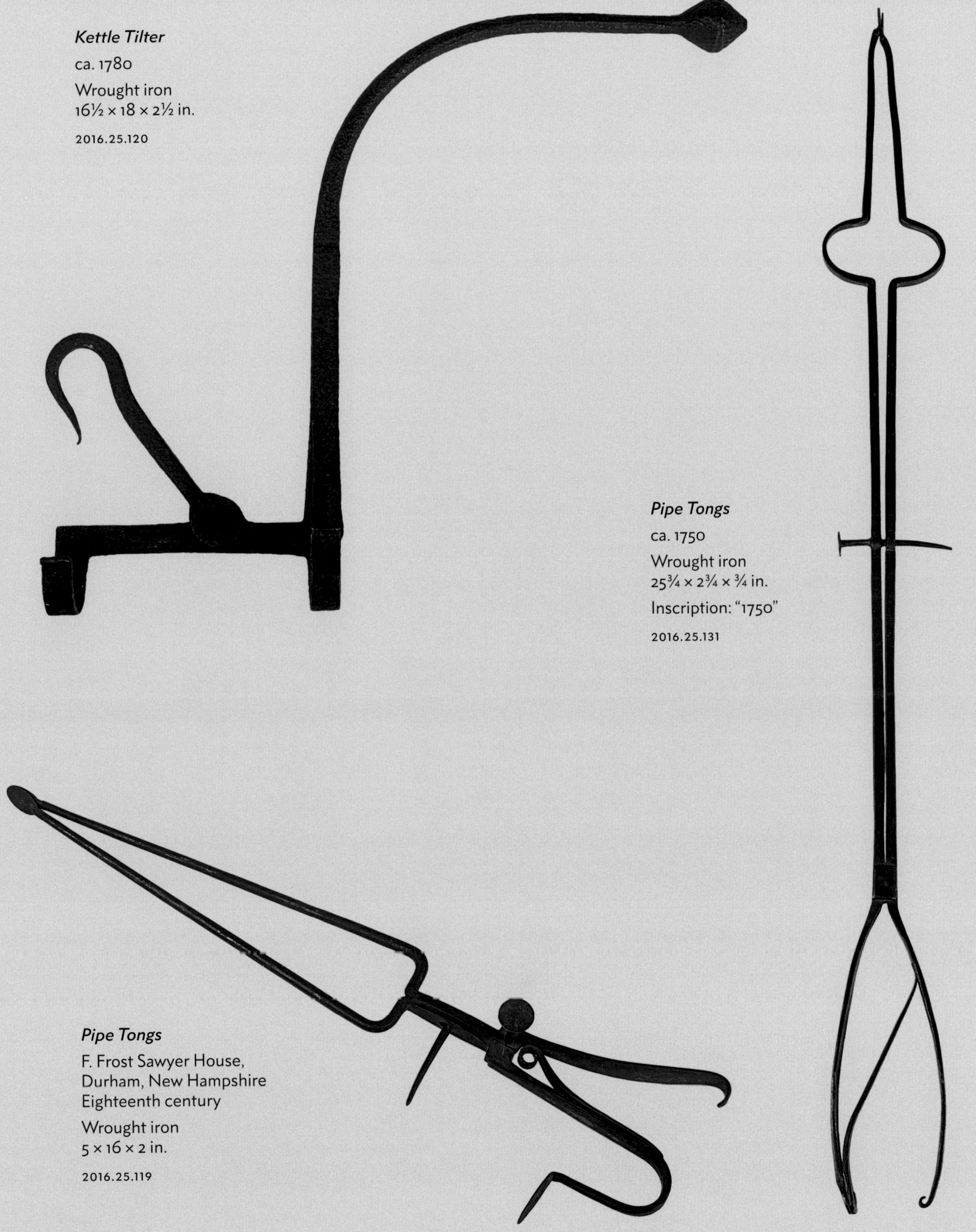

Kettle Tilter

ca. 1780

Wrought iron

16½ × 18 × 2½ in.

2016.25.120

Pipe Tongs

ca. 1750

Wrought iron

25¾ × 2¾ × ¾ in.

Inscription: "1750"

2016.25.131

Pipe Tongs

F. Frost Sawyer House,
Durham, New Hampshire
Eighteenth century

Wrought iron

5 × 16 × 2 in.

2016.25.119

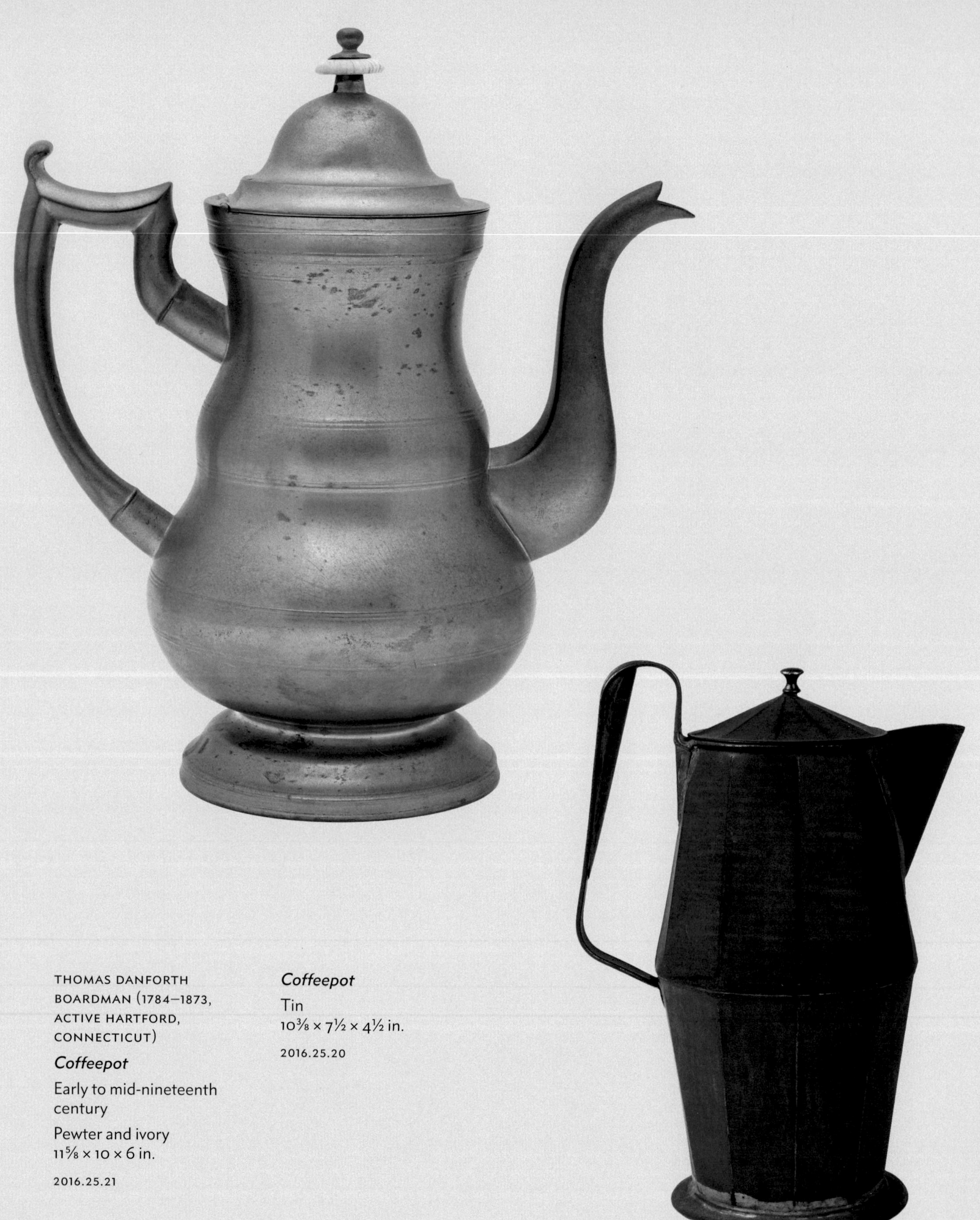

THOMAS DANFORTH BOARDMAN (1784–1873, ACTIVE HARTFORD, CONNECTICUT)

Coffeepot

Early to mid-nineteenth century

Pewter and ivory
11⅝ × 10 × 6 in.

2016.25.21

Coffeepot

Tin
10⅜ × 7½ × 4½ in.

2016.25.20

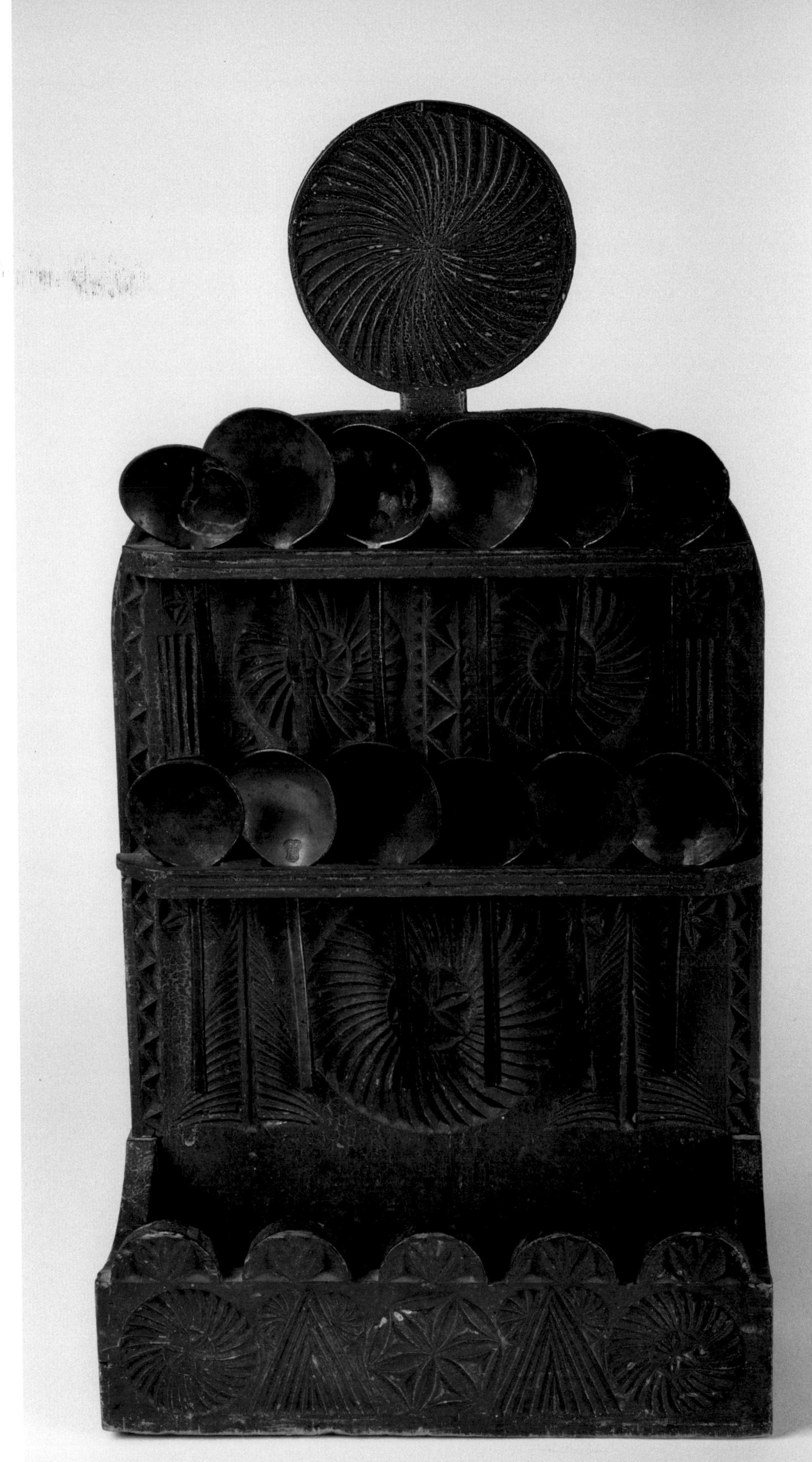

Chip-Carved Spoon Rack

Possibly Hudson River Valley or Connecticut
ca. 1760

Probably pine and blue paint
24 × 12½ × 5½ in.

L2015.41.101

CERAMICS

This and the following spread contain American stoneware and redware ceramics made for everyday kitchen use. During the eighteenth and nineteenth centuries, these were among the most common kitchen items and frequently listed in probate records. Jars might have held pickled fruits, like pears or plums, or shellfish, including oysters and mussels, to which vinegar was added for preservation. They could have also held molasses, homemade beer, cider, or rum, a potent liquor made from molasses that New Englanders imbibed in great quantities.

These ceramics fell into two types: redware, an earthenware fired at a low temperature, and stoneware, fired at a higher temperature with fewer impurities and more silica. Potteries all over the Northeast turned out low-cost earthenware items, like this redware jar with its variegated green and red glazes. Besides chipping easily, redware is too porous to hold liquids without the addition of toxic lead-based glazes. As early as 1778, the British physician James Hardy warned about the dangers of lead poisoning from earthenware vessels, especially those that held acidic foods containing vinegar. By contrast, stoneware is nonporous and uses a safe, salt-based glaze with a distinctive orange-peel texture.

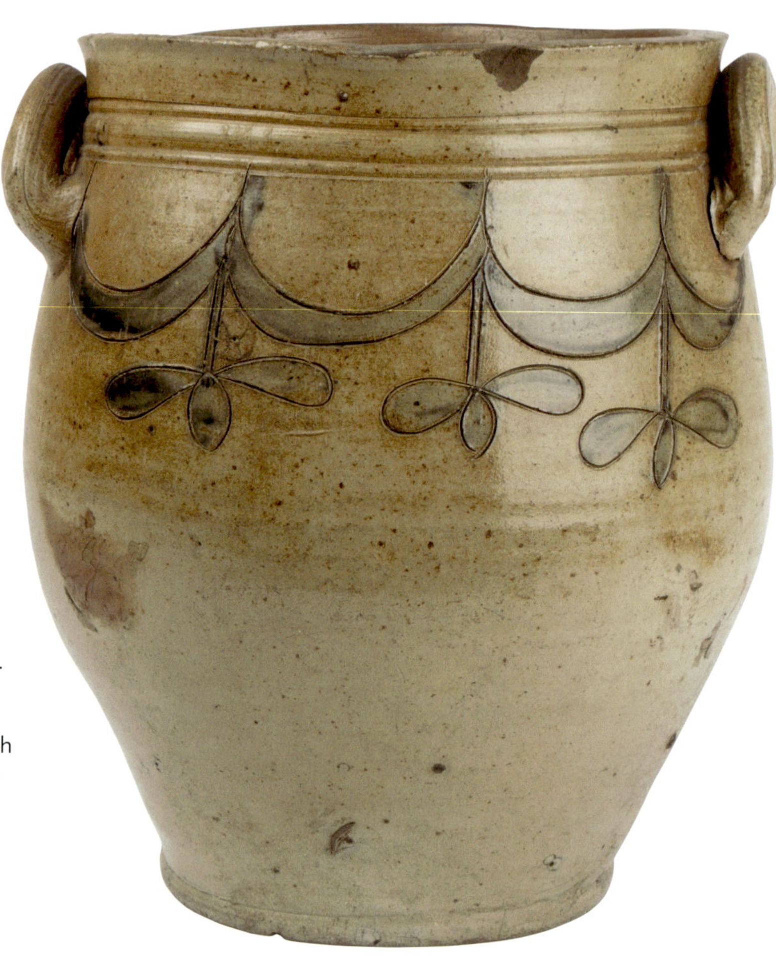

Swag- and Tassel-Decorated Jar

Possibly New York State
ca. 1810

Stoneware
13¾ × 11½ in.

2016.25.12

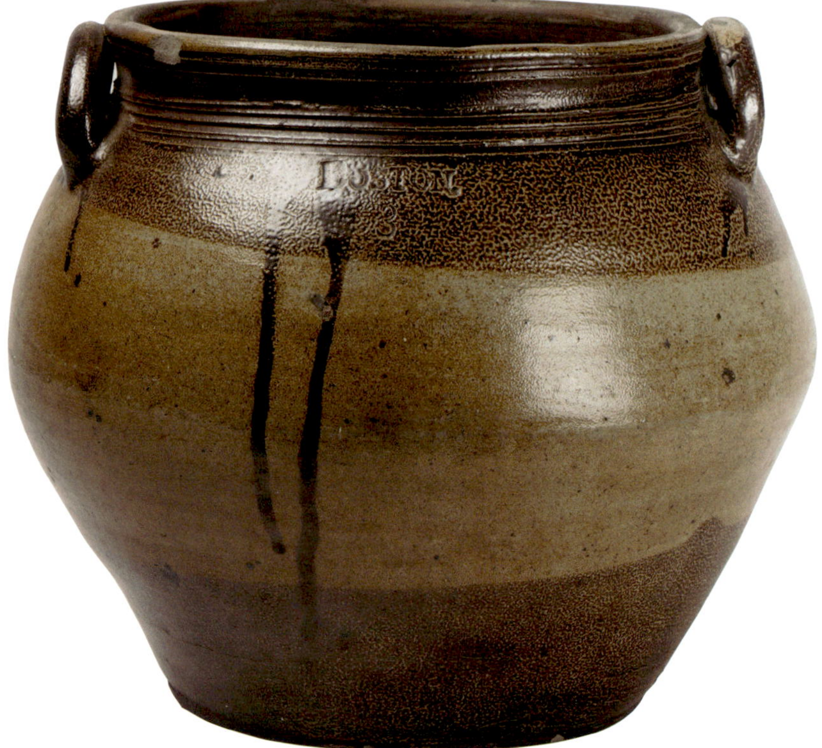

Jar

Boston
ca. 1804

Stoneware
10¾ × 12½ in.

Inscription: "BOSTON / 3"

2016.25.8

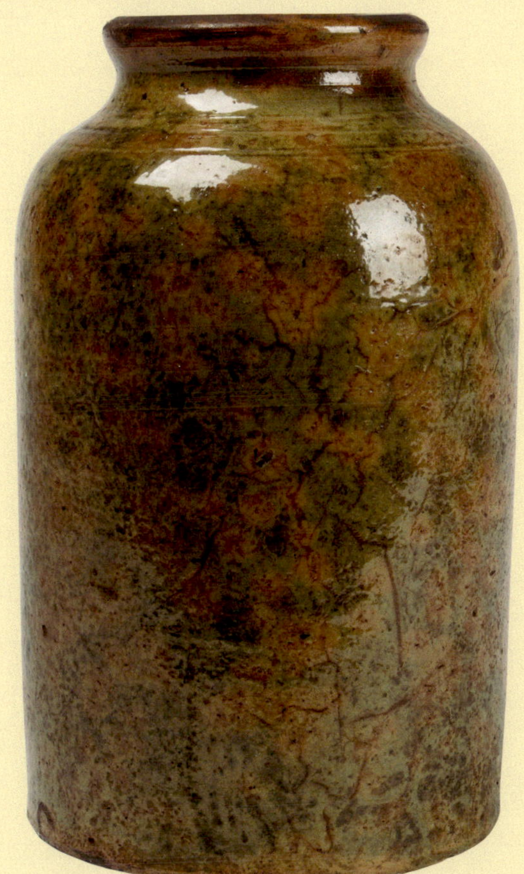

Jar

Albany area, New York
ca. 1840

Redware
12½ × 7¾ in.

2016.25.11

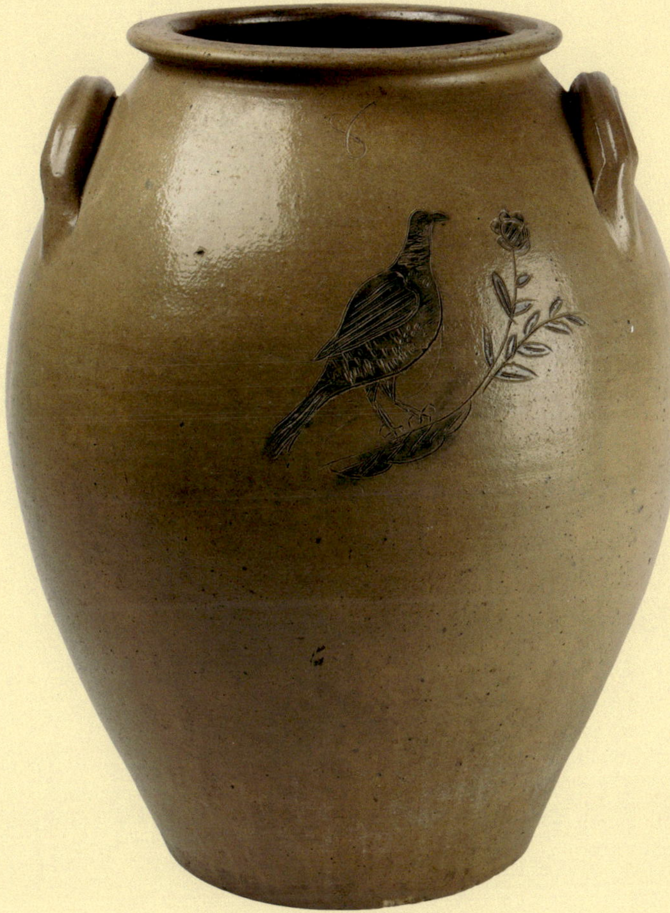

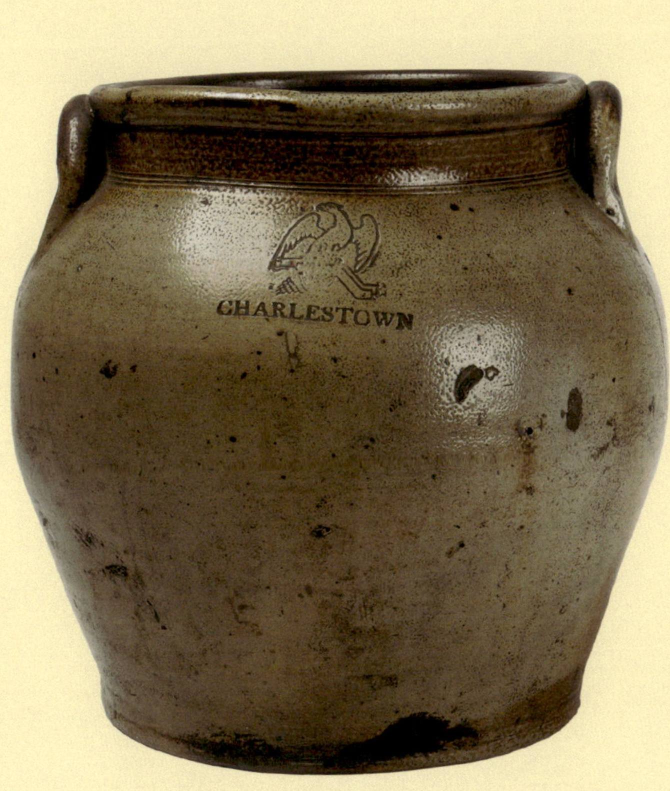

Jar

Charlestown, Massachusetts
ca. 1810

Stoneware
11¾ × 12 in.

Inscription:
"CHARLESTOWN"

2016.25.13

Jar

Connecticut or New York
ca. 1820

Stoneware
17⅜ × 13½ in.

2016.25.15

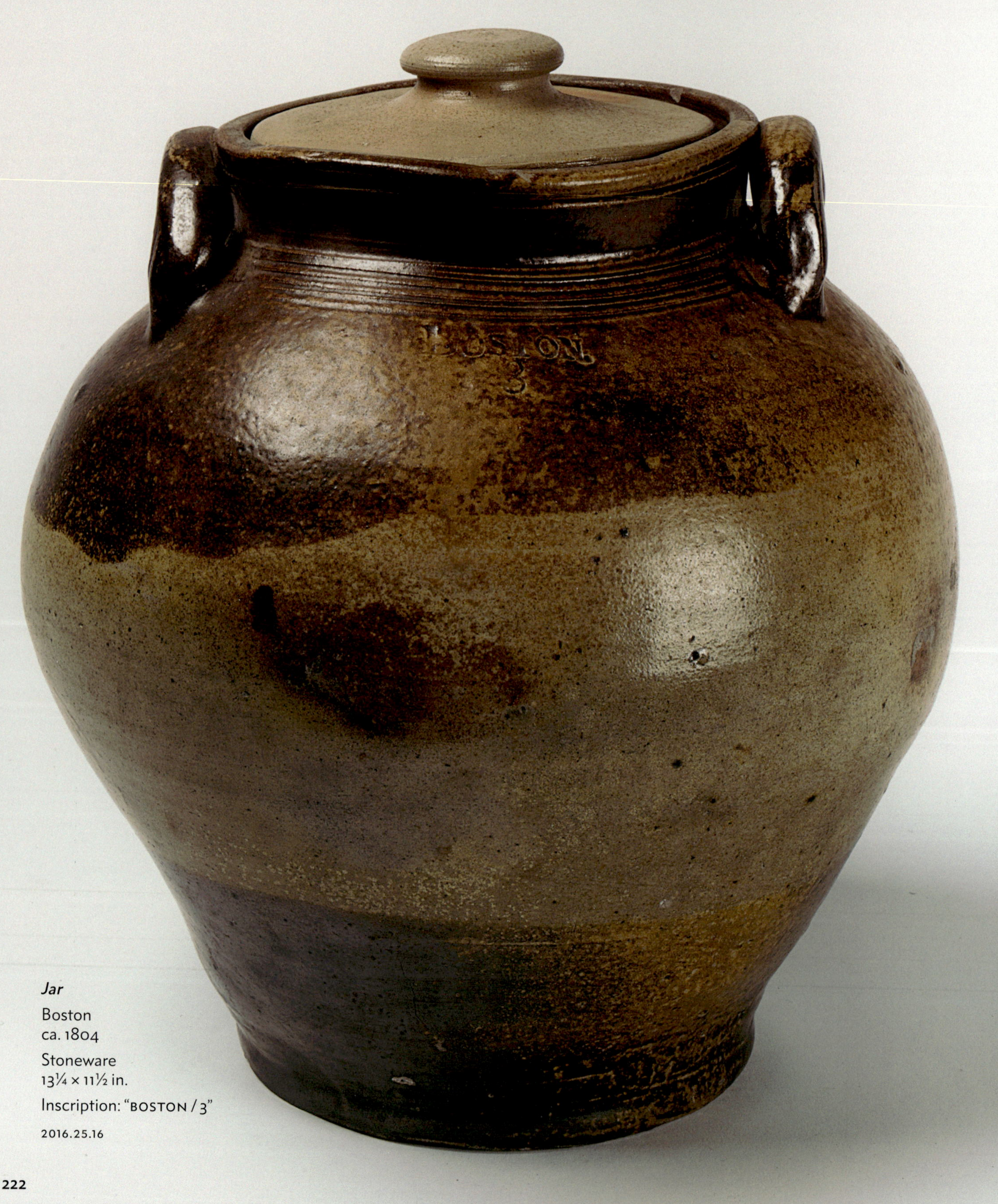

Jar
Boston
ca. 1804
Stoneware
13¼ × 11½ in.
Inscription: "BOSTON / 3"
2016.25.16

SLAVERY IN NEW ENGLAND

These jugs probably held rum or its principal ingredient, molasses, a product made by slaves on the sugar plantations of the West Indies. New Englanders exported rum to Africa, Africa sent slaves to the Caribbean, and the Caribbean shipped molasses to New England in the Triangular Trade. The traffic in molasses and rum meant that New Englanders enriched themselves from slavery, while some participated in the slave trade.

In colonial New England, there were sizable numbers of slaves who were Native Americans or of African descent. In 1750, slaves made up 14 percent of Rhode Island's population, while New York City in 1771 had around twenty thousand. Unlike slaveholders in the South or the Caribbean, where plantations had hundreds of slaves, the average New England slaveholder had only one or two, and many worked in skilled trades like ironworking, shipbuilding, weaving, and tailoring. After the American Revolution, the slave population of New England decreased, but the cotton mills that sprang up depended on cotton from Southern plantations. The wealth of New England continued to derive from an inhumane and horrific system. Also, racist laws blocked political rights of freed people. In 1814, Connecticut limited suffrage to white males, and Rhode Island did the same in 1822.

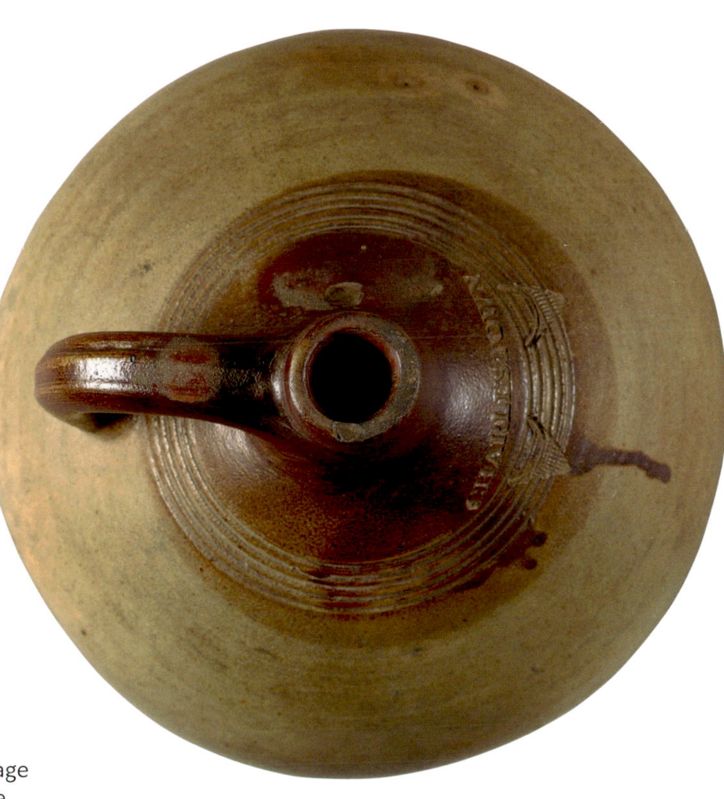

Jug

Charlestown, Massachusetts
ca. 1810

Stoneware
14½ × 11 in.

Inscription: "CHARLESTOWN"

2016.25.17

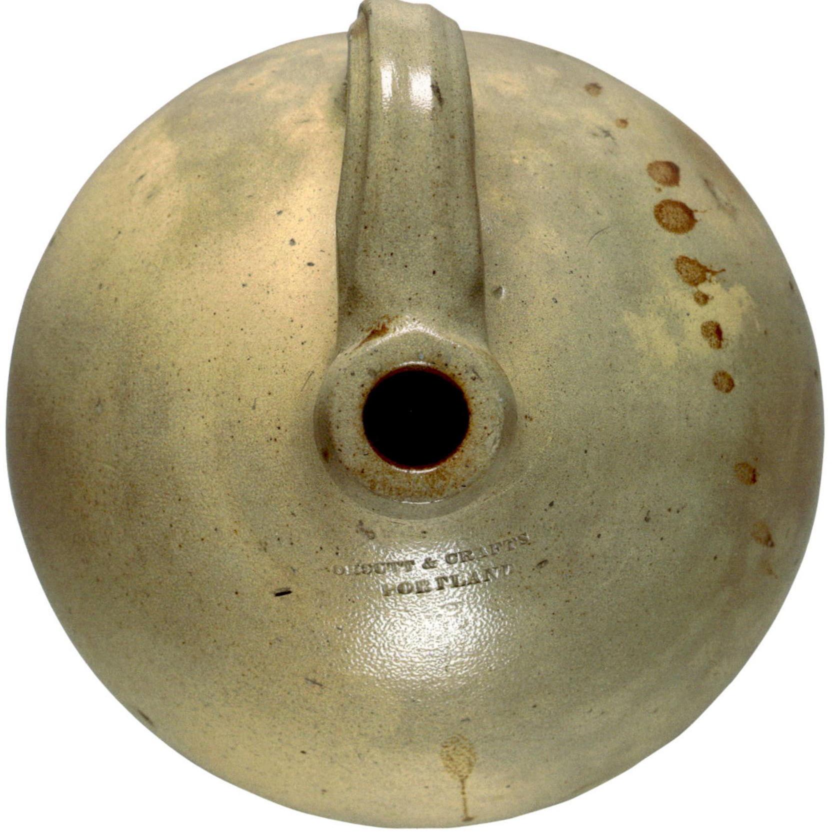

ORCUTT & CRAFTS POTTERY

Three-Gallon Jug

Portland, Maine
ca. 1835–37

Stoneware
15 × 11 in.

Inscription: "ORCUTT & CRAFTS / PORTLAND / 3"

2016.25.14

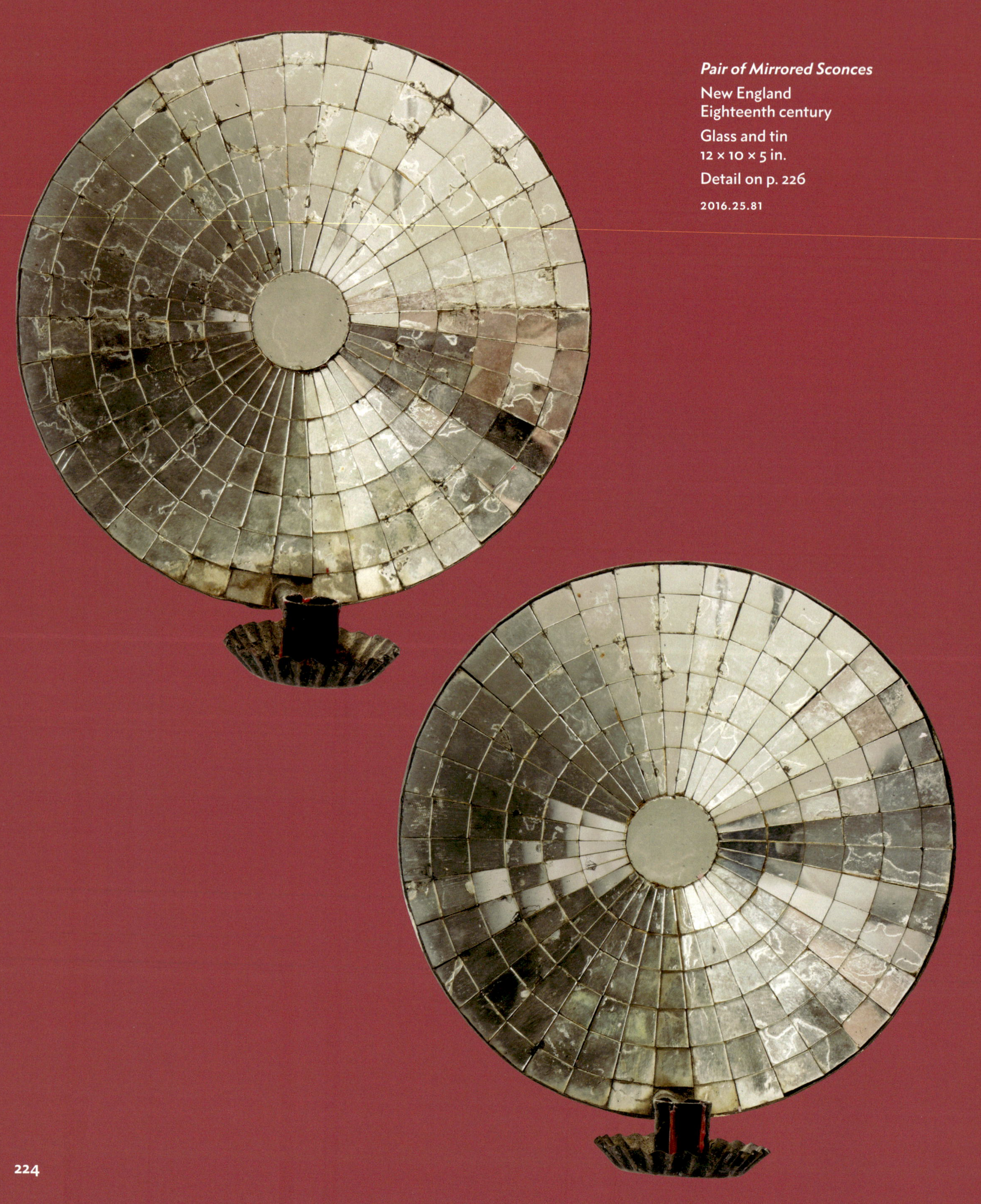

Pair of Mirrored Sconces
New England
Eighteenth century
Glass and tin
12 × 10 × 5 in.
Detail on p. 226
2016.25.81

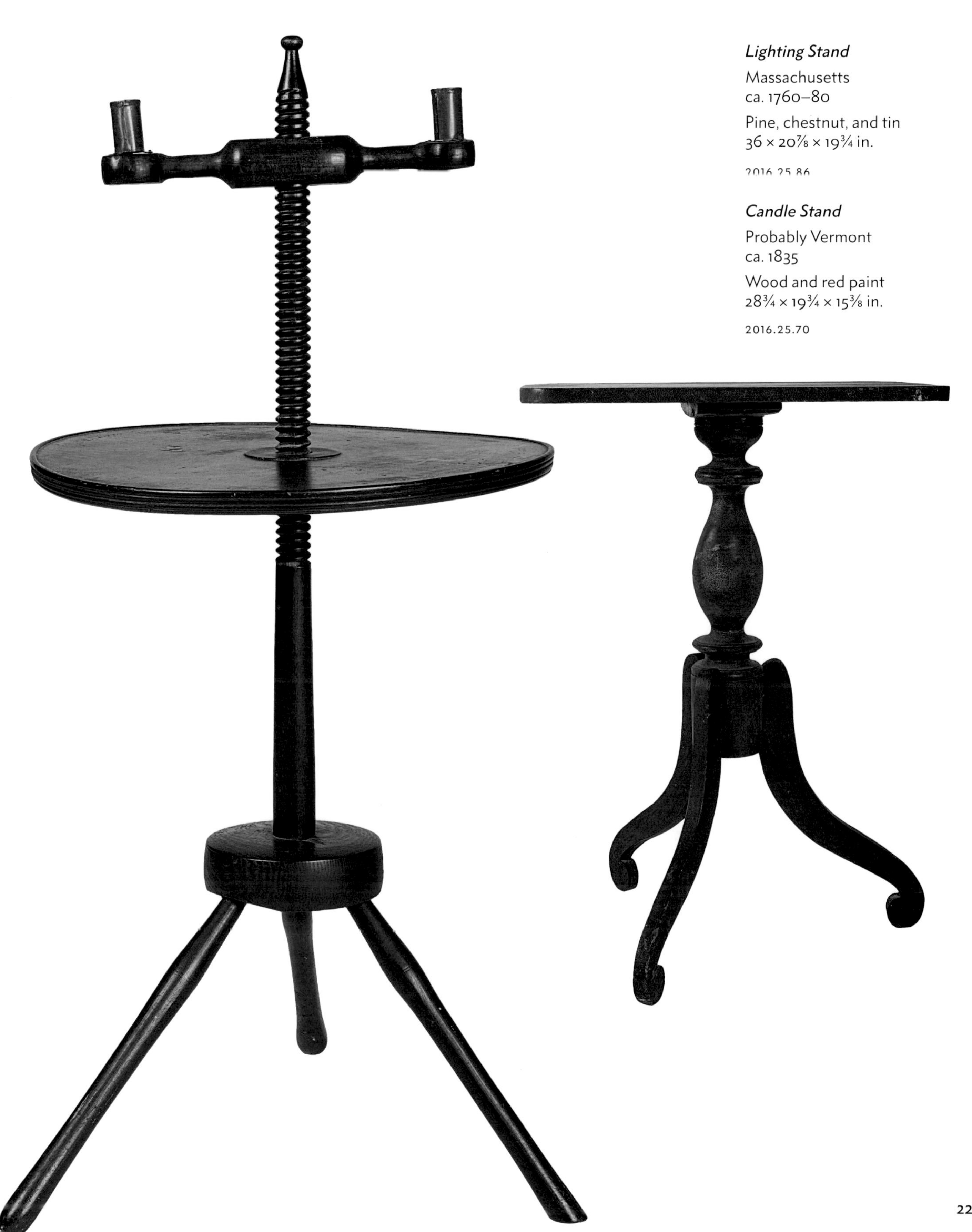

Lighting Stand
Massachusetts
ca. 1760–80
Pine, chestnut, and tin
36 × 20⅞ × 19¾ in.
2016.25.86

Candle Stand
Probably Vermont
ca. 1835
Wood and red paint
28¾ × 19¾ × 15⅜ in.
2016.25.70

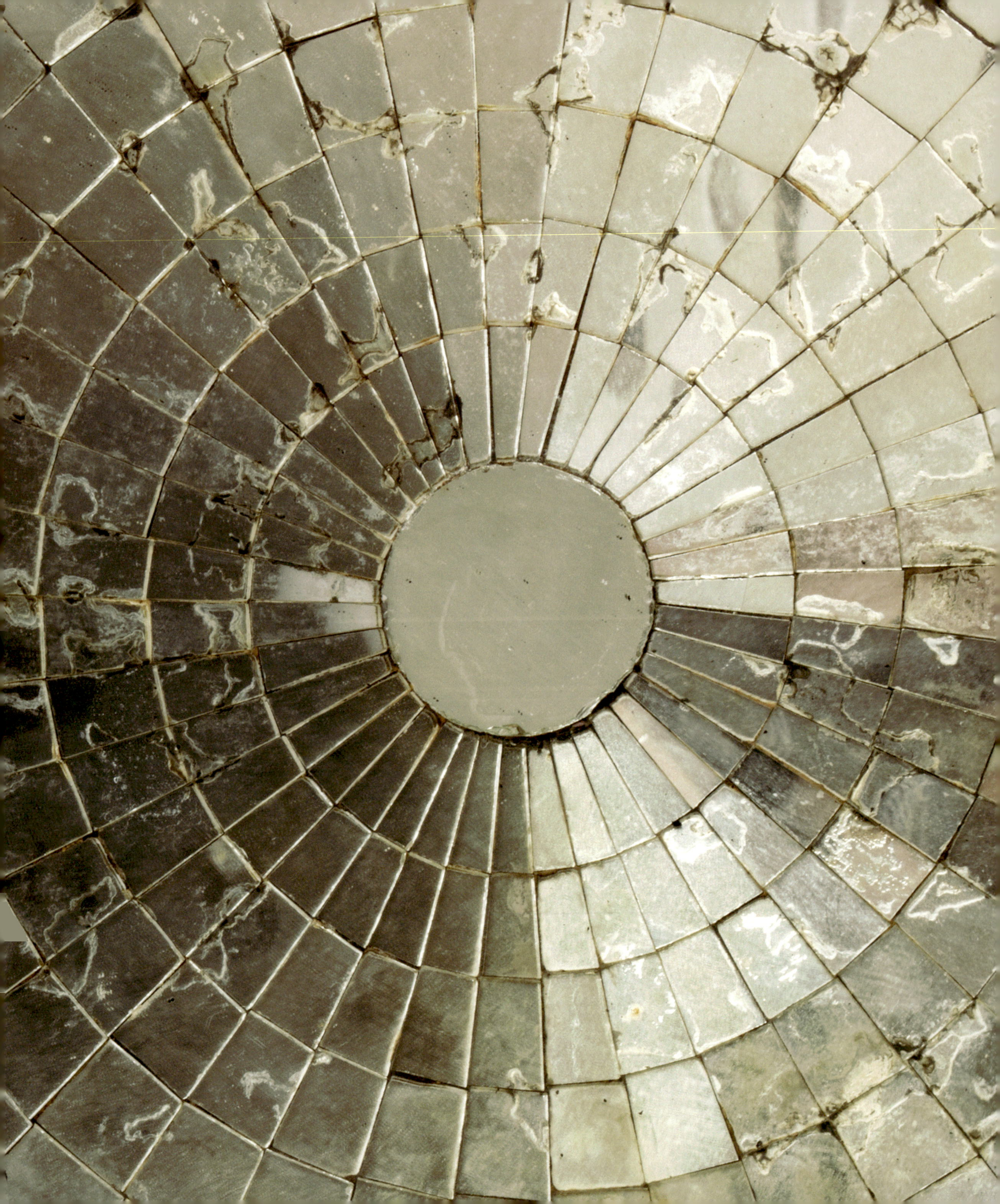

Mirrored Sconce (detail)

See p. 224

Adjustable Candle Lamp

ca. 1810

Tin and sand
11½ × 8½ × 6 in.

2016.25.82

Adjustable Candle Lamp and Snuffer

ca. 1800

Tin and sand
23¾ × 6¼ in.

2016.25.83

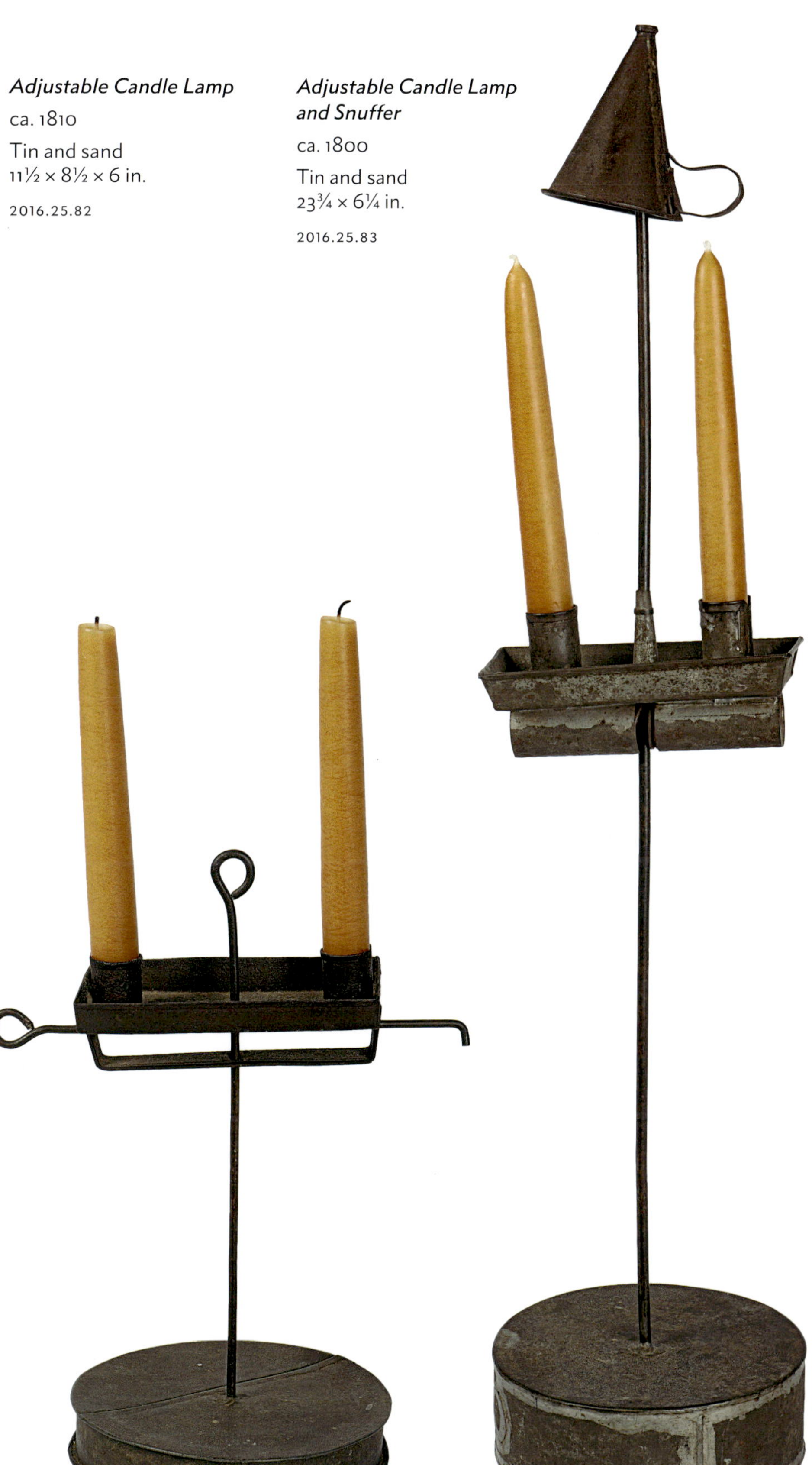

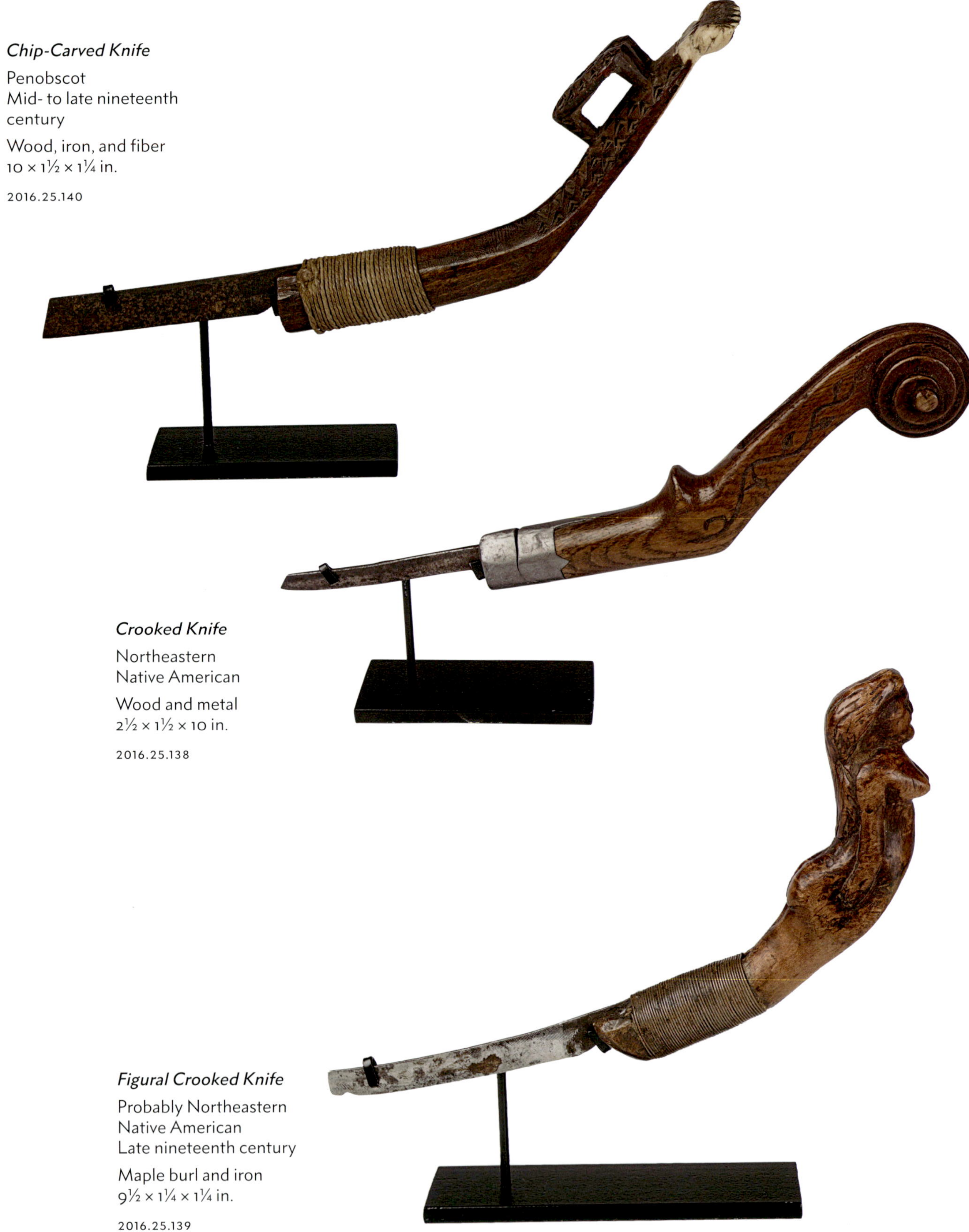

Chip-Carved Knife

Penobscot
Mid- to late nineteenth century

Wood, iron, and fiber
10 × 1½ × 1¼ in.

2016.25.140

Crooked Knife

Northeastern
Native American

Wood and metal
2½ × 1½ × 10 in.

2016.25.138

Figural Crooked Knife

Probably Northeastern
Native American
Late nineteenth century

Maple burl and iron
9½ × 1¼ × 1¼ in.

2016.25.139

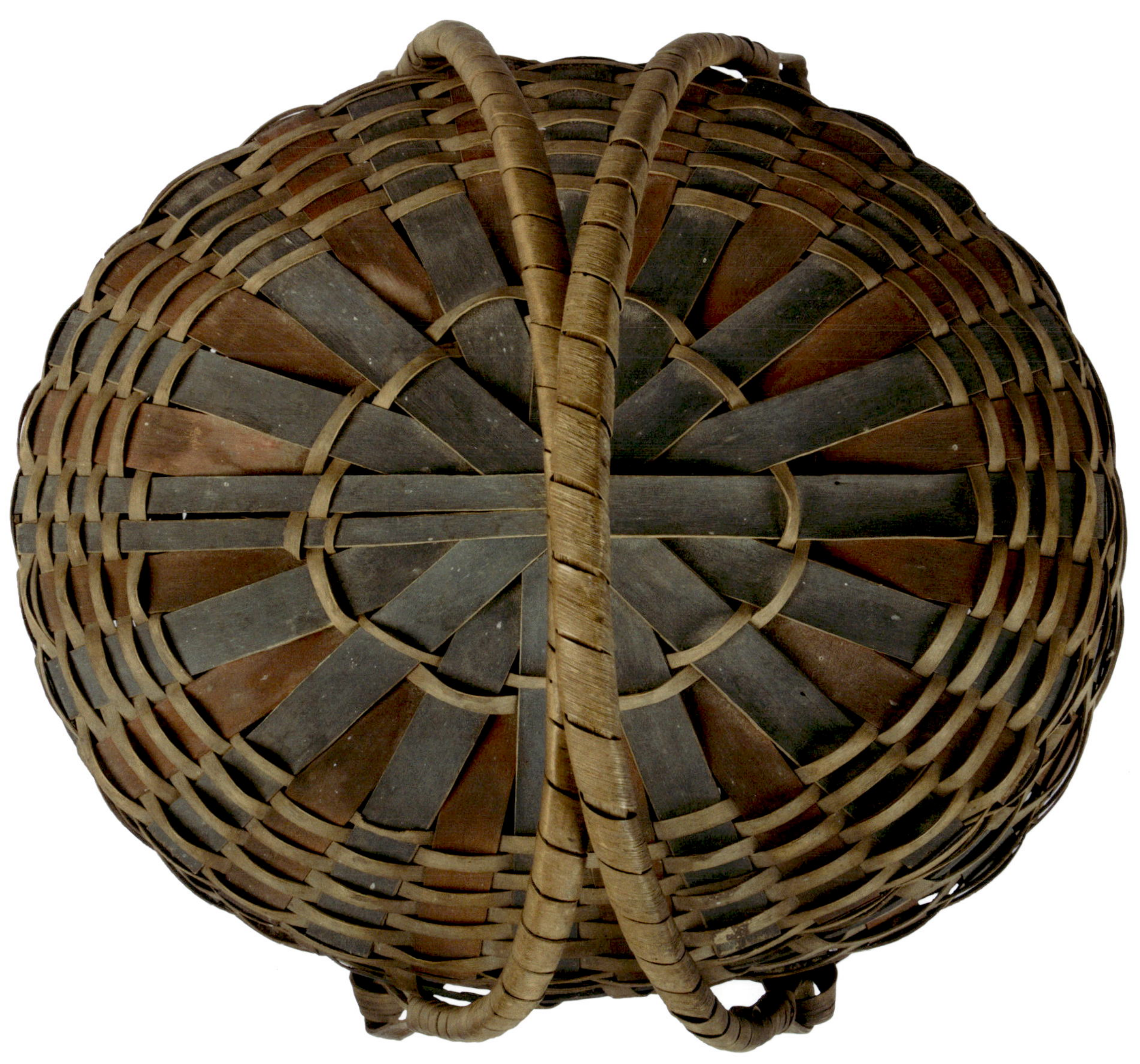

BASKETMAKING

Today in Maine and nearby areas, Native American people have vibrant practices in basketmaking and other craft traditions. Organizations like the Maine Indian Basketmakers Alliance and the Abbe Museum share the work of Passamaquoddy, Mi'kmaq, Maliseet, and Penobscot artists. In the early nineteenth century, Native American basketmakers who peddled their wares from door to door were already a fixture across New England. In face of the dispossession of their land, discrimination, and few economic opportunities, baskets woven mostly by women from freely available wood and grasses offered a way to earn money. They filled Northeastern homes, holding clothes, tools, sewing, hats, cheese, and fruits.

Few baskets can be attributed to an artist or even a group. In the Fielding Collection, a tricolor ash splint basket, however, is initialed "J.H.S.," as are about a dozen other known examples. J.H.S. was purportedly Mohegan. On the following page, two other splint baskets have colored, stamped, and drawn patterns, which are typical.

Baskets are only one kind of container. Waterproof and naturally antiseptic, birchbark containers (pp. 231, 233) held food and liquids, including maple syrup. Colored porcupine quillwork (p. 231) remains a specialty of the Mi'kmaq. Soaking the hollow quills makes them pliable and good for weaving.

J. H. S.

***Basket* (view from above)**

Mohegan
ca. 1880

Ash splint and dye
14 × 12 × 10½ in.

Inscription: "J.H.S."

2016.25.50

Splint Woven Basket

Maine
Late nineteenth century

Wood splint and pigment
7¼ × 12⅛ × 11⅞ in.

2016.25.24

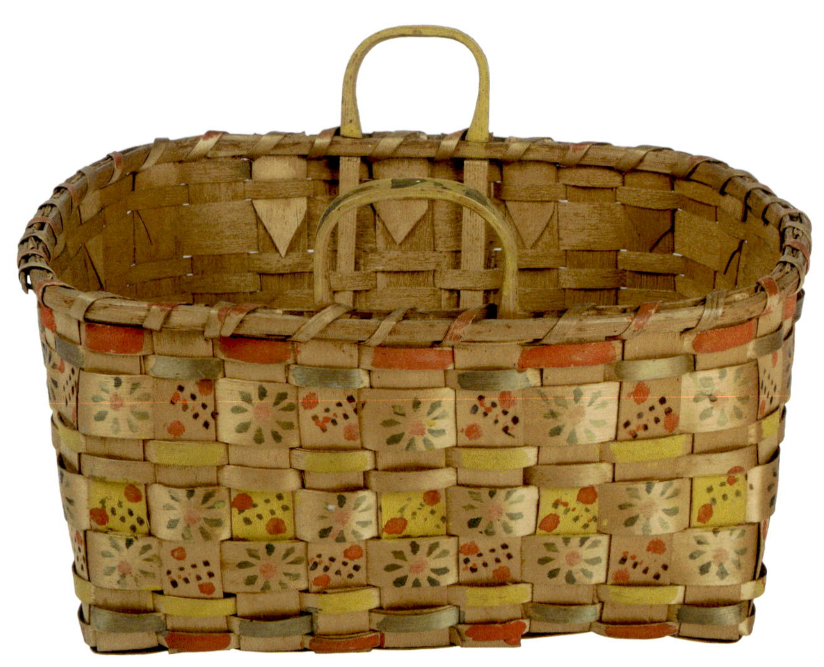

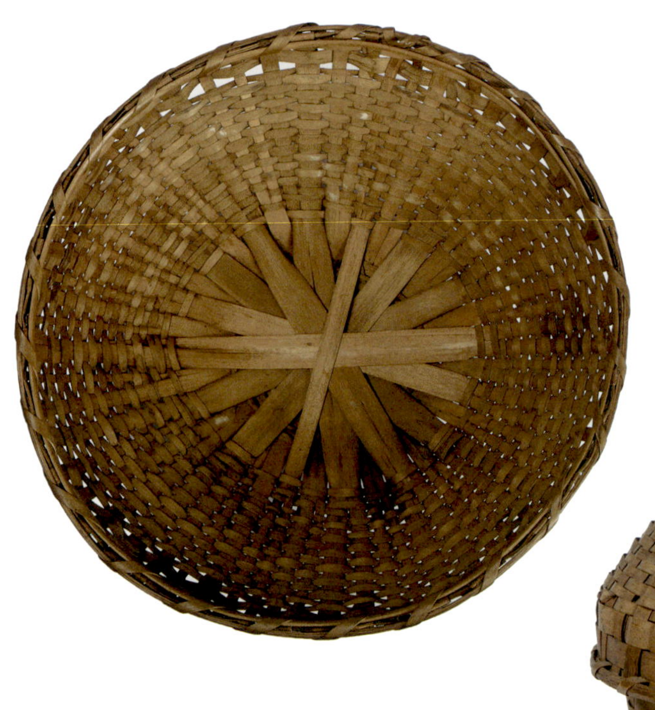

Basket (and lid interior)

New England area,
Native American
ca. 1832

Woven ash splint and pigment
Basket: 7½ × 12⅞ × 13½ in.
Lid: 5⅞ × 14½ × 13¾ in.

2016.25.25

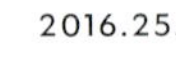

Bark-Covered Container

Mid-nineteenth century

Elm bark, spruce root, and black pigment
$4\frac{1}{8} \times 3\frac{1}{2} \times 6\frac{1}{2}$ in.

2016.25.23

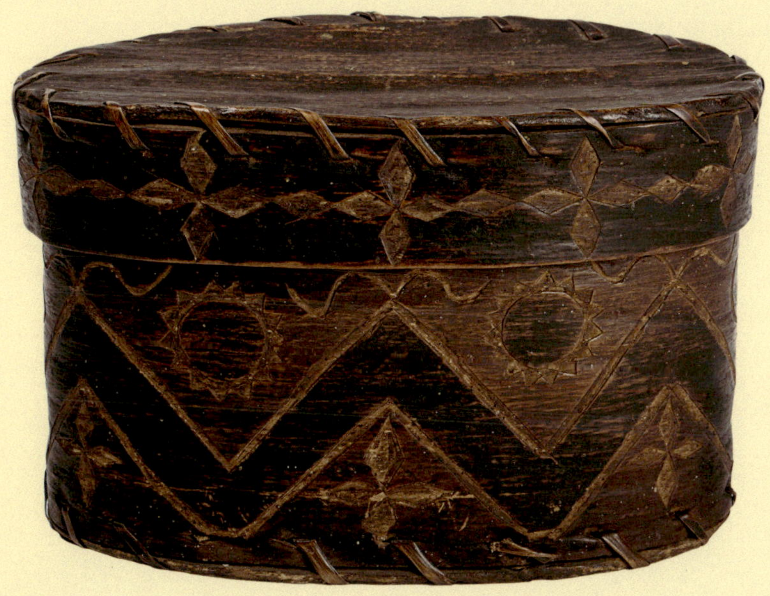

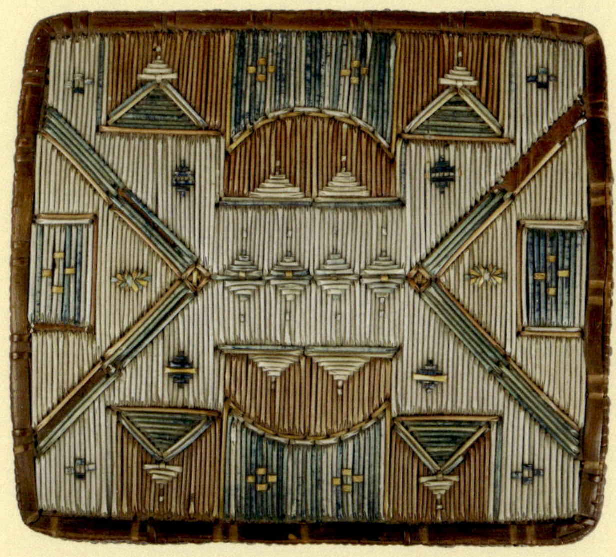

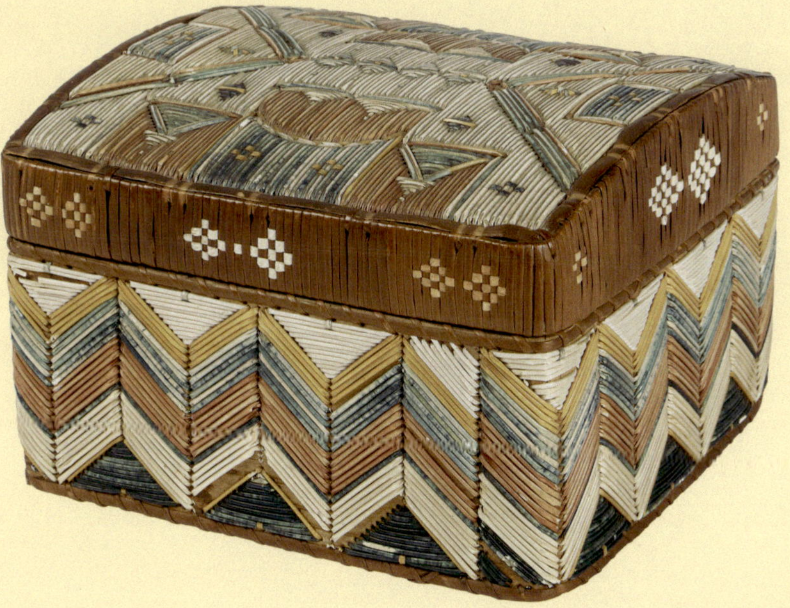

Quillwork Box

Mi'kmaq
ca. 1850

Wood, birchbark, porcupine quills, and natural aniline dye
$3\frac{7}{8} \times 5\frac{7}{8} \times 5\frac{1}{4}$ in.

2016.25.27

GNARLY

A burl is an abnormal, wart-like tree growth caused by a virus or fungus. Rather than the typical parallel bands found in wood, the burl grain pattern is irregular. This makes it unusually resistant to warping, cracking, and wear—an ideal material for kitchen bowls like these. Because they are hewn by hand rather than turned on a lathe, it is likely that they were made by a Native American craftsperson.

Finely textured burl veneers, like those on the Fielding Collection chest of drawers (see pp. 60–61 for a detail), also embellished furniture surfaces. Burls form on trees in mature forests, which were common in North America but far rarer in heavily logged Europe. For this reason, burl woods were a luxury in Europe, but far more common in the colonies.

Oval Bowl

Ash burl, carved
8 × 20 × 16⅝ in.

L2015.41.55

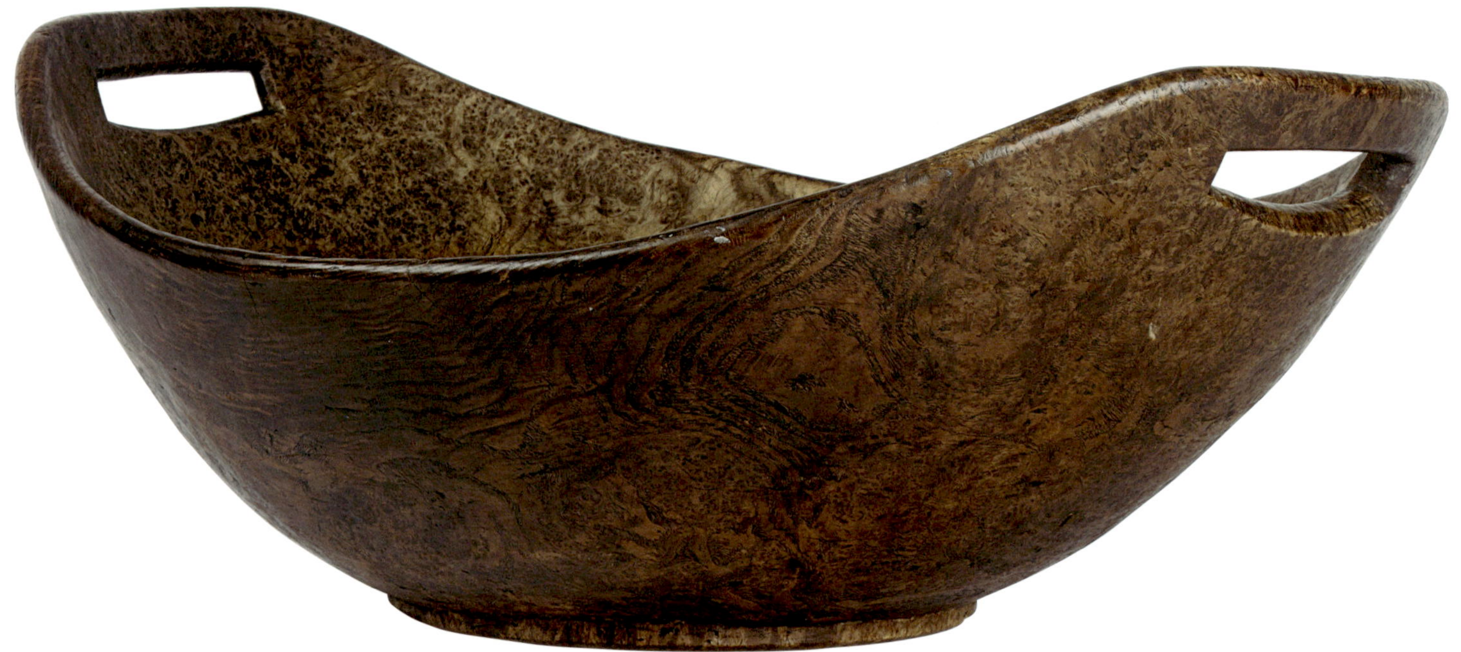

Small Makuk

Probably Ojibwe
Late eighteenth to early nineteenth century

Birchbark and spruce root
6 × 5 × 5 in.

2016.25.48

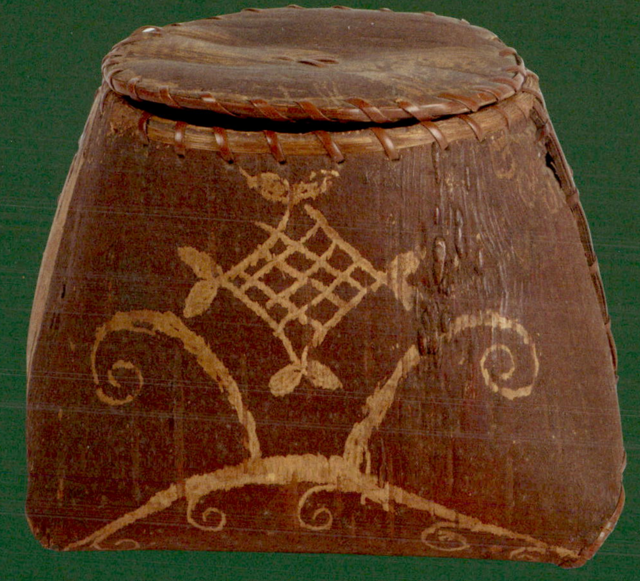

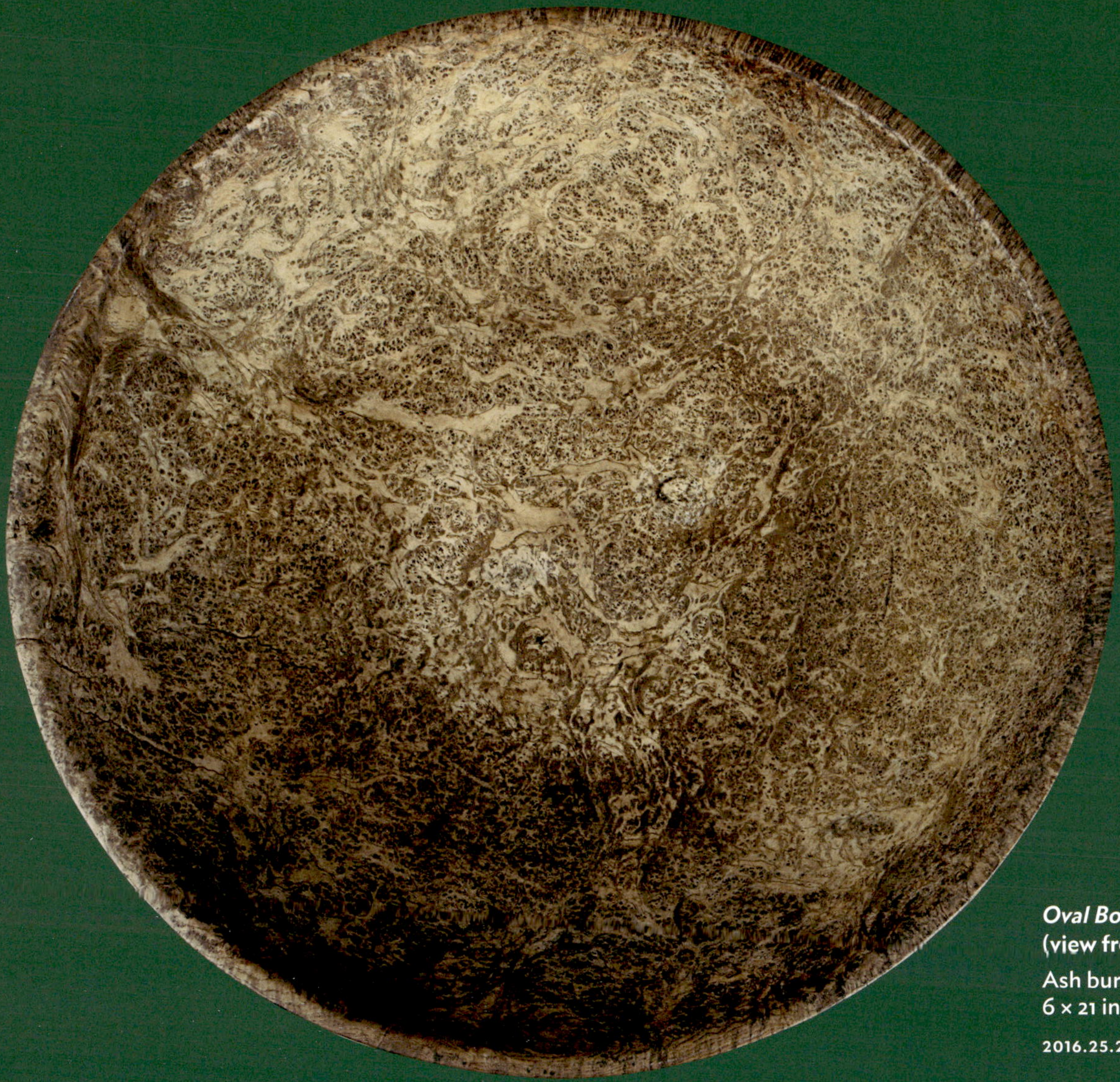

Oval Bowl
(view from above)

Ash burl, carved
6 × 21 in.

2016.25.22

SALMON BREWSTER
(1802–1887)

Bucket

Maine
Nineteenth century

Wood, metal, and paint
8⅝ × 11¾ × 11⅛ in.

Inscription: "J. BAGNALL & SONS"

2016.25.118

SALMON BREWSTER
(1802–1887)

Bucket

Maine
Nineteenth century

Wood, metal, and paint
13⅛ × 12½ × 12⅛ in.

Inscription: "SB"

L2015.41.188.2

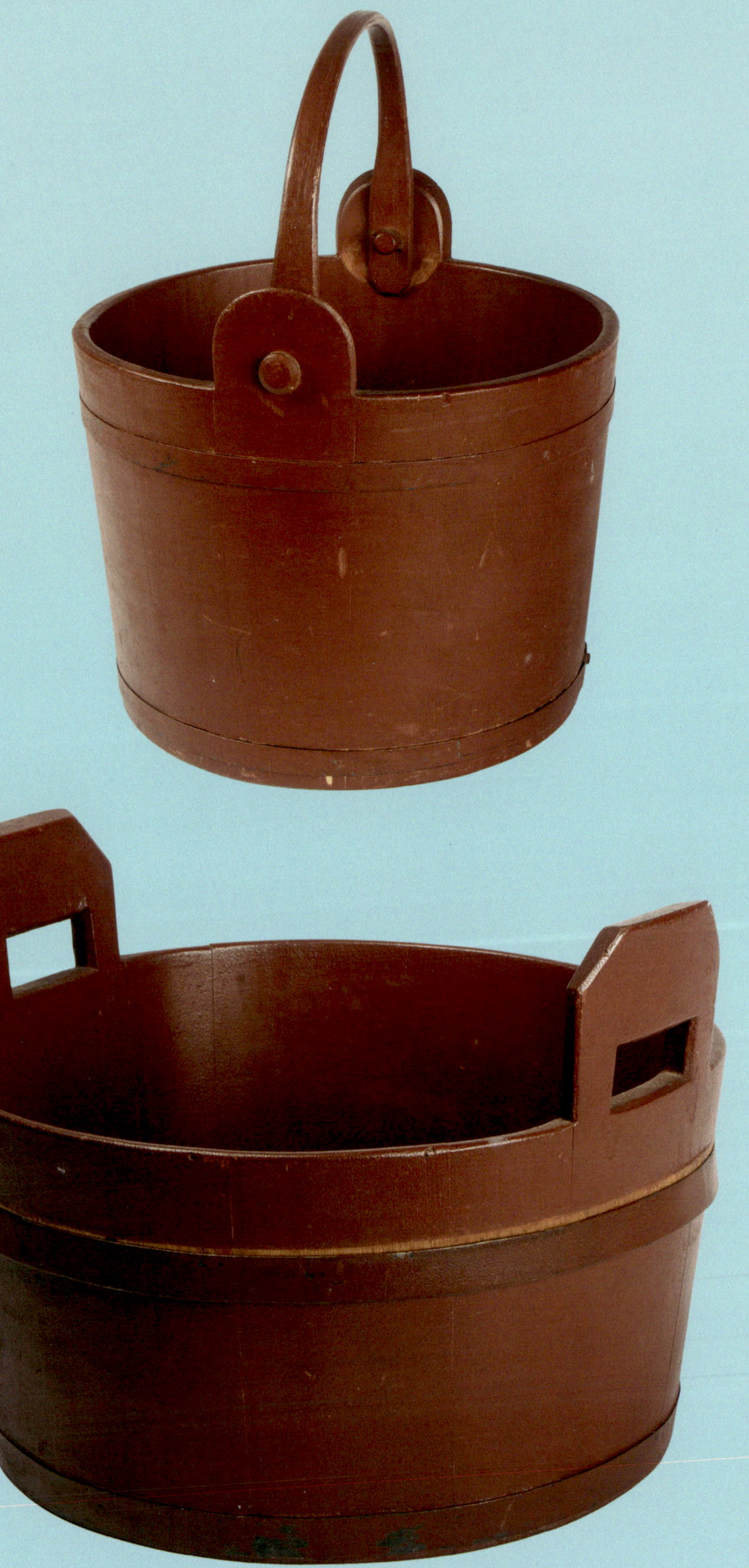

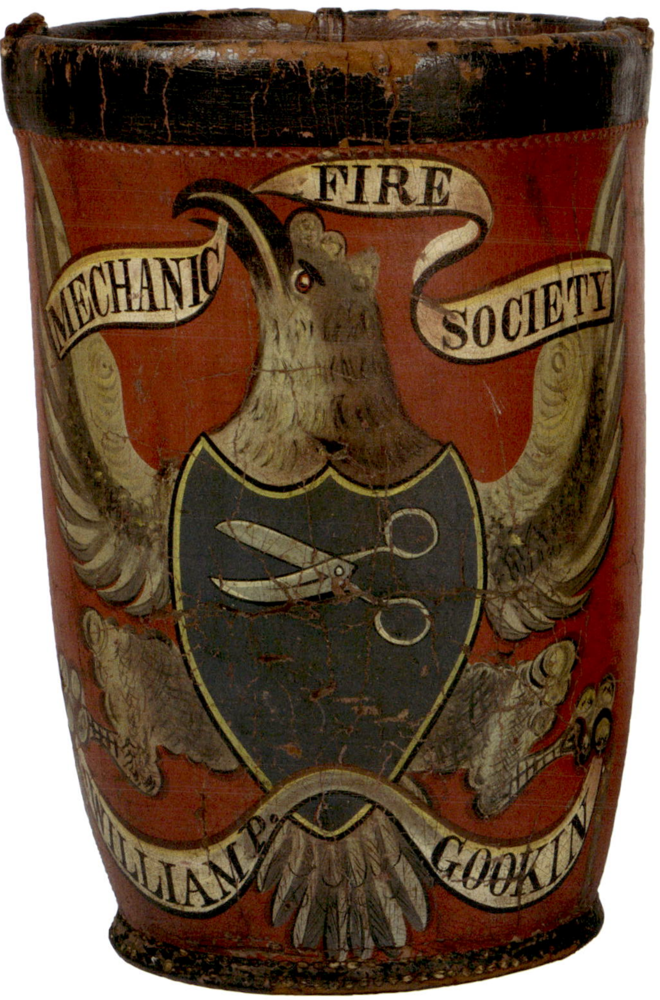

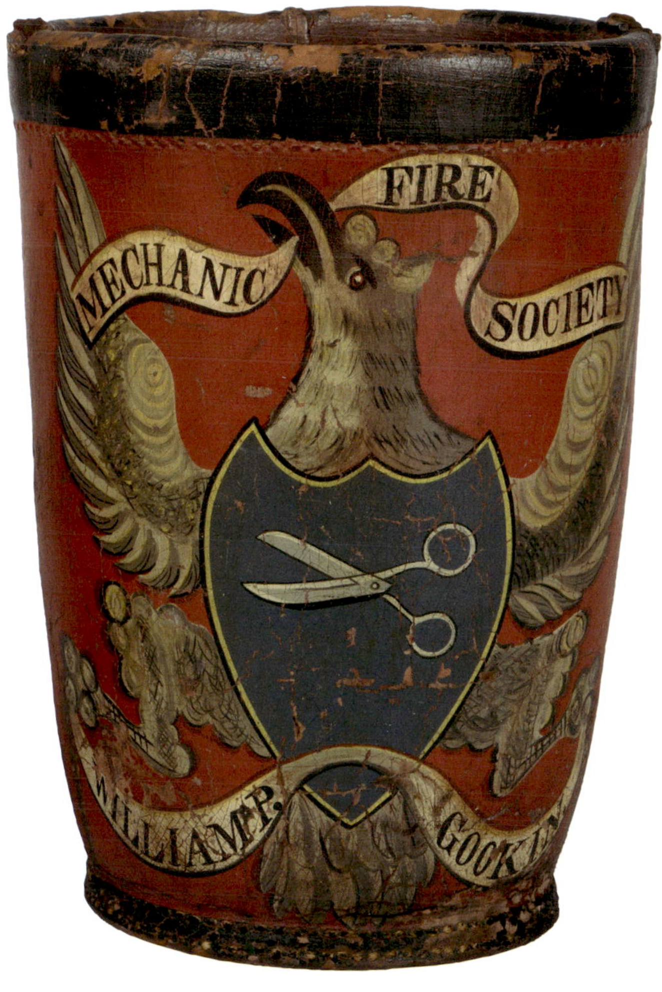

FIRE!

During a period when open flames were needed for cooking, lighting, and heating, fire posed a perennial danger. Volunteer firefighters patrolled city streets looking for uncontrolled fires and organized bucket brigades to douse flames. Portsmouth, New Hampshire, saw serious fires in 1802, 1806, and 1813, the last destroying 108 buildings. These two leather fire buckets come from Portsmouth's Mechanic Fire Society, a volunteer firefighting organization. They bear the name William P. Gookin (1813–1857) and have shears to signal his trade, a draper. Fire buckets had names on them to facilitate their return to the owner after the mayhem of a blaze. Gookin joined the society in 1839 and rose through the ranks, eventually becoming its president in 1854.

Pair of Fire Buckets

Portsmouth,
New Hampshire
ca. 1839

Leather and paint
12¼ × 8⅜ × 8¾ in.

Inscription: "Mechanic Fire Society / William P. Gookin"

L2015.41.189

JOHN YOUNG

Powder Horn

New England

1777

Horn

3 × 13 in.

Inscription: "JOHN YOUNG / 1777"

2016.25.49

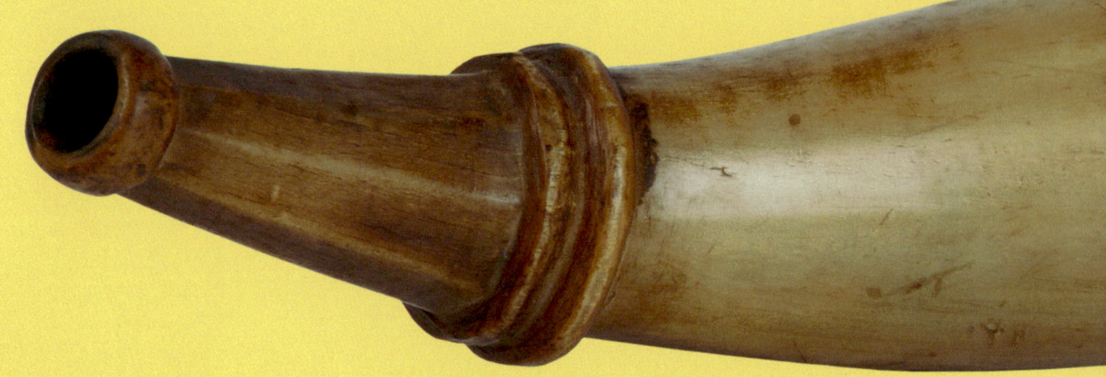

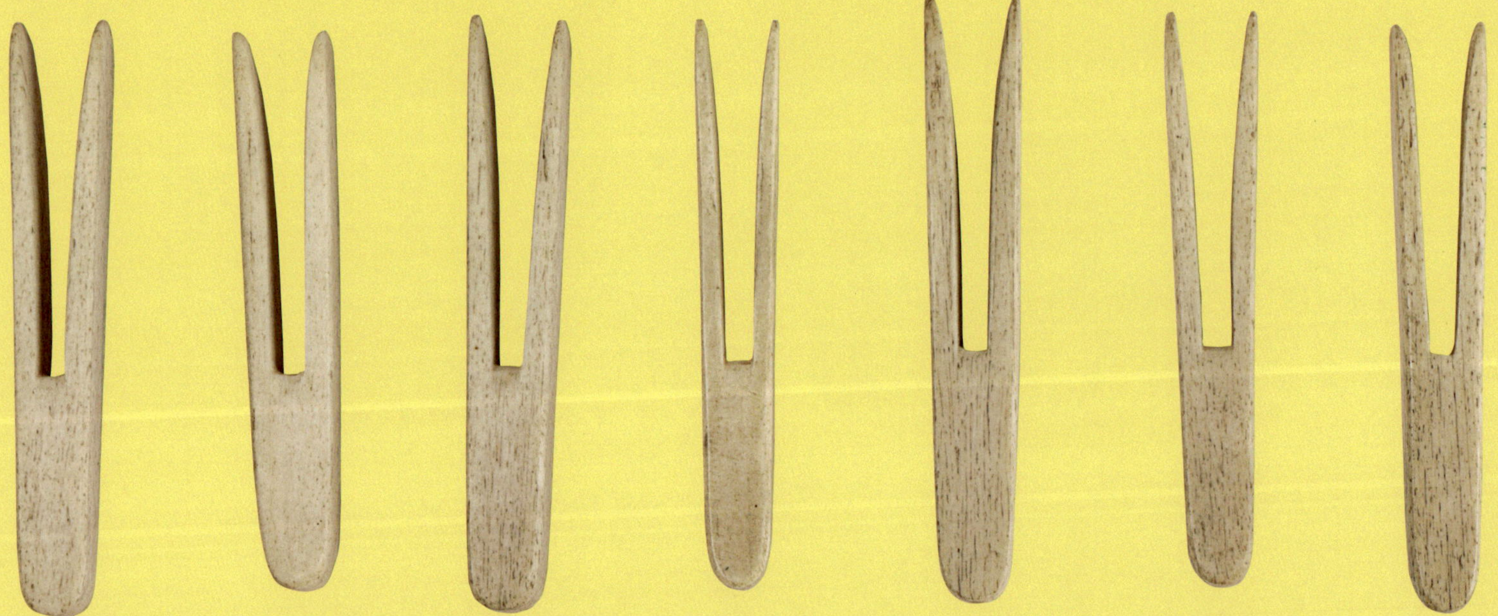

Clothespins

ca. 1825

Whalebone

Each: 3¾ × ½ × ⅝ in.

2016.25.146

BONE AND HORN

In between sighting, killing, and butchering whales, sailors had to pass the time—ports of call being months apart and home thousands of miles away. On seeing another ship in the open ocean, they might gam, or pull up alongside it, to gossip and trade. Some ships had small libraries for readers, while scrimshanders carved elaborate scrimshaw. Besides busks, sailors made practical items, like these clothespins, or this elegant seam rubber probably used for pressing down the seams on tough sailcloth.

Powder horns made from ox, buffalo, or cattle held gunpowder, keeping it secure and dry. The narrow opening fed gunpowder—a mixture of saltpeter (potassium nitrate), charcoal, and sulfur—into the gun barrel. Besides his name, John Young etched the date and game animals, including squirrels and a boar, that he might have shot while carrying this horn.

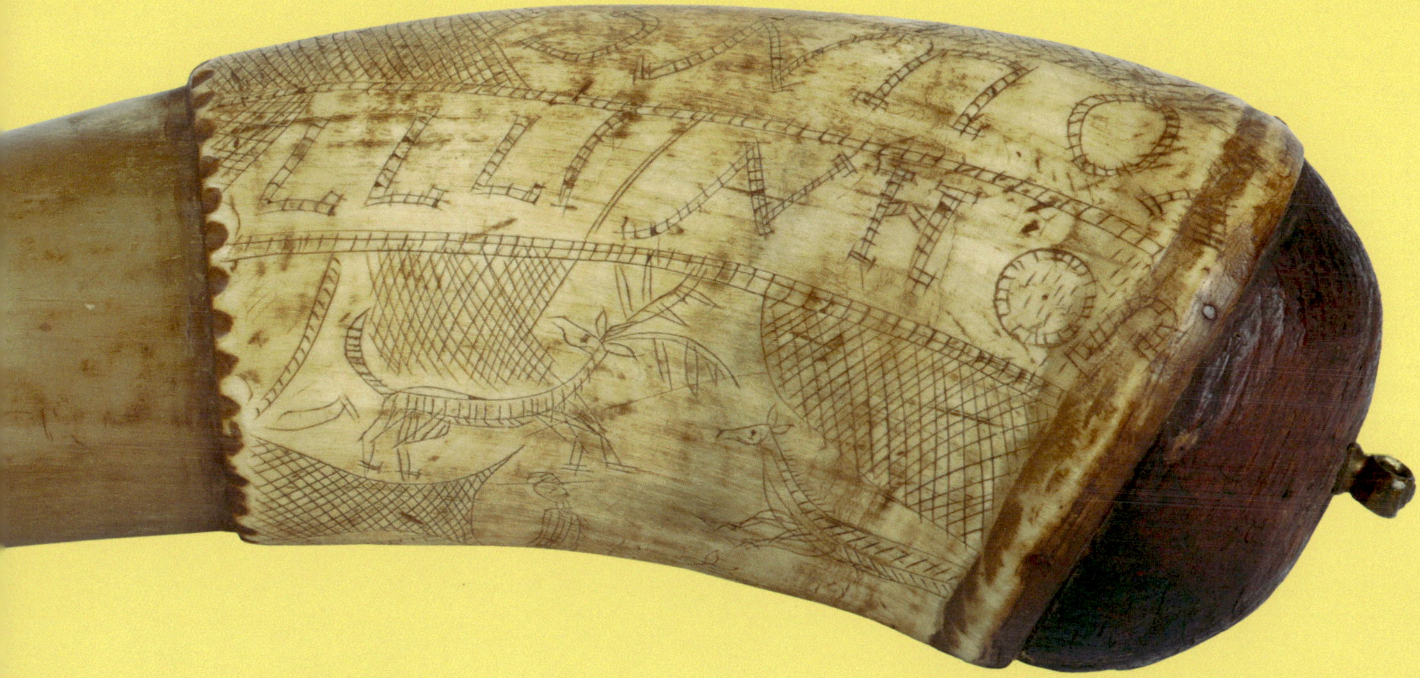

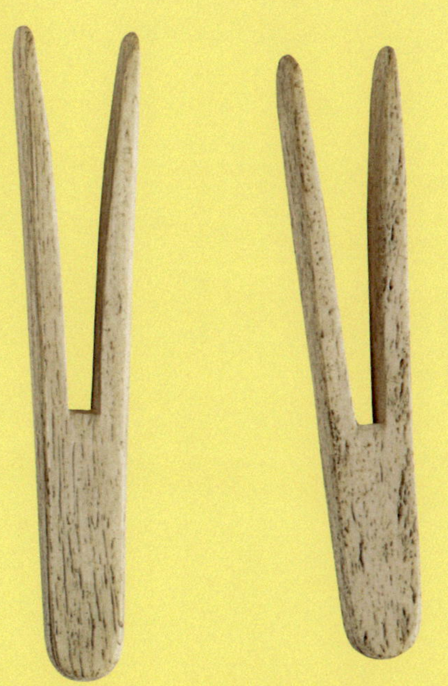

Seam Rubber

Whalebone
5½ × 2⅛ × ½ in.

2016.25.147

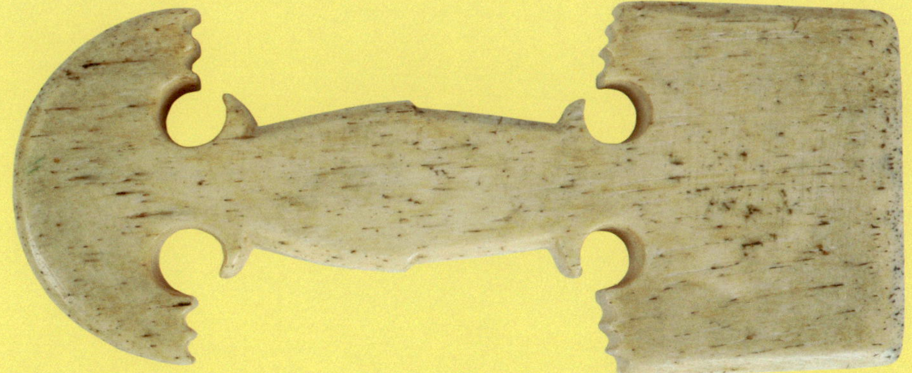

CLOSE TO THE HEART

A busk slides into a pocket in a woman's corset located on the sternum. Busks and whalebone-reinforced corsets entered European aristocratic fashion in the beginning of the sixteenth century. From the start, busks were tokens of romantic affection inscribed with hearts, birds, and sometimes poetry. These scrimshaw examples, embellished by sailors with plants, birds, and radiating patterns, were gifts to women they rarely saw. Sailors spent years away from home. Birds and plants could be symbols of fecundity. Carried close to the body, busks acted as constant reminders of the absent companion.

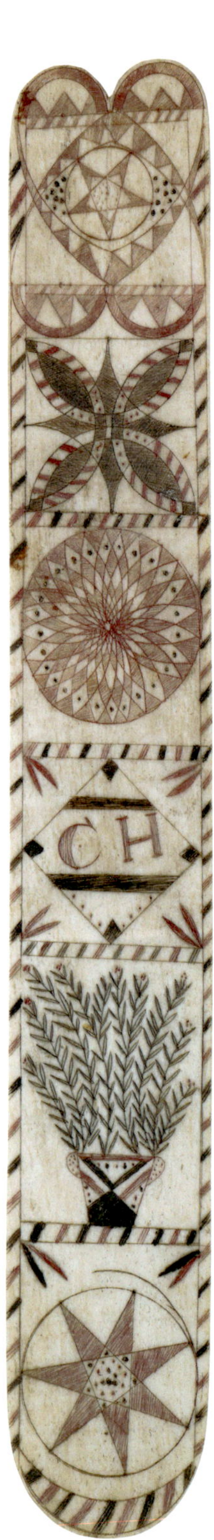

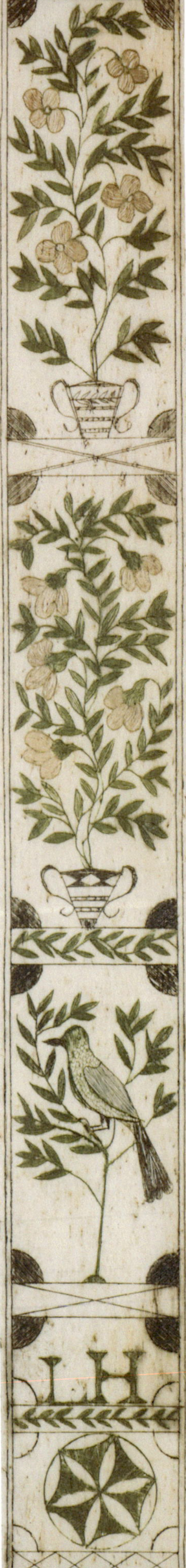

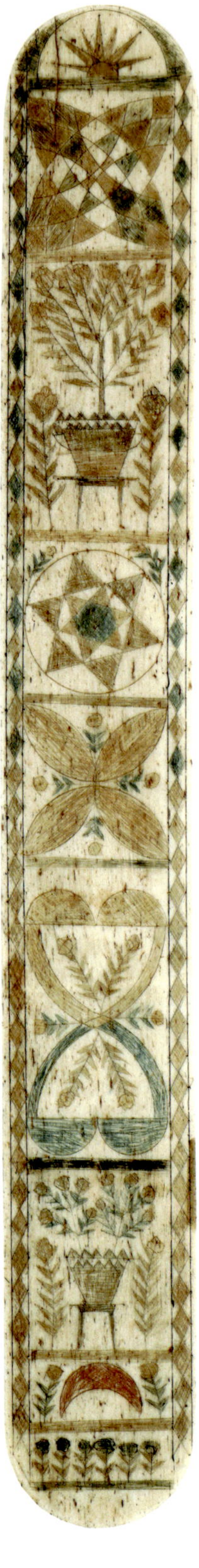

LEFT TO RIGHT:

E. WARREN

Scrimshaw Busk

Whalebone and pigment
13 1/1 × 2 in.

Inscription: "C H"

2016.25.4

Scrimshaw Busk

New England
ca. 1835

Whalebone and pigment
14 × 1½ in.

Inscription: "LH"

2016.25.2

Scrimshaw Busk

ca. 1825

Whalebone and pigment
13¼ × 1¼ in.

2016.25.3

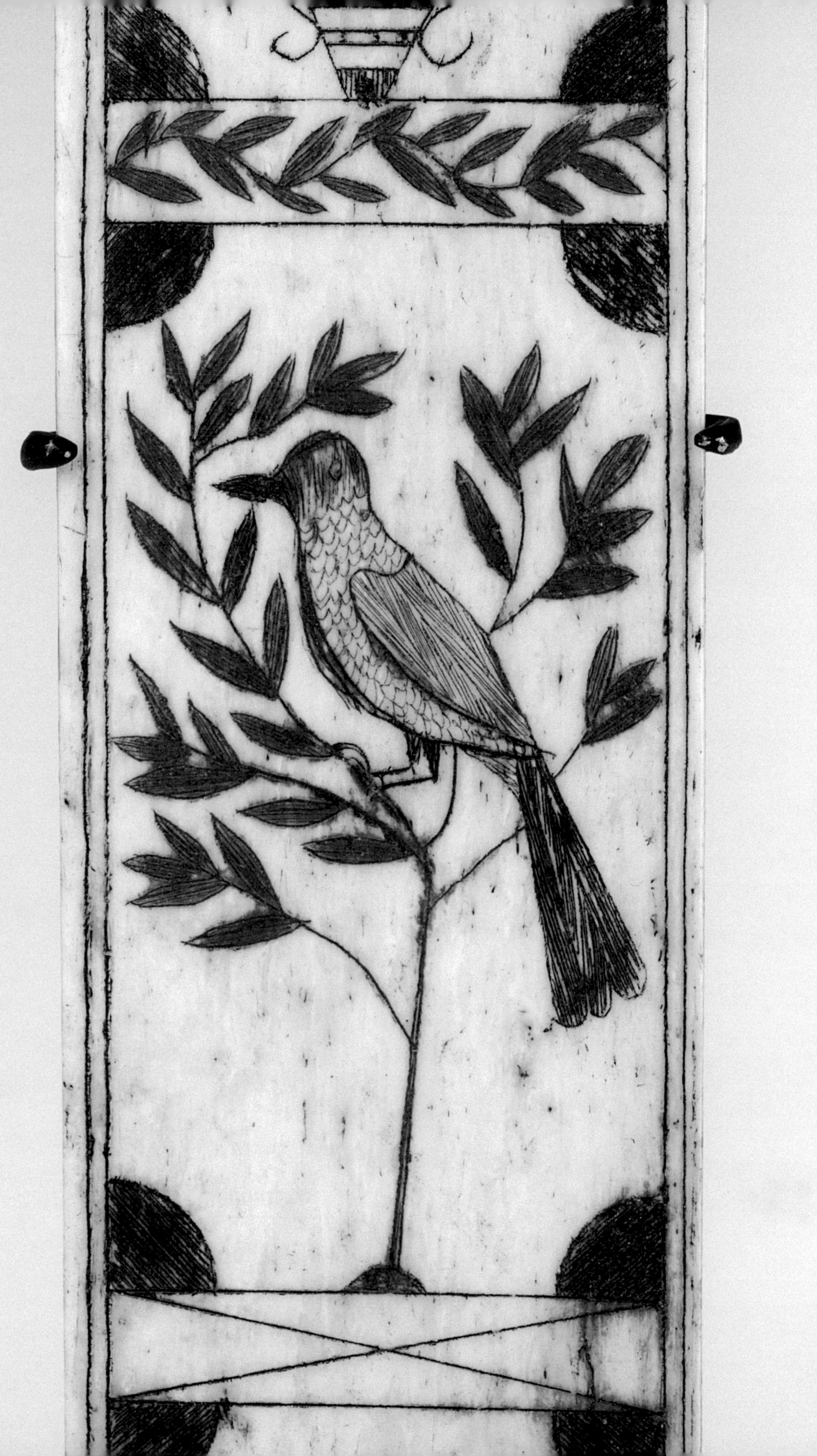

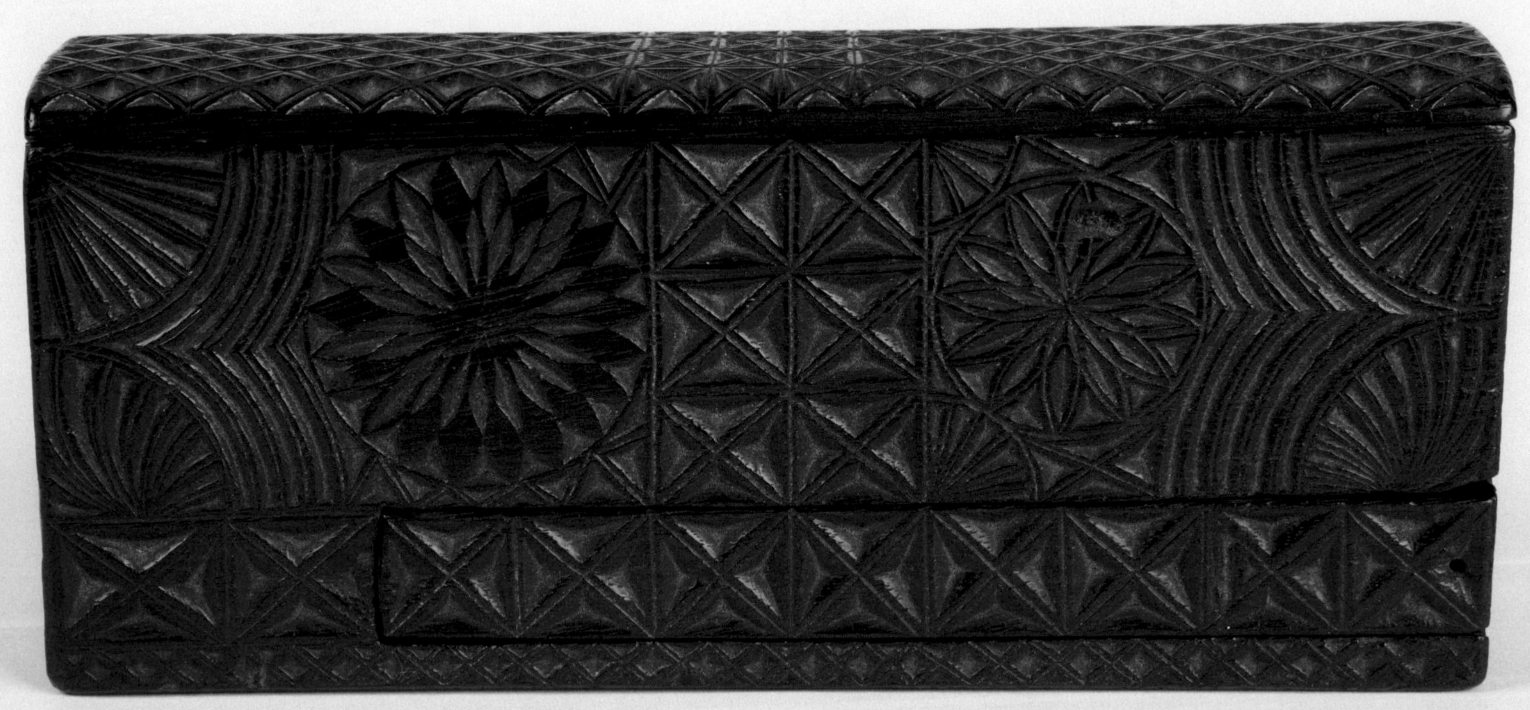

Chip-Carved Box

Second half of nineteenth century

Wood
$3\frac{1}{4} \times 8 \times 2\frac{1}{4}$ in.

L2015.41.52

COLD FEET

Before the widespread use of central heating in homes, railways, and public buildings, foot warmers provided portable heat. They could be low-tech, a hot brick or a water bottle. This example, however, with its delicate twisted wrought-iron handle and intricate circular patterns, is exceptional. The metal cup held hot coals. Perforations let in oxygen for combustion and allowed heat to escape. A metal hook holds the door shut to contain the coals.

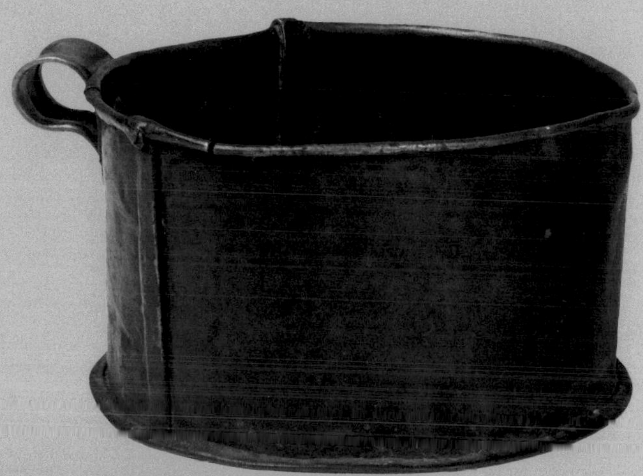

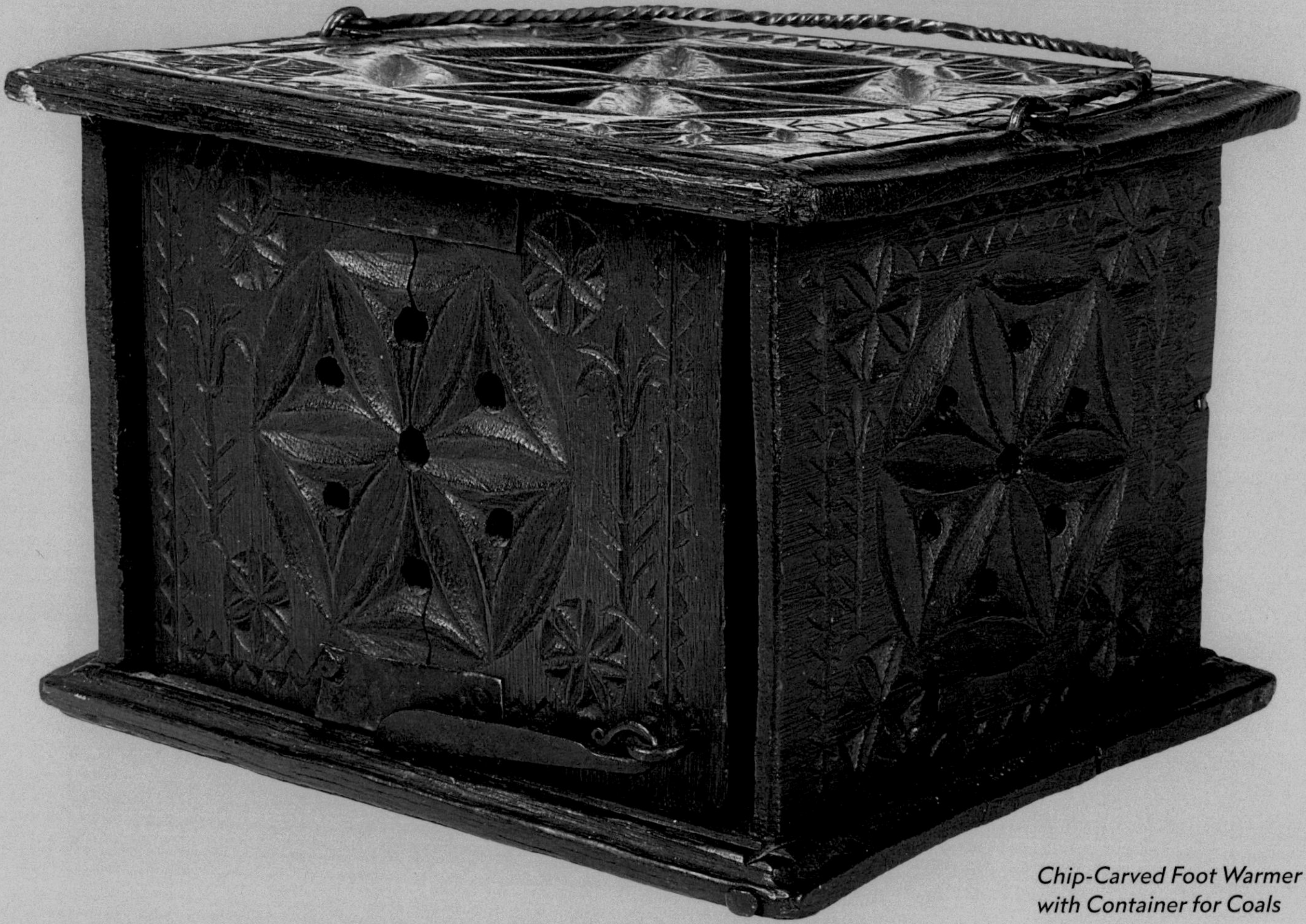

Chip-Carved Foot Warmer with Container for Coals

Eastern Massachusetts
ca. 1720

Oak, iron, and tin
Foot warmer:
6½ × 9½ × 7$\frac{3}{16}$ in.

Container: 3¼ × 5 in.

L2015.41.29

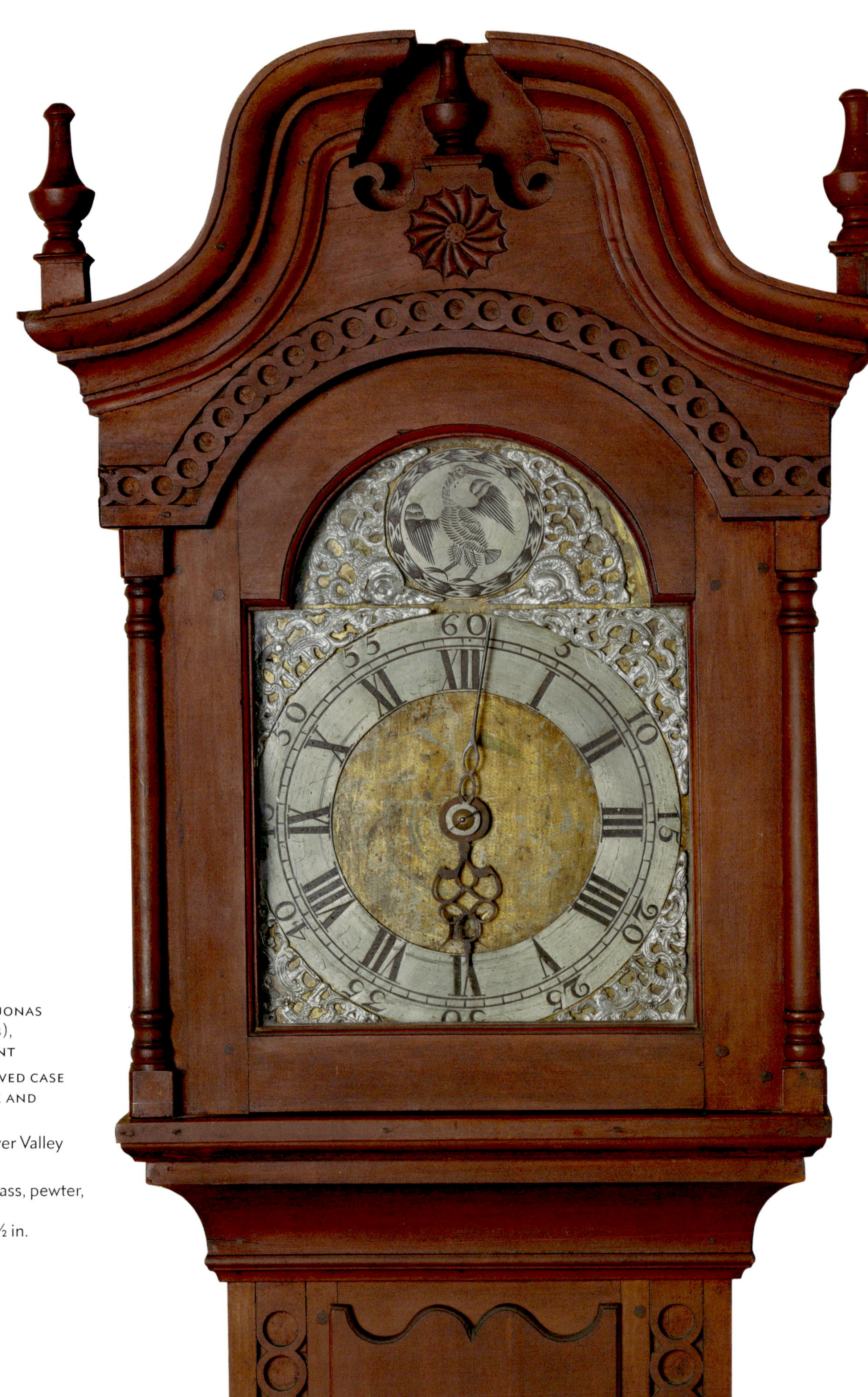

Tall Case Clock

ATTRIBUTED TO JONAS FITCH (1741–1808), CLOCK MOVEMENT

UNKNOWN, CARVED CASE WITH FRETWORK AND TURNED FINIALS

Connecticut River Valley
ca. 1775–1800

Cherrywood, brass, pewter, and glass
88¼ × 19¼ × 10½ in.

2016.25.19

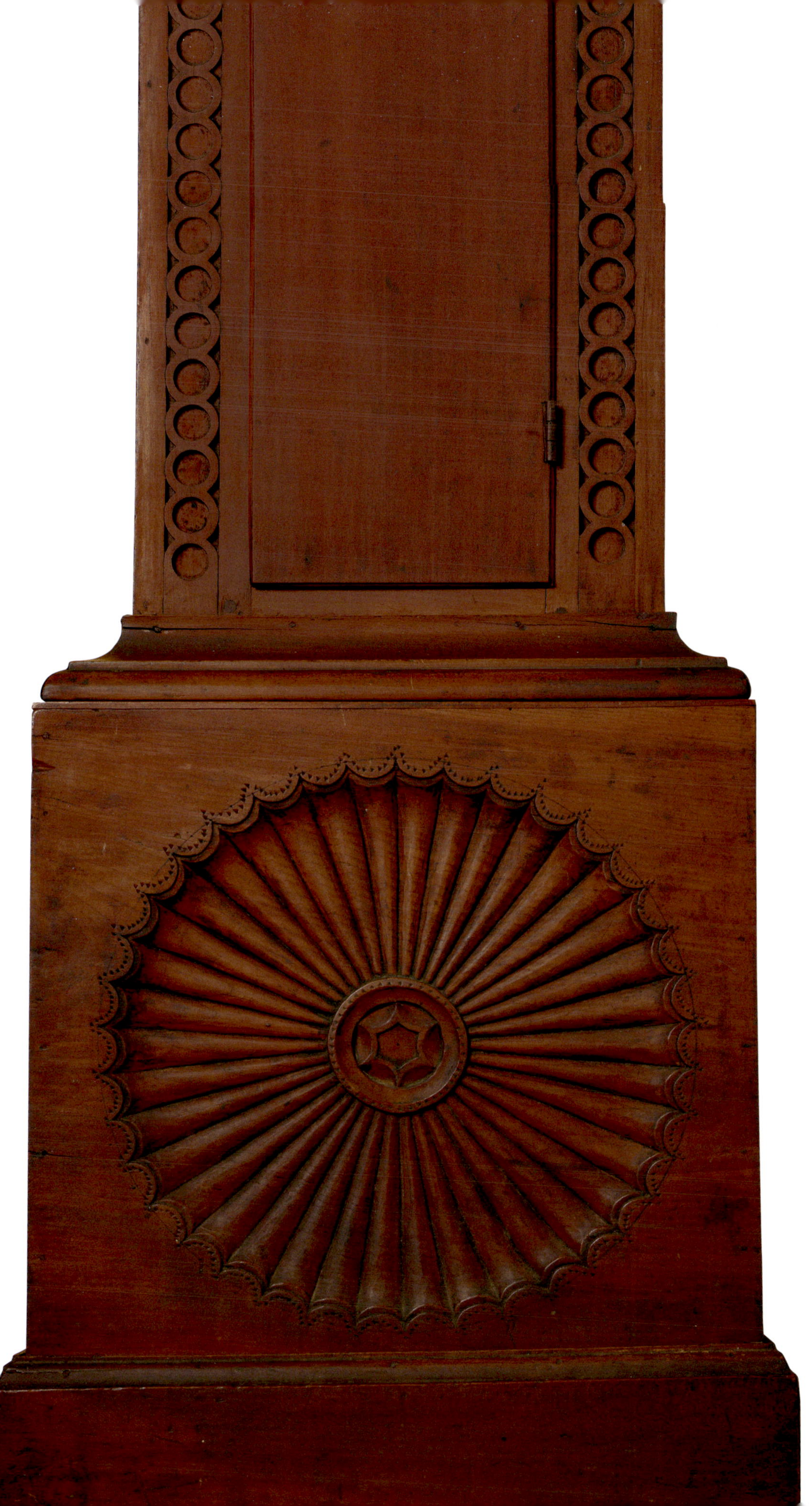

KEEPING TIME

Clocks were an expensive consumer item whose diffusion into homes marks the increasing affluence of Americans during the eighteenth and nineteenth centuries. In 1668, Boston saw its first public clock, put there by the selectmen. Scholars Philip Zea and Robert C. Cheney have noted that between 1685 and 1735, a dozen clock repairmen were active in Boston, a town of around four thousand. Brass clockworks were imported until the mid-eighteenth century, but repairs to these finicky machines had to be done locally. By 1798, 8 percent of Connecticut households owned a clock, a fact that is known because the U.S. Congress imposed a clock tax and did a census. Timekeeping devices became still more common in households after Simon Willard patented his wall-mounted banjo clock in 1802. He eventually produced around five thousand examples.

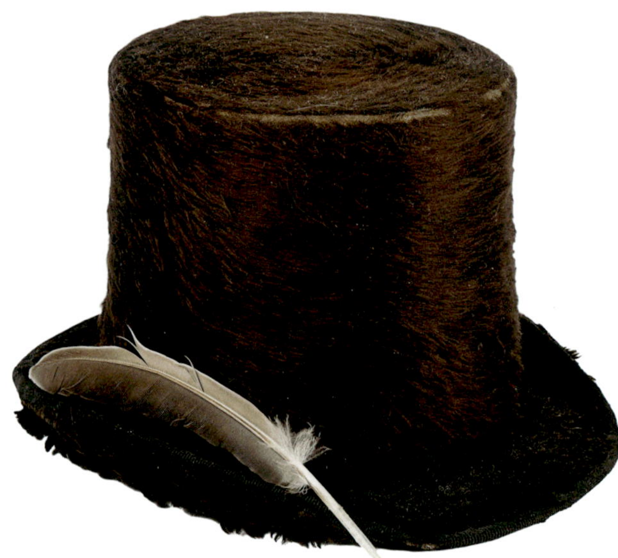

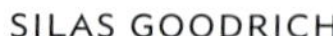

COLLINS & FAIRBANKS

Top Hat

Boston
ca. 1835

Silk-lined beaver-skin hat
4 × 6 × 5 in.

Inscription (inside hat): "EXTRA QUALITY / TRADEMARK / COLLINS & FAIRBANKS, 383 WASHINGTON ST. / OPP. FRANKLIN / BOSTON / REGISTERED"

2016.25.75

SILAS GOODRICH

Bandbox

Boston
ca. 1835

Printed wallpaper on pasteboard
4 × 7 × 6 in.

Inscriptions (lid, silkscreened): "FROM / PETER HIGGINS'S / HAT AND CAP / ESTABLISHMENT, / NO. 1 CITY WHARF, / BOSTON."; (underside of lid, printed paper label) "SILAS GOODRICH, / Manufacturer of / BAND BOXES, / Hat, Store Muff & Fancy Boxes, / OF EVERY DESCRIPTION, / 25 Court Street, Boston. / Entrance through S.H. Gregory & / Co's Paper Hanging Store."

2016.25.76

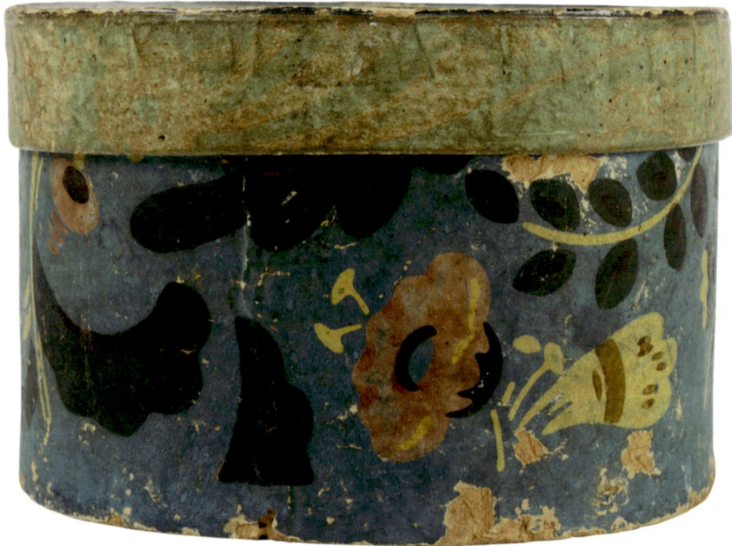

TOP HATS

Starting in the 1790s, top hats became a fashion necessity for well-off men and remained part of a man's formal attire until the 1940s. Like all fashions, their look changed over time, from these brown and black hats with curving brims to the tall stovepipe hats associated with Abraham Lincoln. Made by Boston hatter Collins & Fairbanks, the hats shown here were sold in mass-produced pasteboard boxes. The smaller hat above is probably a sample.

Jacob Maentel (1778–1863), a German immigrant painter active in Pennsylvania and later Indiana, pictured a jaunty John Mays in his hat shop in Schaefferstown, Pennsylvania. The white, brown, and black hats, which narrow toward the hat band, date this image to the late 1820s or early 1830s, when D'Orsay and Regent styles ruled. Beaver-fur top hats went out of fashion by the 1850s, when silk became the covering of choice.

JACOB MAENTEL (1778–1863)

Portrait of Hatter John Mays of Schaefferstown, Pennsylvania

ca. 1830

Watercolor, gouache, ink, and pencil on paper
Framed: 18 × 15 in.

2016.25.102

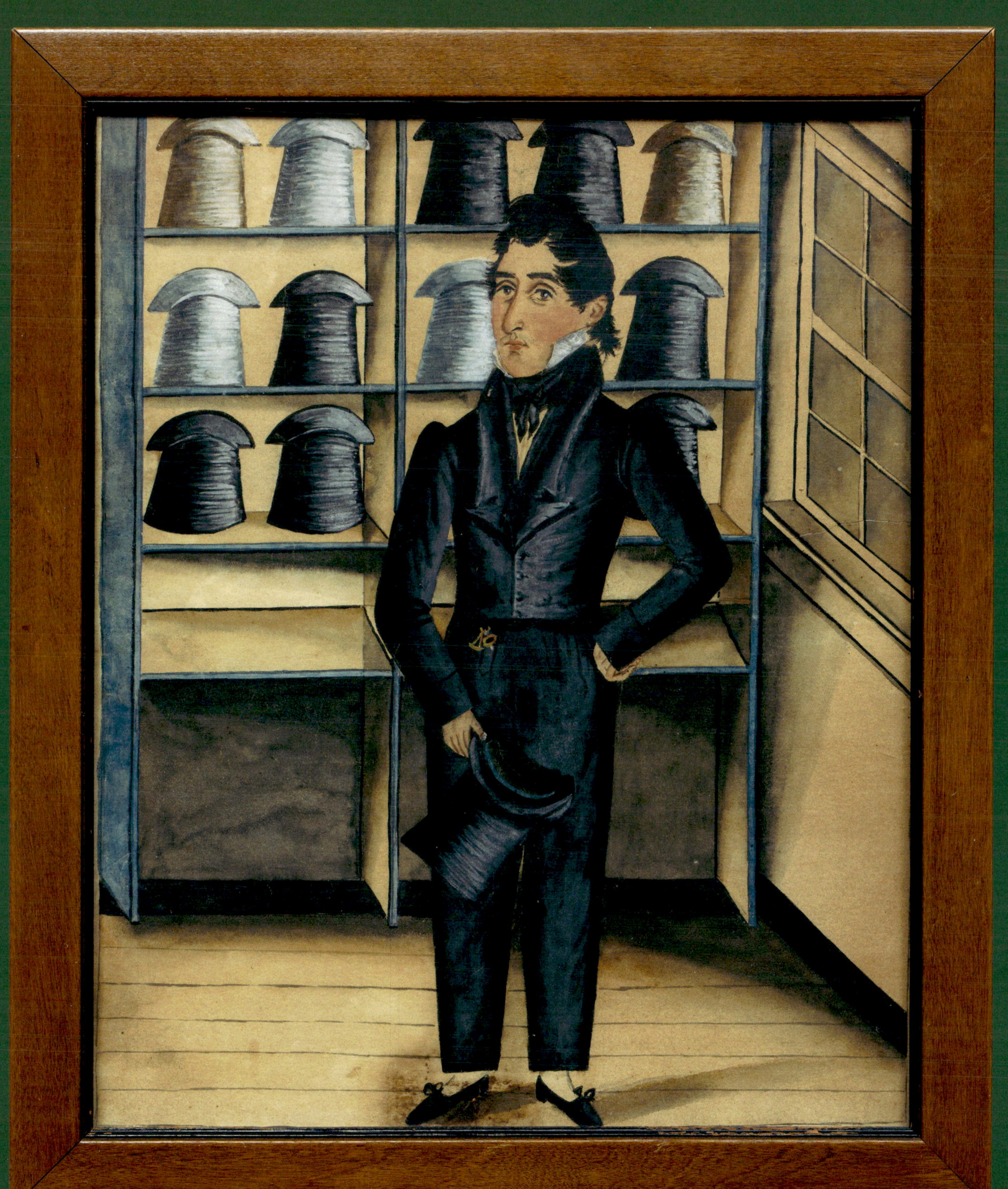

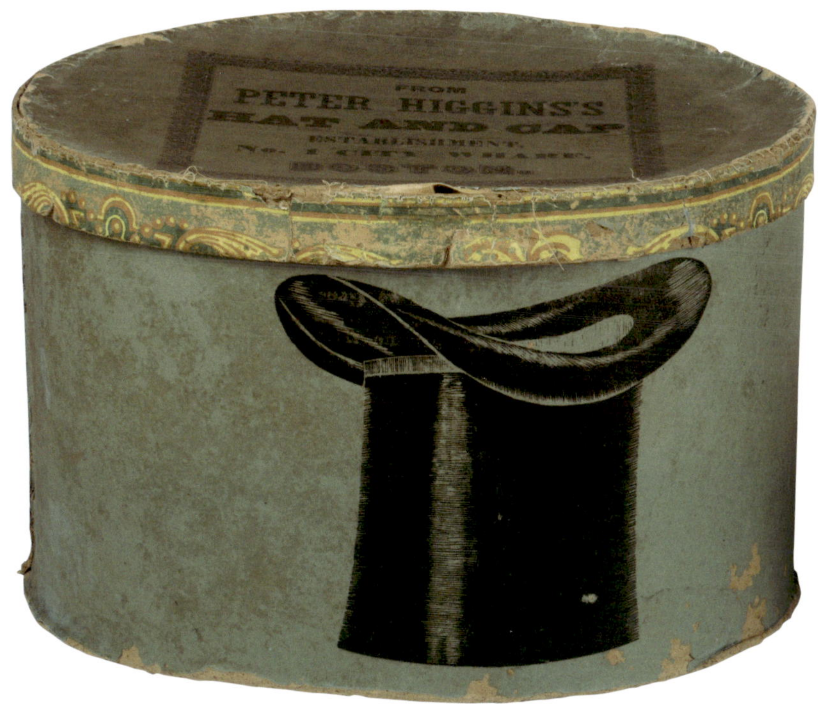

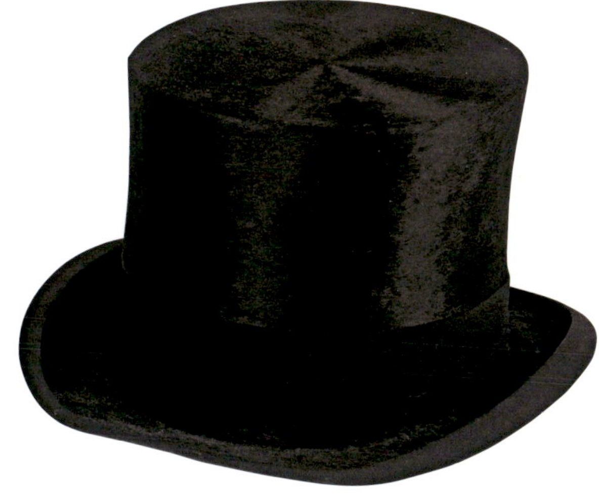

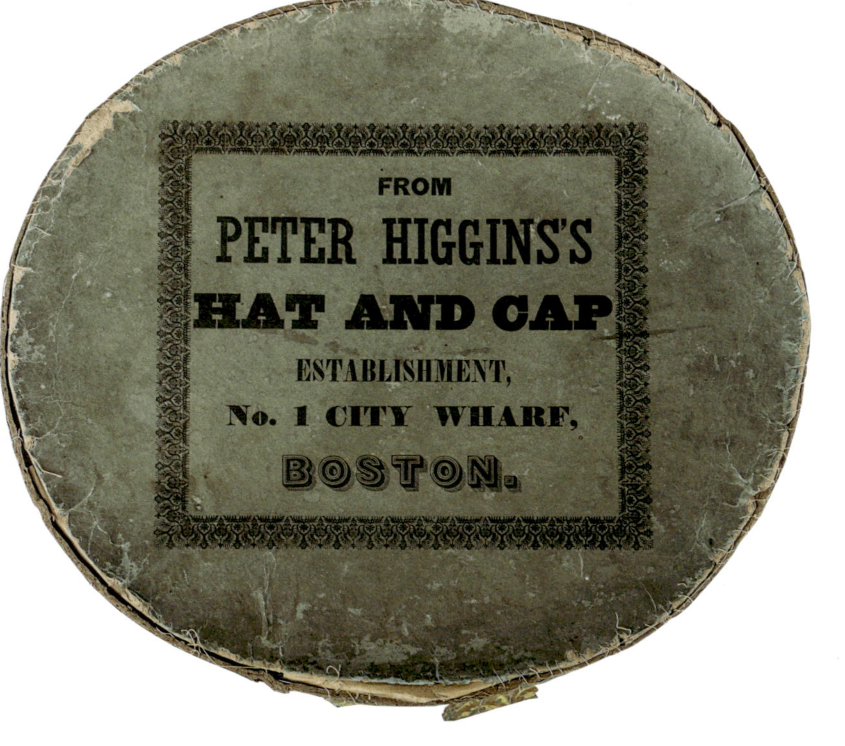

SILAS GOODRICH

Bandbox

Boston
ca. 1835

Printed wallpaper on pasteboard
9 × 14 × 13 in.

Inscription (lid, silkscreened): "FROM / PETER HIGGINS'S / HAT AND CAP / ESTABLISHMENT, / NO. 1 CITY WHARF, / BOSTON."

2016.25.78

COLLINS & FAIRBANKS

Top Hat

Boston
ca. 1835

Silk-lined beaver-skin hat
6 × 11 × 10 in.

Inscription (inside hat): "EXTRA QUALITY / TRADEMARK / COLLINS & FAIRBANKS, 383 WASHINGTON ST. / OPP. FRANKLIN / BOSTON / REGISTERED"

2016.25.77

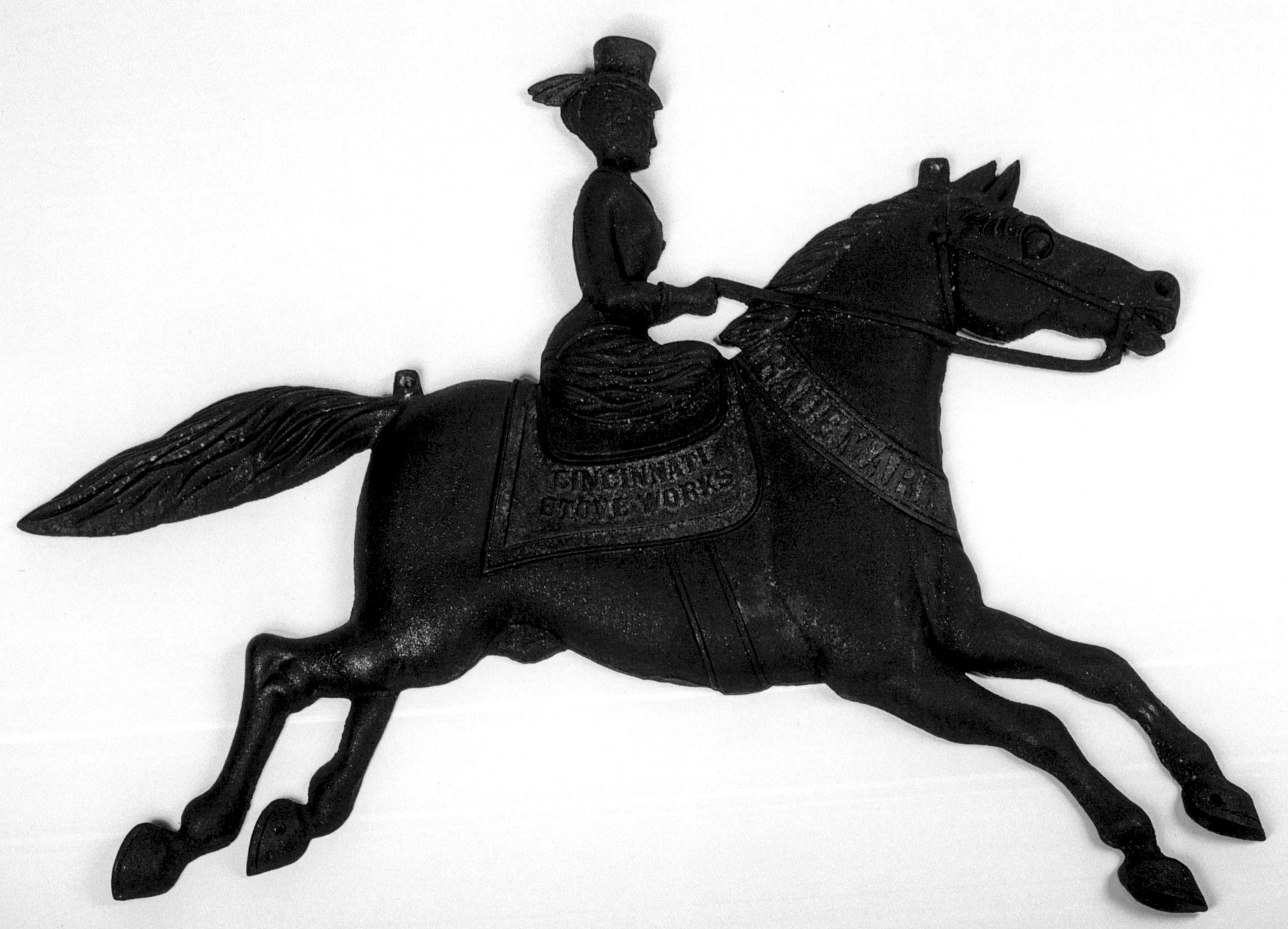

Equestrian Trade Sign for the Cincinnati Stove Works

ca. 1901

Cast iron and paint
27½ × 40½ × 2½ in.

Inscription:
"CINCINNATI STOVE WORKS / TRADEMARK"

2016.25.95

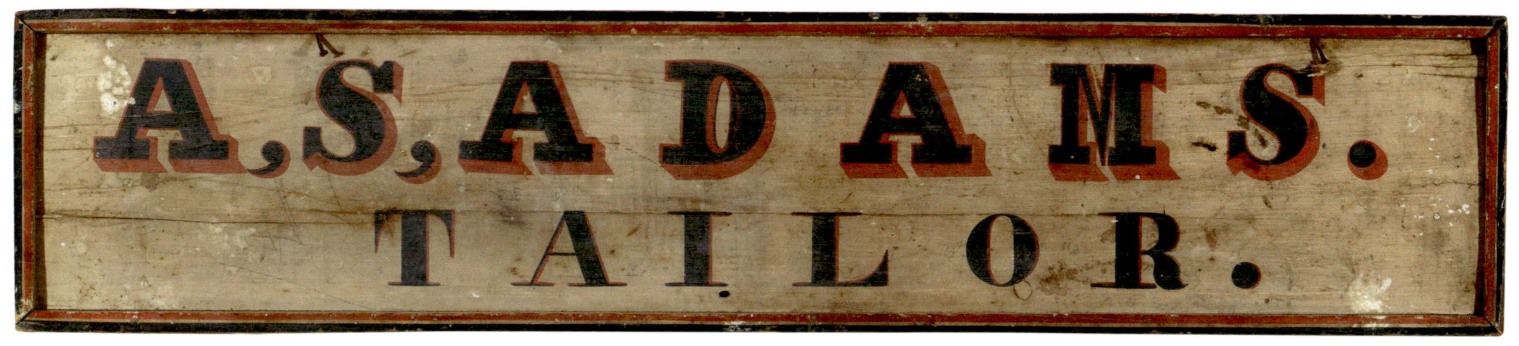

Sign for A,S,Adams. Tailor.

New England
ca. 1840

Wood and paint
12⅞ × 58½ × 1⅞ in.

Inscription: "A,S,ADAMS. / TAILOR."

2016.25.96

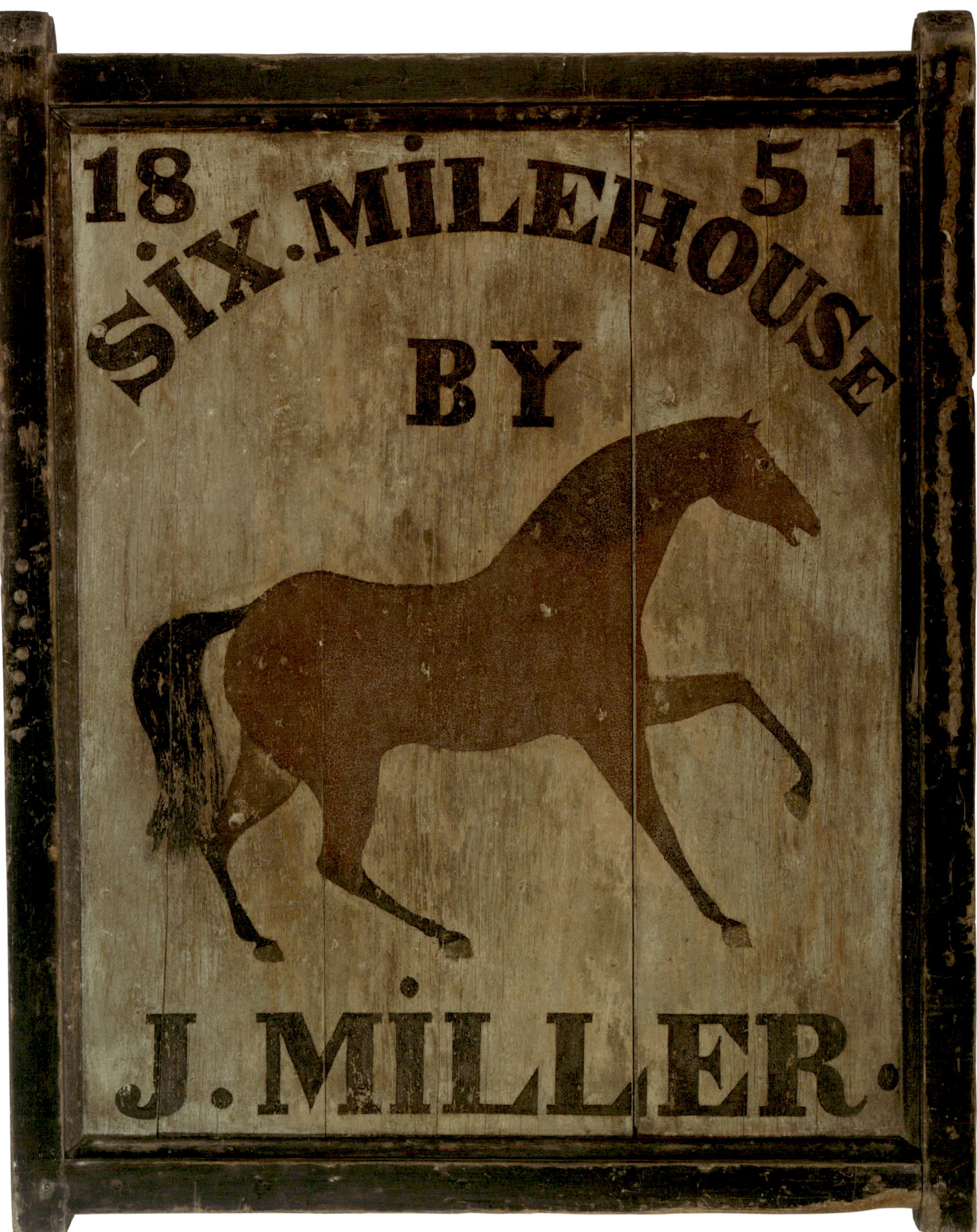
18 51
SIX.MILEHOUSE
BY
J.MILLER.

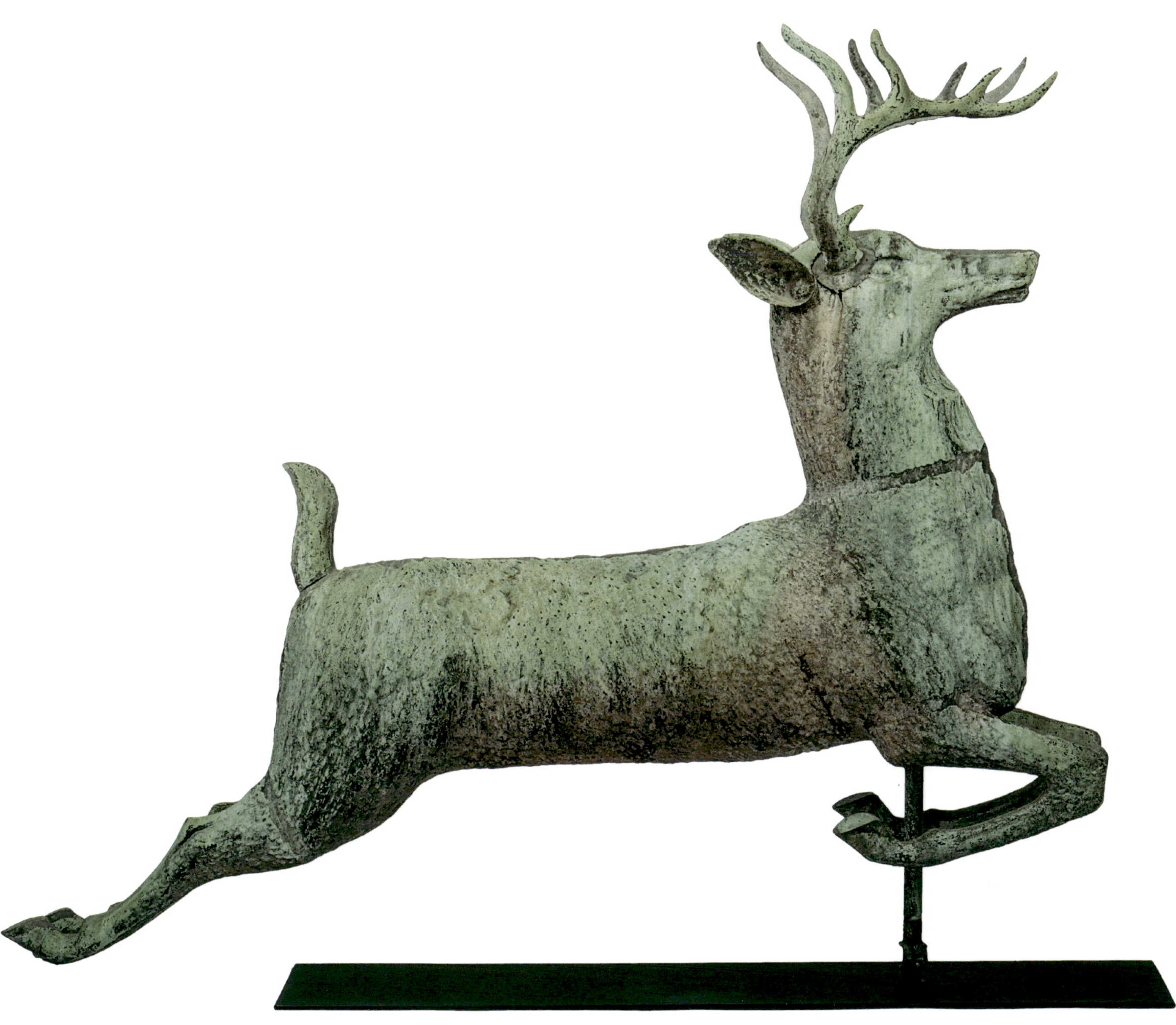

"Six Mile House"
Tavern Sign

Montgomery County, Ohio

Wood and paint
52 × 40 × 4 in.

Inscription: "1851 / six.
MiLEHOUSE / BY / J.MiLLER."

L2015.41.136

Ten-Point Leaping Stag
Weather Vane

ca. 1880

Molded copper and
lead-filled antlers
32 × 39 × 9 in.

L2015.41.132

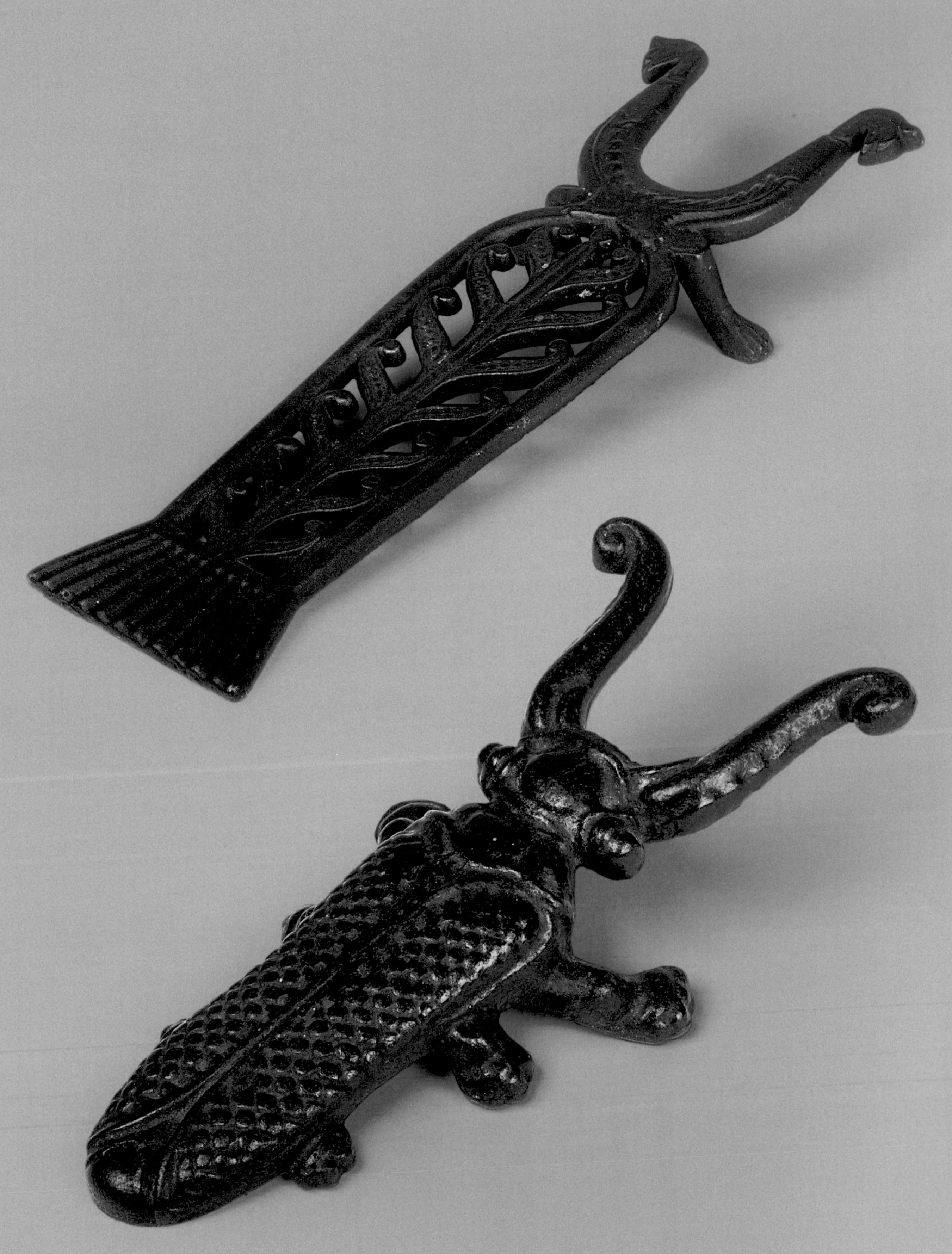

Acknowledgments

This catalogue is the result of the farsighted generosity and capacious vision of Jonathan and Karin Fielding. It has been an absolute delight to work with them and the collection over the years. I hope this volume reflects their passion and curiosity.

I want to acknowledge those who helped us reach the milestone of this catalogue, especially those who contributed to the hugely successful opening of the Jonathan and Karin Fielding Wing at The Huntington in October 2016. The Advancement team, especially Randy Shulman, Vice President for Advancement, has done much work with the Fieldings to ensure the wing's construction and now the catalogue's publication. Frederick Fisher and Partners designed the Fielding Wing, a stunning modernist addition to the Virginia Steele Scott Galleries of American Art. Fred Fisher and his team, including Trevor Behner and Nathan Prevendar, also laid out the thoughtful inaugural installation.

At The Huntington, the building project and installation was overseen by Kevin Salatino, former Hannah and Russel Kully Director of the Art Collections, Laurie Sowd, former Vice President for Operations, and Jessica Todd Smith, former Virginia Steele Scott Chief Curator of American Art. In Facilities, Jerry Eaton, Larry Gaudy, and Tony Ceccia kept an eye on construction details. Alex Moran, Lana Johnson, Lindsey Hansen, and Sharon Robinson ably coordinated a talented crew of preparators, including Gregg Bayne, Tom Cabbell, Anders Lansing, Adam Maron, Pat Pickett, Amy Sampson, and Jacob Yanes. Kamil Beski fabricated mounts. Graphic design was provided by Meghan Moran and Christian Mounger. Kimberly Chrisman-Campbell helped develop content for labels, with assistance from intern Jacqueline Gufford. Hal Nelson, former Curator of American Decorative Arts, contributed labels, and Jean

Bootjack
New York
ca. 1850
Cast iron
2¼ × 14⅝ × 5⅜ in.
2016.25.115

Bug Bootjack
ca. 1850
Cast iron
3 × 11 × 5½ in.
2016.25.116

Patterson copyedited the gallery text. Lindsay Ash and Anna Engstrom worked with Antenna International to produce a strong audio guide. In the Communications and Marketing department, Susan Turner-Lowe and her team publicized the exhibition to a wide audience. In the Botanical division, Scott Kleinrock, Seth Baker, and Kelly Fernandez have created beautiful plantings around the Fielding Wing's entrance. Conservation services were provided by Christina Varvi, Laura Telford, Sarah Giffin, Ben Brandfon, and Lily Doan of Rosa Lowinger and Associates. Additionally, Cara Varnell, a textile conservator, and Catherine Keaveney, a furniture conservator, supplemented the outstanding Huntington team that included Andrea Knowlton, Kristi Westberg, Christina O'Connell, and Annie Wilker. Hilah Loewenstein, Assistant to Karin Fielding, responded to countless queries.

This catalogue could not have been completed without the unstinting support of two Huntington staff members. Jean Patterson, as Managing Editor, kept the entire project moving forward and worked her editorial magic time after time. She deserves special recognition for her efforts. Lindsey Hansen ably and efficiently coordinated the installation and now the catalogue. John Sullivan's great team in Imaging Services, including Manuel Flores and Devonne Tice, provided several thousand images to choose from. Elizabeth (Elee) Wood, former Curator/Educator, Fielding Collection for Early American Art, reviewed the essays with her characteristic thoughtfulness and creative eye. Lily Allen assisted authors with research and queries.

The contributors' sparkling essays do justice to the collection. Many thanks to John Demos, Jonathan and Karin Fielding, Robin Jaffee Frank, Stacy Hollander, Sumpter Priddy, Elizabeth (Liz) Warren, and David Wheatcroft. At Lucia | Marquand, Adrian Lucia, Meghann Ney, Kestrel Rundle, Brynn Warriner, Jeremy Linden, and Leah Finger shepherded this project. Ryan Polich's strong design and Melissa Duffes's editorial review contributed to the catalogue's success.

Many others provided indispensable support. Catherine Hess, as Interim Director of the Art Collections, and Steve Hindle, as Interim President of The Huntington, offered able guidance. On her arrival in October 2018, Christina Nielsen, Hannah and Russel Kully Director of the Art Museum, embraced the project and gave strong support to move it forward. The library staff, under the leadership of Sandra Brooke, Avery Director of the Library, located numerous books and references.

These acknowledgments must end by turning back to the Fieldings. Throughout our many conversations about contributors, design, layout, photography, and all the details that make up the catalogue, I was grateful for such thoughtful and inspiring collaborators. Their exceptionally keen eye for artistic quality is on display in this catalogue, which they generously underwrote. Their desire to share the collection shaped this catalogue and everything we do with the Fielding Collection at The Huntington.

James Glisson
June 2019

Index

Pages with illustrations are indicated with italics. Works are grouped under type or function, and also under the maker's name if known or probable. If no name is given, the creator is unknown.

Adams, A. S.
  Sign for A, S, Adams, Tailor, 249
Addison, Joseph, 89, 94
African Americans, 35, 152, 223
Albers, Josef: Homage to the Square series, 51
Ames, Asa: *Portrait of Susan Ames, 32,* 34, *jacket front*
Ames, Susan
  Portrait of Susan Ames (Asa Ames), *32,* 34, *jacket front*
Amish, 49–51
  quilts, 49, 116–19
andirons, 147
  Pair of Hessian Grenadier Andirons, 213–14, jacket back
  Pair of Shield Front Andirons, 213
Andrews, Abigail M., 123–24, 129n11
  Sampler, 123, *123*
Andrews, Lucy, 124
antiques, early American, 33–35, 44, 55, 68–69
  and auctions, 11–12, 14–15, 33, 35, 68
  and connoisseurship, 46–47
  dealers in, 52, 55–56
  and fakes, 35–36
  market for, 68–69
  and museums, 68
  See also individual types; individual periods and styles; Fielding Collection; folk art
Antiques Roadshow, 203
Arts and Crafts movement, 8, 94

Barber, Martha, 123
barber poles, 25
  Barber Pole, 26
Bard, James: *The Steamboat "Peter Crary," 38–39,* 40
Barr, Alfred H., 44
baskets, 25, 229
  Basket, 230
  Basket (J. H. S.), 229, *229*
  depictions of, 35, 90, 116, 126, 151
  by J. H. S., 229
  Native American, 229
  Red Shaker Carrier, 98
  Shaker, 100
  Splint Woven Basket, 230
beadwork
  Native American, 109, 124
  Niagara Beadwork Hat, 10, 11–12, 124
  Niagara floral style, 124
bedcovers, 109, 116
  Jacquard coverlet, 87
  See also quilts
bedsteads, 62–63, 93
Beecher, Catharine, 177
Beecher, Henry Ward, 144
  Norwood; or Village Life in New England, 144
Bicentennial, 33, 36
blanket chests, 49, 65
  Blanket Chest, 43, 44–46, 49
  Grain-Painted "Matteson" Blanket Chest, 84, 87
  Lift-Top Blanket Chest (Elisha Morse), *24*
  Six-Board Blanket Chest, 51
  Six-Board Chest, 87, *88*
  See also chests of drawers
Boardman, Thomas Danforth: *Coffeepot, 218, jacket front*
bootjacks and boot scrapers
  Boot Scraper, 2–3, 208, 214
  Bootjack, 252
  Bug Bootjack, 252
  Devil Bootjack, 2, 209–10, jacket front

Boston, Massachusetts, 8, 25, 53, 56, 59, 63, 76, 82, 120, 139, 143, 144, 148, 162, 175, 180, 182, 190, 205, 206, 220, 221, 243, 244, 247
Boston rocking chairs, 90
clocks in, 243
furniture makers in, 31
Boston & Sandwich Glass Co.: *Lamps*, *12*
boxes
Arch-Decorated Box, *104–5*
Bandbox (Silas Goodrich), *244*
Bandbox (Silas Goodrich), *247*
Bark-Covered Container, *231*
Blue Box with Oyster-Shell Graining and Ivory Keyhole, 90, *102*
Blue Smoke-Decorated Box, *102*
Box with Painted Geometric Design, *93*, 94
Chip-Carved Box, *240*
Chrome Yellow Oval Box, 100, *100*, *jacket front*
Decorated Box, *102–3*
Decorated Box, *103*
Decorated Box, *107*
Decorated Document Box (attrib. Elijah and Elisha North), *106*
Dome-Top Trunk, 90, *107*
Flat-Top Diagonally Decorated Box, *102–3*
Green Dash-Decorated Box, *105*
Painted and Decorated Dome-Top Box, *106–7*
Painted Dome-Top Box, 90, *105–6*
Quillwork Box, *231*
Red-Spotted Box with Shallow Dome Top, *104*
Sailor's Trinket Box, *98*
Scrimshaw Oval Box with Inlaid Five-Point Star, *99*
Shaker boxes, 100
Shaker Boxes, 100, *101*
Small Makuk, *233*
Stenciled Box, *96*
Swirl-Decorated Box, *43*, 44
Writing Box, *103–4*
See also baskets; blanket chests; painted furniture
Brader, Ferdinand A.: *The Property of Daniel and Sarah Leibelsperger, Fleetwood, Berks County, Pennsylvania*, 142, *156–57*
Brewster, Sir David, 91–93
The Kaleidoscope: Its History, Theory and Construction, 90
A Treatise on the Kaleidoscope, 92
Brewster, John, Jr., 172, 183n1, 189
Portrait of Henry Sayward, *188*, 189
portraits by, 183–84n1
Portraits of Elizabeth Stone Coffin and Major David Coffin, 31, 142, *170*, 171–75, *172*, 184n1
Brewster, Royal, 172
Brewster, Salmon
Bucket, *234*
Bucket, *234*
Brewster, William, 172
broilers, 211
Broiler, *212*
Broiler, *216*
Broiler with Grease Collector, *2*, *212*
Large Broiler, *2*, *212*
Browne, Alexander, 89
buckets, 62, 100
Bucket (Salmon Brewster), *234*
Bucket (Salmon Brewster), *234*
fire buckets, 141, 153n3, 235
Pair of Fire Buckets, *235*
Bullard, Dr., 144
Bullard, Eunice, 144
burl carvings, 232
Figural Crooked Knife, *228*
Oval Bowl, *232*
Oval Bowl, *233*
Burnham, Simeon
Simeon Burnham & Lucy Smith Family Record, *198*
busks, 236, 238
Scrimshaw Busk, *238*
Scrimshaw Busk, *238–39*
Scrimshaw Busk (E. Warren), *238*
candle molds, 29, 52
Candle Mold, *31*
candle stands, 26
Candle Stand, 29, *29*, *jacket front*
Candle Stand, *225*
candleholders, 26, 29, 52
See also candle stands; candlesticks; lamps; lighting stands; sconces, lighting
candles, 12, 26–29, 52
candlesticks, 25
Candlestick, *28*
Caverly, Azariah
The Azariah Caverly Family (attrib. Joseph H. Davis), 179, *179*
Caverly, Charles, 141, 180
Family Portrait of Charles and Comfort Caverly and Their Son Isaac (Joseph H. Davis), 31, 141, 171, 175–79, *177*
Caverly, Comfort, 141, 177–80
Family Portrait of Charles and Comfort Caverly and Their Son Isaac (Joseph H. Davis), 31, 141, 171, 175–79, *177*
Caverly, Cyrus, 177, 180
Caverly, Eliza, 179
The Azariah Caverly Family (attrib. Joseph H. Davis), 179, *179*
Caverly, Eliza Jane, 177, 185n21
Caverly, George
The Azariah Caverly Family (attrib. Joseph H. Davis), 179, *179*
Caverly, Isaac, 141, 175–77, 180
Family Portrait of Charles and Comfort Caverly and Their Son Isaac (Joseph H. Davis), 31, 141, 171, 175–79, *177*
Caverly, Sarah
The Azariah Caverly Family (attrib. Joseph H. Davis), 179, *179*
Caverly Cemetery, 177
Caverly family, 178–79
ceramics, 220
See also redware; stoneware
chairs, 19, 25, 26, 59, 62–69
armchairs, 19, 63
Banister-Back Side Chair, *82–83*
benches and stools, 62, 66
Carver Chair, *64*
Chair, *54*
chair-tables, 62
Child's Ladder-Back Armchair, 72, *72*
Corner Chair, *73*, *jacket front*
great chairs, 63–68
painted, 90, 144
rocking chairs, 90
settees, 62
Side Chair (attrib. John Gaines III), *79*
side chairs, 59, 66
Slat-Back Armchair, 72, *80*
See also Windsor chairs
Chamberlain, Jacob
A Record of the Family of Ensign Jacob Chamberlain of Alton, in the County Strafford, and State of New Hampshire, *201*
Chambers, Thomas G.: *The "Benjamin Franklin,"* *161*
Chandler, Gardiner, 154n9
Chandler, Samuel, 154n9
Chandler, Winthrop, 154nn9–10
Landscape with Riding and Walking Figures, a River, and a Village (Overmantel), 143–44, *144–47*, 147
overmantels by, 143–44, 154n8
portraits by, 143, 154n9
portraits of Samuel and Prudence Waters, 143
Chapin, Eliphalet: *High Chest of Drawers* (attrib.), 16, *17*, *jacket front*
Cheney, Robert C., 243
chests of drawers
Chest on Chest (attrib. shop of Samuel Dunlap), *67*
Federal Lift-Top Chest of Drawers, 16, *57*, *71*
High Chest of Drawers, 57–59, *58*, *60–61*, 232
High Chest of Drawers (attrib. Eliphalet Chapin), 16, *17*, *jacket front*

highboys, 68
  See also blanket chests
children, 177, 179–80, 182–83
  child's chair, 72, *72*
  deaths of, 171, 173, 180–83, 185n31, 189
  games and toys of, 182–83
  and pets, 178, 182
children in portraits, 34, 175–83, 205
  The Azariah Caverly Family (attrib. Joseph H. Davis), 179, *179*
  Boy with a Book and a Flute, *199*
  Children in Pink and Blue (Mrs. Moses Russel), *191*
  Family Portrait of Charles and Comfort Caverly and Their Son Isaac (Joseph H. Davis), 31, 141, 171, 175–79, *176*
  Four Portraits of Children (Edwin Plummer), 40, *187*
  Girl with Flowers, *165*
  Little Girl in a Windsor Armchair (attrib. Sheldon Peck), *189*
  Portrait of Cynthia Mary Osborn (Samuel S. Miller), 31, 153, 171, *180*, 181–83, *186*
  Portrait of Henry Sayward (John Brewster Jr.), *188*, 189
  Portrait of Susan Ames (Asa Ames), *32*, 34, *jacket front*
  A Portrait of Two Children (Sturtevant J. Hamblin), *207*
  Portraits of Boy and Girl (Prior-Hamblin School), *205*
chimney boards. *See* fireboards
Chippendale style, 16, 55
  and collectors, 68–69
clocks, 243
  banjo clocks, 243
  Tall Case Clock (attrib. Jonas Fitch), *242–43*, *jacket back*
  Tall Case Clock (Riley Whiting), 40–46, *41–42*, 90
Coffin, David, 172–73, 175–77, 183–84n1
  Portraits of Elizabeth Stone Coffin and Major David Coffin (John Brewster Jr.), 31, 142, *170*, 171–75, 183–84n1
  portraits of David and Elizabeth Coffin (William Jennys), 184n1
coffeepots
  Coffeepot, *218*, *jacket front*
  Coffeepot (Thomas Danforth Boardman), *218*, *jacket front*
Coffin, Dorcas, 172
  married Royal Brewster, 172
Coffin, Ebenezer Stone, 173
Coffin, Elizabeth Stone, 172–77, 184n14
  children of, 173, 175, 184nn6 and 7
  portraits of David and Elizabeth Coffin (William Jennys), 184n1
  portraits of, 171–75, 183–84n1, 184n12
  Portraits of Elizabeth Stone Coffin and Major David Coffin (John Brewster Jr.), 31, 142, *170*, 171–75, 183–84n1, 184n12
Coffin, Nathaniel, 173, 184n6
Coffin, Paul, 172
Collins & Fairbanks, 244
  Top Hat, 244, *244*
  Top Hat, *246–47*
Comb, *202*
Connecticut, 15, 19, 31, 57, 68, 90, 96, 136, 143, 164, 194, 218, 219, 221, 223, 243
  clocks in, 243
  Connecticut River Valley, 16, 242
  East Windsor, 16
  furniture workshops, 31, 56, 72
  Hampton, 172
  Hartford, 56, 189
  Lisbon, 72, 78
  New London, 55
  Winchester, 41
  Woodstock, 154n9
Custis, John, Colonel, 148

daguerreotypes, 15, 181
  Young Woman with Rose, 181, *181*
Davidson, Archibald, 87
Davidson, Marshall B., 26
Davis, Joseph H., 178
  The Azariah Caverly Family (attrib.), 179, *179*
  Family Portrait of Charles and Comfort Caverly and Their Son Isaac, 31, 141, 171, 175–79, *177*
De La Rue, Thomas, 89, 150, 151
  printing playing cards, 151, 155n25
Dearstyne, James, 113
delftware tiles, 148, 154n19
Demos, John, 20, 31
Deyo, Jacob
  Jacob Deyo–Ruth Smith Family Record, 194, *194–95*
dower chests. *See* blanket chests
Doyle, William M. S., 190
Dunlap, Samuel: *Chest on Chest* (attrib. shop of), *67*

Eager, Winthrop
  Acrostic "Portrait" Dedicated to Winthrop Eager (H. Wilcox), 194, *196–97*
Edison, Thomas Alva, 29
education, of women, 113, 121, 123, 151, 177
Ellis, A., 15–16, 34
  Portrait of Albert G. Gilman, *6*, 15–16, 34, *jacket back*
Emerson, Nehemiah, Captain, 120–21
Empire style, 56

fakes and reproductions, 35–36, 68
family registers, 124, 194
  Acrostic "Portrait" Dedicated to Winthrop Eager (H. Wilcox), 194, *196–97*
  Elijah E. Norton and Sally Martin Marriage Certificate (William Johnson, Esq.), *200*
  Jacob Deyo–Ruth Smith Family Record, 194, *194–95*
  A Record of the Family of Ensign Jacob Chamberlain of Alton, in the County Strafford, and State of New Hampshire, *201*
  Simeon Burnham & Lucy Smith Family Record, *198*
  Tracy Family Register ("Heart and Hand Artist"), 194, *198*
Fancy movement, 44–46, 68, 85–90
  definitions of, 85–88, 95n4
  demise of, 94–95
  and kaleidoscope, 90–94
fancy painting, 86, 87, 159
Federal style, 16, 44, 56, 119
Fellows, Elisabeth:
  Pocketbook, 119–21, *120–21*
Fielding Collection, 25–26, 31, 37, 40, 46, 49, 52, 53, 55–56, 68, 87
  formation of, 11–14, 34–36
firebacks, 31, 211
  Adam and Eve Fireback, *162*
fireboards, 142, 143, 147
  Fireboard, 147–48, *163*
  Fireboard, 148, *149*
  paintings on, 147–48
Fish, Elvira
  Portrait of Elvira Fish (possibly Ezra Wood, "Puffy Sleeve Artist"), 40, 190, *190*
Fish, Samuel
  Portrait of Samuel Fish (possibly Ezra Wood, "Puffy Sleeve Artist"), 40, 190, *190*
Fitch, Jonas: *Tall Case Clock* (attrib.), *242–43*, *jacket back*
foot warmers, 241
  Chip-Carved Foot Warmer with Container for Coals, *241*
folk art, 34–40
  affected by technology, 40
  decoration or simplicity, 49, 52, 94
  definition of, 36, 85
  exhibitions, Museum of Modern Art, 44
  rural compared to urban, 40–44, 52, 56–57

furniture, 36, 55–57, 62
cabinetry, 68
and Colonial Revival, 68
furniture making, 56–57, 59
machine made, 65, 68, 88
original surface of, 46–48
reproductions of, 68
wood for, 56–57, 68
workshops, 15, 72, 85
See also individual furniture types; antiques, early American; Fancy movement; painted furniture

Gaines, John, III: *Side Chair* (attrib.), *79*
Gerdts, William H., 151
Gibbons, Euell, 36
Gilbert, Betsy Brownell
Portrait of Betsy Brownell Gilbert (Ammi Phillips), *202*
Gilman, Albert G.
Portrait of Albert G. Gilman (A. Ellis), *6*, 15–16, 34, *jacket back*
Goodrich, Silas
Bandbox, *244*
Bandbox, *247*
Gookin, William P., 235
Gottlieb, Adolph, 44
Greenwood, John: *The Greenwood-Lee Family*, 120, *120*

Hamblin, Joseph, 205
Hamblin, Rosamond, 205
Hamblin, Sturtevant J., 205
A Portrait of Two Children, *207*
Hamlen, Mary Craig, 123, 129nn7 and 9
Sampler, *122*, 123, 129n8
Hardy, James, 220
Harvard College (Harvard University), Cambridge, Mass., 26, 172, 129n22
Hatch, Helen E.: *Folk Art Crazy Quilt*, 116, *134*
hats, 124, 244
glengarry hat, 12, 124
Niagara Beadwork Hat, *10*, 11–12, 124
See also top hats
"Heart and Hand Artist": *Tracy Family Register*, 194, *198*
Hepplewhite style, 56
Hewins, James, 126
Hewins, Mary Peters, 129n22
Geometric Hearth Rug (attrib.), 37, *37*, 126, *132–33*
Hilling, John, 154n4, 159
paintings on burning of Bath's Old South Church, 142, 154n4
Before the Burning of Old South Church in Bath, Maine (attrib.), *158*
The Burning of Old South Church in Bath, Maine (attrib.), *159*
Hitchcock, Lambert, 90
Holyoke, Edward, 26–29
Hooper, Eunice, 129n5
Sampler, 123, *131*
samplers, 123
Hooper, Hannah: samplers, 123
Hopkins, Milton W.: *Girl with Flowers*, *165*
Horse Tool, *211*
Humphrey, Heman, 90
Huntington Library, Art Museum, and Botanical Gardens, San Marino, California, 20
American galleries, 25
Fielding Wing, 25–26, 253
Jonathan and Karin Fielding Collection of Folk Art, 8, 20, 22, 25
Virginia Steele Scott Galleries of American Art, 7, 25

Illinois
Chicago, 203
DuPage County, 203
Indians. *See* Native Americans
ironwork. *See* kitchen and hearth tools

J. H. S.: *Basket*, 229, *229*
Jacobean style, 55
Jennys, William: portraits of David and Elizabeth Coffin, 184n1
Johnson, Martha, 100
Johnson, William: *Elijah E. Norton and Sally Martin Marriage Certificate*, *200*
Judkins, Samuel and Eunice
Portrait of Samuel and Eunice Judkins, Ulster County, New York (Sheldon Peck), 203, *204*

kaleidoscopes, 85, 90–94
as design tool, 92–93
and quilts, 92–94
keeping rooms, 62
Kentucky, 121
kitchen and hearth tools, 52, 63, 211, 220
Cheese Ladder, *214–15*
Chip-Carved Spoon Rack, *219*, *jacket back*
Fry Pan with Long Handle, *215–16*
Heart-Shaped Trivet, *3*, *211*
Hearth Fork, *3*, *215*
Ice Tongs, *9*
Kettle Tilter, 211, *217*
Mackerel Plow, *215*, *jacket back*
Oven Peel, 211, *215*
Pierced Spatula, *3*, *211*
Skimmer, *216*
See also andirons; broilers; coffeepots; pipe tongs; toasters
knives
Chip-Carved Knife, *228*
Crooked Knife, *228*
Figural Crooked Knife, *228*
Know-Nothings, 154n4, 159
Kopp, Joel and Kate, 125

Ladies Art Company, 113
lamps, 12, 29, 52
Adjustable Candle Lamp, *227*
Adjustable Candle Lamp and Snuffer, *227*
Betty Lamp, 29, *30*
camphine lamps, 12, 29
Lamp (William Webb), *28*
Lamps (Boston & Sandwich Glass Company), *12*
oil lamps, 26, 29, 52
See also lighting devices
landscapes, 31, 142–43, 149
Family Mansion of David Thayer, 142, *142*
Fancy, 141
Landscape with Riding and Walking Figures, a River, and a Village (Overmantel) (Winthrop Chandler), 143–44, *144–47*, 147
Overmantel: Coastal Landscape, 147, *160*
in portraits, 142, 174–75
as portraits of houses and lands, 142–43
The Property of Daniel and Sarah Leibelsperger, Fleetwood, Berks County, Pennsylvania (Ferdinand A. Brader), 142, *156*
by self-taught artists, 142, 153
See also overmantels; paintings
Leibelsperger, Daniel and Sarah
The Property of Daniel and Sarah Leibelsperger, Fleetwood, Berks County, Pennsylvania (Ferdinand A. Brader), 142, *156*
lighting devices, 12, 26–29, 52
Ratchet Lighting Device, 12, *15*
See also candles; candlesticks; lamps; lighting stands; sconces, lighting
lighting stands
Lighting Stand, 29, *30*, *jacket front*
Lighting Stand, 29, *30*, *jacket front*
Lighting Stand, *225*
Rush Holder, *28*
Lincoln, Abraham, 244
Linnaeus, Carl, 148
Locke, John, 179

Maentel, Jacob, 244
Portrait of Hatter John Mays of Schaefferstown, Pennsylvania, 34, *34*, 244, *245*
Maine, 7, 11, 14, 15, 37, 41, 64, 72, 107, 167, 178, 206, 229, 230, 234
Alfred, 189
Augusta, 123, 129n9
Cony Female Academy, 123, 129n7

Bath, 159
burning of Old South Church, 142, 154n4, 159
Bridgton, 198
Buxton, 172
Fielding house in, 11, 14
Maine Indian Basketmakers Alliance, 229
Mount Vernon, 7
Native Americans in, 229
New Portland, 25
Paris, 97,
Paris Hill, 102
Portland, 205
Stevens Plains (now Westbrook), 106
Winterport, 134
mantelpieces
from Snow Hill, Surry County, Virginia, 86, *86*
See also overmantels
Martin, Sally
Elijah E. Norton and Sally Martin Marriage Certificate (William Johnson, Esq.), *200*
Martineau, Harriet, 90
Maryland, 152
Baltimore, 110
Massachusetts, 15, 40, 73, 82, 135, 136, 187, 197, 225
Amherst, 129n20
Cambridge, 181
Mount Auburn Cemetery, 181
Cape Ann, 149
Charlestown, 181, 221, 223
furniture workshops, 31, 72
Hawley, 129n20
Marblehead, 123, 129n5, 131
Medfield, 129n22
Newburyport, 172, 174, *175*, 183n1, 184n12
Norfolk County, 37, 132
Northampton, 56
Old Sturbridge Village, 126
Plymouth, 73
Salem, 56
Sharon, 129n22
Sutton, 143
Worcester, 154n9
See also Boston; Harvard College
Mays, John
Portrait of Hatter John Mays of Schaefferstown, Pennsylvania (Jacob Maentel), 34, *34*, 244, *245*
metalwork. *See individual types*; kitchen and hearth tools
Miles, Jasper P.
Portrait of Hannah Spear, 190, *192*
Portrait of Stephan Spear, 190, *193*
Miller, Ann Wait, 180
Miller, Elvira Wait, 181
Miller, Robert, 180
Miller, Samuel S., 180–81
Portrait of Cynthia Mary Osborn, 31, 153, 171, *180*, 181–83, *186*
portraits of children, 180
mirrors, 91–94
looking-glass tablets, 153n3
Moon, Emily Quail, 110
Moon, Mary Seeds, 110, 129n1
Lone Star Quilt (attrib.), 110, *111*, *back endpapers*
Morse, Elisha: *Lift-Top Blanket Chest*, *24*
murals, 147, 154n14

Nadelman, Elie, 44
Native Americans, 12, 124, 223, 228, 229, 230, 232
basket making, 229
beadwork, 109, 124
First Nations, 124
Haudenosaunee (Iroquois), 12, 124
Maine Indian Basketmakers Alliance, 229
Mi'kmaq, 229, 231
Mohegan, 229
and Niagara souvenirs, 12
Ojibwe, 233
Penobscot, 228, 229
porcupine-quill work, 229
Wabanaki, 124
nativism, 154n4, 159
Neal, John, 141–42, 149, 153, 153n3
needlework, 31, 119
appliqué, 110, 119, 124–26
broderie perse, 110
canvas work, 119–21, 124
depictions of, *120*
embroidery, 12, 113, 119–21
flowers and fruit in, 151
knitted socks, 51
pattern books, 151
See also beadwork; pockets; pocketbooks; quilts; rugs; samplers; yarn making
New Hampshire, 31, 44, 66, 135, 141, 147, 178, 198, 200, 204
Canterbury, 100
Durham, 198, 217
furniture makers, 47, 56
Hampton, 51
Portsmouth, 56, 79, 235
New Jersey, 14, 19, 20
New York, 14, 20, 141, 148, 253
Bainbridge, 142
furniture makers, 31
New York City, 25, 56, 151, 152, 223
Niagara Falls, 12, 124
North, Elijah and Elisha: *Decorated Document Box* (attrib.), *106*
Norton, Elijah E.
Elijah E. Norton and Sally Martin Marriage Certificate (William Johnson, Esq.), *200*
Nutting, Wallace, 68, 70

Ohio, 164, 190
Holmes County, 116, 118
Montgomery County, 251
Orcutt & Crafts Pottery: *Three-Gallon Jug*, *223*
ornamental painting, 87, 90, 94, 143, 148, 150
Osborn, Cynthia Mary, 181
Portrait of Cynthia Mary Osborn (Samuel S. Miller), 31, 153, 171, *180*, 181–83, *186*
overmantels, 143, 147, 154n9
Landscape with Riding and Walking Figures, a River, and a Village (Overmantel), 143–44, *144–47*, 147
Overmantel: Coastal Landscape, 147, *160*

painted furniture, 49
Fancy, 31, 44, 68, 86
faux painting, 16, 44
fumée effect, 44, 148
graining, 44, 57, 86, 90, 144
marbling, 86, 144, 148
rocking chairs, 90
scumbling, 90
Windsor chairs, 19, 47, 72
paintings, 141–43, 153n3
based on European works, 143–44
deception or trompe-l'oeil, 143
interior mural paintings, 147, 154n14
by self-taught artists, 142–43, 153
See also landscapes; portraiture; still lifes
Peale, Charles Willson, 15, 149, 154n20
Peale, Raphaelle, 149
Peck, Sheldon, 203
Little Girl in a Windsor Armchair (attrib.), *189*
Portrait of Samuel and Eunice Judkins, Ulster County, New York, 203, *204*
Untitled (Portrait of a Young Man with Red Curtain), 203, *203*
Pennsylvania, 14, 33, 49, 139, 190
Berks County, 7, 119, 142, 156
Lancaster County, 49, 74, 116, 117–18
Lehigh County, 114
Lenhartsville, 117
Pennsylvania Germans, 49, 119, 244
Philadelphia, 8, 25, 53, 56, 81, 143, 148
Charles Willson Peale's museum, 149
the Columbianum, 149, 154n20
Schaefferstown, 34, 244
western oil wells, 29
pets, 178, 182
in portraits, *176*, 178
Puppies, *168*
Phelps, Almira Hart: *Familiar Lectures on Botany*, 151
Phillips, Ammi, 15
Portrait of Betsy Brownell Gilbert, *202*
Portraits of a Man and Woman, Members of the Van Keuren Family, *13*, 15, 40

Phillips, Augustine Washington, 125, 129n20
and *Yarn-Sewn Rug*, 125, *167*
pipe tongs, 211
Pipe Tongs, *217*
Pipe Tongs (Sawyer House), *217*
Plaque with Bas Relief of a Man and Woman, *206*
Plater, Sophia, 152
Plummer, Edwin: *Four Portraits of Children*, 40, *187*
pocketbooks, 109, 113
Pocketbook (Elisabeth Fellows), 119–21, *120–21*
worked, 120–21
pockets, 113, 119–20, 121
Pair of Pockets, 119, *130*
Poe, Edgar Allen, 94
Poonah painting, 150–51, 155n26
and *La Belle Assemblée*, 151
Porter, Rufus, 153
A Select Collection of Valuable and Curious Arts, and Interesting Experiments, 144–47
portraits
The Azariah Caverly Family (attrib. Joseph H. Davis), 179, *179*
Boy with a Book and a Flute, *199*
Children in Pink and Blue (Mrs. Moses Russel), *191*
Family Portrait of Charles and Comfort Caverly and Their Son Isaac (Joseph H. Davis), 31, 141, 171, 175–79, *177*
Four Portraits of Children (Edwin Plummer), 40, *187*
Girl with Flowers (Milton W. Hopkins), *165*
The Greenwood-Lee Family (John Greenwood), 120, *120*
Little Girl in a Windsor Armchair (attrib. Sheldon Peck), *189*
Portrait Miniatures of a Sea Captain and His Wife, 173, *174*
Portrait of Albert G. Gilman (A. Ellis), *6*, 15–16, 34, *jacket back*
Portrait of Betsy Brownell Gilbert (Ammi Phillips), *202*
Portrait of Cynthia Mary Osborn (Samuel S. Miller), 31, 153, 171, *180*, 181–83, *186*
Portrait of Hannah Spear (Jasper P. Miles), 190, *192*
Portrait of Hatter John Mays of Schaefferstown, Pennsylvania (Jacob Maentel), 34, *34*, 244, *245*
Portrait of Henry Sayward (John Brewster Jr.), *188*, 189
Portrait of Samuel and Eunice Judkins, Ulster County, New York (Sheldon Peck), 203, *204*
Portrait of Stephan Spear (Jasper P. Miles), 190, *193*
Portrait of Susan Ames (Asa Ames), *32*, 34, *jacket front*
A Portrait of Two Children (Sturtevant J. Hamblin), *207*
Portrait of a Woman with a Bowl of Cherries, 142, *164*
Portraits of Boy and Girl (Prior-Hamblin School), *205*
portraits of David and Elizabeth Coffin (William Jennys), 184n1
Portraits of Elizabeth Stone Coffin and Major David Coffin (John Brewster Jr.), 31, 142, *170*, 171–75, 184n1
Portraits of a Man and Woman, Members of the Van Keuren Family (Ammi Phillips), *13*, 15, 40
Portraits of Samuel and Elvira Fish (possibly Ezra Wood, "Puffy Sleeve Artist"), 40, 190, *190*
portraits of Samuel and Prudence Waters (Winthrop Chandler), 143
Untitled (Portrait of a Young Man with Red Curtain) (Sheldon Peck), 203, *203*
Young Woman with Rose, 181, *181*
portraiture, 15, 31, 37, 141–43, 149, 171–83
gender-specific attributes, 172–75, 179
of married couples, 31, 40, 171–75, 143, 183–84n1, 190
mechanical device for profiles, 178
memorial, 171
miniatures, 173–74, 190
occupational, 34
painters, 15, 154n9, 189–90, 205
pets in, 178
posthumous, 171, 180–82
silhouettes, 40, 190
watercolor profiles, 40, 178
See also children in portraits; daguerreotypes; portraits
potteries, 16, 19, 148, 220, 223
powder horns, 236
Powder Horn (John Young), 236, *236–37*
Prince, James, 172
family portraits by John Brewster, 183–84n1
Prior, William Matthew, 205
Prior-Hamblin School, 205
Portraits of Boy and Girl, *205*
Proctor, Joseph, 35, 152
Still Life with a Basket of Fruit, Flowers, and Cornucopia (attrib.), 35, *140*, 151–53
"Puffy Sleeve Artist." *See* Wood, Ezra

Queen Anne style, 55
quilts, 31, 36, 109–19, 151
and abstraction, 33, 44, 52
album quilts, 110
Amish, 49, 51, 116–19
with appliqué, 110, 119, 124
Berks County quilts, 119
with *broderie perse*, 110
with chintz, 110
construction of, 110, 113, 116–17
crazy quilts, 116
fabric for, 109–10, 117, 119
in Fielding Collection, 11, 110
friendship quilts, 110–12
and *Godey's Lady's Book*, 113
as group activities, 113
and the kaleidoscope, 92–94
Lancaster County quilts, 51, 117–18
market for, modern, 33–34
patterns
Bulls Eye, 119
center medallion, 49
Diamond in the Square, 49–51, 117–18
Geese in Flight, 112
Jacob's Ladder, 112
Log Cabin, 113–16
Pineapple Log Cabin, 116
Wild Goose Chase, 112
Windmill Blades, 116
pieced quilts, 33, 100, 112–13, 119
foundation piecing, 113–16
patterns, 112–13
quilting bees, 113
red-and-white quilts, 110, 119
show quilts, 116
quilts illustrated
Album Quilt, *108*, 110
Bars Quilt, 116–18, *116*
Diamond in the Square Quilt, 49, *50*, 51–52, 117–18
Drunkard's Path Quilt, *91*
Folk Art Crazy Quilt (Helen E. Hatch), 116, *134*
Geese in Flight Quilt, 112, *138*
Jacob's Ladder Quilt, 112, *114*
Log Cabin Quilt, 113–16, *139*
Lone Star of Bethlehem Quilt, *137*
Lone Star Quilt (attrib. Mary Seeds Moon), 110, *111*, *front endpapers*
Lone Star Quilt Top—Red and White, *118*, 119
Lone Star Quilt—Red, White, and Blue, *92*, *back endpapers*

Red and White Garden Maze Quilt, *118–19*, 119
Red Friendship Quilt, 110–12, *112–13*
Quilt with Concentric Circles, *117*, 119
Wild Goose Chase Quilt, 112, *115*

Raphael: *Madonna of the Goldfinch*, *182*
redware, 220
Jar, *221*
Rhode Island, 72, 73
Providence
Friends' Boarding School (now Moses Brown School), 123
and slavery, 223
Smithfield, 124, 129n11
Woonsocket Falls
D. Warren's school, 123
Ring, Betty, 121–23
rugs, 31, 94, 124–26, 151
bias shirring for, 126
Flower Basket Rug, *125*, 126, *166*, *169*
Geometric Hearth Rug (attrib. Mary Peters Hewins), 37, *37*, 126, *132–33*
geometric hearth rugs, 126
hooked, 37
Pictorial Hearth Rug, 124, *126–28*
shirring for, 125–26
yarn-sewn, 37, 124, 126
Yarn-Sewn Rug, 125, *167*
Russel, Mrs. Moses: *Children in Pink and Blue*, *191*

S. W. Chandler & Bro. Lithographers: *A North-east View of the Town & harbour of NewburyPort* (after Ben. Johnson), 174, *175*
samplers, 113, 119, 121–23, 151
family record, 123
by Hannah Hooper, 123
from Marblehead, Massachusetts, 123
Sampler (Abigail Andrews), 123, *123*
Sampler (Eunice Hooper), 123, *131*
Sampler (Mary Craig Hamlen), *122*, 123, 129n8
schoolgirl, 119, 121–23, 129n8
verse inscriptions, 123, 129n9
Sayward, Henry, 189
Portrait of Henry Sayward (John Brewster Jr.), *188*, 189
Schranks, 47–49
Painted Schrank, *4*, *46*, 47, *48*, 49, 90, *jacket back*
sconces, lighting
Lighting Sconces, *27*
Pair of Mirrored Sconces, 12, *224*, *226*
self-taught artists, 14–15, 142–44, 153, 178
settees, 62
Windsor Low-Back Settee, *74–75*, *jacket back*
Sewall, Samuel, 143
sewing. *See* needlework
Seymour, James, 144
Sheraton style, 56
Shakers (United Society of Believers in Christ's Second Appearing), 100
boxes by, 100
Chrome Yellow Oval Box, 100, *100*, *jacket front*
Red Shaker Carrier, *98*
Shaker Boxes, 100, *101*
signs, 159, 190
Barber Pole, 25, *26*
Equestrian Trade Sign for the Cincinnati Stove Works, *248*, *jacket back*
Sign for A, S, Adams, Tailor, *249*
"Six Mile House" Tavern Sign, *250*
Sigourney, Lydia, 177
slavery, 144, 223
Smith, Mary Emerson, 121
Smith, Lucy
Simeon Burnham & Lucy Smith Family Record, *198*
Smith, Ruth
Jacob Deyo–Ruth Smith Family Record, 194, *194–95*
Smith, Sukey Jarvis: sampler, 123
Spear, Hannah
Portrait of Hannah Spear (Jasper P. Miles), 190, *192*
Spear, Stephan
Portrait of Stephan Spear (Jasper P. Miles), 190, *193*
spinning wheels, 62
Spinning Wheel, 136, *136*, *jacket back*
Steward, John, 189
Stewart, Alexander, 143
Stewart, George, 152
Stickley, Gustav, 94–95
still lifes, 31, 35, 142, 148–51
and botany, 148–51
Fruit and Flowers, 152, *152*
in portraits, 173
prints, 3, 149–50
by self-taught artists, 142, 153
Still Life with a Basket of Fruit, Flowers, and Cornucopia (attrib. Joseph Proctor), 35, *140*, 151–53
Still Life with Fruit Theorem Painting, 89, *89*, 150–51, *150*
See also fireboards; theorem paintings
stoneware, 16–19, 220
jars, 220, *220–23*
Jar, 16–19, *20–21*
Jug, *223*
Swag- and Tassel-Decorated Jar, *220*
Three-Gallon Jug (Orcutt & Crafts Pottery), *223*
Westerwald stoneware, 19

tables, 62–63
circular and oval, 66
Dressing Table, *63*
dressing tables, 68
Gateleg Table with Drop Leaves, 62, *76–77*
One-Drawer Stand, *97*
Splayed-Leg Table, *44–45*, *47*
textiles, 36, 87, 109–28, 173
dyes, 119, 126
mills, New England, 109
printed, 36, 110
See also beadwork; needlework; pocketbooks; pockets; quilts; rugs; samplers; yarn making
Thayer, David
Family Mansion of David Thayer, 142, *142*
theorem paintings, 31, 89, 150, 155n25
The Artist, or, Young Ladies' Instructor in Ornamental Painting, Drawing, &c, 150
and Oriental tinting, 150
pouncing for, 150–51
stencils used for, 89, 150–51
See also Poonah painting; still lifes
Thomas, Sallie B., 121
toasters, 211
Toaster, *210*
Toaster with Shoulder Handle, *210*
top hats, 244
Bandbox (Silas Goodrich), *244*
Bandbox (Silas Goodrich), *247*
Top Hat (Collins & Fairbanks), *244*
Top Hat (Collins & Fairbanks), *246–47*
Tracy, Ebenezer, Sr., 19, 72
High-Back Windsor Armchair with Writing Arm (attrib.), *18*, 47, 72, *78*, *jacket front*
Tracy family
Tracy Family Register ("Heart and Hand Artist"), 194, *198*
trade signs. *See* signs
Trollope, Frances, 143

Van Keuren family
Portraits of a Man and Woman, Members of the Van Keuren Family (Ammi Phillips), *13*, 15, 40
Vermont, 43, 46, 105, 203, 204, 225
New Shaftsbury, 85
Virginia
Surry County, Snow Hill house, 86–87, 95n2
Williamsburg, 148

Warren, E.: *Scrimshaw Busk*, *238*
Washington, George, 29

Waters, Ebenezer, 143, 154n8
Waters, Prudence and Samuel
portraits by Winthrop Chandler, 143
weather vanes
Ten-Point Leaping Stag Weather Vane, *251*, *jacket front*
Webb, William: *Lamp*, *28*
whalebone carving, 236
Clothespins, 236, *236–37*
scrimshaw, 236–38
Scrimshaw Oval Box with Inlaid Five-Point Star, *99*
Seam Rubber, 236, *237*
See also busks
whaling, 29, 236
Wheatcroft, David, 14, 55
conversation with, 29, 33–53
Whiting, Riley
Tall Case Clock, 40–46, *41–42*, 90
Whitman, Walt, 26, 31
"Chants Democratic and Native American," 25–26
Whittier, Mollie Mary, 121
Wilcox, H.: *Acrostic "Portrait" Dedicated to Winthrop Eager*, 194, *196–97*
Willard, Simon, 243
William and Mary style, 55–56
Williams, Andy, 35
Windsor chairs, 19, 66, 72
Birdcage Windsor Armchair, *73*
Comb-Back Windsor Armchair with D Seat, *81*
High-Back Windsor Armchair with Writing Arm (attrib. Ebenezer Tracy Sr.), *18*, 47, 72, *78*, *jacket front*
painted, 19, 47, 72
Windsor Continuous Armchair, 47, *47*, *82*
Windsor Continuous Armchair, *82*
Windsor Low-Back Settee, *74–75*, *jacket back*
Windsor Armchair, *72*
writing armchairs, 19
Wise, Captain and Mrs. William
portraits by John Brewster, 183n1
Wolcott, Erastus, 16
Wolcott, Samuel and Jerusha, 16
women
attributes in portraits, 173–75
education of, 113, 121–24, 151, 155n27, 177
as maternal, 172–73, 177, 180, 183
as spiritual and moral guardians, 121, 172, 175–77, 180
Wood, Ezra ("Puffy Sleeve Artist"), 40
Portraits of Samuel and Elvira Fish (possibly), 40, 190, *190*
wood harvesting, 56
Wootton, John, 144
Worcester, Joseph E., 87, 95n4
Wordsworth, William, 177, 178, 179

yarn making, 62, 136
looms, 136
Niddy-Noddy, *135*, 136
Spinning Wheel, 136, *136*, *jacket back*
Yarn Rack, *135–36*, 136
Yarn Winder, 62, *135*, *jacket back*
See also needlework; rugs, yarn-sewn; samplers
Young, John: *Powder Horn*, 236, *236–37*

Zea, Philip, 70, 243

Illustrations and Photo Credits

Jacket front and flap, clockwise from lower-left corner: *Devil Bootjack*, 2016.25.114 (pp. 209–10); *Ten-Point Leaping Stag Weather Vane*, L2015.41.132 (p. 251); *Coffeepot*, 2016.25.21 (p. 218); *Candle Stand*, 2016.25.80 (p. 29); *Corner Chair*, 2016.25.62 (p. 73); *Lighting Stands*, 2016.25.92.1,.2 (p. 30); *Portrait of Susan Ames*, L2015.41.183 (p. 32); *Coffeepot*, 2016.25.20 (p. 218); *High Chest of Drawers*, L2015.41.97 (p. 17); *High-Back Windsor Armchair with Writing Arm*, L2015.41.112 (p. 18); *Chrome Yellow Oval Box*, L2015.41.27 (p. 100)

Jacket back and flap, clockwise from lower-left corner: *Spinning Wheel* (detail), 2016.25.145 (p. 136); *Windsor Low-Back Settee*, L2015.41.100 (pp. 74–75); *Chip-Carved Spoon Rack*, L2015.41.101 (p. 219); *Painted Schrank*, 2018.10 (p. 4); *Yarn Winder*, 2016.25.148 (p. 135); *Mackerel Plow*, 2016.25.136 (p. 215); *Hessian Grenadier Andiron*, 2016.25.6 (pp. 213–14); *Tall Case Clock*, 2016.25.19 (pp. 242–43); *Equestrian Trade Sign for the Cincinnati Stove Works*, 2016.25.95 (p. 248); *Portrait of Albert G. Gilman*, L2015.41.173 (p. 6)

Front endpapers: *Lone Star Quilt* (detail), L2018.3.1 (p. 111)

Back endpapers: *Lone Star Quilt—Red, White, and Blue* (detail), 2016.25.58 (p. 92)

Pp. 2–3, clockwise from lower-left corner: *Devil Bootjack*, 2016.25.114 (pp. 209–10); *Broiler with Grease Collector*, 2016.25.123 (p. 212); *Large Broiler*, 2016.25.122 (p. 212); *Heart-Shaped Trivet*, 2016.25.133 (p. 211); *Pierced Spatula*, 2016.25.130 (p. 211); *Hearth Fork*, 2016.25.134 (p. 215); *Boot Scraper*, 2016.25.117 (p. 214)

Principal photography by John Sullivan and Manuel Flores

Additional photography by Fredrik Nilsen: pp. 6, 17, 34, 38–39, 41–42, 58, 60–61, 67, 89, 130, 140, 149–50, 164, 170, 172, 204, 245

Funding for this publication was provided by Jonathan and Karin Fielding. Additional funding was made possible through a Director's Designated grant from The Rose Hills Foundation, made in honor of John Light.

Published in conjunction with the long-term installation *Becoming America: Highlights from the Jonathan and Karin Fielding Collection* at The Huntington Library, Art Museum, and Botanical Gardens

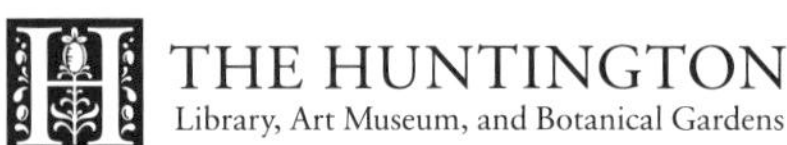

Published by The Huntington Library,
Art Museum, and Botanical Gardens
1151 Oxford Road
San Marino, CA 91108
www.huntington.org
(626) 405-2100

Distributed by Yale University Press
302 Temple Street
P.O. Box 209040
New Haven, CT 06520-9040
www.yalebooks.com/art

Produced by Lucia | Marquand, Seattle
www.luciamarquand.com

Designed by Ryan Polich
Typeset in Grad and Metro Nova Pro by Brynn Warriner
Content editing by Melissa Duffes
Proofreading by Bruno George
Color management by iocolor, Seattle
Printed and bound in China by Artron Art Group

For The Huntington:
Volume editor: James Glisson
Extended captions: James Glisson
Managing editor: Jean Patterson
Rights and reproductions: Lindsey Hansen
Editorial assistants: Lindsey Hansen, Elizabeth (Elee) Wood, and Lily Allen
Indexer: Kathleen M. Friello

The Fielding Wing, completed in October 2016, was made possible by:
Jonathan and Karin Fielding

And the generosity of the following donors:
The Ahmanson Foundation
Robert N. Essick
The Fletcher Jones Foundation
Sharon and John Light
Margot and Mitch Milias
Lisa and Tim Sloan
David and Joan Traitel

With additional support from:
Nancy Berman and Alan Bloch
The Philip and Muriel Berman Foundation
Maribeth and Hal Borthwick
The Ralph M. Parsons Foundation

Library of Congress Cataloging-in-Publication Data
Names: Glisson, James, editor. | Henry E. Huntington Library and Art Gallery, organizer, host institution.
Title: Becoming America : highlights from the Jonathan and Karin Fielding collection of folk art / essays by John Demos, Jonathan and Karin Fielding, Robin Jaffee Frank, James Glisson, editor, Stacy C. Hollander, Sumpter Priddy, Elizabeth V. Warren, David Wheatcroft.
Description: San Marino, California : Huntington Library, Art Museum, and Botanical Gardens, 2020. | Includes index.
Identifiers: LCCN 2019019922 | ISBN 9780300247565 (hardback)
Subjects: LCSH: Folk art—United States—Exhibitions. | Fielding, Jonathan E.—Art collections—Exhibitions. | Fielding, Karin.—Art collections—Exhibitions. | Art—Private collections—United States—Exhibitions. | BISAC: ART / Folk & Outsider Art. | DESIGN / Decorative Arts. | ART / Collections, Catalogs, Exhibitions / Permanent Collections.
Classification: LCC NK805 .B43 2020 | DDC 745.0973—dc23
LC record available at https://lccn.loc.gov/2019019922

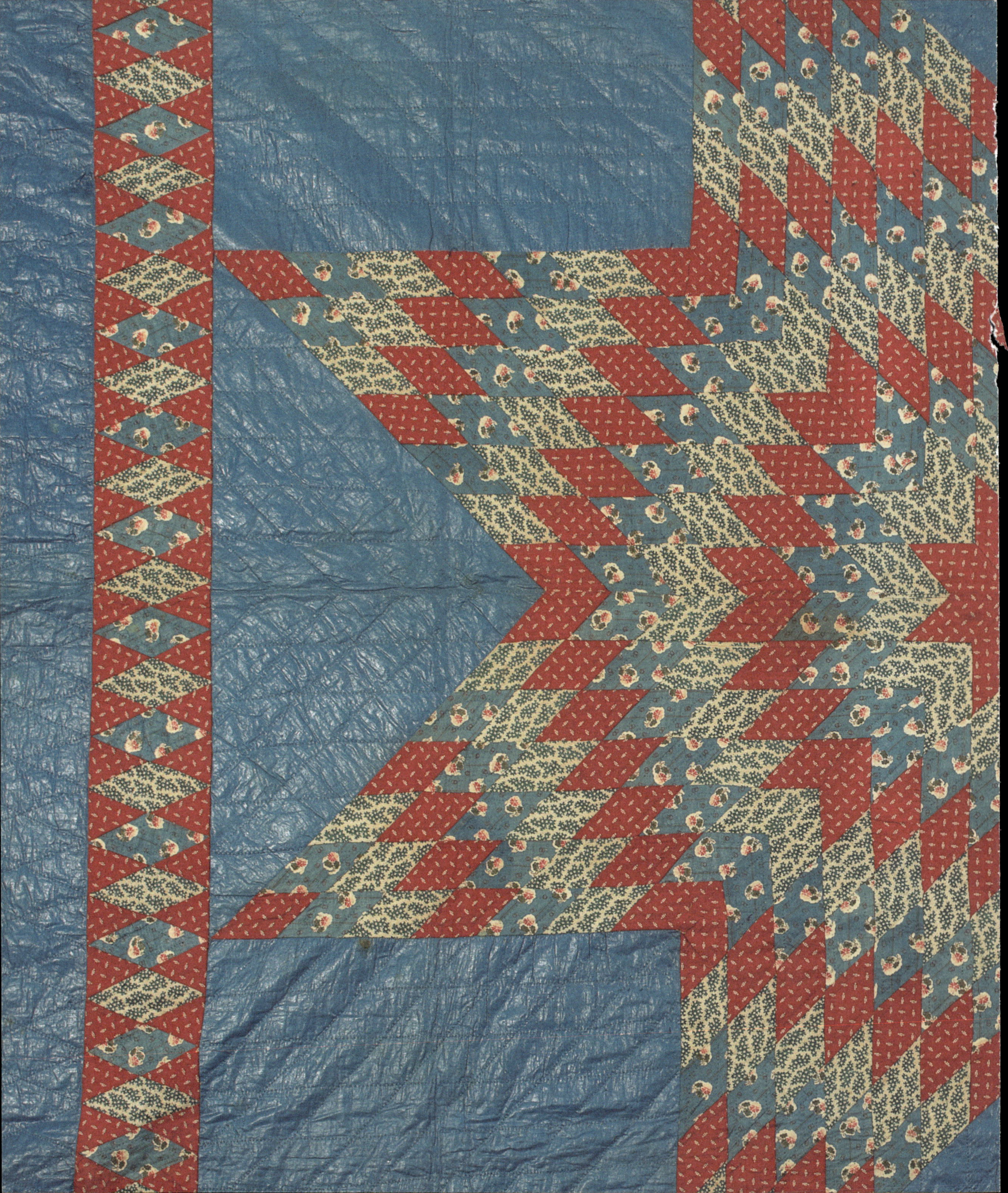